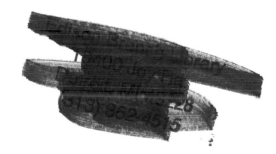

ENCYCLOPEDIA OF AFRICAN AMERICAN WOMEN WRITERS

ENCYCLOPEDIA OF AFRICAN AMERICAN WOMEN WRITERS

Volume 1

Edited by Yolanda Williams Page

GREENWOOD PRESS
Westport, Connecticut • London

Library of Congress Cataloging-in-Publication Data

Encyclopedia of African American women writers / edited by Yolanda Williams Page.
  p. cm.
Includes bibliographical references and index.
ISBN 0-313-33429-3 (set : alk. paper)—ISBN 0-313-34123-0 (vol 1 : alk. paper)—
ISBN 0-313-34124-9 (vol 2 : alk. paper)   1. American literature—African American authors—
Encyclopedias.   2. American literature—Women authors—Encyclopedias.   3. American
literature—20th century—Encyclopedias.   4. African American women authors—Biography—
Encyclopedias.   5. African American women—Encyclopedias.   I. Page, Yolanda Williams.
PS153.N5E49   2007
810.9'896073—dc22   2006031193

British Library Cataloguing in Publication Data is available.

Library of Congress Catalog Card Number: 2006031193
ISBN-10: 0-313-33429-3 (set)   ISBN-13: 978-0-313-33429-0
         0-313-34123-0 (vol. 1)   978-0-313-34123-6
         0-313-34124-9 (vol. 2)   978-0-313-34124-3

First published in 2007

Greenwood Press, 88 Post Road West, Westport, CT 06881
An imprint of Greenwood Publishing Group, Inc.
www.greenwood.com

Printed in the United States of America

∞

The paper used in this book complies with the
Permanent Paper Standard issued by the National
Information Standards Organization (Z39.48–1984).

10 9 8 7 6 5 4 3 2 1

To my two favorite beaus, David and William

CONTENTS

PREFACE

Since its inception, the African American literary tradition has been very vital to African American culture. Historically not only has the literature provided insight into various aspects of the African American experience, but it has also served as a source of activism. For example, during the colonial period it was used to prove that blacks, like writers of nonAfrican descent, could successfully produce a variety of belletristic and practical genres of writing; thus giving lie to the justification for the enslavement of black people. Later, during the reconstruction era the literature was used to emphasize African Americans' similarities to other educated Americans and to protest their exclusion from the American mainstream. Today, it continues to serve as a political and social conduit, the majority of it being used to promote ideas, philosophies and causes, while the rest is simply written with the purpose to entertain or as a platform for the author to express himself.

Although the preponderance of African American literature that exists is written by African American males, African American women writers have also produced an impressive body of the literature. In fact, the tradition began with a black woman, Lucy Terry whose ballad poem "Bars Fight" was recited for a century before it was published in 1855. Although some works by African American women were published near or at the turn of the twentieth century, when they enjoyed modest popularity, the vast majority of it was published during the Harlem Renaissance and in the years after the 1970s, as women writers, in general, gained increased access to the marketplace.

The *Encyclopedia of African American Women Writers* provides a comprehensive reference to literature by African American women. One hundred sixty-eight writers are included in this sourcebook. While this work is by no means exhaustive, it does provide coverage of many African American women writers. Many of them are established and canonized, others are emerging, while some are obscure, forgotten writers that this author seeks to bring to the critical attention of contemporary students and scholars. This work is an extensive study of the well-known, not so known and unknown African American women writers from 1746 to present; it provides a thorough examination of their lives, major works and the critical reception of that work.

While this sourcebook's focus is writers of African American descent, Caribbean authors such as Michelle Cliff, Edwidge Danticat, and Jamaica Kincaid have been included because they are closely identified with the African American literary tradition; the themes of their writing resonate aspects of African American life and experience. In addition, their inclusion iterates that the experience of the African Diaspora is not exclusive.

The *Encyclopedia of African American Women Writers* is not the first work of its kind, but it fills an important information gap in that it is genre inclusive. That is, the entries include women who write in a variety of belletristic forms: autobiography, drama, essay, fiction and poetry. Also included are cultural/literary theorists and children/young adult writers.

The *Encyclopedia of African American Women Writers* has been written so that the user will find it helpful no matter his stage of research. Advanced high school students, undergraduates and users of community college and public libraries will all find the information accessible. The book includes an alphabetical list of authors as well as a chronological list of authors, a list of authors by genre, and a list of authors and awards. Too, graduate students and seasoned scholars in the initial stage of research will find this text useful, for each entry includes primary and secondary sources. Entries are written in chapter format and consist of five parts: (1) heading-which includes the writer's name, year of birth and year of death (if applicable); (2) biographical narrative-which consists of a concise writer biographical profile; (3) majors works-which consists of a discussion of the writer's works. Motifs and themes are also highlighted; (4) critical reception-which consists of critical response to the author's work; and (5) bibliography which-consists of a list of the author's work and a list of studies of the author's work. Entries vary in length from 750 words to 5000 words.

ACKNOWLEDGMENTS

There are many to whom I am indebted for the completion of this book. I thank George Butler at Greenwood Press for considering this a worthy project. Thanks to my Dillard University family for providing me a research award that allowed me to complete the preliminary work on this project. Thanks also to my undergraduate assistant, La-Chandra Pye, for helping with the administrative aspects of this project. I especially express gratitude to the contributors of this book. Without you this project would not have come to fruition. Lastly, I thank my friends and family, especially my mother and my sister, for their words of encouragement and support.

LIST OF AUTHORS BY GENRE

Autobiography
Maya Angelou
Annie Louise Burton
Lucille Clifton
Angela Y. Davis
Lucy Delaney
Kate Drumgoold
Zilpha Elaw
Julia A. J. Foote
Juanita Harrison
bell hooks
Mattie Jane Jackson
Rebecca Cox Jackson
Harriet Jacobs
Elizabeth Hobbs Keckley
Adrienne Kennedy
Jarena Lee
Audre Geraldine Lorde
Anne Moody
Pauli Murray
Eliza Potter
Mary Seacole
Notzake Shange
Amanda Berry Smith
Susie King Taylor
Era Bell Thompson

Biography
Elizabeth Laura Adams
Octavia Victoria Rogers Albert
Anna Julia Hayward Cooper
Shirley Graham DuBois
Pauli Murray
Ann Plato
Henrietta Cordelia Ray

Children's Literature
Candy Boyd (Marguerite Dawson)
Gwendolyn Brooks
Jeannette Franklin Caines
Lucille Clifton
Alexis DeVeaux

Eloise Greenfield
Virginia Hamilton
Carolivia Herron
bell hooks
Amelia E. Johnson
Sharon Bell Mathis
Patricia McKissack
Louise Meriwether
Opal J. Moore
Connie Porter
Fatima Shaik
Ellen Tarry
Mildred D. Taylor
Mildred Pitts Walter
Brenda Wilkinson

Criticism
Joanne Braxton
Barbara T. Christian
Sarah Webster Fabio
Beverly Guy-Sheftall
bell hooks
Toni Morrison
Claudia Tate
Gloria Wade-Gayles

Drama
Maya Angelou
Marita Bonner
Olivia Ward Bush-Banks
Alice Childress
Pearl T. Cleage
Kathleen Conwell Collins
J. California Cooper
Alexis DeVeaux
Rita Dove
Shirley Graham DuBois
Mari Evans
Julia Fields
Patricia Joann Gibson
Mercedes Gilbert
Angelina Weld Grimké

Rosa Guy
Lorraine Hansberry
Zora Neale Hurston
Angela Jackson
Elaine Jackson
Mae Jackson
Gayl Jones
June Jordan
Adrienne Kennedy
May Miller
Suzan-Lori Parks
Aishah Rahman
Sonia Sanchez
Ntozake Shange
Anna Deavere Smith
Katherine Davis Chapman Tillman
Shay Youngblood

Essay
Clarissa Minnie Thompson Allen
Tina McElroy Ansa
Doris Jean Austin
Toni Cade Bambara
Marita Bonner
Olivia Ward Bush-Banks
Octavia Butler
Barbara Chase-Riboud
Alice Childress
Barbara T. Christian
Pearl T. Cleage
Eugenia W. Collier
Anna Julia Hayward Cooper
Edwidge Danticat
Angela Y. Davis
Rita Dove
Mari Evans
Nikki Giovanni
Jewelle Gomez
Angelina Weld Grimké
Virginia Hamilton
Frances Ellen Watkins Harper
Pauline Elizabeth Hopkins (Sara A. Allen)
Gayl Jones
June Jordan
Jamaica Kincaid
Audre Geraldine Lorde
Paule Marshall
Louise Meriwether

Opal J. Moore
Gertrude Bustill Mossell
Gloria Naylor
Ann Petry
Ann Plato
Ann Allen Shockley
Ellease Southerland
Maria W. Stewart
Lisa Teasley
Era Bell Thompson
Katherine Davis Chapman Tillman
Alice Walker
Margaret Walker
Ida B. Wells-Barnett
Fannie Barrier Williams

Etiquette Book
Madame Emma Azalia Smith Hackley

Memoir
Toi(nette) Marie Derricotte
bell hooks
Dori Sanders
Era Bell Thompson

Mystery
Barbara Neely

Novel
Clarissa Minnie Thompson Allen
Tina McElroy Ansa
Doris Jean Austin
Nikki Baker
Toni Cade Bambara
Candy Dawson Boyd
Gwendolyn Brooks
Linda Beatrice Brown
Bebe Moore Campbell
Barbara Chase-Riboud
Alice Childress
Pearl T. Cleage
Michelle Cliff
Kathleen Conwell Collins
J. California Cooper
Edwidge Danticat
Rita Dove
Grace Edwards-Yearwood
Jessie Redmon Fauset
Patrice Gaines
Marita Golden

Jewelle Gomez
Joyce Hansen
Frances Ellen Watkins Harper
Pauline Elizabeth Hopkins (Sara A. Allen)
Zora Neale Hurston
Angela Jackson
Amelia E. Johnson
Gayl Jones
June Jordan
Jamaica Kincaid
Pinkie Gordon Lane
Nella Larsen
Kristin Hunter Lattany
Andrea Lee
Helen Elaine Lee
Paule Marshall
Terry McMillan
Louise Meriwether
Mary Monroe
Toni Morrison
Gloria Naylor
Suzan-Lori Parks
Ann Petry
Connie Porter
Alice Randall
Jewell Parker Rhodes
Dori Sanders
Fatima Shaik
Ann Allen Shockley
Ellease Southerland
Barbara Summers
Lisa Teasley
Katherine Davis Chapman Tillman
Mary Elizabeth Vroman
Alice Walker
Margaret Walker
Dorothy West
Sherley Anne Williams
Harriet E. Wilson
Sarah Elizabeth Wright
Shay Youngblood

Novella
Ruth D. Todd

Poetry
Maya Angelou
Gwendolyn Bennett
Joanne Braxton

Gwendolyn Brooks
Linda Beatrice Brown
Olivia Ward Bush-Banks
Barbara Chase-Riboud
Pearl T. Cleage
Michelle Cliff
Lucille Clifton
Wanda Coleman
Eugenia W. Collier
Jayne Cortez
Margaret Esse Danner
Doris Davenport
Toi(nette) Marie Derricotte
Alexis DeVeaux
Rita Dove
Alice Dunbar-Nelson
Mari Evans
Sara Webster Fabio
Julia Fields
Patrice Gaines
Mercedes Gilbert
Nikki Giovanni
Marita Golden
Jewelle Gomez
Rosa Guy
Frances Ellen Watkins Harper
Frenchy Jolene Hodges
Safiya Henderson-Holmes
bell hooks
Pauline Elizabeth Hopkins (Sara A. Allen)
Angela Jackson
Mae Jackson
Amelia E. Johnson
Georgia Douglas Johnson
Helen(e) Johnson
Gayl Jones
June Jordan
Audre Geraldine Lorde
Naomi Long Madgett
May Miller
Arthenia J. Bates Millican
Opal J. Moore
Gertrude Bustill Mossell
Harryette Mullen
Beatrice Murphy
Pauli Murray
Brenda Marie Osbey
Pat Parker

Ann Petry
Ann Plato
Henrietta Cordelia Ray
Carolyn Marie Rodgers
Mona Lisa Saloy
Sonia Sanchez
Ntozake Shange
Ellease Southerland
Lucy Terry
Joyce Carol Thomas
Katherine Davis Chapman Tillman
Gloria Wade-Gayles
Alice Walker
Margaret Walker
Marilyn Nelson Waniek
Phillis Wheatley
Sherley Anne Williams
Sarah Elizabeth Wright

Science Fiction
Octavia Butler

Short Fiction
Mignon Holland Anderson
Tina McElroy Ansa
Toni Cade Bambara
Gwendolyn Bennett
Marita Bonner
Olivia Ward Bush-Banks
Octavia Butler
Michelle Cliff
Wanda Coleman
Eugenia W. Collier
Kathleen Conwell Collins
J. California Cooper
Edwidge Danticat
Edwina Streeter Dixon
Rita Dove
Alice Dunbar-Nelson
Mari Evans
Carolyn Ferrell
Julia Fields
Jewelle Gomez
Angelina Weld Grimké
Frances Ellen Watkins Harper
Carolivia Herron
Frenchy Jolene Hodges
Zora Neale Hurston
Amelia E. Johnson

Adrienne Kennedy
Jamaica Kincaid
Nella Larsen
Kristin Hunter Lattany
Andrea Lee
Paule Marshall
Victoria Earle Matthews
Colleen J. McElroy
Patricia McKissack
Louise Meriwether
Arthenia J. Bates Millican
Mary Monroe
Opal J. Moore
Toni Morrison
Barbara Neely
Diane Oliver
Ann Petry
Carolyn Rodgers
Ann Allen Shockley
Ellease Southerland
Barbara Summers
Lisa Teasley
Ruth D. Todd
Mary Elizabeth Vroman
Dorothy West
Paulette Childress White
Shay Youngblood

Slave Narrative
Harriet Ann Jacobs
Lucy Delaney
Mattie Jane Jackson
Elizabeth Hobbs Keckley
Mary Prince

Travel Literature
Juanita Harrison
Andrea Lee
Colleen McElroy
Nancy Prince
Mary Seacole

Young Adult Literature
Rosa Guy
Joyce Hansen
Sharon Bell Mathis
Joyce Carol Thomas
Mildred Pitts Walter
Brenda Wilkinson

CHRONOLOGICAL LIST OF AUTHORS

The dates to the right of the author's name indicate the date of the author's initial publication.

Lucy Terry (1746)
Phillis Wheatley (1767)
Mary Prince (1831)
Maria W. Stewart (1831)
Jarena Lee (1836)
Zilpha Elaw (1840)
Ann Plato (1841)
Nancy Prince (1850)
Rebecca Cox Jackson (1857)
Mary Seacole (1857)
Frances Ellen Watkins Harper (1859)
Eliza Potter (1859)
Harriet E. Wilson (1859)
Harriet Ann Jacobs (1861)
Mattie Jane Jackson (1866)
Elizabeth Hobbs Keckley (1868)
Julia A. J. Foote (1879)
Clarissa Minnie Thompson Allen (1885)
Octavia Victoria Rogers Albert (1890)
Amelia E. Johnson (1890)
Lucy Delaney (1891)
Ida B. Wells Barnett (1892)
Anna Julia Hayward Cooper (1892)
Victoria Earle Matthews (1893)
Henrietta Cordelia Ray (1893)
Amanda Berry Smith (1893)
Katherine Davis Chapman
    Tillman (1893)
Gertrude Bustill Mossell (1894)
Kate Drumgoold (1898)
Olivia Ward Bush-Banks (1899)
Alice Dunbar-Nelson (1899)
Pauline Elizabeth Hopkins
    (Sara A. Allen) (1900)
Angelina Weld Grimké (1900)
Susie King Taylor (1902)
Ruth D. Todd (1902)
Fannie Barrier Williams (1902)

Annie Louise Burton (1909)
Madame Emma Azalia Smith
    Hackley (1916)
Georgia Douglas Johnson (1918)
May Miller (1920)
Gwendolyn Bennett (1923)
Jessie Redmon Fauset (1924)
Helen(e) Johnson (1926)
Dorothy West (1926)
Marita Bonner (1927)
Nella Larsen (1928)
Mercedes Gilbert (1931)
Shirley Graham DuBois (1932)
Zora Neale Hurston (1934)
Juanita Harrison (1937)
Ann Petry (1939)
Ellen Tarry (1940)
Elizabeth Laura Adams (1941)
Naomi Long Madgett (1941)
Margaret Walker (1942)
Gwendolyn Brooks (1945)
Beatrice Murphy (1945)
Alice Childress (1949)
Rosa Guy (1954)
Sara Elizabeth Wright (1955)
J. California Cooper (1956)
Pauli Murray (1956)
Lorraine Hansberry (1958)
Paule Marshall (1959)
Margaret Esse Danner (1962)
Julia Fields (1962)
Adrienne Kennedy (1963)
Pat Parker (1963)
Mary Elizabeth Vroman (1963)
Kristin Hunter Lattany (1964)
Ellease Southerland (1964)
Diane Oliver (1965)
Louise Meriwether (1967)

Alice Walker (1967)
Mari Evans (1968)
Sarah Webster Fabio (1968)
Audre Geraldine Lorde (1968)
Anne Moody (1968)
Carolyn Marie Rodgers (1968)
Lucille Clifton (1969)
Jayne Cortez (1969)
Mae Jackson (1969)
June Jordan (1969)
Sharon Bell Mathis (1969)
Arthenia J. Bates Millican (1969)
Sonia Sanchez (1969)
Mildred Pitts Walter (1969)
Maya Angelou (1970)
Nikki Giovanni (1970)
Toni Morrison (1970)
Ann Allen Shockley (1970)
Pearl T. Cleage (1971)
Angela Y. Davis (1971)
Patricia Joann Gibson (1971)
Frenchy Jolene Hodges (1971)
Elaine Jackson (1971)
Toni Cade Bambara (1972)
Eugenia W. Collier (1972)
Pinkie Gordon Lane (1972)
Aishah Rahman (1972)
Paulette Childress White (1972)
Sherley Anne Williams (1972)
Jeannette Franklin Caines (1973)
Alexis De Veaux (1973)
Virginia Hamilton (1973)
Mildred D. Taylor (1973)
Joyce Carol Thomas (1973)
Angela Jackson (1974)
Barbara Chase-Riboud (1974)
Ntozake Shange (1974)
Gayl Jones (1975)
Brenda Wilkinson (1975)
Mignon Holland Anderson (1976)
Octavia Butler (1976)
Joanne Braxton (1977)
Wanda Coleman (1977)
Edwina Streeter Dixon (1977)
Toi(nette) Marie Derricotte (1978)
Eloise Greenfield (1978)
Beverly Guy-Sheftall (1979)

Gloria Wade-Gayles (1979)
Barbara T. Christian (1980)
Michelle Cliff (1980)
Kathleen Conwell Collins (1980)
Doris Davenport (1980)
Rita Dove (1980)
Jewelle Gomez (1980)
Joyce Hansen (1980)
Marilyn Nelson Waniek (1980)
bell hooks (1981)
Andrea Lee (1981)
Harryette Mullen (1981)
Barbara Neely (1981)
Gloria Naylor (1982)
Marita Golden (1983)
Jamaica Kincaid (1983)
Brenda Marie Osbey (1983)
Claudia Tate (1983)
Linda Beatrice Brown (1984)
Colleen J. McElroy (1984)
Mary Monroe (1985)
Bebe Moore Campbell (1986)
Doris Jean Austin (1987)
Candy Dawson Boyd (1987)
Terry McMillan (1987)
Fatima Shaik
Grace Edwards-Yearwood (1988)
Patricia McKissack (1988)
Tina McElroy Ansa (1989)
Opal J. Moore (1989)
Suzan-Lori Parks (1989)
Barbara Summers (1989)
Shay Youngblood (1989)
Safiya Henderson-Holmes (1990)
Mona Lisa Saloy (1990)
Dori Sanders (1990)
Nikki Baker (1991)
Carolivia Herron (1991)
Connie Porter (1991)
Anna Deavere Smith (1992)
Jewell Parker Rhodes (1993)
Edwidge Danticat (1994)
Carolyn Ferrell (1994)
Patrice Gaines (1994)
Helen Elaine Lee (1994)
Lisa Teasley (1997)
Alice Randall (2001)

ELIZABETH LAURA ADAMS (1909–1982)

BIOGRAPHICAL NARRATIVE

Biographer Elizabeth Laura Adams is remarkable for more than the fact that she converted to Catholicism in the early years of the twentieth century. It is remarkable that she recorded her experience as a spiritual biography that highlighted pivotal events of her life in the context of her spiritual awakening and her subsequent attempts to achieve a certain level of validation as an African American Catholic. Equally important is Adams's tenacity and fortitude in the face of the obstacles of isolation and ignorance that she had to overcome as an African woman and a writer in order to bring attention to her struggles. Carla Kaplan, editor of the most recent reprint of Adams's narrative and other works, provides a rich sociohistorical context in which to read Adams's work and a valuable literary-critical overview. Kaplan rightly argues that Adams's text demonstrates the same double-voiced strategy that is common in the African American narrative tradition. "[Adams's] story of acquiescent, obedient girlhood is laced with private, sometimes coded rebellion. Her frailty and passivity mask resolve and determination. Even her use of the conversion narrative, an often formulaic genre . . . functions in coded, or double-voiced ways" (xviii).

Elizabeth Laura Adams was born on February 9, 1909, in Santa Barbara, California, to Lula Josephine Holden Adams, a teacher at the Los Angeles School of Art and Design, and Daniel Adams, a Los Angeles headwaiter. Upon her marriage to Daniel Adams, Lula became a full-time mother and homemaker. The eldest of two children, Adams became the only child after the death of her infant brother. The Adams family lived a comfortable, middle-class existence; however, they were careful not to encourage self-indulgence in their daughter. For example, in *Dark Symphony*, the author uses an analogy to describe the success of their discipline. "By the time I was nine years of age my parents had trained me to respond to their commands by a gesture. If they had placed me in a circus I would have won out in competition with a well-trained seal without the slightest effort" (Adams 60). They "trained" Adams to be self-sacrificing and an exemplary Christian.

Adams came of age during the Depression years and, to some extent, records her experience in the context of that time of national economic depression. Her parents loved her, but they would not shield her from the hard facts of life. Adams experienced the deaths of her infant brother, great-grandmother, and grandparents, all within a short length of time. Her parents' response to her significant emotional and psychological distress was to demand that she "face the cruel realities of life" (Adams 37). The Adams's parental focus on discipline and restraint extended to the child's encounters with racism, which started in grade school. Adams's mother practiced a Christian refinement of Booker T. Washington's strategy of accommodation, to the extent that her response to her daughter's "awakening of racial consciousness" was to insist that if she could not "love [her] enemies," then she would not openly rebel. Adams's father was less "forgiving" and told his daughter that during his own youth he had physically fought back when a white person had called him a "nigger"; however, he bowed to his wife's discretion and encouraged his daughter's passivity.

The Adams's strict discipline was tempered by their encouragement of their daughter's imagination and musical abilities. In her autobiography, Adams credits her teachers (and later friends and clergy) for recognizing and encouraging her propensity for dreaming and creativity. In junior high school, she began developing skills as a musician and a writer and had aspirations to become a concert violinist, but illness forced her to turn away from the physically demanding challenges of public music career. During this time, Adams had begun to attend the Catholic Church, but the premature death of her father influenced Adams's turn to religion in earnest.

After formerly rejecting Adams's requests to join the Catholic Church, her mother granted permission for her to join the Church after her graduation from high school. However, even the Catholic Church was not immune to racial prejudice. In *Dark Symphony* Adams recounts one such instance when she took Holy Communion at the altar rail and noticed how the clergyman wiped the chalice before passing it to the white communicants. Having experienced prejudice in the Catholic Church, Adams reflects on prejudice in other churches: "I wondered: What about God—dogmas and creeds? . . . What sort of God would lay down a lot of rules and then not make a way for them to be observed" (126)? Despite these social issues and theological concerns, Adams converted to Catholicism and later enrolled in convent classes with the intention of becoming a nun.

By the mid-1930s, Adams had made preparations to join the convent, but again, she had to relinquish this dream in order to aid her mother, who by this time had separated from her abusive second husband. Adams supported her mother until her death in 1952. During this same period, Adams began to publish poetry in the Catholic journal, *Torch*. She also published short "religious musings" in *Sentinel of the Blessed Sacrament* and poetry in the *Westward*. In 1940, she began publishing her "spiritual autobiography" in serial form under the title "There Must Be a God . . . Somewhere." This series ran from 1940 to 1941. In 1942, she published the entire autobiography with a Catholic press under the title *Dark Symphony*. According to Kaplan, "the book became a best seller among Catholics and was translated into Dutch and Italian, in addition to being published in Great Britain. Adams sold nearly 15,000 copies and received over $5,000 in royalties. For a while, she even received fan mail that was published in the Catholic press" (xvii).

Adams makes the point in her narrative that not all white people and not all Catholics were prejudiced or insensitive. "Her affiliations with the Catholic community, with publishers and editors of the Catholic publications like *Torch* and the Blessed Martin Guild may have provided Adams with not only 'tranquillity,' but also a way to fight for racial justice without seeming 'controversial' or ill-mannered" (Kaplan xli). During the mid-1930s, probably close to the publication of "There Must Be a God . . . Somewhere," Adams became a "Franciscan Tertiary, a member of what is called The Third Order, one who while secular takes vows to live by moderation, temperance and daily prayer and to remain in his or her current state—whether married or unmarried" (Kaplan xix). She had long admired the work of Tertiaries such as the Sister of Social Services in Los Angeles, California, for their work in the community.

Dark Symphony, published in 1942, was the literary high point of Adams's public career. However, her sporadic illness and her mother's illness and dependency after her divorce from her second husband made it difficult for Adams to pursue a full-time writing career. In the ten-year period following publication of the book, Adams spent much of her time caring for her mother and pursuing a variety of jobs, including that of a domestic worker, office worker, and service-industry employee. After 1952, Adams seemed to have faded from public view, with the exception of brief mention in *The National Catholic Almanac* in 1942 and 1943 under the listings of "contemporary authors" and "Recommended Books," respectively, and mention (through 1959) in *The Almanac*'s "Gallery of Living Catholic Authors" section. Kaplan notes that Adams was "living in Santa Barbara, California as late as 1970 and perhaps as late as 1980" (Kaplan xxii). Recent findings reveal that Adams died on September 9, 1982.

MAJOR WORKS

Dark Symphony belongs to the tradition of spiritual autobiography, dating back to St. Augustine's *Confessions* (sixth century) and including the conversion narrative of Olaudah Equiano's eighteenth-century prototype for the African diasporic slave narrative. Within the tradition of African American women's spiritual narratives, Adams's narrative can be considered along with nineteenth-century evangelists Zilpha Elaw and Jarena Lee and twentieth-century writer Estella Conwill Majozo. Beyond the formal properties of the spiritual narrative (which may not strictly obtain), all of these writers believe they were "called" to serve God and spread the Gospel in some capacity, whether in the secular world or the religious world. To some degree they all express the conviction that their writing is an emancipatory act, in the sense that they use their voices and their "representative" lives for the purpose of enlightenment. Elaw, Lee, and Adams were all officially affiliated with the Church in some capacity, their differences in religion or denomination notwithstanding.

Dark Symphony is conservative in tone, and, as Carla Kaplan has observed, not readily identifiable as a "New Negro" or "Harlem Renaissance" product, in spite of Adams's identification as a member of "the New Negro" generation. The earlier serialized version, "There Must Be a God . . . Somewhere" (1940–1941), demonstrates a stronger racial and gendered identity, as evidenced by the explicit subtitle, "A Colored Convert's Spiritual Autobiography." According to Kaplan, in the earlier version, as well as Adams's earlier work in general, there is an "interesting formal and imaginative playfulness." On the other hand, there is also a "hard-edged grimness . . . which accords with the realism of the New Negro writing. Kaplan suggests that the deliberate blandness of the latter version can be attributed to the author's acquiescence to the editorial staff and their concerns with commercial viability and avoidance of perceived controversy.

The differences between the earlier version and the book-length version are apparent from the first line. The former opens: "The majority of newspapers and magazine articles about my people are written by authors of other races. Now and then a broad-minded Caucasian editor permits a Negro to sketch the lives of our people, but most writers are men" (Adams 212). Compare this passage to the opening lines of *Dark Symphony*: "My life, as a very small child, was filled with happiness. I saw only the beauty of rose coloured dawns. No clouds were visible to darken my path" (Adams 7).

Race pride and the sense of outrage against social and political injustices that are common to writings of the New Negro era are more apparent in the earlier narrative, as well as in earlier essays such as "She Talks Like We Do," written in epistolary form and addressed to "Sister Aloysius" and the "Sisters of the Dominican Sisters of the Perpetual Rosary." In the latter prose piece, Adams expresses her gratitude to the Sisters and explains why their continued support is necessary: "The Negro either becomes spiritual and decides to keep his or her vision upon the Compassionate Face of the Savior and tries not to mind the stumbling blocks . . . the suffering and pain that living in this world brings . . . or the Negro loses faith" (261). For Adams, these "stumbling blocks" are often acts of insensitivity or ignorance. She cites the experience that provides the title for the essay. "I can recall how hurt I was one day while working in the home of one who was fair to hear her say to her guest (and nodding in my direction): 'She talks like we do' " (263).

Adams's last known creative piece is a prose poem, "The Last Supper" (1943), "as told to her by a Caucasian priest" (266). Significantly, it features a "doomed" character who is identified as both a "convict" and a "Prince," but perhaps most telling is the fact that the character is also a "New Negro." The priest relates the story of his brief acquaintance with Joseph, an African American man, convicted of murder and condemned to die. As his counselor and Confessor, the priest is disturbed by Joseph's seeming indifference to his fate. The warden's description of this "convict" is significant for its contradiction: "Prince of Prisoners, and a Catholic strayed from his faith" (272).

Given what he has learned about Joseph, the priest recollects what he knows about the race, and confesses that he can find no egregious fault with them and, in fact, admires the work of poet, Paul Laurence Dunbar, "Singer of songs—dreamer of dreams" (270). In response to the priest's recollection, the warden describes Joseph as "the type of Colored youth / Known today as *The New Negro*. / To no man has he confided the secrets of his soul." The priest is therefore surprised when Joseph asks him to hear his confession. Joseph does not confess to murder, but he does confess the need to "forgive an enemy" and proves himself to be knowledgeable of the Holy Sacraments and by quoting "verbatim several passages from the Confessions of Saint Augustine" (276). After Joseph has been executed the priest learns the truth: "A year later a man of another race / Pleaded guilty to the murder charge / For which Joseph had paid / The penalty with his life" (281). As a kind of personal penance, the priest asks the Bishop to send him to a parish where he "can work among the Colored."

The poem is not didactic, even though the poet deliberately characterizes the unrepentant Joseph as representative of the New Negro who was no longer willing to acknowledge a kind of a priori guilt in order to be "accepted." It is an object lesson on the tragedy that can result from racial prejudice or, in its contemporary manifestation, "racial profiling."

CRITICAL RECEPTION

Critical responses to *Dark Symphony* were divided along racial lines. White critics praised the work for its cautious, conservative tone that seemed to urge cultural and racial rapprochement through Christian faith and perseverance. African American critics, especially those familiar with the ideological positions held by well-known New Negro writers, were of the opinion that Adams "fell short of being a Catholic Dunbar or Johnson" (xlix). The sometimes-stilted language and euphemistic representations of characters and events did not sound "authentic" as an African American woman's voice. Kaplan remarks, "There was no natural or ready-made audience for her. Negotiations both divided audiences and controversies over African Americans and the Catholic church must have sometimes felt like 'marching' through land mines. No wonder that Adams's African American contemporaries sometimes questioned whether she was truly up to the task and whether her voice came through, strongly and clearly as her own" (xlix).

In *Witness to Freedom: Negro Americans in Autobiography*, Rebecca Chalmers Barton places several writers under the topic "Experimenters." In support of this designation, she argues that these particular narratives of the 1930s and 1940s fore-ground the search for "individual self-expression. The value contained in being true to one's self outweighs any considerations of race" (Barton 87). Barton's observation does not appreciate Adams's divided allegiances: her ideological allegiance to New Negro writers and rhetoric; her allegiance to the Catholic Church and within the Church, the Sisters with whom she identified and aspired to emulate; and African American women who worked as domestics and industrial workers in a nation that had historically and culturally devalued them.

Even Adams's identification of herself as a New Negro is complex. She cites Elise Johnson McDougal, Langston Hughes, and Alain Locke, African American intellectuals who defined New Negro from a sociohistorical and political perspective. Adams also cites Edwin R. Embree, a white sociologist and author of *Brown America*, to support her arguments. His interpretation of "the New Negro" and his demand for ethical treatment of the "new race" is based, in part, on "blood admixture" that is a byproduct of the institution of slavery in the United States and accounts for the "Negro's" mixed lineage. Adams interpreted New Negro as a "thinking Negro" by conflating the cultural and political definitions of Alain Locke and the cultural-biological-based theory of Embree. Though she was not alone in her opinion (W.E.B. DuBois and Zora Neale Hurston, in their writings, expressed similar views), Adams's theories did not make her popular with African American critics of her day.

BIBLIOGRAPHY

Works by Elizabeth Laura Adams

"The Art of Living Joyfully." *Torch* (December 1942): 29.
"Children under Fire." *Torch* (November 1943): 29.
"Consecrated." *Westward* (October 1936): 29–32.
"The Country Doctor." *Torch* (May 1942): 31.
Dark Symphony. New York: Sheed & Ward, 1942.
"The Finding of Soul." *Sentinel of the Blessed Sacrament* (October 1930): 97–101.
"Hypocrisy." *Torch* (June 1942): 24.
"The Last Supper." *Torch* (June 1943): 9–12.
"Our Colored Servants." *Torch* (September 1941): 16–17.
"She Talks Like We Do." *Interracial Review* (October 1940): 153–54.
"The Summons." *Torch* (May 1941): 16, 32.
"There Must Be a God . . . Somewhere." *Torch* (October 1940): 4–6; (November 1940): 19–20, 30; (December 1940): 9–10; (January 1941): 16–18; (February 1941): 10–11; (March 1941): 23–24, 29. (Serialized.)
"Until I Found You." *Westward* (July 1936): 30–31.
"Yes, I'm Colored." *Westward* (October 1938): 24–25.

Studies of Elizabeth Laura Adams's Works

Barton, Rebecca Chalmers. *Witness for Freedom: Negro Americans in Autobiography.* New York: Harper & Brothers, 1948, 123–24.
Braxton, Joanne M. *Black Women Writing Autobiography: A Tradition within a Tradition.* Philadelphia: Temple University Press, 1989, 140.

Brignano, Russel A. *Black Americans in Autobiography.* Chapel Hill, NC: Duke University Press, 1983, 3.

David, Jay. *Growing Up Black.* New York: William Morrow, 1968, 60–70.

Dwyer, Joseph. Rev. of *Dark Symphony. Torch* (June 1942): 27.

Kaplan, Carla. "Introduction," "I Wanna March," and "*Dark Symphony* and Other Works." In *African American Women Writers, 1910–1940,* edited by Henry Louis Gates, Jr., and Jennifer Burton, xvii–lvii. New York: G. K. Hall, 1996.

LaFarge, John. "One God for All." Rev. of *Dark Symphony. A Catholic Review of the Week* (May 30, 1942): 215.

Lewis, Theophilus. Rev. of *Dark Symphony. Interracial Review* (May 1942): 20–81.

Mathews, Geraldine O. *Black American Writers, 1773–1949: A Bibliography and Union List.* Boston: G. K. Hall, 1975.

Russell-Robinson, Joyce. "Elizabeth Laura Adams." In *African American Authors, 1745–1945,* edited by Emmanuel S. Nelson. Westport, CT: Greenwood Press, 2000.

Scally, Mary Anthony. *Negro Catholic Writers, 1900–1943: A Bio-Bibliography.* Detroit: Walter Romig, 1945, 19–23.

Tarry, Ellen. Rev. of *Dark Symphony. Catholic World* (July 1942): 504–5.

Hermine Pinson

OCTAVIA VICTORIA ROGERS ALBERT (1853–1889)

BIOGRAPHICAL NARRATIVE

Octavia Victoria Rogers Albert, biographer, was born to slave parents on December 24, 1853, in Oglethorpe, Georgia. The Reconstruction efforts enabled Albert to enter Atlanta University, where she studied to become a teacher. In 1873, she taught in Montezuma, Georgia; it was there she met Dr. Aristide Elphonso Peter Albert, a fellow teacher three years her senior and her future husband. They were married in 1874 and possibly had two daughters, Laura and Sarah (Gardner 16), although some sources refer to Laura as their only daughter (Ravi 7). In 1878, the Alberts moved to Houma, Louisiana. There, they opened their house to former slaves, providing not only food but also lessons in reading and writing and some solace through the readings of the Bible. The Alberts moved to New Orleans in late 1879. While living in Oglethorpe, Albert was a member of the African Methodist Episcopal Church but converted to the Methodist Episcopal Church in 1875. She died on August 19, 1889.

MAJOR WORKS

Albert's only book, *The House of Bondage*, was initially serialized in *Southwestern Christian Advocate*, a major regional Methodist Episcopal newspaper, where it first appeared in 1890, several months after her death. As her husband and daughter Laura indicate in the book's preface, New Orleans received the stories with great enthusiasm and numerous letters flooded the editor's office, insisting that the stories be published in book form. *The House of Bondage* is, in the words of Albert's husband, "a panoramic exhibition of slave-life, emancipation, and the subsequent results" and "an unpretentious contribution to an epoch in American history that will more and more rivet the attention of the civilized world as the years roll around" (v).

The book consists of first-hand accounts of several former slaves, Aunt Charlotte, Uncle John and his wife, Lorendo, Aunt Sallie, Uncle Stephen, Uncle Sephas, and Colonel Douglass Wilson, who relate not only their own experiences but also the experiences of many others. Two major themes can be discerned in the text: the suffering of slaves and the importance of religion. While Catholic religion undergoes uncompromising criticism in Albert's book, "'Merican or Protestant religion" is presented as a source of hope and resistance (38). The slaves' narratives address spousal and family separation so common during slavery and the slaves' brutal treatment in the hands of their masters and mistresses. Attention is drawn also to the issues related to the Reconstruction period, namely ex-slaves' alcoholism, homelessness, lack of education, and continuing separation of their families as well as the Ku Klux Klan, the Black Codes of 1865, and the deficient assistance to the ex-slaves from the churches in the South.

CRITICAL RECEPTION

While parts of Nanette Morton's dissertation address Albert's *The House of Bondage*, Frances Smith Foster offers the only extensive study of this collection of narratives. Foster outlines the similarities and connections between *The House of Bondage* and the works of other African American women authors, namely Frances Harper's *Sketches of Southern Life*, placing Albert within the African American female literary context of the time. Foster also points to the black folk dialect preserved by Albert in her transcription, which contributes to the natural flavor and authenticity of the historical record. Stressing the book's demythologizing character, Foster approaches Albert's work as "an act of appropriation and redesign" (162) and juxtaposes it with Thomas Nelson Page's *In Ole Virginia*, whose sentimentality and romanticizing of slavery that Albert's narrative directly challenges.

BIBLIOGRAPHY

Work by Octavia Victoria Rogers Albert

The House of Bondage or Charlotte Brooks and Other Slaves, Original and Life-like, as They Appeared in Their Old Plantation and City Slave Life; Together with Pen-Pictures of the Peculiar Institution, with Sights and Insights into Their New Relations as Freedmen, Freemen, and Citizens. New York: Hunt & Eaton, 1890.

Studies of Octavia Victoria Rogers Albert's Work

Foster, Francis Smith. "Confrontation and Community in Octavia Victoria Rogers Albert's *The House of Bondage*." In *Literary Production by African American Women, 1746–1892*, written by herself. Bloomington: Indiana University Press, 1993.
————. "Introduction." In *The House of Bondage; or, Charlotte Brooks and Other Slaves*, edited by Frances Smith Foster, i–xlii. New York: Oxford University Press, 1988.
Furman, Jan. "Octavia V. Rogers Albert." In *The Oxford Companion to African American Literature*, edited by William L. Andrews, Frances Smith Foster, and Trudier Harries, 10–11. New York: Oxford University Press, 1997.
Gardner, Eric. "Albert, Octavia Victoria Rogers." In *The Greenwood Encyclopedia of African America Literature*, edited by Hans Ostrom and J. David Macey, 16–17. Westport, CT: Greenwood Press, 2005.
McMickle, Marvin A. *An Encyclopedia of African American Christian Heritage.* Valley Forge: Judson Press, 2002.
Morton, Nanette June. "Houses of Bondage, Loopholes of Retreat: Space and Place in Four African American Slave Narratives." Ph.D. diss., McMaster University, Hamilton, Ontario, 2003.
Ravi, Geetha. "Octavia Victoria Rogers Albert." In *African American Authors, 1745–1945: A Bio-Bibliographical Critical Sourcebook*, edited by Emmanuel S. Nelson, 6–12. Westport, CT: Greenwood Press, 2000.

Iva Balic

CLARISSA MINNIE THOMPSON ALLEN (?–?)

BIOGRAPHICAL NARRATIVE

The oldest of nine children, essayist Clarissa Minnie Thompson Allen was the child of Samuel Benjamin Thompson and Eliza Henrietta Montgomery. Politically active, her father was a delegate to the South Carolina Constitutional Convention, 1865. In addition, he served six years in the state legislature and eight years as a justice of the peace. Eliza Montgomery held a higher position in South Carolinian society and helped to elevate her husband's social standing.

Allen's education consisted of attending the Howard School and South Carolina's State Normal School. For a brief period, she was the first assistant at the Howard School. She also worked at the Poplar Grove School in Abbeville and Allen University in Columbia. The well-rounded young teacher taught every subject from history to algebra. No matter how many publications she had, her primary joy in life was educating. After teaching in her native South Carolina, she moved to Texas, teaching first in Jefferson, 1886, and then in Ft. Worth.

MAJOR WORK

Allen's longest effort is titled *Treading the Winepress; or, A Mountain of Misfortune*. Wanting her work to represent societal issues pertinent to African American families, Thompson created forty-one episodes relating to two aristocratic African American families. Giving Columbia, South Carolina, a fictitious name, Capitolia, her fiction takes place in the city in which the characters' adventures unfold. A love triangle includes Doctor Will deVerne, Lenore "Gypsy" Tremaine, and Gertie Tremaine, the sister of Gypsy. The latter character is the protagonist. Mixed ancestry plays a roll in the plot, as does murder, insanity, and death. Concerning murder and death, Walter Tremaine, a priest and Will's brother, is arrested for murder and found guilty. After all the suffering, Gertie spends her life as a Good Samaritan in Capitolia.

Besides this work of fiction, Allen wrote poetry expressing her tea-totaling beliefs; "A Glass of Wine" appeared in the Texas *Blade*. The *Dallas Enterprise* accepted a novelette, *Only a Flirtation*, for publication. In 1892, an address to a teachers' convention in Ft. Worth, "Humane Education," was published in part in the *Afro-American Encyclopaedia*.

CRITICAL RECEPTION

Criticism of Allen's work appeared after she published the first three chapters of her work, *Treading the Winepress; or, A Mountain of Misfortune*, in a religious paper, *The Christian Recorder*. Those responsible for the newspaper felt her content went against the teachings of the African Methodist Episcopal Church. Never published as a novel, the fiction was serialized in the *Boston Advocate*, 1885–1886. Ann Allen Shockley refers to this serialized effort as "long drawn out episodes [that] spill over with unrequited love, murder, insanity, and death..." (145). Unfortunately, Allen is not well remembered as a fiction writer or poet.

BIBLIOGRAPHY

Work by Clarissa Minnie Thompson Allen

Treading the Winepress; or, A Mountain of Misfortune. Out of print.

Studies of Clarissa Minnie Thompson Allen's Work

Shockley, Ann Allen. "Clarissa Minnie Thompson." *Afro-American Women Writers, 1746–1933: An Anthology and Critical Guide*. Boston: G. K. Hall, 1988, 144–50.
Wallace-Sanders, Kimberly. "Clarissa Minnie Thompson." *Oxford Companion to African American Literatur*em, edited by William L. Andrews, Frances Smith Foster and Trudier Harris. New York: Oxford University Press, 1997.

Elizabeth Marsden

MIGNON HOLLAND ANDERSON (1945–)

BIOGRAPHICAL NARRATIVE

Mignon Holland Anderson, short story writer, was born in Cheriton, Northampton County, Virginia. She earned her B.A. from Fisk University (1966) and her M.F.A. from Columbia University School of the Arts (1970). She began teaching English at the University of Maryland Eastern Shore in 1992.

MAJOR WORKS

Anderson's short story, "In the Face of Fire I Will Not Turn Back," affords the reader entrance into black female consciousness from her beginnings in Africa to mid-twentieth-century America. The lower eastern shore of Virginia provides the setting for Anderson's major works that depict the lives and deaths of African Americans strug gling to survive the harsh realities of an overtly racist society. The structure of her short story collection, *Mostly Womenfolk and a Man or Two*—as indicated by the subtitle "Born a Child to Struggle and to Die" and reflected in the section headings—introduces the reader to several African American characters linked to one another through blood and/or community. The stories depict the loss of African culture and racial unity, resulting from the displacement caused by slavery, that turns the minds of many African Americans "as white and cold as the snows of late winter" (73), causing them to become "convinced that blackness was somehow an affliction because it was easier to think of it that way" (38), easier to appropriate white culture than to fight against racial oppression.

Two of the characters from *Mostly Womenfolk*, the undertaker Turner Allen and his daughter Carrie, reappear in *The End of Dying*, the story of the Allens and their community that continues to depict the fear and degradation—the segregation, verbal abuse, mental and physical torture, even lynchings—experienced by African Americans. Anderson tells the stories of those who cannot speak for themselves, whose stories might otherwise remain untold—those who, like Earl Togan, were lynched, or who, like Carrie Allen, were rendered mute by unspeakable horrors. *The End of Dying* also explores the dangers of African Americans themselves falling victim to racist thinking as Stella Allen struggles with her life-long belief that her looks allow her and her children to be better off than those of her race who are darker skinned. Turner explains to his wife that her beliefs have been tainted by the view of white supremacy, that

White people don't really care about us, anymore than they care about any other coloured folks. "Good hair" and light skin don't mean a thing when you get down to it, except that he's managed to set us against one another, fighting our own little battles of racism within. We are all encouraged to hate ourselves, to be bigots for the racists. You've got to see that. We need unity if we're going to survive. We have to love ourselves. (47)

The text conveys the idea that African Americans must listen to their own voices, not to the voice of white supremacy, and can effectively battle racism only by learning to love themselves, to embrace their history and their race, and to persevere with dignity, to stop the bloodshed as Carrie does when she hears Earl's voice and buries the food intended for Shorty King that she has tainted with arsenic, "the slave's remedy."

CRITICAL RECEPTION

In his review of *Mostly Womenfolk and a Man or Two*, George Kent notes that the form realized by each piece is unique, and generally closer to the form of a tale with the power to "render folk values" than to that of the conventional short story. While Anderson's tales "effectively [evoke] important moments in the emotional and psychological history" of African Americans, their strongest impact is attributable to her subjects' abilities to "express inner beauty" and the "spiritual essence of humanity" even in the face of loss and destruction. Yet, despite her skill and capacity to depict fundamental issues important to African American history in an exceptionally engaging lyrical prose, to date there has been virtually no critical response to Anderson's work.

BIBLIOGRAPHY

Works by Mignon Holland Anderson

The End of Dying. Baltimore: America House, 2001.
"In the Face of Fire I Will Not Turn Back." *Negro Digest* 17 (August 1968): 20–23.
Mostly Womenfolk and a Man or Two: A Collection. Chicago: Third World Press, 1976.

Studies of Mignon Holland Anderson's Works

Kent, George. Rev. of *Mostly Womenfolk and a Man or Two*. *Black Books Bulletin* 4.4 (1976): 52–53.
Tarver. Australia. "Mignon Holland Anderson." *The Oxford Companion to African American Literature,* edited by William L. Andrews, Frances Smith Foster, and Trudier Harris. New York: Oxford University Press, 1997, 103–4.

Teresa Clark Caruso

MAYA ANGELOU (1928–)

BIOGRAPHICAL NARRATIVE

It is impossible to distill autobiographer, dramatist and poet Maya Angelou's artistic contributions down to one particular genre. She is best known for her ability to create beauty out of bleakness; therefore, it is fitting that each of Angelou's texts wrestles with the possibilities of the human soul. With lyrical imagery and insightful reflection, Angelou penetrates the umbrage of twentieth-century questions about black female existence by considering the most intimate aspects of her own experience in light of larger ideological, social, and political movements.

Angelou proclaims that whenever she uses "the first person singular" she is really speaking "about the third person plural" (Russell 8). In fact Angelou's life and career provide a palpable testament both to her ability to transcend prescribed notions of black existence and her own openness to human potential. She is a best-selling author, poet, singer, songwriter, actress, playwright, dancer, producer-director, civil-rights activist, historian, and educator. She is fluent in six languages including Arabic, French, Italian, Spanish, and West African Fanti. Her legendary odyssey has taken her around the globe—from racing cars in Mexico to teaching modern dance and drama at the Rome Opera House in Rome, Italy, and at the Habima Theatre in Tel Aviv, Israel; from working as an editor of the *Arab Observer* in Cairo, Egypt, to writing and teaching in Ghana, West Africa, as a featured editor for the *African Review*, and as assistant administrator at the University of Ghana in West Africa.

Her travels are matched equally by her many achievements. She is a woman of many firsts. As a young adult, she was the first African American to collect fare on the Market Street cable car line in San Francisco. In 1972, she was the first African American woman to write and score a major motion picture, *Georgia Georgia* starring Diana Sands. She is the first African American woman admitted to the Directors Guild of America. She is the first African American with the longest running book on the *New York Times* best-seller list for *I Know Why the Caged Bird Sings* (nonfiction paperback for two years). And in January 1993, Angelou became the first woman and second poet in U.S. history to write and perform an original work for a presidential inauguration, for William Jefferson Clinton the forty-second president of the United States.

Yet, Angelou's magnum opus is her six-volume autobiographical book series which explores her life from childhood to the inception of her critically acclaimed first novel, *I Know Why the Caged Bird Sings*, which was nominated for the National Book Award. She has also published six volumes of poetry among others: *Just Give Me a Cool Drink of Water 'fore I Die* (1971), which was nominated for the Pulitzer prize; *Oh Pray My Wings Are Gonna Fit Me Well* (1975); *And Still I Rise* (1978); *Shaker, Why Don't You Sing?* (1983); *Now Sheba Sings the Song* (1987); and *I Shall Not Be Moved* (1990), and *The Complete Collected Poems of Maya Angelou* (1994).

Born Marguerite Annie Johnson on April 4, 1928, in St. Louis, Missouri, Angelou experienced a tumultuous childhood. She is the daughter of Bailey Johnson, a naval dietician and doorkeeper, and Vivian Baxter, a realtor and nurse, who were divorced by the time she was three years old. As a result, Angelou and her brother Bailey lived in California, Missouri, and rural Arkansas shuffling between their mother and paternal grandmother, Annie Henderson. She and Bailey finally returned to their mother in San Francisco when she was thirteen years of age and remained there until they were on their own. Her life can appropriately be described as being in constant flux. The popular and award-winning *I Know Why the Caged Bird Sings*'s narrative primarily addresses the ten years she lived in Stamps, Arkansas.

In this seminal work, Angelou reveals and explores her childhood experiences with racism in the south and her traumatic sexual assault by her mother's boyfriend at the age of eight years. The latter experience changed the trajectory of her life. After her assailant was convicted and subsequently murdered by her uncles, she refused to speak for five years, retreating into silence and finding refuge in books. As a result, Angelou became an avid reader and observer. These writers and texts became her mentors and teachers. Her subsequent work, as a result, embodies a life-affirming ethos containing bitter honesty about the struggles in her life. In her revelation, she captures a truth that resonates with readers around the world.

The arts became her avenue of expression. She has received numerous honors and awards from various humanitarian, artistic, and academic institutions including nearly fifty honorary degrees, and a lifetime appointment as the Reynolds Professor of American Studies at Wake Forest University in North Carolina. Angelou has also written, produced, directed, and starred in several productions for stage, film, and television. However, it was not until she moved to New York in the late 1950s with the Harlem Writers Guild that Angelou discovered her literary voice.

Interestingly, Angelou's professional career began as a dancer. She studied dance with Pearl Primus in New York and in 1954 Angelou landed her first notable role. Sponsored by the U.S. State Department, Angelou was a featured cast member of George Gershwin's *Porgy and Bess* as Ruby. The production toured twenty-two countries in Europe and Africa through 1955. Subsequently, she soon became a noted actress in the Off-Broadway production of Genet's *The Blacks* in 1960–1961, which won the Obie Award in 1961 for the Best Broadway play. In 1973, Angelou was nominated for a Tony Award for best supporting actress in her Broadway debut in *Look Away*. And in 1977, she received an Emmy nomination for her portrayal of Nyo Boto (Kunta Kinte's grandmother) in Alex Haley's *Roots*.

MAJOR WORKS

Maya Angelou's work and life are enmeshed. Her work is in essence a tapestry of lyrical language that engages an honest, provocative, and hopeful dialogue about "what it is like to be human" (Russell 8). Each novel functions as a large canvas for themes echoed in her poetry, plays, and screenplays. Her primary goal is to evoke critical self-reflection. Angelou openly embraces the beauty, loss, and contradictions of her past. She does this knowing that the little southern girl from Stamps could never have become the renowned Renaissance woman called Maya Angelou without triumphs and defeats. Angelou, in fact, wages her own revolution and dares her readers likewise to survive and transcend socially constructed ideology designed to control self-understanding and socioeconomic mobility. Her artistry raises important questions about self-creation.

The opening volume of her autobiographical series introduces the unifying themes of black womanhood, motherhood, race, self-acceptance, survival, hope, and renewal. Angelou sees her work as an opportunity for her readers to peer into her world and reflect on their own worlds, a point of critical self-reflection that engages one to observe oneself and concomitantly to observe humanity. She believes autobiography is an act of writing about humanity: "So the person who reads my work and suspects that he or she knows me, hasn't gotten the half of the book, because he or she should know himself or herself better after reading my work. That's my prayer" (Russell 8–9). Subsequent volumes in the series continue to integrate several major themes introduced in the first text.

In *I Know Why the Caged Bird Sings* (1970), Angelou reveals the struggles of her childhood in the 1930s and 1940s, growing up doubly marginalized as a young African American female. The title of *Caged Bird* is an allusion to Paul Laurence Dunbar's poem "Sympathy." The poignant story begins as the three-year-old girl along with her four-year-old brother are uprooted and shipped off from California to their paternal grandmother's house in rural Arkansas when Maya and Bailey's parents divorce. In Stamps, grandmother Annie Henderson, who is God-fearing and fiercely independent, raises the two with a stern southern hand. She owns a grocery store and rental property in the small cotton town. She rents to whites. Henderson's strength and resolve in the community provide Angelou with a powerful early example of endurance.

At the age of seven years when Angelou is sent to St. Louis to live with her mother, her childhood comes to an abrupt end. This happens a year later when her mother's frustrated lover, Mr. Freeman, rapes her. After he is tried and convicted, an angry mob incited by his actions murders him. The whole incident summons forth tremendous pain for Angelou. She retreats into silence, a five year self-imposed space. During this time, Angelou struggles with feelings of complicity, bitterness, anger, and shame. She is eventually sent back to Stamps and there, with the help of Momma Henderson and Mrs. Bertha Flowers, she not only speaks again but also finds her literary voice. Mrs. Flowers contributes to this by reading her literary classics. The children are then sent back to their mother in San Francisco. By the time Angelou is sixteen, however, she is pregnant and gives birth to her son, Guy. Her mother, Vivian Baxter, later becomes a central female figure in her life.

Gather Together in My Name (1974) is the second novel in the series. *Gather Together* focuses primarily on Angelou's journey from adolescence to young womanhood and her ability to survive against extenuating socioeconomic circumstances. The narrative begins in her late teens and continues through her early twenties. With the birth of her now two-month-old son, Angelou takes on the responsibility and challenge of providing for him. The story is an honest exploration of juvenile choices with men and a desire to reconcile those choices with an emerging and more mature self-understanding. The episodes follow her experiences as a singer/dancer, a Creole cook, a bordello madam, a prostitute, and a drug user.

The third book, *Singin' and Swingin' and Gettin' Merry Like Christmas* (1976), introduces Angelou as an artist who is deeply conflicted by motherhood. The story narrates the five years after *Gather Together*, following her into marriage with Tosh Angelos and onto the European stage in *Porgy and Bess*. After three years, her marriage dissolves, and she turns all her attention to the stage. Angelou, however, finds life as an artist too difficult to bear in the absence of her son. She eventually returns home.

The Heart of a Woman (1981) introduces a more seasoned Angelou now nearing thirty. In this text, she explores woman as a self-conscious artist, emphasizing creativity.

The narrative chronicles the beginning of her writing career and her developing political activism. She joins the Harlem Writers Guild and becomes committed to her craft. As she enters the New York artistic community, she personally commits herself to the civil rights movement. Her efforts garner an appointment by Dr. Martin Luther King, Jr., as the Northern Coordinator for the Southern Christian Leadership Conference (SCLC). Angelou is now a stronger and more composed woman and mother, free of the self-doubt disclosed in previous texts.

In her fifth installment, *All God's Children Need Traveling Shoes* (1986), Angelou makes Ghana her home for four years as a writer and editor. She finds herself in a community of African Americans who have migrated to the new independent Ghana under Kwame Nkrumah's rule. She integrates into the fabric of her new country and her new romantic relationship. Her journey is an exploration of blackness both as an African and an Afro-American. In the absence of the white/black dichotomy, which is indicative of the American experience, she finds herself coming to grips with her own notions of American racism and oppression. Here again her experiences as mother follow the trajectory of the life of her now maturing young son who is nearing adulthood. The novel ends with her leaving Guy in Ghana as she begins her journey back to the United States. Guy remains in Ghana to complete his college degree.

A Song Flung Up to Heaven (2002) is the sixth volume and culmination of the series that began in 1970. Here Angelou's experience with grief and sadness over the climate in black America leads her to an important moment in her writing career. The story begins as Angelou returns to the United States from Ghana to work with Malcolm X. Upon returning to California to visit her mother, she is informed that Malcolm X has been assassinated. In an effort to cope with the devastating news, Angelou continues working in the arts, but soon takes a job and moves to Watts in Los Angeles, California. While in Watts conducting market research on African American women, she witnesses the Watts riots of 1965. Three years later Angelou is recruited by King to work on his campaign with SCLC; however, she is confronted with yet another moment of despair. King is assassinated. Angelou becomes inconsolable and isolates herself. It is only when her dear friend, James Baldwin, cajoles her into attending a dinner that she finds a moment of clarity. At this event emerges the idea for *Caged Bird*. This narrative ends with the opening lines of her now classic tale.

CRITICAL RECEPTION

Although Angelou has gained a reputation as a popular poet with "And Still I Rise" and "Phenomenal Woman," two poems that have become a part of popular consciousness, her poetry and screenplays are less well known. Most critics regard Angelou as one of the great voices in contemporary American literature and her work an important contribution to the American literary landscape. By far, critics study her work as a feminist and political text. Although, *I Know Why the Caged Bird Sings* is still the most critically studied and praised in the series.

Some critics argue that the episodic nature of subsequent texts in the series lends itself to open dialogue (an evolution of self), while others have argued that the loose narrative development impedes understanding. Sondra O'Neale in "Reconstruction of the Composite Self: New Images of Black Women in Maya Angelou's Continuing Autobiography," suggests the seeming mendacity of the events recorded help create openness and continuity across the series with the reappearance of characters and themes (34). This openness empowers Angelou to fashion a new self. Pierre Walker likewise argues that the form of the text is the vehicle through which Angelou politicizes the text, both the form and content cohere, and the seeming episodic nature of the text includes valuable juxtapositions. He argues that "to ignore form in discussing Angelou's book, therefore, would mean ignoring a critical dimension of its important political work" (92).

Whatever conclusion one draws about Maya Angelou, the woman, it is clear that her life not only represents the journey of a woman but has major implications as well for the civilization in which she lived. She personifies the peculiar experience of a people. Moreover, because of the background of the civilization in which she lives, her heroic journey is a celebration of the human spirit. Her risky truth-telling, wrapped in poetic song, is a unique gift to the world, and her personal experience preserved in her novels will continue to tell the story why the caged bird sings.

BIBLIOGRAPHY

Works by Maya Angelou

Fiction
All God's Children Need Traveling Shoes. New York: Random House, 1986.
Gather Together in My Name. New York: Random House, 1974.
The Heart of a Woman. New York: Random House, 1981.
I Know Why the Caged Bird Sings. New York: Random House, 1970.
Singin' and Swingin' and Gettin' Merry Like Christmas. New York: Random House, 1976.
A Song Flung Up to Heaven. New York: Random House, 2002.

Poetry
The Complete Collected Poems of Maya Angelou. New York: Random House, 1994.
Just Give Me a Cool Drink of Water 'fore I Die. New York: Random House, 1971.
Oh Pray My Wings Are Gonna Fit Me Well. New York: Random House, 1975.
Shaker, Why Don't You Sing? New York: Random House, 1983.
And Still I Rise. New York: Random House, 1978.

Plays
Ajax, 1974.
And Still I Rise, 1976.
Cabaret for Freedom, 1960.
Gettin' Up Stayed on My Mind, 1967.
The Least of These, 1966.
Moon on a Rainbow Shawl, 1988.

Studies of Maya Angelou's Works

Bloom, Harold, ed. *Maya Angelou's* I Know Why the Caged Bird Sings. Philadelphia: Chelsea House, 1998.
Bloom, Lynn Z. "Maya Angelou 4 April 1928– ." In *Dictionary of Literary Biography*, vol. 38. Detroit: Gale Research Company, 1985, 3–11.
Braxton, Joanne M., ed. *Maya Angelou's* I Know Why the Caged Bird Sings: *A Casebook*. New York: Oxford University Press, 1999.
Christian, Barbara T. "Angelou." In *Contemporary Authors*. New Revision Series, Detroit: Gale Research Company, vol. 19, 1987.

Coulthard, A. R. "Poetry as Politics: Maya Angelou's Inaugural Poem, 'On the Pulse of Morning.'"
   Notes on Contemporary Literature 28.1 (1998): 2–5.

Courtney-Clarke, Margaret. *Maya Angelou: The Poetry of Living.* Foreword by Oprah Winfrey.
   New York: C. Potter, 1999.

Elliot, Jeffrey M., ed. *Conversations with Maya Angelou.* Jackson: University Press of Mississippi,
   1989.

Estes-Hicks, Onita. "The Way We Were: Precious Memories of the Black Segregated South."
   African-American Review 27.1 (Spring 1993): 9–18.

Gottlieb, Annie. "Angelou." In *Contemporary Authors.* New Revision Series, Detroit: Gale Research Company, vol. 19, 1987.

Jaquin, Eileen O. "Maya Angelou (1928–)." In *African American Autobiographers: A Source
   Book*, edited by Emmanuel S. Nelson. Westport, CT: Greenwood Press, 2002.

Juncker, Clara, and Edward Sanford. "Only Necessary Baggage: Maya Angelou's Life Journeys."
   Xavier Review 16.2 (1996): 12–23.

Lupton, Mary Jane. "Singing the Black Mother: Maya Angelou and Autobiographical Continuity." *Black American Literature Forum* 24.2 (Summer 1990): 257–75.

———. "'Spinning in a Whirlwind': Sexuality in Maya Angelou's Sixth Autobiography." *MAWA
   Review* 18.1–2 (2003): 1–6.

McPherson, Dolly. *Order Out of Chaos: The Autobiographical Works of Maya Angelou.* New
   York: Peter Lang, 1990.

Moallem, Minoo, and Iain A. Boal. "Multicultural Nationalism and the Poetics of Inauguration."
   In *Between Woman and Nation: Nationalisms, Transnational Feminisms, and the State*,
   edited by Caren Kaplan, Norma Alarcon, and Minoo Moallem, 243–63. Durham, NC: Duke
   University Press, 1999.

O'Neale, Sondra. "Reconstruction of the Composite Self: New Images of Black Women in Maya
   Angelou's Continuing Autobiography." In *Black Women Writers (1950–1980): A Critical
   Evaluation*, edited by Mari Evans, 25–36. Garden City, NY: Anchor Press/Doubleday, 1984.

Russell, Sandi. "Maya Angelou," *Women's Review* (December 1985): 8–9.

Saunders, James. "Breaking Out of the Cage: The Autobiographical Writings of Maya Angelou."
   Hollins Critic 28.4 (October 1991): 1–11.

Smith, Sidonie. "The Song of a Caged Bird: Maya Angelou's Quest after Self-Acceptance."
   Southern Humanities Review 7 (1973): 365–75.

Tangum, Marion, and Marjorie Smelstor. "Hurston's and Angelou's Visual Art: The Distancing
   Vision and the Beckoning Gaze." *Southern Literary Journal* 31.1 (Fall 1998): 80–96.

Tinnie, Wallis. "Maya Angelou." In *The History of Southern Women's Literature*, edited by
   Carolyn Perry and Mary Louise Weaks. Baton Rouge: Louisiana State University Press,
   2002.

Walker, Pierre. "Racial Protest, Identity, Words, and Form in Maya Angelou's *I Know Why the
   Caged Bird Sings*." *College Literature* 22.3 (October 1995): 91–108.

Joi Carr

TINA McELROY ANSA (1949–)

BIOGRAPHICAL NARRATIVE

Having been born in Macon, Georgia, it is no wonder that essayist, novelist and short story writer Tina McElroy Ansa is a southern writer. She is known for works of fiction that not only capture the imagination of her readers but also bear record of small town African American life from the 1950s through the twenty-first century. Each of her four novels is set in the fictional town of Mulberry which no doubt pays homage to her hometown and her home state of Georgia. Ansa was sent to Catholic school and then to Spelman College in Atlanta, Georgia. It was at Spelman College under the tutelage of renowned scholar Gloria Wade Gayles that Ansa officially claimed her identity as a writer though her love and talent for narrative were established at the feet of her elders when she was a small child.

Beginning in 1971 Ansa's early journey as a writer marked her as a journalist and editor for newspapers like the *Atlanta Journal* and *Constitution* and the *Charlotte Observer*. In 1978 she married filmmaker Joneé Ansa and the family later took up permanent residence on St. Simons Island, Georgia. In the early 1980s Ansa became a full time freelance writer and her work has appeared in magazines, journals, and anthologies of both fiction and nonfiction. Spelman College, Brunswick College, and Emory University are among the sites of her guest lectures and workshops. In 2004 Ansa established the Sea Island Writers Retreats. The Retreats are a series of workshops held on historic Sapelo Island, Georgia, and are designed to provide encouragement and resources for writers of African American literature. Ansa was named the 2005 recipient of the Stanley W. Lindberg Award. Named for the esteemed editor of the *Georgia Review*, the Lindberg award recognizes the author for her contribution to Georgia's literary landscape.

MAJOR WORKS

Ansa's most well-known work is her 1989 novel *Baby of the Family*. It has the distinction of being named a Notable Book of the Year by the *New York Times Book Review* in both 1989 and 1990. The novel also won the Georgia Author Series Award as well as the best book recommendation by the American Library Association in 1989. *Baby of the Family* establishes Ansa as a writer of southern gothic fiction. It depicts the birth and childhood of Lena McPherson, the only female child of a middle-class African American family in 1950s Georgia. Lena is born with a caul over her face which is an indication of psychic abilities. In fact, Lena is plagued with her ability to see ghosts and understand supernatural events. In her mother's attempt to move beyond African American folk beliefs and traditions, Lena is ill equipped to handle her special abilities and suffers ridicule from her peers and a lack of understanding from her family. Although Lena's family does not always embrace her uniqueness, they fill her life with love and she is basically well adjusted and grows up to be quite successful. In *The Hand I Fan With* (1996) the author revisits Lena who in her mid-forties is having a torrid affair with a ghost. Prevalent in both books is love and respect for the agrarian nature of the south. Ansa spends a great deal of time detailing the ficitional town of Mulberry. Not only are its inhabitants vividly drawn but also the inanimate objects like the river or The Place (the juke joint owned by Lena's father) become characters in their own right.

Ugly Ways published in 1993, is Ansa's second novel. Again set in the town of Mulberry it is the story of the Lovejoy sisters who go home to bury their mother. Unlike the McPherson family, the Lovejoys are dysfunctional. The three Lovejoy daughters have been emotionally abandoned by their mother and left to rear and nurture each other. Set in the last decade of the twentieth century, *Ugly Ways* is the antithesis of the strong black mother tale so common to writings by African Americans. It is possible in this novel to see the repercussions when the African American woman chooses not to lend herself to her family. This is particularly devastating for a trio of girls who have a father who is physically present but unable to bridge the generational and gender gaps to help rescue his daughters. When the reader meets the Lovejoy sisters they are burying not only their mother but also their past.

Thematically *Ugly Ways* is typically Ansa as she chooses to have Mudear still present in the narrative as a spirit. While the girls arrange their mother's funeral, Mudear is ever presenting commenting back as the girls work out their fears, frustration, and pain. However, Mudear's ephemeral presence does little to endear her to the audience. Thus, Ansa is committed to depicting a variety of characters interacting in and reacting to a variety of circumstances. The novel does much to expand the African American literary canon's possibilities for presentations.

In 1997 Ansa published her third novel that continues the saga of Lena McPherson. In *The Hand I Fan With* Lena is a woman in her mid-forties who makes up in wealth and influence what she lacks in family and love life. As a middle-aged woman, Lena finds herself the only surviving member of the McPherson family. Her parents and her two brothers have died and Lena is single and without children. Lena's penchant for seeing not only ghosts but also people's true intentions has prevented her from finding true love and the novel opens as she staves off her loneliness with charity work and financial acquisitions. Tickled by breezes when there is no wind blowing and by invisible hands beneath the water of her pool Lena discovers love in *The Hand I Fan With*.

Ansa's fascination with the spiritual world and Lena's connection to it is highlighted when Lena's love turns out to be a ghost. Herman, who has been dead at least a century, is able to give Lena all that she has been missing. He is her friend, confidant, supporter, and, of course, lover. Herman connects Lena not just to the supernatural but also to the physical as he not only awakens corporeal passion but also ignites in her a zest for life. Herman teaches Lena to garden and encourages her at the end of the novel when she must deliver her favorite horse's foal. The conflict of the novel, besides the fact that Lena is having a torrid affair with a ghost, comes in the way the townspeople respond to Lena's new beau. Although no one has seen the new man, they feel the repercussions of Lena's decision to live her own life.

Seemingly written in response to the wave of disconnected, beauty- and consumer-crazed young people driving the culture at the beginning of the new millennium, *You Know Better* (2002) is Ansa's fourth novel. Again set in Mulberry it is the story of the three generations of Pines women, Lily, Sandra, and LaShawndra. Lily is the quintessential African American matriarch who, despite her own teenage pregnancy, manages to go to school, marry, and bring up her daughter. Sandra, too, has an out of wedlock pregnancy and instead of doting on her daughter, LaShawndra, she virtually ignores her and leaves the rearing of the child to Lily. Unsure of anything except a short skirt and a good time, LaShawndra is intent on hitching a ride out of Mulberry and away from the trouble she has caused. Once again the novel's protagonists have close encounters with departed spirits. This time the ghosts of three former Mulberry residents intervene to help each Pines woman heal and move forward. Each ghost, Miss Moses, Nurse Bloom, and Liza Jane, acts as a mirror to help the women face their mistakes and is a catalyst to help them move past the painful experiences in their lives. In addition to Ansa's signature ghosts in the machine is the idea that each woman must understand the past in order to move forward. Each woman seems to be missing a part of herself because she is missing some connection with the past. Ansa often returns to this theme of connect-edness in her novels as a critique of what is problematic in African American personal and family life.

CRITICAL RECEPTION

Much of the criticism surrounding Ansa's work places her firmly within the realm of the southern writer. Elena Shakhovtseva writes of Ansa, "among her clearly Southern themes . . . are . . . the interrelation of past and present, the importance of roots, family ties, and gender roles in black communities" (1). If southern writing and southern African American writing is defined by its love of the idiosyncrasies and idioms that form southern life, then Ansa's writing definitively falls within the category. In addition to her fascination with the south and earth themes like seasons, water, soil, and vege-tation is Ansa's delight in the language of the African American south. Reared in the middle of the century, Ansa occupies a position that bridges the old and new south. She can hear the echoing voices of the grandchildren of slaves as well as the beat of the new millennium south, and the amalgamation is apparent in her writing.

There is not yet an enormous body of criticism regarding Ansa's work. As a Geor-gian who must share the state with writers like Alice Walker and Flannery O'Connor, her place in the pantheon of southern writers is yet to be seen. According to Carol P. Marsh-Lockett, "Ansa's work has been well received. Her works are widely read and taught and bear the hallmarks of enduring American classics" (22). Although Ansa's work is not primarily concerned with the struggle of being black in America or even in the south, her novels still bear witness and record to African American existence. Acknowledging that not all African American families suffer financially or are in a constant battle against racism, Ansa is concerned with what may be more subtle enemies. In each of her novels the spirits who come to deal with the living bring them news from the past. Whether the ghosts remind the protagonists of the fortitude and perseverance of their ancestors, or the strength and dignity that is their legacy, these intervening spirits preach a connectivity without which the African American family cannot survive.

The tendency for Ansa to animate her novels with dead folk is symptomatic of the relationship many African Americans had and continue to have with those who have passed out of physical life. Harkening back to Afrocentric ideologies that extend con-nections between people beyond death, Ansa's characters and her readers do not seem too terribly disturbed at the constant inference of the dead in the affairs of the living. In this sense the author's work links her characters and her audiences with cultural roots that extend at least as far as slavery and arguably all the way back to Africa.

BIBLIOGRAPHY

Works by Tina McElroy Ansa

Baby of the Family. New York: Harcourt, 1989.
The Hand I Fan With. New York: Doubleday, 1996.
Ugly Ways. New York: Harcourt, 1994.
You Know Better. New York: HarperCollins, 2002.

Studies of Tina McElroy Ansa's Works

Bennett, Barbara. "Making Peace with the (M)other By." In *The World Is Our Culture: Society and Culture in Contemporary Southern Writing*, edited by Jeffery Folks and Nancy Summers Folks, 186–200. Lexington: University Press of Kentucky, 2000.
Green, Tara T. "Mother Dear: The Motivations of Tina Ansa's Mudear." *Griot: Official Journal of the Southern Conference on Afro-American Studies, Inc.* 21.1 (Spring 2002): 46–52.
Grooms, Anthony. "Big Bad Mudear." *Callaloo* 17.2 (Summer 1994): 653–56.
Shakhovtseva, Elena. "The Gothic in the Black South Novels of Tina McElroy Ansa." *Speaking in Tongues: The Magazine of Literary Translation*. Online journal of the Institute for Foreign Languages, Far Eastern National University. Vladivostok, Russia. http://spintongues.vladivo stok.com?Shakhovtseva3.htm (accessed February 2005).
Town, Caren J. "A Whole World of Possibilities Spinning Around Her: Female Adolescence in the Contemporary Southern Fiction of Josephine Humphreys, Jill McCorkle, and Tina Ansa." *Southern Quarterly: A Journal of the Arts in the South* 42.2 (Winter 2004): 89–108.
Warren, Nagueyalti. "Echoing Zora: Ansa's Other Hand in *The Hand I Fan With*." *CLA Journal* 46.3 (March 2003): 362–83.

Tarshia L. Stanley

DORIS JEAN AUSTIN (1949–1994)

BIOGRAPHICAL NARRATIVE

Doris Jean Austin was raised in Mobile, Alabama, until she was six years old in a household with her mother Tommie Letitia Austin and grandmother Rebecca Stallwork. Later, the family moved to Jersey City on Belmont Avenue where she attended School 12 and Lincoln High School. There, she received inspiration from her English teacher, Rev. Ercell F. Webb, who encouraged her to write and who also performed her first marriage ceremony. Her mother and grandmother fashioned her life perspective for family tradition of church attendance, church loyalty, and morality by being a part of the Monumental Baptist Church. It was also where she found the characters for her first book, *After the Garden*. This book was noted favorably by the *New York Times Book Review*. Another major work was an anthology Austin coedited, *Street Lights: Illustrating Tales of the Urban Black Experience*. Doris Jean Austin was a journalist, critic, news writer, and novelist and has published in fiction and essay collections internationally. She conducted workshops in Advanced Fiction at Columbia University's School of writing from 1989 to 1994. Austin was a member of the famous Harlem Writers Guild, which she cofounded. According to Maya Angelou, the Harlem Writers Guild was a "loosely formed organization, without dues or membership cards, had one strict rule: any guest could sit in for three meetings, but thereafter, the visitor had to read from his or her own work in progress" (41). In 1984 Austin and fifteen other writers left this group and formed The New Renaissance Writers Guild, fashioned after the young writers of the Harlem Renaissance. Austin saw this group as a way to be a literary force, feeling supported, with members calling each other on a regular basis, borrowing money and other amenities that served to make a close knit community with fellow writers like Arthur Flowers and Terry McMillan. Like the Harlem Renaissance young writers Langston Hughes, Zora Neale Hurston, and others who created the journal *Fire!!* they felt that they had to venture out on their own to prove their convictions: "There has to be a criterion of excellence: we have to make sure we have some power" (*Interview* 107). During that same time, Austin received a PEN Writer's Fund grant and the DeWitt Wallace/Reader's Digest Fellowship Award, among other honors, and spent a highly productive two months at the McDowell's Artist's colony. Doris Jean Austin was also a newscaster for NBC radio, but felt that it was "quick and chilly" and eventually harmful for a writer of fiction (*Interview* 107). Austin was a writer for *Amsterdam News*, *Essence*, and *New York Times Book Review*. She died of liver cancer in 1994.

MAJOR WORKS

Austin's only novel, *After the Garden*, is a tightly woven work of fiction that dares its audience not to feel its deep reverberations of wicked idealism and tainted relationships of its main character, Alzina, as she struggles to balance her need for true love and loyalty to her grandmother who has shaped her point of view in the garden. In the novel Austin develops authentic characters who draw the reader into their lives because the reader understands them. The main character, Elzina, is interesting because she is complex and ambivalent. On one hand, she loves Jessie, but she does not love who he is because who he is goes against everything for whom her grandmother has programmed her.

However, her emotional well-being is tied up with loving Jessie. Like so many grandmothers, Rosalie Thompkins also wants so deeply for her grandchild that everything she lives and breathes is for her. She bargains with God, "Safe passage home to Alabama 'fore I die, and let me see Elzina grown . . . and graduated from a good southern college, please Lord. Amen" (12). This statement, along with Rosalie's resistance/compliance is the underlining principal affecting all of her relationships. Elzina believes she is destined for better things in life; even though she marries Jesse, they continue to live with her grandmother where their lives are tainted daily by this unanswered prayer. Jesse cannot access entry to his manhood: money to open up his own business, even though it is available. Having a child does not add to the marriage, either; Elzina is obsessed about the safety of her son, not that different from how her grandmother expressed concern about her. So, when one of Jesse's sisters, Ollie Mae, is late coming back with the child, it gives Elzina a chance to tell the James family how she really feels, ". . . A James ain't shit" (186). This pinnacle moment in the novel sends the rest of the events into a tailspin: Jesse's indiscretion resulting in the birth of a daughter, his accidental death, and Elzina's nervous breakdown. Her education/renewal begins when she discovers this illegitimate daughter and understands that their connection is what both of them need to survive through life's pains. Austin's style of writing is not storybook, idyllic metaphors, but journals of struggles, tough choices, and disappointments, laced with reality and hope.

Part of the grandmother's story is excerpted from *After the Garden* in the anthology, *Black Southern Voices*, titled "Heirs and Orphans." Early in the story, as a child, Rosalie witnesses her house being burned down with her parents in it. Nevertheless, she and her cousin Moses escape the wicked men seeking their lives; throughout her life she is motivated by constantly hearing her father's voice urging her, "Run baby. You run away from here" (197). Although upon first impression it appears the theme is children's lives altered tragically by the whim of evil men who deny them the right to liberty and the pursuit of happiness, it is really about the memory of the father's voice urging Rosalie to find another path.

"Room 1023" which appears in the anthology edited by Austin, *Street Lights: Illuminating the Tales of the Urban Black Experience*, captures the dire plight of Lelah Vanessa Frederick (Alexander) who is in a woman's hotel, waiting on a check from her soon-to-be ex-husband so that she will not be evicted from her room. She tries to tell the manager that the check is in the mail, but he is not convinced. This tale also shows glimpses of females in contemporary urban America. There is a Cantonese woman who feels that American women are living less than they should be living, while she fails to see that she has assimilated and is less than she was in her culture. There is a clerk in the hotel held together by her sponsors (hotel manager and wife) and can only see her way to being a good citizen. Leland's situation is augmented by the lives of these woman; it may be a man's world, but she takes control momentarily by defying the eviction notice as she defied her husband's demand not to leave; she had all of the comforts of home with him, except she had lost herself. As she lays in waiting under the bed, with no where to go, room 1023 represents the womb where life is enclosed from the outside world tempo-rarily, but her birth is imminent and seems to be beyond her control. Facing the outside world can be painful; however, it is also the consequence of birth, living, and rebirth.

CRITICAL RECEPTION

The *Library Journal*'s review of the anthology *Streetlights* recommends "Room 1023" as one of the best stories; the reviewer feels most of the others are not appealing. The *Publishers Weekly*, on the other hand, states that nearly every story is artful, sensitive to language, contains highly developed metaphors, and puts the aesthetics and the politics side by side. The two reviewers also assessed Austin's major work, *After the Garden*. The *Library Journal* felt that it was graphic and realistic and should be highly recommended for all fiction collectors. The *Publishers Weekly* felt that even though the voices of the characters were convincing, "strong and appealing, the story line is too heavy for them to carry gracefully." They add, however, that the story still has many virtues. The *New York Times Book Review* gives the book a most complimentary review. The reviewer feels that it is eloquent and has many other qualities, including a "very unfirst-novel-like control of technique." He lauds Austin's ability to make her audience see the characters as authentic inside and out.

BIBLIOGRAPHY

Works by Doris Jean Austin

After the Garden. New York: New American Library Penguin Inc., 1987.
"An Almost Perfect Romance." *Essence* 21.10 (February 1991): 56.
"Heirs and Orphans." In *Black Southern Voices*, edited by John Oliver Killens and Jerry Ward, Jr., 192–98. New York: Penguin Group, 1992.
"Looking for Home." In *Breaking Ice: An Anthology of Contemporary African American Fiction*, edited by Terry McMillan. New York: Penguin Books, 1990.
"The Men in My Life." *Essence* 23.7 (November 1992): 44.
"Mind: Taming the Demons." *Essence* 23.1 (May 1992): 106.
Street Lights: Illuminating Tales of the Urban Black Experience. New York: Penguin Books, 1996

Studies of Doris Jean Austin's Works

"After the Garden," *Kirkus Review* 55 (May 15, 1987): 739.
"After the Garden," *Publishers Weekly* 231 (June 12, 1987): 72.
Browne, Phiefer. "Doris Jean Austin." *The Oxford Companion to African American Literature*, edited by William L. Andrews, Frances Smith Foster, and Trudier Harris. New York: Oxford University Press, 1997.
King, Christine. "After the Garden." *Library Journal* 112 (July 1987). 34.
Masello, David. "Harlem Revival." *Interview* 16 (January 1986): 107.
Nelson, Emmanuel S., ed. *Contemporary African American Novelists: A Bio-Bibliographical Critical Sourcebook*. Westport, CT: Greenwood Press, 1997.

Imani Lillie B. Fryar

NIKKI BAKER (1962–)

BIOGRAPHICAL NARRATIVE

Nikki Baker is a pseudonym for novelist Jennifer Dowdell. Although it is known that Baker was born in 1962, other biographical information is purposefully limited. Inquiries to the author requesting biographical information remain unacknowledged. However, interested readers will find readily that Baker's chosen genre is African American lesbian detective fiction, showcasing African American characters in complicated personal and professional situations.

MAJOR WORKS

Baker's major works include four detective novels, which form the Virginia Kelly Series: *In the Game* (1991), *The Lavender House Murder* (1992), *Long Goodbyes* (1993), and *The Ultimate Exit Strategy* (2001). Virginia Kelly, Baker's protagonist in the four novels, is a successful professional working as a stockbroker at an investment firm located in the Midwest. Kelly is a savvy, sexy, well-educated lesbian African American sleuth whose accolades provide her with the social capital she needs to work effectively within the system to solve murder mysteries. *An Encyclopedia of Gay, Lesbian, Bisexual, Transgender, and Queer Culture* notes that "[c]rime fiction has a long tradition of female investigators, but the lesbian mystery novels that proffer an amateur investigator are unimaginable without the kinds of intervention into the workplace that feminism made in the 1970s[,]" of which Baker's *In the Game* is given as an example of such fiction (Munt). *In the Game* explores the possibilities for an African American woman working from a position of elevated socioeconomic status. In fine, Baker's female protagonist finds that she must intervene on behalf of close personal friends who are prime suspects in murder cases for which there seems to be little, if any, hope of genuine criminal investigation. Lesbian politics are central in Baker's published fiction, and her characters interact romantically across racial, social, and economic boundaries.

In addition, Baker has published two novellas in anthologies published by Third Side Press: "Film Noir," published in *Out for Blood: Tales of Mystery and Suspense by Women* (1995) and "Negatives" in *Out for More Blood: Tales of Malice and Retaliation by Women* (1996).

CRITICAL RECEPTION

Baker's body of work can be described as black, lesbian detective fiction. While scholarly responses to Baker's writing are scant, academic interest is growing. Critical receptions to her writing may be found in academic critiques that discuss marginalized texts, but Baker is discussed more freely and frequently and openly in mainstream media sources. Diane Anderson, Editor of *Curve Magazine*, wrote about Baker while at *Girlfriends Magazine* prior to 1998, and there are *Publishers Weekly* critiques of Baker's fiction on Amazon.com. Within the genre of detective fiction, Baker's writing exists in a narrow, highly specific space. Denise Hamilton's announces Nikki Baker's presence on the fiction scene in her essay from the *Los Angeles Times* titled "Black Women Writers Put Their Brand on the Suspense Genre." When Hamilton states "[t]hen there is author Nikki Baker, whose sleuth is a [B]lack lesbian," she is using Baker as an example of a writer whose characters stand apart from the cultural stereotypes that inform detective fiction on varying cultural levels (Hamilton).

As a publishing interest, Baker has been well received and published by such notable feminist and lesbian presses as Third Side Press, Naiad, and Bella Books, Incorporated. At present, her novels are out of print but are available in both new and used editions from online booksellers, and her work is well known to writers of detective fiction. Given the cultural studies discussions in the early 1990s regarding the cloistered nature of gay and lesbian communities thriving at the same time Baker began publishing her novels, characters like Virginia Kelly are symbolic of lively, intellectual discussant groups.

BIBLIOGRAPHY

Works by Nikki Baker

"Film Noir." In *Out for Blood: Tales of Mystery and Suspense by Women*, edited by Victoria A. Brownworth, 23–58. Chicago: Third Side, 1995.
In the Game. Tallahassee: Bella, 1991.
The Lavender House Murder. Tallahassee: Bella, 1992.
Long Goodbyes. Tallahassee: Bella, 1993.
"Negatives." In *Out for More Blood: Tales of Malice and Retaliation by Women*, edited by Victoria A. Brownworth and Judith M. Redding, 215–36. Chicago: Third Side, 1996.
The Ultimate Exit Strategy: A Virginia Kelly Mystery. Tallahassee: Bella, 2001.

Studies of Nikki Baker's Works

Hamilton, Denise. "Black Women Writers Put Their Brand on the Suspense Genre." *Paula Woods' Noir Wave*, January 1, 2006, http://www.woodsontheweb.com/Bio/noir_wave.htm (accessed January 31, 2006).
Klein, Kathleen Gregory. *Great Women Mystery Writers: Classic to Contemporary*. Westport, CT: Greenwood Press, 1994.
Munt, Sally R. "Mystery Fiction: Lesbian, The Urban Dystopia." *GLBTQ, Inc.: An Encyclopedia of Gay, Lesbian, Bisexual, Transgender, and Queer Culture*, January 6, 2006, http://www.glbtq.com/literature/myst_fic_lesbian,4.html (accessed January 31, 2006).

Kimberly Downing Braddock

TONI CADE BAMBARA (1939–1995)

BIOGRAPHICAL NARRATIVE

Novelist, short fiction writer and essayist Miltona Mirkin Cade, the author of *Gorilla, My Love* (1972), *The Sea Birds are Still Alive* (1977), *The Salt Eaters* (1980), *If Blessing Comes* (1987), *Those Bones Are Not My Child* (2000), and the editor of *The Black Woman: An Anthology* (1970) and *Tales and Stories for Black Folks* (1971), went through several name changes before finally deciding to call herself Toni Cade Bambara. Throughout her life she was referred to as Hanifa, Tonal Coda, or Karma Bene Bambara, but the story of how Toni Cade Bambara ultimately *re-named herself* exemplifies what it means to be an artist, particularly a female artist and artist of color, in America:

> Toni Cade Bambara—the minute I said it, I immediately inhabited it, felt very at home in the world. This was my name. It is not so unusual for an artist, a writer, to name themselves; they are forever constructing themselves, are forever inventing themselves. That's the nature of that spiritual practice. ("Deep Sightings and Rescue Missions" 206)

Born and raised in New York, Bambara often sought, with her art, as with her life, to show how important self-definition is for marginalized people. As a child, Bambara was comfortable expressing herself, in part because of her mother, a woman Bambara saw as having "a tremendous respect for . . . the activity of the mind and the privacy of imagination" (Chandler 346). At a young age, Bambara was also a frequent visitor at the Harlem branch of the New York Public Library, where she often encountered and was inspired by poet Langston Hughes (Goodnough D10).

Bambara attended Queens College and received her B.A. in theater arts in 1959. Afterward, Bambara studied in Paris and Italy and received a master's degree from City College of New York in 1964. Bambara served as director of the Colony Settlement House in Brooklyn and taught at several universities including Rutgers University, Duke University, and Spelman College. Over the course of her lifetime, she contributed to a wide variety of periodicals, including the *Negro Digest*, *Prairie Schooner*, *Liberator*, and the *New York Times*.

Later in life, Bambara developed a strong interest in film. Bambara became a filmmaker and a film critic and lecturer. She worked with independent filmmaker Louis Massiah, on *The Bombing of Osage Avenue*, winner of a 1986 Academy Award for best documentary. Bambara's final project was *W.E.B. DuBois: A Biography in Four Voices*, a documentary that was directed by Massiah and written by Bambara, Wesley Brown, Thulani Davis, and Amiri Baraka.

In 1995, Bambara died of cancer in a Philadelphia hospital.

MAJOR WORKS

The Black Woman: An Anthology is a groundbreaking work that includes short stories by Alice Walker and Paule Marshall and poems by Nikki Giovanni and Audre Lorde. *The Black Woman* also contains three essays by Bambara herself: "On the Issue of Roles," "The Pill: Genocide or Liberation," and "Thinking about the Play: The Great White Hope." *The Black Woman* explores a wide range of subjects, including sexism, motherhood, and education. The diverse material of the writers, who engage, enrich, and sometimes contradict each other, makes for a scattered but powerful collection. In the foreword to *This Bridge Called My Back: Writings by Radical Women of Color*, a feminist anthology edited by Cherrie Moraga and Gloria Anzaldua, Bambara writes that it is important that women of color "break through the diabolically erected barriers" and "hear and see each other" (vi). And, Bambara's own anthology seems to reflect that belief, as *The Black Woman* seems a conscious effort to find women from wondrously varied walks of life. These black women define themselves as teachers, counselors, writers, opera singers, social workers, mothers, poets, wives, actresses, travelers, ski-enthusiasts, commercial artists, and cosmic forces (323–27). Moreover, these writers differ stylistically, and the tone often switches even when the writers are examining the same subject.

For example, Gail Stokes's "Black Man, My Man, Listen!" is addressed to black men and reads as a personal and impassioned plea to black men for "comfort" and "reassurance." Stokes's essay expresses emotions ranging from helpless frustration ("I try to make you a man") to passionate anger ("I told them you were now a man!"). This work is immediately followed by a contrasting piece by Jean Carey Bond and Patricia Perry. While both Stokes and Bond and Perry explore black heterosexual relationships, Bond and Perry's essay "Is the Black Male Castrated?" is the more analytical discussion, with its detailed exploration of the array of stereotypes that both black men and black women have had to face. Bambara is clearly comfortable with this juxtaposition of divergent voices: if there is any connection at all among Bambara's selected writers, it is in their awareness of race, gender, and social class, and the sense of urgency that seems to inform through their work. These black women realize that they are in the midst of a historical moment, and they also recognize the importance of defining who they are and how they see the world. In all cases, the writers' words are never mild and serve as clarion calls to action; these are women determined to "make revolution irresistible" ("Foreword" viii).

Told almost entirely in the first person and linked by a funny, tough-talking narrator, Hazel, *Gorilla, My Love* is an achievement. Although *Gorilla, My Love* features glimpses into the life of an adult or near-adult Hazel ("My Man Bovanne" and "The Johnson Girls," for example), most of the collection is told in the voice of a young African American girl. Keeping in mind Bambara's deep love and appreciation of black dialect and culture, it is apparent that Bambara uses black English and African American nicknames to create a sense of community in her stories. In an article written for the *New York Times* about J. L. Dillard's *Black English: Its History and Usage in the United States*, Bambara argues that

Black English is . . . a fusion of a West African deep-base structure with an overlay of African retained and European absorbed and Asiatic and Indian borrowed features; a language that has structural affinities and historical profiles similar to Black French, Black Dutch, Black Portuguese and other "bridge" systems throughout the world; the language habitually used to perceive, record, remember, transmit, abstract, recall, and relate by at least 80 percent of black Americans . . . ("Black English" BR3)

Thus, it is fitting that "Gorilla, My Love," Bambara's often anthologized title story, begins with a discussion on the significance of the name that the black community has given one of the characters: "That was the year Hunca Bubba changed his name. Not a change up, but a change back, since Jefferson Winston Vale was the name in the first place" (13). "Gorilla, My Love" examines life from the perspective of Hazel, a girl who constantly seeks truth in a confusing world of grown-up half-truths and lies, in a land where adults are continuously "playin change-up and turnin you round every which way so bad" (20).

In "Gorilla, My Love," Hazel, who lives in a vibrant African American community that gives everyone a nickname, actually experiences two forms of betrayal. First, Hazel's uncle discards the community nickname. The uncle associates the community's nickname with immaturity; and because he plans on getting married, he is "usin his real name now" (18). The community's nicknames—"Baby Jason," "Big Brood," and Hazel and her friends derisively call the movie matron "Thunderbuns"—are not always complimentary, but they do reveal how people in the community see and identify with one another. Hazel, who attends a school with white teachers who "don't like me cause I won't sing them Southern songs or back off when they tell me my questions are out of order," sees the importance of the community nicknames and refuses to view her uncle's name change as progress. Hazel recognizes the community nickname as a way of knowing someone's true and private self, of sharing a deeper spiritual connection with another. Therefore, the name change not only symbolizes a change in Hazel's relationship with her uncle and the emergence of scary, unfamiliar adulthood, but also suggests a departure from the community and a movement toward a larger world that is dangerous, uncertain, and sometimes tragic. For Hazel, the rejection of the Hunca Bubba moniker is an abandonment of both her and the community in which they live. "I'm a new somebody" (20), proclaims Hazel's uncle, the recently renamed Jefferson Winston Vale, and perhaps he is. Published in *Redbook* in 1971, "Gorilla, My Love," seems to subtly explore, through the loss of the community nickname, the idea of African Americans becoming a "new somebody" in an era where the black pride of the 1960s mingled with the promises of integration.

"Raymond's Run," which appeared earlier in *Tales and Stories for Black Folks*, centers around a race among the neighborhood children. In "Raymond's Run," Bambara allows the community to become a source of strength. Hazel, the narrator, known alternately as "Squeaky" and "Mercury" by members of her community, is determined to win the race. Although Hazel recognizes that she is a part of the community, she remains slightly at odds with it; Hazel partakes in frequent fights with the children in her neighborhood. Once again, Bambara demonstrates the role of the community through the community nickname. The community nickname suggests closeness and familiarity, and when an adult that Hazel does not like calls her Squeaky, her community nickname, she automatically challenges him:

Then here comes Mr. Pearson with his clipboard and his cards and pencils and whistles. . . . We used to call him Jack and the Beanstalk to get him mad . . .

"Well, Squeaky," he says, checking my name off the list and handing me number seven and two pins. And I'm thinking he's got no right to call me Squeaky, if I can't call him Beanstalk.

"Hazel Elizabeth Deborah Parker," I correct him. (28)

At the end of "Raymond's Run," we see the potential for friendship between two girls who were once competitors. Most likely, this potential arises due to a change within Hazel; while the majority of the story had been focused on Hazel's desire for individual achievement, by the story's end, Hazel understands the importance of helping her mentally retarded brother, and she finally moves outside the realm of the individual and into a holistic community space. Hazel's heightened sensitivity to those around her allows her to recognize, finally, a connection between herself and another young female runner who belongs to the same neighborhood.

Likewise, the opening lines of another story in *Gorilla, My Love*, "The Lesson" reveal the strength of the community: "Back in the days when everyone was old and stupid or young and foolish and me and Sugar were the only ones just right, this lady moved on our block with nappy hair and proper speech and no makeup." Sylvia, the narrator of this story, uses black dialect that shows that she knows, understands, and is a part of this community, while oddly, Miss Moore, the teacher with the "proper speech," is somewhat separated from it. Miss Moore's well-meaning attempts to connect with the children of the community are slightly complicated by her inability to belong to the community of adults. Also, Miss Moore does not belong to a church in the community, and this is "one of things the grownups talked about when they talked behind her back like a dog" (87–88). Yet it is Miss Moore's longing to help the community and connect with it on some level that ultimately allows the black adults to grant her entry into their children's lives. And the children do experience intellectual growth as a result of Miss Moore's actions. After Miss Moore takes the lower-income neighborhood children on a visit to the expensive F.A.O. Schwarz toy store, they become aware of the lack of equality in their lives. They begin thinking revolutionary thoughts:

"I think," say Sugar pushing me off her feet like she never done before, cause I whip her ass in a minute, "that this is not much of a democracy if you ask me. Equal chance to pursue happiness means an equal crack at the dough, don't it?" (95)

In "The Lesson," black English plays an important role in that it "emphasizes the children's distance from mainstream white bourgeois culture and power" (Heller 279). Furthermore, Bambara allows Sylvia to use black English to "express her self-confidence, assertiveness, and creativity as a young black woman" (Heller 279). Interestingly, Bambara's decision to have the characters who are most connected to the black community use black English but still have negative feelings about blackness ("And she was black as hell") gives her characters a greater degree of complexity (87). Thus, Bambara's use of black English helps to define her characters and suggests the multi-faceted aspects of the black American experience.

Still, Bambara explores the intricacies of black English not only in "The Lesson," but also in nearly all of the stories in *Gorilla, My Love*. The characters in Bambara's *Gorilla, My Love* continuously use black English and community nicknames to define themselves in relation to each other and to find their own individualized voices. And along with these unique voices, comes a certain expectation of truth: "Cause if you say Gorilla, My Love, you suppose to mean it" (17).

The Salt Eaters, Bambara's acclaimed novel, examines the life of Velma Henry, a Civil Rights Worker who attempts suicide due to her perception of hopelessness and a lack of unity within the black community. The novel itself seems to mock any idea of unity or wholeness. Told from a wide range of perspectives, the novel seems to ask, in varying degrees: "Whatever happened to Third World solidarity?" (91). Minnie Ransom, the flashy "fabled healer of the district" tries to save Velma (1) and convince her of the need for wholeness and unity in her life. Minnie Ransom, a woman "known to calm fretful babies with a smile or a pinch of the thigh . . . to dissolve hard lumps in the body that the doctors at the county hospital called cancer" (113), represents the best of the black community and what can happen if marginalized communities try to heal themselves. Thus, it is "Minnie Ransom's healing energy" that "is necessary to bring Velma back from fragmentation to wholeness" (Collins 39). Over and over again, Minnie asks Velma if she wants to face the world, if she can "afford to be whole" (106), and, at the very end of the novel, the answer appears to be yes. The novel ends with Velma making a crucial decision. Velma has "[n]o need of Minnie's hands now so the healer withdraws them . . . just as Velma, rising on steady legs, throws off the shawl that drops down on the stool a burst cocoon" (295). The novel's ending, while hopeful, also suggests that Velma has had and will have many battles ahead of her:

Velma would remember it as the moment she started back toward life, the moment when the healer's hand had touched some vital spot and she was still trying to resist. . . . And years hence she would laugh remembering she'd thought that was an ordeal. She didn't know the half of it. Of what awaited her in years to come. (278)

The Salt Eaters is a book filled with characters who want to overcome boundaries of race, gender, and class, but who also acknowledge that this may be a near impossible task. Indeed, in *The Salt Eaters*, "Toni Cade Bambara fuses the poetics and politics of postmodernism to create a text exploding with power, yet with a message that is balanced precariously between despair and hope" (Collins 35).

Those Bones Are Not My Child, Bambara's posthumous novel, deals with the Atlanta Child Murders of the 1970s and 1980s. Described as a "masterly if not yet fully balanced work" (Birkerts 17), Bambara examines the lives of Zala and Spence Rawl when their child Sonny disappears. Zala and Spence embark on a desperate search to find their son, and the novel chronicles Zala's "transformation from shocked mother to the empowered activist who confronts government agencies that trivialize Sonny's disappearance" (Benjamin 338). Writer Shanna Greene Benjamin suggests that a "distressed tone" haunts the book, and Bambara admits that *Those Bones Are Not My Child* was a difficult work to write because of the subject matter and the fact that she had several other projects on hand: "In 1981 and 1982, I set the project aside several times" (673). Still, Bambara's descriptions of her obsessions with this case . . . reveal the cost of acting as interviewer, investigator, journalist, essayist, and ultimately fiction writer, pushing herself to complete a work she did not want to write" (Taylor 259).

Perhaps the most significant aspect of Bambara's legacy is her work in the short story genre. In the essay "Salvation Is the Issue," Bambara acknowledges her love for the short story:

Of all the writing forms, I've always been partial to the short story. It suits my temperament. It makes a modest appeal for attention, allowing me to slip up alongside the reader on her/his blind side and grab'm. (43)

While Bambara was indeed a master of the short story, this might have been a mixed blessing. As Bambara herself explained, " . . . the major publishing industry, the academic establishment, reviewers, and critics favor the novel" ("Salvation Is the Issue").

Writing for the *National Observer*, Anne Tyler gives Bambara a mixed review that seems to arise partly from the nature of short story collections themselves. Tyler commends Bambara's use of black English but observes that "collections of a single person's stories are a dangerous business. You may, in fact, begin to find tedious a writer whose stories, taken singly, you've always admired. This is so with Toni Cade Bambara's new collection *The Sea Birds Are Still Alive*" (23).

CRITICAL RECEPTION

Most of Bambara's critical praise arises from the way she uses black English to tell rich, believable, and often humorous stories. *New York Times* critic C.D.B. Bryan writes that " 'Toni Cade Bambara tells me more about being black through her quiet, proud, silly, tender, hip, acute, loving stories than any amount of literary polemicizing could hope to do' " (quoted in Goodnough). However, while Bambara's use of black English creates lively, interesting narratives, some critics wonder if the vivid language masks her characters' real anguish. Literary scholar Mary Helen Washington expresses appreciation for "the power of Bambara's characters," but she also wonders if there might not be "almost too much bravado in these first-person narratives—a blurring of the problems and the grief" (353).

Critics are also impressed by the way that Bambara intersperses an activist mindset into her writings. Critic Elizabeth Muther describes *The Black Woman* as a "pathbreaking, intimate, and incendiary" anthology (447) and she argues that Bambara's female characters "are not diminutive characters, to be outgrown with the coming of age of the movement. Rather, through their precocious insight they anticipate the resistance strategies and forms of collective self-affirmation that will be essential to the survival of community" (449). Furthermore, Bambara offers a glimpse into everyday, working or middle-class black family life, and in these portrayals, Bambara's writing is at its most human, its most complex. Hazel, the narrator of *Gorilla, My Love*, matures as a character in part because she exists in "the liberating and nurturing space of a harmonized and functional African American family" (Muther 449). And, in *These Bones Are Not My Child*, "Bambara creates a persuasive psychological ambiguity... in which the full intensity and complication of family life emerge" (Birkerts 17).

In the preface to *Deep Sightings* Morrison writes, "I don't know if she knew the heart cling of her fiction. Its pedagogy, its use, she knew very well, but I have often wondered if she knew how brilliant at it she was" (ix). Still, if Bambara was unaware of her brilliance, we certainly are. Bambara's work allows us to see the beauty of ourselves, of our own communities, and the language that they exhibit. We are glad for a writer like Bambara, a writer who chose to write "straight-up fiction" that celebrated who and what we are.

BIBLIOGRAPHY

Works by Toni Cade Bambara

"Black English." *New York Times*, September 3, 1972, BR3.
The Black Woman: An Anthology. 1970. Introduction by Eleanor Traylor. Reprint, New York: Washington Square Press, 2005.

"Foreword." In *This Bridge Called My Back: Writings by Radical Women of Color*, edited by Cherríe Moraga and Gloria Anzaldúa. New York: Kitchen Table, Women of Color Press, 1981.

"Gorilla, My Love." In *Gorilla, My Love*, 13–20. New York: Putnam, 1978.

"How She Came by Her Name." In *Deep Sightings and Rescue Missions*, edited by Toni Morrison, 206. New York: Pantheon, 1996.

"The Lesson." In *Gorilla, My Love*, 87–96. New York: Putnam, 1978.

"Raymond's Run." In *Gorilla, My Love*, 28. New York: Putnam, 1978.

The Salt Eaters. New York: Vintage, 1992.

"Salvation Is the Issue." In *Black Women Writers, 1950–1980*, edited by Mari Evans. New York: Doubleday, 1984.

The Sea Birds Are Still Alive. New York: Vintage, 1982.

Tales and Stories for Black Folks. New York: Doubleday, 1971.

Those Bones Are Not My Children. New York: Vintage, 2000.

Studies of Toni Cade Bambara's Works

Benjamin, Shanna Greene. "Those Bones Are Not My Child." *African American Review* 35 (2001): 338–40.

Birkerts, Sven. "Death in Atlanta." *New York Times* 7 (January 2, 2000, late edition): 17.

Chandler, Zora. "Interview with Toni Cade Bambara and Sonia Sanchez." In *Wild Women in the Whirlwind*, edited by Joanne M. Braxton and Andree Nicola McLaughlin. New Brunswick, NJ: Rutgers University Press, 1990.

Collins, Janelle. "Generating Power: Fission, Fusion, and Post Modern Politics in Bambara's The Salt Eaters." *MELUS* 21.2 (1996): 35–47.

Goodnough, Abby. "Toni Cade Bambara, A Writer and Documentary Maker, 56." *New York Times*, December 11, 1995, D10.

Heller, Janet Ruth. "Toni Cade Bambara's Use of African American Vernacular English in 'The Lesson.'" *Style* 37 (2003): 279–93.

Hull, Gloria T. "'What It Is I Think She's Doing Anyhow': A Reading of Toni Cade Bambara's The Salt Eaters." In *Conjuring: Black Women, Fiction, and Literary Tradition*, edited by Marjorie Pryse and Hortense Spillers, 216–32. Bloomington: Indiana University Press, 1985.

Morrison, Toni, ed. "Preface." In *Deep Sightings and Rescue Missions*. New York: Pantheon, 1996.

Muther, Elizabeth. "Bambara's Fiesty Girls: Resistance Narratives." *African American Review* 36 (2002): 447–59.

Taylor, Carole Anne. "Post Modern Disconnection and the Archive of Bones: Toni Cade Bambara's Last Work." *Novel: A Forum on Fiction* 35.2–3 (2002): 258–80.

Traylor, Eleanor. "Music as Theme: The Jazz Mode in the Works of Toni Cade Bambara." In *Black Women Writers (1950–1980)*, edited by Mari Evans. New York: Doubleday, 1984.

Tyler, Anne. "Farewell to the Story as Imperiled Species." *National Observer*, May 9, 1977, 3–4.

Washington, Mary Helen. "Toni Cade Bambara." In *Black-eyed Susans, Midnight Birds*, 353–55. New York: Doubleday, 1990.

Rochelle Spencer

GWENDOLYN BENNETT (1902–1981)

BIOGRAPHICAL NARRATIVE

Gwendolyn Bennett, poet and short story writer, was born on July 8, 1902, in Giddings, Texas, and came to adulthood as the Harlem Renaissance developed and flourished. Bennett made significant contributions to this emerging African American cultural scene as a poet, journalist, and artist, contributions that are now coming to be recognized as significant.

Bennett's parents were teachers and she spent her early years in Nevada and Washington, D.C., while they taught and furthered their educations. When Bennett was seven years old she was in effect kidnapped by her father in a custody dispute and did not see her mother for fifteen years, living meanwhile in Pennsylvania and then Brooklyn, where she graduated from Brooklyn Girls' High School. There Bennett was the first African American to be elected to the school literary and dramatic societies, won art awards and was elected to write the class graduation speech. She began college in arts education at Columbia University and graduated from Pratt Institute in 1924, studying painting and graphic design; Bennett's poetry often shows influence of her visual sensibility in its vivid imagery.

As early as 1923 Bennett's poems began appearing in African American periodicals such as *Opportunity* published by the Urban League, and *Crisis*, the house organ of the NAACP, both important journals in promoting African American cultural expression in the 1920s. Bennett became part of Harlem Renaissance networks with close ties of friendship and aesthetics to those of her own generation such as Countee Cullen, Langston Hughes, and Helene Johnson while also receiving vital support from older figures like W.E.B. DuBois, Jessie Fauset, and particularly James Weldon Johnson and Charles S. Johnson, the publisher of *Opportunity*. These connections remained strong after she left New York to teach art at Howard University in 1924 and while she studied art on a scholarship in Paris from 1925 to 1926.

Returning to Harlem for the summer of 1926, Bennett worked at *Opportunity* and began writing an arts news column she titled "The Ebony Flute." Bennett also joined with Langston Hughes and Wallace Thurman in founding *Fire!!* a short-lived journal serving younger African American artists before returning to Howard that fall.

In 1927 Bennett left Howard for what proved to be an unhappy marriage to Alfred Joseph Jackson. They moved to Eustis, Florida, where Jackson practiced medicine but from this culturally remote location Bennett found herself unable to continue with her "Ebony Flute" columns. She and her husband returned to New York area in 1930 but the Great Depression had muted the Renaissance and Bennett's writing career never fully revived. Her next decades were spent in arts administration and education, first with New Deal arts programs and then progressive community schools. Charges of communist sympathies forced Bennett to leave several posts, and she spent her last years in Kutztown, Pennsylvania, as an antiques dealer with her second husband, Richard Crosscup. Bennett died on May 30, 1981.

MAJOR WORKS

Bennett's most productive literary period coincided with the early years of the Harlem Renaissance and her writing engaged with its political and aesthetic issues, as well as those of Modernism. Pride in racial heritage and in African American forms of creativity show in her typically short lyric poems. The poems also often play with conventional forms, using a loosely structured free verse and take surprising turns, invoking the freedom of the new literary sensibilities. Bennett most frequently published in *Opportunity* and *Crisis*, and her artwork also occasionally appeared on their covers.

Illustrating this new pride in African roots is "Heritage" (1923), whose speaker longs to experience Africa with all her senses and to feel deep connection to the palm trees, to the Nile, and to the people of Africa. "To a Dark Girl" (1923) unapologetically celebrates all aspects of African American beauty, the sources of which are traced to both African queens and African Americans' troubled history in the United States. The conventional diction of "Song" (1925) bursts suddenly into African American folk dialect in its second stanza and celebrates the folk music culture of hymns and banjo music.

"To Usward" (1924) was chosen as the dedication poem for the March 1924 Civic Club dinner for Harlem writers sponsored by *Opportunity*, and consequently became one of Bennett's best-known poems. The dinner was an intergenerational gathering of Harlem Renaissance literary figures that launched New Negro literature and brought African American writers and white publishers together. "To Usward" celebrates this moment and the diversity of forms and tones of the younger artists of the Renaissance. A Chinese ginger jar is used as the poem's central image, reflecting an orientalizing influence from modernism. "To Usward" was published in both *Opportunity* and *Crisis* shortly after presentation.

Even Bennett's most personal poems can often be seen as commenting on larger concerns. In the short lyric "Hatred" (1926) Bennett dissects the emotion using both strictly poetic diction such as "even-tide" and the conventional nature imagery of trees "etched" in a horizon, alongside the language of raw emotion. While presumably describing a personal relationship, Bennett's poem can also be interpreted as expressing a more generalized social anger that would be difficult to express more directly as an African American female. Personal concerns are again combined with cultural commentary in Bennett's "Lines Written at the Grave of Alexander Dumas" (1926), which pays homage to the black author while lamenting a lost love. Poems such as "Nocturne" (1923), "Street Lamps in Early Spring" (1926), and "Fantasy" (1927) use the free verse and imagism of modernist poetry, while their nocturnal themes link Bennett to other Harlem Renaissance poets in seeing this alternative sphere as suggestive of the rich but often masked and equivocal nature of African American experience.

Bennett's creative resistance to conventional poetic structure can be seen in poems such as "Quatrain 2" (1923) and "Sonnet 2" (1927). Both are self-consciously and pointedly titled with the names of poetic forms associated with "high" literature, which Bennett goes on to problematize. "Sonnet 2" starts in Shakespearean sonnet form before suddenly turning to informal and folk diction and lines of varying lengths. The two couplets of "Quatrain 2" are only loosely connected by their nature imagery and use irregular line lengths, meter, and punctuation.

While not much known as a fiction writer, Bennett published two short stories including "Wedding Day." The work centers on Paul Watson, an African American in 1920s Paris who overcomes his distrust of white Americans after falling in love with an expatriate. When Mary flees on their wedding day, leaving a note explaining that she "just couldn't go through with it" the "surprise" ending is ironic, with Bennett's work implying that this racist conclusion is no surprise at all.

Bennett's "Ebony Flute" columns represent a substantial part of her published work and offer a sense of the vibrant flowering of African American culture in many genres in the late 1920s, including African American centers beyond New York. Using her network of contacts and soliciting comment and opinion from her readers, Bennett produced the engaging monthly arts column for *Opportunity* from August 1926 to May 1928. Typically a series of brief notices relayed news of authors, dramatists, artists, and musicians, their publications, performances, and their works in progress. It also included informal reviews, literary group and contest news, and excerpts of correspondence, all interspersed with Bennett's commentary and musings, conveyed with an inclusive and whimsical yet discerning tone.

CRITICAL RECEPTION

Bennett was recognized in her time as a versatile and significant artist and personality of the Harlem Renaissance. James Weldon Johnson and Charles S. Johnson actively mentored her, with the latter describing Bennett as "one of the most versatile and accomplished of the younger poets." Her work appeared in many of the leading anthologies of African American literature of the era including Alain Locke's *The New Negro* (1925), Cullen's *Caroling Dusk* (1927), and James Weldon Johnson's *Book of American Negro Poetry* (1931).

Contemporary anthologies of African American women's and Harlem Renaissance writing have continued to include Bennett, although a separate edition of her work has never been made available; Bennett's relatively few published poems and her early retirement from literature have left her largely unknown. While the significance of Bennett's work and career, including her "Ebony Flute" columns, has been increasingly recognized, contemporary criticism typically discusses her in relation to other Harlem Renaissance figures rather than taking her as solo focus. Sandra Y. Govan is the scholar most noted for her work on Bennett, including a planned biography that would correct a lack for this accomplished and interesting writer.

BIBLIOGRAPHY

Works by Gwendolyn Bennett

"The Ebony Flute." In *Black Writers Interpret the Harlem Renaissance*, edited by Cary D. Wintz, 103–37. New York: Garland, 1996. (Volume 3 of *The Harlem Renaissance 1920–1940*.)
"Heritage" (1923), "To Usward" (1924), "Song" (1925), "To a Dark Girl" (1923), "Fantasy" (1927), "Secret" (1927), "Hatred" (1926), "Nocturne" (1923), "Quatrain 2" (1923), and "Street Lamps in Early Spring" (1926). In *Shadowed Dreams: Women's Poetry of the Harlem*

Renaissance, edited by Maureen Honey, 103–8, 159–61, 222–24. New Brunswick: Rutgers University Press, 1989.

"Lines Written at the Grave of Alexander Dumas" (1926), "Sonnet 1" (1927), and "Sonnet 2" (1927). In *Caroling Dusk: An Anthology of Verse by Negro Poets*, edited by Countee Cullen, 159–62. New York: Harper and Row, 1927.

"Wedding Day" (1926). In *Voices from the Harlem Renaissance*, edited by Nathan Huggins, 191–97. New York: Oxford University Press, 1976.

Studies of Gwendolyn Bennett's Works

Daniel, Walter C., and Sandra Y. Govan. "Gwendolyn Bennett." In *Afro-American Writers from the Harlem Renaissance to 1940*, edited by Trudier Harris, 3–10. Detroit: Gale, 1987. (Volume 51 of *Dictionary of Literary Biography*.)

Jones, Gwendolyn S. "Gwendolyn Bennett." In *African-American Authors 1745–1945: A Bio-Bibliographical Critical Sourcebook*, edited by Emmanuel S. Nelson, 18–23. Westport, CT: Greenwood Press, 2000.

Witalec, Janet, ed. "Gwendolyn Bennett." In *The Harlem Renaissance: A Gale Critical Companion*, 1–34. 3 vols. Detroit: Gale, 2003.

Sue E. Barker

MARITA BONNER (1898–1971)

BIOGRAPHICAL NARRATIVE

One of four children born in Boston to Joseph and Mary Anne Bonner, essayist, short storywriter and dramatist Marita Bonner is increasingly cited as a pioneering and in-fluential woman writer of the Harlem Renaissance. An essayist, short story writer, and playwright, Bonner was one of the first writers of her generation to confront the complex connections of race, gender, and class in the first half of the twentieth century. After excelling in the public school system of Boston's Brookline district, Bonner enrolled at Radcliffe College in Massachusetts in 1918, where she majored in English and Com-parative Literature. Bonner began her own teaching career while still a student at Radcliffe, taking a position at Cambridge High School in Boston.

After her graduation in 1922 Bonner secured two teaching positions in Washington, D.C., first at Bluefield Colored High School and then at Armstrong High School, the first manual training school for African Americans in the city. While in Washington, Bonner lived at two addresses in the affluent, middle-class LeDroit Park, an area favored by writers, educationalists, and other professionals. Bonner was a frequent visitor to Georgia Douglas Johnson's S Street Salon—an important base for Harlem Renaissance writers in Washington; other guests included Jessie Fauset, Angelina Grimké, Alain Locke, Countee Cullen, and Jean Toomer. In 1925 Bonner's autobiographical "On Being Young—a Woman—and Colored" won the essay writing competition of the NAACP's *Crisis* magazine, under the editorship of W.E.B. DuBois. After the success of her first publication, Bonner produced a series of short stories and essays, which appeared in *Crisis* as well as in *Opportunity*, the official journal of the Urban League. Between 1927 and 1929 she also completed work on three original plays, *The Purple Flower* being the most notable and well received.

In 1930 Bonner married accountant William Almy Occomy, and the couple moved to Chicago where they raised three children. Bonner continued to write under her married name, producing her *Frye Street* collection of short stories set against the backdrop of urban, multiethnic life in Chicago. In 1941 Bonner published her final short story, stopped writing, and returned to teaching. She died from injuries sustained during an apartment fire in 1971. After her death Bonner's work largely disappeared from view, until, in 1987, a posthumous edition of her complete works was published under the title *Frye Street and Environs*. The book's material, which includes previously unpublished writing, was taken from the writer's notebooks which had been kept and preserved by Bonner's daughter.

MAJOR WORKS

Following the publication of Marita Bonner's complete works, it is her prize-win-ning essay of 1925, "On Being Young—a Woman—and Colored," that continues to be regarded as her major contribution to African American literature. Its importance lies in the fact that it identifies and then challenges the dynamics that operate *between* race, class, and gender in Harlem society. Bonner highlights a crucial contradiction between the emancipatory promise of an *ultimately masculine* "New Negro," and the disappointing reality of the female urban experience. For Bonner the moral impediments placed on the middle-class woman of all races ensured that her life continued to be defined by paralysis, frustration, and feminine confinement:

For you know that—being a woman—you cannot twice a month or twice a year, for that matter, break away to see or hear anything in a city that is supposed to see and hear too much. That's being a woman. A woman of any color. . . . You decide that something is wrong with a world that stifles and chokes; that cuts off and stunts; hedging in, pressing down on eyes, ears and throat. (1)

After the success of her first essay, Bonner continued to explore ideas of racial and sexual empowerment in her essays, short stories, and plays, anticipating many of the central themes of more familiar writers, including Jessie Fauset and Zora Neale Hurston. However, Bonner's literary preoccupation with racial "passing" as a potent mode of nonidentification suggests that she can be most closely associated with fellow urbanite, Nella Larsen.

Bonner's series of Frye Street stories, written throughout the 1920s and 1930s, mark a narrative shift away from the unfulfilled promises of a Harlem élite toward an increasingly degraded, racially conflicted urbanity. Stories such as "Nothing New" (1926), "Tin Can" (1934), and "The Whipping" (1939) openly reject Harlem's insistence upon bourgeois "uplift" and aspiration. Instead, Bonner's ability to express a sense of dispossession and discord in the urban North establishes her both as an important voice of the Depression era, and as a necessary critic of the mythology of the "New Negro."

CRITICAL RECEPTION

The publication of Marita Bonner's complete works in 1987 saw a gradual proliferation of scholarly interest in her writing and wider cultural significance. While Cheryl Wall's *Women of the Harlem Renaissance* primarily focuses on the work of Jessie Fauset, Nella Larsen, and Zora Neale Hurston, Bonner's work is also illuminated and contextualized in this important study. In her introduction to an emergent tradition of women's writing within Harlem, Wall identifies Bonner's prize-winning essay of 1925 "On Being Young—a Woman—and Colored" as a necessary counterpoint to Alain Locke's seminal study of the same year, *The New Negro*. In *Invented Lives*, Mary Helen Washington pairs the work of Marita Bonner and Nella Larsen in an attempt to foreground the related racial, sexual, and class dynamics of "passing." Maria Balshaw's recent book, *Looking for Harlem*, provides a series of detailed analyses of Bonner's short stories. In a chapter titled "Women in the City of Refuge," Balshaw pays close attention to Bonner's cycle of Frye Street stories, illuminating the writer's critical observations of working-class, multiethnic urbanity. This chapter also makes clear Bonner's removal of a Harlem aesthetic to other centers of black cultural life, in this case Chicago. Although in *Color, Sex and Poetry* Gloria Hull pays little close attention to the detail of Bonner's work, her book does offer some invaluable insights into the personal and cultural dynamics that defined Georgia Douglas Johnson's S Street Salon.

Bonner's work can also now be found in a number of critical anthologies. Most useful are Rita Dandridge's *Black Women's Blues*, Clarence Major's *Calling the Wind*, and Bill Mullen's *Revolutionary Tales*. While Major and Mullen focus specifically on Bonner's importance as a short story writer, Katherine Kelly's *Modern Drama by Women* introduces Bonner's parallel status as a popular and critically acclaimed playwright.

Until recently the range of scholarly articles and essays on Bonner's work has been limited, often placing the writing on the margins of Harlem's more familiar writers. However, there is now a growing body of critical argument directed at Bonner's literary contributions of the 1920s, 1930s, and early 1940s. Allison Berg and Merideth Taylor advance an elegant, theoretically informed account of Bonner's most famous play in their article "Enacting Difference: Marita Bonner's 'Purple Flower' and the Ambiguities of Race." In contrast, Judith Musser's article for *Studies in Short Fiction* explores the impact of Bonner's dedication as a teacher and educationalist on her writing. A good example of an early response to Bonner's critical re-emergence can be found in Sharon Dean and Erlene Stetson's "Flower-dust and Springtime: Harlem Renaissance Women."

BIBLIOGRAPHY

Works by Marita Bonner

Frye Street and Environs: The Collected Works of Marita Bonner, edited and introduced by Joyce Flynn and Joyce Occomy Stricklin. Boston: Beacon Press, 1987.
"On Being Young—a Woman—and Colored." Reprint in *Invented Lives: Narratives of Black Women 1860–1960*, edited by Mary Helen Washington, 168–73. London: Virago Press, 1989.

Studies of Marita Bonner's Works

Balshaw, Maria. *Looking for Harlem: Urban Aesthetics in African-American Literature.* London; Stirling, VA: Pluto Press, 2000.
Berg, Allison, and Merideth Taylor. "Enacting Difference: Marita Bonner's 'Purple Flower' and the Ambiguities of Race." *African American Review* (Fall 1998): 468–81.
Chick, Nancy. "Marita Bonner's Revolutionary Purple Flowers: Challenging the Symbol of White Womanhood." *Langston Hughes Review* 13.1 (Fall/Spring 1994–1995): 21–32.
Dandridge, Rita B. *Black Women's Blues: A Literary Anthology.* New York: G. K. Hall, 1992.
Dean, Sharon, and Erlene Stetson. "Flower-dust and Springtime: Harlem Renaissance Women." *Radical Teacher* 18 (1980): 1–8.
Hull, Gloria T. *Color, Sex and Poetry.* Bloomington and Indianapolis: Indiana University Press, 1987.
Kelly, Katherine E., ed. *Modern Drama by Women, 1880s–1930s: An International Anthology.* New York: Routledge, 1996.
Major, Clarence, ed. *Calling the Wind: Twentieth Century African-American Short Stories.* New York: HarperPerennial, 1993.
Mullen, Bill, ed. *Revolutionary Tales: African American Women's Short Stories, from the First Story to the Present.* New York: Laurel, 1995.
Musser, Judith. "African American Women and Education: Marita Bonner's Response to the 'Talented Tenth.' " *Studies in Short Fiction* 34.1 (Winter 1997): 73–85.
Roses, Lorraine Elena, and Ruth Elizabeth Randolph. "Marita Bonner: In Search of Other Mothers' Gardens." *Black American Literature Forum* 21.1–2 (Spring–Summer 1987): 165–83.
Wall, Cheryl A. *Women of the Harlem Renaissance.* Bloomington and Indianapolis: Indiana University Press, 1995.

Washington, Mary Helen. *Invented Lives: Narratives of Black Women 1860–1960.* London: Virago Press, 1989.

Wilson, Sondra K., ed. *The Crisis Reader: Stories, Poetry and Essays from the NAACP's Crisis Magazine.* New York: Random House, 1989.

Sophie Blanch

CANDY DAWSON BOYD (1946–)

BIOGRAPHICAL NARRATIVE

Candy Dawson Boyd is a children's book author, an activist, an educator, and a literacy advocate. She was born Marguerite Cecille Dawson in Chicago, Illinois, on August 8, 1946. The eldest of three children born to Julian Dawson and Mary Ruth (Ridley), Boyd was raised by her divorced mother in an all black neighborhood in south Chicago. She attended segregated schools until high school and utilized a small segregated library stocked with books discarded from the white library.

After graduating from high school in 1962, Boyd enrolled in Northeastern Illinois State University. Her commitment to social change started when she and several friends tried to stop blockbusting in a nearby Chicago neighborhood. In college her activist activities began to supersede her schoolwork, so Boyd withdrew from college and worked with the civil rights movement. A year later, she returned to college and pursued a degree in education. She graduated with a B.A. degree in 1967. After college, Boyd taught for several years as an elementary school teacher in her Chicago neighborhood.

In 1971, Boyd moved to Berkeley, California, where she taught a multiethnic classroom of students for the first time. Instead of just holding one teaching position, Boyd held several positions simultaneously while she earned her M.A. degree in 1978 and later her doctoral degree in 1982. At the discovery of a paucity of appropriate literature for children, Boyd decided to write books for children. She prepared responsibly by taking classes in writing for children and by reading every children's book in the Berkeley Public Library. She wrote six novels before committing herself almost exclusively to training teachers to teach.

Boyd is director and professor of Reading and Language Arts Program in the School of Education at Saint Mary's College of California. She has become renowned for her devotion to training teachers and developing programs that produce great readers. She lectures and writes articles challenging authors to provide accurate and quality multiethnic literature for all children.

MAJOR WORKS

Unlike most children's books at the time, written in demeaning language depicting African Americans and their neighborhoods negatively, Boyd has written books that are inspiring, positive, and realistic. Her novels focus on the universal themes of love, friendship, striving for excellence, broken dreams, death, rejection, and responsibility for self and others. Her books contradict the widely held perception by the dominant society that the black is lazy and violent. In her first novel *Circle of Gold*, young Mattie believes her widowed mother, who works two jobs, loves her twin brother Matt more. She tries to win her mother's love by struggling to purchase her a gold pin.

At the loss of a best friend from a drunken driving incident in *Breadsticks and Blessings Places*, the major character, Toni, is consumed with grief. With her friend Mattie's help, she is able to recover. Charlie, an entrepreneurial sixth grader in *Charlie Pippin*, has trouble following the school code elects to do her social science report on Vietnam. She discovers her stern father was a Vietnam War hero who lost his dreams after the experience. *Chevrolet Saturdays* deals with divorce and adjustment in a blended family. The protagonist Joey's difficulty dealing with his parents' divorce and his mother's remarriage affect his school performance. In Boyd's books, schools are sites for learning and places for developing responsibility outside the family. Each of her works has episodes at school.

CRITICAL RECEPTION

Candy Boyd has written stories about children experiences in the home, at school, and in the community from the child's perspective. She provides through stories how families survive and prevail despite setbacks and hardships. Her aim is to write realistic stories for children to see themselves and family positively and at the same time dismantle the dominant society's stereotype of the African American. Boyd realized she has initiated that change when a young reader wrote her a letter saying the novel *Fall Secrets* touched her heart. Even though she did not share the character Jessie's race "we are much the same. I feel as if it could be me. . . ." Although *Breadsticks and Blessing Places* was turned down for publication for nine years, the work is a reprieve from the gang violence, broken homes, and despair of many urban, adolescent novels, says reviewer, Gerry Larson. Jerry Flack, a reviewer for *School Library Journal*, says *Charlie Pippin* is a good novel about vital people and important issues. It informs children on the impact the Vietnam War has had on families and it addresses questions not well represented in books for children. Boyd comprehends the impact divorce has on children, says Frances Bradburn of *Chevrolet Saturdays*. Most of all she helps readers of all races and ethnic backgrounds understand the challenge.

BIBLIOGRAPHY

Works by Candy Dawson Boyd

Breadsticks and Blessing Places. New York: Macmillan, 1985. Reprint, *Forever Friends*. New York: Puffin, 1986.
Charlie Pippin. New York: Macmillan, 1987.
Chevrolet Saturdays. New York: Macmillan, 1992.
Circle of Gold. New York: Scholastic, 1984.
Daddy, Daddy Be There. New York: Philomel, 1995.
A Different Beat. New York: Puffin, 1996.
Fall Secrets. New York: Puffin, 1994.
"I See Myself in There: Experiencing Self and Others in Multiethnic Children's Literature." In *The New Press Guide to Multicultural Resources for Young Readers*, edited by Daphane Muse. New York: New Press, 1997.
"Multiethnic Literature as Story." *Yearbook (Claremont Reading Conference)*, 1991, 24–39. *School Library Media Annual (SLMA)*, 1991, 9, 49–59.

Studies of Candy Dawson Boyd's Works

Bradburn, Frances. Rev. of *Chevrolet Saturdays*. *Wilson Library Bulletin* 68 (January 1994): 119.
Cooper, Ilene. Rev. of *Fall Secrets*. Booklist 91 (September 15, 1994): 135.
Flack, Jerry. Rev. of *Charlie Pippin*. *School Library Journal* 33 (April 7, 1987): 92.
Larson, Gerry. Rev. *Breadsticks and Blessing Places*. *School Library Journal* 32 (September 1985): 142.

Bennie P. Robinson

JOANNE BRAXTON (1950–)

BIOGRAPHICAL NARRATIVE

Literary critic and poet Joanne "Jodie" Margaret Braxton was born in Lakeland, Maryland, on May 25, 1950, to Mary Ellen Weems Braxton and Harry McHenry Braxton, Sr. Braxton graduated from Northwestern Senior High School in Hyattsville, Maryland, earned a B.A. from Sarah Lawrence College, and obtained a Ph.D. in American Studies from Yale University. Her doctoral dissertation, "Autobiography by Black American Women: A Tradition Within a Tradition" (1984), is an early version of her ground breaking critical study *Black Women Writing Autobiography: A Tradition Within a Tradition* (1989), which offers a trenchant analysis of the Afra-American experience as expressed in slave narratives, autobiographies, and subgenres of the field of autobiography.

Braxton is a dedicated teacher, fruitful scholar, and an accomplished poet and playwright. She is currently the Frances L. and Edwin L. Cummings Professor in the English and American Studies Departments at The College of William and Mary. She has received several awards honoring her classroom performance, including the Thomas Jefferson Teaching Award, the William and Mary Alumni Teaching Fellowship, and The Outstanding Virginia Educator Award. Her scholarly writings and edited volumes include the aforementioned *Black Women Writing* (1989), *Wild Women in the Whirlwind: Afra-American Culture and the Contemporary Literary Renaissance* (with Andrée Nicola McLaughlin) (1990), *The Collected Works of Paul Laurence Dunbar* (1993), *Maya Angelou's I Know Why the Caged Bird Sings: A Casebook* (1998), and *Monuments of the Black Atlantic: Slavery and Memory* (2004). She is a frequent contributor of poetry and reviews to magazines and periodicals such as *Presence Africaine*, *Massachusetts Review*, and the *Journal of Black Poetry*. Her creative works include a volume of poetry titled *Sometimes I Think of Maryland* (1977), and a play written in conjunction with her work with the Middle Passage Project at The College of William and Mary that celebrates the survival of African people in the New World, titled *Crossing Deep River: A Ritual Drama in Three Movements*. Braxton's uncompromising efforts to enrich the lives of people of African descent have won her widespread recognition and numerous awards. She is currently writing two new plays.

MAJOR WORKS

While Braxton studied autobiography under Charles T. Davis and John Blassingame, her affinity and fascination with autobiography stemmed from her close relationships with the elders of her family, particularly her family's matriarchs. Braxton's love affair with autobiography began in childhood as she sat at her grandmother's knee listening to "ghost stories and preacher tales, as well as lullabies and nursery rhymes" (Black Women Writing Autobiography, 3–4). Learning about her family history and genealogy in this manner paved the way for her intellectual study because she not only listened to the stories but also came to understand her connection to them and used this knowledge to *see* the experience of black womanhood that was hidden behind a veil of race, gender, and color prejudice.

Braxton's childhood connection to black women's stories as both outsider (because she would never live these particular experiences) and insider (because she is black and female) is reflected in the thesis of *Black Women Writing Autobiography*. Throughout the book, she argues that black American women enjoy a "confluence of culture and con-sciousness" (208) and a "mystic sisterhood" of shared language, frame of reference, and allusion (1). The three-part study traces this bond from accounts by nineteenth-century enslaved and freeborn women to ones by modern black women, examining the birth and development of the figure of the "outraged mother" who wields sassy language as a weapon against racial discrimination and gender oppression.

In *Wild Women in the Whirlwind*, Braxton extends this argument in her role as editor and contributor. As editor, she gathered essays by and about women of African descent that analyze the Afra-American literary renaissance and acknowledge its rich cultural history, effectively continuing the matrilineal sisterhood established in her earlier work. As contributor, she proves the validity of black women's written and oral traditions as she revisits the trope of the outraged mother.

In recent years, Braxton's love for and celebration of the Afra-American experience have been channeled into new scholarly and creative endeavors, especially through the establishment of The Middle Passage Project in 1995 at The College of William and Mary, which serves to explore the "history and memory surrounding the transatlantic slave trade, its resounding effects on Africans in the Americas, and its representation in literature and the humanities." The Middle Passage Project is multifaceted and has components ranging from research and lectures to curriculum development, workshops, and artistic performances.

CRITICAL RECEPTION

Critics of Braxton's work praise her resolute call to correct black and feminist literary criticism by demanding a redefinition of African American autobiography to include images of women and their oral and written expressions, such as diaries, jour-nals, reminiscences, and memoirs. Wilma King calls *Black Women Writing Autobiog-raphy* a pioneering contribution to African American feminist scholarship. When *I Think of Maryland* was released, Gwendolyn Brooks hailed it for its economy, courage and genuine expression of youthful energy. Her recent scholarship and work continues this quest, as it demands that the experiences of all people of African descent get the attention they deserve.

BIBLIOGRAPHY

Works by Joanne Braxton

"Asserting Selfhood: The Harlem Renaissance Remembered (Book Review)." *New Republic*, November 4, 1972, 27–30.
Black Women Writing Autobiography: A Tradition Within a Tradition. Philadelphia: Temple University Press, 1989.

The Collected Works of Paul Laurence Dunbar. Charlottesville: University Press of Virginia, 1993.

"Crusader for Justice: Ida B. Wells." In *African American Autobiography: A Collection of Critical Essays,* edited by William L. Andrews, 90–112. Englewood Cliffs, NJ: Prentice Hall, 1993.

"Introduction." In *The Work of the Afro-American Woman,* edited by N. F. Mossell. New York: Oxford University Press, 1988.

"Living Down to Expectations: Schoolgirls (Book Review)." With Julia K. Brazelton. *The Women's Review of Books* 12 (1995): 20–21.

Maya Angelou's I Know Why the Caged Bird Sings*: A Casebook.* New York: Oxford University Press, 1998.

Monuments of the Black Atlantic: Slavery and Memory, edited with Maria Diedrich. Muenster, Germany: LIT, 2004.

"Silences in Harriet 'Linda Brent' Jacobs's *Incidents in the Life of a Slave Girl.*" In *Listening to Silences: New Essays in Feminist Criticism,* edited by Elaine Hedges and Shelley Fisher Fishkin, 146–55. New York: Oxford University Press, 1994.

Sometimes I Think of Maryland. New York: Sunbury Press, 1977.

"A Song of Transcendence: Maya Angelou." In *Maya Angelou's* I Know Why the Caged Bird Sings, edited by Harold Bloom, 93–110. Philadelphia: Chelsea House, 1998.

Wild Women in the Whirlwind: Afra-American Culture and the Contemporary Literary Renaissance, edited with Andrée Nicola McLaughlin. New Brunswick: Rutgers, 1990.

Studies of Joanne Braxton's Works

Evans, Gaynelle. "Frustration over Sexual, Racial Oppression Unleashed in 'Wild Women.' " *Black Issues in Higher Education* (April 1990): 22.

King, Wilma. "Black Women Writing Autobiography: A Tradition Within a Tradition." Rev. of *Black Women Writing Autobiography: A Tradition Within a Tradition,* edited by Joanne Braxton. *Journal of Southern History* 57 (1991): 523–24.

Sadoff, Dianne F. "Black Women Writing Autobiography." Rev. of *Black Women Writing Autobiography: A Tradition Within a Tradition,* edited by Joanne Braxton. *American Quarterly* 43 (1991): 119.

Sundquist, Eric J. "Words Walking Without Masters." Rev. of *Wild Women in the Whirlwind,* edited by Joanne Braxton and Andrée McLaughlin. *New York Times Book Review,* February 25, 1990, 11.

Wilentz, Gay. "Affirming Critical Difference: Reading Black Women's Texts." Rev. of *Changing Our Own Words,* edited by Cheryl A. Wall; and *Wild Women in the Whirlwind,* edited by Joanne Braxton and Andrée McLaughlin. *Kenyon Review* 13 (1991): 146–51.

Tanya N. Clark

GWENDOLYN BROOKS (1917–2000)

BIOGRAPHICAL NARRATIVE

Poet, novelist and short story writer Gwendolyn Brooks is known and celebrated as a wordsmith who embraced and experimented with words in her poetry in order, ultimately, to shape them so that others would clearly comprehend their import. This was not only the way that she *did* poetry, but also the way that she described herself; she did not mince words. When, for example, her biographer asked her in a 1990 interview if she would embrace the term "African American" in lieu of the term "Black" to describe herself, Brooks responded, "I am a *Black*," because it was this term that made her both "African and American" alike and that connected her to blacks throughout the diaspora.

Although Brooks makes a distinction between her earlier poetic ethos and the one that existed after her introduction to the Black Power Movement in 1967, the one trope that travels throughout all of her writing is her gift of responding to the human experience through black subjects. From the 1945 poem "The Mother," which describes a black tenement mother's relationship to her aborted child to the 1990 poem "Winnie" that describes Winnie Mandela's relationship to her husband and his cause, Brooks has captured the desires and emotions of her subject in poetic form and has invited us into her creative world.

Brooks was born in Topeka, Kansas, to Keziah Corinne Wims who went back to her hometown to deliver her first of two children because of her desire to give birth in the presence of her own mother. It was Brooks's mother who taught both children eight basic tenets of successful living including being dutiful to others—it was Keziah's wont to say, "If you know yourself, you know other people"—and empathizing with other people. It was also Keziah who told Brooks that she was "going to be the lady Paul Laurence Dunbar!" and insisted that her talented daughter approach both James Weldon Johnson and Langston Hughes when they separately visited local churches in Chicago, so that they could see Brooks's work.

Brooks's father, David Anderson, rounded off Brooks's loving household in that he was a humble and soft-spoken janitor who surrounded his children with edifying books and song and who encouraged his children to submit to the only church that mattered, that of simple kindness. There is no doubt that these wonderful nuggets of living spilled eloquently into Brooks's poetry and her life. She was so grateful to his influence that by the time she wrote *The Bean Eaters* in 1960, she hurried and finished the collection so that she could dedicate it to her father before his death.

In 1938, under the tutelage of Chicago socialite Inez Cunningham Stark, a reader for *Poetry* magazine, Brooks joined a group of up-and-coming Chicago artists and scholars, among them Margaret Taylor Goss Burroughs who operates the African American Cultural Center in Chicago, William Couch, a scholar of African American drama and author of *New Black Playwrights* (1968), Margaret Danner a poet that Brooks describes as under-recognized, and poet Henry Blakely, whom Brooks married and had two children. Although Blakely never sent out his own work and therefore never experienced fame as did Brooks, she points out that he always "encouraged me in my writing all along"—a fact that she acknowledges even when they briefly separated in 1969. It was with these artistic comrades in a Chicago South Side Community Arts Center that Brooks honed some of her writing skills and much of the work she produced during this time ended up in her first collection of poems, *A Street in Bronzeville* (1945).

Although Brooks's first publication occurred when she was thirteen years old, a poem that was published in *American Childhood* magazine in 1930 when her influences were English and American romantic poets such as William Wordsworth, John Keats, William Cullen Bryant, and Henry Wadsworth Longfellow, it was not until the 1940s that audiences began to see influences of modern poets like T. S. Eliot and Ezra Pound. It was Brooks's knowledge of all these forms that, no doubt, informed her own poetic style and form. In 1943, she won the Midwestern Writer's Conference Poetry award but it was not until the creation of *Annie Allen* in 1949, that she garnered the Pulitzer Prize, the first ever awarded to a black person. Of this poem, Brooks is most proud, not so much the content as the form by acknowledging that she was "impressed with the effectiveness of technique" in this poem, which is written in precise iambic pentameter.

In the midst of her creative production, Brooks met Emily Morrison, whose words helped shape the poet that some have defined as one of the greatest American poets. Morrison told Brooks "not to write disconnectedly about such things as love, death, and the mysteries of life, but to center [her] ideas in the background [she] really knew something about." As a result, Brooks wrote a stream of books that focused on what she knew—namely people who fleshed out her life in Chicago: *Maud Martha* (1953), a fictional autobiography, and her only novel: *Bronzeville Boys and Girls* (1956), which was about those who lived in what was politically and commonly referred to as Chicago's Black Belt; and *The Bean Eaters* (1960), which included one of her most anthologized and poignant poems, "We Real Cool." Along with these publications came awards and teaching jobs that allowed her to reach the community she was building her entire poetic career upon—people and their experiences.

This was also true in her later works as they were in her earlier works, even when she met some young, progressive black male poets who were committed to the revolution in 1967. While attending a conference at Fisk University, Brooks encountered, among others, Don L. Lee, who later changed his name to Haki Madhubuti. Although Brooks attributes her creative growth in part to him because he was one of the innovators who ushered her into a more black-centered conversation and consciousness, he along with others respected Brooks and her work and made that clear at the conference. Eventually, their influence was not only seen in the form and content of Brooks's poetry—from structured form to free verse—it was also this group of artists who encouraged Brooks to subscribe and use black publishers for her work after 1967. It was this medium that allowed Brooks to reach the very people who informed her poems from the beginning— black people—and to explain the human experience as an extension of the black experience, a feature that makes her work relevant to all who read it today.

Brooks died December 3, 2000, at the age of 83.

MAJOR WORKS

Keziah Brooks's characterization of her daughter's fate of being the lady Paul Laurence Dunbar should not be analyzed lightly. Though neither Brooks nor her mother elaborate on what that meant, it only takes reading Brooks's poetry to see that, like

Dunbar, Brooks was invested in capturing the emotional upheaval, physical struggle, and material reality of black people. Brooks is able to take the form that Dunbar initiated and elevate it to another artistic level in that her poems present a more realistic view of diversity and complexity of black people and thus the human experience. Her women, for example, are more than the stereotypical matriarch, whore, or bitch that one expects. In "The Mother," Brooks describes a woman who aborted multiple children but not without some regret and sadness. Though we never understand exactly why she decided to "kill" the children, we accept her pain of losing them. Where the mother is un-apologetically flawed, Brooks gives us a heroine in characters like Annie Allen in the "Anniad." The title very purposely reminds any literary scholar of Homer's "Iliad" and Virgil's "Aeniad" in that Brooks creates a war situation in which the eventual antagonist, Tan Man, is sent to fight. But in the midst of the poem, we see that the real war is Annie's thoughts concerning Tan Man and her love for him that has eclipsed the love that she has for herself. We find that in the end, Annie trusts her construction of Tan Man as being a destructive force in her life so by abandoning her fantasies of Tan Man, she finds herself. In turn, she wins her own personal "war" by finding peace and fulfillment within herself. Brooks points out that her 1988 poem, "Song of Winnie" (from *Gottschalk and the Grande Tarantelle*), marked a "very significant change in my writing"; it is one of Brooks's longer poems that goes into the mind of a young Winnie Mandela. She thinks about the long years that her husband, Nelson, spent in prison cut off from so much and how she was left to uphold his image and political ideals. In the end, Winnie tries to put the love she has for her people ahead of the love she has for herself.

Brooks also gives us insight into her own life by providing the autobiographical novel *Maud Martha* and her autobiography *Report from Part One*. What is most significant about both works is the strong detection of transformation that both heroines go through. In addition to dealing with the ugliness of racism, classism, and sexism, *Maud Martha* ultimately tells the story of a black girl who advances from romantic dreams to achieve completeness as a woman. When Maud Martha meets her future husband, Paul, she laments the fact that she has only one real feature that would make him marry her: "I am what he would call—sweet" (52). Her sister Helen, on the other hand, had beauty from the beginning. As a child, Maud realized that though Helen is only two years older and matches Maud in weight, height, and thickness, Helen has features that Maud could never match: "the lashes, the grace, the little ways with the hands and feet" (2, 3). Even as a teenager, one of the neighborhood boys looks past Maud's "sweetness" for Helen's beauty. He invites one of them into his car and when Maud mistakes his invitation as one meant for her, he replies, "I don't mean you, you old black gal . . . I mean Helen" (34, 35). But despite her dark skin and indelicate features, when Paul meets Maud, he wants to marry her. Maud makes it through her marriage, her life, and her existence not because Paul finally comes around and recognizes her inner beauty but because of a kind of understanding that was fostered in her when she had to deal with her family's awe of Helen's beauty:

> Helen was still the ranking queen, not only with the Emmanuels of the world, but even with their father—their mother—their brother. She did not blame the family. It was not their fault. She understood. They could not help it. They were enslaved, were fascinated, and they were not at all to blame. (35)

But it is in her nonfictional autobiography that we are truly able to appreciate her transformation from one who did not know her own power in this world to one who embraces it fully. The preface sets up the framework when she is quoted as describing this new, more confident black who responds to prejudices and discrimination with dignity and as far as Brooks is concerned, "Your *least* pre-requisite toward an understanding of the new black is an exceptional doctorate which can be conferred only upon those with the proper properties of bitter birth and intrinsic sorrow" (13). In this one statement, Brooks identifies power in those that had been previously rendered powerless. She acknowledges the possibilities in growing up black and disfranchised and not the drawbacks. As one flips through the book and encounters the photos that mark significant shifts in her life—from her childhood to those moments that mark the height of her artistic production—we view the flowering of a woman who has come into her own. Her prose celebrates what she always knew—that black is beautiful and it always was.

Brooks's approach to diversity also finds its way into her discussion of black men, whom she respectfully critiques in her work as well. In the *Bean Eaters*, Brooks uses one of her most infamous poems "We Real Cool" to give voice to a group of young men that society could forget about because they are not participating in mainstream America in traditional ways. Instead, they spend their time playing hard and dying young. The most poignant feature about this poem is that Brooks asserts their subjectivity by ending each line with the word "We" so as to show that even they matter. She also celebrated the uniqueness in other black men in her poems in *In the Mecca*, titled "Medgar Evers" and "Malcolm X." Both depictions celebrate the incomparable contributions of the two important black men while staying true to the theme of rebirth that is suggested in the title of the collection. In her 1983 book she devotes her energy and time to the only black mayor of Chicago to date in "Mayor Harold Washington; and, Chicago, the I Will City." The fact that she captures the strengths of such a varied group of men—each social actors but in different ways—highlights her desire to be both responsible and analytical of those blacks who are impacting society.

Her work also reports the varied ills that plague black children. In "The Life of Lincoln West," Brooks begins by chronicling the angst that the dark-skinned and "ugly" little boy encounters every time he is in someone else's midst—whether they are black or white. His father cannot stand to look at him and his teacher both pities and is repulsed by him. But it is the comment of a white stranger that impacts Lincoln the most because it is he that identifies Lincoln as a "real" monkey and thus a "true" representation of blackness. When this stranger refers to Lincoln as a real black person, it is this moniker that comforts Lincoln and grants him the place that he most appreciates and covets. Brooks travels to Africa to depict another tragic tale of the boy in "The Near-Johannesburg Boy," who recounts the anger of growing up in a country that he cannot call his own because of his despised skin-color. Although there are clearly many blacks in this poem and, thus, in this place outside of Johannesburg (perhaps Soweto, suggests Brooks in the introductory epigraph), they do not make up enough to combat the injustice system that is South Africa.

CRITICAL RECEPTION

While many of Brooks's earlier critics as well as Brooks herself may view 1967 a year in which her political and social interests shifted to include "blacker" themes, one look at her work, demonstrates a writer who has always been aware of the political timber of her poems. In an interview with Claudia Tate in 1983, Tate says to Brooks that her "earlier works, *A Street in Bronzeville* and *Annie Allen*, don't seem to focus directly on heightened political awareness" suggesting that her later work does. To this Brooks responds, "Many of the poems, in my new and old books, are 'politically aware'; I suggest you reread them. You know, when you say 'political,' you really have to be exhaustive." When Tate follows up with the question later in the interview whether or not any of Brooks's early work assumed "the blatant, assertive, militant posture we find in the 'new black poetry' of the early seventies," Brooks with even more conviction than before shoots back, "Yes, ma'am. I'm fighting for myself a little bit here, but not overly so, because I certainly wrote no poem that sounds like Haki's [Madhubuti] 'Don't Cry, Scream' or anything like Nikki's 'The True Import of Present Dialogue, Black v. Negro,' which begins: 'Nigger / Can you kill / Can you kill?' But I'm fighting for myself a little bit here because I believe it takes a little patience to sit down and find out that in 1945 I was saying what many of the young folks said in the sixties" (*Conversations* 106). Brooks advocates for her awareness and begins the conversation for critics to acknowledge that there exists more continuity in her work than earlier critics, like Tate, recognize.

Joyce Ann Joyce extends the idea that Brooks's evolution was in line with a developing sensibility that accentuates continuity in her essay "Gwendolyn Brooks: Jean Toomer's November Cotton Flower." In focusing on the strength of Brooks's poetry to express herself creatively in the normally confining world of literary production, Joyce notes that "[having] bloomed under the light of Robert Hillyer's First Principles of Verse, Brooks brought to modern American poetry her own peculiar sensibility which manifests at once the embodiments of both Wallace Stevens's blue guitar and the African griot's drum. Even though they have the visual and stylistic attributes of a Euro-American poetic tradition, her earlier ballads, free verse poems, and the sonnets reveal the same feelings of racial integrity and record the same malaises of racism as those poems published after 1967 when Brooks's blackness confronted her 'with a shrill spelling of itself'" (*On Gwendolyn Brooks*, 246). In order to clarify her point, Joyce points to various early works such as "The Mother," "When You Have Forgotten Sunday: The Love Story," "Ballad of Pearl May Lee," "To those of My Sisters Who Kept Their Naturals," "Horses Graze," "Infirm," and "The Near-Johannesburg Boy," which all—old and new alike—fulfill "Africanist" criteria from which Joyce obtains her reference in her own book titled *Warriors, Conjurers, and Priests: Defining African-Centered Literary Criticism* (Chicago: Third World Press, 1994).

This conversation gains even more momentum when white critics explore her work. In the 1996 essay "Whose Canon? Gwendolyn Brooks: Founder at the Center of the 'Margins,'" Kathryne V. Lindberg notes that "Brooks did not radically change her poetic themes. Even obvious modulations in her line and other organizing musical techniques are, on the whole, unremarkable. . . . Certainly the texture of her poems, her palette of allusions and affiliations, has shifted from the white Anglo-American canon, but *In the Mecca* (1968), which Haki Madhubuti plausibly claims "'blacked its way out of the National Book Award'" (*RFPO* 21), is as remarkable for its range of verse forms as for its direct treatment of race and class oppression" (*Say That The River Turns,* 285). She does a judicious reading of *Annie Allen* and *Maud Martha* as it relates to the later *Primer for Blacks* in order to prove that though Brooks may focus more on blacks in her later poetry, she "is always aware of 'the People' and her public; that is, of race, of being racialized, and of the need to seize the power and tools of representation" (288). In turn, white feminist critic Sheila Hassell Hughes writes in her article "A Prophet Overheard: A Juxtapositional Reading of Gwendolyn Brooks' 'In the Mecca'" that while "Brooks' determination to write 'to blacks'" leaves "no easy entrance for the white reader" in "In the Mecca," the poem speaks to so many more people because it is "much more than a depiction of a particular place [the black belt of Chicago's South side]" in that Brooks issues "a call for liberation, represented as a communal construction out of that ruined place" (273), suggesting that it is the liberation that appeals most to the whole of Brooks's audience—even whites.

Many critics make strong arguments to recognize Brooks's early poetry as less self-aware than her latter poetry as did Claudia Tate. One of the most interesting is the recent article by James D. Sullivan titled "Killing John Cabot and Publishing Black: Gwendolyn Brooks' *Riot*," where he makes the assertion that by moving out of the white publishing arena into a specifically black one, Brooks's *Riot* should be viewed differently because "[the] material qualities of the artifact, therefore, are designed to establish an African American context for both interpreting and judging the poem" (562) in ways that differ from her earlier work. Though Sullivan's argument warrants further investigation, it seems more accurate to view all of Brooks's work as connecting to anyone who is invested in promoting a political agenda that brings out the best of any destructive, racialized situation.

BIBLIOGRAPHY

Works by Gwendolyn Brooks

Aloneness. Detroit: Broadside Press, 1971.
Annie Allen. New York: Harper, 1949.
The Bean Eaters. New York: Harper & Brothers, 1960.
Beckonings. Detroit: Broadside Press, 1975.
Black Steel: Joe Frazier and Muhammad Ali (1971).
Blacks. Chicago: Third World Press, 1987.
A Broadside Treasury. Detroit: Broadside Press, 1971.
Bronzeville Boys and Girls. Reprint, New York: Amistad, 2007.
Children Coming Home. Chicago: David Co., 1991
Family Pictures. Chicago: Broadside Press, 1971.
Gottschalk and the Grande Tarantelle. Chicago: Third World Press, 1989.
In the Mecca. New York: Harper Collins, 1968.
Jump Bad. Reprint, Detroit: Broadside Press, 1991.
Maud Martha. Reprint, Chicago: Third World Press, 1992.
Mayor Harold Washington and Chicago, the I Will City. Chicago: Brooks Press, 1983.
Primer for Blacks. Chicago: Third World Press, 1991.
Report from Part Two. Reprint, Chicago: Third World Press, 1993.
Riot. Detroit: Broadside Press, 1969.
Selected Poems. New York: Harper, 1963.
A Street In Bronzeville. New York: Harper, 1945.
The Tiger Who Wore White Gloves, or What You Really Are, You Really Are. Chicago: Third World Press, 1974.
To Disembark. Chicago: Third World Press, 1981.
Very Young Poets. Chicago: Third World Press, 1992.
The Wall. Detroit: Broadside Press, 1967.
We Real Cool. Detroit: Broadside Press, 1966.
Winnie. Reprint, Chicago: Third World Press, 1991.
The World of Gwendolyn Brooks. New York: Harper Collins, 1971.

Studies of Gwendolyn Brooks's Works

Brown, Patricia L., Don L. Lee, and Francis Ward, eds. *To Gwen, with Love*. Chicago, Johnson, 1971. *Colorado Review* n.s. 19.1 (Spring and Summer 1989).

Davis, Arthur P. "The Black and Tan Motif in the poetry of Gwendolyn Brooks." *CLAJ* 6 (December 1960).

———. *From the Dark Tower: Afro-American Writers 1900–1960*. Washington, DC: Howard University Press, 1974.

———. "Gwendolyn Brooks: Poet of the Unheroic." *CLAJ* 7 (December 1963).

Gabbin, Joanne V. "Blooming in the Whirlwind: The Early Poetry of Gwendolyn Brooks." In *The Furious Flowering of African American Poetry*, edited by Joanne Gabbin. Charlottesville: University of Virginia Press, 1999.

Gayles, Gloria Wade. *Conversations with Gwendolyn Brooks*. Jackson: University Press of Mississippi, 2003.

Hughes, Sheila Hassell. "A Prophet Overheard: A Juxtapositional Reading of Gwendolyn Brooks' 'In the Mecca'" *African American Review* 38.2 (Summer 2004), 257–280.

Kent, George E. *A Life of Gwendolyn Brooks*. Lexington: University Press of Kentucky, 1990.

Kufrin, Joan. "Gwendolyn Brooks." In *Uncommon Women*, 35–51. Piscataway, NJ: New Century Publishers, 1981.

Loff, Jon N. "Gwendolyn Brooks: A Bibliography." *College Language Association Journal* 17 (September 1973): 21–32.

Madhubuti, Haki R., ed. *Say That the River Turns: The Impact of Gwendolyn Brooks*. Chicago: Third World Press, 1987.

Mahoney, Heidi L. "Selected Checklist of Material by and about Gwendolyn Brooks." *NALF* 8 (Summer 1974).

Melhem, D. H. *Gwendolyn Brooks: Poetry and the Heroic Voice*. Lexington: University Press of Kentucky, 1987

———. "Gwendolyn Brooks: Humanism and Heroism." In *Heroism in the New Black Poetry: Interviews and Interviews*, 11–38. Lexington: University Press of Kentucky, 1990.

Miller, R. Baxter. *Langston Hughes and Gwendolyn Brooks: A Reference Guide*. Boston: G. K. Hall, 1978.

Mootry, Maria K., and Gary Smith. *A Life Distilled: Gwendolyn Brooks, Her Poetry and Fiction*. Urbana: University Press of Illinois, 1987.

Shaw, Harry B. *Gwendolyn Brooks*. Boston: Twayne, 1980.

Wright, Stephen Caldwell. *The Chicago Collective: Poems for and Inspired by Gwendolyn Brooks*. Sanford, FL: Christopher-Burghardt, 1990.

———. *On Gwendolyn Brooks: Reliant Contemplation*. Ann Arbor: University of Michigan Press, 1996.

Bridget Harris Tsemo

LINDA BEATRICE BROWN (1939–)

BIOGRAPHICAL NARRATIVE

Novelist and poet, Linda Beatrice Brown was born on March 14, 1939, in Akron, Ohio, to Raymond R. and Edith Player Brown. She married Harold E. Bragg in 1962 and had two children, Willa B. ("Lali") and Christopher P. Brown, before her divorce and subsequent marriage to Vandorn Ninnant. In 1961, Brown received her B.A. from Bennett College, a liberal arts college for women in Greensboro, North Carolina. She earned her M.A. at Case Western Reserve and completed her Ph.D. at Union Graduate School in Cincinnati, Ohio. In 1970, Brown began teaching at the University of North Carolina; she moved to Guilford College in 1986, and in 1992 she took a position at Bennett College, her alma mater, where she held the Willa B. Player Chair in Humanities and served as a Distinguished Professor.

Brown is the recipient of several awards, including *Who's Who in American Colleges and Universities* (1961), Woodrow Wilson Fellowship (1961–1962), Kent State Teaching Fellowship (1962–1964), *Outstanding Young Women of America* (1972), and various literary prizes. She was a contributing member at the 1975 Bread Loaf Writer's Conference. A novelist, poet, and lecturer, Brown's work is represented in several anthologies, including *Beyond the Blues* (1960), *A Living Culture in Durham* (1987), *Edge of Our World* (1990), *The Rough Road Home* (1992), *O Henry Festival Stories* (1995), and *Store of Joys* (1997). She has also contributed to numerous publications including *Encore, Guilford Review, Ebony Junior, Writer's Choice, Black Scholar, Cricket Magazine*, and *Religion and Intellectual Life*.

MAJOR WORKS

Brown's work, rich with metaphor and imagery, covers several genres. She first began writing poetry—her first poem was published when she was nineteen years old—turning to fiction many years later when she started writing her first novel while her composition students were taking an exam. Brown's portrayal of internal conflict, drawn from various aspects of African American experience, reflects her belief that history has a profound effect on the individual story. In a 1976 interview, Brown noted that "one of the responsibilities of the black poet is to make political statements." In addition to the political issues, other subjects of her poetry and fiction include African American culture, relationships between men and women, and the special strengths of African American women.

Brown's nonfiction addresses these same themes. *The Long Walk* tells the story of Willa B. Player, Brown's maternal aunt, and her successful service as the first female African American president of a fully accredited four-year liberal arts college. In *Forget-Me-Not*, Brown provides text on the history and use of memory jugs and their commemorative role in African and African American culture. Just as *The Long Walk* was created from numerous interviews with graduates and faculty of Bennett College, memory jugs use fragments to create a story, an essential act that reflects Brown's belief that "without memory we do not know who we are."

Brown's first novel, *Rainbow Roun' Mah Shoulder*, won a contest (with subsequent publication) sponsored by the North Carolina Cultural Arts Coalition for the best book by a North Carolina writer. Like many of Brown's poems, *Rainbow Roun' Mah Shoulder* celebrates African American women, their stories, and their efforts toward self-empowerment and freedom from oppression. The spiritual, intuitive side of the female is represented in Florice Rebecca Lentenielle's knowledge of herbs, her sight or "knowing," and her ability to heal others. Florice's story is interspersed with biological remarks about Lepidoptera that begin to appear shortly into the first chapter: "Lepidoptera develop by a complete metamorphosis which is characterized by four distinct stages. The egg hatches into larvae which feeds grows and molts several times before transforming into a pupa." These biological references serve as a parallel to Florice's own transformation, the changes in her life, her initial reluctance to and eventual acceptance of her God-given powers of sight and healing. Like the caterpillar that molts, allowing for future growth, Rebecca Florice goes through many stages in her life: Mac leaves, she starts a new life with Alice Wine, she has an affair with Robert, Robert leaves. Like a butterfly, Florice grows out of her fear to embrace her powers, but in the end, like a moth flying into the fire, she extinguishes herself in giving life back to Robert. In Florice, Brown portrays the ultimate mother figure: gentle and nurturing—cooking and caring for all the girls at the college, saving Harriet, nurturing Maye and Alice Wine—yet strong enough to exact judgment by beating Ole Bubba. Florice's powers, symbolized by the rainbow hanging on her arm, are both a burden and a comfort. She struggles with these powers, eventually accepting God's dangerous, but wonderful gifts, and passes them on to Ronnie, who will carry the rainbow on her shoulder, keeping the ancestral link intact through female tradition.

The importance of such links and of history's effect on the individual can also be seen in Brown's second novel, *Crossing Over Jordan*, the story of three generations of women, Story Temple Green, her mother Sadie, and her daughter Hermine, a family traumatized by Story's father whose feelings of impotence and rage brought on by the effects of slavery and its lingering legacy of racism are visited upon the females. What first appears as a lack of love in both Sadie and Story is really a conscious withholding, a way to educate their daughters in an effort to allow those daughters freedom from the cycle of oppression. The women are bound to those who came before them and to each other like a pattern in a slave quilt. And, like the story in the quilt, whether they write it, like Sadie who wrote hers on the backs of recipes, or tell it, each woman's story is essential for understanding, forgiveness, and freedom from the trauma born of oppression.

Brown's influences include the Romantic poets, Gwendolyn Brooks, Robert Frost, Don Lee, Langston Hughes, Ralph Emerson, Richard Wright, Alice Walker, Maya Angelou, and Toni Morrison.

CRITICAL RECEPTION

To date, Brown's work has received little critical attention beyond mixed reviews. Critics were ambivalent about Brown's poetry and the blend of poetic passages with narrative in *Rainbow Roun' Mah Shoulder*. Though lauded for its portrayal of the manifestation of the devastation and scars of slavery through generations of African Americans, *Crossing Over Jordan* was heavily criticized for insufficient development:

the characters lack complexity and dimension, preventing readers from empathizing with her characters.

BIBLIOGRAPHY

Works by Linda Beatrice Brown

Brown, Linda Beatrice. Video recording. Raleigh: North Carolina State University, 1991.
Crossing Over Jordan. New York: Ballantine, 1995.
"Holding Back the Nothing." In *Forget-Me-Not: The Art and Mystery of Memory Jugs*, edited by Brooke Davis Anderson, Linda Beatrice Brown, and Robert Farris Thompson. Winston-Salem: Winston-Salem State University, 1996.
The Long Walk: The Story of the Presidency of Willa B. Player at Bennett College. Greensboro, NC: Bennett College, 1998.
A Love Song to Black Men. Detroit: Broadside Press, 1974.
Rainbow Roun' Mah Shoulder. Chapel Hill, NC: Carolina Wren Press, 1984. (Reprinted by Ballantine in 1989.)

Studies of Linda Beatrice Brown's Works

Andrews, William L., Frances Smith Foster, and Trudier Harris. *The Oxford Companion to African American Literature.* New York: Oxford University Press, 1997, 103–4.
Brookhart, Mary Hughes. "Spiritual Daughters of the Black American South." In *The Female Tradition in Southern Literature*, edited by Carol S. Manning. Urbana: Illinois University Press, 1993.
Edgar, Kathleen J., ed. "Linda Beatrice Brown." *Contemporary Authors* 148 (1996): 62–63.
Prenshaw, Peggy Whitman. "A Conversation with Seven Fiction Writers." *Southern Quarterly: A Journal of Arts in the South* 29.2 (Winter 1991): 69–93.
Smith, Virginia W., and Brian J. Benson. "An Interview with Linda Brown Bragg." *College Language Association Journal* 20 (1976): 75–87.
Weil, Eric. "Inner Lights and Inner Lives: The Gospel According to Linda Beatrice Brown." *North Carolina Literary Review* 1.1 (1992): 106–14.

Teresa Clark Caruso

ANNIE LOUISE BURTON (1858–1910)

BIOGRAPHICAL NARRATIVE

Daughter of a white planter and a slave woman, autobiographer Annie Burton was born circa 1858 on a plantation near Clayton, Alabama. When her mother ran away after being whipped in 1862, Burton spent the final years of the Civil War in the care of her mistress. Reunited with her mother in December 1865, Burton lived with her siblings and two children adopted by her mother on a plantation located just miles from the place of her enslavement. Although she had earned minimal wages selling fruit and picking cotton to help her family subsist, Burton's first job came the following year as a nanny for Mrs. E. M. Williams, a music teacher and wife of a prominent attorney. It was during her time with this family that Burton was taught not only to cook and do housework, but also to read and write. Burton spent the next ten years of her life working in Eufaula, Alabama, and Macon, Georgia, where she attended school intermittently.

Upon her mother's death, Burton assumed the additional responsibility of caring for three small children, requiring her to pursue better employment opportunities in the north, where in 1879, she relocated to Boston. Despite the limitations of a domestic role that became a form of low-wage servitude for many, Burton cultivated her skills and used them as a foundation from which to achieve financial freedom. In 1884, Burton became a successful restaurateur and supplemented her income by transforming her residence into a boarding house. With money earned from these ventures, Burton was able to send her nephew to Hampton College in Virginia and return to Boston, where she married Samuel H. Burton in 1888. At the age of 43, Burton began taking classes at the Franklin Evening School where her headmaster, Frank Guild, requested that students begin an assignment that would later inspire Burton to write the story of her life, *Memories of Childhood's Slavery Days*.

MAJOR WORKS

Published in 1909, Burton's *Memories of Childhood's Slavery Days* is an auto-biographical narrative divided into eight sections. Although Burton's first section "Recollections of a Happy Life" begins by describing "happy, care-free childhood days on the plantation," her nostalgia is tempered by stories of pitiless hunger, separation of slave families, and the brutal lynching of African American men at the hands of vengeful whites. The remaining vignettes trace Burton's developing understanding of self-worth, education, and pecuniary compensation, and record the unshakable determination of a woman unmoved by the societal conventions of gender, race, or class.

Considered by Burton to be a sequel, her second segment is didactic in nature and emphasizes stories of Christian charity and benevolence. These themes reflect Burton's spiritual conversion following a period of critical illness in 1875, when she promised to dedicate her life to God if He restored her health. Burton's prose affirms her commitment to keep this promise, exuding optimism and providing solace and strength to her readers.

Yet, she insists that her work is a product of divine inspiration, and that her role is "something of the type of Moses." Accompanying these first two components are a composition on Abraham Lincoln, two shorter prose pieces, an essay by Dr. P. Thomas Stanford titled "The Race Question in America," and a collection of her "Favorite Poems" and "Favorite Hymns." These last pieces form tangible elements of self-representation meant to inspire her readers and affirm her belief in education and spirituality as vehicles to achieve success.

Burton also published a short biography of sixteenth U.S. President Abraham Lincoln in 1909.

CRITICAL RECEPTION

While Burton's voice sustains the tenor of her literary forebears, she has not garnered the critical attention bestowed upon more recognized figures such as Sojourner Truth, Harriet Jacobs, and Lucy Delaney. Reading Burton alongside other postbellum slave narrative writers such as Kate Drumgoold, William Andrews notes the recurrence of themes extolling black motherhood and the virtuous, indomitable spirit of the African American woman. Yolanda Pierce views Burton's work as a narrative of resistance that challenges proscribed social roles for African American women following Emancipation and one that defies stereotypical representations of black womanhood. These examinations reveal the depth of Burton's work and provide a rationale for continuing research into the life and work of this unique entrepreneur.

BIBLIOGRAPHY

Works by Annie Louise Burton

Abraham Lincoln. Boston: Ross Publishing Company, 1909.
Memories of Childhood's Slavery Days. Boston: Ross Publishing Company, 1909.

Studies of Annie Louise Burton's Works

Andrews, William L. "Introduction." In *Six Women's Slave Narratives*, xxix–xli. New York: Oxford University Press, 1988.
Pierce, Yolanda. "Her Refusal to Be Recast(e): Annie Burton's Narrative of Resistance." *Southern Literary Journal* 36.2 (2004): 1–12.

Gabriel A. Briggs

OLIVIA WARD BUSH-BANKS (1869–1944)

BIOGRAPHICAL NARRATIVE

Born on May 23, 1869, in Sag Harbor, New York, dramatist, essayist and poet Olivia Ward was the daughter of Eliza Draper and Abraham Ward, both from families of long-time free blacks. When Olivia Ward was nine months old, her mother died and her father remarried, sending her to Providence, Rhode Island, to live with her aunt, Maria Draper. While in high school, Ward began penning poetry, much of which reflects and lauds her mixed Montauk and African American heritages and the idea of biracial identity. In 1889, Ward married Frank Bush, and over the next few years she focused on raising and providing economically for her two daughters, Marie and Rosamund. In 1899, four years after her divorce, Ward published *Original Poems*, a small volume of verse praised by Paul Laurence Dunbar. A handful of the works from *Original Poems* appeared in the then leading paper for African Americans, *Voice of the Negro*, and others were reprinted in the *Boston Transcript*. By the turn of the century, Ward Bush was both contributing regularly to *Colored America* and serving as the official historian for the Montauk nation. She held the latter position, participating in pow wows and other tribal gatherings, until she married Anthony Banks and moved to Chicago. This move allowed her to concentrate on her writing in a more arts-oriented community. In 1914, she published her second, larger collection *Driftwood*. A mixture of poetry and prose, it was welcomed more enthusiastically by critics than her previous effort. While in Chicago, Bush-Banks became an advocate of the "New Negro Movement," serving as a settlement house activist and exploring communism. She also instructed drama and developed her own "Bush-Banks School of Expression," a nexus for writers, musicians, actors, and artists of color. In the 1930s, Olivia Ward Bush-Banks moved to New York, participated for three years in the Works Progress Administration (WPA), and accepted a position as arts editor for the *New Rochelle Westchester Record-Courier*. Her friends included Langston Hughes, Countee Cullen, Paul Robeson, Julia Ward Howe, and W.E.B. DuBois. She died in 1944.

MAJOR WORKS

In *Original Poems*, Olivia Ward Bush-Banks explores several recurring themes: the grand but ambivalent character of nature, the necessity of—and solace found in—faith in God, and a continuing quest for racial justice and harmony which would not preclude diversity. In many of her poems, the reader senses nostalgia for something lost—the language of the Montauk people, the purity of the agrarian way of life, or American opportunities for peace and equality. Her early writing is frequently romantic and pastoral, whereas her later writing is often satirical, socially critical, and politically charged. In *Driftwood*, she memorializes those who have fought for equality in the United States, including Crispus Attucks, Abraham Lincoln, Frederick Douglass, William Lloyd Garrison, and Harriet Beecher Stowe, and in one prose piece, "Hope," she disparages lynching and the denegration of persons of color. She dedicates "The Moaning of the

Tide" to Paul Laurence Dunbar for uplifting African Americans, and in an unpublished one-act play, *Shantytown Scandal*, she explores the implications of the Depression Era on people of color. Other socially conscious stories from the 1930s which never received copyrights include her "Aunt Viney" tales, a series of humorous anecdotes about a dialect-using, advice-wielding Harlem wise-woman who predates and foreshadows Langston Hughes "Jesse B. Semple" character (Guillaume 34). Bush-Banks left over sixty works unpublished at her death, the majority of which appear in *The Collected Works of Olivia Ward Bush-Banks*, a 1991 volume edited by her descendent, Bernice Forrest Guillaume.

CRITICAL RECEPTION

Very little criticism of Olivia Ward Bush-Banks's work exists, especially from her time. Upon reading *Driftwood*, Paul Laurence Dunbar remarked that it "should be an inspiration to the women of our race." A December 1938 letter from Carter G. Woodson, editor of the *Negro History Bulletin*, also praised her poetry. From the past century, only Bernice Forrest Guillaume and Marie Blue Bennis have explored Bush-Banks beyond biography, revisiting the themes of racial dualism, pride, and identity in—and the social and literary implications of—Bush-Banks's writing.

BIBLIOGRAPHY

Works by Olivia Ward Bush-Banks

The Collected Works of Olivia Ward Bush-Banks, edited by Bernice Forrest Guillaume. New York: Oxford University Press, 1991.
Driftwood. Providence, RI: Atlantic Printing Co., 1914.
Memories of Calvary. Philadelphia: A.M.E. Book Concern, 1915.
Original Poems. Providence, RI: Louis A. Basinet Press, 1899.

Studies of Olivia Ward Bush-Banks's Works

Altman, Susan. "Olivia Ward Bush Banks." In *The Encyclopedia of African-American Heritage*. New York: Facts on File, 1997.
Bennis, Marie Blue. "Reclaiming a Multicultural Heritage: Race, Identity, and Culture in the Life and Literary Works of Olivia Ward Bush-Banks." DAI, Section A: *The Humanities and Social Sciences* 61.2 (August 2000): 607.
Bush, Theresa G. *Black American Writers Past and Present: A Biographical and Bibliographical Dictionary, Volume One*. Metuchen, NJ: Scarecrow Press, 1975.
Daniels, John. *In Freedom's Birthplace: A Study of the Boston Negroes*. 1914. Reprint, New York: Negro University Press, 1968.
Grant, Nathan L. "Olivia Ward Bush-Banks." In *American National Biography, Vol. 4*. New York: Oxford University Press, 1999.
Guillaume, Bernice F. "Character Names in *Indian Trails* by Olivia Ward Bush (Banks): Clues to Afro Assimilation in Long Island's Native Americans." *Afro-Americans in New York Life and History* 10.2 (1986): 45–53.
———. "The Female as Harlem Sage: The 'Aunt Viney's Sketches' of Olivia Ward Bush-Banks." *Langston Hughes Review* 6.2 (1987): 1–10.

———. "Olivia Ward Bush: Factors Shaping the Social and Cultural Outlook of a Nineteenth-Century Writer." *Negro History Bulletin* 43 (1980): 32–34.

Hatch, James V., and Omanil Abdullah. *Black Playwrights, 1823–1977: An Annotated Bibliography of Plays*. New York: Bowker Press, 1977.

Matthews, G. S. *Black American Writers 1773–1949: A Bibliography and Union List*. Boston: G. K. Hall, 1975.

Porter, Dorothy B. *North American Negro Poets: A Checklist of Their Writings*. Hattiesburg, MS: The Book Farm, 1945.

Schomburg, Arthur A. *A Bibliographical Checklist of American Negro Poetry*. New York: Doran Co., 1916.

Shockley, Ann Allen. *Afro-American Women Writers 1746–1933: An Anthology and Critical Guide*. Boston: G. K. Hall, 1988.

Susan M. Stone

OCTAVIA BUTLER (1947–2006)

BIOGRAPHICAL NARRATIVE

Often referred to as the "grand dame" of science fiction, Octavia Butler is the first, if not the only, successful female African American writer of science fiction and fantasy, making a dramatic change in the predominantly white male landscape of the genre. She has published twelve novels as well as a collection of short stories and critical essays.

Octavia Estelle Butler was born in Pasadena, California, on July 22, 1947. Her father having died when she was very young, and herself an only child, Butler was brought up by her mother in a racially mixed community, one that was united by a common day-to-day struggle to make ends meet. Although not having to contend with the more formal and harsh aspects of segregation, Butler experienced the burden of racism through the experiences of her mother who worked as a housemaid and learned to recognize the required heroism of the so-called ordinary life, a recognition that becomes manifest in her fiction.

Writing since she was ten years old, Butler is often quoted as ascribing her own turn to speculative fiction to an episode at the age of twelve, when her frustration with a particularly bad film on television led to the emerging conviction that she could do better. Described as a shy girl and often lonely, Butler increasingly turned to her writing for comfort and company. In 1968 Butler received her Associate of Arts degree from Pasadena City College. She went on to attend California State University, Los Angeles, and the University of California, Los Angeles, but attributes her growth as a writer mainly to independent programs such as the Open Door Program of the Screen Writers Guild of America and the Clarion Science Fiction Writers Workshop.

After publishing a number of short stories, Butler's *Patternmaster* (1976) was published to significant critical acclaim, a text that became the first of five novels in her Patternist series. She has also published the Xenogenesis series, consisting of three texts, and two of an initially planned six Earthseed novels. In addition to these and to *Bloodchild and Other Stories*, a collection of shorter writing, Butler's neo-slave narrative *Kindred* (1979) is possibly the most widely known novel, if arguably the least rigidly science-fictional of her work. In 2005, Butler's final novel, *Fledgling*, was published. There, writing about vampires, she explores more explicitly the gothic traditions which were addressed subtly in her earlier works.

MAJOR WORKS

Butler's contribution to the domain of speculative fiction goes far beyond her racial or gendered identity. Butler's rich oeuvre singularly participates in the generic discourse while simultaneously challenging many of its defining characteristics. Herself wary of rigid stylistic categorizations, Butler comments that

A good story is a good story. If what I'm writing reaches you, then it reaches you no matter what title is stuck on it. The titles are mainly so that you'll know where to look in the library, or as a marketing title, know where to put it in the bookstore so booksellers know how to sell it. It has very little to do with actual writing. (Sanders)

While refraining from any overt focus on purely generic concerns (preferring a tight narrative to extraneous descriptions of the alternate realities she creates, for example), Butler's texts manipulate the imaginative foundation of her narratives to contend with key individual, social, and cultural paradigms. Although rarely political in any dogmatic or didactic sense, it is precisely through her subtly understated concern with issues of genre, gender, and race, and their constant thematic presence throughout, that illuminates Butler's particular literary treatment of them.

In her Patternist series Butler explores different patterns of evolution for the human race. She imagines a possibility of apparent regression, through the aggressive and animal-like Clayarks in *Patternmaster*. This model of gradual but extreme degeneration becomes complicated as Butler offers a redeeming quality both in the underlying humanity of the Clayarks's early days, described in *Clay's Ark* (1984), and in their rather desperate intelligence with which they survive and exist in constant contest with the "mutes" and telepaths. Allegorizing the processes of *othering*, which characterize the history of American racism, Butler further disrupts the fundamental presumption of human supremacy (a supremacy based on the defining capacity of the human mind and spirit), in *Survivor* (1978). Describing a culture of racist intolerance and fear within the human community of religious missionaries that has established a colony among an alien species, Butler demonstrates the possible limitations and dangers of such psychosocial patterns.

The imagined progress possible in human evolution is described in *Mind of My Mind* (1977). The narrative describes the development of a telepathic matrix, the ur-pattern, which links the members to one another and to the patternmaster. The progress associated with these enhanced mental capabilities (powers which overpower physical ones, as healers can control the body with their minds) is challenged, however, as Butler illuminates the devastating price of their development, a price exacted through violence and articulated through models of hierarchy and subservience. *Wild Seed* (1980) tells the story of Anyanwu and Doro, the two forebears of a new race. Anyanwu is a maternal figure and a healer whose body can take the shape of virtually any living being. Doro, on the other hand, is an autocratic character who must feed by killing as he appropriates the body of his opponents. The narrative follows the progress of Doro's long-lasting project to create a new race, a project whose power structures unmistakably echo the socio-cultural history of slavery. Thus Butler demonstrates the inevitable abuse of power concomitant with its progressive possibilities. The shifting relationship between these protagonists through the generations manifests the primary tension of a mind-body binary, a binary that informs all of these humanoid races, and serves as the conceptual and thematic crux of the Patternist series.

The aforementioned paradigm of a tangible psychology, as manifest in a physically binding telepathic pattern, and an intangible physicality, as it is literally translated into an alien form, is reconfigured in *Kindred* (1979). Apparently moving away from the style and content characteristic of Butler's other texts, *Kindred* can be read as a neo-slave narrative as it renegotiates the tropes and structures central to this form. This move into other literary forms notwithstanding, the reader soon learns that time-travel is the essential premise of the narrative. In the novel, Dana Franklin, a young African American woman newly married to Kevin, a white man, is transported back and forth from Los Angeles, in 1976, to a nineteenth-century slave plantation in Maryland. Dana quickly discovers that her journey through time is directly related to the life of Rufus Weylin, a slave owner and distant ancestor. The link between them is an absolutely vital one as she is called back through time and space at moments when his life is endangered and moves forward when her own is threatened.

Dana's own crucial role in ensuring the beginning of her own family line must be fulfilled before her return to 1976 can become permanent, a role that comes at a costly physical and ideological sacrifice. Explaining this decision, Butler comments that "I couldn't really let her come all the way back. I couldn't let her return to what she was, I couldn't let her come back whole...Antebellum slavery didn't leave people quite whole" (Kenan 498). Butler never explains the mechanism for time travel but develops it as a literary conduit which links twentieth-century African American experience not only to the horrors but also to the complexities (personal, social, economic, and cultural) of slavery. The parallel existence that Dana begins to experience demonstrates the "contemporaneity of history" (McKible), on one hand, but also the impossibility of historical representation, on the other. Finding herself at a public whipping, Dana is profoundly distressed and genuinely surprised by this gap. "I had seen people beaten on television and in the movies. I had seen the too-red blood substitute streaked across their backs and heard their well-rehearsed screams. But I hadn't lain nearby and smelled their sweat or heard them pleading and praying shamed before their families and themselves" (36). The protagonist must take an active role in conceiving her past for her present to be at all possible or for this past to be real in any true sense. Thus, embracing the literary freedom afforded her by the genre of science fiction in which she participates, Butler stretches the realism of her narrative to include a literal temporal journey so that she may be able to depict the reality of a virtually unimaginable experience of slavery, and to contend with its contemporary reverberations.

The rigid political economy of reproduction during slavery and its implications on gendered roles, identities, and definitions become reconfigured in Butler's award-winning short story "Bloodchild" and in her Xenogenesis series. Reprinted as *Lilith's Brood* (2000), the three novels take place in a postapocalyptic universe, centuries after a war that killed most of Earth's inhabitants and made it virtually uninhabitable. Into this setting Butler introduces the Oankali, powerful alien beings who survive symbiotically through genetic exchange with primitive peoples. Traveling across the galaxies, through time, the Oankali are in perpetual flux: by collecting and combining genetic structures of indigenous populations with those of their own, they gradually alter each irrevocably and continue evolving, a pattern they impose on humans for the duration of the novels.

In *Dawn* (1987), the first of the series, to ensure optimal cooperation in a procreative project that cloaks the disturbing resonance of the political economy of slavery with evolutionary concerns of survival, the Oankali select and train Lilith Iyapo, an African American woman who lost her husband and son in the war, to mediate between other humans and themselves. Significantly named after the mythologically subversive feminine archetype, a mother of demons, Butler's Lilith eventually becomes the human progenitor of a mixed species. Depicting the gradual emergence of this new species in *Adulthood Rites* (1988) and *Imago* (1989), Butler's Oankali embody a dramatic transgression of expected boundaries of gendered identities. Not only do they become identified with a particular gender only as they grow into procreative maturity, but they have a third gender—the ooloi, who are neither male nor female. In "Bloodchild," Butler similarly depicts a human-alien coexistence that relies on altered cultural and physical (as well as political) roles, which defined by reproductive processes. In exchange for protection and relative autonomy, and in what gradually approximates a nurturing symbiotic relationship, the alien Tlic population exacts a price of at least one son from each human family. These boys serve as host bodies for alien eggs that are torn out by a female Tlic in a "blood ritual." Through these disruptions of normative cultural expectations and through their echoes in the changing sexual and social behavior of the humans in these texts, Butler explores the possibilities theorized in contemporary gender discourse.

In her Earthseed series, Butler constructs a dystopian vision of the near future in America. Depicting a social, economic, political, and cultural apocalypse and its aftermath, in her two parables, respectively, Butler has moved from the alien constructs of her earlier works to a narrative scope that is more grounded in a naturalist tradition. Positioning herself in the tradition of dystopian fiction, this nearly recognizable context serves to highlight those destructive themes of human behavior being explored. Butler's parables retain the strong African American female protagonist characteristic of Butler's writing but her vision focuses on a much nearer and bleaker future.

Participating in current critical ecological, urban, and sociological discourses, *Parable of the Sower* (1993) and *Parable of the Talents* (1998) envision a war-torn, violence-ridden earth and a community of people who struggle to survive. Guiding this community is Lauren Olamina, a young woman who, across the two novels, is transformed into a messiah figure, leading her people to salvation. The Earthseed texts resonate scriptural writing as they narrate Olamina's growth into maturity as a woman and as a leader, and her gradual development of the Earthseed religion. The theological premise of the texts is a relatively straightforward humanist one that, although it ultimately promises a destiny in the stars, is firmly grounded in the practicalities of life. Through this destiny of displacement, Butler's novels investigate constructs of self and community, examining alternate models of behavior under conditions of distress and emergency. Moreover, reminiscence of the relationship of the Oankali to their environment, Earthseed demonstrates the absolute imperative to achieve a balance of coexistence with the landscape (physical as well as cultural).

Finally, both texts are narrated through a series of journal entries by various characters, a decision which lends an autobiographical tone to the texts. By introducing these intradiegetic narrators in a process that is simultaneously personal and private—in the journals and public—in their implicit publication, Butler thematizes the very structure of the novels and reflects on the effects which sociopolitical crises can have on the very notion of self as well as on the narratives of history. Examining the narrative structure of the novels inevitably reveals the combined influence of journals with travel narratives, while simultaneously revisiting the tradition of the slave narrative. Through the quintessential American version of the journey and the travel narrative, Butler's novel repositions the function and nature of some of the central themes of modern American literature: family, religion, society, home, politics, love, and death.

Butler returns to these themes in *Fledgling*, the last novel published before her untimely death. This first-person narrative follows Shori Matthews, a pre-pubescent 53-year-old vampire with the appearance of a human child, as she recovers from a near-fatal injury and must contend with complete memory loss to rediscover her past and understand who is trying to kill her. As Shori learns to survive by reuniting with her people, the Ina, and by establishing symbiotic relationships with humans around her, relationships that become fital for her and for her symbiants, it becomes clear that she is the successful product of genetic experiments, combining Ina with African American blookdlines, to adapt the Ina to the changing needs of their environment. Blood, which so often serves metonymically to signal both race and history, becomes—through the vampire romance genre—a literal means through which Butler reconfigures the bases of contemporary western society. Here, family, community, history, and biology are explored, not as static or predetermined objects, but as dynamic variables that open new possibilities for human interaction.

CRITICAL RECEPTION

Butler's first published story "Crossover," in 1971, received limited critical notice. *Patternmaster*, her first published novel, on the other hand, established her as a serious writer of science fiction. Butler has received numerous awards recognizing the importance of her work in the field of science fiction and in literature. In 1984, Butler's short story "Speech Sounds" won the prestigious Hugo Award as best short story of that year. The following year Butler's "Bloodchild" won both the 1985 Hugo and the 1984 Nebula awards as best novelette—two of the most valued awards in the genre. Butler received widespread recognition in 1995 when she became the first writer of science fiction to be awarded the five-year MacArthur Fellowship which rewards creative people who push the boundaries of their fields. The second novel in her latest series, *Parable of the Talents*, won the 1999 Nebula for Best Novel, and in the year 2000 Butler was awarded the PEN Center West Lifetime Achievement Award.

Despite her unquestioned standing in the field of speculative fiction, there is an astonishing dearth of full-length critical work published on Butler's writing. Ruth Salvaggio's important 1984 article, "Octavia Butler and the Black Science-Fiction Heroine," on the Patternist novels focuses on identity constructs, arguing that Butler's fiction not only challenges preexisting hierarchies but also, through the empowered black female protagonists, disrupts the very structure of systemic hegemony. This hierarchical infrastructure is further eroded in Elyce Rae Helford's 1994 essay. Concentrating primarily on "Bloodchild," Helford illuminates the power structures intrinsic to processes of labeling and identity constructions, and examines how—and to what end—Butler's texts are located on the intersection of high art and popular culture. Helford's article offers a significant precursor to Madhu Dubey's "Books of Life: Postmodern Uses of Print Literacy," in *Signs and Cities*, one of the most recent and more acute readings of Butler's first Earthseed novel. Here Dubey meticulously positions Butler's work within a critical African American literary tradition, which she then reinserts into a postmodern discourse on modern humanism and print culture. Dubey demonstrates how Butler reconfigures the printed text as a rehabilitative force that engages in a productive (and empowering) dialogue with the possibilities and the problems of postmodern cultural and political contexts.

BIBLIOGRAPHY

Works by Octavia Butler

Adulthood Rites. New York: Questar, 1988.
Bloodchild and Other Stories. New York: Seven Stories Press, 1995.

Clay's Ark. New York: Aspect, 1984.

Dawn. New York: Aspect, 1987.

Imago. New York: Aspect, 1989.

Kindred. 1979. Reprint, Boston: Beacon Press, 2003.

Mind of My Mind. New York: Aspect, 1977.

"The Monophobic Response." In *Dark Matter: A Century of Speculative Fiction from The African Diaspora*, edited by Sheree R. Thomas. New York: Aspect, 2001. First published, *Journeys* PEN/Faulkner Foundation. Rockville, MD: Quill & Brush, 1996.

Parable of the Sower. London: The Women's Press, 1995. First Published, New York: Four Walls Eight Windows, 1993.

Parable of the Talents. London: The Women's Press, 2001. First Published, New York: Seven Stories Press, 1998.

Patternmaster. New York: Aspect, 1976.

Survivor. New York: Doubleday, 1978.

Wild Seed. New York: Aspect, 1980.

Studies of Octavia Butler's Works

Allison, Dorothy. "The Future of Female: Octavia Butler's Mother Lode." In *Reading Black, Reading Feminist: A Critical Anthology*, edited by Henry Louis Gates, Jr., 471–78. London: Penguin Books, 1990. First published, *Village Voice*, December 19, 1989, 67–68.

Barr, Marleen S., ed. *Envisioning the Future: Science Fiction and the Next Millennium*. Middletown, CT: Wesleyan University Press, 2003.

Crossley, Robert. "Critical Essay." In *Kindred*. Boston: Beacon Press, 2003.

Doerksen, Teri Ann. "Octavia E. Butler: Parables of Race and Difference." In *Into Darkness Peering: Race and Color in the Fantastic*, edited by Elisabeth Anne Leonard, 21–34. London: Greenwood Press, 1997.

Doughton, Sandi. "Octavia Butler—Science Fiction Author." *Seattle Times* (May 16, 2004).

Dubey, Madhu. *Signs and Cities: Black Literary Postmodernism*. Chicago: University of Chicago Press, 2003.

Govan, Sandra Y. "Connections, Links, and Extended Networks: Patterns in Octavia Butler's Fiction." *Black American Literature Forum* 18.2 (1984): 82–87.

Helford, Elyce Rae. " 'Would You Really Rather Die Than Bear My Young?': The Constructions of Race, Gender, and Species in Octavia E. Butler's 'Bloodchild.' " *African American Review* 28.2 (1994): 259–71.

Kenan, Randall. "An Interview with Octavia E. Butler." *Callaloo* 41.2 (Spring 1991): 495–504.

Luckhurst, Roger. " 'Going Postal': Rage, Science Fiction, and the Ends of the American Subject." In *Edging into the Future: Science Fiction and Contemporary Cultural Transformation*, edited by Veronica Hollinger and Joan Gordon, 142–56. Philadelphia: University of Pennsylvania Press, 2002.

McKible, Adam. "These Are the Facts of the Darky's History: Thinking History and Reading Names in Four African American Texts." *African American Review* 28.2 (Summer 1994): 223–35.

Roberts, Robin. "Gender and Science Fiction." *MFS (Modern Fiction Studies)* 50.3 (2004): 734–39.

Salvaggio, Ruth. "Octavia Butler and the Black Science-Fiction Heroine." *Black American Literature Forum* 18.2 (1984): 78–81.

Sanders, Joshunda. "The Africana QA: Octavia Butler." *AOL Black Voices*, February 24, 2004, http://archive.blackvoices.com/articles (accessed February 25, 2004).

Shinn, Thelma J. "The Wise Witches: Black Women Mentors in the Fiction of Octavia E. Butler." In *Conjuring: Black Women, Fiction, and Literary Tradition*, edited by Marjorie Pryse and Hortense J. Spillers, 203–15. Bloomington: Indiana University Press, 1985.

Weixlmann, Joe. "An Octavia Butler Bibliography." *Black American Literature Forum* 18.2 (1984): 88–89.
White, Donna R. "Introduction." In *Dancing with Dragons: Ursula K. Le Guin and the Critics.* New York: Camden House—Boydell & Brewer Inc., 1999, 1–6.

Keren Omry

JEANNETTE FRANKLIN CAINES (1938–2004)

BIOGRAPHICAL NARRATIVE

Author of acclaimed books about children and their families, Jeanette Caines was born and raised in Harlem and attended school in New York City. She grew up in a religious Baptist family, joined the Lutheran church, but then returned to the Baptist church. Her husband's name is Alan, and her children are Kevin and Abby (who are also the main characters in her book titled *Abby*). Caines was inspired to read and write after she read Jesse Jackson's book *Call Me Charley*. She worked for many years in Harper & Row's Juvenile Book Department. Caines has also been a member of the Coalition of One Hundred Black Women's Council for Adoptable Children and the Negro Business and Professional Women of Nassau County (New York). She was a member of the Board of Directors of the Salvation Army and the Council of Christ Lutheran Church in Nassau County. Caines resided in Freeport, Long Island (New York), before moving to Charlottesville, Virginia. In 2004, the year of her death, Caines received a Lifetime Achievement Award from Motheread and Fatheread of the Virginia Foundation.

MAJOR WORKS

In Caines's first book, *Abby* (1973), the title character, Abby, reads her baby book with her older brother, Kevin, and her mother. She learns that she was born in Manhattan and was adopted when she was eleven and a half months old. Reading her baby book gives Abby a sense of belonging within her family, and her mother's compilation of Abby's baby book makes the girl feel welcome and part of the family. She accepts adoption and even wants the family to adopt a brother for her and Kevin. Kevin takes pride in his sister and wants to bring her to his class for show and tell. Caines manifests how this adoption leads to a cohesive family unit.

Just Us Women (1982) concerns a road trip to North Carolina that the narrator will take with her Aunt Martha. In a segment, the young narrator mentions that she remembers things for her forgetful aunt, who absentmindedly takes two road maps with her in case she loses one and who forgot the map and their lunch on the kitchen table last time. This is a road trip for females only; they can take their time and shop or look around without men telling them to stop dawdling. The story embraces sisterhood and camaraderie between the females, who gain autonomy by leaving the controlling men home. She anticipates that the men will be jealous and will demand, upon their return, to know what took them so long; she conjectures, "we will just tell them we had a lot of girl talk to do between the two of us. No boys and no men—just us women" (32).

Chilly Stomach (1986), an important and progressive children's book, concerns a girl, Sandy, who experiences a chilly stomach whenever her Uncle Jim visits. Uncle Jim tickles Sandy and kisses her on the lips. As an adolescent, the narrator distinguishes between the loving kisses of her parents and the inappropriate kisses of her Uncle Jim, causing her to ask to sleep over at her friend Jill's house. Sandy confides in Jill that her uncle is acting inappropriately toward her, and Jill indicates that she will tell her mother and that Sandy should confide in her own parents. Sandy has been reluctant to tell her parents because she is afraid that they will dislike her for telling on her uncle. At the conclusion, Sandy makes the right decision—to tell her parents what her Uncle Jim has done to her. This action suggests that Caines is directing her young readers who are experiencing the same dilemma to come forward and help themselves.

In *I Need a Lunch Box* (1988), the nameless narrator is jealous because his older sister, Doris, is getting a lunch box because she will be entering the first grade, while he, who is too young for school, will not be receiving one. He contemplates that he would put his crayons, marbles, bug collection, or toy animals in it, indicating that he is perhaps not ready for one because he does not understand its purpose. In a beautiful and imaginative touch, Caines shows the narrator dreaming of having five lunch boxes, each of a different color, for each day of the week; the lunch boxes walk in a parade. His father, understanding his desire (he calls it a need) for a lunch box, buys him one so that he can be like his sister. The story deftly covers a significant theme in childhood development—the pangs of frustration and hurt that young children experience when their older siblings can acquire things and do activities that they, because they are too young, cannot.

CRITICAL RECEPTION

Critical reception of Caines's work has been positive. Critics like the sensitive way that she handles touchy issues, such as adoption and divorce. For her excellent work, Caines has received the National Black Child Development Institute's Certificate of Merit and Appreciation.

Caines books have, unfortunately, not received the attention that they deserve. The books have received good reviews (aside from *Chilly Stomach*) and portray positive African American role models and portray African American culture in a positive light. Maia Angelique Sorrells enjoys the open endings: "Often Caines' books end without a resolution to the problem. This encourages thought and discussion and facilitates effective communication and problem solving between parents and children" (116). Some critics have complained, however, that *Chilly Stomach* should not be read by young children because of the subject matter (sexual abuse of a little girl) and because the ending lacks a clear resolution to Sandy's dilemma. The other books have received positive reviews for the author's gentle humor, the healthy relationships between parents and children, tackling serious subjects (such as adoption, divorce, and the pangs of being unable to do what older siblings do), and for being excellent role models for African American children. Caines says, "I think it's important that I'm listed as a black writer, that the illustrations in my books are of black children. There aren't many books about black kids, there aren't many black authors going around talking to kids" (Raymond 25).

BIBLIOGRAPHY

Works by Jeannette Franklin Caines

Abby. New York: Harper & Row, 1973.
Chilly Stomach. New York: Harper & Row, 1986.

Daddy. New York: Harper & Row, 1977.
I Need a Lunch Box. New York: Harper & Row, 1988.
Just Us Women. New York: Harper & Row, 1982.
Window Wishing. New York: Harper & Row, 1980.

Studies of Jeannette Franklin Caines's Works

Commire, Anne, ed. "Jeanette Caines." In *Something about the Author: Facts and Pictures about Authors and Illustrators of Books for Young People*, vol. 43. Detroit: Gale, 1986, 52–53.

Hile, Kevin S., ed. "Jeanette Franklin Caines." In *Something about the Author: Facts and Pictures about Authors and Illustrators of Books for Young People*, vol. 78. Detroit: Gale, 1994, 23–25.

Raymond, Allen. "Jeannette Caines: A Proud Author, with Good Reason." *Early Years* 13.7 (March 1983): 24–25.

Rollock, Barbara. "Jeannette Franklin Caines." In *Black Authors & Illustrators of Children's Books: A Biographical Dictionary*, 2nd ed., 32. New York: Garland, 1992.

Sorrells, Maia Angelique. "Jeanette Franklin Caines." In *Oxford Companion to African American Literature*, edited by William L. Andrews, Frances Smith Foster, and Trudier Harris, 116. New York: Oxford University Press, 1997.

Ward, Martha, et al., eds. "Jeantte Franklin Caines." In *Authors of Books for Young People*, 3rd ed., 105. Metuchen, NJ: Scarecrow Press, 1990.

Eric Sterling

BEBE MOORE CAMPBELL (1950–)

BIOGRAPHICAL NARRATIVE

Novelist and playwright Bebe Moore Campbell has also authored children's books. Her essays, articles, and excerpts appear in many anthologies. She was born in Philadelphia, Pennsylvania, in 1950, the only child of Doris and George Moore. After her parent's divorce, she grew up in both the north and the south, spending school months with her mother and grandmother, and summer months with her father.

Campbell attended the University of Pittsburgh, graduating in 1972 with a Bachelor of Science degree in Elementary Education. She taught school for five years before becoming dissatisfied with her chosen career, and began attending writing workshops where she nurtured her love of writing.

Campbell gained her first publication when a fiction piece appeared in *Essence* magazine. She went on to write a nonfiction book, *Successful Women, Angry Men: Backlash in the Two-Career Marriage* (1986), and followed up with her memoir, *Sweet Summer: Growing Up with and without My Dad* (1990).

Campbell published her first novel, the critically acclaimed *Your Blues Ain't Like Mine*, in 1992. She has since penned three best-selling novels: *Brothers and Sisters*, one of *New York Times*'s most notable books of 1992; *Singing in the Comeback Choir*; and *What You Owe Me*, *Los Angeles Times*'s "Best Book of 2001."

Campbell's first children's book, *Sometimes My Mommy Gets Angry*, won the National Alliance for the Mentally Ill (NAMI) Outstanding Literature Award for 2003. Several of her essays and articles have appeared in such publications as *Ms. Magazine* and the *New York Times*. She is also a regular morning commentator on National Public Radio.

The mother of two currently resides in Los Angeles with her husband.

MAJOR WORKS

Campbell's fiction is heavily influenced by her personal experiences and displays her fascination with human relations. Having grown up in both the north and south, the author witnessed firsthand the effects of racial segregation. The Emmett Till murder happened when she was just five years old and inspired *Your Blues Ain't Like Mine*, which chronicles the events following and a racially divided community's reaction to the brutal murder of fifteen-year-old Armstrong Todd, an African American.

Watching the fallout of the Rodney King beating and the LA riots that ensued was the basis for her second novel, *Brothers and Sisters*, about the blossoming friendship between Esther, a black woman, and Mallory, a white woman, in the midst of LA's racial tension.

Campbell focused more on healing with the novels *Singing in the Comeback Choir*, where a woman deals with the aftermath of her husband's affair, and *What You Owe Me*, where the descendant of an African American entrepreneur fights to receive what was stolen from her mother in a bad business venture years prior.

Having watched a close loved one suffer from mental illness, Campbell was moved to address the issue in her most recent works. The children's book *Sometimes My Mommy Gets Angry* is about a little girl whose mother is mentally ill, and *72 Hour Hold*, Campbell's most recent novel, focuses on a single mother whose daughter struggles with bipolar disorder. Campbell's stage play *Even with the Madness* also explores the theme of mental illness, debuted in New York in 2003.

CRITICAL RECEPTION

Campbell's most critically acclaimed novels are her first two, *Your Blues Ain't Like Mine* and *Brothers and Sisters*, both of which focus heavily on race relations. Much of this acclaim, however, is from reviews. A few academic analysis of her work exist.

Although most of the reviews praise Campbell's ability to write about the delicate issue of race, Clyde Edgerton of the *New York Times* finds merits in Campbell's use of point of view. In 1992, about *Your Blues Ain't Like Mine*, he writes, "[m]uch of the power of this novel results from Ms. Campbell's subtle and seamless shifting of point of view." About *Brothers and Sisters*, *Publishers Weekly* said in 1994 that "[a]droitly using the great racial divide of Los Angeles, this absorbing novel explores the intricacies of experience, knowledge and bias which perpetuate inequalities and segregated lives."

In addition to various recognition and awards, Campbell has also received praise for her other novels, a children's book, and a recent stage play.

BIBLIOGRAPHY

Works by Bebe Moore Campbell

Brother and Sisters. New York: Berkeley Books, 1994.
72 Hour Hold. New York: Penguin Putnam, 2005.
Singing in the Comeback Choir. New York: Penguin Putnam, 1998.
Sometimes My Mommy Gets Angry. Illustrated by E. B. Lewis. New York: Penguin Putnam, 2003.
Successful Women, Angry Men: Backlash in the Two-Career Marriage. New York: Penguin Putnam, 1986.
Sweet Summer: Growing Up with and without My Dad. New York: Berkeley Books, 1990.
What You Owe Me. New York: Penguin Putnam, 2001.
Your Blues Ain't Like Mine. New York: Ballantine, 1992.

Studies of Bebe Moore Campbell's Works

Peacock, Scot, et al., eds. *Contemporary Authors: New Revision Series* 81. Farmington Hills, MI: Gale, 1999, 83–85.
Russell-Robinson, Joyce. "Bebe Moore Campbell (1950–)." In *Contemporary African-American Novelists: A Bio-Bibliographic Critical Sourcebook*, edited by Emmanuel S. Nelson, 76–81. Westport, CT: Greenwood Press, 1999.

Tenille Brown

BARBARA CHASE-RIBOUD (1939–)

BIOGRAPHICAL NARRATIVE

Barbara Chase-Riboud is an artist as well as a poet and novelist. She was born on June 1939 in Philadelphia, Pennsylvania, the only daughter of Charles Edward Chase and Vivian May West. In 1946, she enrolled at the Fletcher Memorial Art School. Then, she became a student at the Philadelphia Museum School of Art. She also attended the Philadelphia Academy of Music.

Chase-Riboud began writing poetry in 1950, enrolled at the Philadelphia High School for Girls and finally graduated summa cum laude. In 1957, she graduated from Tyler School of Fine Arts in Elkins Park, Pennsylvania. One year later, she studied at the American Academy in Rome. Moreover, during her stay in Italy, she decided to spend three months traveling and studying art in Egypt. Chase-Riboud returned to the United States in 1959 and attended Yale University where she studied design and architecture. After receiving her master's degree, she moved to London in 1960.

She arrived in Paris in 1961. There, she married French photographer Marc Riboud. She traveled throughout Europe and, in 1963, she made a trip to the Soviet Union.

Her first son David Charles was born in 1964, and the following year she visited the People's Republic of China. Her poems written at that time reflect her previous visits to China as well as Egypt. Her second son Alexis Karol was born in 1967. Later, Chase-Riboud divorced her first husband in 1981 and married Sergio Tosi, an Italian publisher, art expert/historian.

MAJOR WORKS

Chase-Riboud's literary career started with a book of poetry, *From Memphis to Peking* (1974). In the 1960s, she exhibited her works not only in Europe but also in West Africa. Thereafter, throughout the 1970s, her art pieces were displayed in the United States and Europe.

Chase-Riboud's *Sally Hemings* (1979) propelled her to the front stage of the literary scene. She published *Valide: A Novel of the Harem* in 1986. Her third novel *Echo of Lions* (1989) was inspired by the story of a former African slave. The prequel to *Sally Hemings*, *The President's Daughter* was completed in 1994.

Most recently, Riboud's *Hottentot Venus: A Novel* (2003) tells the tragic story of South African Sarah Baartman who was taken to London by an English surgeon.

The idea of writing *Sally Hemings* came from her interest in the story of an African American slave who became romantically involved with Thomas Jefferson. In *Valide: A Novel of the Harem*, she relates the enslavement of an American Creole girl by Algerian pirates in 1802.

Portrait of a Nude Woman as Cleopatra (1987) uses Plutarch's description of Cleopatra and the events in her life. Riboud's poem is a melologue, a combination of both male and female voices imitated by one person and a recitation with musical accompaniment.

CRITICAL RECEPTION

Following the publication of *Sally Hemings* (1979), Chase-Riboud received the Janet Heidinger Kafka prize for best historical novel. The text leads to Chase-Riboud being praised for the breadth of her historical research on the lives of African slaves, slave traders, and slave narratives in the nineteenth century. Specifically, she has received rave reviews for skillfully weaving fictional characters and scenes into her historical fiction. An article in the *New York Tribune* explains that "the sadness captured in the final pages of this novel is a testimonial to the sensitiveness of an important novelist." Likewise, a review in the *San Francisco Chronicle* highlights that "Chase-Riboud is a scrupulous historical researcher who writes movingly of the horrifying, murderous brutality of the slave trade. Her descriptions of the starvation, mass suicides and insanity stir us in a way that a mere historical account could never match." *Essence* magazine shows that "the historical backdrop gives . . . a rare glimpse into the lives of free Black men and women in the pre-Civil War era and a place for her brilliant depiction of John Quincy Adams."

In 1997, the film *Amistad* by Steven Spielberg was inspired by Chase-Riboud's *Echo of Lions* (1989). Alex Haley wrote, "*Echo of Lions* is a brilliant dramatization of the most gripping, significant and epic saga that a century of slave ships ever produced."

Chase-Riboud won the Carl Sandburg prize for a book of poetry titled *Portrait of a Nude Woman as Cleopatra*. Furthermore, the French government awarded her the Knighthood in Arts and Letters in 1996. More recently, the Black Caucus of the American Library Association named *Hottentot Venus: A Novel* (2003) "Best Fiction Book of 2004." Interestingly, *Africa Rising* (1998), her eighteen-foot bronze memorial sculpture, was also inspired from her desire to restore Sarah Baartman's human dignity.

Finally, Barbara Chase-Riboud has been the subject of a number of books published internationally from the 1970s until the late 1990s and she has also been featured in many periodicals.

BIBLIOGRAPHY

Works by Barbara Chase-Riboud

Echo of Lions. New York: Morrow, 1989.
From Memphis to Peking: *Poems*. New York: Random House, 1974.
HottentotVenus: A Novel. New York: Doubleday, 2003.
Portrait of a Nude Woman as Cleopatra. New York: Morrow, 1987.
The President's Daughter. New York: Random House, 1994.
Sally Hemings: *A Novel*. New York: Random House, 1979.
Valide: *A Novel of the Harem*. New York: Morrow, 1986.

Studies of Barbara Chase-Riboud's Works

Cohen, Roger. "Judge Says Copyright Covers Writer's Ideas of a Jefferson Affair." *New York Times* (August 15, 1991).
Davis, Thadius M., and Trudier Harris, eds. *Dictionary of Literary Biography: Afro-American Fiction Writers After 1955*, vol. 33. Farmington Hills, MI: Thomson Gale, 1984.
Farris, Phoebe, ed. *Women Artists of Color: A Bio-Critical Sourcebook to 20th Century Artists in the Americas*. Westport, CT: Greenwood Press, 1999.

Jansen, Anthony, and Peter Selz, eds. *Barbara Chase-Riboud, Sculptor.* New York: Harry N. Abrams, 1999.
McKee, Sarah. "Barbara (Dewayne Tosi) Chase-Riboud." In *Contemporary African American Novelists: A Bio-Bibliographical Critical Sourcebook,* edited by Emmanuel S. Nelson. Westport, CT: Greenwood Press, 1999.
Witzling, Mara R., ed. *Voicing Today's Visions: Writings by Contemporary Women Artists.* New York: Universe Publishing, 1994.

Ginette Curry

ALICE CHILDRESS (1916–1994)

BIOGRAPHICAL NARRATIVE

Although Alice Childress enjoyed a career as a novelist, playwright, director, actress, and activist that spanned four decades, the details of her early life are elusive and Childress's reticence in discussing her private life further obscures her personal narrative. Alice Herndon Childress was born on October 12, 1916, in Charleston, South Carolina, to Florence White, a seamstress, and Alonzo Herrington. After her parents' separation, her maternal grandmother, Eliza Campbell White became her legal guardian and Childress subsequently moved from Charleston to Harlem in 1925. She would later emphasize the significance of this move and of White's influence on her life in an interview with Elizabeth Brown-Guillory identifying the change as "a very fortunate thing that happened" (Brown-Guillory 67).

Even as Childress's mother continued to play a limited role in her life until her death in the early 1930s, her grandmother was her primary caregiver and teacher. White introduced her to a variety of experiences at a young age including giving her walking tours of the city and churches in Harlem as well as exposing her to art galleries as she continued her early education at P.S. 81, Julia Ward Howe Junior High, and Wadleigh High School. White encouraged her granddaughter to use her imagination and Childress linked the use of imagination to writing. In interviews with Roberta McGuire and Clayton Holloway, Childress recounts how she and her grandmother would look out from their apartment window, choose a person on the street and create an oral narrative about that person—who he or she was, where he or she lived, what his or her family was like, what he or she did for a living. Childress would then write the narrative, and she credited these childhood experiences with her grandmother or getting "involved in the life of people" as one of the significant influences on her career as a writer (Maguire 33; Holloway 8). In addition to writing, she was beginning to act in plays at school, demonstrating an interest in acting that she would continue throughout her life (Maguire 34).

The promising changes in Childress's life that began in 1925 came to a halt in the early 1930s when both her mother Florence and her grandmother Eliza died. Ultimately, their deaths meant the end of her formal education and the beginning of work to support herself. It is during this period following the deaths of her mother and grandmother around 1933 through 1941 that enormous changes took place in Childress's life. She met Alvin Childress, a Mississippi native who came to New York to find work in the theater, and married him. In November 1935 their only daughter, Jean, was born.

Although she took on new responsibilities as a mother and wife, Childress continued to pursue her interests in both acting and writing, and the American Negro Theatre (ANT) served as the launching site for her long career in theater. Childress was central to the establishment of ANT along with cofounders Abram Hill, Frederick O'Neal, Ruby Dee, and Ossie Davis. She made her first appearance as an actress as Dolly in Abram Hill and John Silvera's *On Strivers Row* in 1940 at ANT, and appeared in several productions with the company alongside her husband. In 1944, they both appeared in Philip Yordan's *Anna Lucasta*, which moved to Broadway in August of that year and ran there for 957 performances, earning Childress a Tony award nomination for her performance (Dugan 147). Behind the scenes, she excelled in administrative work and served the company in every capacity with the exception of working as stage manager. However, by the late 1940s the Childress's marriage encountered difficulties due in part to Alvin Childress's move to the West Coast to begin work on the television situation comedy *Amos 'n' Andy* which was the first to have an all-black cast. The development of the program from radio to television and the airing of the controversial show reignited an ongoing debate within the African American community about race and representation. Organizations like the National Association for the Advancement of Colored People (NAACP) maintained that the narrow representations of black identity in the show were stereotypical, demeaning, and ultimately detrimental to political and social change, while others, particularly the program's actors including Alvin Childress, did not believe that the representations were harmful. This ideological difference seemingly influenced the eventual dissolution of their marriage. Though Childress would later challenge the black middle-class ideologies of groups like the NAACP that sought in some instances to distance itself from such images, she was also disturbed by the reading of the images as representative of all definitions of black identity and this perspective on representations of African American identity clearly influenced her work. Ironically, in 1949 Alvin Childress won the title role of Amos and, during the same year at ANT, she staged, directed, and starred in her first play, *Florence*, which contests stereotypical images of black domestic workers. By 1957, she divorced Alvin Childress and married composer Nathan Woodard on 17 July of the same year.

The early 1950s to the mid-1960s marked a writing boom for Childress. She staged three more plays: *Just a Little Simple* in 1950, *Gold through the Trees* in 1952, and *Trouble in Mind* in 1956 which won an Obie Award for Best Original Off Broadway Play, making Childress the first woman to win the award. Even as she wrote and produced plays, she also penned a column for Paul Robeson's newspaper *Freedom* where she worked with Lorraine Hansberry who wrote Childress's first stage review for the paper. Selections from Childress's column called "One a Month" were later collected for her book *Like One of the Family* published in 1956 and it was excerpted in the *Baltimore Afro-American* for sixty-two weeks in 1956 and 1957. Over the next two decades, she staged eight plays including *Wedding Band* in 1966 and published the novel *A Hero Ain't Nothin' but a Sandwich* in 1973, for which she is best known, which garnered several awards recognizing the best in young adult fiction.

In the last twenty years of her life, Childress continued to write, staging three plays and publishing two novels. Her last completed work *Those Other People* was published in 1989 and the following year her only child, Jean, died of cancer. Childress was working on a book about the life of her grandmother when she died of cancer in Queens, New York, on August 14, 1994.

MAJOR WORKS

The realist mode of representation that drives all of Childress's work draws upon characters whom she described in a 1984 essay as "the have-nots in a have society, [who are] seldom singled out by mass media, except as source material for derogatory humor and/or condescending clinical, social analysis" (Childress 250). Focusing primarily on representations of African American women, many of the characters in her work recuperate standard racial stereotypes, challenge gender roles, and raise questions about class status and class mobility within the African American community through themes of race and racial discrimination, gender equity, regional stereotypes, and class stratification.

In *Florence*, a play that was written in one night and grew out of Childress's frustration at the scarcity of roles for African Americans that portrayed more than one-dimensional stereotypes, Mrs. Whitney, the mother of two adult daughters, Florence and Marge, meets out of work white actress Mrs. Carter en route to New York to bring her daughter Florence back home to the south and to discourage her from attempting to become an actress. After two exchanges between the women in a segregated train station and Mrs. Carter's refusal to grant the legitimacy of the multiple facets of African American identity that Mrs. Whitney attempts to detail for her, Mrs. Whitney decides to support her daughter's decision to pursue an acting career in New York because as she tells the porter, Mr. Brown, Florence "can be anything in the world she wants to be! That's her right."

Childress's Obie-award-winning *Trouble in Mind* raises related questions around African American identity and what constitutes that identity. The plot hinges on the production of a play called *Chaos in Belleville* and how the actors who will appear in the play negotiate their need for gainful employment alongside the racial politics and representations put forth in the play. Written, produced, and directed by white men, the play trades in standard racial, gender, and regional stereotypes. However, Willetta Mayer, the play's protagonist, refuses to play the role as it is written and her confrontation with the play's director lays bare how deeply his own notions of African American identity are informed by stereotypes.

An interracial relationship set in early twentieth-century Charleston drives the plot of *Wedding Band*. It is the story of Julia (a black seamstress) and Herman (a white baker) who have maintained a long-term relationship but are prohibited by law from marrying. As Herman falls ill and is dying, Julia is forced to confront Herman's racist mother, members of a black community who question her commitment to it due to her relationship with Herman, and her own relationship to both her racial and regional identities. Rather than continuing to view their relationship as one that transcends or is blind to racial difference, by the end of the play she acknowledges the weight and significance of their respective histories and what they bring to bear on their relationship.

CRITICAL RECEPTION

Though generally Childress's work was well received by critics, one recurring issue in much of the criticism of her work is the concern that the social protest flattens characterization and style in her work. While on one hand critics appreciate the significance of the social problems her texts underscore, on the other, they are concerned with the "sermonizing" of her work.

Critics of the original production of *Trouble in Mind* applauded the play for its themes of racial stereotypes and racial identity. Harry Raymond argued in the *Daily Worker* that the play had "an important point of view about the problems of the Negro in the theatre" and further that Childress provides the audience with "some sound thoughts on one of the major social problems in the field of American culture (Raymond 48). Characterization was also often a noted strength of much of her work and in this play Willeta was viewed as exemplary in troubling both racial and gender stereotypes. Gayle Austin asserted in "Black Woman Playwright as Feminist Critic" that Childress had sketched "some alternative images of black women, three dimensional characters with weaknesses and strengths" (Austin 53). Despite these accolades, for some critics there were concerns that detracted from the play's strengths. Doris Abramson argued that the play has "interesting characters and dialogue, though both tend to ring false whenever they are saturated with sermonizing" (Abramson 49). However, several critics found that the play's themes were relevant years after its original production. In her assessment of it in a 1979 *Village Voice* article, Sally R. Sommers suggested that the play speaks to both U.S. social history and the history of African American drama, "the best parts of the play, its multi-leveled language and seething, funny role reenactments, prefigure the tough black style of the '60s plays naturalistic dramas that hit hard, inset with sermon-like arias for solo performers" (Sommers 17). Linda Armstrong praised the play's ideological perspective and Childress's efforts to complicate African American identity in her review appearing in the *New York New Amsterdam News* in April 1998 saying, "[she] is careful to present a variety of views and justify them" (Armstrong 30).

The critics who dared to review *Wedding Band* had similar impressions of the play. It was widely disregarded by critics and producers when it was written because its controversial themes of interracial marriage and miscegenation were still illegal in some states. When a production of the play was aired on ABC in 1973, the several Southern affiliates banned its broadcast and it was nearly three years before the play's first stage production at the University of Michigan. Like Childress's *Florence* and *Trouble in Mind*, *Wedding Band* was optioned for production on Broadway, but was never staged there. Despite the controversy, the *New York Times*'s Richard Eder found the characters particularly compelling, calling them "rich and lively" and he further made a case for the power of the plays themes stating that the play poses what he terms the old question of whether or not race is a category or humanity or a division of it. In response, he contends that while that question is old, "it takes on the freshness of new life in the marvelous characters that Miss Childress has created to ask it" (Eder 14). Harold Clurman reiterated the strength of Childress's characterization and its timeliness in his 1972 review in the *Nation* that "[t]he fact that black and white interrelationships have somewhat changed since 1918 does not make the play less relevant to the present. Constitutional amendments and laws do not immediately change people's emotions; the divisions and tensions which *Wedding Band* dramatizes still exist to a far more painful extent than most of us are willing to admit" (Clurman 475).

Though prolific during her long career, there has been limited academic critical inquiry into Childress's work. As critic Olga Dugan and others have argued, Childress's oeuvre necessitates reconsideration in terms of its contribution and significance to the "literary and theatrical histories of how drama functions in American culture and society" (Dugan 146).

BIBLIOGRAPHY

Works by Alice Childress

Black Scenes. New York: Doubleday, 1971.
"Florence." In *Wine in the Wilderness: Plays by African American Women from the Harlem Renaissance to the Present*, edited by Elizabeth Brown-Guillory. Westport, CT: Greenwood Press, 1990.

A Hero Ain't Nothin' but a Sandwich. London: Coward, 1979.

Let's Hear It for the Queen: A Play. Music by Woodward. Illustrated by Charles Lilly. New York: Coward, 1975.

Like One of the Family: Conversations from a Domestic's Life. Boston: Beacon Press, 1986.

Many Closets. New York: Coward, 1987.

Mojo and String: Two Plays. New York: Dramatists Play Service, 1971.

Rainbow Jordan. New York: Coward, 1981.

A Short Walk. New York: Coward, 1979.

Those Other People. New York: Putnam, 1989.

"Trouble in Mind." In *Black Theatre: A Twentieth Century Collection of the Work of Its Best Playwrights*, edited by Lindsay Patterson. New York: Dodd, 1971.

Wedding Band: A Love/Hate Story in Black and White. New York: Samuel French, 1973.

When the Rattlesnake Sounds: A Play. Illustrated by Charles Lilly. New York: Coward, 1975.

Wine in the Wilderness: A Comedy-Drama. New York: Dramatists Play Service, 1972.

Studies of Alice Childress's Works

Abramson, Doris E. *Negro Playwrights in the American Theatre, 1925–1959*. New York: Columbia University Press, 1969.

Armstrong, Linda. Review of *Trouble In Mind*. New York. New Amsterdam News, 1998.

Austin, Gayle. "Alice Childress: Black Woman Playwright as Feminist Critic." *Southern Quarterly* 25 (Spring 1987). 53–62.

Billingslea-Brown, Alma Jean. "The Blight of Legalized Limitation in Alice Childress's Wedding Band." In *Law and Literature Perspectives*, edited by Bruce L. Rockwood and Roberta Kevelson, 39 51. New York: Peter Lang, 1996.

Brown, Janet. *Feminist Drama: Definition and Critical Analysis* Metuchen, NF Scarecrow Press, 1979, 56–70.

Brown-Guillory, Elizabeth. *Their Place on the Stage: Black Women Playwrights in America*. Westport, CT: Greenwood Press, 1988.

Burke, Sally. *American Feminist Playwrights: A Critical History*. New York: Twayne/London: Prentice Hall, 1996, 144 52.

Clurman, Harold. Review of *Wedding Band. The Nation, 1972.*

Curb, Rosemary. "An Unfashionable Tragedy of American Racism: Alice Childress's *Wedding Band*." *MELUS* 7 (Winter 1980): 57–68.

Dugan, Olga. "Telling the Truth: Alice Childress as Theorist and Playwright." *Journal of Negro History* 81 (Winter–Fall 1996): 123–36.

———. *Useful Drama: Variations on the Theme of Black Self-Determination in the Plays of Alice Childress*. New York: University of Rochester Press, 1998.

Eder, Richard. Review of *Wedding Band. New York Times, 1973.*

Ely, Melvin Patrick. *The Adventures of Amos n Andy: A Social History of an American Phenomenon*. New York: Free Press, 1991.

Holloway, Clayton. "The Alembic of Genius: An Interview with Alice Childress." *Xavier Review* 17.1 (1997): 5–22.

Jennings, La Vinia Delois. *Alice Childress*. New York: Twayne Publishers, 1995.

Maguire, Roberta S. "Alice Childress." *Twentieth Century Dramatists*. Ed. Christopher Wheatley. Detroit: Thomson Gale, 2002: 30–39.

Reuben, Paul P. "Chapter 8: American Drama." *Alice Childress. PAL: Perspectives in American Literature—A Research and Reference Guide*. http://www.csustan.edu/english/reuben/pal/chap8/childress.html (accessed February 2003).

Raymond, Harry. Review of *Trouble in Mind. Daily Worker* 1955.

Schroeder, Patricia R. "Re-Reading Alice Childress." In *Staging Difference: Cultural Pluralism in American Theatre and Drama*, edited by Marc Maufort, 323–37. New York: Peter Lang, 1995.

Sommers, Sally R. Review of *Trouble in Mind*. *Village Voice,* 1999.

Turner, Beth. "Simplifyin': Langston Hughes and Alice Childress Re/member Jesse B. Semple." *Langston Hughes Review* 15 (Spring 1997): 37–48.

Vojta, Barbara Rothman. *In Praise of African-American Women: Female Images in the Plays of Alice Childress*. New York: New York University Press, 1993.

Wiley, Catherine. "Whose Name, Whose Protection: Reading Alice Childress's Wedding Band." In *Modern American Drama: The Female Canon*, edited by June Schlueter, 184–97. Rutherford, NJ: Fairleigh Dickinson University Press, 1990.

Carol Bunch Davis

BARBARA T. CHRISTIAN (1943–2000)

BIOGRAPHICAL NARRATIVE

Barbara T. Christian was author and editor of several books and published many articles and reviews in scholarly journals and magazines. She was born in St. Thomas, Virgin Islands, in 1943. At fifteen, she attended Marquette University in Milwaukee, Wisconsin, graduating cum laude in 1963. While earning a Ph.D. from Columbia University in contemporary British and American Literature, Christian taught at the College of the Virgin Islands, Hunter College in New York City, and City College of New York, in the SEEK (Search for Education, Elevation, and Knowledge) program for talented under-privileged students. Completing her Ph.D. with distinction in 1970, Christian joined the faculty of the University of California, Berkeley, in 1971, where she spent her entire career. She was key in founding the Department of Afro-American Studies, serving as chair from 1978 to 1983; she was also instrumental in forming the Ph.D. program in Ethnic Studies, which she chaired from 1986 to 1989, and the alternative University Without Walls that served people of color, from 1971 to 1976. In a career of "firsts," she was the first African American woman awarded tenure at Berkeley in 1978 and full professorship in 1986. She was the first African American to win the university's Distinguished Teaching Award in 1991, and she was also awarded the prestigious Berkeley Citation for achievement and service in 2000.

MAJOR WORKS

Considered a groundbreaking and influential scholar of black women's writing, an outstanding and generous teacher and mentor, and an exceptionally committed contributor to her academic and civic community, Christian is perhaps best known in academic circles for two books of literary criticism, *Black Women Novelists: The Development of a Tradition, 1892–1976* (1980) and *Black Feminist Criticism: Perspectives on Black Women Writers* (1985). The first volume appeared at a time when few critics had acknowledged the renaissance of African American women writing in the 1970s. Christian described and discussed the origins of black women's writing and traced stereotypes of black women in literature from 1892. The work included a close examination of the work of Toni Morrison, Paule Marshall, and Alice Walker, and is considered a significant piece of American literary history and one of the cornerstone texts of black feminist literary scholarship; in fact, many consider this work not just the first of its kind but the genesis of the field as well. *Black Feminist Criticism*, a collection of essays analyzing the writing of African American women from nineteenth to the late twentieth century was equally significant, creating the academic ground upon which much criticism of African American women writers is based. Perhaps equally significant was her much cited and frequently anthologized essay "The Race for Theory," which urged scholars to maintain their focus on the writing itself, because, she insisted, "I know from literary history that writing disappears unless there is a response to it" (77). In addition to her analysis and promotion of the black female literary tradition, Christian's investigation of the intersections of race, class, and gender in black women's lives and writing has been useful to literary and cultural critics. Her efforts to elucidate and foster African American literature and research have had a lasting impact on the evolution of the disciplines of African American and feminist literary history and scholarship.

CRITICAL RECEPTION

Because of the significance of her academic work, which included, in addition to the major books, nearly 100 published articles and numerous speeches at national and international conferences, Christian was highly sought after as a mentor by aspiring students of African American literature and culture. Tributes to her work at University of California at Berkeley indicate that she was beloved by students, who flocked to her classes in droves and sought support at her home in Berkeley, which they report was a comfortable gathering place for scholars, students, admirers, progressives, and artists. They note that Christian's intellectual passion crossed disciplines and produced significant work, such as the book *Female Subjects in Black and White: Race, Psychoanalysis, Feminism* (1997), which she edited with Elizabeth Abel and Helen Moglen. Christian was recognized outside of the university as well; she worked in the local community on issues ranging from police brutality to American foreign policy. She twice won the Louise Patterson African American Studies Award in 1992 and 1995; she was awarded the City of Berkeley Icon award for her community service in 1994, the Modern Language Association MELUS award for her contributions to ethnic and African American scholarship, and the Gwendolyn Brooks Center award in 1995. Her intellectual rigor, combined with her political commitment and interpersonal generosity made her a much beloved community member, mentor, and colleague.

BIBLIOGRAPHY

Works by Barbara T. Christian

Black Feminist Criticism: Perspectives on Black Women Writers. New York: Pergamon, 1985.
Black Women Novelists: The Development of a Tradition, 1892–1976. Westport, CT: Greenwood Press, 1980.
"But What Do We Think We're Doing Anyway: The State of Black Feminist Criticism(s) or My Version of a Little Bit of History." In *Changing Our Own Words: Essays on Criticism, Theory and Writing by Black Women*, edited by Cheryl Wall, 58–74. New Brunswick, NJ: Rutgers University Press, 1989.
Female Subjects in Black and White: Race, Psychoanalysis, Feminism, edited by Elizabeth Abel and Helen Moglen. Berkeley: University of California Press, 1997.
"The Race for Theory: Science, Technology and Socialist Feminism in the 1980s." In *Feminisms*, edited by Sandra Kemp and Judith Squires, 69–78. Oxford: Oxford University Press, 1997.

Studies of Barbara T. Christian's Works

"Barbara Christian, 56, Leader in Modern Literary Feminism." *New York Times* 1 (July 9, 2000, late edition): 31.
"Barbara Christian." *University of California: In Memoriam* (2001). Available from the Online Archive of California: http://ark.cdlib.org/ark:/13030/hb987008v1 (accessed March 30, 2005).

"Barbara T. Christian." *Contemporary Authors Online* (May 23, 2001). Reproduced in Biography Resource Center. Farmington Hills, MI: Gale, 2005. http://galegroup.com/servlet/BioRC (accessed March 30, 2005).

"Barbara T. Christian." *Contemporary Black Biography.* V. 44. Detroit: Gale, 2004. Reproduced in Biography Resource Center. Farmington Hills, MI: Gale, 2005. http://galegroup.com/servlet/ BioRC (accessed March 30, 2005).

"Barbara T. Christian." *Feminist Writers.* St. James Press, 1996. Reproduced in Biography Resource Center. Farmington Hills, MI: Gale, 2005. http://galegroup.com/servlet/BioRC (ACCESSED March 30, 2005).

Bowles, Gloria. "Tribute: Barbara T. Christian (1943–2000)." *NWSA Journal* 13.2 (Summer 2001).

Goldberg, David Theo. "Obituary: Barbara Theresa Christian, 1943–2000." *Social Identities* 6.4 (2000).

Spencer, Suzette. "Introduction to Barbara Christian's 'The Past Is Infinite.' " *Social Identities* 6.4 (2000).

Sharon L. Barnes

PEARL T. CLEAGE (1948–)

BIOGRAPHICAL NARRATIVE

Essayist, novelist, poet, and playwright Pearl T. Cleage was born on December 7, 1948, in Springfield, Massachusetts, to Doris Graham Cleage, a teacher, and Albert B. Cleage, Jr., a minister and civil rights activist. When she was a young child, her family moved to Detroit, Michigan, where her father started his own church. Cleage considers her childhood home a writer's paradise. Scattered throughout the house were books by Langston Hughes, Richard Wright, and Ossie Davis alongside works by Simone de Beauvoir, Margaret Sanger, and Arthur Miller. From an early age, Cleage found herself engaged in lively political debates with her parents and their friends. Further, her parents often took her to museums, the theater, and other live cultural events that spurred Cleage's love for language and performance.

In 1966, Cleage graduated from Detroit public schools and began her college education at Howard University in Washington, D.C., where she majored in playwriting and dramatic literature. In 1969, she married Michael Lomax, an Atlanta politician, and moved from D.C. to Atlanta. She enrolled in Spelman College while in Atlanta and graduated in 1971 with a degree in drama. Later she joined the faculty there as a writer and playwright. Cleage and Lomax have one child, Deignan Njeri. They divorced in 1979. In 1994, Cleage married Zaron W. Burnett, Jr., a writer and director for the Just Us Theater Company, where Cleage serves as artistic director. She currently resides in Atlanta's historic Southwest neighborhood with her husband and her cat.

MAJOR WORKS

Cleage's first love is playwriting. "I still believe that theatre has a ritual power to call forth the spirits, illuminate the darkness and *speak the truth to the people*" (in Preface, *Flyin' West and Other Plays*). Her most often produced plays, *Flyin' West* and *Blues for Alabama Sky*, were commissioned by the Atlanta-based Alliance Theatre, *Flyin' West* in 1992 and *Blues for Alabama Sky* in 1995.

Flyin' West takes its story from an historical fact. According to the Playwright's Note, in 1860 The Homestead Act offered 320 acres of "free" land to U.S. citizens willing to settle in the Western states. By 1890, a quarter of a million unmarried or widowed women were running their own farms and ranches, many of them African American (*Flyin' West* 6).

Flyin' West tells the story of two sisters who have acquired the deeds to their land, but who must rescue a third sister who is being physically abused and swindled out of her land by her free-loading, mulatto, passing husband. The play ends happily, and so more than just providing exposure of this little-known aspect of African American women's history, *Flyin' West* demonstrates how women can come together to provide strength and protection to each other, one of Cleage's favorite and recurring themes.

Cleage explains in "Why I Write: An Introduction" that she came to this raison d'etre on the morning of her forty-first birthday when she heard the news about a misogynist lone gunman in Montreal who had killed fourteen women and wounded thirteen others. Coming after a series of encounters with students, friends, and colleagues all suffering the wounds of domestic violence, the news about the gunman clarified for Cleage that in order to maintain hope, all of her writing must be about combating the growing despair she saw in herself and her African American sisters. "I am writing," she says, "to understand the full effects of being black and female in a culture that is both racist and sexist..." (*Deals with the Devil* 7). She has never strayed from this commitment. From her earliest plays to her latest novel, Pearl Cleage tells the hard truths about life for African American women, and more importantly provides a vision for sisterhood and survival.

But Cleage's message does not always come with a happy ending. In *Blues for Alabama Sky*, the protagonist Angel Anderson, a blues singer turned prostitute during the depression, has given up all hope of ever escaping Harlem and its poverty until she meets Alabama, a religious zealot who falls in love with her because she looks like his dead wife. Angel agrees to marry Alabama in order to escape the city and her desperate economic plight, even though she does not love him. But Alabama is not the savior that Angel imagined, and, instead of providing escape, Alabama murders Angel's best ally and leads her to spiritual and emotional destruction. Although at the end of the play Angel is worse off than in the beginning, the play still reinforces one of Cleage's most important messages: women need each other. Women who are isolated will have to compromise their principles and their lives, something which can never be an option.

Although a prolific and successful playwright, in the mid-1990s, Cleage turned from playwriting to fiction. On April 25, 2005, at a reading at Books and Company in Dayton, Ohio, Cleage explained that she made the shift because she had a specific story that she wanted to tell, and the story did not fit within the parameters of a dramatic production. "There were too many characters, too many scenes, and the story would take longer than two hours to tell," she explained.

Cleage's first novel, *What Looks Like Crazy on an Ordinary Day*, was published by Avon Books in 1997. It tells the story of successful business woman Ava Johnson, who when she finds out she is HIV positive, decides to return to her hometown of Idlewood, Michigan, before heading off to a new life in San Francisco. What she thinks is a quick visit turns into a life-long commitment. Although the novel tackles some heavy issues such as AIDS, teenage motherhood, crack, joblessness, and low self-esteem, it remains surprisingly upbeat and funny.

The successful first novel was followed by a less successful second and third novel, *I Wish I Had a Red Dress* and *Some Things I Thought I'd Never Do*. But Cleage's fourth and latest novel, *Babylon Sisters*, finds Cleage reconnected with her gutsy genius.

Babylon Sisters explores the power of truth through the character of a single mother, Catharine, and her sixteen-year-old daughter, Phoebe, who is bent on finding her father. Catharine, who runs a successful business helping immigrant women find jobs, has kept the truth about Phoebe's father from her daughter for too many years to give it up now. But the truth is inevitably going to come out, and in this story the outcome is as surprising as the secret.

CRITICAL RECEPTION

Mark Marino of offoffoff.com in a review of *Hospice*, one of Cleage's first plays, said, "The themes are heavy but the show is a joy to watch." This sentiment has been repeated extensively in the reviews of Cleage's work. "Though there are some potentially over-the-top emotional moments, the integrity of the characters and the world of the play are held," said Freda Scott Giles in a 1997 review of *Bourbon at the Border*, a play about the devastating effects of Freedom Summer on an African American couple still struggling with the horrendous emotional repercussions of their experience twenty-five years later.

Cleage gained national attention as a playwright beginning in 1992 with the production of her play *Flyin' West*, which premiered at the Alliance Theatre in Atlanta and has subsequently been produced at a number of regional theatres across the country and at the Kennedy Center in Washington, D.C. *Flyin' West* was followed by *Blues for Alabama Sky* and *Bourbon at the Border* which have added to her reputation and popularity as a playwright.

When her first novel, *What Looks Like Crazy on an Ordinary Day*, was chosen by television personality Oprah Winfrey as her first on-air Book Club selection, Cleage gained national acclaim as a fiction writer. *What Looks Like Crazy* became a *New York Times* best seller and won the BCALA Literary Award. Cleage has received numerous other awards in recognition of her work, including the Bronze Jubilee Award for Literature in 1983 and the outstanding columnist award from the Atlanta Association of Black Journalists in 1991.

Cleage's success manifests from her self-proclaimed mission as a writer to tell the truth. From her earliest plays through her latest novel, she does just that with "passion and humor, anger and wit, idealism and dignity" (Monroe).

BIBLIOGRAPHY

Works by Pearl T. Cleage

Babylon Sisters. New York: One World/Ballantine, 2005.
The Brass Bed and Other Stories. Chicago: Third World Press, 1991.
Deals with the Devil and Other Reasons to Riot. New York: Ballantine, 1993.
Flyin' West and Other Plays. New York: Theatre Communications Group, 1999.
Hospice. New Plays for the Black Theater, edited by Woodie King, Fr. Chicago: Third World Press, 1989.
I Wish I Had a Red Dress. New York: William Morrow, 2002.
Mad at Miles: A Black Woman's Guide to Truth. Southfield, MI: Cleage Group, 1990.
Some Things I Thought I'd Never Do. New York: One World/Ballantine Books, 2003.
We Don't Need No Music. Detroit: Broadside Press, 1972.
What Looks Like Crazy on an Ordinary Day. New York: Avon Books, 1997.

Studies of Pearl T. Cleage's Works

Giles, Freda Scott. "The Motion of Herstory: Three Plays by Pearl Cleage." *African American Review* (Winter 1997): 709–12.
Marino, Mark. "Death of a Diva." May 30, 2002. www.offoffoff.com.
Monroe, Steve. "Black Women as Pioneers." *American Visions* October/November 1994.

Paige, Linda Rohrer. "Pearl Cleage." In *Significant Contemporary American Feminists: A Biographical Sourcebook*, edited by Jennifer Scanlon, 67–72. Westport, CT: Greenwood Press, 1999.

"Pearl Cleage." *Essence* (March 2005): 135.

Peterson, Jane T., and Suzanne Bennett. "Pearl Cleage." In *Women Playwrights of Diversity: A Bio-Bibliographical Sourcebook*, 90–93. Westport, CT: Greenwood Press, 1997.

Robert, Tara. "Pearls of Wisdom." *Essence* (December 1997).

Washington, Elsie B. "Pearl Cleage." *Essence* (September 1993).

Adrienne Cassel

MICHELLE CLIFF (1946–)

BIOGRAPHICAL NARRATIVE

Michelle Cliff has penned three novels as well as several books of poetry and a collection of short stories. She was born in Jamaica on November 2, 1946. Her family migrated to the United States and moved into a Caribbean neighborhood in New York City during her childhood. Cliff traveled back and forth to Jamaica and was educated in Jamaica, the United States, and Britain. She attended Wagner College in New York and Warburg Institute of the University of London, where she wrote a dissertation on the Italian Renaissance. Cliff's novels are *Abeng*, *No Telephone to Heaven*, and *Free Enterprise*.

MAJOR WORKS

Michelle Cliff's primary literary preoccupation is with the recovery and rewriting of the lost histories of slavery, colonization, and women's resistance in the Caribbean islands and the United States from the perspective of the African diaspora. The project of rewriting black women's histories is inextricably linked to the quest of rearticulating black female identity, a theme evident in the tribulations of Clare Savage, Cliff's light-skinned heroine in *Abeng* and *No Telephone to Heaven*. Cliff attempts to locate black women's identity at the shifting intersections of race, color, class, and sexual orientation. Clare Savage, Cliff's heroine, comes to terms with her identity as the racially mixed, descendant of African slaves and white plantation owners. However, as she grows into womanhood Clare identifies herself with her grandmother and her mother's relatives in the Jamaican countryside, the rhythms of agricultural life, and the African rituals, persisting in the pre-Christian folk memories of the island, rather than her urban, lighter-skinned, paternal relatives. Clare's adolescence in New York allows her to establish solidarity with civil rights and the anti-Vietnam movements in the United States and connect these to the struggles against poverty and underdevelopment in postcolonial Jamaica.

In Cliff's novels the personal questions of identity get explored in the context of the history of African slavery and colonization as well as the contemporary realities of neocolonialism and global poverty. In representing women like Nanny in *Abeng* and Mary Ellen Pleasant in *Free Enterprise*, she attempts to re-inscribe women who participated in armed resistance to slavery into the archives of history, at a time when globalization is erasing the lived history of slavery from the islands and fetishizing these places and histories.

Michelle Cliff employs a variety of narrative linguistic methods to achieve her complex literary and philosophical project. She is particularly skilful in her use of multiple perspectives, which fracture a teleological time sequence and constantly juxtapose the present with the past. She is also very effective in mingling Jamaican dialect with standard English, succeeding in giving voice to marginalized languages in the Afro-Caribbean novel.

CRITICAL RECEPTION

Michelle Cliff's literary oeuvre has received widespread and enthusiastic critical attention. Her works have been studied from a variety of critical approaches including those of transnational feminism, postcolonial theory, queer theory, and African American and African diaspora studies. Her work has inspired many critical articles in scholarly journals and critical anthologies as well as a monograph.

BIBLIOGRAPHY

Works by Michelle Cliff

Abeng. New York: Plume, 1984.
Bodies of Water. New York: Dutton, 1990.
Claiming an Identity They Taught Me to Despise. Watertown, MA: Persephone, 1980.
Free Enterprise. New York: Dutton, 1993.
The Land of Look Behind: Prose and Poetry. Ithaca, NY: Firebrand, 1985.
No Telephone to Heaven. New York: Dutton, 1987.
The Store of a Million Items: Stories. Boston: Houghton Mifflin, 1998.

Studies of Michelle Cliff's Works

Agosto, Noraida. *Michelle Cliff's Novels: Piecing the Tapestry of Memory and History.* New York: Peter Lang, 1999.
Edmondson, Belinda. "Race, Writing, and the Politics of (Re) Writing History: An Analysis of the Novels of Michelle Cliff." *Callaloo* (Winter 1993): 180–91.
Lionnet, Francoise. "Of Mangoes and Maroons: Language, History, and the Multicultural Subject of Michelle Cliff's Abeng." In *De/Colonizing the Subject: The Politics of Gender in Women's Autobiography,* edited by Sidonie Smith and Julia Watson, 321–45. Minneapolis: University of Minnesota Press, 1992.
Macdonald-Smyhte, Antonia. *Making Homes in the West Indies: Constructions of Subjectivity in the Writings of Michelle Cliff and Jamaica Kincaid.* New York: Routledge, 2001.
Needham, Anuradha Dingwaney. *Using the Master's Tools: Resistance and the Literature of the African and South Asian Diasporas.* New York: St. Martin's Press, 2000.
Raiskin, Judith. "Inverts and Hybrids: Lesbian Rewritings of Sexual and Racial Identities." In *The Lesbian Postmodern,* edited by Laura Doan, 156–72. New York: Columbia University Press, 1994.

Lopamudra Basu

LUCILLE CLIFTON (1936–)

BIOGRAPHICAL NARRATIVE

Author of more than twenty children's books and over 100 anthologies of poetry, Thelma Lucille Sayles Clifton was born in Depew, New York, in 1936. Her family migrated North to find work, but their lives in the South were not forgotten. Lucille grew up with stories of her southern heritage, including tales of her great great grandmother Caroline, a slave brought to America from Dahomey, West Africa.

Lucille's parents, although not well educated, provided their children with books and instilled a love of the learning process in their offspring, especially in Lucille. She was the first of her family to attend college. At Howard University, on a full scholarship, Lucille met notable African American authors Sterling Brown, LeRoi Jones (later Amiri Baraka), and Toni Morrison, who would later become her editor at Random House.

After losing her scholarship due to poor grades, Lucille returned to New York and attended Fredonia State Teachers College but did not graduate. In 1958, she married Fred Clifton, a yogi, who went on to receive his Ph.D. and establish an ashram. During the early years of their marriage, Lucille worked as a claims clerk, gave birth to six children, and wrote poetry. The death of her mother in 1959 at the early age of forty-four affected Clifton greatly and became a catalyst for many of her later poems.

In 1969, Clifton asked poet Robert Hayden to help her publish her poetry. He passed Clifton's poems on to poet Carolyn Kizer, who entered them in the YMCA Poetry Center Discovery Award Contest. Clifton won the award and her volume *Good Times* was published by Random House. Also an author of children's books, Clifton saw her *Some of the Days of Everett Anderson* published the next year.

The next decade was an active time for Clifton. She published *An Ordinary Woman* in 1974, which along with *Two-Headed Woman* (1980), explores the spirituality of her world. A memoir based on the stories her father told her of their ancestors, *Generations*, was published in 1976. Clifton served as Maryland's Poet Laureate from 1979 to 1982. A quiet period ensued after the death of her husband at age forty-nine in 1984. It was not until 1987 that two more volumes of poetry were published: a retrospective collection, *Good Woman*, and *Next*, a collection of lamentations and dirges for those who have been lost. Between 1994 and 2004, Clifton has faced numerous challenges and losses. She was diagnosed with cancer in 1994, underwent a kidney transplant; lost her daughter, Fredrica, to a brain tumor; and her son, Channing, to heart failure. Her personal journey has always been a central theme in her work. Her journey to self-awareness along with a concern for "social justice, African American history, and the innate strength of womanhood" (Holladay, *Wild Blessings*, 13) inform most of Clifton's most recent poetry in *Quilting* (1991), *The Book of Light* (1993), *The Terrible Stories* (1996), and *Blessing the Boats* (2000).

Clifton has taught at many institutions including the University of California at Santa Cruz and Columbia University. She taught at Duke University as the William Blackburn Distinguished Visiting Professor, and in 1999 was appointed to the Hilda

C. Landers Chair in the Liberal Arts at St. Mary's College of Maryland. Clifton has also received much recognition for her poetry. Her awards include several Pulitzer Prize nominations, a lifetime achievement award from the Lannan Foundation, being named a fellow of the Academy of American Poets, and many book awards.

MAJOR WORKS

Best known for her poetry, Clifton is also a respected author of children's books. Her series of books based on the life of a young African American boy named Everett Anderson begins with the 1970 *Some of the Days of Everett Anderson*. Everett Anderson, always referred to by his full name, is a six-year-old boy who lives with his mother in an inner city neighborhood. The eight books that form the series are told in verse and demonstrate many of the themes present in Clifton's poetry: the strength of family, self-love, and pride. The child and his mother have very little, but who they are is not based on what they have—another persistent motif. The 1984 *Everett Anderson's Goodbye* won the Coretta Scott King Award. Other children's titles include *The Black BC's* (1970), an alphabet book that praises the contributions of African Americans, and *Sonora Beautiful* (1981), whose protagonist is a white girl.

Clifton's first volume of poetry, *Good Times*, expands upon the motifs of her children's books, and addresses themes that appear in later volumes: spirituality, details of the lives of African American women and their bodies, and the importance of family and identity. The often-anthologized "Good Times" sets the celebratory tone of the volume. "I wish to celebrate and not be celebrated," Clifton has frequently told interviewers. The poem is representative of the celebration of the small events that make for celebration in the inner city—paying the weekly insurance premium, hitting it big in the numbers game, paying the rent.

Good News about the Earth was Clifton's second poetry collection. Three sections make up the book: "About the Earth" and "Heroes" are devoted to poems addressing race and racism. In these poems, Clifton apologizes for her "whiteful ways" and joyfully accepts her black identity. The final section is titled "Some Jesus" and contains a series of biblically inspired poems that are Afrocentric. Later, *Two-Headed Woman* presents a series of poems about Mary, and *Book of Light* contains the Lucifer poems.

An Ordinary Woman and *Two-Headed Woman* are often paired in critical assessments of Clifton's work. In these two volumes, the themes introduced in earlier works become the touchstone of the books. The often-autobiographical poems explore Clifton's growing awareness of herself as a spiritual black woman. Poems about female bonding between African American women in *Ordinary Woman* ("Sisters" and "Leanna's Poem") are countered by several poems, such as "Ms. Ann," that demonstrate the divide between black and white women, making bonding between them nearly impossible. In the second section, "I Agree with the Leaves," Clifton introduces Kali, a Hindu goddess who is depicted as a black female with four arms carrying implements of both creation and destruction. The narrator of the Kali poems identifies with the goddess, acknowledging that they are sisters. Nominated for a Pulitzer Prize, *Two-Headed Woman* continues the themes found in *Ordinary Woman* and includes many poems about Clifton's mother, Thelma, who died when Clifton was pregnant with her first child. Like the terrifying image of Kali, the two-headed woman is a weird, Janus-like figure whom the narrator must claim as sister. The first part of the book focuses on "Body Poems," such as "Homage to My Hips" and "Homage to My Hair." The poems are light in tone and celebratory of the joys of being a woman. The second section, "I Was Born with Twelve Fingers," is more mystical and includes the Mary poems.

Clifton's *Next* was released at the same time as the collection *Good Woman: Poems and a Memoir, 1969–1980*, which was considered for a Pulitzer and included the memoir *Generations*. Many of the poems in *Next* are more global in nature, exploring defining moments in history and identifying with the participants. Clifton writes about the Jonestown massacre, Gettysburg, and Nagasaki. Other poems in the volume address issues closer to home with a section of elegies told from the deceased's point of view.

In 1991, *Quilting: Poems 1987–1990* appeared. Each section of the book is given the name of a quilting pattern. Leslie Ullman said in her review of *Quilting* that the section titles "supply a visual metaphor for the vibrant wholeness of vision the book achieves through its many patterns of speech and points of focus" (quoted in Holladay, *Wild Blessings*, 49). The poems utilize the black vernacular and poetic patterns of sermons, folk tales, and slave spirituals. The section "Log Cabin" laments the struggles and celebrates the triumphs of both the unknown and well known. A poem on an unidentified slave rubs shoulders with one on Nelson and Winnie Mandela. Two companion poems based on plantation visits fill in the gap that surrounds a reference to aunt Nanny's bench in "Slave Cabin, Sotterly Plantation, Maryland, 1989." Clifton offers a life for aunt Nanny that corrects the omission made by the plantation docent of details of the lives of the slaves whose work made the plantation possible.

Three sections comprise the *Book of Light*. The first, "Reflection," continues the themes introduced in *Quilting* of the poet's identity as an aging woman, gaining in wisdom what she is losing in physicality. The final section, "Splendor," contains the sequence of Lucifer poems that present Lucifer, not as a devil, but as a humanized figure who has been separated from his brother, God (Holladay, *Wild Blessings*, 56). *The Terrible Stories*, which followed *Book of Light*, is colored by her experiences of breast cancer. The mood of the volume is darker and more introspective than her earlier works. A shamanic figure of a fox appears in a sequence of poems with whom the speaker identifies in "all its beauty and vulnerability" (Holladay 58).

Clifton's most recent volume, *Blessing the Boats: New and Selected Poems, 1988–2000* was a National Book Award winner. The first section of new poems includes "Jasper, Texas," an account of James Byrd's death as he is dragged behind a truck. The section ends with a retelling of the founding of the United States in a less than glorious manner. The volume is praised for its continued demonstration of the African American oral tradition.

CRITICAL RECEPTION

Much has been made of Clifton's simple style of writing. Alicia Ostriker calls her a "minimalist poet." Helen Houston is among those critics who liken Clifton to Gwendolyn Brooks, Walt Whitman, and Emily Dickinson in her style. "Her poems are spare in form, deceptively simple in language, complex in ideas, and reflective of the commonplace, the everyday." Influenced by the Black Arts Movement of her early writing career, Clifton developed such stylistic features as "concise, untitled free verse lyrics of mostly iambic trimeter lines, occasional slant rhymes, anaphora and other forms of repetition, puns and allusions, lowercase letters, sparse punctuation, and a lean lexicon of rudimentary but evocative words" (*Oxford Companion to African American Literature*). Mari Evans remarks that her poetry "reflects optimism, an emphasis on the 'qualities which have allowed us to survive,' and the belief that we have the ability to make things better." Evans also cites Clifton as saying, "I use a simple language. I have never believed that for anything to be valid or true or intellectual or 'deep' it had to be first complex." Audrey McCluskey also praises Clifton's language as simple and avoiding abstractions (138).

Joyce Johnson believes the success of the "leanness" of Clifton's poetry depends on what critic Stephen Henderson defines as mascon images: compressed images that offer African American archetypes "which evoke a powerful response in the [reader] because of their direct relationship to concepts and events in the collective experience" (quoted in Joyce 71). Terms like "inner city" evoke a positive sense of home that is defined by all the experiences of the people who have lived there in a way that the negative term "ghetto" does not.

Preeminent Clifton scholar Hilary Holladay has noted that although Clifton was born in New York, she has spent most of her life in Maryland. The influence of living in the South, along with the stories of her ancestors who lived in Virginia, informs her poetry ("Black Names"). The subjects of her writings include a deep exploration of her own ancestors, slave and free, and those nameless African Americans whose contributions to the building of the South have been marginalized or even forgotten. The companion poems, "At the Cemetery, Walnut Grove Plantation, South Carolina, 1989" and "Slave Cabin, Sotterly Plantation, Maryland, 1989" published in *Quilting*, are attempts by Clifton to right the injustice of not only slavery but the erasure of the lives of the slaves altogether. In both the poems, tour guides at two plantations Clifton is visiting are ignorant about the presence and the day-to-day lives of those blacks who were an intrinsic part of the plantations. In "At the Cemetery" the narrator discovers that although there is a record of the names of male slaves, the female slaves were not considered valuable to have been recorded.

This namelessness offends Clifton and in both poems she draws attention to how names that others call us do not define us as long as we can remember our own names. Names and what they signify is a frequent theme in Clifton's work. In her memoir *Generations*, great great grandmother Caroline refuses to reveal her Dahomey name; like Aunt Nanny in "Slave Cabin," she keeps her true name to herself and is known publicly by the name she is given by her white owners. In a sequence of poems about Lucifer, in *The Book of Light*, Clifton explores the character of Lucifer, but also ponders the nature of his name, which like Lucille, means "light."

Jean Anaporte-Easton comments that "the distinctive quality of Clifton's voice comes from her ability to ground her art in an imagery of the body and physical reality." Clifton has many poems that celebrate her body, in all of its manifestations from youth to middle age. In a discussion of Clifton's lyric poetry, Mark White applauds Clifton's refusal to denigrate the beauty of a womanly African American body to conform to the "Euro-American obsession with boniness, girlishness, and female frailty." She also does not pull back from confronting the devastating toll breast cancer and kidney failure have had on her body. In *Terrible Stories*, a sequence of poems forms the section "From the Cadaver."

Audrey McCluskey and Edward Whitley both agree that Clifton's memoir, *Generations*, is imbued with the spirit of Whitman. McClusky's discussion of the memoir foregrounds the celebratory, self-discovery of the work; Whitley concentrates on how Clifton replaces the individuality that is at the heart of "Song of Myself" with the more "generational sense of self based around an expanding African American family" (37).

Clifton's almost psychometric ability to understand allows her to write poems that, though centered in the world of an African American woman, exhibit an awareness of the struggles and triumphs of all people, not only of this generation but also of those which have come before.

BIBLIOGRAPHY

Works by Lucille Clifton

All Us Come Cross the Water. New York: Holt, Rinehart & Winston, 1973.
Amifika. New York: Dutton, 1977.
The Black BC's. New York: Dutton, 1970.
Blessing the Boats: New and Selected Poems, 1988–2000. Brockport, NY: BOA Editions, 2000.
The Boy Who Didn't Believe in Spring. New York: Dutton, 1973.
Dear Creator: A Week of Poems for Young People and Their Teachers. Garden City, NY: Doubleday, 1997.
Don't You Remember? New York: Dutton, 1973.
Everett Anderson's Christmas Coming. New York: Holt, Rinehart & Winston, 1971.
Everett Anderson's Friend. New York: Holt, Rinehart & Winston, 1976.
Everett Anderson's Goodbye. New York: Holt, Rinehart & Winston, 1983.
Everett Anderson's Nine Month Long. New York: Holt, Rinehart & Winston, 1978.
Everett Anderson's 1-2-3. New York: Holt, Rinehart & Winston, 1977.
Everett Anderson's Year. New York: Holt, Rinehart & Winston, 1974.
Generations. New York: Random House, 1976.
Good News about the Earth: New Poems. New York: Random House, 1972.
Good, Says Jerome. New York: Dutton, 1973.
Good Times: Poems. New York: Random House, 1969.
Good Woman: Poems and a Memoir, 1969–1980. Brockport, NY; St. Paul, MN: BOA Editions, 1987.
The Lucky Stone. New York: Delacorte, 1979.
Mercy. Brockport, NY: BOA Editions, 2004.
My Brother Fine with Me. New York: Holt, Rinehart & Winston, 1975.
My Friend Jacob. With Thomas DiGrazia. New York: Dutton, 1980.
Next: New Poems. Brockport, NY; St. Paul, MN: BOA Editions, 1987.
One of the Problems of Everett Anderson. New York: Holt, Rinehart & Winston, 2001.
An Ordinary Woman. New York: Random House, 1974.
Quilting: Poems, 1987–1990. Brockport, NY: BOA Editions, 1991.
Some of the Days of Everett Anderson. New York: Holt, Rinehart & Winston, 1970.
Sonora Beautiful. New York: Dutton, 1981.
The Terrible Stories: Poems. Brockport, NY: BOA Editions, 1996.
Three Wishes. New York: Viking, 1976.
The Times They Used to Be. New York: Holt, Rinehart & Winston, 1974.
Two-Headed Woman. Amherst: University of Massachusetts Press, 1980.

Studies of Lucille Clifton's Works

Anaporte-Easton, Jean. "Healing Our Wounds: The Direction of Difference in the Poetry of Lucille Clifton and Judith Johnson." *Mid-American Review* 14.2 (1994): 78–87.
Bernard, Mark. "Sharing the Living Light: Rhetorical, Poetic, and Social Identity in Lucille Clifton." *CLA Journal* 40.3 (March 1997): 288–304.

Bryant, Thelma. "A Conversation with Lucille Clifton." *SAGE: A Scholarly Journal on Black Women* 2.1 (Spring 1985): 52.

Evans, Mari, ed. *Black Women Writers (1950–1980): A Critical Evaluation*. Garden City, NY: Anchor-Doubleday, 1984.

Glaser, Michael. "I'd Like Not to Be a Stranger in the World: A Conversation/Interview with Lucille Clifton." *Antioch Review* 58.3 (Summer 2000): 310–29.

Holladay, Hilary. "Black Names in White Space: Lucille Clifton's South." *Southern Literary Journal* 34.2 (Spring 2002): 120–34.

———. "'I Am Not Grown Away from You': Lucille Clifton's Elegies for Her Mother." *CLA Journal* 42.4 (June 1999): 430–44.

———. "'Our Lives Are Our Line and We Go On': Concentric Circles of History in Lucille Clifton's *Generations*." *Xavier Review* 19.2 (1999): 18–29.

———. "Song of Herself: Lucille Clifton's Poems about Womanhood." In *The Furious Flowering of African American Poetry*, edited by Joanne V. Gabbin, 281–97. Charlottesville: University Press of Virginia, 1999.

———. *Wild Blessings: The Poetry of Lucille Clifton*. Baton Rouge: Louisiana State University Press, 2004.

Houston, Helen R. "Lucille Clifton." In *The Oxford Companion to Women's Writing in the United States*, edited by Cathy N. Davidson. New York: Oxford University Press, 1995.

Hull, Akasha. "Channeling the Ancestral Muse: Lucille Clifton and Dolores Kendrick." In *Female Subjects in Black and White: Race, Psychoanalysis, Feminism*, edited by Elizabeth Abel, Barbara Christian, and Helene Moglen, 330–48. Berkeley: University of California Press, 1997.

———. "In Her Own Images: Lucille Clifton and the Bible." In *Dwelling in Possibility: Women Poets and Critics on Poetry*, edited by Yopie Prins and Maeera Shreiber, 273–95. Ithaca, NY: Cornell University Press, 1997.

Johnson, Dianne. "The Chronicling of an African-American Life and Consciousness: Lucille Clifton's Everett Anderson Series." *Children's Literature Association Quarterly* 14.3 (Winter 1989): 174–78.

Johnson, Joyce. "The Theme of Celebration in Lucille Clifton's Poetry." *Pacific Coast Philology* 18.1/2 (November 1983): 70–76.

Kallet, Marilyn. "Doing What You Will Do: An Interview with Lucille Clifton." In *Sleeping with One Eye Open: Women Writers and the Art of Survival*, edited by Marilyn Kallet and Judith Ortiz Cofer, 80–85. Athens: University of Georgia Press, 1999.

Lazer, Hank. "Blackness Blessed: The Writings of Lucille Clifton." *Southern Review* 25.3 (Summer 1989): 760–70.

"Lucille Clifton." *The Oxford Companion to African American Literature*, edited by William M. Andrews et al. New York: Oxford University Press, 1997.

Mance, Ajuan M. "Re-Locating the Black Female Subject: The Landscape of the Body in the Poems of Lucille Clifton." In *Recovering the Black Female Body: Self-Representations by African American Women*, edited by Michael Bennett and Vanessa D. Dickerson, 123–40. New Brunswick, NJ: Rutgers University Press, 2001.

McCluskey, Audrey T. "Tell the Good News: A View of the Works of Lucille Clifton." In *Black Women Writers (1950–1980): A Critical Evaluation*, edited by Mari Evans, 139–49. Garden City, NY: Anchor-Doubleday, 1984.

Miller, James. "Lucille Clifton." In *Heath Anthology of American Literature*, vol. II, 4th ed., edited by Paul Lauter, 2700–701. Boston: Houghton Mifflin, 2002.

Ostriker, Alicia. "Kin and Kin: The Poetry of Lucille Clifton." *American Poetry Review* 22.6 (November–December 1993): 41–48.

Peppers, Wallace R. "Lucille Clifton." In *Dictionary of Literary Biography, Volume 41: Afro-American Poets Since 1955*, 55–60. Detroit: The Gale Group, 1985.

Rushing, Andrea B. "Lucille Clifton: A Changing Voice for Changing Times." In *Coming to Light: American Women Poets in the Twentieth Century*, edited by Diane W. Middlebrook and Marilyn Yalom, 214–22. Ann Arbor: University of Michigan Press, 1985.

Wall, Cheryl A. "Sifting Legacies in Lucille Clifton's *Generations*." *Contemporary Literature* 40.4 (Winter 1999): 552–74.

White, Mark B. "Sharing the Living Light: Rhetorical, Poetic, and Social Identity in Lucille Clifton." *CLA Journal* 40.3 (March 1997): 288–304.

Whitley, Edward. " 'A Long Missing Part of Itself': Bringing Lucille Clifton's *Generations* into American Literature." *MELUS* 26.2 (Summer 2001): 47–64.

Patricia Kennedy Bostian

WANDA COLEMAN (1946–)

BIOGRAPHICAL NARRATIVE

A Los Angeles native, Emmy-award winner Wanda Coleman has written over 2,000 poems, 100 short stories, and given more than 500 dramatic performances. Coleman was born in Watts and raised in what she has depicted as a black, middle-class Ozzie and Harriet family. Her father was an entrepreneur and her mother worked for Ronald Reagan as a seamstress. Coleman's occupations have varied. She has worked as a medical secretary, journalist, scriptwriter for the daytime soap opera *Days of Our Lives*, magazine editor, and recording artist. Although Coleman has worn and continues to wear many hats, she is mostly known as a prolific poet. She has received fellowships from the Guggenheim Foundation and the National Endowment for the Arts and, in 1999, Coleman was the winner of the Lenore Marshall Poetry Prize.

MAJOR WORKS

Most of Coleman's poetry is informed by her Los Angeles social, political, and economic surroundings. She writes about the oppression blacks have faced and are faced with in America. Themes of female persecution, alienation, exploitation, the inequitable class structure of America, male/female dichotomies, and internalized rejection are often discussed in her somewhat contemplative poetry. No matter the angle or critique she may proffer in her works, Coleman's poetry and short stories quite often produce a cathartic effect on her readers. Her poetic language is simultaneously thought provoking, sensual, and violent as she draws attention to issues of power and subordination in both men and women—black and white. Her language often takes the form of the modernist stream of consciousness technique in which her words mimic the chaos and fluidity of the human thought process. Her poet personas encompass a plethora of characterizations, dilemmas, and voices from the rape victim to the rapist, from themes of intraracial prejudice to black empowerment interests of the radical Black Panther organization, and from the incessant cries of the crack baby to the black woman standing her ground in the racist and sexist society in which she lives. Whatever the predicament or social commentary she offers in her poetry, Coleman portrays these incidences honestly and sympathetically.

In her frequently anthologized poem, "Women of My Color," Coleman describes the physical act of fellatio in the first few lines. Often criticized for her explicit sexual language and imagery, this sexual act that she illustrates quickly turns into a discussion on sexual politics. "Going down" begins to signify more than a sexual act or performance of sexual favors. "Going down" symbolizes the inferior position women have been socially subjected to within patriarchal systems of oppression. In this poem, Coleman takes the reader through a variety of male gazes—both black and white— wherein black women are viewed stereotypically and stripped of any individuality or autonomy. Like the blues tradition in which problems are presented without proffering a viable solution, the woman in the poem gives no method of solving her present situation, but she does intimate hope and optimism in an otherwise pessimistic poem.

CRITICAL RECEPTION

In many of Coleman's poems, her language demonstrates her desire to eschew "professionalizing" poetry and her disdain for poetic convention, or restraints, that permeate academic writing. Although she has been heavily criticized for her explicit sexual imagery, derogatory language, and unconventional grammatical structure, Coleman still has not received the attention that her poetry merits.

In "Doing Battle with the Wolf: A Critical Introduction to Wanda Coleman's Poetry," Tony Magistrale discusses the deficiency of scholarly and critical interpretations of Coleman's works. Discussing Coleman's past omission from the academic canon of black poets, he states:

She is a radical feminist who produces poems that are not similar in tone, style, or subject matter to the technically elegant and solipsistic verse that is currently being produced by graduates of advanced writing programs. (539)

Coleman's works are "technically elegant." Her word configurations, double entendres, and keen articulation of empathy for her poet persona(s) reveal this elegance and her status as a valuable poet of and for the people.

BIBLIOGRAPHY

Works by Wanda Coleman

Bathwater Wine. Santa Rosa: Black Sparrow Press, 1998.
Hand Dance. Santa Rosa: Black Sparrow Press, 1993.
Mad Dog Black Lady. Santa Rosa: Black Sparrow Press, 1979.
Mercurochrome: New Poems. Santa Rosa: Black Sparrow Press, 2001.
A War of Eyes and Other Stories. Santa Rosa: Black Sparrow Press, 1988.

Study of Wanda Coleman's Works

Magistrale, Tony. "Doing Battle with the Wolf: A Critical Introduction to Wanda Coleman's Poetry." *Black American Literature Forum* 23.3 (1989): 539–54.

Terri Jackson Wallace

EUGENIA W. COLLIER (1928–)

BIOGRAPHICAL NARRATIVE

Eugenia W. Collier has written several articles, essays, short stories, and poems. Born on April 6, 1928, in Baltimore, Maryland, Eugenia Collier has spent much of her life in Baltimore. Her father, Harry Maceo, was a physician and her mother, Eugenia Williams, was an educator. Collier had three sons with ex-husband, Charles Collier.

She graduated from Howard University in 1948, and later earned a Master of Arts from Columbia in 1950, then a Ph.D. from University of Maryland in 1976. Collier taught at the University of Maryland (Baltimore County), Howard University, and Atlanta University; she also taught and chaired in the English Department at Morgan State University before retiring in 1996. Earlier in her career, Collier worked as a caseworker for the Baltimore Department of Welfare.

Collier's articles, essays, short stories, and poems have appeared in such periodicals as *African American Review, Callaloo*, College Language Association Journal, the *New York Times*, and *Phylon*. In 1972 she coedited an anthology, *Afro-American Writing: An Anthology of Prose and Poetry*, with Robert A. Long; in 1994 she wrote a book of short stories, *Breeder and Other Stories*, and wrote a one-act play, *Ricky*. Her short story *Marigolds* won the Gwendolyn Brooks Award for Fiction in 1969. Collier was also awarded the Outstanding Educators of America Award from 1972 to 1975 and the Distinguished Writers Award from Middle Atlantic Writers Association in 1970. She has been a member of the College Language Association, Association for the Study of Negro Life and History, Middle Atlantic Writers Association, and the African American Writers Guild.

MAJOR WORKS

Most of Collier's writings challenge the role of African Americans in literature. In her creative works and staunch critiques, she often raises tough questions. She writes passionately about language in her stories and addresses issues and concerns of poorer blacks, particularly urban blacks. In a moving tribute to mentor and friend Sterling Brown, she says he was the "liaison between [characters] and the unreachable world of artists, and scholars" ("Sterling's Way" 885). Collier acknowledges the disconnection between scholars and the world that exists outside of the institution. Many of her stories in *Breeder* bridge these notions of connectedness. In one short story, "Rachel's Children," a professor moves from the north to the south onto a haunted slave plantation and immediately notices the disparaging economic conditions. In another story, "Present for Sarah," a retired professor slips into a state of depression and paranoia fueled by alcoholism and aging.

Collier drew from her own experiences as a social worker in her short story, "Ricky" (also based on the one-act play). The main character, Vi, patterns a social worker and admonishes the bureaucratic, insensitive, and neglectful social system after she attempts to care for a troubled young relative, Ricky. Collier writes, "... [judges, social workers, probation officers] seemed unrelated to the real trauma of the young lives whose direction was now in their hands" (Breeder 27). A failed justice system is also to blame in "Dead Man Running," where an accused drug-dealing murderer is released from custody while on another side of town a toddler is gunned down playing in front of his home and a teenage girl is found killed execution style. In other stories, "Journey Through Woods" and "The Caregiver," Collier addresses the overwhelming challenges of caring for ailing relatives and the damage and devastation that wreak havoc on the relative that feels the greatest sacrifice: the caregiver.

CRITICAL RECEPTION

In a 1972 essay written for the *New York Times*, Collier blasted the then-new television sitcom, *Sanford & Son*. She accused the popular television show of being more reflective of white contemporary culture than black culture and examined the roles of the main characters. The show perpetuated minstrel stereotypes under the guise of humor. The main characters, Fred and Lamont, were not reflective of real blacks and the show's form of humor only depicted contemporary American culture. There was no tragedy behind the humor rather; selfishness, immaturity, and bigotry were depicted.

In response to the essay, a critic accused Collier of being a separatist followed by a barrage of angry rebuttals sent to the editor. Collier was described as racist, banal, and ignoring advances that had been made in media with African American representation. She remained critical of misrepresentations of blacks and challenged readers to demand and expect more.

In a 1974 review based on the film *Conrack*, Collier lamented the trite image of the white savior that comes to rescues ignorant blacks. She argued that the film avoided real-life depictions of the poor blacks in the Sea Islands and was culturally void. Collier always sought authenticity and honesty in work and believed in the power of serious writers.

Breeder has been praised for showing the multilayered dimensions of black women: common themes such as dysfunctional family relationships, senility, poverty, failed social systems, and drug abuse. The title alone suggests that Collier was thinking beyond black and female as she repeatedly raised the notion that women indelibly hold families together by embracing the spoils of community despite repeated pitfalls. While one critic stated that Collier's writing was flat and didactic, she charged that blacks have to take care of each other first.

BIBLIOGRAPHY

Works by Eugenia W. Collier

Afro-American Writing: An Anthology of Prose and Poetry, edited with Robert A. Long. University Park: Pennsylvania State University Press, 1985.
Breeder and Other Stories. Baltimore: Black Classic Press, 1994.
Hurl. Detroit: Broadside Press, 1974.
Impressions in Asphalt: Images of Urban America in Literature. With Ruthe T. Sheffey. Southern Pines, NC: Scribner, 1969.
"Sterling's Way." *Callaloo* 21.4 (Fall 1998): 884–87.

Studies of Eugenia W. Collier's Works

Kaganoff, Peggy. "Forecasts: Paperbacks." *Publishers Weekly* 241 (January 17, 1994): 427.
Moore, Opal J. "A Bill of Wrongs: Stories for the Children." *Black Issues in Higher Education* 14.2 (March 20, 1997): 34.
Peterson, Bernard L., Jr. *Contemporary Black American Playwrights and Their Plays*. Westport, CT: Greenwood Press, 1988.

T. Jasmine Dawson

KATHLEEN CONWELL COLLINS (1942–1988)

BIOGRAPHICAL NARRATIVE

Dramatist, novelist and short stry writer Kathleen Conwell Collins (also known as Kathleen Conwell or Kathleen Collins Prettyman) managed to change the face and content of black womanist film during the forty-six years of her short life. She was born in Jersey City, New Jersey, on March 18, 1942, to Frank and Loretta Conwell. Her father, Frank Conwell, worked as a mortician and afterward became the principal of a high school that is now named after him. He later became the first African American state legislator in New Jersey. After graduating from Skidmore College in Sarasota Springs, New York, Collins followed her father's political lead and became involved in the Student Nonviolent Coordinating Committee's (SNCC) thrust to help register voters in the South.

After obtaining her degree in philosophy and religion in 1963, Collins furthered her education at the Sorbonne in Paris, France. There she became interested in telling stories through film. She received the Master of Arts degree in 1966 through the Sorbonne's Middlebury graduate program. She then returned to the United States and began her writing career, while working on the editorial and production staff of WNET Radio in New York.

Collins's first short stories reflected her experiences in SNCC, France, and the dilemmas of a young married woman. In 1974, shortly after her marriage to Douglass Collins ended, Collins joined the faculty of City College at the City University of New York as a professor of film history and screenwriting. In fact, it was her students, particularly Ronald Gray, who encouraged her to pursue a script she had previously abandoned. Adapting Jewish writer Henry H. Roth's fiction to film, Collins became the first African American woman to write, direct, and produce a full-length feature film. The screenplay turned film *The Cruz Brothers and Mrs. Malloy*, which is about the struggle of three Puerto Rican brothers to survive in a small country town, won first prize in the Sinking Creek Film Festival.

Losing Ground followed in 1982 and won first prize at the Figueroa da Foz International Film Festival in Portugal. Other films to her credit include *Madame Flor* (1987) and *Conversations with Julie* (1988). Her films have been shown on the Learning Channel and the Public Broadcasting Station.

Among her plays are *In the Midnight Hour* (1981); *The Brothers* (1982), which was a finalist for the Susan Blackburn International Prize in Playwriting and voted one of the Best Plays of 1982 by the AUDELCO Awards Committee; and *The Reading*, a one-act play about the conflict between white and black women, commissioned by the American Place Theatre (1984). She also penned *Begin the Beguine* (1985), a collection of one-act plays produced at the Richard Allen Center for Culture and Arts in New York, a play about the first Black aviatrix, Bessie Coleman; *Only the Sky Is Free* (1985); *While Older Men Speak* (1986); and *Looking for Jane*. In 1987, Collins married Alfred E. Prettyman and completed her screenplay *Madame Flor*. In spring 1988, Collins completed a novel,

Lollie: A Suburban Tale, and by the summer another screenplay, *Conversations with Julie*, which is about a mother and daughter coming to terms with separation.

In 1983 Collins was reacquainted with Alfred Prettyman, whom she had met years earlier. The two married four years later. Within one week of their marriage, Collins learned she had cancer. She died in 1988, survived by her husband; her daughter Nina; her two sons, Asa Hale and Emilio; a stepdaughter, Meryl Prettyman; and a stepson Evan Prettyman.

Although Collins wrote and produced a number of plays and films in her lifetime, one gets the feeling that she was only just beginning when she succumbed to cancer. Her influence extends to other black filmmakers such as Euzhan Palcy and Julie Dash who both honor her fearlessness and presence as a writer and filmmaker. Her work has been described as postmodern, iconoclastic, and experimental (Williams 39).

MAJOR WORKS

Many of Collins's plays are no longer in print. Readily available at many university libraries are the screenplay *Losing Ground* and the dramas published in other anthologies, *The Brothers* and *In the Midnight Hour*. Her plays employ such themes as marital malaise, male dominance and impotence, freedom of expression, and the unglorified plight of the black middle class. Her protagonists are typically self-reflective women who move from a state of subjugation to empowerment. Collins's plays followed the "Blaxploitation" era and a number of plays and films that focused on the rise of blacks from poverty or "ghetto" life. She met a great deal of criticism because many feel that her plays have not been black centered or have lacked the requisite positive representations of black life. Despite such disapproval, Collins continued to write about the complexities of black life, some of which has little, if anything, to do with race. In *Reel Women* Part 4 Collins commented: "I have a sense of going my own way, and I don't really think much about whether it's going against the grain. I don't really want to spend a lot of time worrying about how I am perceived by other people" (quoted in *Columbia World of Quotations Online*).

The original screenplay, *Losing Ground*, led to the first independent feature film by an African American woman filmmaker. The "comedy drama" as the author describes it, set in New York, centers around a married couple, Sara, a professor of Western philosophy, and her artist-husband, Victor. Sara is a consummate philosophy professor, fixated on examining ecstasy from a rational perspective while her husband Victor is more concerned about ecstasy in a more experiential manner. Sara's students point out to her how lucky she is to have a husband in addition to her other good qualities. While Victor is a "genuine Negro success" (130), Sara struggles against becoming the stereotypical tragic mulatto. Sara is orderly, straightforward, practical, and logical. Victor counts on that. He is passionate, irreverent, and vulgar. Though Sara knows that her husband is a flirt and engages in extramarital affairs, she claims in conversation with her mother that she is jealous of his freedom, his ability to let go without inhibition and not the fact that he inserts his "thing" inside other women. This declaration is dismantled when Sara becomes annoyed by and then enraged by Victor's flirtations with Celia, a young and vivacious Puerto Rican woman, in her presence.

Sara's students convince her to step out of her conventional box and play Frankie, in an archetypal reinterpretation of the Frankie and Johnnie story. It is through the drama that Sara begins to grapple seriously with her practical, rational, philosophical learnings and begins to seek in a realistic way the ecstasy that up until now she only writes about.

The philosophy Sara pursues in the classroom and in her scholarship undergirds the drama and the lessons the protagonist learns comes out of a realization that she has operated both in the classroom and in her home in a masculinist, limiting world. She resists both when she figuratively shoots Johnnie in the play within the play at the end of the drama.

The Brothers, named by Theatre Communications Groups as one of twelve outstanding plays of the 1982 season, was first presented at the American Place Theatre on March 31, 1982, under the direction of Billie Allen. The temporal scheme of the drama runs from February 1, 1948, the assassination of Mahatma Gandhi, to April 5, 1968, the assassination of Martin Luther King, Jr. The play opens with Gandhi's assassination and the decision of thirty-one-year-old two-time Olympic champion Nelson, the youngest of the brothers, to remain in his bed forever. He declares that the "Negro life is a void" (302). The Edwards brothers, Lawrence, Franklin, Jeremy, and Nelson, and the one sister, Marietta, were reared to be proud and unlimited by the fact of their blackness. They were coached by their cruel and unrelenting father to pursue "whiteness" and white dreams.

The Brothers is a complex drama centered on the Edwards men, but focused on the Edwards women. For although titled *The Brothers*, it is the women who take center stage and are involved in all the play's action. The men are only glimpsed through the women's comments and remembrances, and the men are so endowed with the speed, tenacity, and will of the Edwards men that their presence fills a room even though they are never seen on stage. The audience meets them off camera, in snatches of the others' conversation, but knows them as intimately as their wives know them.

The brothers are central and essential in the women's lives. The wives' and sisters' conversations, actions, and attitudes are all restricted to the brothers' needs, wants, and dispositions. One, Caroline, works as a maid to put her husband, Lawrence, through school. Lawrence is an unscrupulous real-estate agent who will stop at nothing to get the deal he wants. He treats Caroline no better for it. Their marriage is unstable and unpredictable, made worse by the loss of their child Laura. Lillie, Franklin's first wife, dies from an unnamed disease; she wastes her potential sitting by the phone waiting for calls of death. At the time of her death, Franklin is a mortician studying to become a teacher; later, he becomes a politician. To avoid having his mother-in-law gain custody of his children, Franklin marries Letitia, a thirty-eight-year-old virgin when they meet, whom he belittles and embarrasses because she does not measure up to Lillie's stature or grace. Witty Danielle, Nelson's wife, used to the high life of partying and drinking, cannot forgive Nelson for breaking his promise to give her the world. The reader never meets Aurora, Jeremy's wife, because as Letitia points out she is the only one who had the sense enough to get away from them. There is only one sister in the Edwards family, Marietta; she is unmarried because she believes her father would find her love interest too black in skin color and in aspiration.

The brothers are so caught up in brooding over what being a Negro means, and Marietta is so caught up in her brothers, that they take no note of the history taking place all around them. They make little notice of Gandhi's or King's assassination, and one gets the sense that they have wasted the last twenty years on themselves.

In the Midnight Hour is an unusual drama with a twelve-hour time span. Set in 1962, Harlem, New York, the drama focuses on the Daniels family members and their own personal dreams (literal and figurative). Each family member—Ralph, Lillie, Anna, and Ben—wishes to paint a canvass with his or her memories and hold forever with him or her the good times in the family parlor where they talked, danced, entertained, and were entertained by their regular guests, Floyd, a rejected priest, turned itinerant philosopher, and Chips, the pianist.

Ralph, the father, is obsessed with finding the truth. Recovering from years of depression and rage, he firmly believes, as his psychiatrist teaches, anger is the only truth. He carves figurines, tables, chairs, dollhouses, and so on with wood believing that one can carve out the right life in the same manner that he skillfully carves with a carving knife.

Lillie, good-natured wife and mother, lives in the past of her own dreams, to an extent. She forgives Ralph for the years he psychologically absents himself from their marriage and determines to affect the perfect disposition for the perfect mother and wife for picture-perfect moments with her family and its closest friends.

Twenty-year-old Anna, nurtured for greatness, has just been introduced to the civil rights movement and is enthralled by the idea of doing something magnanimous to help others.

Ben, the eighteen-year-old son, rides an emotional roller coaster, possibly spun into action by his memories of racial awareness when he was a teenager, when he and his father were "ace boon coons" but he had not been taught that there were "Negro reasons" for some of the things he experiences. Ben and Anna marshal Christine, a young Barnard student from Boston, into their lives and she serves to balance out and lend something a little more grounded, mundane, and ordinary to the Daniels household.

In the middle of the play—in the middle of the night—the playwright ushers us into a scene that takes place in both the present and the far future. In the illusory, derivative properties of dream, by the end of this scene the audience is slightly disoriented but is given insight to the future for this family of dreamers—Ralph's therapist-god commits suicide and topples Ralph's progress; Lillie loses her son, and as a result, the good times and perfect picture she wants to create fade away; Anna, in searching for the genuine trust and love she shared with her brother and in her quest to do something spectacular and different, goes through several marriages and babies to end up a lonely and cynical person. Each family member's fate punctuates Ben's "present" story to Christine about his experience with Bucky Rogers and Walter Duffy, his private school classmates, whose visit to Harlem when they were fifteen made him painfully aware of their differences.

In the closing scene of the drama, after Ben upsets Christine by foolishly jumping from a pier, we are left with a sense that it is Ben's anger that will ultimately lead to his and the family's ruin in the future.

Inspired by Lorraine Hansberry's aesthetics, Collins wrote life as she saw it and did not allow herself to be fettered by constraints placed on African American writers. She looked at African Americans as human subjects not race subjects. When her plays did focus on issues of race, she rendered what she felt were honest portrayals of black life and not portrayals which exaggerated or posed overly positive aspects of black existence in America while ignoring the often negative and daunting realities. Rather than seeing black problems as simple manifestations of white oppression, through her writing, Collins suggests that much of it has to do with the internal dialogue and pressures people impose on themselves. Her plays are deeply psychological in nature. She integrates certain elements of her personal life into her plays and invites audience members to go beyond the surface meaning of things and think about the values and the attitudes imposed on them by society and how they choose to deal with them.

CRITICAL RECEPTION

Though Collins's plays deal with some of the deeper, psychological issues involved in individuals' lives and though she has won numerous awards and fellowships for her work, there has been little critical commentary on her plays. There is no doubt that she is a pioneering African American filmmaker and playwright, ushering in an era of Black women filmmakers such as Julie Dash who was her student at CUNY and Euzhan Palcy. John Williams mentions her influence in his exploration and review of black women filmmakers in *Cineaste*, "Re-creating their media image: two generations of black women filmmakers" Williams points out that though critical reception was less than positive in regards to much of Collins work, she paved the way for a generation of black woman filmmakers. He contends that Collins wrote dramas and produced feature films that wrote against what she saw as the "phallocentric conventions of white Hollywood cinema" (38). He also writes that the few critics who "deigned to comment on [*Losing Ground*] were less than receptive to its originality (39). He further argues that most critics "simply did not know how to comment on *Losing Ground*'s subversive vision of black culture. Some even took issue with the very notion of a "black female philosophy professor" as entailing too much of a willing suspension of disbelief" (39).

In "Dialogic Modes of Representing Africa(s): Womanist Film" Mark A. Reid, like Williams, acknowledges Collins's work and its influence. He reads *Losing Ground* as a womanist texts and notes that "Collins speaks of an 'imperfect synthesis' of the African American condition" (386).

In the *New York Times* review of *The Brothers*, while commenting on the weaknesses of the play's dialogue and limiting form, Frank Rich writes, "Miss Collins is a promising writer. She is capable of passions both tender and angry; she can be funny; she is also, to borrow a line form her text, 'fond of the sound of words'" (C13).

The fact that there has been little critical attention to Collins work does not diminish the quality of her work. She was a playwright writing life as she saw it, perhaps a bit ahead of her critical moment. In the words of actress-director and friend to Collins, Seret Scott, [we] cannot resolve [Collins's] leaving.

BIBLIOGRAPHY

Works by Kathleen Conwell Collins

Begin the Beguine (1985). No publication information available.
The Brothers. In *Nine Plays by Black Women*, edited by Margaret B. Wilkerson, 293–346. New York: Mentor, 1986.
In the Midnight Hour. In *The Women's Project*, edited by Julia Miles, 35–83. New York: Performance Arts Journal Publications and American Place Theatre, 1980.
Looking for Jane (1986). No publication information available.
Losing Ground: An Original Screenplay. In *Screenplays of the African American Experience*, edited by Phyllis Rauch Klotman, 119–85. Bloomington: Indiana University Press, 1991.
Only the Sky Is Free (1985). No publication information available.
The Reading (1984). No publication information available.
While Older Men Speak (1986). No publication information available.

Studies of Kathleen Conwell Collins's Works

Brown, Janet. *Taking Center Stage: Feminism in Contemporary U.S. Drama*. Metuchen, NJ: Scarecrow Press, 1991.

Campbell, Loretta. "Reinventing Our Image: Eleven Black Women Filmmakers." *Heresies* 4.4 (1983): 58–62.

Nicholson, David. "A Commitment to Writing: A Conversation with Kathleen Collins Prettyman." *Black Film Review* 5.1 (1988–1989): 6–15.

Reid, Mark A. "Dialogic Modes of Representing Africa(s): Womanist Film." *Black American Literature Forum* 25.2 (Summer 1991): 375–88.

Rich, Frank. "Theatre: Black Anguish in 'Brothers.' " *New York Times*, April 6, 1982, C13.

Williams, John. "Re-creating Their Media Image: Two Generations of Black Women Filmmakers." *Cineaste* 20.3 (Summer 1993): 38–42.

Chandra Tyler Mountain

ANNA JULIA HAYWARD COOPER (1858–1964)

BIOGRAPHICAL NARRATIVE

Anna Julia Hayward Cooper, biographer and essayist, was born in 1858 in Raleigh, North Carolina, to Hannah Stanley, a slave, and George Washington Hayward, her white owner. In 1865, she entered St. Augustine's Normal and Collegiate Institute and, by 1868, was tutoring fellow students. She married George A. C. Cooper in 1877. Following her husband's untimely death in 1879, she earned a B.A. and an M.A. in mathematics from Oberlin College, excelling in the "gentlemen's courses."

In 1892, Cooper published *A Voice from the South by a Black Woman of the South*, a collection of essays, treatises, and reflections based largely on her personal experience. After teaching at St. Augustine's and Wilberforce University, she joined the faculty of "M" Street School (later Dunbar High School) in Washington, and was named principal in 1901. She became a target for the Tuskegee Machine, however, and lost her principalship in 1906 when she refused to eliminate the school's classical curriculum in favor of vocational training. Rehired in 1910, she remained at "M" Street until 1930 when she retired and became president of Frelinghuysen University, an evening school for working blacks. Cooper so believed in providing educational opportunities for the lower classes that when Frelinghuysen suffered financial reversals, she held classes in her own home.

In 1925, at the age of sixty-seven, Cooper earned her doctorate from the Sorbonne, University of Paris, completing two theses: *Le Pèlerinage de Charlemagne: Voyage à Jérusalem et à Constantinople* (1925), a translation of a medieval tale, and *L' Attitude de La France a L' Êgard de L' Esclavage Pendant La Révolution* (1925), a historical study of French racial attitudes. Even in her later years, Cooper exemplified education as a lifelong process by writing, publishing, speaking, and participating in community outreach programs into the 1950s. Her later works included *Equality of the Races and the Democratic Movement* (1945), *Personal Recollections of the Grimké Family* (1951), and *The Third Step* (after 1945). Active in the Pan-African movement, black women's clubs, and Colored Social Settlement efforts, Cooper also cofounded the Colored Women's League and the Colored Women's YWCA. In testimony to her scholarly work, Cooper was the only woman elected to the American Negro Academy. She died February 27, 1964, in Washington, D.C.

MAJOR WORKS

Throughout Cooper's works appears a concurrent passionate sense of racial pride and a concern for equal treatment and equal opportunity, particularly in education. In *A Voice from the South by a Black Woman of the South* (1892), the work that defines her as a feminist and racial theorist, Cooper identifies her "Raison D'être" as the silence of the Black Woman of America who has yet to speak about racial issues. The text's two-part division ("Soprano Obligato," focusing on the individual black woman's voice, and "Tutti ad Libitum," concerning the larger black community) emphasizes the oppressed position of women, especially black women, in America and the factors that perpetuate that oppression. These thoughtful scholarly pieces, praising the progress of African Americans only one generation removed from slavery, illustrate her extensive knowledge of both history and contemporary society. Her well-reasoned arguments urge the black woman to take her rightful place as the social force upon which the fate of black society rests. Of particular interest is "Woman versus the Indian," an essay in which Cooper challenges both black men and white feminists to participate in uplifting the black woman.

In her 1925 dissertation, *L' Attitude de La France a L' Égard de L' Esclavage Pendant La Révolution* (published in the United States as *Slavery and the French Revolutionists*), Cooper meticulously documents the horrors of slavery in the French Caribbean colonies, connecting conditions there with those in France and in the United States and recounting the rebellion to end slavery. She pictures all involved committing atrocities and engaging in intrigues without regard for the suffering of others, and she suggests that the evils of the slave system create similar evils within the slaves and that slavery could have been easily abolished if the desire to end it had existed.

Le Pèlerinage de Charlemagne: Voyage à Jérusalem et à Constantinople (1925), a translation of a medieval text into modern French, garnered much praise from academics and quickly made its way into French language classrooms. It remained unpublished in the United States despite Cooper's attempts to donate the copyright to Oberlin College.

The two volumes of *Personal Recollections of the Grimké Family* (1951), a testimony to her long-lasting friendship with Charlotte Forten Grimké, contain letters, poems, essays, and sermons by members of the Grimké family, interspersed with Cooper's personal reminiscences and commentary.

CRITICAL RECEPTION

Controversy and disagreement characterize contemporary critical views of Cooper's only readily accessible work, *Voice*: either Cooper is considered a pivotal figure in nascent African American feminist theory, or she is seen as too closely tied to the "Cult of True Womanhood" and, thus, not a majority voice. For Charles Lemert, despite its white feminist language, *Voice* is "the first *systematic* . . . insistence that no one social category can capture the reality of the colored woman" and prefigures contemporary discussions regarding the inadequacies of categories "to capture . . . the complexities of a woman's social experiences" (14, 16). In her introduction to the Schoemberg edition of *Voice*, Helen Washington contends Cooper seems detached from "a black and female past" while identifying "black womanhood as the vital agency for social and political change in America" (xxxi). Washington attributes the "neglect" of Cooper's "embryonic black feminist analysis" to its being "by and about women" and asserts that although *Voice* critiques both genders, Cooper is unable to identify with "ordinary black working women" (xxviii, xlvi). Likewise, Stephanie Athey argues that Cooper adopted the language of white female sovereignty arguments to construct her own arguments for racial "regeneration," expanding the meaning of eugenic terminology, while inadvertently contradicting her purposes. In a similarly conflicted view, Elizabeth Alexander disdains Cooper's "essentialist" approach, yet praises her for creating a "new space between . . . the slave narrative . . . and . . . political essays," a communal voice that "conflates . . . single authorship with collective voice and responsibility" (65, 79, 62).

At least partially because W.E.B. DuBois quoted Cooper without acknowledging her as his source, some critics compare the two. Hanna Wallinger deems them intellectual equals and attributes Cooper's lesser fame to gender restrictions. For Wallinger, the "scholarly and argumentative" essays in *Voice* provide "occasional glimpses at the author's personal experience, and reveal a strong sense of irony and deep concern for the knowledge of the subject" (268).

Recent criticism has also addressed pedagogy and rhetorical strategies. Cathryn Bailey grounds Cooper's importance in her valuing a liberal education and insists that Cooper's rhetorical skill allowed her to manipulate the language of white feminists to claim womanhood for African American women. Bailey attributes contradictory views of Cooper to strong convictions and sensitivity to audience. Both Karen Johnson and Frances Richardson Keller recognize Cooper's impact on education theory and praise her for emphasizing lifelong learning. Indeed, Keller claims Cooper originated the community college concept of education for all, regardless of class and gender.

Cooper's self-publishing suggests the negative impact of her professional disagreements with the Washington, D.C., school system and has made her later works virtually inaccessible. Her dissertation, her reminiscences, and her later essays have thus garnered little critical attention, yet all remain important texts that reveal Cooper's keen intellect, her view of racism as an obstacle to social progress and human happiness, and her determination to uplift her race, especially through educational opportunities.

BIBLIOGRAPHY

Works by Anna Julia Hayward Cooper

Personal Recollections of the Grimké Family. 2 vols. United States: Privately printed, 1951.
Slavery and the French Revolutionists (1788–1805). Translated from *L' Attitude de La France a L' Égard de L' Esclavage Pendant La Révolution* by Frances Richardson Keller. Lewiston: Mellen, 1988.
The Third Step. N.p.: Privately published, 1945(?).
A Voice from the South. Introduction by Mary Helen Washington. New York: Oxford University Press, 1988.
The Voice of Anna Julia Cooper, edited by Charles C. Lemert and Esme Bhan. Lanham: Rowman, 1998.

Studies of Anna Julia Hayward Cooper's Works

Alexander, Elizabeth. "'We Must Be about Our Father's Business': Anna Julia Cooper and the Incorporation of the Nineteenth-Century African-American Woman Intellectual." In *In Her Own Voice: Nineteenth-Century American Women Essayists*, edited by Sherry Lee Linkon, 61–80. New York: Garland, 1997.
Athey, Stephanie. "Eugenic Feminisms in Late Nineteenth-Century America: Reading Race in Victoria Woodhull, Frances Willard, Anna Julia Cooper, and Ida B. Wells." *Genders On-Line Journal* 31 (2000). www.genders.org/.
Bailey, Cathryn. "Dedicated in the Name of My Slave Mother to the Education of Colored Working People." *Hypatia* 19 (2004): 56–73.
Baker-Fletcher, Karen. *A Singing Something: Womanist Reflections on Anna Julia Cooper.* New York: Crossroad, 1994.
Behling, Laura L. "Reification and Resistance: The Rhetoric of Black Womanhood at the Columbian Exposition, 1893." *Women's Studies in Communication* 25 (2002): 173–97.
Gable, Leona C. *From Slavery to the Sorbonne and Beyond: The Life and Writings of Anna J. Cooper.* Northampton: Smith College Press, 1982.

Hutchinson, Louise Daniel. *Anna J. Cooper: A Voice from the South*. Washington, DC: Smithsonian, 1981.

Johnson, Karen A. *Uplifting the Women and the Race: The Educational Philosophies and Social Activism of Anna Julia Cooper and Nannie Helen Burroughs*. New York: Garland, 2000.

Keller, Frances Richardson. "An Educational Controversy: Anna Julia Cooper's Vision of Resolution." *NWSA Journal* 11 (1999): 49–67.

Logan, Shirley Wilson. *"We Are Coming": The Persuasive Discourse of Nineteenth-Century Black Women*. Carbondale: Southern Illinois University Press, 1999.

May, Vivian M. "Thinking from the Margins, Acting at the Intersections: Anna Julia Cooper's *A Voice from the South*." *Hypatia* 19 (2004): 74–91.

McCaskill, Barbara. "Anna Julia cooper, Pauline Elizabeth Hopkins, and the African American Feminization of DuBois's Discourse." In *The Souls of Black Folk: One Hundred Years Later*, edited by Dolan Hubbard, 70–84. Columbia: University of Missouri Press, 2003.

Wallinger, Hanna. "The Five Million Women of My Race: Negotiations of Gender in W.E.B. DuBois and Anna Julia Cooper." In *Soft Canons: American Women Writers and Masculine Tradition*, edited by Karen L. Kilcup, 262–80. Iowa City: University of Iowa Press, 1999.

Gloria A. Shearin

J. CALIFORNIA COOPER (19??–)

BIOGRAPHICAL NARRATIVE

Having published a total of six collections of short stories and four novels, Joan California Cooper entered the literary field as an award-winning playwright. She was born in Berkeley, California, in an undisclosed year, undisclosed because "a woman who will tell her age will tell anything." She has one daughter, Paris Williams, and she now lives in Portland, Oregon. She is a self-proclaimed semi-recluse who is private to the point of eccentricity, choosing not to entertain visitors nor disclose such personal facts as her age. In a process that is described as organic, she listens to her characters and writes them in bed, in longhand, during the first hours of the morning. One of Cooper's creative muses is history. Cooper also credits an active imagination from years of playing in an imaginary world of paper dolls and being fascinated with fairy tales as her other muses. In 1984 she published her first collection of short stories, *A Piece of Mine*.

MAJOR WORKS

By far, Cooper's most frequently discussed innovation is her textual language. One finds her characters and, correspondingly, her readers on a porch shelling peas or shooting the breeze with a narrator who cajoles, orders, and tells tales. Her tales engage rape, racism, miscegenation, oppression, the joys and ills of marriage, the emptiness of wealth, and just plain old life while simultaneously balancing those topics with others: truth, love, happiness, satisfaction, the power of choice, the merits (and demerits) of family, and the universality of the human experience. The stories may end happily or not, but there is always justice at the end. Cooper's narrative characters are predominantly females from a variety of backgrounds who act as the conduits through which the readers receive the story, and they are always aware of their audience. One example is the narrator in "A Shooting Star" who calls attention to herself and the role of her audience as active participants: "Now, you don't know me. And, I know that *you* know that nobody knows everything. . . . But, it seems to me, and I already told you I don't know everything, that nowadays sex is making the world go round" (*The Future Has a Past* 1). The italicized "you" expresses the text's insistence that someone is listening as opposed to just reading, but the text is aware that it will be read as well. For example, in "Swimming to the Top of the Rain" and "Loved to Death," Cooper uses a modernist technique that supplements the written text with symbols. In "Swimming," the narrator says of her sister who does not attend their mother's funeral, "Middle didn't come, but sent $10.00" (*Homemade Love* 7). The use of similar symbolic representation in "Loved to Death" appears more logical since the narrator is addressing her notebook, but it is still a visual interruption of a profoundly oral and aural text that is enriched by being read aloud.

In "Too Hep to Be Happy!" the eighty-one-year-old narrator, Ida Walker, actually invites the reader-listener into her home. Walker says, "*Sit on down over there. Make yourself comfortable. I'm gonna roll out these rolls and pop them in the oven for us to make our acquaintance by. I'm a good cook!*" (*A Piece of Mine* 79). This italicized address occurs early in the story, and it is a visual and aural divergence from the story in progress that Walker is already telling to her listener. The story is interspersed with Walker's self-interruptions to comment on her rolls, and, by the story's end, she and the reader are buttering up and eating her fresh baked rolls. Her pleasure in an element as simple and yet scrumptious as homemade rolls is juxtaposed against the moral of the story, which is that being afraid of life's chances and guarding one's self too closely can be the road blocks to a life filled with love and happiness. Walker's subject, Lester, a man whose soul is quite depleted and empty, is outside of the rich culture that enjoys the hot butter of rolls and a good chat with a passerby. The story reminds the reader-listener of the words of the communal voice that narrates Gloria Naylor's *Mama Day*: "Think about it: ain't nobody really talking to you. . . . Uh, huh, listen. Really listen this time: the only voice is your own." The difference with Cooper is that the reader is convinced that the only voice is not her own since the book really does talk. The innovation of an aural text is completely Cooper's as it builds on the technique of Zora Neale Hurston's speakerly text, so named by Henry Louis Gates, Jr. What Cooper creates, however, is a preacherly text best articulated through her novels.

The interactive narrators of Cooper's short stories also articulate the elements of didacticism that pervade and are characteristic of her stories. Though the didacticism of Cooper's stories clearly draws on that of the early nineteenth-century sentimentalists, hers is clearly separated by its situation in the African American folk tradition of "mother wit." The allegorical naming and mother wit of the narrators espoused through plain talk are the tools used to communicate a didacticism based on the Ten Commandments. In the now anthologized "He Was a Man! (But He Did Himself Wrong)," the narrator is a neighbor who tells the story of overweight Della and her skinny husband Smitty. Smitty is a verbally and physically abusive husband who treats his wife more like a mule of the world. One evening after an extremely difficult day for Della, Smitty comes home to find Della asleep when he expects to find his dinner done. She accidentally hits him when he beats her and he leaves. As a result of mourning her abandonment, Della loses weight and consequently attracts a man who comes to love her for who she is. In a whirlwind of events, Smitty ends up hanging himself in a noose similar to one he has previously prepared for Della, and she marries her new man and lives happily ever after as her weight increases back to her 200 pounds of joy. As all of Cooper's stories have a moral, the narrator's emphasis is not that Della finds a new life because she loses the weight that has intimidated Smitty but that Della is able to give the love and happiness that Smitty could have had to someone else because she is finally able to value herself.

Another example of Cooper's didacticism is in a story whose title signifies on Flannery O'Connor's "The Life You Save May Be Your Own," "The Life You Live (May Not Be Your Own)." Narrated by Molly, the story is of Molly and Isobel who grow up in different types of families but marry equally emotionally abusive men and become neighbors. The women are denied the possibility of friendship by the lies of Isobel's husband Tolly. After Tolly dies and Molly's husband abandons her, the ladies are free to pursue their friendship and discover themselves for themselves. They move onto land that Isobel has purchased with insurance money from Tolly's death and become self-sufficient women who make wise choices for their own lives. Molly narrates the story while bestowing tidbits of wisdom on the reader like "People with plenty money don't get peace just cause they have money" (*Some Soul to Keep* 61). However, financial security is a key factor that drives many of the choices of Cooper's female characters, and as Molly and Isobel attain it, they also learn the power of self-love that is a sign of liberation in Cooper's texts. When Molly's husband Grady returns after the younger woman he has left to pursue cheats on him, she tells the reader, "I didn't WANT him. Nomore, ever again, in this life, or no other life. I didn't love him. I loved me" (*Some Soul to Keep* 65). As Wolfgang Karrer points out, Cooper writes using a "womanist model," and it appears in this story as Molly does not reject men at all. She says at the story's end, "I know if I got a man there would be just that much more to love" (65). As in many of Cooper's other short stories, the women in "The Life You Live" signify on literary ancestors like Alice Walker's Celie and Zora Neale Hurston's Janie in their presentation of alternative readings of the characters' situations and what can be learned from them. Cooper's link to Hurston is present in many ways.

Hurston is cited as the literary foremother of many writers, but few match her wit, style, and love of dialect and folklore more than J. California Cooper. Cooper's settings are typically Southern and "just outside the city" locales that are rich with remnants of folk culture. As Victoria Valentine records in her review, Cooper "could very well have begun *In Search of Satisfaction* with 'Come sit on da porch; I gotta story tuh tell.' " This claim immediately calls up images of Hurston's porch tale, *Their Eyes Were Watching God*. Her capacity to recreate the oral in the literary is by far her strongest connection to Hurston. Cooper is undeniably linked to Hurston in her use of the speakerly text, the orality found in African American literature that convinces the reader that someone is actually speaking to her.

One Cooper text that incorporates orality and a number of Cooper's textual innovations and signals an important shift in her body of work is *In Search of Satisfaction*. Using a Greek chorus style of narration, the novel describes the interwoven lives of the allegorically named (a characteristic of Cooper's short stories and novels) Krupt (corrupt), Befoȩ (suggesting a family cycle), and Josephus (like the biblical Joseph attacked by Potipher's wife) families, families entangled by a web created in slavery. The characters are black, white, rich, poor, and all in search of some form of satisfaction. The novel is a revisionary text of the African American tradition and the American sentimental genre of the eighteenth and nineteenth centuries. The revision creates a mulatto text that blends two historically distinct cultures and their traditions into one text on the ironies of American racial politics. While redefining the tropes of sentimental literature, the novel also engages the liberatory themes of the African American experience in American history. As the text exposes the irony of America's greatest shame, its legacy of slavery, it does so in the form and structure of a sermon. Just as the oral quality of the written word characterizes the speakerly text, Cooper's *In Search of Satisfaction* is preacherly in its evocation of the oral and aural imagery of a heard sermon, an interesting point of irony since preachers are not revered in the novel.

Cooper's didactic theology is best portrayed through the character of Hosanna, whose allegorical name means "praise." Hosanna begins without a belief in God, but by the novel's end she has a firm belief in Him and His providence. Although the tendency would be to read Cooper's work as a reinforcement of Christian values, it is more a critique of them. Most of the traditional Christians are characterized as hypocritical at best, while more value is given to the characters whose lives suggest that they live, rather than preach, the Christian dogma. Hosanna comes to the conclusion toward the novel's end that it is not Christianity that is to blame for society's woes but people's failure of it. Cooper's critique of failed morality revisits traditional values and challenges the characters and readers to rise above their common complacency and hypocrisy and live them.

Although the characters are from different racial and economic backgrounds, Cooper clearly points out that the characters' choices are what lead them to or away from any type of satisfaction. Cooper extends her critique and lesson in humanity in her latest novel as well.

In *Some People, Some Other Place*, an unborn female child takes on the role of griot as she narrates the multigenerational story of her ancestors and the multiethnic neighbors that her mother, Eula Too, will meet in a town called Placeland on Dream Street. The story centers around Eula Too and opens with her family's flight from the South in the years after slavery and the events that lead to Eula Too's asexual employment in a brothel. As the novel shifts its focus from character to character who either lives or will come to live on Dream Street, it continually critiques American social and economic history while continuing to engage the themes and motifs for which Cooper is known. The stories surrounding Eula Too are well balanced in their engagement of the issues faced by different ethnicities and genders. However, the most remarkable element is the ancestral presence of the unborn narrator.

Although Cooper joins other African American female writers in her use of a dead narrator in her first novel, *Family*, she separates herself with the use of the unborn narrative persona. As critics note the limitations of a dead narrator like *Family*'s Cora, the use of the child is a strategy that allows more narrative freedom and disrupts the paradigm of expected narratological practices. In an expression of her timelessness and freedom, the narrator states, "I have been able, almost in the twinkling of an eye, to look back through time, down upon the world and even at the ancestors I will have, if I decide to be born" (1). This narrative presence who is omniscient and omnipresent, decreasingly so as the novel leads to her conception, delivers didactive prose, suggesting a wisdom that is born in some ancient place, hence the first of many word plays on "some other place." The narrator's reliability is also unquestionable since she is unborn, and as she states, "incorruptible." The narrative technique in her latest novel marks Cooper's continual growth as a novelist and author.

CRITICAL RECEPTION

Critical commentary in the form of essays, articles, and books on Cooper's work has been oddly scarce since she has been writing for over twenty-five years, but it is becoming increasingly more visible. In 1990, Cooper received only a passing mention in *Wild Women in the Whirlwind: Afra-American Culture and the Contemporary Literary Renaissance*. By 1992, Barbara Marshall publishes an essay that provides an Afrocentric analysis of Cooper's first three collections of stories based on the work of Molefi Asante. She deals with female bonding, communal mothering, healing, and transcendence above adversity as correlatives to elements found in African culture. In so doing, she argues against Cooper's own insistence on the intentional universality of her work, but Marshall is still one of the first to devote serious scholarship to Cooper's texts, even to the extent that a chapter in her dissertation engages a number of Cooper's stories. In the following year, Wolfgang Karrer publishes an essay that examines the structure of "When Life Begins!" which is most noted for its adherence to its self-announced structure in the shape of a "Y." The beginning of Karrer's essay provides a useful introduction to Cooper's work and the characteristics of her short stories. Karrer's analysis of the story focuses on the symmetrical structure and narrative control that Cooper wields throughout the story as well as the gendered aspects that underlie her use of a "womanist model."

Following Karrer, both Trudier Harris (2001) and Angelyn Mitchell (2002) devote chapters in their books to Cooper's *Family*, and Cynthia Bryant (2005) devotes a full study to much of Cooper's body of work. Harris critiques the model of the strong black woman found in African American literature and culture, and she discusses the role that Cora plays in the novel as a woman so strong that her spirit remains after death to watch over her children. Cora is a mother trying to follow in her mother's footsteps and commits suicide to avoid slavery. She tries to kill all of her children too, but fails, and her spirit remains and tells the reader their story. Cora's daughter, Always, emerges as the protagonist who eventually subverts the slave system in a way that is beneficial to her community and realizes alternative possibilities that her mother could not see. Always's acts of subversion lead Mitchell to critique the novel as a liberatory novel that challenges history through its focus on the family. Incorporating the ideas of Harris, Mitchell, and others, Bryant provides an in-depth analysis of Cooper's texts as healing narratives. Bryant's close readings of four of the short story collections and the novels *Family* and *The Wake of the Wind* are thorough and useful in providing a functional paradigm for understanding the texts. The anthologizing of some of Cooper's stories and the recent publication of the studies of Harris, Mitchell, and Bryant represent a growth and increase of critical interest in Cooper's work that will hopefully continue.

BIBLIOGRAPHY

Works by J. California Cooper

Family. New York: Doubleday, 1991.
The Future Has a Past. New York: Doubleday, 2000.
Homemade Love. New York: St. Martin's Press, 1986.
In Search of Satisfaction. New York: Doubleday, 1994.
The Matter Is Life. New York: Doubleday, 1991.
A Piece of Mine. 1984. Reprint, New York: Anchor, 1991.
Some Love, Some Pain, Sometime. New York: Doubleday, 1995.
Some People, Some Other Place. New York: Doubleday, 2004.
Some Soul to Keep. New York: St. Martin's Press, 1987.
The Wake of the Wind. New York: Doubleday, 1998.

Studies of J. California Cooper's Works

Bryant, Cynthia Downing. "Storytelling from the Margins: The Healing Narratives of J. California Cooper." Ph.D. diss., Louisiana State University, 2004. *DAI* 65.10 (2005): 3804. AAT3151822.
Harris, Trudier. *Saints, Sinners, and Saviors: Strong Black Women in African American Literature*. New York: Palgrave, 2001.
Karrer, Wolfgang, and Barbara Puschmann, eds. *The African American Short Story, 1970–1990*. Trier: Wissenschaftlicher Verlag Trier, 1993.
Marshall, Barbara J. "Kitchen Table Talk: J. California Cooper's Use of Nommo—Female Bonding and Transcendence." In *Language and Literature in the African American Imagination*, edited by Carol Aisha Blackshire-Belay. Westport, CT: Greenwood Press, 1992.
Mitchell, Angelyn. *The Freedom to Remember*. New Jersey: Rutgers University Press, 2002.

Adrienne Carthon

JAYNE CORTEZ (1936–)

BIOGRAPHICAL NARRATIVE

Poet, activist, and musician Jayne Cortez was born in Fort Huachuca, Arizona, on May 10, 1936. While the Fort Huachuca army base where her father was stationed provided Cortez's family with a close sense of community, it also afforded Cortez her first experience with segregation; she went to school with African American and Native American children while white children "went to white schools" (Melhem, "Melus" 72). At the age of seven she and her family moved to San Diego, where they lived for a year, and then to West Los Angeles where her classmates were African American and Japanese American children. Cortez and her family later moved to Watts in South Los Angeles. Of her integrated and predominantly white junior high school, Cortez states, "We had integration and segregation and domination at the same time. Blacks were a small minority. When a white kid called me 'nigger,' I had to jump up and beat the hell out of him or her. . . . My mother was always at the school" (Melhem, "Melus" 72). Cortez studied drawing, painting, and design at Manuel Arts High School in Los Angeles, as well as piano, bass, cello, and the music theory that would influence and permeate her poetry. She later attended Compton Junior College although financial difficulties forced her to drop out. Cortez married jazz musician Ornette Coleman in 1954 when she was eighteen years old. Two years later she gave birth to their son, Denardo Coleman, and divorced Ornette Coleman in 1964.

In the 1960s she participated in the civil rights movement in Mississippi, an experience that has marked her work. Cortez herself has reflected:

The Civil Rights Movement heightened my level of awareness, affected my work as a writer and helped expand my range of choices. It gave me a humanistic focus for my growth and development as a person and an artist. I learned how to transform material from that experience into art. The events of that time also connected me to other struggles, and to the language of struggle. I would say that those events have given me a lifetime of work. (Ballard 68)

In 1964, Cortez founded the Watts Repertory Theater. Cortez left California and moved to New York in 1967. Taking control of the publication of her own work, Cortez established Bola Press in 1972 where most of her books have been published. Sculptor Melvin Edwards, whom Cortez married in 1975, has illustrated all of her books, which have been translated into twenty-eight different languages to date. Apart from producing poetry, recording music and jazz-inspired renditions of her poetic works, and performing publicly, the prolific and steadfastly political Cortez has continued her public work that has consistently been politically inspired. In 1991 she founded the Organization of Women Writers of Africa (OWWA) with Ghanaian writer Ama Ata Aidoo. This nonprofit organization concentrates on the literary advancement and development of women writers from Africa and the African diaspora, and also undertakes literacy projects for young people. Jayne Cortez currently serves as president of the OWWA.

MAJOR WORKS

Jane Cortez emerged from the Black Arts Movement, a movement that broke from political strategies that employed protest and petition and made the revolutionary dash toward Black Power. While some critics such as Don. L. Lee have rightly cautioned that the "Black Aesthetic cannot be defined in any definite way. To accurately and fully define a Black Aesthetic would automatically limit it" (232), the language and form of the poetry that emerged from the Black Arts Movement has frequently been described as revolutionary and angry, a powerful outcry that reflected the rage of the time and gave voice to the human rights struggle through methods often described as "surreal." Accordingly, Penelope Rosemont has included Cortez as a surrealist in her much-lauded 1998 international anthology, *Surrealist Women*. Although Cortez has been frequently described as a surrealist, she has described her work to critic D. H. Melhem as "superrealism," which Melhem defines as a vision of reality that goes "beyond the intellectual and unconscious aspects of surrealism" and into "a divine and infernal realism" (*Heroism* 181). It is this black experience—its politics, its joys, its tragedies and the contradictions—both divinely and hellishly real so as to be read as *surreal*, that makes up the subject matter in Cortez's work which has been recognized with the American Book Award, the International African Festival Award, and the Langston Hughes Award for Excellence in the Arts and Letters.

The year 1969 marked the publication of Cortez's first book of poetry, *Pissstained Stairs and Monkey Man's Wares*, a work that was written for, originally performed by, and (when published as a collection) later dedicated to the Watts Repertory Theatre Company. Controversial for its homophobic poem "Race," Cortez's first collection of poetry nevertheless established her as a poet who seamlessly integrated African American musical traditions, black speech, black politics (and arguably, the controversial politics of the Black Arts Movement), with poetic experimentation. This first work contains several poems that pay tribute and respond to the works and musical contributions of artists such as Bessie Smith, Billie Holliday, John Coltrane, Ornette Coleman, and Charlie Parker, among others. Of these important musicians as subject matters, T. J. Anderson III observes, "Cortez's references to African American musicians are a means of acknowledging the critical role African American music has played in the spiritual and historical development of the black community" (124).

The creative impetus for her 1971 collection *Festivals and Funerals*, Cortez noted to Melhem, was the subconscious, through which, she describes, she creates poetry that is ritual, festive, and transformative. These transformations, festivals, and rituals are accompanied by jazz-inspired rhythms that continue to drum out pan-Africanist observations. Cortez's vision, Anderson III contends, makes "her less of a regional poet and instead one of a larger geopolitical constituency" (127). Cortez continues to scathingly reflect upon these pan-Africanist concerns two years later in *Scarifications* (1973). The poem "I Am New York City" has been one poem in this collection that has received attention for the way Cortez personifies the city and makes it markedly feminine, all the while injecting the jazz and blues for which Cortez, at this point, becomes known. By this time, Jayne Cortez is indeed regarded as a gifted and original jazz poet. Consider, for instance, Stanley Crouch's thoughts on Cortez: "She's got bop, boogie, blues and the new Black Music flowing through her lines—she achieves those sounds and rhythms and, thereby, comes up with a prismatic, swinging sound as varied in color as the everglades" (Fuller 340).

Given Cortez's poetic musicality, it was inevitable that she would record her published poems in jazz arrangements. In 1973 Cortez recorded a version of "I Am New York City" with bassist Richard Davis, which was later released in the 1974 recording *Celebrations and Solitudes*. In 1977 Cortez published her next book of poetry, *Mouth on Paper*, a collection of poems that combines the physical and the visual, the spoken with the written, and includes music that gleans from the call and response tradition.

The 1984 collection *Coagulations* contains poems from her three prior publications and also offers new poetry. Although *Coagulations* marked the first time that Cortez uses an outside publisher, she continued to release recorded work such as the 1986 *Maintain Control* and the 1990 *Everywhere Drums* through her company Bola Press. The poem, "Everywhere Drums" is found one year later in her next publication *Poetic Magnetic* (1991), in which she combines poetry, technology, music, and the Yoruba language. Cortez released the recording *Women in (E) Motion* the following year; it contains poems from her prior publications.

Two years later she followed with the collaborative *Fragments: Poetry of Jayne Cortez and the Sculpture of Melvin Edwards* (1994) in which Cortez and husband Edwards combine the visual with the poetic—he with his steel sculptures and she with her poetic battle cry. This is followed by the 1996 collection *Somewhere in Advance of Nowhere*, which contains many poems that, according to Anderson III, reveal "the complexity of being African American" (143).

The 2002 publication *Jazz Fan Looks Back* is a collection of Cortez's previously published jazz and music poetry that spans from 1968 to 2000. Some of the poetry from this collection is included in Cortez's 2003 recording *Borders of Disorderly Time*, a work that offers contributions from musicians such as Ron Carter and James "Blood" Ulmer. While Cortez has been anthologized and presented primarily as a jazz poet, it is important to stress that the music and the poetry are necessarily political, for as Aldon Lynn Nielsen has noted, for poets such as Jayne Cortez, "moving to an avant-gard poetics was never motivated by the desire to evade the political imperatives of race and class. For them a radical politics and a radical poetics were virtually inseparable" (*Black Chant* 254).

CRITICAL RECEPTION

Reactions to the poetry, music, and performance of Jayne Cortez, while overwhelmingly positive, have ranged from the laudatory to the conspicuously silent. Cortez has frequently been called a revolutionary, brave, and a truth speaker. Penelope Rosemont, for instance, has called her "one of the strongest surrealist voices of our time . . . a brave example of the true poet in a period in which so much intellectual life is dominated by cowardice, confusion, hypocrisy, and shame" (358). Cortez's unabashed and forthright writing has also been called "raw" and recognized as a breaking of the boundaries of both acceptable language and acceptable subject matter. Perhaps the tacit notion of the limits of acceptability and decorum are precisely the "hypocrisy" of which Rosemont writes, but the space between the acceptable and the outrageous has occasionally led to contradictory assessments of her poetic and political trajectory. Note, for example, Jon Woodson's observation that Cortez's poetry testifies "to her active participation, as an artist, in the struggle for human freedom" (71), while, a few sentences later, he describes Cortez's poem "Race," in the 1969 publication, *Pissstained Stairs and the Monkey Man's Wares* as one of her most successful poems in the collection and a poem "which bitterly condemns black male homosexuality in unflinching detail" (71).

These contradictions in reading have for the most part gone unmentioned. On occasion, Jayne Cortez herself has gone unmentioned and has been conspicuously absent in articles about jazz poetry. To one such slight in a *New York Times* article, Ishmael Reed responded: "An article about jazz fiction-writing that fails to mention Langston Hughes, Bob Kaufman, Al Young, Xam Cartier, Sarah Fabio, Quincy Troupe, Ted Joans, Eugene Redmond, Yusef Rahman, Larry Neal, Charels Wright, Babs Gonzales, Amiri Baraka and Jayne Cortez is worthless. Worthless!" (2: 4).

Writers such as Kevin Meehan have observed that when Cortez is anthologized in canonical collections such as the Norton Anthology, she is "cleaned up" for public consumption through the inclusion of a single and representative work such as "Trane" (a lament for John Coltrane), rather than a poem such as "Rape" that documents the rape of Inez Garcia and prison rape of JoAnne Little in the 1970s. "What really separates the two poems, in my view," Meehan argues, "is the fact that 'Trane' mutes its institutional criticism, whereas 'Rape' calls attention to the jailhouse as a site of institutionalized racist and sexist violence" (46).

The preference of Cortez's jazz poetry over more political and violent works is seemingly established with the reception of her first publication *Pissstained Stairs and the Monkey Man's Wares* which tended to concentrate on Cortez's musical subject matter. Nikki Giovanni pronounced in 1969 that Cortez could "wail from Theodore Navarro and Leadbelly to Ornette and never lose a beat and never make a mistake. She's a genius and all lovers of jazz will need this book—lovers of poetry will want it" (35), and Eugene Redmond praised her work as "rich in its interweavings of music and indexes of struggle" (406).

Festivals and Funerals received attention for Cortez's "musical daring" and technical dexterity (Redmond 415), while *Scarifications* was recognized for treating "new subjects" such as the Vietnam War, the Attica revolt, and police brutality with irony, a technique that Jon Woodson observes, played down "the escalation of violence" (72).

Mouth on Paper, *Firespitters*, and *Poetic Magnetic* are each lauded for Cortez's ability to seamlessly combine musicality with poetry, and each collection is praised for Cortez's further development as an artist by critics such as T. J. Anderson III. Kimberly Brown, however, illumines Cortez's ability to write "in connection with—not in opposition or subordination to—her black male counterpart" in Coagulations (75).

More recent criticism, while still immersed in the analysis of Cortez's musicality within her poetry, has highlighted the political implications of Cortez's words. David Mills advises in his review of *Somewhere in Advance of Nowhere*:

Think of Cortez as a revolutionary hosting mutual of mau mau's wild kingdom. But the kingdom is The World Bank. Or think of her as an urban shaman imbuing her poetry with the magic realism of Carlos Castaneda's Yaqi Indian adventures in an attempt to liberate people from oppression of the flesh. (31)

Kimberly Brown posits a theory of scarification that borrows from Cortez's publication *Scarifications*. Cortez's poetry, Brown explains, "serves as an excellent example of how one can theorize through scars," because she creates an "ethnopoetics that blurs the lines between lived experience and theory" (69). Brown's theorization of Cortez's poetry perhaps predates the 2002 *Publishers Weekly* review of Cortez's *Jazz Fan Looks Back* foretelling the academic attention that Jayne Cortez's work has been receiving.

BIBLIOGRAPHY

Works by Jayne Cortez

Borders of Disorderly Time. New York: Bola Press, 2003.

Celebrations and Solitudes. New York: Strata East, 1974.

Coagulations: New and Selected Poems. New York: Thunder's Mouth Press, 1984.

Everywhere Drums. New York: Bola Press, 1990.

Festivals and Funerals. New York: Bola Press, 1971.

Find Your Own Voice. New York: Harmolodic/Verve/Polygram, 1998.

Firespitter. New York: Bola Press, 1982.

Fragments: Poetry of Jayne Cortez and the Sculpture of Melvin Edwards. New York: Bola Press, 1994.

Jazz Fan Looks Back. Brooklyn: Hanging Loose Press, 2002.

Maintain Control. New York: Bola Press, 1986.

Merveilleux Coup De Foudre: Poetry of Jayne Cortez & Ted Joans. France: Handshake Editions, 1982.

Mouth on Paper. New York: Bola Press, 1977.

Pissstained Stairs and the Monkey Man's Wares. Los Angeles: Phrase Text, 1969.

Poetic Magnetic. New York: Bola Press, 1991.

Scarifications. New York: Bola Press, 1973.

Somewhere in Advance of Nowhere. New York: High Risk Books, 1996.

Taking the Blues Back Home. New York: Harmolodic/Verve/Polygram, 1996.

There It Is. New York: Bola Press, 1982.

Unsubmissive Blues. New York: Bola Press, 1979.

Women in (E) Motion. Schauburg, Bremen: Radio Bremen Jazzredaktion, 1992.

Studies of Jayne Cortez's Works

Anderson III, T. J. "Hot House: Jayne Cortez and the Music of Illumination." In *Notes to Make the Sound Come Right—Four Innovators of Jazz Poetry*. Fayetteville: University of Arkansas Press, 2004.

Bullard, Audreen. "Voices of the 90s." *New Crisis* 106.1 (January/February 1999): 68–73.

Bolden, Tony. *Afro-Blue: Improvisations in African American Poetry and Culture*. Urbana: University of Illinois Press, 2004.

———. "All the Birds Sing Bass: The Revolutionary Blues of Jayne Cortez." *African American Review* 35.1 (Spring 2001): 61–71.

Boyd, Herb. "Everywhere Drums." *Black Scholar* 21.4 (Fall 1991): 41.

Brown, Kimberly N. "Of Poststructuralist Fallout, Scarification, and Blood Poems." In *Other Sisterhoods: Literary Theory and U.S. Women of Color*, edited by Sandra Kumamoto Stanley, 63–85. Urbana: University of Illinois Press, 1998.

Chrisman, Robert. "Jayne Cortez & the Firespitters: Taking the Blues Back Home." *Black Scholar* 27.1 (Spring 1997): 65–66.

Feinstein, Sascha. "From 'Alabama' to a Love Supreme: The Evolution of the John Coltrane Poem." *Southern Review* 32 (Spring 1996): 315–27.

Fuller, Hoyt W. "The New Black Literature: Protest or Affirmation." In *The Black Aesthetic*, edited by Addison Gayle, Jr., 327–48. Garden City: Anchor Books, 1972.

Giovanni, Nikki. "Pisstained Stairs and the Monkey Man's Wares." *Negro Digest*, December 19, 1969, 35.

"A Jazz Fan Looks Back." *Publishers Weekly* 249.17 (April 29, 2002): 66.

Lee, Don L. "Toward a Definition: Black Poetry of the Sixties." In *The Black Aesthetic*, edited by Addison Gayle, Jr., 222–33. Garden City: Anchor Books, 1972.

Macnie, Jim. "Jazz Blue Notes." *Billboard*, August 31, 1996, 87.

Meehan, Kevin. "Spiking Canons." *Nation*, May 12, 1997, 42–46.

Melhem, D. H. *Heroism in the New Black Poetry: Introductions and Interviews.* Lexington: University Press of Kentucky, 1990.

———. "MELUS Profile and Interview: Jayne Cortez." *MELUS* 21.1 (Spring 1996): 71–79.

Mills, David. "Somewhere in Advance of Nowhere." *Black Book Review*, February 28, 1997, 31.

Newson-Horst, Adele S. "Jazz Fan Looks Back." *World Literature Today* 77.2 (July–September 2003): 102.

Nielsen, Aldon Lynn. *Black Chant: Languages of African-American Postmodernism.* Cambridge: Cambridge University Press, 1997.

———. "Capillary Currents: Jayne Cortez." In *Integral Music: Languages of African American Innovation*, edited by Aldon Lynn Nielsen, 175–93. Tuscaloosa: University of Alabama Press, 2004.

———. "Capillary Currents: Jayne Cortez." In *We Who Love to Be Astonished: Experimental Women's Writing and Performance Poetics*, edited by Laura Hinton and Cynthia Hogue, 227–36. Tuscaloosa: University of Alabama Press, 2002.

Poetry in Motion. Dir. Ron Mann. Perf. Jayne Cortez. Sphinx Productions, 1985.

Redmond, Eugene B. *Drumvoices: The Mission of Afro-American Poetry, A Critical History.* Garden City: Anchor Books, 1976.

Reed, Ishmael. Letter. "Names of the Missing." *New York Times* 2 (September 19, 1999, late edition): 4.

Rosemont, Penelope. "Jayne Cortez." In *Surrealist Women: An International Anthology*, edited by Penelope Rosemont, 358–63. Austin: University of Texas Press, 1998.

Ruffin, Kimberly N. " 'Freedom of Expression' Meet Jayne Cortez." *Footsteps* 7.2 (March–April 2005): 27.

"Somewhere in Advance of Nowhere." *Publishers Weekly* 243.23 (June 3, 1996): 74.

Woodson, Jon. "Jayne Cortez." In *Dictionary of Literary Biography, Volume 41: Afro-American Poets since 1955*, edited by Trudier Harris and Thadious M. Davis, 69–74. Detroit: The Gale Group, 1985.

Ruth Blandón

MARGARET ESSE DANNER (1910–1984)

BIOGRAPHICAL NARRATIVE

Margaret Esse Danner, poet and community activist, author of five volumes, two recordings, editor of two volumes, and widely anthologized, uses strong visual images to introduce the art and culture of Africa and African Americans to her readers. In bridging the past, present, and future in her poems, Danner shows a relation to Western poetic tradition. Later in life, Danner wrote that "Down through the years, differing cultural life has been most successfully introduced through poetry. Kipling's *Gunga Din* and Longfellow's *Hiawatha* are famous examples. The interest in my published poetry proves that this can still be the case." Ahead of her time, Danner introduced the beauty of African art and culture, long obscured by Western civilization as "primitive and exotic," that she might "reawaken" African Americans "to reclaim another spark of [their] incomparable heritage" ("Chicago Art Scene 1967"), that all her readers might cherish and celebrate the value and significance of African culture and arts.

Danner records her birthplace in "Chicago Art Scene 1967 Just as Our African Ancestors Did," writing "here, in Chicago, about five blocks from where I was born" (*Iron Lace* 1968). Detroit also claims her. Certainly, Danner enjoyed rebirths of her spirit in both places. In a personal letter to a spiritual advisor, Danner writes, "I, Margaret Danner, was born January 12, 1910, at night, or early morning before sunup." Her parents, Caleb and Naomi Esse Danner, followed the Great Migration north from their home in Pryorsburg, Kentucky, where some say Danner was born, perhaps even before 1910. Danner married Cordell Strickland, with whom she had her daughter Naomi. Later, Danner married Otto Cunningham. Sterling Montrose Washington, Jr., Naomi's son, inspired Danner's "Muffin" poems. Danner died in Chicago on January 1, 1984. Memorial services were held on February 5, 1984, at the DuSable Museum in Chicago, with her family in attendance. Memorials were also held in Detroit, Memphis, and Richmond, cities where Danner had held the position of artist-in-residence, and in Los Angeles, where her sister lived.

MAJOR WORKS

Danner won her first poetry prize in the eighth grade for "The Violin." Danner said, "I wrote a poem about wanting to be a violin. The teacher was so impressed that she gave me a violin. But I didn't want one; I wanted to be one." Images of the Stradivarius and Guarnerius violins appeared in later poetry.

Continuing with her writing, Danner joined the South Side Community Art Center (SSCAC) in Chicago and met there with the Writers' Group, which included Margaret Goss Burroughs and Gwendolyn Brooks. SSCAC participants brought and read their poetry to one another and criticized each other strongly. Burroughs recalls that she and Danner "were sisters in creativity. Always, she encouraged the development and pres- ervation of black culture from the founding of the South Side Art Center in 1941 to the founding of DuSable Museum twenty years later. . . . She was the first life member of the S.S.A.C." Burroughs reminded me that the poetry workshops were conducted by Inez Cunningham Stark, a wealthy poet and editor of *Poetry* magazine. Perhaps this connection with Stark influenced Danner's opportunity to work at *Poetry* later.

Also influential in opening doors for Danner was the second prize she won in the 1945 Poetry Workshop of the Midwestern Writers Conference held at Northwestern. Gwendolyn Brooks had won first prize in the 1943 conference; Danner's prize in 1945 set up a spirit of friendly competition between them that encouraged their writing.

Under editor Paul Shapiro, Danner worked on *Poetry*, a magazine of modern poetry, appearing first as Margaret Cunningham, editorial assistant, in October 1952 (Vol. LXXXI). This volume contains three of her "Far from Africa" poems: "1. Garnishing the Aviary" (176), "2. Dance of the Abakweta" (177–78), and "3. The Visit of the Professor of Aesthetics" (178–79), published under the name of Margaret Danner. The star next to Danner's name indicates this is her first appearance in the magazine: a brief biographical sketch under "Contributors" identifies Danner as a student of arts and archaeology at Roosevelt College (220). In Volume LXXXIV, Shapiro is still editor and Margaret Cunningham editorial assistant; in this volume, the fourth "Far from Africa" poem, "Etta Moten's Attic," appears (320–21) under the name of Danner. In the next volume, Danner, not Cunningham, is listed as editorial assistant under Shapiro. She continued as editorial assistant under Shapiro and then under editor Henry Rago in October 1955. In December 1955, she became assistant editor and continued through June 1956, marking a first for an African American in this position of the avant-garde magazine, which published the modern poets of the time.

The four "Far from Africa" poems gave Danner the recognition and awards that enabled her to see the Exhibition of African Art in Paris and to read her poetry at the World Festival of Negro Art in Dakar, Senegal, Africa, in 1966. In 1950 Danner received grants from the Women's Auxiliary of Afro-American Interests and the African Studies Association, and a John Hay Whitney Fellowship. She won the Harriet Tubman award in 1951, the Native Chicago Literature Prize in 1956, and a grant from the American Society of African Culture in 1960. In 1956, in its "Contribution of the Negro" in "Patterns in American Culture," the University of Michigan chose Danner as one of the ten top African American poets. Her poetry appeared in *Poetry, Chicago Magazine, Negro Digest, Voices, The Negro History Bulletin, Black World, Clear Views, World Order*, and *South and West*.

According to Danner, she worked at *Poetry* magazine "in order to master the techniques of poetry." Dudley Randall credits Hayden, Brooks, Tolson, and Danner with bringing "black poetry abreast of its time by absorbing and mastering the techniques of T. S. Eliot, Hart Crane, and Ezra Pound," the modern poets published in *Poetry*.

Danner uses both African and western symbols in her poetry, from the violin in her early work to the Ashanti stool, the sandalwood stork hairpin, and the iron Senufo bird, which becomes the iron lace lady. Her colors range from tangerine to western pastels, as Arthur Pfister notes in his roast of Danner. "Irony lace" is another chosen theme: "molded latticed," "iron fences," and "metal lace" in "The Small Bells of Benin." "Life, to me, is a pattern of lace," Danner says in "Valentine (nineteen sixty-six)." "Today Requires a Lace of Truths" includes "the lace that Truths / form," and "I Welcome Lace" has "the power of lace," "the clouds form lace patterns," "many lace patterns," "lacebranched," and "lace has the strength / of immortality." In "Inheritance for Muffin," Danner leaves "eclectic laces and lattices of writings." "The Slave and the

Iron Lace" blends intricate patterns. Finally, looking "into each different face," in "Through the Varied Patterned Lace," Danner is "exalted to recognize His Grace / shimmering through the varied patterned lace." Danner also writes of the mask, as in "To a Mounted Ivory Masque Pin," "The Bondman and My Senufo Masque," "And He Carves These 'Dudes,'" "And Through the Caribbean Sea," and "To the Bronze Masque." As Barksdale points out in "Margaret Danner and the African Connection," Danner is concerned with the African continuum but writes with "a verbal brilliance that is both bedazzling and enlightening" and has a "superb gift of imagery." Also, he tells that her concern "goes beyond her colorful imagistic description of African art and sculpture" to "historical events and the monumental ironies and gaping inequities that powered those events."

Marked-up proofs of some of her poems and correspondence in 1959 with Rago and his secretary, discussing her offer of a trip to Africa from the John Hay Whitney Fellowships Committee, are held in the Special Collections Research Center of the University of Chicago Library. Danner called her association with *Poetry* one of the most rewarding experiences of her life. The four "Far from Africa" poems are the most often anthologized of her work.

Danner felt obliged to leave her sixteen-year-old daughter and husband Otto Cunningham to take a Poet-in-Residence position at Wayne State in Detroit in 1961–1962, the first of several positions she held as Poet-in-Residence. Not having a degree in higher education, the only teaching positions open to her were poet-in-residence, which Danner considered a great honor. Finances were always a problem; however, her husband was supportive of her work and assisted with a stipend while she was in Detroit. An article in the *Detroit Free Press* noted that "After a series of July lectures at McGregor Memorial Building, she will sail for Africa," but that trip would be put off until later. Instead, seeking a place to live and write, Danner approached Rev. Theodore S. Boone, pastor of King Solomon Church, and persuaded him to let her use an empty parish house to establish a community arts center, which she did from 1962 to 1964.

Five or six poets came to the monthly meetings on Sunday evenings to read their work to each other. The late Ron Milner shared the house for awhile. Danner and Dudley Randall often worked together there on their poems for *Poem Counterpoem*. Others regularly there included poet Naomi Long Madgett and Arthur and Carolyn Reese, teachers and civil rights activists. In her unpublished memoirs, Madgett tells that the lovely old house was beautiful but in need of repairs, including a furnace, but they "were glad to have this meeting place and to huddle together good-naturedly in front of the fireplace in cold weather." Poets that came to visit Danner include Robert Hayden, Hoyt Fuller, and Owen Dodson.

Two special guests at Boone House were the Dutch author Rosey Pool on May 11, 1963, for a lecture and reading celebrating the publication of her *Beyond the Blues*, and Langston Hughes on February 8, 1964. Later that year, Ron Milner encouraged Danner to go to New York to record poetry with Hughes. Hughes had published much already and was given widespread recognition as a poet before he met Danner, then in the early stages of her career. However, he was not condescending but kind and agreed to record the poetry with her. Because Milner was interested in getting to New York to see some plays he rode to New York with Danner and sat in Hughes's hotel room with her to do the recording. After the second session, Danner felt sabotaged as Hughes had used more time to read than she had. But back in Detroit, Motown did all of the editing, adding music that changed the aesthetics of the reading. The recording was not published until after the death of Hughes. Motown Record Corporation published *Poets of the Revolution* in 1970 on the Black Forum label BB 453. Danner's poems for the recording are now archived with those of Hughes at the Beinecke Rare Book and Manuscript Library, Yale Collection of American Literature.

Hughes also visited Danner's home in Chicago and included her "Far from Africa" poems in *New Negro Poets: USA*. Danner later responded to Hughes's kindness by writing several poems featuring him.

After returning from Africa and France, Danner became the poet-in-residence at Miles College in Birmingham in 1967, at Virginia Union University in Richmond in 1968–1970, and LeMoyne-Owen College in Memphis from 1971 to 1975. Always interested in encouraging the arts, Danner also joined the Memphis branch of the National League of American Pen Women, the Society of Afro American Culture, Contemporary Artists, Memphis Cable TV, the National Council of Teachers of English, and Poets in a Bottle.

Danner wrote a lovely tribute to her friend in "Samuel Allen's Soul Dances." Allen recalls a poetry gathering in Atlanta where an extraordinary event with Danner occurred. No warning of stormy weather had been given. That night they were gathered inside, and immediately after Danner read the lines, "and God called forth thunder," there was a loud roll of thunder. All were amazed. After the shock, they laughed a nervous laughter, wondering, "What powers does this poet have?" Allen wrote the "Introduction" to *The Down of a Thistle*, in which he warns that "In many of these poems, exquisite and complex, an image is established, deftly explored, paralleled or interlaced with another to establish, finally, a complex labyrinth through which the poet moves toward deviance and transcendence: to give the reader a succession of poems stamped with a central compelling image" (9). Danner layers her poetry, allowing her readers to savor slowly the complex meanings of her exquisite images.

CRITICAL RECEPTION

Barksdale, Stetson, and Aldridge have given the most recent critical attention to Danner. Miller writes an extensive headnote on Danner in *Call and Response* and points out that Danner deserves additional critical attention.

In her preface to her poetry in *The Forerunners*, Danner says, "I believe that my dharma is to prove that the Force for Good takes precedence over the force for evil in mankind. To the extent that my poetry adheres to this purpose it will endure" (48). In 2005, composer Valerie Coleman used Danner's poems "The Painted Lady" and "Through the Caribbean Sea" in her *The Painted Lady* for Hartford Symphony for Soprano and Orchestra. Danner would have been delighted to know of her continuing contributions to the arts.

BIBLIOGRAPHY

Works by Margaret Esse Danner

Brass Horses. Richmond: Virginia Union University Press, 1968.
The Down of a Thistle: Selected Poems, Prose Poems, and Songs. Waukesha, WI: Country Beautiful, 1976.

For Malcolm: Poems on the Life and the Death of Malcolm X. With Dudley Randall. Detroit, MI: Broadside Press, 1967.

Impressions of African Art Forms. Detroit, MI: Broadside Press, 1960.

Iron Lace. Millbrook, NY: Kriya Press, 1968.

Not Light, Nor Bright, Nor Feathery. Detroit, MI: Broadside Press, 1968.

Poem Counterpoem. With Dudley Randall. Detroit, MI: Broadside Press, 1966.

Regroup. Richmond: Virginia Union University Press, 1969.

To Flower. Nashville, TN: Hemphill Press, 1963.

Writers of the Revolution. With Langston Hughes. Black Forum (BB 453), 1970.

Studies of Margaret Esse Danner's Works

Adoff, Arnold, ed. *The Poetry of Black America: Anthology of the 20th Century*. New York: Harper & Row, 1973.

Aldridge, June M. "Benin to Beale Street: African Art in the Poetry of Margaret Danner." *CLA Journal* 2 (December 31, 1987): 201–9.

———. "Langston Hughes and Margaret Danner." *Langston Hughes Review* 3.2 (Fall 1984): 7–9.

———. "Margaret Esse Danner." In *Afro-American Poets Since 1955,* edited by Trudier Harris and Thadious M. Davis, 84-89. Detroit: Thomson Gale, 1985.

Barksdale, Richard, and Keneth Kinnamon, eds. *Black Writers of America: A Comprehensive Anthology*. New York: Macmillan, 1972.

Barksdale, Richard K. "Margaret Danner and the African Connection." In *Praisesong of Survival Lectures and Essays, 1957–89*. Urbana: University of Illinois Press, 1992.

Breman, Paul, ed. *You Better Believe It. Black Verse in English from Africa, the West Indies, and the U.S.* Kingsport, TN: Penguin, 1973.

Hayden, Robert, et al., eds. *Afro-American Literature: An Introduction*. New York: Harcourt Brace Jovanich, 1971.

Henderson, Stephen, ed. *Understanding the New Black Poetry*. New York: Morrow, 1973.

Johnson, Patricia L. Brown, et al., eds. *To Gwen with Love*. Chicago: Johnson Publishing Co., 1971.

King, Woodie, Jr., ed. *The Forerunners Black Poets in America*. Washington, DC: Howard University Press, 1981.

Miller, Ruth, ed. *Blackamerican Literature 1760–Present*. Beverly Hills, CA: Glencoe Press, 1971.

Pfister, Arthur. *Granny Blak Poet (in Pastel) for Mrs. Margaret Danner*. Detroit: Broadside Press #35, 1970.

Randall, Dudley, ed. *The Black Poets*. New York: Bantam, 1971.

Stetson, Erlene, ed. *Black Sister: Poetry by Black American Women, 1746–1980*. Bloomington: Indiana University Press, 1981.

Taft, Claire. "'Her Blood Sings'. Margaret Danner's *Impressions of African Art Forms*." *Langston Hughes Review* 12.2 (Fall 1993): 45–49.

Claire Taft

EDWIDGE DANTICAT (1969–)

BIOGRAPHICAL NARRATIVE

For novel, essay, and short story writer Edwidge Danticat, who was born in Haiti in 1969 and raised (like her protagonist, Sophie Caco, in *Breath, Eyes, Memory*) by her aunt and uncle until she was sent for by her parents in Brooklyn at the age of twelve, the valences of "home" are scattered, ambivalent, polylocal, and migratory. In a lecture presented at the Inter-American Development Bank's Cultural Center in Washington, D.C., in 1997 (later published under the title "*AHA!*"), Danticat notes that her family's trajectory to the United States was mapped in several journeys by individual family members, but that this was a "somewhat typical migration pattern," adding "typical for many people I know" (40).

Danticat's father, André Danticat, who migrated in 1971 when Edwidge was two years old, later sent for his wife Rose when the author was four. She was raised by an aunt and uncle in Haiti from the age of four until she was twelve, when she herself migrated to the United States. (Joseph Dantica, an eighty-one-year-old Baptist minister and the uncle who raised his niece Edwidge Danticat, recently died while detained without cause by U.S. Department of Homeland Security officials in Miami as the elderly man tried to enter the United States through the Miami international airport after fleeing political violence during the Haitian crisis of 2004.)

As a child growing up in Haiti in the late Duvalier period, and as a Haitian immigrant to the United States in 1981 (five years before the imposed exile of Jean-Claude Duvalier), Danticat's narratives must be examined in the larger historical frames of Haitian-American relations and the Haitian diaspora. Danticat, like writer Dany Laferrière, is a "migratory subject,"[1] one whose *haïtiennité*[2] is mapped in diaspora, which forms a virtual—if not geographical—"tenth department."

Though she initially felt ostracized by virtue of language and nationality from her peers in Brooklyn, Danticat went on to master the language (English) that she initially struggled to acquire, and her education has been a distinctly literary one: she finished a Bachelor of Arts in French literature from Barnard College and a Master of Fine Arts in Creative Writing from Brown University. An early draft of *Breath, Eyes, Memory* served as Danticat's M.A. thesis. The public emergence and critical acclaim of Danticat as a Haitian American writer in the last decade marked a new point of (anglophone) crossing for Haitian diasporic writers. Unlike her literary predecessors—writers as diverse as Jacques Roumain, Jacques-Stéphen Alexis, Marie (Vieux) Chauvet, René Depestre, Gérard Étienne, Emile Ollivier, and even her older contemporaries, Lilas Desquiron and Dany Laferrière—Danticat writes and publishes in English.

Though marked by the influences of French and Kreyòl, Danticat's texts are translations of neither. She is one of an emergent, but still small group of Haitian writers to depart from a literature written in Haiti's mother tongues (Kreyòl and Français), one of the first, and certainly the most important, to write in English. In 1995, at the young age of twenty-six, Danticat won the Pushcart Short Story Prize, became a finalist for the National Book Award for *Krik? Krak!* and received awards from the journal the *Caribbean Writer*, as well as *Seventeen* and *Essence* magazines, for her fiction. In 1999, she won the American Book Award. In January 2005, Danticat won the inaugural award for The Story Prize for *The Dew Breaker*, which was also a finalist for the 2004 National Book Critics Circle Award and the 2005 PEN/Faulkner Prize. That Danticat is such a critically lauded and precociously young writer only further speaks to her significance as a trans-American writer.

Danticat published her first novel, *Breath, Eyes, Memory*, in 1994, the year that the U.S. government began sending troops to Haiti in order to secure Jean-Bertrand Aristide's return to power after the democratically elected president was deposed by a brutal military coup led by Général Raoul Cédras and was sent into exile only seven months after his election in September 1991. The period from 1991 to 1994 witnessed a massive exodus of Haitian refugees, referred to as "boat people" (*boat peuples/bòt pipol*), an appellation that had earlier been used to describe Vietnamese refugees. Initially, the United States systematically returned the refugees to Haiti; later, however, the refugees were housed in camps at the U.S. military base on Guantánamo Bay in Cuba while asylum cases were reviewed.

Danticat's second literary work, *Krik? Krak!* (a collection of short stories), was published in 1995, the year that also saw the beginning of the withdrawal of U.S. troops from Haiti (although U.N. troops remained) and the democratic election of René Preval, Aristide's successor and political ally. In 1998, Danticat published the novel *The Farming of Bones*, a historical novel that revisits the Trujillo regime in the Dominican Republic and the massacre of thousands of Haitian cane laborers under Generalissimo Trujillo's command. In 2002, Danticat published a nonfiction travel narrative *After the Dance: A Walk through Carnival in Jacmel* and a young adult's novel *Behind the Mountains: The Diary of Célianne Esperance.*

In 2004, Danticat published *The Dew Breaker*, a novel told through interwoven short stories, about a Duvalierist torturer who has found exile in Haiti's diaspora in Brooklyn, and thus, escaped punishment for his crimes against the Haitian people. As editor, Danticat has also importantly contributed to the shifting landscapes of American literatures: in 2000, she edited *The Beacon Best of 2000. Great Writing by Women and Men of All Colors and Cultures*; and in 2001, she edited *The Butterfly's Way: Voices from the Haitian Dyaspora in the United States*, the first anthology to focus exclusively on Haitian American literatures. Danticat's literary texts uniquely reflect the trans-American experiences of Haitian refugees and *dyasporas*. Teacher as well as writer, Danticat has taught at the University of Miami and New York University. Cinematically, Danticat has also collaborated on filmic projects with directors Jonathan Demme and Patricia Benoît, serving as associate producer for both *Courage and Pain* (1996), the documentary film about Haitian torture victims that was directed by Benoît and produced by Demme, and the documentary film *The Agronomist* (2003), which was directed by Demme and which recounted the life and political assassination of Jean Dominique in 2000.

Danticat has also been a visible activist within the United States to protest the impact of U.S. foreign policies, as well as state and local policies, on both Haitian Americans and on her home country Haiti, marching in New York, for instance, to protest police violence against Haitian American men (Patrick Dorismond, Abner Louima) by the New York City Police Department (NYPD). By doing so, Danticat participates in transnational forms of social justice activism, organizing to protest U.S. action or inaction about Haitian political problems, using the media, community resources, and constitutionally protected rights of free speech and assembly to pressure federal, state, and local governments to alter policies and effectuate change both within the diasporic context and at home in Haiti. Glick Schiller and Fouron discuss such transnational forms of grassroots activism in *Georges Woke Up Laughing*, asserting that long-distance nationalists create subaltern political forms through participation in "transnational movements for global justice" (272).

MAJOR WORKS

Danticat's *Breath, Eyes, Memory*, published in 1994, explores many themes common in American ethnic literatures—adolescent alienation, migration, traumatic uprooting from a childhood in the Caribbean (for Danticat's protagonist Sophie Caco, in Haiti), and the challenges of establishing new relations in the United States. The novel recounts the difficult process of coming-of-age in diaspora; Sophie has a fractious relationship with her mother; she is in exile from her homeland; she remains haunted by an unknown paternal origin—Sophie is the fatherless daughter of a raped mother, a fact that she learns only later in life; she experiences recurrent dreams of being chased, captured, and confined; and through the protagonist, Danticat explores the ambivalent identifications and dis-identifications with mother, motherland, and diaspora through daffodils and other botanical forms.

Danticat's short story collection *Krik? Krak!* (1995) is comprised of nine short stories intricately woven together through recurrent characters and motifs such as violence, survival, hope, migration, terror, love, and hate; the collection ends with the poetic "Epilogue: Women Like Us," like Haiti's nine administrative departments and its diaspora or "tenth department." The book opens with the short story "Children of the Sea," a short story about love, loss, and violence in which two lovers are separated by political chaos and migratory flight; the book ends with the lyrical poetic prose of "Epilogue: Women Like Us," in which the storyteller and writer pays homage to her ancestors, the "kitchen poets" who "slip phrases into their stew and wrap meaning around their pork before frying it" (219–20).

The book begins in Haiti with refugees taking flight for Florida's coastal waters; it ends in the United States with Haiti's diasporic daughters remembering their mothers and their motherland. In between fall eight interlocking stories—"Nineteen Thirty-Seven," "A Wall of Fire Rising," "Night Women," "New York Day Women," "Between the Pool and the Gardenias," "The Missing Peace," "Seeing Things Simply," and "Caroline's Wedding"—that sing of hope and despair, of love and loss, of faith and broken promises, and each weds its readers to Haiti's history, culture, and politics.

The Farming of Bones, Danticat's second novel, explores the brutal 1937 "Haitian Massacre" of Haitian cane laborers working on sugar cane corporations in the Dominican Republic. In 1937, the Dominican dictator Generalissimo Rafael Trujillo, or "Jeffe" as he was commonly known, ordered the slaughter of thousands (some scholars estimate scores of thousands) of Haitian cane laborers working in the Dominican Republic; as the massacre began, many fortunately had a narrow escape, fleeing the state military violence and crossing the Massacre River and Haiti's eastern border. Within this historical narrative, Danticat weaves the love story of Amabelle Désir and Sebastien Onius; the grief experienced by Amabelle as a small girl when she loses her parents as they perilously assay crossing the Massacre River; the complicated daughter-and-sister-like relationship of Amabelle first with Valencia and her father; the *restavèk*, or servant, relationship with Señora Valencia and her husband Señor Pico Duarte; and the filial relationships between those who work on the sugar cane corporations and flee the massacre. The novel (a first-person fictional account of an historical event) echoes Jacques-Stéphen Alexis's *Compère Général Soleil* (*General Sun, My Brother*) in its depictions of the 1937 Haitian Massacre.

Danticat's most recent book *The Dew Breaker*, published in early March 2004 (just days after the forced resignation and departure of President Aristide from the country on an American military jet), is a novel that also unfolds in short story form about a former member of the Volunteers for National Security (VNS), the *Miliciens*, more popularly known as the infamous tonton macoutes, who tortured political prisoners in the Casernes Dessalines Military Barracks and at the Fort Dimanche Prison, renowned for its crimes against humanity and its routine torture of Duvalier's enemies, political prisoners, or dissidents. The character's narrative biography thus parallels that of a contemporary exiled torturer, Emmanuel "Toto" Constant who was on the CIA payroll and who with CIA money created the violent death squad FRAPH, which tortured and killed Lavalas supporters during the *defakto* regime from 1991 to 1994. The nine individual stories comprising the novel reveal psychologically complex, nuanced, and often interrelated portrayals of the "Dew Breaker" and his family's secretive, isolated life in East Flatbush, Brooklyn, since fleeing Haiti during the first Duvalier regime. The multilayered portrait of the "Dew Breaker" grows through haunting voices and multiple narrative perspectives, offering often oblique or indirect snapshots, as his survivors and those close to them give testimony in diaspora to unborn infants, dead aunts, answering machines, tape recorders, strangers, and ultimately, to Danticat's readers.

The plots of six stories—"The Book of the Dead"; "Seven"; "Water Child"; "The Book of Miracles"; "The Bridal Seamstress"; and "The Funeral Singer"—all unfold in Haiti's Tenth Department, or its diaspora, scattered from Brooklyn to Tampa, while three are set in Haiti ("Night Talkers"; "Monkey Tails"; and the title story "The Dew Breaker"). Even these three stories recount diasporic returns to Haiti (as in "Night Talkers"), or exilic flights to the North American diaspora from Haiti (as in "Monkey Tails" and "The Dew Breaker") following traumatic experiences of violence (suffered or committed) or feared violence (retaliation) The nine stories also cover a wide time span—from the late reign of "Papa Doc" Duvalier (circa 1967) to the *Dechoukaj*, or uprooting, overturning the reign of his son "Baby Doc" Duvalier (1985–1986), to the post-1991 period with strewn references to the terror organization FRAPH, to its notorious leader "Toto" Constant (granted asylum by the U.S. government in 1994), and to victims of NYPD violence, Abner Louima (brutalized in 1997) and Patrick Dorismond (killed on March 16, 2000); perhaps unsurprisingly, or not, there are no direct references to either of the two Lavalas-affiliated and democratically elected Haitian Presidents of the contemporary era, René Préval (1995–2000) or Jean Bertrand Aristide (1990–1991; 1994–1995; 2001–2004).

CRITICAL RECEPTION

Danticat's literary texts have been the focus of several dissertations: foregrounding the interrelations between Danticat's, Julia Alvarez's, and Michelle Cliff's literary writings, Ortiz (2000) positions the texts within a decisively Caribbean frame that explores their writings as autoethnographic; Braziel (2000) places Danticat's writings in conversation with other Haitian diasporic (notably, Dany Laferrière) and Vietnamese diasporic writers in the post–Vietnam War and post-Duvalier periods; Hewett (2002) examines Danticat's texts within an African diasporic frame alongside the writings of Buchi Emecheta and Julie Dash; Robinson (2003) probes Danticat's writings in relation to both other Caribbean writers and to the Caribbean landscape as traumatized or wounded; Rossi (2004) places Danticat's literary texts within emergent black women's writings in the United States; Schleppe (2004), however, locates Danticat within the category of postcolonial francophonie writing.

As revealed in the dissertations, classification (whether by nationality, ethnicity, or language) of Danticat's writings—as American, Ethnic American, African American, Haitian American, Haitian, Caribbean, Antillean, Anglophone, and Francophone—has remained problematic in scholarly criticism on her writings. Chancy (1997) and Dash (1998) were among the earliest of Danticat's critics: while Chancy contextualizes Danticat within a tradition of Haitian women writers, Dash reads Danticat as an "other American" writer within the regional literary landscapes first charted in the writings of Martí, Césaire, Glissant, Walcott, and others. N'Zengou-Tayo (1998, 2000), Kekeh-Dika (2000), the collaborative efforts of N'Zengou-Tayo and Wilson (2000), Larrier (2001), and Saint-Éloi (2001) all explore Danticat as a francophone Antillean writer, although these critics also openly acknowledge and pay close critical attention to her *haïtiennité* or Haitianness.

Gyssels (2000, 2002), Poon (2000), Braziel (2000, 2003), Brice-Finch (2001), and Tabuteau (2002) explore Danticat's writing through diasporic lenses, Haitian or comparative Caribbean. Poon (2000) and Braziel (2003) comparatively analyze Danticat's and Jamaica Kincaid's diasporic narratives. Tabuteau (2002) compares Danticat to George Lamming, a Caribbean diasporic writer of an older generation. Like Braziel (2000), Mardorossian (2002) and Anatol (2004) complicate the rubric of "exile" literature through a theorization of "migrant" literatures, the latter reading Caribbean migrants as "ex-isles" rather than "exiles."

Working largely within an American ethnic lens that examines Anglophone diasporic writings in the United States, Charters (1998), Shea (1999), Shemak (2002), Johnson (2003), Strehle (2003), and Ink (2004) provocatively analyze Danticat's literary interventions in the history of Hispaniola—specifically the Haitian Massacre of 1937 and border wars between Haiti and the Dominican Republic, the two countries on the island—although this conflict has also been examined by the Belgian-based scholar Kathleen Gyssels (2002). Ortiz (2000), Johnson (2003), and Ink (2004) explicitly compare Danticat's and Dominican American writer Julia Alvarez's literary portrayals of Rafael Trujillo's regime in the Dominican Republic.

Gerber (2000), Cornejo (2000), Goldblatt (2000), Jurney (2001), Loichot (2004), Francis (2004), and Putnam (2004) all explore the feminist dimensions of Danticat's writings. Horn (2001) explores Danticat as an "intimate reader," as well as writer of literature. Samway (2003–2004) and Squint (2004), following the critical lead of Robinson (2003), examine landscapes in relation to questions of genre in Danticat's literature. Shakleton (2003) adopts the story "Caroline's Wedding" to articulate an anthropological study of Haitian transnationalism. For interviews with Danticat, see Shea (1996), Anglesey (1998), Wachtel (2000), Wucker (2000), and Alexandre and Howard (2002).

NOTES

1. Carole Boyce Davies uses migration to examine the transitory and mobile nature of diasporic subjectivities, while underscoring the subjective experiences of migration in her groundbreaking study *Black Women Writers and Diaspora*.

2. Myriam Chancy defines *haïtiennité* as textual inscriptions of Haitian identity within literary texts (*Framing Silence*).

BIBLIOGRAPHY

Works by Edwidge Danticat

After the Dance: A Walk Through Carnival in Jacmel. New York: Crown Publishing, 2002.

"AHA!" In *Becoming American: Personal Essays by First Generation Immigrant Women*, edited by Meri Nana-Ama Danquah, 39–44. New York: Hyperion, 2000.

Beacon's Best of 2000: Great Writing by Women and Men of All Colors and Cultures. Boston: Beacon Press, 2000.

Behind the Mountains: The Diary of Célianne Esperance. New York: Orchard Books, 2002.

Breath, Eyes, Memory. New York: SoHo Press, 1994.

The Butterfly's Way: Voices from the Haitian Dyaspora in the United States. New York: SoHo Press, 2001.

"Carnivalia." *Transition: An International Review* 12.3 [93] (2002): 40–49.

The Dew Breaker. New York: Alfred A. Knopf, 2004.

The Farming of Bones. New York: SoHo Press, 1998.

Krik? Krak! New York: SoHo Press, 1995.

"No Greater Shame." *Haitian Boston Reporter* (May 2003). Reprint, In *Haiti: A Slave Revolution, 200 Years after 1804*, edited by Pat Chin, Greg Dunkel, Sara Flounders, and Kim Ives. New York: International Action Center, 2004.

"Preface." Special Issue: "Haiti, 1804–2004: Literature, Culture, and Art." *Research in African Literatures* 35.2 (Summer 2004): III–VIII, 1–206.

Studies of Edwidge Danticat's Works

Alexandre, Sandy, and Ravi Y. Howard. "My Turn in the Fire: A Conversation with Edwidge Danticat." *Transition: An International Review* 12.3 [93] (2002): 110–28.

Anatol, Giselle Liza. "Caribbean Migration, Ex-Isles, and the New World Novel." *The Cambridge Companion to the African American Novel*. Ed. Maryemma Graham. Cambridge, England: Cambridge University Press, 2004, 70–83.

Anglesey, Zoe. "The Voice of the Storytellers: An Interview with Edwidge Danticat." *MultiCultural Review* 7.3 (September 1998): 36–39.

Bell, Beverly. *Walking on Fire: Haitian Women's Stories of Survival and Resistance*. Ithaca, NY: Cornell University Press, 2001.

Boyce Davies, Carole. *Black Women, Writing and Identity. Migrations of the Subject*. London and New York: Routledge, 1994.

Braziel, Jana Evans. "*Daffodils, Rhizomes, Migrations*: Narrative Coming of Age in the Writings of Edwidge Danticat and Jamaica Kincaid." *Meridians: Feminism, Race, Transnationalism* 3.2 (March 2003): 110–38.

———. "Nomadism, Diaspora and Deracination in Contemporary Migrant Literatures." Ph.D. diss., University of Massachusetts, Amherst, 2000.

Brice-Finch, Jacqueline. "Edwidge Danticat: Memories of Maäfa." *MaComère: Journal of the Association of Caribbean Women Writers and Scholars* 4 (2001): 146–54.

Chancy, Myriam J. A. *Framing Silence: Revolutionary Novels by Haitian Women*. New Brunswick, NJ: Rutgers University Press, 1997.

Charters, Mallay. "Edwidge Danticat: A Bitter Legacy Revisited." *Publishers Weekly* 245.33 (August 17, 1998): 42–43.

Cornejo, Josefina. "La afirmacion de la sexualidad femenina: Memoria y exilio en *Breath, Eyes, Memory*." In *Exilios Femeninos*, edited by Pilar Cuder Dominguez, 355–64. Huelva, Spain: Instituto Andaluz de la Mujer—Universidad Huelva, 2000.

Dash, J. Michael. *The Other America: Caribbean Literature in a New World Context*. Charlottesville and London: University Press of Virginia, 1998.

Francis, Donette A. " 'Silences Too Horrific to Disturb': Writing Sexual Histories in Edwidge Danticat's *Breath, Eyes, Memory*." *Research in African Literatures* 35.2 (Summer 2004): 75–90.

Gerber, Nancy F. "Binding the Narrative Thread: Storytelling and the Mother-Daughter Relationship in Edwidge Danticat's *Breath, Eyes, Memory*." *Journal of the Association for Research on Mothering* 2.2 (Fall–Winter 2000): 188–99.

Glick Schiller, Nina, and Georges Fouron. *Georges Woke Up Laughing: Long-Distance Nationalism and the Search for Home*. Durham and London: Duke University Press, 2001.

Goldblatt, Patricia. "Finding a Voice for the Victimized." *MultiCultural Review* 9.3 (September 2000): 40–47.

———. "The Implausibility of Marriage." *MultiCultural Review* 10. 3 (September 2001): 42–48, 73.

Gyssels, Kathleen. "Haitians in the City: Two Modern Day Trickster Tales." *Jouvert: A Journal of Postcolonial Studies* 7.1 (Autumn 2002): 34 paragraphs.

———. " 'Schild en vriend' in de Dominicaanse republiek: Edwidge Danticat over het bloedbad van Massacre." *Streven* 67.6 (June 2000): 518–25.

Hewett, Heather Anne. "Diaspora's Daughters: Buchi Emecheta, Julie Dash, Edwidge Danticat and the Remapping of Mother Africa." Ph.D. diss., University of Wisconsin, Madison, 2002.

Horn, Jessica. "Edwidge Danticat: An Intimate Reader." *Meridians: Feminism, Race, Transnationalism* 1.2 (Spring 2001): 19–25.

Ingberg, Pablo. "Edwidge Danticat: *La fiebre de contar*." *Suplemento Cultura La Nacion*, February 27, 2000, 8.

Ink, Lynn Chun. "Remaking Identity, Unmaking Nation: Historical Recovery and the Reconstruction of Community in *In the Time of the Butterflies* and *The Farming of Bones*." *Callaloo: A Journal of African Diaspora Arts and Letters* 27.3 (Summer 2004): 788–807.

Johnson, Kelli Lyon. "Both Sides of the Massacre: Collective Memory and Narrative on Hispaniola." *Mosaic: A Journal for the Interdisciplinary Study of Literature* 36.2 (June 2003): 75–91.

Jurney, Florence Ramond. "Exile and Relation to the Mother/Land in Edwidge Danticat's *Breath Eyes Memory* and *The Farming of Bones*." *Revista/Review Interamericana* 31.1–4 (January–December 2001).

Kekeh-Dika, Andrée-Anne. "Entre ville et village: Quelles destinées pour le féminin chez Edwidge Danticat?" In *La Ville plurielle dans la fiction antillaise anglophone: Images de l'interculturel*, edited by Corinne Duboin and Eric Tabuteau, 59–67. Toulouse, France: PU du Mirail, 2000.

Larrier, Renée. " 'Girl by the Shore': Gender and Testimony in Edwidge Danticat's *The Farming of Bones*." *Journal of Haitian Studies* 7.2 (Fall 2001): 50–60.

Loichot, Valerie. "Edwidge Danticat's Kitchen History." *Meridians: Feminism, Race, Transnationalism* 5.1 (2004): 92–116.

Mardorossian, Carine M. "From Literature of Exile to Migrant Literature." *Modern Language Studies* 32.2 (Fall 2002): 15–33.

N'Zengou-Tayo, Marie-José. "Children in Haitian Popular Migration as Seen by Maryse Conde and Edwidge Danticat." In *Winds of Change: The Transforming Voices of Caribbean Women*

Writers and Scholars, edited by Adele S. Newson and Linda Stong-Leek, 93–100. New York: Peter Lang, 1998.

———. "Le vodou dans la representation littéraire de la migration des *boat-people* haïtiens." In *Haïti: Le Vodou au troisième millénaire*, 143–64. Sous la direction de Frantz-Antoine LeConte. Montréal: Les Éditions du CIDHICA, 2002.

———. "Rewriting Folklore: Traditional Beliefs and Popular Culture in Edwidge Danticat's *Breath Eyes, Memory* and *Krik? Krak!*" *MaComère: Journal of the Association of Caribbean Women Writers and Scholars* 3 (2000): 123–40.

———. "Women, Literature and Politics: The Haitian Popular Migration as Viewed by Marie Thérèse Colina and the Haitian Female Novelists." In *Moving Beyond Boundaries*, vol. 2, *Critical Responses*. edited by Carole Boyce Davies and 'Molara Ogundipe-Leslie. London: Pluto Press, 1995.

N'Zengou-Tayo, Marie-José, and Elizabeth Wilson. "Translators on a Tight Rope: The Challenges of Translating Edwidge Danticat's *Breath, Eyes, Memory* and Patrick Chamoiseau's *Texaco*." *TTR: Traduction, Terminologie, Redaction: Etudes sur le Texte et Ses Transformations* 13.2 (2000): 75–105.

Ortiz, Lisa Marie. "Modes of Autoethnography: Genealogical, Autobiographical, and Historical Recovery in the Novels of Alvarez, Cliff and Danticat." Ph.D. diss., Wayne State University, 2000.

Poon, Angelia. "Re-Writing the Male Text: Mapping Cultural Spaces in Edwidge Danticat's *Krik? Krak!* and Jamaica Kincaid's *A Small Place*." *Jouvert: A Journal of Postcolonial Studies* 4.2 (Winter 2000): 30 paragraphs. http://social.chass.ncsu.edu/jouvert/ (accessed February 28, 2005).

Putnam, Amanda. "Mothering the Motherless: Portrayals of Alternative Mothering Practices within the Caribbean Diaspora." *Canadian Woman Studies/Les Cahiers de la Femme* 23.2 (Winter 2004): 118–23.

Robinson, Kim Dismont. "Probing the Wound: Re-Membering the Traumatic Landscape of Caribbean Literary Histories." Ph.D. diss., University of Miami, 2003.

Rossi, Jennifer Christianna. "Souls across Spaces: Ambiguity as Resistance and a New Generation of Black Women Writers." Ph.D. diss., State University of New York, Buffalo, 2004.

Saint-Éloi, Rodney. "L'Ecriture Bizango: Edwidge Danticat, le go-between." *Notre Librairie: Revue des Littératures du Sud* 147 (January–March 2001): 58–61.

Saint-Louis, Loretta. "Migration Evolves: The Political Economy of Process and Form in Haiti, the U.S. and Canada." Ph.D. diss., Boston University, 1988.

Samway, Patrick S. J. "A Homeward Journey: Edwidge Danticat's Fictional Landscapes, Mind-scapes, Genescapes, and Signscapes in *Breath, Eyes, Memory*." *Mississippi Quarterly: The Journal of Southern Cultures* 57.1 (Winter 2003–2004): 75–83.

Schleppe, Beatriz Eugenia. "Empowering New Identities in Postcolonial Literature by Franco-phone Women Writers." Ph.D. diss., University of Texas, Austin, 2004.

Shakleton, Mark. "Haitian Transnationalism: Edwidge Danticat's 'Caroline's Wedding': A Case Study of Literary Anthropology." *Suomen Antropologi/Antropologi i Finland/The Journal of the Finnish Anthropological Society* 28.2 (May 2003): 15–23.

Shea, Renee H. "The Dangerous Job of Edwidge Danticat: An Interview." *Callaloo* 19.2 (Spring 1996): 382–89.

———. "Edwidge Danticat." *Belles Lettres* 10.3 (Summer 1995): 12–15.

———. "'The Hunger to Tell': Edwidge Danticat and *The Farming of Bones*." *MaComère: Journal of the Association of Caribbean Women Writers and Scholars* 2 (1999): 12–22.

Shemak, April. "Re-Membering Hispaniola: Edwidge Danticat's *The Farming of Bones*." *MFS: Modern Fiction Studies* 48.1 (Spring 2002): 83–112.

Squint, Kirstin. "Exploring the Borderland between Realism and Magical Realism in *Krik? Krak!*" *Eureka Studies in Teaching Short Fiction* 5.1 (Fall 2004): 116–22.

Strehle, Susan. "History and the End of Romance: Danticat's *The Farming of Bones*." In *Doubled Plots: Romance and History*, edited by Susan Strehle and Mary Paniccia Carden, 24–44. Jackson: University Press of Mississippi, 2003.

Tabuteau, Eric. "American Dream, Urban Nightmare: Edwidge Danticat's *Breath, Eyes, Memory* and George Lamming's *In the Castle of My Skin*." *Alizés: Revue Angliciste de la Réunion* 22 (June 2002): 95–110.

Wachtel, Eleanor. "A Conversation with Edwidge Danticat." *Brick* 65–66 (Fall 2000): 106–19.

Wucker, Michele. "Edwidge Danticat: A Voice for the Voiceless." *Americas* 52.3 (May–June 2000): 40–45.

———. *Why the Cocks Fight: Dominicans, Haitians, and the Struggle for Hispaniola*. New York: Hill and Wang, a Division of Farrar Straus Giroux, 1999.

Jana Evans Braziel

DORIS DAVENPORT (1949–)

BIOGRAPHICAL NARRATIVE

Born January 29, 1949, in Gainesville, Georgia, contemporary writer/performance poet Doris Davenport is an iconoclastic figure who resists being pigeonholed into a specific categorization of writers. Davenport, raised in the Appalachian foothills in the small town of Cornelia, Georgia, a place where "red Georgia clay sticks to everything inside and out," experienced a rare type of "open-mindedness" in a 1950s grade school classroom in the South (quoted in Montgomery 155). Davenport attributes this openness and Cornelia's lack of "visible boundaries" as an influence on her poetry. The oldest of seven children raised in a single-parent home, Davenport credits the guidance received from her beloved teacher, "Miz Cooke," who taught her the importance of balancing the duties and responsibilities between home and schoolwork (156).

Davenport attended Paine College in Augusta, Georgia, graduating cum laude with a B.A. in English in 1969. She acknowledges her experiences at Paine College as an influence in establishing her "value systems" and "love of learning and reading" (Montgomery 155). Davenport later received an M.A. in English from State University of New York at Buffalo in 1971 and a Ph.D. in literature from the University of Southern California in 1985. In addition to writing, Davenport has taught as an assistant professor of English at the University of North Carolina in Charlotte and at Stillman College in Tuscaloosa, Alabama, where she presently resides. Davenport's diverse "areas of academic expertise" include African American literature/multiethnic literature; contemporary critical theory (ethnic-feminist), pedagogy in/of education; women's studies, and creative writing (poetry).

Davenport has written several books of poetry, the first few being self-published as a result of being rejected by alternative presses (lesbian, feminist, African American) because of what has been described as the "bitter tone" of her poetry (Montgomery 156). Titles include, *it's like this* (1980), *eat thunder & drink rain* (1982, second printing 1983), *Managia Il Touna & Bebi La Pioggia* (Italian translation of *eat thunder & drink rain* (1988), *Voodoo Chile: Slight Return* (1991), *The Cornelia Book* (1992), and *Madness like Morning Glories* (2005). In addition, her poems have been published in *Black American Literature Forum* and *Callaloo*.

MAJOR WORKS

Davenport's works espouse both lesbian and feminist views and also chronicle the life of African Americans, particularly in "Affrilachia," a term coined by poet Frank X Walker, "to convey the particular experiences of African Americans from the Appalachians" (Miller 97). Using both Affrilachia and also other places which chronicle her own biographical happenings, Davenport transports readers on an "odyssey" as she revisits sites of personal and collective memory and experience—an odyssey that leaves the reader spellbound by her eloquence (Miller 97).

Most who read Davenport's poetry are asked to confront complexities, whether historical, racial, sexual, or familial, while encountering mythological allusion and occasional nods to canonical poets as she reworks recognizable lines in paradoxical and clever approach. Themes in Davenport's poetry include, but are not limited to, issues of lesbian sexuality in a predominantly heterosexual world, giving voice to those silenced (especially oppressed voices in her hometown region of south Georgia), and the "indignities of institutionalized slavery" and its lingering effects on blacks in the South (Montgomery 157). Davenport passionately explores "areas of deep aesthetic, cultural, and social / political aversion that often lead to antagonisms between black and white women"—aversions resulting in a gulf that is not easily overcome because of "centuries of racial / psychological conditioning" (Miller 99). There is also a sardonic tone to some of her poetry that gives cause for an acknowledging chuckle to those who can relate to Davenport's blunt treatment of certain themes. For example, in "Teaching Composition in California / With My Grandfather near Death in Georgia," Davenport explores the conflict of dealing with the death of a loved one while confronting what becomes seemingly mundane and frustrating ordeals of daily life. Davenport writes,

Today is rather cruel
breeding students out of
rubrics like flies out of
summer and me with no
raid . . . (5)

CRITICAL RECEPTION

Critics note that Davenport's poetry promotes healing by "removing illusion" and confronting the harsh realities of past injustices in a truthful, straightforward, and sometime uncomfortable manner for the reader (Montsomery 157). In "Coming Home to Affrilachia: The Poems of doris davenport" (from *Her Words*, 2002), James Miller notes that Davenport's resistance to "easy classification" of her work has, at times led to "critical neglect" because of "her unwillingness to claim convenient, tailor-made identities" (96). It is indeed this "unwillingness" that makes Davenport's persona enigmatic and her poetry exciting. In another biographical entry written on Davenport in *Contemporary Lesbian Writers of the United States* (1993), Helena Louise Montgomery notes that at that time "Davenport's three self-published works ha[d] not received any formal critical attention to date" (158). This has not been the case in the twelve years hence. Davenport's works have gone from scant recognition and rejection by editors to national exposure and publication by a major university press. Critics *are* taking note of her poetry; some calling her works "iconoclastic" (Miller 96).

Montgomery argues that Davenport's poetry "can transport her readers from a very painful time in history, make them feel the consequences of a particular event, and then take them right into the most private room of their homes," a technique grounded in an honest approach to "past or present social ills existing within the lesbian or heterosexual communities" (158). Janet St. John notes of Davenport's most recent work, *Madness like Morning Glories*:

Davenport's background in performance poetry comes through strongly in this unique collection highlighting the voices of Afrilacians, that is, African Americans in Appalachia. She re-creates the voices of a Georgia community in a narrative of personal histories told from different perspectives. Each poem brings to life a person who adds insight into every facet of life, from family ties to family troubles, witchcraft to gossipy exchanges. Davenport is a storyteller who loves to wear the many hats of her characters as she weaves her embroiled tale. She understands true spoken language as well as poetic structure and technique.

St. John is just one of many critics who laud Davenport's marriage of unique style and regional themes.

In addition to poetry, Davenport's critical essays and book reviews have appeared in numerous anthologies and journals, including *Azalea, Day Tonight / Night Today, Lesbian Studies: Present and Future, This Bridge Called My Back: Writings by Radical Women of Color, MELUS, Mid-American Review, Listen Here: Women Writing in Appalachia, Out of the Rough: Women's Poems of Survival and Celebration*, and *Bloodroot: Reflections on Place by Appalachian Women Writers*. Some of these works have incited criticism, particularly one essay that critic James Taranto claims espouses "anti-white" racist sentiments, especially in respect to Davenport's depiction of the physicality of white "wimmin." In "The Pathology of Racism: A Conversation with Third World Wimmin" (from *This Bridge Called My Back*), Davenport's description of white women as "esthetically ... repulsive" has been the cause of outcry from some who bemoan not only because of what Davenport writes in the essay, but also because of the essay's inclusion on college syllabi (Taranto). Taranto takes umbrage to one particular passage where Davenport writes,

Esthetically (and physically) we frequently find white wimmin repulsive. That is, their skin colors are unaesthetic (ugly, to some people). Their hair, stringy and straight, is unattractive. Their bodies, rather like misshapen lumps of whitish clay or dough, that somebody forgot to mold in-certain-areas (quoted in Taranto).

However, it should be noted that Taranto does not only decry Davenport's "anti-white racism," he also denounces works by other authors that make their way into college curricula, especially essays that discuss feminist, environmentalist, and homosexual topics and issues.

Doris Davenport is clearly a poet/activist who champions causes she is passionate about through her poetry, while at the same time is a chronicler of the voices and experiences of her hometown people. Davenport's groundbreaking poetry, with its stylistic richness and "bitter tones," will find a way into the college classroom, enriching those who allow themselves to journey with Davenport into her world to explore her passions and confront perhaps their own prejudices. In doing so, they will come to know the genius of Doris Davenport and become moved by the experience.

BIBLIOGRAPHY

Works by Doris Davenport

"Black American Poetry in the Eighties: Book Reviews." *Black American Literature Forum* 17.4 (Winter 1983): 177–79.
"Black Lesbians in Academia: Visible Invisibility." In *Lesbian Studies: Present and Future*, edited by Margaret Cruikshank, 9–11. Old Westbury, NY: Feminist Press, 1982.

"Claiming Another Identity: Wimmin's Spirituality." *Day Tonight/Night Today* 3 (June/July 1981): 15–18.

"Dinner with the Orishas—Almost." *Callaloo* 16 (October 1982): 125–26.

eat thunder & drink rain. Los Angeles: Self-published, 1982. Second print, Iowa: City Women's Press, 1983.

it's like this. Los Angeles: Self-published, 1980.

Madness Like Morning Glories. Baton Rouge: Louisiana State University Press, 2005.

Managia Il Touna & Bebi La Pioggia (Italian translation of *eat thunder & drink rain*). Introduction and translation by Franco Meli. Milano: Cooperativia Libraria I.U.L.M. Scrl, Archipelago Edizioni, 1988.

"Music in Poetry: If You Can't Feel It/You Can't Fake It." *Mid-American Review* 10.2 (June 1990): 57–64.

"The Pathology of Racism: A Conversation with Third World Wimmin." In *This Bridge Called My Back: Writings by Radical Women of Color*, edited by Cherríe Moraga and Gloria Anzaldúa, 85–90. New York: Kitchen Table Press, 1984.

"Pedagogy and/of Ethnic Literature: The Agony and the Ecstasy." *MELUS* 16.2 (1989–1990): 51–62.

"A Signifying Short Story." *Azalea* 3.3 (Fall 1980): 25.

"Teaching Composition in California / With My Grandfather Near Death in Georgia." *Black American Literature Forum* 18.1 (Spring 1984): 5.

Voodoo Chile: Slight Return. Charlotte, NC: Soque Street Press, 1991.

Studies of Doris Davenport's Works

Miller, James. "Coming Home to Affrilachia: The Poems of Doris Davenport." In *Her Words: Diverse Voices in Contemporary Appalachian Women's Poetry*, edited by Felicia Mitchell, 96–106. Knoxville: University of Tennessee Press, 2002.

Montgomery, Helena Louise. "Doris Davenport." In *Contemporary Lesbian Writers of the United States*, edited by Sandra Pollack and Denise D. Knight, 155–59. London: Greenwood Press, 1993.

St. John, Janet. Rev. of *Madness Like Morning Glories. Booklist Online.* April 17, 2005. http://www.amazon.com/gp/product/product-description/0807129917/ref=dp_proddesc_0/104-7318024-7799954?%5Fencoding=UTF8&n=283155 (accessed February 28, 2005).

Taranto, James. "College Campuses Crawling with Crazies: a Report on Political Correctness, Back when It Was Still News." *New York City Tribune*, July 13, 1990, http://home.nyc.rr.com/taranto/crazies.htm (accessed April 10, 2005).

Denise R. Shaw

ANGELA Y. DAVIS (1944–)

BIOGRAPHICAL NARRATIVE

A political activist and philosopher, Angela Yvonne Davis was born in Birmingham, Alabama, on January 26, 1944. Experiencing the Ku Klux Klan's racist terrorism in close proximity she became politically active from high school onwards. She graduated *magna cum laude* from Brandeis University (1965), was a graduate student at the Frankfurt Institute under Theodor Adorno, and gained her doctorate under Herbert Marcuse's supervision, University of California, San Diego. By twenty-four, Davis was a philosophy professor at UCLA and an activist academic. Her commitment to communist revolutionary ideas, involvement with the Black Panther Party, and the politics of Black Liberation led to her dismissal by the University of College Regents in 1969

An active campaigner to free the Soledad Brothers, the police named Davis as an accomplice in Jonathan Jackson's failed kidnapping attempt at Marin County Hall of Justice (August 7, 1970) as his gun was registered to her. Charging the defendants with the killings from police fire, Davis was on the FBI's Ten Most Wanted List, accused of murder, conspiracy, and kidnapping. After two months underground and the biggest fugitive hunt in history she was captured on October 13, 1970.

Her custody sparked the international Free Angela Davis movement and she formed the National Alliance Against Racist and Political Oppression, which still exists today. The cold war cocktail of non-American communism and a Black Panther "anti-white" association consolidated Davis as a dangerous figure for the authorities and she potentially faced the death penalty.

Cleared of the fraudulent charges by an all-white jury on June 4, 1972, Fidel Castro provided a Cuban base for her to write *Angela Davis: An Autobiography* (1974). Her prison experiences led to a lifelong commitment to prison reform writing and public speaking, pioneering analyses of the oppressive interfaces of racism and capitalism in black history and the politics of sexism. Currently professor in the History of Consciousness (1994) at the University of California, Santa Cruz (Californian Republican senators objected), Davis is a member of the Advisory Board of the Prison Activist Resource Center and a leading expert on penal institutional racism. She is on the boards of the National Political Congress of Black Women and the National Black Women's Health Project.

MAJOR WORKS

The impediments to black people's advancement characterizing American society and its institutions make the broad spectrum of Davis's achievements all the more extraordinary. Anticapitalistic sentiment underpins her work. From her first challenges to the chauvinism of black liberation politics, "Reflections on the Black Woman's Role in the Community of Slaves" (1971), to contemporary critique on the role the United States plays in globalized economic and ideological warfare, *Abolition Democracy:*

Beyond Prisons, Torture and Empire (2005), she remains a powerful model worldwide for black consciousness and antiracist feminism.

Davis's writing is canonical in black studies and feminist thought. She works within a Hegelian-Marxist view of world history. Marxist ideology is her interpretative framework for addressing issues of postslavery black criminalization, feminism, aesthetics, and culture. As a political prisoner, she spearheaded *If They Come in the Morning* (1971) noting that the political prisoner's threat is due to "his persistent challenging—legally or extra-legally of fundamental social wrongs." *Women, Race and Class* (1981) retrieves black women's achievements in the nineteenth-century Suffrage and Club movements. Debunking the shibboleth, "Am I not a woman and a sister?" Davis argues that gains by white women have been at the expense of black people's franchise from slavery onwards. Foregrounding race and class she makes further distinctions between black and white women's groups in relation to rape, birth control, and housework.

The Angela Y. Davis Reader (1998) places her alongside Wittgenstein, Hegel, Irigaray, and Lyotard in the Blackwell Publishers series, testifying to her status as one of the century's preeminent theorists in Marxism, feminism, and antiracism. Selections reveal the trajectory of her philosophical thought. A lecture from her 1969 UCLA course, "Recurring Philosophical Themes in Black Literature," which is a Hegelian application to issues of black enslavement and freedom, can be read alongside "From the Prison of Slavery to the Slavery of Prison" (1998), which identifies the ideological linking of criminality to blackness.

In "Black Women and the Academy" (2004) she offers an uncompromising assertion that black women cannot define themselves in opposition to Latina, Asian, and Native American women and so reproduce forms of domination that were a template to their own oppression at the hands of white hegemony.

In her critical commentary and activism regarding post–September 11 America, globalization, race, feminism, and the prison industrial complex of America, Davis continues to expand understanding of power in society.

CRITICAL RECEPTION

Huey Newton noted after her arrest in 1970, "Angela has given her energy and devotion to the people's cause . . . in a way that sets an example for people everywhere" (Rhodes 357). This continues to inform her landmark contributions to race and social justice thinking, "a reminder of how dictatorial the Police State can suddenly become towards minorities if it is not vigilantly monitored by free patriots" (Burns 2001).

Davis's writing reorients thinking to identify uniquely black-centered concerns. She functions as a point of continuity in liberation politics between the 1960s to the new millennium as a chronicler and contributor to "progressive movements in radical philosophy and politics, emphasizing prison intellectualism, Marxism, antiracism, feminism, cultural studies and activism" (James 20). A review of *Women, Race and Class* concludes, "Certainly her book should provide direction for resurgence and continuing momentum in both the women's and civil rights movements" (Shields 361).

While one reviewer of the *Reader* asks, "Would she have achieved her intellectual authority without her earlier political celebrity, the integration of elite universities, the growth of the black studies movement, and the academic development of cultural studies?" (Richards 132), Davis herself is not without self-irony regarding her status as political renegade and icon. Decontextualized, depoliticized, and inserted into visual popular culture, "it is both humiliating and humbling to discover that a single generation after the events that constructed me as a public personality, I am remembered as a hairdo" (Davis, "Afro Images," 37).

As a public figure, Davis faces an ongoing iconographic representation, which overshadows her contributions to as a political intellectual. Her defence of affirmative action was denounced by a College Regent as "your record as a revolutionary is not merely disturbing but it may impair your effectiveness as a member of the faculty of one of this nation's most highly respected academic institutions" (James 22) thus revealing the full circle of conservative aversion to Davis's politics and her continued defining, articulating, and legitimizing of black people's concerns despite ideological restrictions.

The scope of her polemic, ranging from the recognition of black Marxist and communist women activists, to correctives to the race hierarchies of feminism and the cultural contributions of black artists, to addressing female sexuality, abortion rights, the commodification of black popular culture, and reductive imaging of resistance struggles, reveal Davis's substantial role in expanding "social thought and political theory" (James 21).

BIBLIOGRAPHY

Works by Angela Y. Davis

Abolition Democracy: Beyond Prisons, Torture and Empire. Open Media, 2005.
"Afro Images: Politics, Fashion, and Nostalgia." *Critical Inquiry* 21.1 (Autumn 1994): 37–39, 41–43, 45.
Angela Davis: An Autobiography. New York: Random House, 1974.
The Angela Y. Davis Reader, edited by Joy James. Malden, MA; Oxford: Blackwell Publishers, 1998.
Are Prisons Obsolete? New York: Seven Stories, 2003.
"Black Women and the Academy." In *The Black Studies Reader,* edited by Jacqueline Bobo, Cynthia Hudley, and Claudine Michel, 91–99. London; New York: Routledge, 2004.
Blues Legacies and Black Feminism: Gertrude "Ma" Rainey, Bessie Smith and Billie Holiday. New York: Partheon Books, 1998.
If They Come in the Morning: Voices of Resistance. London: Orbach and Chambers, 1971.
"Reflections on the Black Woman's Role in the Community of Slaves." *Black Scholar* 3.4 (December 1971).
Women, Culture and Politics. New York: Random House, 1984.
Women, Race and Class. New York: Random House, 1981.

Studies of Angela Y. Davis's Works

The Angela Davis Case: The Legal Background. London: United States Information Source, 1972.
Aptheker, Bettina. *The Morning Breaks: The Trial of Angela Davis.* New York: International Publishers, 1975.
Burns, Alex. Disinformation, http://www.disinfo.com/archive/pages/dossier/id91/pg1/disinformation. March 4, 2001 (accessed February 15, 2005).
Rhodes, Jane. "Black Radicalism in 1960s California: Women in the Black Panther Party." In *African American Women Confront the West 1600–2000,* edited by Quintard Taylor and Shirley Ann Wilson Moore, 346–62. Norman: University of Oklahoma Press, 2003.

Richards, Phillip M. "Brickbats in the Cause of Equality." *Journal of Blacks in Higher Education* 22 (Winter 1998–1999): 132–34.

Schiller, Naomi. "A Short History of Black Feminist Scholars." *Journal of Blacks in Higher Education* 29 (Autumn 2000): 119–25.

Shields, Portia H. "Review." *Journal of Negro History* 51.3 (Summer 1982): 359–61.

Deirdre Osborne

LUCY DELANEY (1830–1890)

BIOGRAPHICAL NARRATIVE

Autobiographer Lucy Delaney was born Lucy Ann Berry in St. Louis, Missouri, the daughter of slaves. Following the death of her first owner in a duel, her father was sold south, and her mother, Polly Berry, planned an escape for the remaining family. After Lucy's older sister Nancy reached Canada, Polly attempted an escape of her own; though she reached Chicago, she returned for fear of reprisals against her daughter. Polly later successfully sued for her freedom by proving that she had been born free, but kidnapped in her childhood by slave-catchers.

In 1842, Lucy showed herself to be increasingly defiant as well as unskilled at housework, and owner D. D. Mitchell threatened to sell her down the river. She fled to her mother, who filed suit in court for Lucy's freedom on the grounds that the child of a freeborn could not be legally enslaved. After Lucy spent seventeen months in jail awaiting the outcome, the suit succeeded, freeing her at the age of fourteen.

Lucy married Frederick Turner in 1845 while visiting Nancy in Toronto, and the couple moved to Quincy, Illinois. However, Turner died soon after in the explosion of a steamboat boiler. Ironically, the boat was named for the lawyer who had won Lucy's freedom, future U.S. Attorney General Edward Bates. In 1849, Lucy married Zachariah Delaney and remained happily married to him for at least forty-two years. They had four children, none of whom lived to twenty-five.

In her later years, Delaney was elected president of the Female Union, the first organization exclusively for African American women, and of the Daughters of Zion.

MAJOR WORKS

Lucy Delaney is chiefly remembered for her 1891 slave narrative, *From the Darkness Cometh the Light, or, Struggles for Freedom.* Delaney's mother is overwhelmingly the dominant character, and the text takes its shape as much from her life story as from Delaney's. Delaney's father, by contrast, is scarcely described and never named.

Delaney opens with her mother's kidnapping and enslavement, and then discusses her own, initially happy childhood as a slave. However, with the death of her first owner and the selling of her father, Lucy's family rebels against their increasingly strict masters. First Lucy's mother, then Lucy herself, defies her owners at risk of being sold down the river. Roughly a third of the narrative is devoted to the trial, which releases Lucy from slavery, then movingly reunites her with her mother as a free woman.

Like many postbellum slave narratives, Delaney's work does not focus so much on the horrors of slavery, but rather on the strength and potential of African American people. Delaney's mother continuously teaches her courage in the face of adversity. Upon the death of Delaney's first husband, for example, her mother offers her no consolation but "cast your burden on [the] Lord," arguing that he is better off in Heaven than he would be in slavery like Delaney's father. When Delaney's four children die before adulthood, she remembers the same consolation despite her bitterness: they "were born free and died free!" By recounting her public accomplishments at the end of the narrative, Delaney shows that she has lived up to her mother's vision of being an active participant in American democracy. In closing, she presents her narrative as an answer to the question, "Can the negro race succeed, proportionately, as well as the whites, if given the same chance and an equal start?" In light of her own accomplishments in the face of adversity, her answer is clearly "Yes."

CRITICAL RECEPTION

Criticism on *From the Darkness Cometh the Light* remains scarce, as the work was only reissued in 1988. In William L. Andrews's introduction to the edition, he discusses how Delaney's narrative, like those of Mattie Jackson and Annie Burton, celebrates the "herculean efforts of slave mothers to keep their families together," as well as how these mothers pass on "an empowering sense of self-respect." P. Gabrielle Foreman describes the text as an attempt to recover "black female motive will and active desire," and also suggests that the proto-feminist teacher "Lucille Delaney" in Frances E. W. Harper's 1892 *Iola Leroy* is based, in part, on the narrative of the real-life Delaney.

BIBLIOGRAPHY

Work by Lucy Delaney

From the Darkness Cometh the Light, or, Struggles for Freedom. Six Women's Slave Narratives. Oxford: Oxford University Press, 1988.

Studies of Lucy Delaney's Work

Andrews, William L., ed. "Introduction." In *Six Women's Slave Narratives*. Oxford: Oxford University Press, 1988.
Barrett, Lindon. "Self-Knowledge, Law, and African-American Autobiography: Lucy A. Delaney's *From the Darkness Cometh the Light*." In *The Culture of Autobiography: Constructions of Self Representation*, edited by Robert Folkenflik, 104–24. Stanford: Stanford University Press, 1993.
Foreman, P. Gabrielle. " 'Reading Aright': White Slavery, Black Referents, and the Strategy of Histotextuality in *Iola Leroy*." *Yale Journal of Criticism* 10.2 (1997): 327–55.
———. "Who's Your Mama?: 'White' Mulatta Genealogies, Early Photography, and Anti-Passing Narratives of Slavery and Freedom." *American Literary History* 14.3 (2002): 505–39.

Dave Yost

TOI(NETTE) MARIE DERRICOTTE (1941–)

BIOGRAPHICAL NARRATIVE

Poet Toi Derricotte was born on April 12, 1941, in Detroit, Michigan, the only child of Benjamin Sweeney Webster and Antonia Baquet Webster. Although she, her parents, and her paternal grandmother could pass for white, Derricotte was reared in a black community and has always considered herself African American. As she explains in her memoir, *The Black Notebooks*, blackness is less a skin color than "an attribute out of the body, slightly, like a halo" (182).

Despite her own light complexion, an early childhood in an upscale Detroit suburb, and a private Catholic education, Derricotte quickly perceived that being white brought privileges to which she was not titled as a black person. "All my life," she writes, "I have passed invisibly into the white world, and all my life I have felt that sudden and alarming moment of consciousness when I remember I am black" (*Black Notebooks* 25).

Derricotte's early bonds were with women: her mother, her grandmother, and a favorite aunt who worked in a print shop and brought her the scraps on which she first experienced "the realness of marks on paper" (Derricotte, "Interview"). Her father was an overbearing perfectionist and physically abusive alcoholic whom Derricotte has compared to the character in Sylvia Plath's "Daddy"; her ironfisted grandfather owned a funeral home where she spent many unsupervised hours "thinking about death" (Derricotte, "Interview").

Derricotte began writing poetry as a child, motivated by Billie Holiday's singing, her own mother's made-up songs, the ritual and music of the Catholic mass, and a need to express repressed feelings of fear, depression, and anger. In her early teens, she shared her writing with an older cousin, who called her poems "morbid." In high school and college, several Catholic nuns encouraged her poetic endeavors. Later, in graduate school, she was mentored by Pulitzer Prize–winner Galway Kinnell, whom she refers to as "the teacher I loved and respected the most" (Derricotte, "Interview").

In 1961, Derricotte gave birth to her only child, Anthony, in a home for unwed mothers. A subsequent marriage to the father lasted only two years. In 1965, she completed her B.A. in special education from Wayne State University and began her career as a teacher. Her marriage in 1967 to a "recognizably black" bank executive, Bruce Derricotte, ended amicably after thirty years.

From 1974 to 1988, Derricotte served as New Jersey poet-in-residence, published two books of poetry (1978, 1983), and completed her M.A. in English literature and creative writing at New York University (1984). Since then she has continued to publish award-winning prose and poetry and has filled academic posts at Old Dominion University (1988–1990), George Mason University (1990–1991), New York University (1992), Mills College (1998–1999), and Xavier University (the Delta Sigma Theta Endowed Chair, 1999–2000). Derricotte is currently a professor at the University of Pittsburgh and president of the board of directors of Cave Canem, a highly successful organization she cofounded in 1996 to establish a nurturing writers' community for emerging and established African American poets.

MAJOR WORKS

In both her poetry and prose, Derricotte probes the vulnerability of a self shaped by family betrayal as well as larger social forces. Always in search of "the truth, however painful" (*Black Notebooks* 141), Derricotte translates her deeply personal conflicts as an African American woman into narratives about the human experience. Repeatedly woven into her interrogations of race, victimization, survival, motherhood, and sex is the trope of a lost or broken self, seeking truth through language.

Derricotte's major publications include four poetry collections and a literary memoir. *The Empress of Death House* (1978) frankly examines female sexuality, motherhood, and, ultimately, the nature of love. In the iconoclastic *Natural Birth* (1983; 2000), Derricotte revises the shame (in 1961) of an out-of-wedlock pregnancy into a paean to motherhood. The poet refers to her third volume, Captivity (1989), as "a lot of scary poems" exploring the psychological bondage of race, class, and family. In *Tender* (1997), Derricotte imposes a nonlinear but tightly controlled form on familiar subjects. Reviewing *Tender* for the *Library Journal*, Ellen Kaufman writes, "these poems probe being at its root—sexually, spiritually, emotionally, and intellectually—and recount how violence—both physical and mental—ravages the self" (104).

The most prominent emotions in Derricotte's early poems are fear, loneliness, and anger. In "Poem for My Father," a daughter remembers her father's mind as "Blacker than burned-out fire. / Blacker than poison" (2–3). More recently, Derricotte has experienced a major shift from negative emotions to the positive force of love. "Something in me has flipped," she says ("Interview"), and the opening lines of "my dad and sardines" (2004) seem to confirm a significant change in her perspective: "my dad's going to give me a self / back. / I've made an altar called / "the altar for healing the father & child" (1–4).

The Black Notebooks, Derricotte's only published prose book to date, is the product of twenty-five years of journal writing, in which Derricotte tries to "unforget" fifty years of excruciating experiences that imposed a self so shameful she nearly committed suicide. Although other personal and social issues surface, it is Derricotte's struggle to locate her true self within her racial identity that predominates.

According to Derricotte, who considers herself primarily a poet, the driving forces behind her writing are an insistence on clarity—"not only clarity in form and language, but clarity in embodying our human nature, our 'truth'—and on the integral connection between beauty, function, and drama" (*Black Notebooks* 19). For her, "revision is what makes a poem a poem"; and what makes a poem a *great* poem is "the [perfect] tension between subject and form" (Derricotte, "Interview").

CRITICAL RECEPTION

Derricotte's international literary success is reflected in her numerous prestigious awards, including a Guggenheim (2004), the first Dudley Randall Award for National Contributions to Literature (2001), the Distinguished Pioneering of the Arts Award from United Black Artists (1993), two NEA fellowships (1985, 1990), the Folger Shakespeare Library Poetry Book Award (1990), the Pushcart Prize (1989, 1998), and the Lucille

Medwick Memorial Award from the Poetry Society of America (1985). In 2004, she was inducted into the African American Writers Hall of Fame at Chicago State University. Her biographical profile appears in *African American Autobiographers* (Greenwood), *Contemporary Authors* (Gale), *Twentieth-Century African American Poetry* (Chadwyck-Healey), and *Who's Who among African Americans* (Gale). Poet Sharon Olds has called Derricotte "one of the most beautiful and necessary voices in American poetry today."

Derricotte's literary memoir, *The Black Notebooks* (1997), was nominated for the Pen Martha Albrand Award and received both the Anisfield-Wolf Book Award and the American Library Association Black Caucus Award for Nonfiction. It was also named a 1998 Notable Book of the Year by the *New York Times*. A French edition was published in 2000. Her fourth volume of poetry, *Tender,* received the 1998 Paterson Poetry Prize.

Derricotte has been guest poet and reader at over a thousand universities and theaters. More than a thousand of her poems have been published in literary journals and magazines, and she is included on numerous professional Web sites. Her writing, anthologized as early as 1982, appears with increasing frequency in literary collections.

BIBLIOGRAPHY

Works by Toi(nette) Marie Derricotte

"Aunt Carrie." In *Memory of Kin: Stories about Family by Black Writers*, edited by Mary Helen Washington. New York: Doubleday, 1991.

"Black Catholics: Cultural Exiles, Literary Exiles." In *Daily Fare: Essays from the Multicultural Experience*, edited by Kathleen Aguero. Athens: University of Georgia Press, 1993.

The Black Notebooks: An Interior Journey. New York: Norton, 1997. Reprint, 1999.

Captivity. Pitt Poetry Series. Pittsburgh: University of Pittsburgh Press, 1989. Reprints, 1991, 1993, 1995.

"Emergence." In *The Grand Permission: New Writings on Poetics and Motherhood*, edited by Patricia Dienstfrey and Brenda Hillman. Middletown: Wesleyan University Press, 2003.

The Empress of the Death House. Detroit: Lotus, 1978.

"My Mother." In *Double Stitch: Black Women Write about Mothers and Daughters*, edited by Patricia Bell-Scott. Boston: Beacon, 1991.

Natural Birth. Crossing Press Feminist Series. Trumansburg: Crossing Press, 1983. Repub. with expanded introduction, Ithaca, NY: Firebrand Press, 2000.

Noire, la coleur de ma peau blanche. Translated by Phillippe Moreau. Kiron Editions du F, 2000.

"A Sistah Outsider." In *Life Notes: Personal Writings by Contemporary Black Women*. New York: Norton, 1994.

Tender. Pitt Poetry Series. Pittsburgh: University of Pittsburgh Press, 1997.

Studies of Toi(nette) Marie Derricotte's Works

Bennett, Juda. "Black by Popular Demand: Contemporary Autobiography and the Passing Theme." *A/B: Auto/Biography Studies* 17 (2002): 262–75.

DeMott, Benjamin. "Passing: A Black Poet and Teacher Chronicles Life in a White World." *New York Times* (November 2, 1997).

Hodges, John, ed. "Seers." Videocassette 3 of *Furious Flowers: Conversations with African American Poets*. San Francisco: California Newsreel, 1998.

Kaufman, Ellen. Rev. of Tender. *Library Journal* 123 (1998): 104.

Lee, Don. "Toi Derricotte: Contributor Spotlight." *Ploughshares* 69 (1996): 208–11.

Melnick, Patrice. "Interview with Toi Derricotte: Saturday, November 6, 1999." *Xavier Review* 20 (2000): 12–20.

Rowell, Charles H. "Beyond Our Lives: An Interview with Toi Derricotte." *Callaloo* 14 (1991): 654–64.

Samuels, Ellen. "My Body, My Closet: Invisible Disability and the Limits of Coming-Out Discourse." *GLQ* 9 (2003): 233–55.

Shanley, Katherine. "Distinct Traditions: Myths and Voices of the Many Americas." *PSA News: Newsletter of the Poetry Society of America* 44–45 (1994): 18–23.

Karen S. Sloan

ALEXIS DE VEAUX (1948–)

BIOGRAPHICAL NARRATIVE

Alexis De Veaux, a playwright, poet, children's author, journalist, activist, illustrator, artist, biographer, and educator, was born in New York City on September 24, 1948. She and her eight siblings were raised by her mother, Mae De Veaux who was supported by state aid. Her father, Richard Hill, was incarcerated for most of her childhood and died in 1975. Ruby Moore Hill, Alexis's paternal grandmother, and James De Veaux, Sr., her maternal grandfather, assisted in the raising of De Veaux and her siblings. Together they formed a strong extended family for survival. When Alexis was fifteen her mother moved the family from Harlem to the South Bronx.

De Veaux received a B.A. from State University of New York Empire State College in 1976. She earned both her M.A. (1989) and her doctoral degree (1992) in American Studies, specializing in Women's Studies, at the State University of New York at Buffalo.

Early in her career, De Veaux became involved in community-based work. She was an instructor of English for the WIN Program of the New York Urban League and a creative-writing instructor for the Frederick Douglass Creative Arts Center in New York City. In 1972, she was a community worker for the Bronx Office of Probation and a reading and creative-writing instructor for New York City's Project Create. In 1975, DeVeaux served as the cultural coordinator of Black Expo for the Black Coalition of Greater New Haven, Connecticut. The same year, she cofounded the Coeur de l'Unicorne Gallery and with actress Gwendolyn Hardwick formed the Flamboyant Ladies Theatre Company (1977–1984). De Veaux also created the Gap Tooth Girlfriends Writing Workshop (1980–1984), which produced two volumes of original poetry and fiction.

After graduating from college, De Veaux taught at several colleges. She has held positions at Sarah Lawrence College in New York, Vermont College of Montpelier University in Vermont, the Owen Dutson Visiting Scholar in the Department of English and Theater at Wabash College in Crawfordville, Indiana, and later visiting assistant professor in Women's Studies in the Department of American Studies at State University of New York at Buffalo where she currently is associate professor and chair of the Women's Studies Department.

From 1978 to 1990, De Veaux was a contributing editor and editor-at-large at *Essence* magazine and she continues to write for it regularly. As an activist, in her political essays published in *Essence* she reveals her support for the political and social liberation of black and third-world women. In "Zimbabwe: Women Fire" she chronicles the contributions of Zimbabwean women in the struggle for independence and the role they played in the establishment of Mugabe as president, but was outraged when, after the war, those women were alienated from the society they had helped to liberate. In her article "Blood Ties," she attacks with a vengeance the government of Haiti and Papa Doc and son, Baby Doc Duvalier, over the extreme poverty that plagued the tiny island of Haiti. De Veaux pleads with black Americans to develop an active consciousness toward the plight of the oppressed Haitians. Her interest in issues confronting black women appears not only in her political journalism and essays but in her fiction as well.

MAJOR WORKS

Love, self-identity, oppression, and the concept of sisterhood are the main focus of De Veaux's work. Her writing style is unconventional. Her experiment with language is daring and original. She writes using slang, no capital letters, unexpected syntactical strategies, and unusual typography as well as prose that contracts into poetry and again expands into prose to communicate with her readers. The setting for De Veaux's works is Harlem. Two of her short stories, "The Riddle of Egypt Brownstone" and "Remember Him a Outlaw," have as their main character poor working-class black girls growing up in a harsh urban environment in Harlem. They are the narrators of the stories. They live in public housing enclosed by artificial parks and graffiti covered walls. They are preyed on by men. Both narrators experience a dual reality in their lives. Both Egypt of "The Riddles of Egypt Brownstone" and Lexie in "Remember Him a Outlaw" are college-bound women who have escaped the ghetto world they are talking about and at the same time still very much affected by that world. They are both insiders and outsiders.

Egypt lives with her mother and she sees her father annually on her birthday when he buys her a present. Her story is dominated by two sexual encounters. The first involves her and insists on sexual favors in return for keeping the theft a secret. The second sexual encounter occurs in college when she accepts her French teacher, Madame duFer from Martinique, proposition to enter a lesbian affair and provides her luxurious apartment as a quiet place to study and live.

Lexie of "Remember Him a Outlaw" has an $8,000 scholarship to college in up state New York. Her Uncle Willie is a survivor on the streets and very proud of Lexie. He is killed while delivering drugs for her father. She asks to remember him in both the first and the last sentence of the story. In both stories, neither Egypt nor Lexie has separated or dismissed their history. De Veaux personifies objects in both stories, describing cars and buildings as hung over, windows that give voice to lovers' desires, the rap of the ball against the pavement and the hospital wall, coins that run on the side walk when dropped, and coins that have freedom that is taken away when Uncle Willie squashes them under his boots. These suggest that all characters in both works are incapable of change except for Egypt and Lexie.

In her other short story, "The Adventures of the Dread Sisters," the setting is on a bridge between Brooklyn and uptown New York. The characters are stalled in a traffic jam on their way to a political rally. The bridge symbolizes her characters' movements from stasis to action. The central character is not only the fifteen-year-old narrator but also a collective character of both the narrator and Nigeria. Nigeria, an artist and political activist, has rejected the conventional role of wife and mother, but adopted the fifteen-year-old narrator and her sister, Toni. Together they have created a family. Toni has a Hollywood name; she likes boys, likes straightened hair, and sleeps in late on Saturdays. The narrator and Nigeria have African names, Rastafarian hairstyles, chosen political work, and the love of women. They therefore declare themselves the dread sisters. The narrator and Nigeria's choices suggest opposition to the dominant society. De Veaux uses a different narrative strategy. She tells her story through a collective protagonist; her plot displaces the accepted gender roles, and she verbalizes alternatives to the dominant institution's concept of the traditional nuclear family. In *Spirit in the Streets*, a poetic prose narrative, De Veaux captures the black experience in Harlem. This work portrays episodes in the lives of various poor people who endure multiple forms of exploitation. The author also recounts some historical events such as the Attica Prison rebellion. De Veaux's illustrations, mixture of text and typography, is highly effective in this work.

In the play *The Tapestry*, first performed in 1975 and broadcast on public television in 1976, De Veaux has reimaged the black female self in contrast to those of the dominant society. In protest against the practiced standards of imaging the black woman in literature as either a white man's concubine, a prostitute, a domineering mammy who ruled the roost, the over-sexed, empty-headed floozy, or the tragic mulatto without a voice or self-identity, De Veaux has created a woman who is independent, makes her own decisions, and prepares herself for the future professionally. Jet, the heroine and law student studying for her exams, goes through the painful process of declaring her autonomy and defines herself on her terms. She rejects her lover Axis's definition of her in relationship to his sexual needs. She also refuses to let her mother define her by not accepting her demand to leave school to help care for her siblings and to eventually become a wife and mother. Both choices are limited aims according to Jet. She resolves the conflict of duty to others and her fulfillment to self by moving away from that world of sexual double standards which stifles individuality and pursues a career as a lawyer. "Each generation must go beyond the previous generation's aspirations," she says to Lavender, her best friend who has an affair with Axis. Jet's determination to proceed with her plans of a career as a lawyer to be able to leave her mark in the world in spite of the opposition she faced from her parents and Axis is her female stance (Paul 55). She plans to promote black equality after graduation. Jet refers to this intent as delivering to society a new set of rules (Splawn 519). Her wrestling with her conflict via her nightmares is cleverly portrayed in the scene with the chorus composed of Reverend Paradise, the parish priest, Jet's parents, and the rest of the parish congregation.

No is a collage of poems, music, and motion. Women in lesbian relationships are discovering themselves and expanding their avenues of self-expression.

An Enchanted Hair Tale and *Na-Ni* are two juvenile books written by De Veaux. *Na-Ni*, also illustrated by De Veaux, is a child's eye view of evil forces in the African American community. On the day welfare checks are delivered, Na Ni a nine-year-old girl sits on the stoop on 133rd street in Harlem waiting for the mailman. She is planning all the things she can do with a new bike, which do not ride but flies, her mother has promised to buy. A thief steals the check from the mailbox and Na Ni's dream is thwarted. In her pain and disappointment, she poetically tells the thief that it is her he steals from, a child that, like him, is black. The illustrations are like wire sculptures that along with the poetics of the text in black English convey the feelings of loss and disappointment. In *Enchanted Hair Tale* a little boy named Sudan is ridiculed and ostracized by his friends for his strange hairstyle. He is unhappy until he accepts his difference and appreciates his hairstyle with a little intervention from an adult. This is an example of the author using the English language to take something considered derogatory and transforming it into something powerful, acceptable, and positive.

Don't Explain: A Song of Billie Holiday is a prose poem written for young adults who recounts the life of the jazz singer. Billie is always striving to improve her art of singing in spite of all her difficulties and hardships doing her troubled life.

De Veaux's latest work, *Warrior Poet: A Biography of Audre Lorde*, is a story of survival and loss of an American literary icon. Lorde created a mystic identity for herself and De Veaux demystifies her iconic status. The book reveals that Lorde was an angry woman who battled depression, racism, sexism, and later cancer. She is also a woman of contradictions. She loved white women and she hated them. She disliked white people, but dated a Jewish man before coming out as a lesbian and for seven years was married to a white gay man who fathered her two children. She chose a white female partner for seventeen years and later an African American partner in St. Croix whom she spent the last six years of her life with as she battled cancer. As a writer, Lorde was remarkable. She became the first African American and first woman to be designated the New York State Poet.

CRITICAL RECEPTION

In spite of a prolific career as a fiction writer, poet dramatist, and literary critic, and an international published author in Spanish, Japanese, Dutch, and Serbo-Croatian languages, Alexis De Veaux's works have received little critical attention outside the gay and lesbian and black presses. The performance of *No* at the Henry Street Settlement Theater in 1981 ignited a series of competitive reviews. In the *Amsterdam News*, reviewer Salaam overlooked the dramatic quality of the play and attacked DeVeaux political position (36). However, Rhea Mandulo of the same paper urged the public to see the work. She found the play's worth in its ability to deal poetically, dramatically, and soul searchingly with a very personal point of view (27). On the other hand, the most appreciative comments on *No* come from Mel Gussow of the *New York Times*. He states that *No* has the potential to be the successor to Shange's outstanding production of *For Colored Girls* performed at the same theater (14).

Warrior Poet reads like a suspense novel according to Martha Miller. De Veaux "draws on personal journals, private archives of Lorde's estate, and interview members of Lorde's family and friends, but does not analyze the material. She provides us with mundane events and leaves critical gaps. Although Lorde's teaching is documented nothing is provided about the students she taught or her life at the university where she worked" (42). Ann Burns in *Library Journal* praised De Veaux's treatment of Lorde. "She left no stone unturned" in delicately handling the life of someone like Lorde who has family and good friends left behind (77). Her Children's book *Na-Ni* and *The Enchanted Hair Tale* were honorable mention on the Coretta Scott King Book Awards List.

BIBLIOGRAPHY

Works by Alexis De Veaux

"Adventures of the Dread Sisters." In *Jo's Girls: Tomboy Tales of High Adventure, True Grit, and Real Life*, edited by Christine McEwen, 53–58. Boston: Beacon Press, 1997.
"Alice Walker: Rebel with a Cause." *Essence* (September 1989): 56–58.
"Blood Ties." *Essence* 13 (January 1983): 62–64, 121.
Blue Heat, Poems. Brooklyn, NY: Diva Publishing, 1985.
"Bold Type: Renaissance Woman." *Ms* 5 (May/June 1995): 73.
Circles. New York: Frederick Douglass Creative Arts Center, March 1973; and Westchester Community College Drama Festival, New York, May 1973.
"Creating Soul Food: June Jordan." *Essence* 11(April 1981): 82, 138–50.

"Dear Aunt Nanadine." In *Afrekete: An Anthology of Black Lesbian Writing*, edited by Catherine E. McKinley and L. Joyce DeLaney, 79–88. New York: Anchor Books, 1995.

"Do Be Bo Wow!" *Essence* (October 1985): 54–65.

Don't Explain: A Song of Billie Holiday. New York: Harper & Row, 1980.

An Enchanted Hair Tale. New York: Harper & Row, 1987; paperback reissue, 1991.

"Ethical Vegetarian." In *Streetlights: Illuminated Tales of the Urban Black Experience*, edited by Doris Jean Austin and Martin Simmons, 83–92. New York: Penguin Books, 1996.

"Forty Fine: A Writer Reflects on Turning Forty." *Essence* (September 1990): 57.

"Going South: Black Women and the Legacies of the Civil Rights Movement." *Essence* (May 1985): 1.

Li Chen/Second Daughter First Son. New York: Ba Tone Press, 1975.

Na-Ni. New York: Harper & Row, 1973.

"New Body, New Life: Dealing with Black Women's Health Issues." *Essence* (June 1988): 57–58.

"Nina's Back!" *Essence* (October 1985): 72–73.

No. New York City, New Federal Theater, 1981.

"Out: Lighting the Path; Brave Lesbian Writers of an Earlier Era Made a Way Out of No Way for the Others Who Would Follow." *Black Issues Book Review* (January/February 2005): 48–49.

"Remember Him a Outlaw." In *Children of the Night: The Best Short Stories by Black Writers, 1967 to the Present*, edited by Gloria Naylor, 152–62. Boston: Little, Brown, 1995.

"Renegade Spirit: Standing up for Gay and Liberation in the Reagan Era." *Village Voice* (June 1984): 8.

A Season to Unravel, New York, St May's Playhouse, January 25, 1979.

"Sister Love." *Essence* 14 (October 1983): 83–84, 150, 155.

Spirits in the Street. New York: Doubleday, 1973.

Tapestry. New York City, Harlem Performance Center, May 1976; and KCET-TV (PBS-New York), 1976.

The Tapestry. Nine Plays by Black Women Playwrights, edited by Margaret Wilkerson, 135–95. New York: New American Library, 1986.

"The Third Degree: Black Women Scholars Storming the Ivory Tower." *Essence* (April 1995): 68–70.

"Walking into Freedom with Nelson and Winnie Mandela." *Essence* (June 1990): 47, 48–53.

Warrior Poet. A Biography of Audre Lorde. New York: W W Norton, 2004.

"Zimbabwe: Woman Fire." *Essence* 12 (July 1981): 72–73, 111–12.

Studies of Alexis De Veaux's Works

Barrios, Olga. "From Seeking One's Voice to Uttering the Scream: The Pioneering Journey of African American Women Playwrights Through the 1960's and 1970's." *African American Review* 37.4 (2003): 611–28.

Burns, Ann. Rev. of *Warrior Poet: A Biography of Audre Lorde*. *Library Journal* (March 1, 2004): 77.

Enekwechi, Adaeze, and Opal Moore. "Children's Literature and the Politics of Hair in Books for African American Children." *Children's Literature Association Quarterly* 24.4 (Winter 1999–2000): 195–200.

Gomez, Jewelle L. "Alexis De Veaux, 1948– ." In *Contemporary Lesbian Writers of the United States: A Bio-Bibliographical Critical Sourcebook*, edited by Sandra Pollack and Denise D. Knight, 174–80. Westport, CT: Greenwood Press, 1993.

Gussow, Mel. "No." *New York Times*, June 6, 1981, 14:1.

Kraft, Marion. "Alexis De Veaus: The Riddles of Egypt Brownstone." In *The African American Short Story 1970–1990*, edited by Wolfgang Karrer and Barbara Puschmann-Nalenz, 75–88. Trier: Wissenschaftlicher, 1993.

Mandulo, Rhea. Rev. of *No*. *Amsterdam News*, June 20, 1981, 27.

Miller, Martha. "A Poet Who Saw Unity in Oppression." Rev. of *Warrior Poet: A Biography of Audre Lorde. Gay & Lesbian Review Worldwide* (May/June 2004): 41–42.

Paul, Lourdes. "Alexis De Veaux's *The Tapestry:* a Female Stance." In *Literature and Politics in Twentieth Century America*, edited by J. L. Plakkoottam and Prashant K. Sinha, 50–56. Hyderabad: American Studies Research Center, 1993.

Ramsey, Priscilla R. "Alexis De Veaux." In *Dictionary of Literary Biography, v38. Afro-American Writers After 1955: Dramatist and Prose Writers*, edited by Thadious M. Davis and Trudier Harris, 92–97. Detroit: Gale Research Company, 1985.

Salaam, Yusef A. Rev. of *No. Amsterdam News*, May 16, 1981, 36.

Splawn, P. Jane. "Re-Imaging the Black Woman's Body in Alex De Veaux's *The Tapestry.*" *Modern Drama* 40.4 (Winter 1997): 514–26.

Washington, Mary Helen. *Black-Eyed Susans/Midnight Birds*: *Stories by and about Black Women*. New York: Anchor Books, 1989.

Bennie P. Robinson

EDWINA STREETER DIXON (1907–2002)

BIOGRAPHICAL NARRATIVE

Currently, the life and work of Edwina Streeter Dixon, a short story writer, remain largely unexamined. Census records of 1920 indicate that Edwina Streeter was born in Chicago in 1907 and that she was according to the census notes, "mulatto." Her father (whose name on the records is illegible) was born in Tennessee. Her mother, Abigail, was born in Ohio. According to the records, Dixon had two sisters—Gloria and Georgia—and one brother, whose name is also illegible. The 1930 census indicates that Streeter had by then married Albert Dixon and had had a daughter, Joyce.

MAJOR WORK

Dixon published "Pa Sees Again" in the *Afro American*. Because of limited access to microfilm, it is not known when she published this story in the *Afro American*. "Pa Sees Again" was republished in Ford and Fagget's famous anthology *Best Short Stories By Afro-American Writers (1925–1950)*.

"Pa Sees Again" is the story of a married couple—the Stones—who, now in their sixties, confront a new conflict late in their lives. Sam, the husband, has gone blind. When the story opens, he has been blind for six months. His spouse—the nameless narrator—has suggested that he move to and attend a school for the blind. She has researched the school and believes it will help Sam cope with his blindness and help him discover new possibilities. Blindness has rendered Sam a broken, defeated man, and he is at first reluctant to leave his home and his spouse for the school. Eventually, however, he agrees with her. The next morning on the bus, as they make their way to the school, two more characters enter the story: a blind boy and his mother. They play a central role in the ensuing climax, Sam's epiphany, and the denouement. "Pa Sees Again" is a compelling short story informed by a rich metaphor: blinding insight.

CRITICAL RECEPTION

Dixon has yet to receive critical attention. She is mentioned in one bibliography and only briefly—as someone who published a story in the *Afro American*—in a larger article about African American women short story writers.

BIBLIOGRAPHY

Work by Edwina Streeter Dixon

"Pa Sees Again." In *Best Short Stories by Afro-American Writers, 1925–1950*, edited by Nick Aaron Ford and H. L. Faggett. Boston: Meador Pub. Co., 1969.

Studies of Edwina Streeter Dixon's Work

Mullen, Bill. " 'Revolutionary Tale': In Search of African American Women's Short Story Writing." In *American Women Short Story Writers: A Collection of Critical Essays*, edited by Julie Brown, 191–207. New York: Garland Pub., Inc., 1995.

Potter, Vilma Raskin. *A Reference Guide to Afro-American Publications and Editors 1827–1946.* Ames: Iowa State University Press, 1993.

Kevin L. Cole and Katherine Madison

RITA DOVE (1952–)

BIOGRAPHICAL NARRATIVE

Rita Dove is the author of eight books of poetry, a book of short stories, a novel, and a verse drama. Her first two poetry books, *The Yellow House on the Corner* (1980) and *Museum* (1983), received critical acclaim. Her third poetry collection *Thomas and Beulah* (1986) was awarded the Pulitzer Prize in 1987, the second Pulitzer Prize for poetry awarded to an African American, after Gwendolyn Brooks. In 1993 Dove was the youngest poet to be named the United States poet laureate and the first African American. She held this post for two years from 1993 to 1995.

Born on August 28, 1952, to a middle-class family in Akron, Ohio, Dove is the oldest daughter and second of four children of Ray A. Dove, the first black chemist at Goodyear Tire and Rubber Company, and Elvira Elizabeth Hord, a housekeeper and housewife. In a family that encouraged education, Dove read many books as a child, studied music, and wrote. One of Dove's favorite childhood memories includes writing a chapter a week on a novel she called "Chaos" which used her school spelling words chronologically from a list.

Dove graduated high school in 1970 among the top 100 high school seniors nationally of that year. She visited the White House as a President Scholar, though President Nixon refused to shake hands with students that year because they protested the Vietnam War. At Miami University in Oxford, Ohio, Dove considered studying pre-law or German, changed her major four times and finally stayed with English. She graduated summa cum laude, Phi Beta Kappa, Phi Kappa Phi, and as a National Achievement Scholar with a B.A. in 1973. After graduation, she worked as a secretary at a construction firm.

In 1974–1975, she attended the University of Tübingen in West Germany on a Fulbright Scholarship studying modern European literature. She completed an MFA from the University of Iowa Writers' Workshop in 1977. Upon graduation, she was offered a tenure-track assistant professor position at Florida State University, but turned it down. Instead she followed fellow University of Iowa student, German novelist Fred Viebahn, to Oberlin College in Ohio where he taught German literature and directed plays. She took classes, sewed, wrote, and completed her first book of poetry *The Yellow House on the Corner* (1980). They married in 1979 and both began freelance writing in Berlin and Israel.

In 1981 Dove taught at Arizona State University. In 1982 she became a writer-in-residence at Tuskegee Institute. Dove's daughter, Aviva Chantal Tamu Dove Viebahn, was born in 1983. In 1987–1988, Dove was approved for sabbatical and with her family visited the Yugoslavian islands, Mexico City, and Berlin. In 1988 she had residency at Bellagio, Italy, sponsored by the Rockefeller Foundation. Also as a Mellon Fellow, she spent time at the National Humanities Center in North Carolina. Due to allergies and a longing for dramatic seasonal changes, Dove and her family moved to Virginia. In 1989 she began teaching at the University of Virginia. In 1993 the University of Virginia appointed her to an endowed chair as Commonwealth Professor of English. Dove currently lives near Charlottesville, Virginia. She writes in a cabin in her backyard using two types of desks because she prefers to move around while she works. One desk is a standard sit-down desk. The other, built by her father, is a desk one utilizes while standing up (Alexander 13). In her spare time she sings, practices the viola da gamba, and ballroom dances with her husband.

During her career, Dove has received numerous honors such as a Guggenheim Fellowship (1983), the Lavan Young Poets Award from the Academy of American Poets (1986), the General Electric Foundation Award for Younger Writers (1987), the Pulitzer Prize for *Thomas and Beulah* (1987), the Charles Frankel/National Humanities Medal (1991), the Ohioana Award for *Grace Notes* (1991), the Harvard University Phi Beta Kappa poetry award (1991), the Literary Lion citation from the New York Public Libraries (1991), the National Association for the Advancement of Colored People (NAACP), Great American Artist Award (1993), a Woman of the Year Award from *Glamour Magazine* (1993), named Poet Laureate (1993), the Distinguished Achievement medal from Miami University (1994), the Renaissance Forum Award for Leadership in the Literary Arts from the Folger Shakespeare Library (1994), the Carl Samberg Award from the International Platform Association (1994), the Heinz Award in the Arts and Humanities (1996), the Charles Frankel Prize National Humanities Medal (1996), the Sara Lee Frontrunner Award (1997), the Barnes & Noble Writers for Writers Award (1997), the Levinson Prize from *Poetry* magazine (1998), a nomination for the National Book Critics Circle Award for *On the Bus with Rosa Parks* (2000), and the Duke Ellington Lifetime Achievement Award (2001). She received with her husband the John Frederick Nims Translation Award from *Poetry* (1999). The governor of Mark Warner appointed Dove as the Poet Laureate of the Commonwealth of Virginia (2004). With Queen Noor of Jordan, Anderson Cooper, Mike Nichols, and John Glen, Dove was awarded the Common Wealth Award of Distinguished Service (2006).

She has also been awarded honorary doctorate degrees from Miami University (1988), Knox College (1989), Tuskegee Institute (1994), University of Miami (1994), Washington University in St. Louis (1994), Case Western Reserve University (1994), University of Akron (1994), Arizona State University (1995), Boston College (1995), Dartmouth College (1995), Spelman College (1996), University of Pennsylvania (1996), Norte Dame (1997), Northeastern University (1997), University of North Carolina (1997), and State University of New York at Brockport (2000).

Dove has served in many literary and service capacities to promote the arts. For example, she worked with the National Endowment for the Arts and Schomburg Center for Research in Black Culture in New York. In 1987 she was the president of the Associated Writing Programs (AWP). In 1991 she served as judge for several poetry competitions including the Walt Whitman Award of the Academy of American Poets, the Pulitzer Prize for Poetry, and the National Book Award Poetry. She was reappointed as the Special Consultant in poetry for the Library of Congress for 1999–2000. She also holds editorial positions with *Callaloo*, *Gettysburg Review*, and *TriQuarterly*.

MAJOR WORKS

Rita Dove has written on numerous subjects and incorporated many themes. As she explains in an interview, "To me the scariest and the most essential thing about writing poetry is that there are a thousand ways to do it. And there are a thousand paths to explore, each leading in a different direction" (Alexander 7). Her works have explored such directions as history, memory, myth, music, art, dance, autobiography, biography, and African American experience. Dove includes historical figures, religious individuals, archaeology relics, artists, musicians, and literary characters in her works. Perhaps more importantly, she incorporates individuals into her works who have been ignored by history due to their race, gender, or class. Thus, her works encompass reflections on the Great Migration, the Black Arts Movement, and the civil rights movement as well as what it was like growing up African American, female, and middle class in Akron, Ohio.

Five-sectioned *The Yellow House on the Corner* (1980) focuses on themes of romance, travel, and slavery. For example, "David Walker (1785–1830)" discusses an abolitionist's death due to his activism. Some poems in this collection focus on famous individuals like a "black arts" movement writer and a musician, "Upon Meeting Don D. Lee in a Dream" and "Robert Schumann, Or: Musical Genius Begins with Affliction," respectively. Dove explains in an interview that the poem "Dusting" from this collection became the impetus for her next collection of poetry.

Thomas and Beulah (1986) was written during Dove's postpartum. In order to write and parent, Dove and her husband divided parenting in four-hour shifts. One parent would write during the first four-hour shift while the other would parent, then the family would come together for four hours, and finally the other parent would write for four hours while the first one watched their daughter. *Thomas and Beulah* is divided into two sections and is based on Dove's maternal grandparents courtship and marriage while discussing the breakdown of public and private realms as well as the history of African Americans who moved from the South to the industrial Midwest. Dove's grandparents migrated from Tennessee to Ohio in the 1920s to find employment. After Dove's grandfather died when she was thirteen, Dove spent weekends listening to her grandmother reminisce. Many of those memories became the basis of this poetry collection. The twenty-three-poem Thomas section begins with the drowning of a best friend. The twenty-one-poem Beulah section covers themes of courtship, marriage, and widowhood. In this collection, Dove chronicles important events in Thomas and Beulah's life such as family, employment, and death. Some poems are linked directly to U.S. history such as "The Event" and "The Zeppelin Factory." *Thomas and Beulah* also utilizes details, symbols, and imagery to convey emotion and meaning. For example, the color yellow is used to connect both sections, a yellow scarf in the Thomas section and a yellow canary in the Beulah section.

Grace Notes (1989) discusses Dove's personal experience as a daughter and a mother of a daughter. Many poems are from a child's perspective and experience, such as "Fifth Grade Autobiography" which captures a family moment while fishing. Both *Grace Notes* and her next collection of poetry, *Mother Love* (1995), discuss coming-of-age incidents and motherhood. *Mother Love*, complete with introduction on the ancient myth of Persephone and Demeter, focuses on maternal themes and images. In this work, Dove writes sonnets of the Shakespearean and Italian form from both Demeter's and Persephone's perspectives. Many of these works probe the bond between mother and daughter, such as "Persephone Abducted" and "Demeter Mourning."

On the Bus with Rosa Parks (1999), also the title of the last section, describes the atmosphere in Montgomery, Alabama, that led to Rosa Parks's act. Several poems in this collection discuss innocence and discovery, often putting the poem's revelation in the last few lines. "Claudette Colvin Goes to Work" tells the story of another woman who refused to give up her seat on a bus. Other poems trace Rosa Parks's life before and after her action, such as "Sit Back, Relax" and "In the Lobby of the Warner Theatre, Washington, D.C."

Dove's newest collection of poetry is *American Smooth* (2004), which was listed on the *New York Times*'s 100 notable books for 2004. The title of the collection describes a particular type of ballroom dance. Divided into five sections, it interweaves literal and metaphorical ballroom dancing with history, emotion, and resistance. Many of the poem titles are dances themselves, like "Samba Summer," "Bolero," and "Fox Trot Fridays." Other verses deal directly with twentieth-century African American experiences with dance. "The Castle Walk" expresses a 1915 black bandleader's frustrations. "Hattie McDaniel Arrives at the Coconut Lounge" tells of the Oscar-winning star's observations in an all white club.

CRITICAL RECEPTION

Rita Dove's work has begun to receive more critical attention. Within the scholarship, many themes are explored. Some works center on Dove herself and her search for imagination freedom (Rampersad). Others explore her representation of race (Baker), gender (Cook and Proitsaki), and class. The second most recent of three complete studies of Dove, *Rita Dove's Cosmopolitanism* by Malin Perira, discusses Dove as part of the new black aesthetic poetics and examines her work in terms of the cultural mulatto, cosmopolitanism, and blackness.

Writers have focused on other aspects within Dove's work such as language and culture (Wallace), historical fragmentation and disclosure (Georgoudaki), enclosure (Wheeler), myth (McDowell), the public and private (Stein), forgotten historical events and individuals (Georgoudaki and Stein), and its universal appeal (Stein, Georgoudaki, Rampersad, Steinman, and Vendler). This is evident in the second comprehensive study of Dove, *Crossing Color: Transcultural Space and Place in Rita Dove's Poetry, Fiction, and Drama* by Therese Steffen. Focusing primarily on Dove's works between the 1970s and 1990s like *Thomas and Beulah* (1986), *Through the Ivory Gate* (1992), and *On the Bus with Rosa Parks* (1999), Steffen asserts that Dove moves beyond culture, race, geography, nationality, and genre because experiences described in Dove's works are universal and cross-cultural.

Other scholars have discussed the form of her works, for example, her cycle poems (Vender, Rampersad, and McDowell), her Shakespeare poems (Erickson), and her montage technique (McDowell and Costello). A third study of Rita Dove by Pat Righelato, *Understanding Rita Dove*, was released in 2006.

BIBLIOGRAPHY

Works by Rita Dove

American Smooth. New York: W. W. Norton, 2004.
"A Black Rainbow: Modern Afro American Poetry." With Marilyn Nelson Waniek. In *Poetry after Modernism*, edited by Robert McDowell, 217–75. Oregon: Story Line Press, 1991.
The Darker Side of the Earth. Oregon: Story Line Press, 1994.
"'Either I'm Nobody, or I'm a Nation.'" *Parnassus: Poetry in Review* 14.1 (1987): 49–76.
Fifth Sunday. Lexington: University of Kentucky, 1985.

Grace Notes. New York: W. W. Norton, 1989.

Mandolin. Ohio: Ohio Review, 1982.

Mother Love. New York: W. W. Norton, 1995.

Museum. Pittsburgh: Carnegie-Mellon University Press, 1983.

Oedipus Rex: A Black Tragedy. Washington, DC: Library of Congress, 1980.

On the Bus with Rosa Parks. New York: W. W. Norton, 1999.

The Only Dark Spot in the Sky. Arizona: Porch Publications, 1980.

The Other Side of the House. Photographs by Tamarra Kaida. Arizona: VARI Studios Pyracantha Press, 1988.

The Poet's World. Washington, DC: Library of Congress, 1995.

Selected Poems. New York: Vintage Books, 1993.

Seven for Luck. Wisconsin: Hal Leonard, 1998.

The Siberian Village. Virginia: Alexander Street Press, 1991.

"Telling It Like It I-S *IS:* Narrative Techniques in Melvin B. Tolson's *Harlem Gallery*." *New England Review and Bread Loaf Quarterly* 8 (Autumn 1985): 109–17.

Ten Poems. Iowa: Penumbra Press, 1977.

Thomas and Beulah. Pittsburgh: Carnegie-Mellon Press, 1986.

Through the Ivory Gate. New York: Pantheon Books, 1992.

The Yellow House on the Corner. Pittsburgh: Carnegie-Mellon University Press, 1980.

Studies of Rita Dove's Works

Alexander, Elizabeth. "An Interview with Rita Dove." *Writer's Chronicle* 38.2 (October/November 2005): 4–16.

Baker, Houston A. "Rita Dove, *Grace Notes*." *Black American Literature Forum* 24 (1990): 574–77.

Booth, Alison. "Abduction and Other Severe Pleasures: Rita Dove's *Mother Love*." *Callaloo* 19 (1996): 125–30.

Cook, Emily Walker. "'But She Won't Set Foot/In His Turtle Dove Nash': Gender Roles and Gender Symbolism in Rita Dove's *Thomas and Beulah*." *College Language Association Journal* 38 (1995): 322–30.

Corn, Alfred. Rev. of *Grace Notes*. *Poetry* 157.1 (October 1990): 37–39.

Costello, Bonnie. "Scars and Wings: Rita Dove's *Grace Notes*." *Callaloo* 14 (Spring 1991): 434–38.

Cushman, Stephen "And the Dove Returned." *Callaloo* 19 (1996): 131–34.

Dungy, Camille. "An Interview with Rita Dove." *Callaloo* 28 (2005): 1027–40.

Edmundson, Mark, ed. "Rita Dove's *Mother Love*: A Discussion." *Callaloo* 19 (1996): 123–42.

Erickson, Peter. "Rita Dove's Shakespeares." In *Transforming Shakespeare: Contemporary Women's Re-visions in Literature and Performance*, edited by Marianne Novy, 87–101. New York: St. Martin's, 1999.

———. "Rita Dove's Two Shakespeare Poems." *Shakespeare and the Classroom* 4.2 (Fall 1996): 53–55.

Georgoudaki, Ekaterini. *Race, Gender, and Class Perspectives in the Works of Maya Angelou, Gwendolyn Brooks, Rita Dove, Nikki Giovanni, and Audre Lorde*. Greece: Aristotle University of Thessaloniki, 1991.

———. "Rita Dove: Crossing Boundaries." *Callaloo* 14 (Spring 1991): 419–33.

Hampton, Janet Jones. "Portrait of a Diasporean People: The Poetry of Shirley Campbell and Rita Dove." *Afro-Hispanic Review* 14 (Spring 1995): 262–76.

Ingersoll, Earl G., ed. *Conversations with Rita Dove*. Jackson: University Press of Mississippi, 2002.

Jones, Kirkland C. "Folk Idiom in the Literary Expression of Two African-American Authors: Rita Dove and Yusef Komunyakaa." In *Language and Literature in the African-American Imagination*, edited by Carol Aisha Blackshire Belay, 149–65. Westport, CT: Greenwood Press, 1992.

Kitchen, Judith, Stan Sanvel Rubin, and Earl G. Ingersoll, eds. "A Conversation with Rita Dove." *Black American Literature Forum* 20 (1986): 227–40.

Lofgren, Lotta. "Partial Horror: Fragmentation and Healing in Rita Dove's *Mother Love.*" *Callaloo* 19 (1996): 135–42.

McDowell, Robert. "The Assembling Vision of Rita Dove." In *Conversant Essays: Contemporary Poets on Poetry*, edited by James McCorkle, 294–302. Michigan: Wayne State University Press, 1990.

Moyers, Bill, ed. "Rita Dove." In *Language of Life: A Festival of Poets*, 109–28. New York: Doubleday, 1995.

Pereira, Malin. *Rita Dove's Cosmopolitanism.* Chicago: University of Illinois Press, 2003.

———. " 'When the pear blossoms / cast their pale faces on / the darker side of the earth': Miscegenation, the Primal Scene, and Incest Motif of Rita Dove's Work." *African American Review* 36 (Summer 2002): 1–17.

Proitsaki, Maria. "Seasonal and Seasonable Motherhood in Dove's *Mother Love.*" In *Women, Creators of Culture*, edited by Ekaterini Georgoudaki and Domna Pastourmatzi, 145–52. Greece: Hellenic Association of American Studies, 1997.

Rampersad, Arnold. "The Poems of Rita Dove." *Callaloo* 9 (Winter 1986): 52–60.

Righelato, Pat. *Understanding Rita Dove.* South Carolina: University of South Carolina Press, 2006.

Schneider, Steven. "Coming Home: An Interview with Rita Dove." *Iowa Review* 19 (1989).

Steffen, Therese. *Crossing Color: Transcultural Space and Place in Rita Dove's Poetry, Fiction, and Drama.* Oxford: Oxford University Press, 2001.

Stein, Kevin. "Lives in Motion: Multiple Perspectives in Rita Dove's Poetry." *Mississippi Review* 23.3 (1995): 51–79.

Steinman, Lisa M. "Dialogues between History and Dream." *Michigan Quarterly Review* 26 (1987): 428–38.

Van Dyne, Susan R. "Sitting the Poet: Rita Dove's Refiguring of Traditions." In *Women Poets of the Americas: Towards a Pan-American Gathering*, edited by Jacqueline Vaught Brogan and Cordelia Chávez Candelaria, 68–87. Indiana: University of Notre Dame Press, 1999.

Vendler, Helen. "The Black Dove: Rita Dove, Poet Laureate." In *Soul Says*, 156–66. Cambridge: Belknap Press, 1995.

———. "Blackness and Beyond Blackness." *Times Literary Supplement* (February 18, 1994): 11–13.

———. "A Dissonant Triad." *Parnassus* 16 (1991): 391–404.

———. "An Interview with Rita Dove." In *Reading Black, Reading Feminist*, edited by Henry Louis Gates, Jr., 481–91. New York: Meridian, 1990.

———. "Rita Dove: Identity Markers." *Callaloo* 17.2 (1994): 381–98.

Wallace, Patricia. "Divided Loyalties: Little and Literary and the Poetry of Lorna Dee Cervantes, Cathy Song, and Rita Dove." *MELUS* 18 (1993): 3–19.

Wheeler, Leslie. "Rita Dove: the House Expands." In *The Poetics of Enclosure: American Women Poets from Dickinson to Dove.* Knoxville: The University of Tennessee Press, 2002.

Wiseman, Laura Madeline. "Rita Dove: A Woman of Many Words." *Empowerment4women* (March/April 2005). Online, April 2005, http://www.empowerment4women.org/respect/ma05_ritadove.html (accessed January 7, 2006).

Laura Madeline Wiseman

KATE DRUMGOOLD (1858?–1898)

BIOGRAPHICAL NARRATIVE

Except for what can be gleaned from her autobiography, little is known about Kate Drumgoold. By her own report, *A Slave Girl's Story*, she was born to married slave parents near Petersburg, Virginia, three years before the Civil War (4). Her earliest years were marred by two major events: the death of her "white mother" (5)—a childless, doting plantation mistress—and the sale of her natural mother to a Georgia planter. After the war, Kate's mother returned to Virginia, collected her surviving children, and moved to Brooklyn, New York, where seven-year-old Kate became a live-in domestic. She also began attending night literacy classes at Washington Avenue Baptist Church where she first heard the Christian rhetoric that permeates her writing.

Despite chronic health problems, Drumgoold was determined to receive a formal education. Through hard work, frugality, and the generosity of family and friends, she completed eleven years of schooling, including three years at Wayland Seminary in Washington, D.C. (1875–1878), and four years at a boarding school in Harpers Ferry, Virginia (1882–1886). After teaching in rural West Virginia for eleven years, Drumgoold had a "break down" (42) and moved back to Brooklyn, where she resumed her work as a domestic and began the "sketch" (3) that would become *A Slave Girl's Story*. Her final manuscript entry, dated March 4, 1897, indicates that Drumgoold was in a precarious state of health. She died sometime in 1898 of unknown causes; neither the exact date of her death nor her burial place is known.

MAJOR WORK

Drumgoold's only known work, *A Slave Girl's Story: Being an Autobiography of Kate Drumgoold*, includes the place and date of publication (Boston, 1898), but no publisher's name or imprint, causing speculation that it may have been self-published. Elizabeth Wright classifies the text as "at once a literacy narrative, a slave narrative, and a migration narrative" because it incorporates accounts of Drumgoold's formal education, her antebellum childhood, and a rambling travelogue. Conversational in tone and—according to its author—addressed to an antislavery audience, the memoir is an effusive apologia for "noble whites" (4), evangelical Christianity, and "the delightful study" of a slave girl's history (24).

Rather than chronologically organized, the autobiography is loosely structured by what Jennifer Fleischner has termed a "cycle of 'loss / illness and recovery' " (143–44). Ignoring boundaries of space and time, the author optimistically addresses a number of paired themes: enslavement and liberation, desire and fulfillment, ignorance and knowledge, alienation and affiliation, and earthly bonds and heavenly rewards.

CRITICAL RECEPTION

Kate Drumgoold's memoir has received little critical attention despite its inclusion in *Six Women's Slave Narratives* (1988) as part of the Oxford University Press Schomburg Series. The first scholarly attention of any note is Jennifer Fleischner's psychoanalytic reading in *Mastering Slavery* (1996), which interprets the narrative as Drumgoold's failed attempt to accept the childhood loss of two "mothers" (147). Elizabeth Wright, in her dissertation (2000), proposes a more liberated Drumgoold using her "life book" to construct a "literate self" (42). Also in 2000, an electronic edition was added to *Documenting the American South* and the *Journal of Black Studies* published results of a 1996 critical literacy experiment that included Drumgoold's memoir. The study's subjects, black university students, generally found Drumgoold's text "too accommodating to whites" (205) and her "oral strategies" confusing.

Despite its artistic flaws, *A Slave Girl's Story* provides a worthwhile retrospective on an African American's childhood memories of slavery, emancipation, and postbellum race relations.

BIBLIOGRAPHY

Work by Kate Drumgoold

Drumgoold, Kate. *A Slave Girl's Story: Being an Autobiography of Kate Drumgoold*. Boston: n.p., 1898.

Studies of Kate Drumgoold's Work

Andrews, William L. "Introduction." In *Six Women's Slave Narratives*, edited by William L. Andrews. Schomburg Lib. 19th-c. Black Women Writers. New York: Oxford University Press, 1988.

Davis, Cynthia J., and Kathryn West. *Women Writers in the United States: A Timeline of Literary, Cultural, and Social History*. New York: Oxford University Press, 1996.

Fleischner, Jennifer. *Mastering Slavery: Memory, Family, and Identity in Women's Slave Narratives*. New York: New York University Press, 1996.

———. "Memory, Sickness, and Slavery: One Slave Girl's Story." *American Imago* 51 (1994): 397–419.

Hine, Darlene Clark, ed. *Black Women in America: An Historical Encyclopedia*. Brooklyn: Carlson, 1993, 356–57.

Horne, Field. *The Saratoga Reader: Writing about an American Village, 1749–1900*. Syracuse: Syracuse University Press, 2004.

Richardson, Elaine. "Critique on the Problematic of Implementing Afrocentricity into the Traditional Curriculum: 'The Powers That Be.' " *Journal of Black Studies* 31 (2000): 196–213.

Wright, Elizabeth J. "Leaving Home: Travel and the Politics of Literacy in United States Women's Fiction and Autobiography, 1898–1988." Ph.D. diss., University of New Mexico, 2000.

Karen S. Sloan

SHIRLEY GRAHAM DUBOIS (1896–1977)

BIOGRAPHICAL NARRATIVE

A playwright, Shirley Graham DuBois (also known as Shirley Graham and Mrs. W.E.B. DuBois) was born Lola Bell Graham in Indiana on November 11, 1896, to Etta Bell Graham and David A. Graham. Her father, an educator and a preacher in the African Methodist Episcopal Church, encouraged her interest in literature and music. Graham married Shadrach McCants in 1921. Upon their divorce in 1927, she made the difficult decision to leave their sons with her parents while she studied music at the Sorbonne, Howard University, and Oberlin College, where she received an M.A. degree. Graham DuBois led the Chicago "Negro unit" of the Federal Theater Project in the mid-1930s, producing several successful musicals. After making significant inroads as a producer, composer, playwright, and biographer, Graham married W.E.B. DuBois in 1951. The couple moved to Ghana in 1961, where W.E.B. DuBois died in 1963. Graham DuBois traveled the globe in support of leftist causes until she died of breast cancer in Beijing.

MAJOR WORKS

Graham DuBois transformed a one-act play, which she had written while she was a student at Oberlin, into *Tom Tom: An Epic of Music and the Negro* (1932), the first all-black opera to be performed on a large scale, while serving as Music Department head at what is now Morgan State University. While Voodoo Man, the opera's protagonist, threatens to confirm white audiences' associations between African Americans and primitivism, the tom tom that links the three settings—an African village during colonization, the plantation south, and 1930s Harlem—constructs a Pan-African consciousness.

Graham DuBois produced a number of dramatic works between 1938 and 1941 while at Yale on a fellowship in creative writing: *I Gotta Home*, *It's Morning*, *Elijah's Ravens*, her radio play *Track Thirteen*, and *Dust to Earth*. *It's Morning* is notable for dramatizing a slave woman's desire to kill her daughter rather than see her sold into slavery. Her biographies are aimed to promote knowledge of African American history. They won her the Julian Messner Award for Best Book Combating Intolerance, the Anisfield-Wolf Award, and an Academy of Arts and Letters Award. She founded *Freedomways* magazine in 1960, and in 1974 published her novel *Zulu Heart*.

CRITICAL RECEPTION

None of Graham DuBois's theater work was published while she was alive, despite successful performances. *Tom Tom*, *Track Thirteen*, *I Gotta Home*, and *It's Morning* can now be found in drama anthologies; additional plays are available in many libraries' electronic databases of black drama. Her career suffered from her controversial support of socialist and communist approaches to economic and racial oppression and from being overshadowed by her husband's work, though critics have recently observed her attention to the complex challenges faced by black mothers (Meier and Perkins), her exploration of double-consciousness, and her modernist use of ambiguity (Horne 61). Gerald Horne's careful biographical study paves the way for additional reevaluations. Graham DuBois's goal was to preserve and celebrate the particularities of African American experience and culture through experiments with dialect and early Afrocentric use of myth, culture, and musical forms.

BIBLIOGRAPHY

Works by Shirley Graham DuBois

Booker T. Washington, Educator of Hand, Head and Heart. New York: Messner, 1955.
Coal Dust (1930), later *Dust to Earth* (1940–1941). No publication information available.
Dr. George Washington Carver, Scientist. With George Lipscomb. New York: Messner, 1944.
DuBois: Pictorial Biography. Chicago: Johnson, 1978.
Elijah's Ravens (circa 1940). No publication information available.
Gamal Abdel Nasser, Son of the Nile. New York: Third, 1972.
His Day Is Marching On: A Memoir of W.E.B. DuBois. Philadelphia: Lippincott, 1971.
I Gotta Home (1939). In *Black Female Playwrights: An Anthology of Plays Before 1950*, edited by Kathy A. Perkins, 211–24. Bloomington: Indiana University Press, 1989.
It's Morning (1940). In *Wines in the Wilderness*, edited by Elizbeth Brown-Guillory. New York: Greenwood Press, 1990.
Jean Baptiste Point de Sable, Founder of Chicago. New York: Messner, 1953.
Julius K. Nyerere. New York: Messner, 1975.
Paul Robeson, Citizen of the World. New York: Messner, 1946.
The Story of Phyllis Wheatley. New York: Messner, 1949.
There Once Was a Slave: The Heroic Story of Frederick Douglass. New York: Messner, 1947.
Tom Tom: An Epic of Music and the Negro (1932). In *The Roots of African American Drama*, edited by Leo Hamalian and James Hatch, 238–86. Detroit: Wayne State University Press, 1991.
Track Thirteen (1940). In *Lost Plays of the Harlem Renaissance, 1920–1940*, edited by James Hatch and Leo Hamalian. Detriot: Wayne State University Press, 1996.
Your Most Humble Servant. New York: Messner, 1949.
Zulu Heart. New York: Third, 1974.

Studies of Shirley Graham DuBois's Works

Boehnlein, James, and Kevin Gladish. "Shirley Graham and the Drama of Cultural Identity." *MAWA Review* 11.2 (1996): 69–75.
Hamalian, Leo, and James V. Hatch. "Shirley Graham." In *The Roots of African American Drama*, 231–37. Detroit: Wayne State University Press, 1991.
Hine, Darlene Clark. "Shirley Graham DuBois." In *Black Women in America*, vol. 1, pp. 357–58. Brooklyn: Carlson, 1993.
Horne, Gerald. *Race Woman: The Lives of Shirley Graham DuBois.* New York: New York University Press, 2000.
Meier, Joyce. "The Refusal of Motherhood in African American Women's Theater." *MELUS* 25.3–4 (2000): 117–39.

Perkins, Kathy A. "The Impact of Lynching on the Art of African American Women." In *Strange Fruit: Plays on Lynching by American Women*, edited by Perkins and Judith Stephens, 15–20. Bloomington: Indiana University Press, 1998.

———. "Shirley Graham." In *Black Female Playwrights: An Anthology of Plays before 1950*, 207–10. Bloomington: Indiana University Press, 1989.

Rebecca Walsh

ALICE DUNBAR-NELSON (1875–1935)

BIOGRAPHICAL NARRATIVE

Alice Dunbar-Nelson was born Alice Ruth Moore on July 19, 1875. She was born in a house on Second Street in New Orleans, Louisiana, a city rich with ethnic and cultural fusions. Her mother Patsy (Patricia) Wright was an ex-slave who worked as a seamstress/washerwoman. Her father, Monroe Moore's occupation was listed on her birth record as a laborer, although according to some sources he was a merchant seaman. Primarily her mother Patsy and her maternal grandmother Mary Wright raised Alice in New Orleans along with her sister Mary Leila, who was five years older. Although not born into the most prosperous neighborhood in New Orleans, her family was middle class for the times. With her racially diverse heritage (a mixture of African, white, and Native American), which allowed her to pass for white, Alice was born into a life that afforded her a somewhat privileged view of her diverse community. There is little documentation available about her early life other than she attended public schools in Louisiana. As a teen, she attended Southern University's high school division, graduating in 1889 at age fourteen. She then entered the teaching program at Straight University (later Dillard University), graduating in 1892. She immediately began teaching in the public school system in New Orleans. It was while teaching in the New Orleans public school system that she began her public career as a writer and civil rights activist.

Shortly after her twentieth birthday in 1895, her first book *Violets and Other Tales* was published under the name Alice Ruth Moore. This fresh work by a young southern woman received generally enthusiastic reviews. Through the publicity surrounding her poetry and an accompanying picture in a Boston magazine, a long-distance epistolary relationship began with the soon to be famous African American poet Paul Laurence Dunbar. Dunbar seeing her picture in the April 1895 issue of the Boston *Monthly Review* magazine began a correspondence that lead to their meeting in February 1897 and culminated with their elopement on March 6, 1898. The romanticism present in her early work is evidenced in her personal life as well, as after one face-to-face meeting with Dunbar, she agreed to become his wife. The next morning Paul Dunbar left for a yearlong trip to England. It was while engaged to Paul Dunbar that she subsequently moved to New York and helped to found the White Rose Mission, which later became the White Rose Home for Girls in Harlem. There she taught evening and Sunday classes as her writing career blossomed. After Dunbar returned from England and shortly after their secret wedding ceremony, the couple moved to Washington, D.C. It was while married to Dunbar that Dunbar-Nelson, under the name Alice Dunbar, published her second book *The Goodness of St. Rocque and Other Stories* (1899). When her marriage to Dunbar ended in 1902, she moved to Wilmington, Delaware, where she taught at Howard High School. After her tumultuous marriage and separation from Dunbar, Dunbar-Nelson chose to continue her education. She studied at Columbia University, the University of Pennsylvania, and Cornell University majoring in psychology and educational testing. While at Cornell she wrote her master's thesis on the influence of Milton on Wordsworth, a portion of which appeared in *Modern Language Notes* (April 1909). In 1910, Dunbar-Nelson entered into a second short-lived marriage with Arthur Callis, a fellow teacher, divorcing a year later. Her third and final marriage was to Robert J. Nelson in 1916, a journalist, politician, and civil rights activist to whom she remained married until her death.

MAJOR WORKS

Dunbar-Nelson's first book, *Violets and Other Tales*, containing poems, essays, and short stories was published in 1895 by the Monthly Review Press. The works in *Violets and Other Tales* are mostly sentimental in theme and reflect a Victorian mentality. The works of poetry and fiction reflect the romanticism prominent in the works of feminine writers of her time. These works illustrate the harshness of unrequited love, jealousy, envy, and the bittersweet taste of revenge. Dunbar-Nelson also displays a wide range of interests when she expounds upon the glory of Flaubert's *Salammbo*. Moreover, she presents a feminist view that is not present in her later book as she asks in her essay "Women," "Why should the well-salaried woman marry?" She eventually points out that the independence a woman achieves through education and being a fiscally responsible single person only enhances her value as a mate, a popular theme for turn-of-the-century feminists. It is interesting to note that the themes within this book stay away, for the most part, from issues of racial inequality, focusing instead on the emotions of lost love and betrayal. This distance from racial issues is a reflection of Dunbar-Nelson's personal fight with the perilous dichotomy of her own racial identity. There are various articles written about her struggles as a light-skinned beauty with hazel eyes and auburn hair, and her perceptions of and conflicts with those of her race with darker skin. Dunbar-Nelson was capable of passing for white and did when it suited her purposes (usually to attend social and culturally uplifting functions). In addition, there is also documentation of her desire and attempts to escape classification as an African American artist, although she actively fought for African American rights throughout her life (Alexander 68–73).

The dedication in her second book *The Goodness of St. Rocque and Other Stories*, published in 1899 reads, "To My Best Comrade, My Husband" who happened at that time to be Paul Laurence Dunbar. Her use of dialect and colloquialism reflects his influence; a tone that was for the most part absent from her first book. In this second book, the exotic Creole milieu of New Orleans and the Louisiana bayous are the principal motifs. One review for the book reads, "delightful Creole stories, all bright and full of the true Creole air of easy going" (Hull xxxii). In this work, a more mature authorial voice presents both new and revised stories. Most notably, in "Little Miss Sophie," a story that appears in both books, Dunbar-Nelson presents a fuller, more descriptive view of the Third District setting; as well, she presents more fully developed characters in her revised work. The tale of "Titee," also from *Violets and Other Tales*, is included in this book, but with an alternate ending. In the first effort, the young protagonist dies and goes on to claim his reward in heaven. In this revised work, despite having done a selfless act, the mischievous Titee not only lives but also returns to his normal behavior. In addition to these revisions, through invoking for the reader the atmosphere of New Orleans and the Creole culture, Dunbar-Nelson skillfully intersperses images of the mystical Creole spiritual beliefs with those of Catholicism, the predominant Christian religion in the region.

Dunbar-Nelson's depictions of Creole life link her with the author Kate Chopin (1850–1904), who was also writing about this unique culture at that time. There are further linkages between Dunbar-Nelson and Chopin's writing in their depictions of women and their problems of understanding or misunderstanding the rules of Creole society. Their depictions of the resultant heartbreak and even disastrous consequences are also analogous. Following the publication of this book Dunbar was never able to put together another commercially acceptable manuscript of her work for a full-length book. Her work became more polemic and rejected at least once on the grounds that "the American public had a dislike for treatment of the "color-line" (Hull xxxvi). Despite these obstacles, Dunbar continued to write and submit articles for publication. In 1920, Dunbar-Nelson edited and published *The Dunbar Speaker and Entertainer, Containing The Best Prose and Poetic Selections by and about the Negro Race, With Programs Arranged for Special Entertainments.* In that same year, she, along with her husband Robert Nelson, founded and edited the *Wilmington Advocate*, a weekly newsletter promoting racial equality. Fortunately, her work continued appearing in the NAACP's and the Urban League's magazines and newsletters, the *Opportunity*, the *Crisis*, *Ebony*, and *Topaz*. In addition, Countee Cullen included three of her most popular poems, "I Sit and I Sew," "Snow in October," and "Sonnet," in his collection of African American poets titled *Caroling Dusk*, published in 1927.

During the 1920s and 1930s, Alice Dunbar-Nelson's prominence was primarily as a political and social activist. Her life as a wife, daughter, and sister, as well as her career during that period, is documented and available for public scrutiny through the publication of her edited diaries, *Give Us Each Day: The Diary of Alice Dunbar-Nelson* (1984). While detailing her life and interactions with her husband, mother, sister, and assorted family members, these diaries also contain descriptions of her interactions with well-known African American public figures, some of whom became friends, like Langston Hughes, James Weldon Johnson, Georgia Douglas Johnson, W.E.B. DuBois, and Mary Terrell. In addition, approximately 2,568 items including manuscripts, pictures, and correspondence are housed in 120 volumes at the Alice Moore Dunbar-Nelson Collection located at the University of Delaware Morris Library Special Collections in Newark, Delaware.

Throughout her life, Dunbar-Nelson played a prominent role in the women's club movement, placing her in the ranks alongside such prominent African American women activists as Mary Church Terrell and Ida B. Wells. Her works have been included in numerous anthologies and collections. Her short story "Summer Session" is included in *Spooks, Spies, and Private Eyes: Black Mystery, Crime and Suspense Fiction* (1995). Her writings are also included in compilations of work by Southern writers, Southern women writers, and Writers of the Harlem Renaissance. Her prose, poetry, and drama are important contributions to the legacy of African American literature. With the publication in 1988 of the Schomburg Collection of her *Works*, and *Give Us Each Day: The Diary of Alice Dunbar-Nelson* published in 1984, her works, including previously unpublished manuscripts, are now accessible to a new generation of readers.

CRITICAL RECEPTION

Although Alice Dunbar-Nelson was a popular writer during her lifetime, twentieth-century literary critics have largely ignored her work. In his essay "Local Color in Louisiana" published in 1985, Thomas Richardson writes, "Even among specialists in

Afro-American literature the memory of Alice Dunbar-Nelson has grown dim" (205). There has, however, been a resurgence of interest in her life and works in the late twentieth century, in part elicited by the work of scholarship connecting Dunbar-Nelson to her contemporary Kate Chopin as well as to African American and feminist issues.

Initial reviews of Dunbar-Nelson's work were racially directed. While generally well received, the criticism for her first book *Violets and Other Tales* (1895) was not so much about its content as for what it symbolized for the advancement of the African American race as a whole. "One reviewer declared the book 'evidence of great intelligence among persons of African birth' " (Alexander 61). This impression of her work is observed in contemporary scholarship through her inclusion (when taught in the classroom) as a poet of the Harlem Renaissance.

Later scholarship on Alice Dunbar-Nelson's body of work locates it as that of a "local-color" writer. Encouraged early in their relationship by the popular Paul Laurence Dunbar to tell "those pretty little Creole stories," Dunbar-Nelson's short stories were particularly descriptive of the culture, social setting, history, and scenery of her New Orleans home. Unfortunately, this type of intimate view of any one particular landscape often serves to pigeonhole writers. In her essay "Varieties of Local Color," Merrill Skaggs remarks, "the local-color label has occasionally been used to denigrate the exceptional fiction of several twentieth-century women" (219). Critics of this genre malign the work as having limited appeal.

However, it is this same intimacy that allows Dunbar Nelson to position the reader within the text. "Although subtly deployed, Dunbar-Nelson's direct addresses to her readers—'you must admit' ("Tony's Wife" *Works* 1, 22) or 'you could not understand' ("La Juanita" 199)—create a particular mediated relationship among narrator, characters, and readers" (3), as noted by Kristina Brooks who in writing on Dunbar-Nelson's use of local-color also writes, "those whom Dunbar-Nelson directly addresses in her short fiction, are those who do not make their homes in New Orleans, the setting for Dunbar-Nelson's stories in two published volumes, or the Upper East side New York neighborhood that serves as a setting for an unpublished volume of her short fiction" (4).

Dunbar-Nelson's coded depictions are interpreted by contemporary scholars like Gloria Hull as being racially ambiguous, and as "separating her from her black experience" (52). Violet Harrington Bryan in her essay, "Race and Gender in the Early Works of Alice Dunbar-Nelson," follows Hull's lead, criticizing the apparent lack of racial themes in Dunbar-Nelson's fiction because her characters' racial identities do not always seem clear (71). In contrast, critics like Brooks feel that by bringing her reader into the setting, through her use of language, real events, and locales, Dunbar-Nelson, while not overtly attacking the inequality of the races, is nonetheless conveying the tragedy, frustration, and life of the Creole of color.

Feminist readings of her work include Mattie Richardson's proposal that Dunbar-Nelson's diary be used to "rethink the political work and effect of the Black women's club movement" (63); Mary Loeffelholz's commentary from *Experimental Lives: Women and Literature, 1900–1945*, where she interprets "I Sit and Sew" as the dramatic monologue of a woman stifled by the "pretty futile seam she works on [. . .]. Adding that the poem's 'impassioned commentary on the narrowness of culturally defined sexual roles' (Hull, 80) is clear, as is the connection it draws between those sex roles and militarism" (184); and Kristin Bloomberg's examination of women's dissatisfaction with their lot in the present and the future in Dunbar-Nelson's "A Modern Undine."

Additional perspectives on Dunbar-Nelson's work and life continue to appear in prominent scholarly journals and important works of criticism. Dunbar-Nelson's poetry and prose feature conventional form with unconventional depth while proffering critical historical, cultural, and social examinations.

BIBLIOGRAPHY

Works by Alice Dunbar-Nelson

The Dunbar Speaker and Entertainer; The Poet and His Song. Naperville: J. L. Nichols, 1920.
The Goodness of St. Rocque and Other Stories. New York: Dodd Mead, 1899.
The Works of Alice Dunbar-Nelson, edited by Gloria T. Hull. New York: Oxford University Press, 1988.
Violets and Other Tales. Boston: Monthly Review Press, 1895.

Studies of Alice Dunbar-Nelson's Works

Alexander, Eleanor. *Lyrics of Sunshine and Shadow: The Tragic Courtship and Marriage of Paul Laurence Dunbar and Alice Ruth Moore: A History of Love and Violence among the African American Elite.* New York: New York University Press, 2001.
Bloomberg, Kristen. *Tracing Arachne's Web: Myth and Feminist Fiction.* Gainesville: University of Florida Press, 2001.
Boyd, Herb, ed. *Autobiography of a People: Three Centuries of African American History Told by Those Who Lived It.* New York: Doubleday, 2000.
Brooks, Kristina. "Alice Dunbar-Nelson's Local Colors of Ethnicity, Class, and Place." *MELUS* 23.2 (Summer 1998): 3–26.
Bryan, Violet H. "Race and Gender in the Early Works of Alice Dunbar-Nelson." In *Louisiana Literature and Literary Figures*, edited by Mathé Allain. Lafayette: Center for Louisiana Studies, University of Louisiana, 2004.
Hardy, Gayle J. *American Women Civil Rights Activists: Biobibliographies of 68 Leaders, 1825–1992.* Jefferson, NC: McFarland, 1993.
Hull, Gloria. *Color, Sex & Poetry: Three Women Writers of the Harlem Renaissance.* Bloomington: Indiana University Press, 1987.
———, ed. *Give Us Each Day: The Diary of Alice Dunbar-Nelson.* New York: W. W. Norton, 1984.
———. "Shaping Contradictions: Alice Dunbar-Nelson and the Black Creole Experience." In *Louisiana Literature and Literary Figures*, edited by Mathé Allain. Lafayette: Center for Louisiana Studies, University of Louisiana, 2004.
———. "Researching Alice Dunbar-Nelson: A Personal and Literary Perspective." *Feminist Studies* 6: 314–20.
Hull, Gloria, Patricia B. Scott, and Barbara Smith, eds. "Researching Alice Dunbar-Nelson: A Personal and Literary Perspective." In *All the Women Are White, All the Blacks Are Men, but Some of Us Are Brave: Black Women's Studies.* Old Westbury, NY: Feminist Press, 1982.
Johnson, A. "Writing within the Script: Alice Dunbar-Nelson's Ellen Fenton." *Studies in American Fiction* 19 (Autumn 1991): 165–74.
Johnson, P. "The Lives and Love of Paul Laurence Dunbar and Alice Dunbar-Nelson." *Black Issues Book Review* 4.2 (March/April 2002): 71–72.
Kein, Sybil, ed. *Creole: The History and Legacy of Louisiana's Free People of Color.* Baton Rouge: Louisiana State University Press, 2000.
Lerner, Gerda. *Black Women in White America: A Documentary History.* New York: Vintage Books, 1972.

Loeffelholz, Mary. *Experimental Lives: Women and Literature, 1900–1945.* New York: Maxwell Macmillan International, 1992.

Marable, Manning, ed. *Freedom on My Mind: The Columbia Documentary History of the African American Experience.* New York: Columbia University Press, 2003.

Richardson, Mattie U. *Journal of Women's History* 15.3 (Autumn 2003): 63.

Richardson, Thomas. "Local Color in Louisiana." In *The History of Southern Literature*, edited by James D. Rubin, Jr. Baton Rouge: University of Louisiana Press, 1985.

Skaggs, Merrill M. "Varieties of Local Color." In *The History of Southern Literature*, edited by James D. Rubin, Jr. Baton Rouge: University of Louisiana Press, 1985.

Staples, B. "She Was Hard to Impress." *New York Times Book Review*, April 14, 1985, 20.

Tylee, C. M. "Womanist Propaganda, African-American Great War Experience, and Cultural Strategies of the Harlem Renaissance: Plays by Alice Dunbar-Nelson and Mary P. Burrill." *Women's Studies International Forum* 20 (January/February 1997): 153–63.

Williams, Ora. "Works by and about Alice Ruth (Moore) Dunbar-Nelson: A Bibliography." *CLA Journal* 19: 322–26.

Denisa E. Chatman-Riley

GRACE EDWARDS-YEARWOOD (1934?–)

BIOGRAPHICAL NARRATIVE

Born and raised in a middle-class family in Harlem, New York, as Grace Faith Edwards, novelist Edwards-Yearwood began writing at the age of seven. The seventy-one-year-old creative-writing teacher now lives in Brooklyn and spends some time living in the Bronx.

As one of forty-five African American published crime fiction writers, Edwards-Yearwood's novels are at the top of reading lists across America. This talented author penetrated the walls of the publishing market by meeting Terry McMillan's agent, who heard an excerpt from *In the Shadow of the Peacock* and in turn put Edwards-Yearwood in contact with the publishers of McGraw-Hill, who published the novel in 1988. This connection led to a successful writing career that has been marked with book releases, tours, and signings, but her career has also distinguished Edwards-Yearwood as a crime fiction writer.

MAJOR WORKS

Edwards-Yearwood has a distinct knack for writing engaging and suspenseful mysteries that captivate her audience and leave them in a state of anticipation for the next novel. Mali Anderson, an astute sleuth who is the central character of the critically acclaimed four-novel Mali Anderson Mysteries, is a former police officer in the New York Police Department who uses her wit and smoothness to navigate through suspense-filled storylines. Edwards-Yearwood highlights Mali Anderson's keen method of solving mysteries, which is an underlying and cohesive thread in the novel series, as well as tracks Mali Anderson's personal development as a character, thus making her multi-dimensional and relatable.

Edwards-Yearwood intrigues the reader by introducing new plots and twists that nurture the murder mystery theme. The plot-thickened storylines are not only centered around the gruesome crimes of the inner city, but the storylines also capitalize on and celebrate the richness of Harlem by intertwining the history of jazz and the nightclubs of years past. Edwards-Yearwood hopes that her discussion of the jazz and night clubs will help her readers gain a sense of what life was like in Harlem during the mid-1900s.

Edwards-Yearwood's novels include her first novel *If I Should Die*, which received an Anthony Award nomination for Best First Book; *A Toast before Dying*, which won the 1999 Fiction Honor Award from the Black Caucus of the American Literary Association; *No Time to Die*; *In the Shadow of the Peacock*, which is the result of her graduate thesis in the creative-writing program at Columbia University, New York; *Do or Die*; and *The Viaduct*, which deviates from her Mali Anderson Mysteries but contains elements of romance, her first writing that mixes love and murder.

Except *In the Shadow of the Peacock* and *The Viaduct*, film and television rights have been sold to CBS for her novels. Edwards-Yearwood also contributed to *Shades of Black: Crime and Mystery Stories by African American Writers* edited by Eleanor Taylor Bland and is completing a romance novel titled *The Blind Alley*.

CRITICAL RECEPTION

Despite the awards Grace Edwards-Yearwood's work has received, very little critical attention has been given to it. One critic, however, does see merit in her work. Jessica Kimball Printz says Edwards-Yearwood's writing "successfully captures the intricate powerplay in intersexual relationships against a backdrop of historical flux" (1066).

BIBLIOGRAPHY

Works by Grace Edwards-Yearwood

Do or Die. New York: Doubleday and Company, Incorporated, 2000.
If I Should Die. New York: Bantam Books, Incorporated, 1998.
In the Shadow of the Peacock. McGraw-Hill, 1988.
No Time to Die. New York: Bantam Books, Incorporated, 2000.
A Toast before Dying. New York: Random House, 1999.
The Viaduct. New York: Doubleday and Company, 2003.

Study of Grace Edwards-Yearwood's Works

Printz, Jessica Kimball. "Marketable Bodies, Possessive Peacocks, and Text as Excess: Edwards
    Yearwood's *In the Shadow of the Peacock*." *Callaloo* 15.4 (1992): 1066–84.

Jasmin J. Vann

ZILPHA ELAW (1790?–1846?)

BIOGRAPHICAL NARRATIVE

An Afro-American Methodist preacher born around 1790, autobiographer Zilpha Elaw forms part of an antebellum tradition of black women evangelists, traveling missionaries, and lay spiritual leaders. Her religious peers of the nineteenth century include Jarena Lee, Julia A. J. Foote, Rebecca Cox Jackson, Amanda Berry Smith, and Sojourner Truth. A freewoman, Elaw is best known for her spiritual autobiography *Memoirs of the Life, Religious Experience, Ministerial Travels and Labours of Mrs. Zilpha Elaw*, published in London in 1846.

A Pennsylvania native, Elaw was exposed to religion by her parents at an early age. After their untimely deaths, she grew up serving as a domestic in the Philadelphia household of a Quaker couple. At fourteen, having taken the Lord's name in vain and suffered a vivid dream of retribution, she began an earnest course of meditation and prayer. She braved paralyzing anxiety, guilt, tears, and other emotions associated with affective piety. Shortly after her initial encounter with area Methodists, Elaw entertained her first vision of Christ while performing daily chores. This direct manifestation of divine love initiated her spiritual conversion. She joined the Methodist Episcopal Society in 1808. Disconnected from her surviving kin (an older brother and a younger sister), often gravely ill, and plagued by lingering doubts, Elaw was "upheld, confirmed, instructed, sanctified, and directed" by the Lord (*Memoirs* 60). As with other religious visionaries, she weathered temptations from Satan, her "unwearied adversary" (83). Through heavenly surrender to Christ, her vacillations of faith were transformed into a simultaneously active and contemplative life.

Zilpha married a fuller, Joseph Elaw, in 1810. The pair encountered difficulties in conjugal life owing to a disparity in their level of religious commitment. Elaw portrays her husband as a nonbeliever and occasionally hostile critic of religion. Although fond of music and dancing, he was ultimately tolerant of his wife's asceticism and exceptional religious fervor. The couple resided just outside of Philadelphia until economic circumstances compelled their relocation to Burlington, New Jersey. In 1812, a daughter, Rebecca, was born.

The camp meeting of 1817 marked a seminal moment of Elaw's religious ascent. Mass revivalism allowed Christians to share wisdom and atone for sins through collective witnessing. At one such event, Elaw was struck down by God and publicly sanctified (i.e., cleansed of sin and filled with the divine spirit). She then felt compelled to preach and administer pastoral care to individuals of both races and various classes. This special calling comprised her "family or household ministry" (71), more or less socially acceptable for churchgoing women of the time. While generally robust, her sense of mission had to be reiterated by both her dying sister and a mysterious voice in order for her to fully embrace the role of sanctified preacher and holy woman.

Joseph's death by tuberculosis in 1823 forced Elaw to revert to domestic work for survival. Awareness of white racism compelled her to open a school for black children where she taught despite poor health. It had been explicitly and repeatedly revealed that she must "preach the gospel and . . . travel far and wide" (82), but she still struggled with her vocation. Later, when sufficiently inspired, she closed the school and set off to preach in Philadelphia and New York, returning home in 1828. At this time, she received intimations through both a heavenly medium and a dream that she would one day visit London, England. This voyage would occur in 1840. In the decade or so prior, she made preaching pilgrimages to the Southern slave states (at risk of being arrested or kidnapped into bondage) and toured such northeastern locales as Baltimore, Washington, Alexandria, Annapolis, New Haven, Hartford, Boston, and Cape Cod. She also ministered throughout the states of Maine, Vermont, and New Hampshire.

Elaw's prayers helped restore the ailing and moribund on more than one occasion. She herself suffered a number of near-death episodes but regained her health through divine grace. Her public ministry, although unlicensed and largely unaffiliated, achieved much in the way of repentance, conversions, and spontaneous fellowship. Gospel rivalries, Presbyterian disapproval, and certain prejudiced individuals were her major stumbling blocks during her travels.

Becoming a grandmother in 1834 did not deter her from leaving home again a year after returning to the Philadelphia area. A persistent cause for brooding, the trip to England finally materialized after a propitious encounter in Providence, Rhode Island. Despite another grave illness, Elaw managed to preach extensively for five years and produce a detailed account of her peripatetic life. While she planned to return to America in 1845, it is unknown whether she did or not. The time and circumstances of her death also remain a mystery.

MAJOR WORK

Elaw's *Memoirs* comprise what is essentially a hybrid text. It illuminates an intensely *personal* journey for the purpose of *public* edification. The central character is a speaking subject liberated by means of strict conformity to Christian beliefs. Bondage takes the form of spiritual temptation and doubt, not the tangible chains of chattel slavery. Her discourse moves away from the primacy of the black body (traditionally the site of political struggle and material reification during the nineteenth century) to the immortal soul, colorless and priceless before the judgment of the Lord.

In terms of literary history, *Memoirs* may interest those acquainted with the legends/ early autobiographies of medieval Christian mystics (among them, the serial traveler Margery Kempe). The same applies to those familiar with the Euro-American genre of Puritan spiritual autobiography. Characteristic similarities emerge in Elaw's writing: intimate communications with the Lord; renunciation of sin and "worldliness"; the (female) body as an index and agent of divine will; the prevalence of supernatural apparitions, voices, clairvoyance, and miracles; attempted corruption by Satan; and the triumph of the subject over nonbelievers, backsliders, and sinners.

Written in elevated diction and with copious recourse to the Scripture, this document is less a sinful woman's confession than a regional and trans-Atlantic travelogue. While politically cognizant (racial prejudice and patriarchal gender bias do arise in context), the work leans more toward *meditatio Christi* than proto-feminist or abolitionist manifesto. Because of its rhetorical sophistication, the ideal reader was educated, Christian, liberal-minded, and probably white, not one of Elaw's colored and illiterate brethren.

Inflected through a deliberate substructure of omissions, understatements, and amplifications, the subject moves almost seamlessly between black and white communities. She heals the sick, humbles the wicked, encourages Christian solidarity, and challenges the pervasiveness of Mammonism and moral flux. It is an intentional irony that the speaker is triply burdened—a "poor and ignorant . . . creature" (75), a "poor, coloured female" (89), and a "poor weak female" (104)—yet stands as one of the divine-elect. This trio of alterity had undeniable political implications, for surely such a choice of messengers subverted existing assumptions about black and female inferiority.

Aside from its biblical allusiveness and metafictional sensitivity to the effects of language ("Take heed of what you read" [52]), *Memoirs* demands critical attention for its portrait of an independent black female and early spiritual leader. At a time when slaves and the less privileged classes of women were virtual prisoners of the home, Elaw privileged her role as traveling evangelist above the more conventional and socially acceptable guises for women: obedient wife, doting mother, and men's intellectual subordinate.

CRITICAL RECEPTION

Declaring Elaw an avatar of "radical spiritual individualism" (3), William L. Andrews introduced his seminal edition of *Memoirs* in 1986 alongside writings by Jarena Lee and Julia Foote. It was after *Sisters of the Spirit*'s release that substantial contemporary scholarship began to emerge on Elaw. She only received perfunctory consideration, if any, in previous studies of black autobiography, likely overshadowed by more charismatic evangelists of her ilk. Furthermore, as has often been the case with early black women's literary production, gaps in knowledge and accessibility were barriers to widespread exposure and study. Among the most recent monographs to treat Elaw is Yolanda Pierce's *Hell without Fires* (2005). It examines such themes as the hermeneutics of biblical retelling, tropes of freedom as they relate to personal and collective spirituality, and generic conventions of Afro-American spiritual writing. Richard J. Douglass-Chin's chapter in *Preacher Woman Sings the Blues* (2001) develops other pertinent issues: Elaw as a "subversive eunuch-subject" (35); her paradoxically healthy poverty ("lack of whiteness, lack of riches, lack of social position" [55]); and the various pedagogical imports of the text. Helpful background into the genre of black spiritual autobiography may be found in Andrews's *To Tell a Free Story: The First Century of Afro-American Autobiography* (Urbana: University of Illinois Press, 1986) and Joanne M. Braxton's *Black Women Writing Autobiography* (Philadelphia: Temple University Press, 1989).

BIBLIOGRAPHY

Work by Zilpha Elaw

Memoirs of the Life, Religious Experience, Ministerial Travels and Labours of Mrs. Zilpha Elaw, an American Female of Colour; Together with Some Account of the Great Religious Revivals in America. 1846. Reprint, *Sisters of the Spirit: Three Black Women's Autobiographies of the Nineteenth Century.* Bloomington: Indiana University Press, 1986, 49–160.

Studies of Zilpha Elaw's Work

Douglass-Chin, Richard J. *Preacher Woman Sings the Blues: The Autobiographies of Nineteenth-Century African American Evangelists*. Columbia: University of Missouri Press, 2001.

Haynes, Rosetta R. "Zilpha Elaw's Serial Domesticity: An Unsentimental Journey." In *Gender, Genre, and Identity in Women's Travel Writing*, edited by Kristi Siegel, 181–91. New York: Peter Lang, 2004.

Hunter, William R. "Do Not Be Conformed Unto This World: An Analysis of Religious Experience in the Nineteenth-Century African American Spiritual Narrative." *Nineteenth-Century Studies* 8 (1994): 75–88.

Moody, Joycelyn. *Sentimental Confessions: Spiritual Narratives of Nineteenth-Century African American Women*. Athens: University of Georgia Press, 2001.

Pierce, Yolanda. *Hell without Fires: Slavery, Christianity, and the Antebellum Spiritual Narrative*. Gainesville: University Press of Florida, 2005.

Nancy Kang

MARI EVANS (1923–)

BIOGRAPHICAL NARRATIVE

Mari Evans is an educator who has also enjoyed a long career as a writer of poetry, children's books, nonfiction, and plays. She was born in Toledo, Ohio, on July 16, 1923. She grew up in the Toledo area and attended the University of Toledo. Although she initially studied fashion design, she eventually switched to creative writing—first short stories, then poetry. Her first professional writing job was as an assistant editor of information systems at a chain-manufacturing plant. Evans tends toward reserve when discussing details of her personal life, although she acknowledges she has been married and divorced and is the mother of two adult sons.

Throughout her long career as an educator, she has taught at Purdue University, Indiana University, Northwestern University, Washington University, Spelman College, the State University at Albany, and Cornell University, where she was distinguished poet-in-residence and an assistant professor in their Africana Studies and Research Center. For her literary contributions she has been awarded many prizes, including the first poetry award presented by the Black Academy of Arts and Letters (1975), an Outstanding Woman of the Year Award (1976), the National Endowment of the Arts Creative Writing Award (1981–1982), and the Alain Locke–Gwendolyn Brooks Award for Excellence in Literature (1995). Evans has also received many fellowships, including the John Hay Whitney Fellowship (1965), a Woodrow Wilson Grant (1968), and residencies at the MacDowell Colony (1975) and Yaddo (1984); she was the Copeland Fellow at Amherst College in 1980.

From 1968 to 1973, she created, hosted, and directed a television show in Indianapolis called *The Black Experience*, one of just three on-air shows about African Americans in the United States at that time. Her film *Remembering Langston: 1968*, a documentary about Langston Hughes, is believed to be the first film by a black filmmaker to so honor the American poet. In 1997, the government of Uganda chose her image to adorn a postage stamp. In 1998, the Chicago State University inducted her into their National Literary Hall of Fame for Writers of African Descent, and in 1999 Martin University awarded her an honorary doctor of humane letters. After several years in Indianapolis, Indiana, Evans now resides in California, where she continues to write.

MAJOR WORKS

With the 1970 publication of *I Am a Black Woman*, Mari Evans received praise for her use of idiomatic speech to celebrate the strengths and document the struggles of African Americans. "Who Can Be Born Black," perhaps her most frequently anthologized poem, closes the collection. In this poem, the speaker of the short, lyrical lines revels in the sheer bliss of being black, even while acknowledging that sometimes being black poses problems. The speaker concludes by wondering how someone could be black and not be jubilant over his or her race. This celebratory tone of racial pride resonates throughout Evans's work, which also includes prose, books for children, and plays.

The celebration of African American identity reflects Evans's participation in the Black Arts Movement, often considered the literary component of the black nationalism of the 1960s and 1970s. This political movement proposed self-reliance, economic independence, and self-respect for African Americans; some members even aspired to a separate country for African Americans. Such slogans as "Black Is Beautiful" and "Black Power" demonstrate these core values. The Black Arts Movement developed after the 1965 assassination of Malcolm X and used all types of literary expression— writing, music, choreography, and drama—to explore the cultural history and contemporary experience of blacks in the United States (sometimes called the diaspora as a way of indicating that Africa was the true homeland). Much of the art produced had strong political foundations: it tried to instill a sense of pride in its audience by establishing connections to African art, clothing, and dance and by encouraging a community-based art, or the Black Aesthetic. Along with fellow writers such as Amiri Baraka, Sonia Sanchez, and Nikki Giovanni, Evans used verse to represent the African American struggle to overcome poverty and racism in *Where Is All the Music?* (1968). Poems like "If There Be Sorrow," "I Would Encompass Millions," and "into blackness softly," from *I Am a Black Woman*, encourage their readers to express their common pain while coming together toward the revolutionary goal of empowerment.

Along with the belief in the revolutionary possibilities of art comes the belief that artists have the power—and the obligation—to help their audience, another dominant theme of Evans's work. In the poem "Speak the Truth to the People" (1970), the speaker extols the necessity of education: without learning, and without sage advice from their leaders, blacks will remain fragmented and victimized. Another poem, "The School-house" (1981), compares a school to a treasure so precious it must be guarded by armed forces. "[O]nce again the poets" (1981) imagines that verse writers, with their talent for observation, possess the ability to prophesize about potential disasters. "Let Us Be That Something" (1981) commends its readers to be role models for young people. Evans's children's books probe equally serious subjects in order to assist and educate. The epistolary *Dear Corinne, Tell Somebody!* (1999) helps children understand abuse by portraying a young girl helping her friend through a difficult time. It also explains what children should do if they are or someone they know is being sexually abused.

To further empower readers, Evans writes in distinctly black idioms and cadences. *Singing Black: Alternative Nursery Rhymes* (1998) attempts to instill self-respect and racial dignity in its readers by telling stories from black history and culture. *Nightstar: 1973– 1978* (1981) contains many poems whose rhythms are derived from the blues, including "Blues in B^b," "Black Queen Blues," "Cellblock Blues," and "Tune for Two Fingers." In *A Dark and Splendid Mass* (1992), Evans poeticizes everyday speech; two poems in this collection, "Oral History: Found Poetry" and "Found Poetry" come directly from ordinary language, from a story told by the speaker's father and from a televised interview with Winnie Mandela upon her release from prison in 1988, respectively. Early poems from *I Am a Black Woman*, as well as *Nightstar*, employ variant spellings and pronunciations: "God" becomes "gaaahd," "the" becomes "d" or "da," and "to" becomes "t." As she explains in her 1980 essay "My Father's Passage," Evans writes "for what will nod Black heads over common denominators . . . how it has been/is/must be, for us" (167).

In "My Father's Passage," Evans also describes reading the poetry of Langston Hughes for the first time: she instantly recognized both a commitment to rendering black experience and a commitment to style. Like her literary predecessor, Evans's poems have a political agenda, as well as attention to traditional poetic concerns, including typography on the page, metaphor, and imagery. The poems in *A Dark and Splendid Mass* demonstrate Evans's use of varying line lengths: some lines are indented and short; some are left justified and long; some poems consist of multiple stanzas; some consist of just one set of lines. She bases the visual layouts on the poems' content and tonality. "Crystal," a word that appears throughout the poems in *I Am a Woman* and *Nightstar*, symbolizes her desire for clarity, or the exact delineation of an idea or experience; indeed, she explores the importance of clarity in her work in her 2005 nonfiction book *Clarity as Concept*. "Let Me Tell You How to Meet the Day" (1992) moves from the abstract—attempts to define "life," "love," and the "self"—to the concrete concluding image of people raising their arms to welcome a new day. Here, as elsewhere throughout Evans's poems, the precisely pinpointed image or experience stands in for optimism: articulation, thus, becomes the first step toward freedom and independence.

CRITICAL RECEPTION

Evans uses "My Father's Passage" to explain her writing goals: "I try for a poetic language that says, 'This is *who* we are, where we have been, *where* we are. This is where we must go. And *this* is what we must do' " (169). Scholarly work on Evans has focused primarily on the political themes and motivations behind her words. As a member of the Black Arts Movement, Evans believes that art is perhaps the best method of not only informing a people of their oppression but also providing the people with a means of escaping their political domination. Like many poets of this time, Evans took Amiri Baraka's 1969 poem "Black Art" as a call to take up the pen and write her people out of their subjugation by white society. To this end, Evans writes primarily for a black audience and sees writing as a form of social resistance.

David Dorsey, in "The Art of Mari Evans," analyzes the didacticism inherent in Evans's work: she imbibes her writing with messages so that her intended audience might benefit from her understanding of oppressive political institutions, including white-controlled media and educational facilities. Throughout her work, Evans teaches her audience to take pride in their cultural heritage. The musical *River of My Song* (1977) incorporates her poems, African music, and the lyrics of Langston Hughes. *I Look at Me!* (1974) portrays a community of black people—bus drivers, doctors, dentists, grocers, and so on—to teach simple vocabulary to young children. From an early age, therefore, children learn to associate blackness with possibility, not with impossibility.

Solomon Edwards, in "Affirmation in the Works of Mari Evans," focuses on the positive themes inherent within Evans's poems, including inspiration, optimism, and celebratory assertions. In poems like "I Am a Black Woman" (1970) and in plays like *Boochie* (1979), Evans transforms the word *black* from a potentially negative racial epithet to a glorious label. Her poetic and dramatic speakers command respect through their very acts of self-definition: rather than let society define them, the speakers repeatedly identify their race as a way of controlling their identities. In this way, *black* becomes equated with strength, pride, respect, and positivity. As Edwards explains, Evans "affirms Black *joie de vivre*" (198).

Some critics compare Evans to other important writers of the Black Arts Movement, including dramatists Ed Bullins and Ntozake Shange, as well as poets Sonia Sanchez and Nikki Giovanni. Other critics, including Joyce Joyce and John Reilly, contrast Evans's poems to those of Gwendolyn Brooks, since both poets attempt to characterize black-ness. Lucille Clifton also explores the multiple meanings of "black" and "woman." Frequently, Evans links words together as a way of heightening their definitions: "saf-fronbrown" ("Apologia," 1970) and "fakefurred" ("Maria Pina & The B & G Grill," 1981). This avant-garde technique connects her to e.e. cummings, a modernist poet who also combined words for poetic effect. Her attention to the visual and tonal effects of her poems shows the inter-movement influence within Black Arts between Evans, Ishmael Reed, Welton Smith, and others. Like the writer Toi Derricotte, Evans prefers self-definition to societal definition, particularly in terms of race and gender, and like the poet Ai, Evans uses dramatic personae to explore universal emotions and common social conflicts. Borrowing rhythms from the blues and jazz has a long history within African American poetry, from Countee Cullen, Sterling Brown, and other poets of the Harlem Renaissance of the 1920s to Evans to Michael S. Harper and Kevin Young. The versi-fication of racial pride, rather than technical innovation, will be Evans's lasting literary legacy.

BIBLIOGRAPHY

Works by Mari Evans

Children's Books
The Day They Made Biriyani (1982).
Dear Corinne, Tell Somebody! Love. Annie: A Book about Secrets. East Orange, NJ: Just Us Books, 1999.
I Look at Me! Chicago: Third World Books, 1974.
J.D. New York: Doubleday, 1973.
Jim Flying High. New York: Doubleday, 1979.
Rap Stories (1974).
Singing Black: Alternative Nursery Rhymes for Children. East Orange, NJ: Just Us Books, 1998.

Critical Work Edited by Mari Evans
Black Women Writers (1950–1980): A Critical Evaluation. New York: Anchor, 1983.

Films and Television Shows
The Black Experience (1968–1973).
Remembering Langston: 1968 (1968).

Nonfiction/Prose
"Blackness: A Definition." *Negro Digest* 19 (November 1969): 19–21.
Clarity as Concept: A Poet's Perspective. Chicago: Third World Press, 2005.
"Contemporary Black Literature." *Black World* 19 (June 1970): 4, 93–94.
"Ethos and Creativity." In *Where We Live: Essays about Indiana*, edited by David Hoppe. Bloomington: Indiana University Press, 1989.
"My Father's Passage." In *Black Women Writers (1950–1980): A Critical Evaluation*, edited by Evans. New York: Doubleday, 1983.

Poetry
A Dark and Splendid Mass. New York: Writers, 1992.
I Am a Black Woman. New York: Writers and Readers Publishing, 1970.

Nightstar: 1973–1978. Irvine: University of California Center for Afro-American Studies, 1981.
Where Is All the Music? London: P. Breman, 1968.

Plays and Musicals
Boochie (1979)
Eyes (1979)
Glide and Sons (1979)
Portrait of Man (1979)
River of My Song (1977)

Studies of Mari Evans's Works

Dorsey, David. "The Art of Mari Evans." In *Black Women Writers (1950–1980): A Critical Evaluation*, edited by Mari Evans, 170–89. Garden City, NY: Anchor Press/Doubleday, 1984.

Edwards, Solomon. "Affirmation in the Works of Mari Evans." In *Black Women Writers (1950–1980): A Critical Evaluation*, edited by Mari Evans, 190–200. Garden City, NY: Anchor Press/Doubleday, 1984.

Joyce, Joyce, and John Reilly. "Mari Evans." *Heath Anthology Online Instructors Guide.* http://college.hmco.com/english/heath/syllabuild/iguide/evans.html (accessed May 30, 2005).

Peppers, Wallace M. "Mari Evans." In *Dictionary of Literary Biography, Volume 41: Afro-American Poets Since 1955*, edited by Trudier Harris and Thadious M. Davis, 117–23. Detroit: Gale Group, 1985.

Reuben, Paul P. "Chapter 10: Late Twentieth Century, 1945 to the Present—Mari Evans." *PAL: Perspectives in American Literature—A Research and Reference Guide.* http://www.csustan.edu/english/reuben/pal/chap10/evans.html (accessed May 21, 2005).

Sedlack, Robert P. "Mari Evans: Consciousness and Craft." *College Language Association Journal* 15 (1972): 465–76.

Jessica Allen

SARAH WEBSTER FABIO (1928–1979)

BIOGRAPHICAL NARRATIVE

Poet, literary critic, and educator Sarah Fabio was born on January 20, 1928, in Nashville, Tennessee. She attended Fisk University, graduating in 1946. While there, she married Cyril Fabio, and the couple went on to have children and eventually the family settled in California. In 1965, Sarah earned a master's degree from San Francisco State College. She then went on to a number of teaching positions, first at Merritt College in Oakland, a focal point of the seminal Black Power Movement. Her involvement in the movement led her to push for African American literature courses being part of the college curriculum. She would later teach at California College of Arts and Crafts, at the University of California at Berkeley (where she created the Black Studies department), and, following her 1972 divorce, at Oberlin College in Ohio, where she stayed until 1974. In 1976, while teaching and studying at the University of Wisconsin, she was diagnosed with colon cancer; consequently, she returned to California to stay with her daughter until her death on November 7, 1979.

MAJOR WORKS

Fabio's most significant work is *Rainbow Signs*, her 1973 collection of poetry comprising seven volumes. Like many of her other works, *Rainbow Signs* addresses a key theme: the need for negotiating the gap between the language of the dominant culture and "the Black mother-tongue" which she feels is "a possible, effective, poetic language" that reflects the African American experience ("A Black Paper" 76). *Jujus: Alchemy of the Blues*, the first volume of *Rainbow Signs*, emphasizes this struggle by placing two versions of the same poem on facing pages: one in standard English and one in dialect. She is also known for blending Western and non-Western literary metaphors and Western metaphors and the reality of black experience.

In addition to her poetry, Fabio also wrote a play (*M.L. King Pageant*) and several essays. These works tend to focus on overcoming racism and the move from slave to self. In "Tripping with Black Writing," for instance, she speaks of the need for writing to encompass "the Black man, his articulation of his experience, and his selfhood" (187).

CRITICAL RECEPTION

A very small body of critical response exists, as Fabio's work was seldom reviewed or commented on. In a largely favorable review of *A Mirror: A Soul*, Johari Amini praises the poems for addressing "the blkexperience of blkpeople" [sic]; he further praises their aurality because they have been produced "to sound like [African Americans] sound" (74). In a tribute appearing in the *Black Scholar* following her death, Carl Mack, Jr., deems her a "dynamic force in the black studies and black poetry movements of the 1960s and 1970s" (84).

BIBLIOGRAPHY

Works by Sarah Webster Fabio

Black Back: Back Black. Oberlin, OH: n.p., 1973.
"'Black Feeling, Black Talk, Black Judgement.' " *Black World* 19 (December 1970): 102–4.
Black Images/Black Resurrection. San Francisco: Julian Richardson, n.d.
"The Black Intellectual and the Crisis in Education in the U.S.A." In *Black Writers and Their Writing 22–24 Jan 1971.* The Ishmael Reed Papers. University of Delaware Library.
Black Is/A Panther Caged. San Francisco: Julian Richardson, n.d.
"A Black Paper: An Essay on Literature." *Negro Digest* 18 (July 1969): 27ff.
"Black Writer's Views on Literary Lions and Values." *Negro Digest* 17 (January 1968): 39.
Boss Soul. Oberlin, OH: n.p., 1973.
Boss Soul. Sound recording. Folkways, 1972.
Dark Debut: Three Women Coming. N.p.: n.p., 1966.
Dark Symphony in Duet: A Celebration of the Word; Seascapes, Love Poems, Tributes, Portraits, Black Talk, Africana. With Thomas L. Gayton. Seattle: University of Washington Black Studies Program, 1979.
Ed. *Double Dozens: An Anthology of Poets from Sterling Brown to Kali.* N.p.: n.p., 1966.
Jujus: Alchemy of the Blues. Oberlin, OH: n.p., 1973.
Jujus: Alchemy of the Blues. Sound recording. Folkways, 1976.
Jujus and Jubilees: Critical Essays in Rhyme about Poets/Musicians/Black Heroes. Oberlin, OH: n.p., 1973.
"Language Arts and Black Bi-Lingualism." *Curriculum Study Commission, Central California Council of Teachers of English* September 26–28, 1969.
A Mirror: A Soul, a Two-part Volume of Poems. San Francisco: J. Richardson, 1969.
M.L. King Pageant. N.p.: n.p., 1967.
My Own Thing. Oberlin, OH: n.p., 1973.
Night Sounds and Other Poems. M.A. thesis, San Francisco State College, 1965.
No Crystal Stair: A Socio-Drama of the History of Black Women in the U.S.A. N.p.: n.p., 1967.
Race Results, USA, 1966. Detroit: Broadside Press, 1967.
Rainbow Signs. 7 vols. N.p.: Phase II, 1973.
Saga of the Black Man. Oakland: n.p., 1968.
Soul Ain't; Soul Is: The Hurt of It All. Oberlin, OH: n.p., 1973.
Soul Ain't; Soul Is. Sound recording. Folkways, 1973.
Together/To the Tune of Coltrane's "Equinox." Oberlin, OH: n.p., 1973.
Together/To the Tune of Coltrane's "Equinox." Sound recording. Folkways, 1977.
"Tripping with Black Writing." In *The Black Aesthetic*, edited by Addison Gayle, Jr., 182–91. Garden City: Doubleday, 1971.
"Who Speaks Negro? What Is Black?" *Negro Digest* 17 (September–October 1968): 33–37.

Studies of Sarah Webster Fabio's Works

Jones, Meta DuEwa. "Jazz Prosodies: Orality and Textuality." *Callaloo* 25 (Winter 2002): 66–91.
Mack, Carl, Jr. "In Memoriam Sarah Webster Fabio—1928–1979." *Black Scholar* 11 (1979): 84.
Rainbow Black: Poet Sarah Fabio. Berkeley: University of California Extension Media Center, 1993.
Ward, Jerry W. "Reading South: Poets Mean and Poets Signify—A Note on Origins." *African American Review* 27 (Spring 1993): 125–26.

Richard A. Iadonisi

JESSIE REDMON FAUSET (1882–1961)

BIOGRAPHICAL NARRATIVE

Born on April 27, 1882, in Camden County, New Jersey, Jessie Redmon Fauset, the youngest of seven children, was a writer, critic, editor, and teacher. Also a highly educated member of DuBois's "Talented Tenth," Fauset graduated Phi Beta Kappa from Cornell University and was fluent in French and well read in British, French, and African American literature. From 1919 to 1926, Fauset served as the literary editor of the *Crisis*, the journal of the civil rights organization, the National Association for the Advancement of Colored People (NAACP). She was hired as the *Crisis*'s literary editor to "promote this first flush of artistic endeavor [and] proved an astute and responsive advocate of others' work. As [literary] editor, Fauset published (some for the first time) those writers who went on to become the most prominent figures of the Harlem movement—[including Claude McKay, Anne Spencer, and Langston Hughes]" (McDowell x). As a patron of the Harlem Renaissance, Fauset published other artists and helped develop "their literary careers by championing their work" (Knopf xxvii). Additionally, she was also known for hosting social gatherings in her home which facilitated discussions of poetry and literature and conversations in French.

As a result of her "high-society" profile, contemporary impressions of Fauset's birth and upbringing have erroneously described her as hailing from an aristocratic (or at least prosperous) family. However, Fauset came from a large and very poor family. Her parents, Redmon Fauset and Annie Seamon Fauset, had seven children and, after her mother's death and her father's remarriage to a widow with three children of her own, another three children were born to her father and stepmother. In spite of this, Fauset's family was educated and cultured and her father, an outspoken Methodist Episcopal minister, instilled in her the desire to achieve success. With her family environment, combined with her own astuteness, Fauset performed very well in the Philadelphia Public School and the Philadelphia High School for Girls, which was well known for its high academic performers. An honor student in high school, Fauset applied to Bryn Mawr College which denied her admission because of her race, but the College sought out a scholarship on her behalf from Cornell University where Fauset attended and, in 1905, graduated with honors. After earning her B.A. degree, Fauset taught briefly in Baltimore and then in Washington, D.C., at the M Street High School from 1905 to 1919. In 1919, she earned an M.A. in French from the University of Pennsylvania.

In 1919, Fauset began to focus on her literary aspirations when she moved to New York and worked as the literary editor of the *Crisis* magazine (1919–1926). She also started writing her own fiction and contributing reviews, stories, and essays to the magazine. During this time, she cofounded (with W.E.B. DuBois) and edited the *Brownies Book: A Monthly Magazine for the Children of the Sun* (1920–1921). This publication, which featured historical biographies of prominent black people and other educational articles, is noteworthy, as Fauset's desire to teach children about their heritage also informs themes and characters in her novels. Additionally, beginning in 1924, with her first novel, *There Is Confusion*, Fauset, who was the most prolific writer of the New Negro movement, went on to publish "more novels than any of the other writers and won the respect of the white literary establishment (they gave her an autograph party at Macy's, the first Black to have this honor)" (Shockley 410). After the publication of her first novel, Fauset studied for six months at the Sorbonne, University of Paris beginning in 1925, and her interest in French literature and travel abroad can be seen in characters and settings in her novels, especially her female characters, who "journey through life, comparing the limitations put upon them as women of color with the comparable "freedom" they encounter in foreign settings" (Griffin 77). This tension is especially predominant in Fauset's last novel *Comedy: American Style* (1933). Fauset also published two other novels, *Plum Bun: A Novel without a Moral* (1929) and *The Chinaberry Tree: A Novel of American Life* (1931). After leaving the *Crisis*, Fauset taught mainly at DeWitt Clinton High School from 1927 to 1944, and then briefly at Hampton Institute from September 1949 to January 1950. During this time, she also lectured, traveled, and wrote poetry. In 1929, she married Herbert Harris, an insurance broker with whom she lived in Montclair, New Jersey, until his death in 1958, after which she moved to Philadelphia with her stepbrother Earl Huff until her own death on April 30, 1961.

MAJOR WORKS

There Is Confusion, inspired by the publication of T. S. Stribling's *Birthright* (1922) which depicted a stereotypical account of the "tragic mulatto," set out to convey a more realistic story of black life including light-skinned, educated blacks whom Fauset and other blacks felt were misrepresented in fictional accounts by whites. The novel is one of her most critically acclaimed, and, like all of her works, attempts to challenge prevailing sociopolitical myths about black people—including the belief in a monolithic black culture—and specifically focuses on women's physical and psychological reactions to the dual oppressions of race and gender in their lives. The novel focuses on two families, the Marshalls of New York and the Byes of Philadelphia. The Marshall family represents a generation of blacks who have transcended slavery to become middle class, while the Bye family involves generations of freeborn Philadelphia blacks who possess merely a "strain of white blood." In a reversal of the established racial order in other literary works, in Fauset's novel, the "white blood" is depicted as being responsible for the faults of Bye family members, including Peter Bye, the man whom Joanna Marshall marries at the novel's conclusion. Fauset uses these two families to stress the significance of racial heritage, including the interconnectedness between blacks and whites. As Thadious M. Davis suggests, "In tracing the complex connections between the black and white Bye families . . . [Fauset] dramatizes recurrent problems of miscegenation, obscured paternity, denial of birthright, and burdens of inherited guilt, which would preoccupy later novelists, such as William Faulkner in *Absalom, Absalom!*" (xi).

In *There Is Confusion*, Fauset, seemingly informed by her life experiences, revises the tale of the tragic mulatto and, moreover, expands roles for women through her female characters. For example, the plot reflects Fauset's upbringing, as its protagonist, Joanna Marshall, desires independence and career success but, with the influence of her mother, does not do so at the expense of devaluing domesticity: Marshall is ambitious and determined—she wants to be an artist and an influential black person—but also chooses to marry at the novel's conclusion. Thus, while the novel concludes with Joanna's commitment to starting a family, as a young girl, when she requests to hear a "story" about "somebody great," she tells her father, "like I'm going to be when I get to be a big girl" (9). This focus on a black woman's attempt to overcome obstacles of race and gender represents a theme in the work overall, wherein the narrative expresses more than just "a child's individual desires; she expresses the long-suppressed dreams of her father, and by extension, of other former slaves" (Davis xi). Although a flawed character (Joanna is both confident and elitist), she works to overcome obstacles and experiences a measure of success in a career as an artist and an influential individual: as the narrator explains, "Joanna was mightily interested in people who had a 'purpose' in life" (16).

The novel also explores the experiences of and connections between black women across class lines as another woman, Maggie Ellersley, is the hardworking daughter of a laundress and boarding house operator, but desires to transcend what she perceives as a "dreary existence" of domestic work. Through her successful accomplishments as a working woman, Maggie also represents expanded career choices for black women as she uses her skills to become a bookkeeper for the Marshall family's catering business, a manager of several beauty shops, and, later, a YMCA worker caring for injured soldiers in France. Eventually, Maggie abandons her career and marries Joanna's brother Phillip, who has been portrayed as a DuBoisian character in his desire to play a leadership role in uplifting black people. His dreams are thwarted, however, after his injuries from serving in World War I leave him in a debilitated condition, from which he succumbs shortly after his marriage to Maggie. The marriage itself, nonetheless, reflects both characters' desire for purposeful lives including Maggie's need to care for others. For example, at one point in the narrative, Maggie expresses her desire for the respectability of home and marriage when she poses this query to another character: " 'can't you see that I want to be safe like other women, with a home and protection?' " (193). Given this, while her marriage at first seems to suggest Fauset's capitulation to impulses contrary to expanding gender opportunities for women, Peter's death frees Maggie to return to her career in business while also giving her an opportunity to have a purposeful life. Overall, these African American women, from different socioeconomic classes, demonstrate the similar gender struggles that African American women experience in their attempts to overcome obstacles of racial oppression, with the additional component of class discrimination.

In her second—and most popular novel—*Plum Bun*, Fauset uses the figure of the mulatto and the passing motif to explore the effects of passing, ultimately demonstrating its disastrous implications. As Jacqueline Y. McLendon argues, Fauset attempts to show that "[blacks'] very belief in the necessity of passing—of attempting to escape the racialized body—is a legacy of slavery" (29). Angela Murray, the protagonist of *Plum Bun*, influenced by her mother's occasional passing for economic and social gains, develops the illusory belief that if she constructs herself to fit into ideals of the typical wealthy white man, she will succeed in gaining a secure and happy station in life. Accordingly, she desires to marry Roger Fielding, a white man, with whom marriage would represent the achievement of a fairy-tale life that her childhood experiences have nurtured in her. Ironically, her plan actually backfires, as her decision to follow this pattern actually closes opportunities for her to realize her desires of home and family. In the process, Angela experiences complete alienation from her family, particularly her dark-skinned sister Jinny. Moreover, Fielding ultimately betrays Angela, stealing her virtue without any consideration of marriage. His rejection, which correlates with

Angela's complete loss of all of her material comforts, brings her back to her race as the novel concludes with Angela's exile to Paris where she works to be self-reliant and vows that "so far as sides are concerned, I am on the coloured [sic] side" (49).

In *The Chinaberry Tree*, a novel with a smaller audience than her first two works, Fauset continues her exploration of race, gender, and class as this narrative focuses on female characters who seek to subvert the existing racial and sexual hierarchies which Fauset exposes as systems of oppression operating in black women's lives. Set in the early twentieth century in Red Brook, New Jersey, the novel centers on protagonist Melissa Paul, who seeks upward mobility through the attainment of marriage and a "traditional" family. Her quest is complicated by her attempts at reconciling the sexual histories of her mother and other female relatives in the novel. Indeed, a major theme and strength of the novel is Fauset's ability to bring together the seemingly irreconcilable tensions between black women's sexual freedom and respectability as the novel explores women's sexuality and their endeavors to maintain control over their bodies, a narratological move which critics have recognized as radical for the historical period in which the work appears. As Deborah McDowell argues, "Fauset introduced several topics into her novels that were hardly typical drawing room conversation topics in the mid-1920s. Promiscuity, exploitative sexual affairs, miscegenation, even incest appear in her novels" ("The Neglected" 87). For example, in *The Chinaberry Tree*, Fauset depicts black women's sexuality in "illicit" affairs with both white and black men while allowing characters such as Melissa to explore traditional, "respectable" relationships. Ultimately, although Melissa initially believes that a traditional relationship should be intraracial, she later understands the freedom associated with one's ability to make decisions about sexual partners or husbands and realizes how racism and gender conditioning have historically oppressed black women in their control of their own bodies and destinies.

In Fauset's final and perhaps most neglected work, *Comedy: American Style*, the author expands her concern with the psychological effects of race and sex oppression on black women's lives as this novel depicts its heroine, Olivia Cary, as the ultimate example of destructive self-hatred and classist behavior, for her intense color-mania brings about a series of events which culminate in her darker-skinned son's suicide and the eventual loss of her entire family, including her own exile to Paris. In this way, the novel is the most poignant example of Fauset's intraracial social commentary as it illustrates the tragic effects of the black community's internalization of white racist beliefs. Indeed, rather than reflect the effects of white racial discrimination on the lives of blacks, *Comedy* focuses exclusively on the demise of the northern Cary family, brought about by their rejection of black cultural traditions and more democratic notions of uplift.

Like her other novels, *Comedy* clearly demonstrates the inevitable deconstruction of the African American family when its members seek distinction based on hierarchies of color, class, and financial standing in an effort to assimilate and integrate into society with whites. Olivia's reaction to the birth of her very-light-skinned daughter, Teresa, exemplifies Olivia's obsession with white skin and desire to escape her race: "It seemed to her that the tenuous bonds holding her ever so slightly to her group, and its station in America, were perceptibly weakened. Every time she appeared in public with the little girl she was presenting the incontestable proof of her white womanhood" (37). A critique of the African American middle class's obsessions with color and class, *Comedy* satirizes its heroine, depicting her as a villainous race-traitor who destroys her entire family in an attempt to escape her racial heritage.

CRITICAL RECEPTION

Initially, Fauset's novels received mixed reviews, and although critical attention to the Renaissance has brought about more awareness of Fauset and her works, she was initially (and to some extent still) judged as conservative even by those critics who demonstrated interest in her work. Early critical readings, for example, concentrate narrowly on Fauset's depiction of African American middle-class characters without attention to her more subversive motives. As Deborah McDowell has observed, "even Fauset's most charitable readers have generally concluded that she was simply an apologist for the African American middle class, and that her most important role in the Harlem Renaissance was that of a midwife" (Introduction ix). Thus, in his *From the Dark Tower: Afro American Writers 1900–1960* (1974), Arthur P. Davis's criticizes Fauset, calling her "the most prolific, and in many ways the most representative of [the] glorifiers of the Negro middle class," and *There Is Confusion* her "fullest and most representative novel" because it renders "more of the typical attitudes and shibboleths held by the New Negro middle class of the 1920s than any of her others" (92).

Recently, scholars have begun to recognize and appreciate the political dimensions of Fauset's work, exposing Fauset's promotion of the African American middle class and her sentimental style as subversive, arguing for example, as does Marcy Jane Knopf, that "Fauset uses sentimentalism to do political work in her fiction . . . to mask a discussion of the plight of black women and to prove that blacks were just as cultured as whites"; Knopf, moreover, praises Fauset for "master[ing] the conventions of the sentimental novel and disrupt[ing] them by examining the intersection of race and sex" (xi). Still, while current critics have begun giving Fauset's works more positive critical attention, ambivalence still exists within the overall body of Fauset scholarship, as even Deborah McDowell, who places Fauset "among the early black feminists in Afro-American literary history," writes that "a curious problem in Fauset's treatment of feminist issues, however, is her patent ambivalence" ("The Neglected" 88). She argues: "She is alternately forthright and cagey, alternately 'radical' and conservative on the 'woman question.'" Similar to many Fauset scholars, however, McDowell's critique is positive overall, particularly with regard to Fauset's exploration of the double bind of race and gender for African American women. As McDowell ultimately concludes, Fauset was a "quiet rebel," who had "strains of feminism" at work in her fiction but may have been constrained because of her awareness of gender discrimination in the publishing and critical arenas ("The Neglected" 99).

Other contemporary critics praise the feminist principles in Fauset's works. As Carolyn Wedin Sylvander, whose work *Jessie Redmon Fauset: Black American Writer* (1981) is the first (and only) book-length study of Fauset and the most comprehensive study of Fauset's life and writings has suggested, "Fauset's strength may lie in her unobtrusive presentation of alternatives for defining the black American woman: more exploratory than dogmatic, more searching than protesting" ("Jessie Redmon Fauset" 85). Importantly, following Sylvander's work on Fauset, a small cadre of other book-length studies have included Fauset in their analysis of her and several other early twentieth-century women writers such as Nella Larsen and Zora Neale Hurston. Thus, while no other book-length studies focus solely on Fauset, those that consider her alongside several of her contemporaries are recuperating Fauset and revising negative readings of her works. One example is the excellent study by Jacquelyn Y. McLendon (mentioned previously). Throughout her work, McLendon revises criticism of Fauset's uses of the mulatto figure, passing, and her focus on the middle class, which have often been read as negative and limiting. Instead, she explores, for example, the mulatto figure as a necessary device to oppose race, gender, and class discrimination. In this way, McLendon's work offers a new paradigm to read Fauset's works and expands the limitations imposed by repeated accounts of the author's seeming conservatism, providing the type of insightful analysis of Fauset's novels needed to continue sustained and substantial critical attention to this important author. Moreover, such literary scholarship helps refocus attention on Fauset's use of the African American middle class as subjects, which is indeed timely in the context of current highly contested debates regarding the African American middle class's seeming desire for class distinction in order to attain social and political equality.

BIBLIOGRAPHY

Works by Jessie Redmon Fauset

"As to Books." Review of *Birthright*, by T. S. Stribling. *Crisis* 24 (June 1022): 66.
The Chinaberry Tree: A Novel of American Life. New York: Frederick A. Stokes, 1931. Reprint, College Park, MD: McGrath Publishing, 1969.
The Chinaberry Tree: A Novel of American Life and Selected Writings. New Foreword by Marcy Jane Knopf. Boston: Northeastern University Press, 1995.
Comedy: American Style. New York: Frederick A. Stokes, 1933. Reprint, College Park, MD: McGrath Publishing, 1969.
Plum Bun: A Novel without a Moral. New York: Frederick A. Stokes, 1929. Reprint, Boston: Pandora, 1985.
There Is Confusion. N.p.: Boni & Liveright, 1924. Reprint, Boston: Beacon, 1989.

Studies of Jessie Redmon Fauset's Works

Allen, Carol. *Black Women Intellectuals: Strategies of Nation, Family, and Neighborhood in the Works of Pauline Hopkins, Jessie Fauset, and Maria Bonner.* New York: Garland, 1998.
Batker, Carol J. "'An "Honest-to-God" American': Patriotism, Foreignness, and Domesticity in Jessie Fauset's Fiction." In *Reforming Fictions: Native, African, and Jewish American Women's Literature and Journalism in the Progressive Era.* New York: Columbia University Press, 2000.
Calloway, Licia Morrow. *Black Family (Dys)Function in Novels by Jessie Fauset, Nella Larsen, and Fannie Hurst.* New York: Peter Lang, 2003.
Davis, Arthur P. *From the Dark Tower: Afro American Writers 1900–1960.* Washington, DC: Howard University Press, 1974.
Davis, Thadious M. "Foreword." In *There Is Confusion* (1924), edited by Jessie Redmon Fauset. Boston: Northeastern University Press, 1989.
du Cille, Ann. *The Coupling Convention: Sex, Text, and Tradition in Black Women's Fiction.* New York: Oxford University Press, 1993.
Griffin, Erica L. "The 'Invisible Woman' Abroad: Jessie Fauset's New Horizon." In *Recovered Writers/Recovered Texts: Race, Class, and Gender in Black Women's Literature*, edited and introduced by Dolan Hubbard. Knoxville: Tennessee University Press, 1997.
Johnson, Abbey A. "Literary Midwife: Jessie Redmon Fauset and the Harlem Renaissance," *Phylon* 34 (June 1978): 153.
Jones, Sharon L. *Rereading the Harlem Renaissance: Race, Class, and Gender in the Fiction of Jessie Fauset, Zora Neale Hurston, and Dorothy West.* Westport, CT: Greenwood Press, 2002.

Knopf, Marcy Jane. "Foreword." In *The Chinaberry Tree and Selected Writings*, edited by Jessie Fauset. Boston: Northeastern University Press, 1995.

Levinson, Susan. "Performance and the 'Strange Place' of Jessie Redmon Fauset's *There is Confusion*." *Modern Fiction Studies* 46.4 (Winter 2000): 825–48.

Lewis, Vashti Crutcher. "Mulatto Hegemony in the Novels of Jessie Redmon Fauset." *CLA Journal* 35.4 (June 1992): 375–86.

McDowell, Deborah. "Introduction." In *Plum Bun: A Novel without a Moral* (1929), edited by Jessie Fauset. Boston: Beacon Press, 1990.

———. "The Neglected Dimension of Jessie Redmon Fauset." In *Conjuring: Black Women, Fiction, and Literary Tradition*, edited by Marjorie Pryse and Hortense J. Spillers. Bloomington: Indiana University Press, 1985.

McLendon, Jacquelyn Y. *The Politics of Color in the Fiction of Jessie Fauset and Nella Larsen*. Charlottesville: Virginia University Press, 1995.

Miller, Nina. "Femininity, Publicity, and the Class Divisions of Cultural Labor: Jessie Redmon Fauset's *There Is Confusion*." *African American Review* 30.2 (Summer 1996): 205–20.

Shockley, Ann Allen. *Afro-American Women Writers 1746–1933: An Anthology and Critical Guide*. New York: New American Library, 1989.

Sylvander, Carolyn Wedin. "Jessie Redmon Fauset." In *The Dictionary of Literary Biography*, vol. 51, pp. 76–86. Detroit: Gale, 1987.

———. *Jessie Redmon Fauset: Black American Writer*. Troy, NY: Whitson, 1981.

Tomlinson, Susan. "'An Unwanted Coquetry': The Commercial Seductions of Jessie Fauset's *The Chinaberry Tree*." In *Middlebrow Moderns: Popular American Women Writers of the 1920s*, edited and introduced by Lisa Botshon and Meredith Goldsmith. Boston: Northeastern University Press, 2003.

Joy R. Myree-Mainor

CAROLYN FERRELL (1962–)

BIOGRAPHICAL NARRATIVE

Short story writer Carolyn Ferrell was born to an African American father and a German mother in Brooklyn, New York and raised on Long Island. She graduated from Sarah Lawrence College in 1984 with a B.A. in creative writing. Ferrell then moved to Germany, teaching high school with the support of a Fulbright Scholarship while playing violin in several orchestras. In 1988 she returned to New York City where she taught adult literacy in the South Bronx and earned an M.A. in Creative Writing from the City College of New York. In 1994, Ferrell's story, "Proper Library" was selected for *The Best Short Stories of 1994* and was later reprinted in *The Best American Short Stories of the Century*. Her first book, *Don't Erase Me*, a collection of eight short stories, received the 1997 *Los Angeles Times* Art Seidenbaum Award, the *Ploughshares* Zacharis Award, and the 1998 *Quality Paperbacks* New Voices award. Her stories have appeared in *Callaloo*, *Fiction*, the *Literary Review*, *Ploughshares*, and *Sojourner: The Women's Forum* and numerous anthologies. In 2004, she received a National Endowment for the Arts grant for prose fiction. Currently a Ph.D. candidate in English at the City University of New York (writing a dissertation on Caribbean, South African, and black German feminist writers), Ferrell teaches creative writing at Sarah Lawrence College and is at work on a novel set on Long Island.

MAJOR WORKS

The stories in *Don't Erase Me* are a set of loosely connected, sparely contextualized vignettes each of which hugs the consciousness of a different teenage narrator. Many of the landscapes follow the trail of Ferrell's own experience—the South Bronx, suburban Long Island, and Germany. The narrators include Lorrie Adams, a gay teenager who has been left back several times in school, even while he teaches younger children out of a math textbook for a class he has not been allowed to enter; an HIV-positive woman whose story unfolds through diary entries running backward in time; high school friends Toya and Bri who are deciding, "should we have babies or become junior-year cheerleaders?" (71); Glory, an alienated transfer student who endures bullying at a suburban school; Hannah, an almost teenager staying with her mother and siblings in a Laguna Beach hotel after her parents had fought; Florence, an African American woman (with one German parent) spending time with extended family in Germany, sent there after graduation by her mother to cut short a high school relationship. Generically, the dense and dreamy inner lives of Ferrell's introspective teenagers mark a striking departure from the gritty realism frequently employed to represent urban life. Ferrell's stories explore with great intimacy the everyday lives of "teenagers who usually don't see themselves reflected in teen magazines or mainstream U.S. culture" (Dobosz 90).

CRITICAL RECEPTION

Published to considerable critical acclaim, Ferrell's stories have struck many critics for their subtle and sensitive characterization. "She inhabits her characters fully, body and soul," writes Elizabeth Searle. Michelle Cliff describes the character-rich texture of Ferrell's work as a "chorus of voices, each story with its own, unique soloist, presented on its own terms" (Cliff 65). Ferrell's style, punctuated by graceful and resonant neologisms and orchestrated with a "keen ear and playful sense of speech rhythms," is described by several critics as taking on the density of prose poetry generating a sense of immersion that "deftly drops her readers into another world" (Whitemore 26) and "allows the reader entry into her characters' lives . . . making the reader listen to voices that speak with subtlety and clarity" (Cliff 65).

BIBLIOGRAPHY

Work by Carolyn Ferrell

Ferrell, Carolyn. *Don't Erase Me.* Boston: Houghton Mifflin, 1997.

Studies of Carolyn Ferrell's Work

Cliff, Michelle. "Urban Renewal." *Village Voice* 42.38 (September 23, 1997): 65.
Dobosz, Ann Marie. Rev. of *Don't Erase Me. Ms* 8.1 (July–August 1997): 90.
Lee, Don. "Carolyn Ferrell, Zacharis Award." *Ploughshares* (Winter 1997–1998). 222–24.
Mayo, Kierna. "Finding Spirit in Troubled Lives." *Emerge* 8.8 (June 1997): 84–85.
Searle, Elizabeth. Rev. of *Don't Erase Me. Ploughshares* 23.2/3 (Fall 1997): 226–27.
Steinberg, Sybil. Rev. of *Don't Erase Me. Publishers Weekly* 244.16 (April 21, 1997): 59.
Whitemore, Katharine. "Phrasemaker in the City." *New York Times Book Review*, September 14, 1997, 26.

Alex Feerst

JULIA FIELDS (1938–)

BIOGRAPHICAL NARRATIVE

A teacher, short fiction writer, poet, and dramatist, Julia Fields also wrote and produced a play titled *All Day Tomorrow* (1966). She was born in Perry County, Alabama. A preacher's kid, she grew up on a farm. Nature and writers such as William Shakespeare and Robert Burns contributed to her early influences. At sixteen, she published her first poem in *Scholastic Magazine*. While at Knoxville College, two of her poems were published in *Beyond the Blues* (1962) (Burger 124). Julia Fields's formal education included a bachelor's degree in English from Knoxville College in Tennessee and a master's degree in English from Middlebury College in Vermont. Following her residency with the racially mixed Bread Loaf Writers Conference, Fields traveled to England and Scotland, where she studied at the University of Edinburgh (Burger 125). She later taught at several high schools and colleges, the latter of which included Hampton Institute and Howard University.

Julia Fields's volumes of poems include *Poems* (1968), *East of Moonlight* (1973), *A Summoning, A Shining* (1976), and *Slow Coins* (1981) (Burger 123). Fields also published the children's book, *The Green Lion of Zion Street* (1988) (Behrmann 96). Like her poems, Fields published short fiction in *Negro Digest*, *Black World*, and *Callaloo*. Her poems also appeared in Langston Hughes's *New Negro Poets, USA* (1964), Robert Hayden's *Kaleidoscope* (1967), and R. Baird Shuman's *Nine Black Poets* (1968) (Burger 125). This nonrevolutionary 1960s writer published a short story titled "Not Your Singing Dancing Spade" (1967), which elicited critical response.

MAJOR WORKS

Fields's most well known works are the short story "Not Your Singing Dancing Spade" and the poem "High on the Hog." "Not Your Singing Dancing Spade" examines challenges related to identity and color; while "High on the Hog" focuses on consumption and citizenship. In the poem the speaker uses food as an extended metaphor to suggest that having survived enslavement and its aftermath, she possesses the right to consume whatever she desires; that is, she possesses all the rights and privileges of American citizenship.

CRITICAL RECEPTION

Described as a little-known writer, Julia Fields's works have received little critical attention (Redmond 318); however, her poems "High on the Hog" and "Testimonials" elicited positive responses. For "High on the Hog" and "Not Your Singing Dancing Spade," Fields received the Seventh Conrad Kent Rivers Memorial Fund Award in 1972 (Burger 127). Writer Clarence Major affirms that Fields's work demands respect and praises her skillful use of imagery (42). Likewise, in their mixed review of *The Green*

Lion of Zion Street (1988), Christine Behrmann and Trevelyn Jones praise Fields's use of imagery but suggest that her juxtaposing informal and formal diction creates an obvious tension in the work (96). Nevertheless, Fields's works, overall, reflect a propensity for truth.

BIBLIOGRAPHY

Works by Julia Fields

"August Heat." *Callaloo* 4 (October 1978): 37–45.
East of Moonlight. Charlotte: Red Clay Books, 1973.
"The Green of Langston's Ivy." *Negro Digest* 16 (September 1967): 58–59.
The Green Lion of Zion Street. New York: Margaret K. McElderry Books, 1988.
"The Hypochondriac." *Negro Digest* 17 (July 1968): 61–65.
"No Great Honor." *Black World* 19 (June 1970).
"Not Your Singing Dancing Spade." *Negro Digest* 16 (February 1967): 54–59.
"The Plot to Bring Back Dunking." *Black World* 22 (August 1973): 64–71.
Poems. Millbrook, NY: Kriya Press, 1968.
Slow Coins. Washington, DC: Three Continents Press, 1981.
"Ten to Seven." *Negro Digest* 15 (July 1966): 79–81.

Studies of Julia Fields's Works

Behrmann, Christine, and Trevelyn E. Jones. Rev. of *The Green Lion of Zion Street* by Julia Fields. *School Library Journal* 34.9 (May 1988): 96.
Broussard, Mercedese. "Blake's Bard." Rev. of *A Summoning, A Shining* by Julia Fields. *Callaloo* 1 (December 1976): 60–62.
Burger, Mary Williams. "Julia Fields." In *Dictionary of Literary Biography, vol. 41, Afro-American Poets Since 1955*, edited by Trudier Harris and Thadious M. Davis, 123–31. Detroit: Gale, 1985.
Hauke, Kathleen A. "Julia Fields." In *The Concise Oxford Companion to African American Literature*, edited by William L. Andrews, Frances Smith Foster, and Trudier Harris, 140–41. New York: Oxford University Press, 2001.
Major, Clarence. *The Dark and Feeling: Black American Writers and Their Work*. New York: Third Press, 1974.
Redmond, Eugene. *Drumvoices: The Mission of Afro-American Poetry: a Critical History*. New York: Anchor Press, 1976.
Rexroth, Kenneth. "New American Poets." *Harpers* (June 1965): 65–71.

Jacqueline Imani Bryant

JULIA A. J. FOOTE (1823–1900)

BIOGRAPHICAL NARRATIVE

Autobiographer Julia A. J. Foote was born in Schenectady, New York, four years before that state abolished slavery in 1827. Her father was born free, but kidnapped and sold into slavery. Her mother was born a slave, and her stories of abuse had a profound impact on her daughter. Eventually Foote's father managed to buy his freedom as well as the freedom of his wife and first child. Foote would be the fourth of eight children.

Foote's father, the only literate member of her family, taught her the alphabet using the family Bible. When she was ten, Foote was hired as a domestic servant by a nearby white family, the Primes. Foote initially regarded Mrs. Prime as a surrogate mother. However, when her mistress falsely accused her of stealing food and whipped her with a rawhide especially purchased for the task, despite her protestations of innocence, Foote angrily dissociated herself from such white hypocrisy. Foote remained with this family for two years and received her only extended formal education at a country school. She was greatly affected by the execution of her schoolteacher, John van Paten, for the murder of his fiancée's best friend. Foote later became an opponent of capital punishment.

Foote returned to her parents in Albany to care for her younger siblings, and at age fifteen she was converted. At age eighteen Foote married a sailor, George Foote—her maiden name is unknown—and moved with him to Boston. By her early twenties Foote had received sanctification (a belief that she was free of sin and able to achieve spiritual perfection) and a call to preach. Both her mother and husband vehemently opposed her public preaching. Her mother told Foote she would rather hear of her daughter's death than her exposure at the pulpit. Her husband threatened to commit her to an insane asylum. Foote persisted in her ministry, and her husband returned to sea. Having no children, the couple lived separate lives until his death in the mid-1850s.

Foote traveled as a preacher from 1845 to the mid-1850s, covering territory ranging from Canada to Ohio. Troubles with her throat forced her into temporary retirement until the late 1860s. When her health improved she returned to the circuit, participating in the religious awakening that swept the Midwest after the Civil War. In 1879 and 1886, respectively, her spiritual autobiography, *A Brand Plucked from the Fire*, was published and reprinted. In 1894 she became the first woman deacon of the A.M.E. Zion Church and later its second woman elder. She died on November 22, 1900.

MAJOR WORK

Julia Foote is the author of only one work, *A Brand Plucked from the Fire* (1879). It borrows from two distinct genres: the fiery rhetoric and politicism of the African American slave narrative (Frederick Douglass, Harriet Jacobs, Olaudah Equiano) and the introspection and evangelism of American spiritual narratives (Michael Wigglesworth, Mary Rowlandson, Elizabeth Hudson, Ann Moore). Foote attacks America for its racism and harsh treatment of African Americans in the chapters "An Undeserved Whipping" and "Indignities on Account of Color." However, Foote is primarily interested in defending her call to preach and encouraging other women who have a vocation. (See chapters 17 and 28: "My Call to Preach" and "A Word to My Christian Sisters.") Foote makes her goal clear in her Preface: "My object has been to testify more extensively to the sufficiency of the blood of Jesus Christ to save all from sin." Foote's autobiography is relatively spare; for example, little attention is given to her siblings or her marriage. Instead, Foote retains her focus on the events and people who influenced her development as a preacher. The title for her work comes from Zechariah 3:2. Chanta Haywood concludes that the title asserts Foote's subjectivity and authority as a writer and preacher. She explains, "[b]y identifying herself as a brand, Foote portrays herself as a legitimate, self-acknowledged subject" (49–50). Thematically, this spiritual autobiography is chiefly concerned with persecution and salvation. As a woman writer, furthermore, Foote imbues her text with themes of woman's place in a patriarchal society and the pursuit of identity. Her travels as a minister supply a questing motif to the text.

CRITICAL RECEPTION

Foote's autobiography has received a fair amount of critical attention. It is most often paired with other narratives by African American women, particularly *The Life and Experience of Jarena Lee* (1836) and *Memoirs of the Life, Religious Experience, Ministerial Travels, and Labours of Mrs. Zilpha Elaw* (1846). Fleischner pairs the book with Kate Drumgoold's *A Slave Girl's Story* (1898) to explore the effect of slavery on the free children of former slaves. She reads Foote's identification with her mother's whipping as a slave with the treatment she received as a servant as the daughter's attempt to repudiate her mother's powerlessness and demand subjectivity. Moody is interested in the orality of the text and also highlights the mother-daughter relationship. She analyzes Foote's protest of the oppression of women theologians by organized religion. Haywood studies the determined professionalism of women preachers of the nineteenth century and places Foote in a rich tradition of black women writers and ministers.

BIBLIOGRAPHY

Work by Julia A. J. Foote

A Brand Plucked from the Fire. 1879. Reprint in *Sisters of the Spirit: Three Black Women's Autobiographies of the Nineteenth Century*, edited by William Andrews, 161–234. Bloomington: Indiana University Press, 1986.

Studies of Julia A. J. Foote's Work

Fleischner, Jennifer. *Mastering Slavery: Memory, Family, and Identity in Women's Slave Narratives*. New York: New York University Press, 1996.

Haywood, Chanta. *Prophesying Daughters: Black Women Preachers of the Word, 1823–1913*. Columbia: University of Missouri Press, 2003.
Moody, Joycelyn. *Sentimental Confessions: Spiritual Narratives of Nineteenth-Century African American Women*. Athens: University of Georgia Press, 2001.

Ann Beebe

PATRICE GAINES (1949–)

BIOGRAPHICAL NARRATIVE

Patrice Gaines, who is best known for her autobiographical works, was born on a military base in Quantico, Virginia, as the eldest of seven children. Although the insulated life on the base initially helped protect her from the harshness of racial discrimination, the family's move to segregated South Carolina when she was ten incited increasing feelings of self-doubt in the young Gaines. Her insecurity continued through her high school years and often informed her romantic relationships with men. Desiring to feel power in her own life, she often chose men who were engaged in lawbreaking or other negative behaviors, but who had reputations that she felt carried respect and weight. At eighteen she became pregnant with her daughter Andrea. Though Gaines's love for her daughter would later cause her to want to drastically change her life, she began using heroin after Andrea was born and spiraled further down into near destruction before she decided to rebuild her life and discover her talent at, and passion for, writing.

Gaines worked as a journalist for twenty-three years, sixteen of which were spent as a reporter for the award-winning *Washington Post*. Her decision to leave the publication in 2001 was motivated by her six-year investigation into a 1985 murder case that revealed many facts about the guilt and sentencing of eight young, black men to prison. She is now a freelance journalist, writing teacher, and public speaker, actively committed to restoring justice, reforming the U.S. judicial system, and changing the prison industry. In 2004 she cofounded The Brown Angel Center, designed to empower women and teenage girls by helping them with their financial, spiritual, and emotional needs and goals.

MAJOR WORKS

Gaines is best known for her riveting memoir, *Laughing in the Dark: From Colored Girl to Woman of Color—A Journey from Prison to Power* (1994). The text not only details her adolescent years trying to come to terms with her identity, feelings of self-hatred, and personal instability, but also chronicles the time she spent in a Charlotte, North Carolina jail on charges of drug possession with the intent to distribute. The book's prologue opens dramatically with Gaines's forehead pressed against the window of her jail cell looking out at her daughter who can neither come inside to visit her nor see her from where she waits outside. It was a pivotal moment for Gaines and also one that initiated her commitment to use her life more purposefully.

Gaines's autobiography is above all a dramatic telling of one woman's desire to persevere against difficult, nearly self-defeating circumstances. It describes her experiences of being sexually assaulted and beaten by a boyfriend and abused repeatedly by a violent husband, her three marriages that ended in divorce, and her search for love from her emotionally distant father. Writing, however, became a refuge for Gaines and served as a place of safety and open communication. She began taking creative writing classes at a community college and was later selected for a program for minority journalists that motivated her to build a career in writing and journalism. Gaines's own transformation is mirrored in the conclusion to the text when she is accepting an award for "Best Commentary" from the National Association of Black Journalists. The award, like the autobiography itself, served as a beginning for the important work of restructuring justice and empowering others ahead.

Gaines's second book, *Moments of Grace, Meeting the Challenge to Change* (1997) documents the changes her own life has undergone as she has sought to redirect it, restructure relationships with family and friends, and stand upon her faith. The text addresses such areas as love, friendship, work, and the opportunities available to all for personal and spiritual growth. It also includes stories from a variety of individuals who chose to move forward with courage and self-love in order to alter the trajectories of their lives.

CRITICAL RECEPTION

Gaines's work has garnered praise from such inspirational writers as Marianne Williamson and Iyanla Vanzant. Her poems "9/11" and "The Peacemakers" have been read on radio stations, and she has served as a commentator on National Public Radio and Pacifica Radio. Her numerous articles have appeared in such publications as *Essence*, *Emerge*, and *Black Enterprise*. She was nominated for the Pulitzer Prize in Journalism, and in 1997 was named the Empatheia Award Winner by Volunteers of America for outstanding community service and excellence in reporting on social issues. She continues to share her work and her life story in detention centers, drug rehabilitation programs, schools, and prisons nationwide.

BIBLIOGRAPHY

Works by Patrice Gaines

Laughing in the Dark: From Colored Girl to Woman of Color—A Journey from Prison to Power. New York: Anchor, 1994.
Moments of Grace, Meeting the Challenge to Change. New York: Crown Press, 1997.

Study of Patrice Gaines's Work

Squazzo, Kelley A. "Patrice Gaines (1949–)." In *African American Autobiographers: A Sourcebook*, edited by Emmanuel S. Nelson, 143–46. Westport, CT: Greenwood Press, 2002.

Amanda J. Davis

PATRICIA JOANN GIBSON (1951–)

BIOGRAPHICAL NARRATIVE

Patricia Joann Gibson, a well-known playwright and story writer, was born in Pittsburgh, Pennsylvania, where she lived with her grandparents until she was five. She has described her upbringing as that of an "only child raised by older people." Though she only spent a short time in Pittsburgh, vivid memories of the landscape and her childhood there—such as being picked up in a nightclub by Nat King Cole while a little girl—shaped her later works. She spent the remainder of her childhood in Trenton, New Jersey. She received her B.A. from Keuka College in 1973. While an undergraduate, Gibson studied drama, religion, and English. While theater arts proved to be her primary genre, she continued her wide-ranging interests, producing works of poetry and short fiction. She obtained an M.F.A. in Theatre Arts from Brandeis University.

Over the past thirty years, Gibson has written over thirty plays, which have been produced in the United States and as far a field as Europe and Africa. In addition, professor Gibson has taught creative writing at Boston College, the Frederick Douglass Creative Arts Center, Rutgers and UC Berkeley, and has held guest lecturer positions at Yale University and the Sudan. She is currently an assistant professor of English at New York City's John Jay College of Criminal Justice. Gibson has also been the recipient of numerous awards, including a playwriting fellowship from the National Endowment for the Arts, a Shubert Fellowship, two Audelco Awards, and the Bushfire Theatre of Performing Arts Seventh Annual "Walk of Fame" award among others.

MAJOR WORKS

While produced widely, many of Gibson's thirty plays are not easily found in print. She is most known for her award-winning play, *Long Time since Yesterday*. The play premiered at the New Federal Theatre on October 10, 1985, under the direction of Bette Howard, and has since been produced more than sixty times. The play is set in New Jersey in the 1980s and examines the lives, recollections, and dreams of a group of old college classmates who have gathered at the funeral of a friend who committed suicide.

Brown Silk and Magenta Sunsets is arguably her second most well-known work, though *Destiny's Daughters: 9 Voices of P. J. Gibson* was released in 2002 to great critical acclaim. Gibson's plays appear in numerous anthologies of contemporary theater and contemporary African American drama. Her work is noted for the resonance and dignity she brings to black women's voices. Her plays and stories often feature well-educated, successful black characters. The playwright has said that too often African Americans are portrayed as desperate, destitute, and even criminal. She strives to undue some of these stereotypes and create a more accurate and positive reflection of African American life.

CRITICAL RECEPTION

Gibson's plays have been critically lauded as resonant and potent dramas with strong roles for African American women. Of her most recent work, *Destiny's Daughters*, Gloria Naylor says, "P. J. Gibson writes of women with a passion and clarity that mesmerizes." Given the contemporary nature of her work and the fact that she is still midcareer, a comprehensive treatment of her role and legacy in contemporary theater would be difficult. Certainly, she is an important figure in African American studies departments and black theater circles; like many playwrights her work and reputation are often limited to a circle of serious dramatists, producers, and students of literature. Of her pivotal role in the dramatic community, Woodie King J., producing director, New Federal Theatre, writes, "When this new anthology by P. J. Gibson arrives in bookstores, black theatres, black studies departments, and community theatres across America will rejoice. I know I will! Gibson is a major voice in black theatre in particular and American theatre in general." Gibson has been a creative, daring, and potent voice in contemporary theater and continues to teach and contribute to the artistic community producing plays, poems, short fiction, and critical essays.

BIBLIOGRAPHY

Works by Patricia Joann Gibson

Brown Silk and Magenta Sunsets. Staged reading at Frederick Douglass Creative Arts Center. 1981.
Deep Roots. World Premiere at the Bushfire Theatre of Performing Arts (Philadelphia). 1998.
Destiny's Daughters: 9 Voices of P. J. Gibson. Bloomington, IN: AuthorHouse, 2002.
Long Time since Yesterday. Produced at the New Federal Theatre under the direction of Bette Howard. 1985.

Studies of Patricia Joann Gibson's Works

Bloom, Harold, ed. "Patricia Joann Gibson." In *Black American Women Poets and Dramatists*. New York: Chelsea House Publishers, 1996.
Hay, Samuel A., ed. "Patricia Joann Gibson." In *African American Theatre: An Historical and Critical Analysis*, pp. 45–6, 60, 121, 125–26. Cambridge: Cambridge University Press, 1994.
Jordan, Casper LeRoy, ed. "Patricia Joann Gibson." In *A Bibliographical Guide to African-American Women Writers*, p. 96. Westport, CT: Greenwood Press, 1993.

Sarah Estes Graham

MERCEDES GILBERT (1889–1952)

BIOGRAPHICAL NARRATIVE

Mercedes Gilbert—novelist, poet, actor, songwriter, and cultural worker—was a daughter of the south who spent her career celebrating the culture of rural black America. Gilbert grew up in Jacksonville and Tampa, Florida, and was the daughter of two business owners. Well educated as a child, she attended Edward Waters College in Jacksonville and later trained as a nurse. Despite her middle-class upbringing, she acquired an affinity for the language of the folk and for writing from her mother, who was active in the church. Church life provided the spark that nurtured Gilbert's interest in writing and performance.

While completing her nursing instruction, Gilbert wrote plays and an unpublished book of poems called *Looking Backward*. She moved to New York in 1916 to work as a nurse, but ended up collaborating with songwriter Chris Smith, who put her poetry to music. She wrote a number of blues songs, including the hit "I've Got the World in a Jug" (1924). As her music career took off, Gilbert also began to perform in films and on stage. She appeared in several all-black silent films, including Oscar Micheaux's *Body and Soul* alongside Paul Robeson. Then came a number of Broadway and Off-Broadway roles, including the female lead in Langston Hughes's *Mulatto* (1936). During the forties, she toured the United States and Canada with a one-woman show of her original material.

MAJOR WORKS

Gilbert's major literary works include three plays—of which only one survives, *Environment*—a collection, *Selected Gems of Poetry, Comedy and Drama* (1931), and a novel, *Aunt Sara's Wooden God* (1938). All of these texts illuminate her interest in the vibrant culture of southern black folklife. In *Selected Gems*, many of her poems are in dialect, but she employed that literary voice to assert the intellectual agility not typically ascribed to speakers of black vernacular English. Her novel built on this theme. In *Aunt Sara's Wooden God*, a celebratory and unapologetic story that revolves around a black community in rural Georgia, we find the hallmarks of the folk romance. Distinctive elements of black folk culture are central elements in the story, including spirituals, the blues, conjuring, superstition, church life, prayers, sermons, work songs, the dozens, dialect, and humor. Langston Hughes, in the foreword to *Aunt Sara*, places Gilbert's work alongside that of Zora Neale Hurston's *Jonah's Gourd Vine* (1934) and praises it for "its little pictures of the rural and small-town life of the South" (vii).

CRITICAL RECEPTION

Critical responses to Gilbert's writing do not universally reflect Hughes's enthusiasm. Few reviews or studies of her work exist, and one critic, John Lovell, Jr., panned the novel in 1939 for its lack of political utility. Gilbert, like Hurston, protested against the New Negro aesthetic. According to Lovell, instead of involving herself in race politics as writers were expected to, Gilbert presented an idealized rural black community. Her text inverts the notion of what constitutes authentic black life and valuable black fiction, a significant move for a woman writer during that time. Since then, critical engagement with Gilbert's texts remains scanty. A noteworthy essay is Susanne B. Dietzel's introduction to the 1997 reprint of *Selected Gems* and *Aunt Sara*.

BIBLIOGRAPHY

Works by Mercedes Gilbert

Aunt Sara's Wooden God. Boston: The Christopher Publishing House, 1938.
"Environment." Reprinted in *Lost Plays of the Harlem Renaissance: 1920–1940*, edited by James V. Hatch and Leo Hamalian. Detroit: Wayne State University Press, 1996.
"I've Got the World in a Jug." 1924. *Viola McCoy: Complete Recorded Works in Chronological Order, Volume 2: 1924–1926*. Document Records DOCD-5417.4. March 2003. http://www.heptune.com/lyrics/ivegotth.html.
Selected Gems of Poetry, Comedy and Drama. Boston: The Christopher Publishing House, 1931.

Studies of Mercedes Gilbert's Works

Azikwe, Marlo D. "Mercedes Gilbert: Romancing the Folk." In *Folklore and Oral Culture in Black Women's Fiction, 1925–1975*. Masters thesis, Rollins College, 2003.
Dietzel, Susanne B. "Introduction." In *Mercedes Gilbert: Selected Gems of Poetry, Comedy and Drama/Aunt Sara's Wooden God*. New York: G. K. Hall, 1997.
Gloster, Hugh. *Negro Voices in American Fiction*. Chapel Hill: University of North Carolina Press, 1948.
Lovell, John, Jr. "Excuses for Negro Novels." Rev. of *Aunt Sara's Wooden God*, by Mercedes Gilbert. *Journal of Negro Education* (January 1939): 73–74.
Roses, Lorraine Elena, and Ruth Elizabeth Randolph, eds. *Harlem's Glory: Black Women Writing 1900–1950*. Cambridge: Harvard University Press, 1996.
———, eds. *Harlem Renaissance and Beyond: Literary Biographies of 100 Black Women Writers 1900–1945*. Boston: G. K. Hall & Co., 1990.
Schraufnagel, Joel. *From Apology to Protest: The Black American Novel*. DeLand, FL: Everett/Edwards, 1973.

Marlo David Azikwe

NIKKI GIOVANNI (1943–)

BIOGRAPHICAL NARRATIVE

Born Yolande Cornelia Giovanni, Jr., on June 7, 1943, in Knoxville, Tennessee, Nikki Giovanni was raised in a predominantly black suburb of Cincinnati, Ohio. She graduated from Fisk University in 1967 and attended graduate school at both the University of Pennsylvania School of Social Work and the Columbia University School of Fine Arts. While an undergraduate she became actively involved in the Black Arts Movement and in the Student Nonviolent Coordinating Committee (SNCC). By 1968 she had published her first book of poetry, *Black Feeling, Black Talk* and soon became a well-known lecturer on behalf of civil rights whose angry rhetoric and plain talk won her standing room only audiences on college campuses. Though she has consistently used her poetry to speak out against racism and to protest war and oppression, she is also known for her lyricism on love and family and for several volumes of children's poetry, beginning with *Spin a Soft Black Song* published in 1971, two years after the birth of her son, Thomas. Giovanni has been called "the Poet of the black Revolution" and "the Princess of black Poetry." She is, indeed, one of the most widely read African American poets in the United States and Europe.

Giovanni began the twenty-first century as a cancer survivor, still writing, teaching, lecturing, and taking advantage of her celebrity to address issues ranging from inequalities in prison sentencing to NASA's Mars mission. During a career spanning three decades, she has taught at a variety of institutions, including Rutgers, Ohio State, Texas Christian, and Virginia Tech, where she was named distinguished professor of black studies in 1987. She is the founder of a publishing cooperative, NikTom, Ltd. She is also an enthusiastic traveler, and a fan of the hip-hop movement, especially of Tupac Shakur, to whom she dedicated *Love Poems* (1997). Her nonfiction works include *Gemini* (1971), subtitled "an extended autobiographical statement," *Racism 101* (1994), and often-quoted dialogues with James Baldwin, Margaret Walker, and, most recently, Queen Latifah. Nikki Giovanni has made several recordings of her poetry set to gospel or jazz music and published an audio compilation of her collected poetry in 2003. In addition to her many literary awards and honorary doctorates, the CD of her collected poems was nominated for a 2004 Grammy.

MAJOR WORKS

Nikki Giovanni's first two volumes of poetry, *Black Feeling, Black Talk* (1968) and *Black Judgement* (1969) contain her most famous militant poems that powerfully exhort black men to fight against oppression. After all, she notes ironically, black men have learned only too well how to die, why not then learn how to kill? These volumes also contain sensual love poems like "Seduction" and nostalgic family poems like "Nikki

Rosa," the source of the popular adage: "Black love is Black wealth." Several of these poems catalogue the violence of the 1960s from the war in Vietnam to the decade's many assassinations and murders. Others celebrate "Beautiful Black Men" or Giovanni's own journey from a happy little girl sitting on her grandmother's front porch to a twenty-five-year-old black female poet whose outspoken verse put her on an FBI watch list.

Throughout the 1970s and 1980s, Giovanni continued to explore these same themes and to reflect on her experience as a mother and her extensive travels in Europe and Africa. The poems of *My House* (1972) and *The Women and the Men* (1975) are a bit more lyrical and personal than her earlier work. Many of these poems affirm the interrelationships between self and community and speak to the roles the poet plays inside and outside the home. Giovanni describes her persona as a woman in control, who cooks what she wants to cook and reigns supreme in her own kitchen. She also expresses her frustration at the failure of the black power movement fundamentally to change the consciousness of most black people.

Cotton Candy on a Rainy Day (1978) marks a further move toward realism and introspection for Giovanni; despite the title, the poems are far from lighthearted. *Those Who Ride the Night Winds* (1983) includes more of the long-verse stanzas she first used to express her anger at the assassination of Martin Luther King, Jr., in *Black Judgement*. These are pieces dedicated to Phillis Wheatley, Lorraine Hansberry, and Rosa Parks, and also to Billie Jean King, John Lennon, and Robert Kennedy. "Writers write from empathy," Giovanni stated in an interview with Claudia Tate. "Experience," she argued, would only provide a few poems, maybe one book. *Love Poems* (1997), a compilation of some of her most popular poems, includes explorations of sexual desire, friendship, and motherhood, some whimsical, some somber. *Quilting the Black-Eyed Pea* (2002) includes poems dedicated to NASA and to new public figures, including the father of tennis stars Venus and Serena Williams. The title poem of this volume compares a trip to Mars with the Middle Passage, arguing that only African Americans can fully appreciate the hardships and significance of such a journey. Bringing together her fascination with space travel, her celebration of black people's survival skills and heroism, and a political critique of persistent white racism from the Fugitive Slave Law to the war on terror, it is a poem that seems the culmination of many of Giovanni's themes and interests.

A full appreciation of Nikki Giovanni must also mention her several volumes of prose and poetry for children. *The Prosaic Soul of Nikki Giovanni* (2003) is a collection of many of her best known essays, including portraits of her grandmother's courage in the face of racism (*Gemini*) and of Native American writer Sherman Alexie, for his frank depictions of Indian life (*Racism 101*). It also contains her perceptive descriptions of Henry Louis Gates, Jr., Toni Morrison, Spike Lee, and Supreme Court Justice Clarence Thomas.

Giovanni began writing poetry for children following the birth of her son. *Spin a Soft Black Song* (1971) and *Ego-Tripping and Other Poems for Young People* (1973) include poems directed explicitly at the dreams of young black boys and their need for heroes and role models. *Vacation Time* (1980) focuses more on a child's sense of discovery and adventure in a lighter, more rhythmic style. She has continued writing poetry for children throughout her career with the goal of providing parents with a positive and enjoyable way of instilling racial pride in their children while communicating the power of their love. Perhaps the best known of all Giovanni's poems, the one that audiences recite with her at the end of her ever-popular public performances, is the exuberant "Ego-Tripping," which claims the fertile crescent and the Sahara desert, Allah and Jesus, gazelles and elephants as the poet's inheritance and legacy in a hyperbolic chant climaxing in mythic flight.

Giovanni has recorded many albums of her poetry, most notably, *The Nikki Giovanni Poetry Collection*, HarperAudio, 2002. A television film, *Spirit to Spirit: The Poetry of Nikki Giovanni*, was produced by the Corporation for Public Broadcasting and the Ohio Council on the Arts in 1986.

CRITICAL RECEPTION

Early in her career Nikki Giovanni was identified as one of the leading black poets of the new black renaissance, most notably by Roderick Palmer in "The Poetry of Three Revolutionists: Don L. Lee, Sonia Sanchez, and Nikki Giovanni" (1971). Much of this early criticism focused on her explicitly political poems that were often dismissed for being either too outspoken or too naive. Few critics commented on the growing lyricism of her poetry or its broadening thematic reach.

Suzanne Juhasz writing in 1976 called for a more feminist reading of Giovanni's poetry and noted that she had clearly matured as a poet from 1968 to 1972. Juhasz sees "power and love" as the great themes in both the political and more personal poems of these years. "Beautiful Black Men," she notes, demonstrates how Giovanni makes good use of her "triple bind" as "poet and woman, poet and black, black and woman." Juhasz also speaks of Giovanni's "irrepressible humor," her use of a "traditionally female vocabulary of cooking and kitchens to underscore her message," and predicts that this young twenty-five-year-old poet will prove a worthy successor to Gwendolyn Brooks.

Margaret B. McDowell writing in 1986 faults academic critics for ignoring "the relationships present between [Giovanni's] poetry and Black speech or Black music" and political critics for underestimating her "affirmation of Afro-American culture and her realistic portrayals of individual Afro-Americans and their experience." McDowell argues that Giovanni's popularity reflects, in fact, "the immediate clarity of lines; the impact of tone, rhythm, and language; and the integrity of the realism" in her portraits. Beyond the "orality" for which she is famous, Giovanni deserves praise, according to McDowell, for the "rich ambiguities and ironies" in the best of her lyrics.

Martha Cook writing in 1990 locates Giovanni in "a rich tradition of Southern poetry . . . in which place functions not only as a vehicle, but also a theme." She praises the poem "Knoxville, Tennessee," written at the height of the civil rights movement, for its effective imagery and for "the simple diction, the soothing alliteration, (and) the short lines" that combine "to create a feeling of love for this place and these people that transcends topical issues." Cook also comments on Giovanni's effective use of literal and metaphorical houses to convey the special significance of "home" to black women searching for a place of their own apart from the houses of patriarchy and bondage, which are their legacy.

Despite the efforts of these scholars, Giovanni's publications generally meet with mixed reviews, and her poetry is not often anthologized. Even so, the enthusiasm of her audiences, the strong sales of her books, and her popularity with young people keep her firmly grounded in the canon.

BIBLIOGRAPHY

Works by Nikki Giovanni

Black Feeling, Black Talk/Black Judgement. New York: Morrow, 1970.
Blues: For All the Changes. New York: Morrow, 1999.
The Collected Poetry of Nikki Giovanni: 1969–1998. New York: Morrow, 2003.
Cotton Candy on a Rainy Day. New York: Morrow, 1978.
A Dialogue: James Baldwin and Nikki Giovanni. Philadelphia: Lippincott, 1973.
Ego-Tripping and Other Poems for Young People. Chicago: Lawrence Hill, 1973.
*Gemini: An Extended Autobiographical Statement on My First Twenty-five Years of Being a Black
     Poet.* Indianapolis, IN: Bobbs-Merrill, 1971.
Love Poems. New York: Morrow, 1997.
My House. New York: Morrow, 1972.
A Poetic Equation: Conversations between Nikki Giovanni and Margaret Walker. Washington,
     DC: Howard University Press, 1974.
The Prosaic Soul of Nikki Giovanni. New York: Perennial, 2003.
Quilting the Black-Eyed Pea. New York: Morrow, 2002.
Racism 101. New York: Morrow, 1994.
Re: Creation. Detroit, MI: Broadside Press, 1970.
Sacred Cows . . . and Other Edibles. New York: Morrow, 1988.
The Selected Poems of Nikki Giovanni, 1968–1995. New York: Morrow, 1996.
Spin a Soft Black Song: Poems for Children. New York: Hill & Wang, 1971.
Those Who Ride the Night Winds. New York: Morrow, 1983.
Vacation Time: Poems for Children. New York: Morrow, 1980.
The Women and the Men. New York: Morrow, 1975.

Studies of Nikki Giovanni's Works

Boldridge, Effie. "Windmills or Giants? The Quixotic Motif and Vision in the Poetry of Nikki
     Giovanni." *Griot* 14.1 (Spring 1995): 18–25.
Brooks, A. Russell. "Power and Morality as Imperatives for Nikki Giovanni and James Baldwin:
     A View of the Dialogue." In *James Baldwin: A Critical Evaluation*, ed. Therman B. O'Daniel.
     Washington, DC: Howard University Press, 1977.
Cook, Martha. "Nikki Giovanni: Place and Sense of Place in Her Poetry." In *Southern Women
     Writers: The New Generation*, edited by Tonette Bond Inge. Tuscaloosa: University of
     Alabama Press, 1990.
Di Christina, S. J. "Tips for Young Readers on Two Poems by Nikki Giovanni." *ELF: Electric
     Literary Forum* 4.3 (Fall 1994): 18.
Fowler, Virginia. *Conversations with Nikki Giovanni.* Jackson: University Press of Mississippi,
     1992.
———. *Nikki Giovanni.* Boston: Twayne, 1992.
Georgoudaki, Ekaterini. "Nikki Giovanni: The Poet as Explorer of Outer and Inner Space." In
     Women, Creators of Culture, edited by Ekaterini Georgoudaki and Domna Pastourmatzi.
     Thessaloniki, Greece: Aristotle Press, 1997.
Giddings, Paula. "Nikki Giovanni: Taking a Chance on Feeling." In *Black Women Writers (1950–
     1980)*, edited by Mari Evans. New York: Anchor-Doubleday, 1984.
Harris, William J. "Sweet Soft Essence of Possibility: The Poetry of Nikki Giovanni." In *Black
     Women Writers (1950–1980)*, edited by Mari Evans. New York: Anchor-Doubleday, 1984.
Josephson, Judith P. *Nikki Giovanni: Poet of the People.* Berkeley Heights, NJ: Enslow, 2003.

Juhasz, Suzanne. " 'A Sweet Inspiration . . . of My People.' " In *Naked and Fiery Forms: Modern American Poetry by Women*. New York: Harper & Row, 1976.

McDonald, Kathlene. "Nikki Giovanni." In *African American Autobiographers: A Sourcebook*, edited by Emmanuel Nelson. Westport, CT: Greenwood Press, 2002.

McDowell, Margaret B. "Groundwork for a More Comprehensive Criticism of Nikki Giovanni." In *Studies in Black American Literary Criticism, II*, edited by Joe Weixlmann and Chester J. Fontenot. Greenwood, FL: Penkevill, 1986.

Palmer, R. Roderick. "The Poetry of Three Revolutionists: Don L. Lee, Sonia Sanchez, and Nikki Giovanni." *College Language Association Journal* 15 (1971): 25–36.

Paul, Jay. "Nikki Giovanni: Overview." In *Contemporary Poets, 6th edition*, edited by Thomas Riggs. Farmington Hills, MI: St. James Press, 1996.

Tate, Claudia. "Nikki Giovanni." In *Black Women Writers at Work*. New York: Continuum, 1983.

White, Evelyn C. "The Poet and the Rapper." *Essence* (May 1, 1999): 122ff.

Jane M. Barstow

MARITA GOLDEN (1950–)

BIOGRAPHICAL NARRATIVE

Novelist, essayist, educator, and activist Marita Golden was born and raised in Washington, D.C. Born on April 28, 1950, she is the only child of her mother. Her mother, a Greensboro, North Carolina native, was a cleaning woman who played the lottery and became wealthy enough to afford many properties. Her father was a taxicab driver. Neither parent had any formal education, but they were very smart people. Golden's mother encouraged her writing talents. At age ten Golden had a letter published in the editorial section of the *Washington Post* and around age fourteen her mother told her that she was going to write books. This was surprising to Golden because she never saw her mother reading. Golden was inspired to write by her father's bedtime stories about African American history and culture.

In 1968 Golden graduated from Western High School and attended American University on a Frederick Douglass Scholarship, a scholarship that was developed as a result of the riots that occurred a year earlier upon the assassination of Dr. Martin Luther King, Jr. The assassination of Dr. King ignited Golden's revolutionary spirit. Convinced that Dr. King's assassination was the manifestation of America's reluctance to embrace equal rights, she was determined to continue the protests and activism of the civil rights movement. While at American University she was very active in the revolutionary fervor of the black power philosophies. She built lasting friendships with charter members of the Student Nonviolent Coordinating Committee from Howard and other local universities. As a student at American University she sat on a panel to help develop an African American Studies program. Upon graduation Golden gained experience as a journalist by interning with the *Baltimore Sun*, and she later became a general assignment reporter there. She then attended Columbia University and graduated with a Master of Fine Arts degree in journalism. Upon graduation she became an editorial assistant and wrote freelance articles in the evenings. By 1975 her articles appeared in large publications such as the *New York Times*, *Washington Post*, and *Essence Magazine*.

While in New York she met and married Femi Ajayi, a native Nigerian, and later moved to Africa with him. While in Nigeria she taught at the University of Lagos and Lagos Comprehensive Girls' School. At age twenty-five, she began writing *Migrations of the Heart: An Autobiography.*

After living in Nigeria for many years, she returned to the United States, residing first in Boston. There she taught English literature and journalism at Roxbury Community College and Emerson College. Longing to return home, Golden moved to Washington, D.C. Discouraged by the number of organizations and literary outlets available to the African American community, Golden founded the African American Writers Guild with friend Clyde McElevene. The organization became a forum in which African American writers could meet, write, and focus their efforts in order to establish a strong literary tradition in the Washington, D.C., area. She continued to stimulate aspiring writers by teaching creative writing at George Mason University, Antioch College, Spelman College, Wayne State University, and Virginia Commonwealth University.

Determined to continue her work as an activist for African American literary traditions, Golden founded the Zora Neale Hurston/Richard Wright Foundation in 1990. The foundation annually rewards talented college writers and encourages the documentation of the African American experience through literature.

Although Golden cultivated positive literary and journalistic feats in District of Columbia, she could not help but become alarmed by the mortality rates among African American males within the district and the surrounding areas. Her spirit of activism was not solely committed to literature. In 1995 Golden wrote *Saving Our Sons*. The book reflects her emotional distress as a mother of a young African American male and her perceptions about the mortality rates of young black men in the District of Columbia.

Golden has received numerous awards, including an honorary doctorate from the University of Richmond and Distinguished Alumni Award from American University. She was honored with the 2002 Authors Guild Award for Distinguished Service to the Literary Community, which recognizes her writing and work as a "literary cultural worker." She also received the Barnes and Noble 2001 Writers for Writers Award presented by *Poets and Writers*. She has been inducted into the International Hall of Fame for Writers of African Descent at the Gwendolyn Brooks Center at Chicago State University. She received the Woman of the Year Award from Zeta Phi Beta in 2003. In addition to her awards and prizes, Golden is on the advisory committee for the Mobil Pegasus Prize for literature. She is a member of the Board of Directors of the Girl Scouts of America, the Authors Guild, and has served as a member of the PEN/Faulkner Board, where she has been a judge.

Golden currently lives in a metropolitan area in Washington, D.C., where she is finishing another novel. She continues to be an activist for literacy and the accurate portrayals of the African American existence in literature as president and CEO of the Zora Neale Hurston/Richard Wright Foundation.

MAJOR WORKS

Golden's works are largely autobiographical, draped in exquisitely crafted prose, laced with vivid images, and saturated with metaphor. The characters within her works are purposeful and their actions and circumstances reflect the complexities of the modern American lifestyle. Her works remain true to the tenets of African American womanist literature, where the heroines seek to discover themselves and identify with some sense of self-fulfillment.

Golden's first work, *Migrations of the Heart* (1983), is sectioned in three parts: "Beginnings," "Journeys," and "Coming Home." The story documents Golden's journey toward self-actualization. In the first portion, "Beginnings," Golden explores her childhood years, the context in which her parents and society defined her. It is in this section that she first rejects the definitions others have placed upon her; she begins to fashion her revolutionary fervor. She refuses to be another "little colored girl" or straighten her hair because it is more acceptable. In light of her political awakening and cultural awareness, she develops strong relationships with other student activists and Africans. Toward the end of the section, she marries Femi Ajayi and moves to Nigeria to pursue a life of love with him. "Journeys" documents her travels to and in Africa, as her idealistic views of her new home begin to fade into the reality of conflicting cultural and personal views of her role as a woman, mother, and wife. Because of the turbulent political climate of Nigeria, her husband is unable to find work. In turn, his masculinity is threatened by Golden's success. The conflicts irrupt in arguments and physical violence within her marriage. She ultimately abandons her husband and returns to the United States. "Coming Home" examines Golden's struggles while attempting to reconnect with herself, both professionally and personally. Although she avoids establishing relationships with men, she finds emotional fulfillment through motherhood and develops close friendships with women who serve as a support system through her difficult times. She acknowledges that there will be other migrations in her life and in the future she will address them with the same certainty and self-actualization that allowed her to succeed in the past.

In 1986 Golden wrote *A Woman's Place*, her first novel. It is a compelling story about a friendship between three African American women—Faith, Serena, and Crystal—to include their professional lives at an Ivy League university in Boston. The story depicts the bonds they share, and is interwoven with the professional challenges and personal decisions each of them makes during the 1960s. In search of personal fulfillment, Faith marries an older Muslim man, converts to Islam, and changes her name to Iesha, only to realize that the realities of gender inequality that she experiences within her marriage are just as pertinent as the race prejudices she experiences in her professional life. Serena commits to a life of social activism and moves to Africa in order to rescue the world from injustice, ignoring a personal means of fulfillment. The third character, Crystal, is a writer who chooses to wed a white man and is confronted with the complex issues of race and rejection in both the black and the white communities.

Golden's second novel, *Long Distance Life* (1989), tells the life of Naomi Reeves Johnson and her generations. The story begins in the 1920s and is laced with memories, history, and strong spiritual overtones. Again, Golden explores her heroine's life as a journey, depicting painful conflicts and implicit determination of Naomi's family. The story begins with Naomi's migration to the north in search of a better life than the one the racially juxtaposed south promises her. Using her skills and wit, Naomi elevates herself into Washington, D.C.'s black middle class, a self-made woman. She marries and has a daughter, Esther. Her husband's untimely death results in Naomi becoming a single, protective mother. Her efforts as an overprotective mother result in her daughter's inability to recognize her self-identity or contribute to society purposefully. In an eager rush to establish her own self, Esther abandons her mother, lover, and child, and moves to the south to become a civil rights activist, whereby acquiring a sense of purpose in a changing society. Later, Esther returns to Washington, D.C., to her lover and the child she left behind. She becomes pregnant again, but her fiancé, Randolph, dies suddenly, leaving her to inherit her mother's feelings of loss. Finally, the novel concludes with Naomi enduring another unexpected loss. Her grandson is murdered by a drug dealer within their community.

Jessie Foster is the heroine of Golden's third novel, *And Do Remember Me* (1992), which examines the self-discovery and reconnections with one's past that are necessary for a more productive future. Jessie Foster escapes the restrictions and abuses that a young black girl experiences in the rural south to fall in love with a civil rights activist, Lincoln. She joins the fight for civil rights and builds a close friendship with Macon. Jessie moves to New York, where she becomes a professional actress, changing her name to Pearl Moon. She quickly discovers that neither her acting career nor her consumption of alcohol can heal the wounds of her childhood. Eventually, Jessie/Pearl stops drinking and builds greater bonds with Macon and Lincoln. She is forced to return to Mississippi to attend her father's funeral and reconnect with the self she abandoned.

Saving Our Sons: Raising Black Children in a Turbulent World (1995) is Golden's response to the horrifying realities that the black urban community faces. Although the book focuses largely on her son, Michael, growing up in Washington, D.C., during the late eighties, it was more of a commentary on the alarmingly high death rates of young African American males in the urban communities. The story questions the community's inability to provide a safe atmosphere for the youth or to nurture two-parent families with both male and female role models.

Golden again explores metrical relationships and identity in her fourth novel, *The Edge of Heaven* (1998). The novel focuses on rebuilding and establishing relationships that have been made distant by forced separation and imprisonment. Showing the love, struggles, and sufferings of three generations of women, Golden examines the issues of guilt, abandonment, and grief that pervade and strengthen bonds between women.

A Miracle Every Day: Triumph and Transformation in the Lives of Single Mothers (1999) demonstrates the miracles of motherhood and the immense resources that children and mothers rely on individually. It shows the resources and strengths of mothers and children and the faith that connects them both.

Don't Play in the Sun: One Woman's Journey through the Color Complex (2004) is Golden's most recent work. It addresses the complexity of complexion, self-identity, and self-worth many young black women face in society. She explores her mother's complex notion of beauty and skin color, along with her own journey to identify beauty and worth, despite society's views and expectations.

In addition to her novels and nonfiction autobiographical works, Golden has edited many anthologies. Among them are *Wild Women Don't Wear No Blues*, which is a collection of African American women's literature that explores relationships, love, and sexuality through essay, prose, and testimony. *Skin Deep: Black Women and White Women Write about Race* is a collection of stories and essays from African American and white American women authors that explores the issues of race within the gender-related roles of mother, wife, and lover. Golden's most recent anthology is *Gumbo: A Celebration of African American Writing*, coedited with author E. Lynn Harris. *Gumbo* is affectionately known as the "literary rent party." Originally compiled to benefit the Hurston/Wright Foundation, the anthology encompasses previously published and new stories from writers ripe with the spirit and grandeur of African American literature.

CRITICAL RECEPTION

Most of Marita Golden's works have received favorable reviews. She has been honored with a number of awards for her writings and lifeworks. These include the 2002 Distinguished Service Award from the Authors Guild, The 2001 Barnes and Noble Writers for Writers Award presented by *Poets and Writers*, an honorary doctorate from the University of Richmond, induction into the International Hall of Fame for Writers of African Descent at the Gwendolyn Brooks Center at Chicago State University, Woman of the Year Award from Zeta Phi Beta, and a Distinguished Alumni Award from American University. Golden is an accomplished author of autobiographical texts and novels. In addition, she has gained acclaim as an editor for three anthologies.

Her autobiographical works, *Migrations of the Heart* in particular, are described as "told in a prose that often seems possessed by some perverse genius" by Deane McWhorter. Mary Carroll refers to *Saving Our Sons: Raising Black Children in a Turbulent World* as "a powerful and eloquent call to action on a critical social problem."

Considering *A Miracle Every Day: Triumph and Transformation in the Lives of Single Mothers*, critics perceive Golden's rebuttal to the social assumption that single-parent households breed social ills was received favorably and applauded for the research within. And the critical receptions of *Don't Play in the Sun: One Woman's Journey through the Color Complex* exceeded readers' expectations. Jewell Parker Rhodes identifies Golden as "a healer, a griot attacking racism and self-hatred with wisdom, a lively spirit, and a generous heart."

The reviews for Golden's novels have been just as favorable as her nonfiction texts. *A Woman's Place* written in 1986 is viewed as a true depiction of the lives of African American women. Susan Wood explains, "Golden makes us believe in her characters and care about them." Critics admire the development of the characters in her second novel, *Long Distance Life*. *And Do Remember Me*, Golden's third novel, received slightly less favorable reviews, yet, according to *Publishers Weekly*, "Golden's portrait of idealism and exhilaration of people coming together in a conflicted time is authentic and engrossing . . ." *The Edge of Heaven*, the fourth novel, is viewed in much the same way as the third and is deemed "compelling" by the same publication.

BIBLIOGRAPHY

Works by Marita Golden

And Do Remember Me. New York: Doubleday, 1992.
Don't Play in the Sun: One Woman's Journey through the Color Complex. New York: Doubleday, 2004.
The Edge of Heaven. New York: Doubleday, 1998.
Gumbo: A Celebration of African American Writing, edited with E. Lynn Harris. New York: Harlem Moon, 2002.
Long Distance Life. New York: Doubleday, 1989.
Migrations of the Heart: An Autobiography. New York: Doubleday, 1983.
A Miracle Every Day: Triumph and Transformation in the Lives of Single Mothers. New York: Doubleday, 1999.
Saving Our Sons: Raising Black Children in a Turbulent World. New York: Doubleday, 1995.
Skin Deep: Black Women and White Women Write about Race, edited with Susan Richards Shreve. New York: Anchor Books, 1995.
Wild Women Don't Wear No Blues. New York: Doubleday, 1993.
A Woman's Place. New York: Doubleday, 1986.

Studies of Marita Golden's Works

Carroll, Rebecca. *I Know What the Red Clay Look Like: The Voice and Vision of Black Women Writers*. New York: Carol Southern Books, 1994.
Davies, Carole Boyce., ed. *Black Women, Writing and Identity: Migrations of the Subject*. London/ New York: Routledge, 1994.
Jackson, Edward M. *Images of Black Men in Black Women Writers 1950–1990*. Lima, OH: Wyndham Hall Press, 1993.
Jordan, Shirley Marie., ed. *Broken Silences: Interviews with Black and White Women Writers*. New Brunswick, NJ: Rutgers University Press, 1993.

DaMaris Hill

JEWELLE GOMEZ (1948–)

BIOGRAPHICAL NARRATIVE

Jewelle Gomez, a poetess and story writer, was born in September 1948 in Boston, Massachusetts. When she was two years old, her parents separated and Gomez moved to Washington, D.C., to live with her paternal grandparents. At the age of eight, she returned to Boston to live with her maternal great-grandmother till the age of twenty-two. Much of Gomez's work is influenced by the oral tradition of both the African American and Native American culture of her grandparents.

Gomez attended Northeastern University on a full scholarship. While there, she was very active in addressing social issues on and off campus. She became involved in the civil rights movement, actively voicing her opinion on issues such as the Vietnam War as well as issues pertaining to race, gender, and sexuality. Moving to Greenwich Village in the 1970s, Gomez earned her master's degree from Columbia University School of Journalism in 1973 on a Ford Foundation Fellowship. During this time she began to explore her lesbian identity, an element that is noticeable in much of her literary works.

Jewelle Gomez was very influenced by the Black Arts Movement and particularly by the self-acclaimed "biomythographer" Audre Lorde. In 1993 Gomez honored Lorde in a memorial written for *Essence* magazine. Like Lorde, Gomez's work reflects an attempt to present an image that embraces all of her identity, including but not limited to her race, gender, and sexuality. Her literature develops and reflects her identification with what she recognizes as her black, feminist, and lesbian self.

Gomez's work has been published in numerous periodicals, including the *Advocate*, *Black Scholar*, *Essence* magazine, *Ms* magazine, the *New York Times*, the *San Francisco Chronicle*, and the *Village Voice*. Much of her work has also been anthologized.

Gomez is not only a writer but is also very active in the literary and artistic community. She was one of the original staff members of one of the first weekly black television shows in the United States, *Say Brother*. She was also on the founding board of the Gay and Lesbian Alliance against Defamation (GLAAD). Gomez has also served as a member of the national advisory of the National Center for Lesbian Rights; Poets and Writers, Inc.; and the Human Sexuality Archives of Cornell University. Currently, Gomez serves as an advisor for the Open Meadows Foundation, a grant funding organization geared toward the empowerment of women and girls. The foundation offers support for projects that are implemented by women and girls which also reflect a cultural and ethnic diversity while promoting social change.

Gomez has made a name for herself both as an author as well as an activist. She was the director of the Literature Program and the New York State Council on the Arts. She was also the executive director of the Poetry Center and American Poetry Archives at San Francisco State University. Gomez, who also works with films, has been active in the film industry, serving as a national advisory board member for Nancy D. Kates film "American Socrates: The Life of Bayard Rustin."

Jewelle Gomez has lectured and made presentations at various colleges and universities, including Hunter College and the Ohio State University. She has established herself not only as a writer, activist, and scholar, but also her continuous contribution to the arts demonstrates her commitment to society. Her work has been acknowledged with a double Lambda Award, which recognizes and honors the best in lesbian, gay, bisexual, and transgender literature. Her book, *The Gilda Stories*, has been adapted into an interpretative dance by the New York–based Urban Bush Women Dance Company. The stage adaptation, which featured original music by Toshi Reagon, was performed in thirteen U.S. cities.

Gomez is currently working on new projects, including a novel that uses humor to look at black activists of the 1960s as they approach and deal with middle age. She has also begun work on a collaborative performance piece dealing with the life of author James Baldwin.

MAJOR WORKS

Jewelle Gomez's most popular work is *The Gilda Stories*, a set of historical narratives that follow the life of a female lesbian vampire from the antebellum period to well into the future. Gomez's visioning of the vampire is very different from traditional renderings. For Gomez the taking of blood does not lead to death; instead, it is a mutual exchange wherein the vampire takes blood and in return leaves the giver with a gift of life. This reimagining of the vampire character can be linked directly to the woman-centered focus of the work, which not only highlights the relationship that women have with each other, but also portrays women as heroes in their own right who have helped to mold and create the world in which we live.

The first narrative in *The Gilda Stories* functions very much like a neo-slave narrative, revisiting the experience of a young female slave who must decide on the value of her freedom. Gomez empowers the young girl, providing her with the agency to determine where her life will take her. This rewriting of the enslaved female is significant as Gomez allows her female character to take control of her own destiny as well as have an impact on the lives of others whom she encounters as she "travels" through America's history.

The Gilda Stories successfully highlights the diversity of experiences that one can have within American society. Gomez points out the connections between women's experiences cross-culturally. Gomez draws a link between the relationship between Bird and the girl, and the marginalized experiences of groups of people who have been rendered "other" by mainstream society. As Bird teaches the girl to read, one of the most significant lessons she learns is that neither Bird's experiences as a Native American woman nor her own as an African American woman are being recorded in the newspapers. This leads to an important question about how history is recorded and the stories and experiences that are often left out of history books.

The Gilda Stories also highlights the experiences of women of different ethnicities, class, and race, showing the interconnectedness of women's experiences in America. The first section of the novel focuses on the experience of a group of prostitutes who struggle to determine a place for themselves in American society, despite the economic pressures they face. Significantly, it is the girl's experience as an enslaved person that is linked to the experiences of these prostitutes. When a man approaches her, thinking that she is a prostitute, the girl likens his gaze to that of slave plantation owners as they looked over slaves on the auction block. Gomez forces readers to make a connection between the limited access that slaves had during that time and the inadequate resources that were available to women.

In the text, the girl becomes Gilda, and the text traces her movement through American history. In doing so, she celebrates the role that women have played in the development of traditions and movements throughout history. One significant moment in the text occurs in the 1920s, when Gilda finds herself amidst the roar of the Harlem Renaissance. In this section, Gomez draws attention to the significant roles women played during the renaissance. The character Eleanor reflects those women who were instrumental in creating an environment that promoted literary creativity. In her characterization of Eleanor, Gomez succeeds in rehistoricizing those women who have been written out of history.

The Gilda Stories is an essential read as it not only refers to women as heroes but also locates those heroes historically, writing women back into a history that has not remembered them.

Oral Tradition is a collection of poems that celebrate Gomez's African American and Native American heritage. Written to be read aloud, these works reflect the oral tradition of each culture. The poems focus on women and their experiences, emphasizing the themes of home, love, and history. Included in this collection, the poem "Gilda Sings: Escape: A Performance Piece in Four Songs" stresses the importance of history and the past.

Don't Explain is a collection of novellas and short stories focusing on the realities of women's lives and experiences. Much attention is paid to issues of sexuality and sexual relationships. The short story "Don't Explain," from which the title of the text comes, celebrates women's communities and the way women support and maintain each other.

Published in 1993, *Forty-three Septembers* reflects Gomez's attempts to reconcile her gender, racial, and sexual identities. Central to the text is Gomez's celebration of her heritage, focusing particularly on the strong influence the women in her life have had on her development as a writer and an activist.

CRITICAL RECEPTION

Jewelle Gomez has received some criticism for her work. Gomez acknowledges that her work attempts to deal with multiple issues, including feminist discourse, which she suggests can often be limited in its perspective. In 1997 Gomez made an appearance at Kalamazoo College, where she was picketed by feminist activists who questioned her use and presentation of sexuality in her literature.

However, much of Gomez's work has received positive reception. Her use of the vampire motif to discuss issues relevant to the social and political experience of women has opened doors for discourse that has often been left unaddressed. Her use of science fiction to perform social criticism has brought questions relevant to the lesbian-black experience to the forefront of academic discourse. Some scholars have characterized Gomez's work as "genre" fiction, in effect minimizing both the literary and social impact of her work. Gomez uses the vampire novel to revision the historical experience of women, specifically lesbians. In critical responses, scholars have acknowledged that one of Gomez's main accomplishments is that within her literature she returns women to their historical positioning, writing them back into a history that they not only witnessed but also helped create.

BIBLIOGRAPHY

Works by Jewelle Gomez

The Best Lesbian Erotica of 1997. San Francisco: Cleis, 1997.
Don't Explain. New York: Firebrand, 1997.
Flamingoes and Bears (1986). Johnson City, TN: Grace Publications, 1996.
Forty-three Septembers. New York: Firebrand Books, 1993.
The Gilda Stories. New York: Firebrand Books, 1991.
The Lipstick Papers (1980), self pubished.
Oral Tradition: Selected Poem Old and New. New York: Firebrand Books, 1995.
Swords of the Rainbow (coeditor). Boston: Alyson Publication, 1996.
"Words." *Hot Wire: The Journal of Women's Music and Culture* 7.2 (May 1991): 12–13, 24.

Studies of Jewelle Gomez's Works

Brinks, Ellen. "Unfamiliar Ties: Lesbian Constructions of Home and Family in Jeanette Witnerson's *Oranges Are Not the Fruit* and Jewelle Gomez's *The Gilda Stories*." In *Homemaking: Women Writers and the Politics and Poetics of Home*, edited by Catherine Wiley and Fiona R. Barens. New York: Garland, 1996.

Brown, Wesley, and Amy Ling, eds. *Imagining America: Stories from the Promised Land*. New York: Persea Books, 2003.

Carbado, Deveon W., Dwight A. McBide, and Donald Weise, eds. *Black Like Us: A Century of Lesbian, Gay, and Bisexual African American Fiction*. San Francisco: Cleis Press, 2002.

Garber, Eric, Mel Keegan, Nina Boal, Tanya Huff, and Dorothy Allison. *Swords of the Rainbow: Gay and Lesbian Fantasy Adventures*. New York: Alyson Publications, 1996.

Gates, Beatrix, ed. *Wild Good: Lesbian Photographs and Writing on Love*. Garden City, NY Doubleday & Company, Incorporated, 1996.

Harris, Laura, and Elizabeth Crocker, eds. *Femme: Feminists, Lesbians, and Bad Girls*. New York: Routledge, 1997.

Karlsberg, Michele, and Karen A Tulchinsky, eds. *To Be Continued*. Ithaca, NY: Firebrand Books, 1998.

Keesey, Pam. *Daughters of Darkness: Lesbian Vampire Stories*. San Francisco: Cleis Press, 1998.

McClune, Lindsay. *On Our Backs: The Best Erotic Fiction*. Boston: Alyson Publications, 2001.

Meyer, Sabine. "Passing Perverts, After All?: Vampirism, (In)Visibility, and the Horrors of the Normative in Jewelle Gomez's *The Gilda Stories*." *FEMSPEC: An Interdisciplinary Feminist Journal Dedicated to Critical and Creative Work in the Realms of Science Fiction, Fantasy, Magical Realism, Surrealism, Myth, Folklore, and Other Supernatural Genres* 4.1 (2002): 25–37.

Thomas, Sherelee. *Dark Matter: A Century of Speculative Fiction from the African Diaspora*. New York: Warner Books Inc., 2004.

Josie A. Brown-Rose

ELOISE GREENFIELD (1929–)

BIOGRAPHICAL NARRATIVE

Eloise Greenfield, who has received numerous awards for her biographies and picture books was born in Parmele, North Carolina. When Greenfield was a child, her family moved to the Langston Terrace Housing Project in Washington, D.C., which she has called "a good growing-up place" because of the warmth and kinship of the extended community. Her home was very close to the library, where Greenfield spent much of her time. Despite these comforting aspects of her early life, Greenfield grew up in a segregated community during the Great Depression and World War II. These factors contributed to her sense of social justice and equality.

Greenfield attended Miner Teachers College. Her first children's book was published when she was in her forties.

MAJOR WORKS

Bubbles (now called *Good News*) was published in 1972. It sets the tone for much of Greenfield's later work: realistic portrayals of loving African American parents working hard to provide for their families, and the children who face life's challenges with a positive outlook. Extended families and grandparents are prominent in her works such as *Grandmama's Joy* and *Grandpa's Face*. Greenfield also cowrote *Childtimes: A Three-Generation Memoir*, sharing stories of her own childhood and those of her mother and grandmother.

Another theme in Greenfield's work is the triumph of African American people throughout history. Her Coretta Scott King Award–winning picture book *Africa Dream* is dedicated "with love to all the children of African descent. May they find in their past the strength to shape their future." The book is about a young woman's dream of visiting "long-ago Africa." The lyrical language reflects the story's dreamlike state, before the scourge of slavery descended on Africa.

Greenfield's skill with descriptive, rhythmic language is also apparent in her works of poetry. Perhaps her best known work is *Honey, I Love and Other Love Poems*. This collection features sixteen poems, each addressing the daily lives and concerns of children. Their overwhelming feel is comfort, enveloping readers in the love displayed by the author. More recently, she published *In the Land of Words: New and Selected Poems* and the whimsical *I Can Draw a Weeposaur and Other Dinosaurs: Poems*.

Greenfield has also written several biographies. In 1973, her biography of Rosa Parks won the first Carter G. Woodson Award for Social Education. She published a middle-grade biography of Paul Robeson, which focused not only on his brilliant career but also on his childhood and young adult life. More recently, her picture book *For the Love of the Game: Michael Jordan and Me* parallels the dreams of a twelve-year-old boy and girl with the life of Michael Jordan. Another unique biography is *Alesia*, a diary cowritten by Alesia Revius, who, at age nine, was paralyzed in a car accident.

CRITICAL RECEPTION

Eloise Greenfield has won more than forty awards and honors for her works. Many of her books have been recognized by the National Council for the Social Studies and the American Library Association. The National Council of Teachers of English gave her the Award for Excellence in Poetry for Children. In 1993 she received the Children's Literature and Social Responsibility Award from the Boston Educators for Social Responsibility. She also holds an honorary Doctor of Education degree from Wheelock College, and has been the recipient of the Hope S. Dean Award from the Foundation for Children's Literature, in addition to the North Star Award for Lifetime Achievement from the Hurston/Wright Foundation. She has also been inducted into the National Literary Hall of Fame for Writers of African Descent.

BIBLIOGRAPHY

Works by Eloise Greenfield

Africa Dream. New York: HarperCollins, 1977.
Alesia. With Alesia Revius. New York: Philomel Books, 1981.
Childtimes: A Three-Generation Memoir. New York: Thomas Y. Crowell, 1979.
For the Love of the Game: Michael Jordan and Me. New York: HarperCollins, 1997.
Good News [formerly *Bubbles*]. New York: Coward, McCann & Geoghegan, Inc., 1972.
Grandmama's Joy. New York: Philomel Books, 1980.
Grandpa's Face. New York: Philomel Books, 1988.
Honey, I Love, and Other Love Poems. New York: HarperCollins, 1978.
I Can Draw a Weeposaur and Other Dinosaurs: Poems. New York: Greenwillow, 2001.
In the Land of Words: New and Selected Poems. New York: Amistad, 2004.
Paul Robeson. New York: Thomas Y. Crowell Company, 1975.
Rosa Parks. New York: HarperCollins, 1973.

Study of Eloise Greenfield's Works

Willis, Eleanor Gervasini. *American Women Who Shaped the Civil Rights Movement Explored Through the Literature of Eloise Greenfield*. http://www.yale.edu/ynhti/curriculum/units/1997/3/97.03.10.x.html.

Elissa Gershowitz

ANGELINA WELD GRIMKÉ (1880–1958)

BIOGRAPHICAL NARRATIVE

Born on February 27, 1880, in Boston, poet, dramatist, essayist, and short fiction writer Angelina Weld Grimké seemed destined from birth to a life of intellect, achievement, and activism. She was the daughter of Archibald Grimké, biracial nephew of the noted abolitionists Sarah Moore Grimké and Angelina Grimké Weld (after whom she was named), and Sarah E. Stanley, writer and member of a prominent white Boston family.

When Grimké was three, her parents separated. Although she initially lived with her mother, Grimké returned to her father when she was seven. Mother and daughter corresponded, but never saw each other again. Grimké's diary records the angst her mother's absence caused, and her frequent treatment of motherhood is likely related to this trauma.

Reared in liberal, upper-class Boston society, Grimké clearly felt psychologically pressured to contribute to her family's heritage. Her relationship with her father, a loving but demanding patriarch, was especially close. Throughout her life, he pushed her to excel, berating her when she fell short of his expectations. Often isolated and lonely as a child, she remained reclusive throughout her life.

Grimké was educated at exclusive schools—Carleton Academy in Northfield, Minnesota; Cushing Academy in Ashburnham, Massachusetts; and the Girl's Latin School in Boston. While her father served as consul in Santo Domingo (1894–1898), she lived with her uncle and aunt, Francis and Charlotte Forten Grimké. Although she loved her aunt—as witnessed in her later poem "To Keep the Memory of Charlotte Forten Grimké"—this tense living arrangement led to Grimké's entering boarding school. She graduated from the Boston Normal School of Gymnastics (now Wellesley College) in 1901 with a degree in physical education. After teaching gym at Armstrong Manual Training School, she became an English teacher at "M" Street School (later Dunbar High School) in 1907. She supplemented her training by taking summer courses in English at Harvard and retired from teaching in 1926 when her father fell ill.

While she never publicly acknowledged her sexual preferences, Grimké's poetry alludes to several lesbian relationships, and a letter documents a youthful affair with the writer Mamie Burrill. Likely her father's disapproval and society's homophobic attitudes caused her to suppress her homosexuality.

Grimké wrote poetry that began appearing in newspapers in the 1890s and penned two race-propaganda dramas: *Rachel* (staged in 1916 by the NAACP Drama Committee, published in 1920) and *Mara* (unpublished). During the 1920s, her work was printed in magazines such as the *Crisis* and *Opportunity* and in several important anthologies, including Countee Cullen's *Caroling Dusk*, but much of her work, especially her highly personal poetry, was never published and is available only in her papers at Howard University's Moorland-Spingarn Research Center.

Devastated by her father's death in 1930, Grimké moved to New York, ostensibly to write. Often ill, she lived there in virtual isolation until her death at the age of seventy-eight. As she became unproductive and even more solitary, Grimké fell into relative obscurity as a writer.

MAJOR WORKS

Grimké wrote poetry, drama, short fiction, and essays and sporadically kept a diary, but her reputation rests largely on a few poems and *Rachel*.

Her poetry includes "elegies, love lyrics, nature lyrics, racial poems, and philosophical poems about the human experience" ("Under the Days," Hull 137). Written in traditional Anglo-American forms such as the sonnet, triolet, and roundel and often told by a male persona, the poems are usually brief; for example, "Epitaph on a Living Woman" with its stark view of ashes is only four lines. Her imagery, which often involves body parts, may be poignantly beautiful (the child hitting the sunlight in "The Black Child"), sensuous (the grass in "Grass Fingers"), grim (the "black-hued gruesome something" in "Trees"), or deadening (the "numbness" in "Ask of Life Nothing, Nothing").

Many poems incorporate a wide palette of colors, some pastels such as lavender and saffron ("Eyes of My Regret"), but particularly black, white, gray, and gold as in "Under the Days." Although most convey a sad, wistful tone, others, such as "Naughty Nan," feature a light, rollicking rhythm. Some—"A Mona Lisa," for example—are covertly lesbian. "El Breso," Grimké's first critically acclaimed love lyric, is probably addressed to a woman. In it, as elsewhere, Grimké omits third-person pronouns, doubtless to avoid gender identification. Although race poems constitute only a small portion of her work, two of the best known are "Tenebris" and "Beware Lest He Awake." Several poems such as "To Clarissa Scott Delaney" honor famous people, but the majority of her poetry ponders the meaning of life and death.

In contrast to most of her poetry, Grimké's drama and fiction explore controversial racial issues, especially black women rejecting motherhood, the effects of lynching, and the economic hardships resulting from racial bias. *Rachel* evoked so much criticism that Grimké publicly denied any intent to promote racial genocide and described her audience as white females and her purpose being to reveal the impact of racial violence on a sensitive young woman.

Rachel combines Grimké's themes of motherhood and despair with recurring images in her poetry—notably roses, babies, and people as puppets of God. Rachel Loving, whose most fervent desire is to produce "little black and brown babies," adopts Jimmy, a little boy whose parents have died of smallpox (143). Rachel's awakened memories of racial discrimination, coupled with the trauma of learning about her father's and brother's lynching, make her question why God allows such oppression. Finally, understanding that black mothers cannot protect their children against the threat of racial violence, Rachel rejects her suitor and her dream of motherhood. Similarly, Mara, the genteel heroine of Grimké's other drama, denounces God for allowing racial discrimination.

Grimké's small corpus of fiction is striking and controversial, especially the two stories that appeared during the early 1920s in Margaret Sanger's *Birth Control Review*. "The Closing Door" continues Grimké's exploration of lynching. In it, Lucy, a motherless young girl taken in by Agnes and Jim Milton, reconstructs the past, recalling the Milton's idyllic marriage and Agnes's subsequent degeneration into madness. While pregnant, Agnes learns her favorite brother has been lynched and gradually isolates herself from family and friends, silently moving away and closing doors. Eventually, unable to accept that she cannot protect her child from the risk of lynching even in the north, Agnes smothers her baby. She dies in a mental institution.

Based, according to Grimké, on an actual event, "Goldie" (rejected by *Birth Control Rreview*'s editor in its original form titled "Blackness") also reconstructs the past. Although the versions differ in details, both concern a man returning to the south to help a woman. In "Blackness," the narrator (a lawyer) discovers his former lover and her husband lynched, her unborn child ripped from her body and mutilated. After strangling the lynch mob's leader, the narrator flees north. His fate remains unknown, but Reed, the listener, believes he has escaped. In "Goldie," Victor Forrest discovers his sister, Goldie, and her husband hanged in the backyard. Learning that Lafe Coleman, who has sexually assaulted Goldie is responsible, he kills Coleman, but is himself lynched.

CRITICAL RECEPTION

Contemporary critic Gloria Hull sees Grimké's poetry as an overt reflection of her "triply disfranchised" life as a homosexual black female who is ever aware of her mixed-race heritage, pressured to perform as one of the talented tenth, and "chained between the real experience" of her lesbianism and the "conventions that would not give [her] voice" ("Under the Days" 77, 79; *Color* 108). Hull describes Grimké's lyrics as "delicate, musical, romantic, and pensive" but "transliterated . . . and double-tongued" ("Under the Days" 77, 79).

Jeanne-Maria Miller describes Grimké as a poet who "worked hard at her craft" and who wrote "carefully worded musical lyrics . . . [often] in free verse" (519). For Miller, Grimké's "instrospective" poems "turn to nature" to illustrate "life, love, and death" in a "dominant note" of sadness (519). Despite Grimké's race themes in drama and fiction, Miller labels her a "raceless" writer in the "genteel" tradition (522).

Lamenting that much of Grimké's work has been "rigorously ignored" because it is "too lesbian and too sentimental," Carolivia Herron considers Grimké the foremost realist prior to Richard Wright. She characterizes Grimké's racial poems as expressing "outrage . . . over racial injustice in general" and as examining "African-American cultural grief" (5). In contrast to those who see motherhood as Grimké's primary theme, Herron thinks children are "almost as significant" (11). She also considers poems such as "To My Father upon His Fifty-fifth Birthday" and "As We Have Sowed" critical of Grimké's father and argues that, despite Grimké's Anglo-American style and rhythm, her depictions of "African-American heroic anguish" are a form of the blues (15, 16).

Grimké's works appear in all three thematic categories of Maureen Honey's *Shadowed Dreams: Poetry of the Harlem Renaissance*—protest, heritage, and love and passion. For Honey, women's poetry of that era—Grimké's included—often used nature as "an objective correlative through which [poets] could articulate their gender oppression as well as that of race, for nature, like them, had been objectified, invaded, and used by men seeking power and wealth" (8). In the Emily Dickinson Electronic Archives, Elaine Upton connects Grimké's poems with Dickinson's, asserting that both poets "tease and fascinate reality." She cites especially the "tension between life in the body and death, in "A Winter Twilight."

Contrasting Grimké's poetic themes with the racial issues predominant in her fiction, nonfiction, and drama, most critics concurrently criticize and praise her skill in dramaturgy. Hull, for example, argues that *Rachel* succeeded because of its "novel and competent treatment of an important topic," but "like closet drama reads better than it acts" (*Color* 122).

Jeanne-Maria Miller cites problems in *Rachel*: a too-obviously "contrived" plot, "artificial" language, and a character too "hypersensitive" for contemporary audiences to accept as realistic (576). James Hatch recognizes potential problems with staging and with using children as main characters, yet he urges modern readers to accept the play's "sentimental style" (138). Despite its flaws, *Rachel* represents a milestone in African American drama: excluding musicals, it is the first play by an African American author to be performed by an African American cast.

James Hatch and Ted Shine consider the play an "experimentation with . . . realism/ naturalism" in the style of Ibsen and Chekhov, two of Grimké's favorite authors (134). They note the "Chekhovian 'inactivity' of her characters" who also "demonstrate strong personal development through their internal motivation for change" and argue that the play effectively addresses issues of economics, race, and personal relationships, including motherhood (134).

Although William Storm values Rachel as a "figure of considerable psychological intricacy and emotional volatility," he contends the play is less racial and more an internal "battle" of "religious doubt and faith" (461, 463). Storm argues that when Rachel characterizes God as enjoying the suffering of African Americans, mocking laughter complicates her question of faith.

Joyce Meier views *Rachel* as "somewhat idealistic" and "overdrawn," but a significant "ironic counterpart to the eugenics movement" (125). Although others criticize Rachel's "vacillation," Meier sees the play's tensions as its "strength," for, through them, Rachel reaches her horrifying vision that the "Christian United States tolerates, even condones, racial violence" (122). According to Meier, the denial of full motherhood for African American women counters racial stereotypes, particularly the black mammy, of D. W. Griffith's 1915 racist film, *Birth of a Nation*.

Situating Grimké's work within a tradition that anticipates the rise of African American feminism, Will Harris argues that *Rachel* features "a dual liberation motif" to emphasize racial problems and to create "substantive, independent African American female presences, and thus propose their sexual equality" (205). For Harris, the play invests significance in the domesticity of African American middle-class women, giving their skills economic power. In a technique used by other African American women playwrights of this period, Grimké pictures the home as insulating women from the outside world. Identifying significant parallels between Rachel and Grimké herself, Patricia Young believes Grimké wrote *Rachel* to continue her family's history of activism ("Shackled" 25).

Calling *Rachel* a "cause celebre in the African-American theatrical community," Patricia Schroeder asserts that the play highlights the opposing view African Americans held regarding the purpose of drama—Locke's art for entertainment stance and DuBois's propaganda approach (94). She traces Grimké's influence on later female playwrights and cites the importance of her work in reversing stereotypes and recovering "African-American women's unrecorded history" (94). Schroeder ties Grimké's techniques, especially the fourth-wall set and causal narrative chain, to those of Henrick Ibsen, August Strindberg, and Gerhart Hauptmann.

Considering a strictly realistic view of *Rachel* too narrow, David Krasner views the plot in allegorical, rather than symbolic, terms. He effectively argues for reading the play through Walter Benjamin's theory of mourning and allegory, citing "the opulence of

[Grimké's] imagery, the overabundance of her passion, and the repetitiveness of her language" and pointing to the continuing mourning in response to racial discrimination (67).

Judith Stephens identifies multiple purposes in *Rachel*: (1) to initiate an interracial dialogue by inviting white mothers to experience the trauma of African American mothers, (2) to criticize white women for their role in perpetuating white male dominance and racial oppression, (3) to highlight the peculiar problems of African American mothers who are excluded from the dominant gender ideology of the day, and (4) to upend the sacred view of motherhood by injecting race. In contrast, Elizabeth Brown-Guillory argues that *Rachel*'s "key issue" is a lack of mothering (191).

Jeanne-Maria Miller draws parallels between *Rachel* and *Mara*, noting that both plays use extensive dialogue, report action, include roses as symbols, denounce God for allowing racial discrimination, and use African American genteel characters to contrast racial mistreatment; she also considers *Mara* a "highly literary work, less overtly a protest play" (517, 578). Patricia Young agrees that *Mara*'s primary purpose is to refute the "stereotype of the African American woman as licentious and untutored," but sees a "type of genocide" afflicting the Marston family who, by the end of the play, lose the last of their seven children (*Mara* 11, 20).

Assessment of Grimké's place in the African American canon continues. Ericka M. Miller notes that, although Grimké was "prolific," critical attention to her "complex and intriguing works" has been sparse and has generally concerned her poetry and *Rachel* (59). Miller's own analysis focuses on Grimké's short fiction, the two short stories that appear in the *Birth Control Review*. These puzzle many critics including Hull, who considers that venue "somehow wrong" ("Under the Days" 80). David Hirsch describes Agnes's act of infanticide in "The Closing Door" as a "sacrifice" (466). He contends that Grimké demonstrates the silencing of a people, and a regeneration of their voice, and that "Goldie" repeats this theme. Emphasizing the importance of both stories, Miller says they "recast a slave narrative in a modern setting," refute assumptions of African American women's excessive fertility, and show black mothers keenly aware that even superior mothering cannot avert racial violence (83, 82).

It is perhaps Miller's and Hull's assessments that suggest how Grimké will continue to be viewed. Miller contends that Grimké's stories "insist upon the inclusion of narratives *by* African American women in discussions *of* African American women in regard to presumed universally understood concepts such as 'violence,' 'motherhood,' and 'freedom'" (97). Hull defines Grimké as "a versatile, socially conscious writer who was particularly concerned with the plight of black people in a racist society and the special problems that faced women" (*Color* 150). Likely, as more of Grimké's works become accessible, her reputation as a feminist, a race spokeswoman, and a writer skilled in multiple genres will continue to grow.

BIBLIOGRAPHY

Works by Angelina Weld Grimké

Rachel. In *Black Theater, U.S.A.: Forty-five Plays by Black Americans, 1847–1974*, edited by James V. Hatch and Ted Shine, 137–72. New York: Free Press, 1974.
Selected Works of Angelina Weld Grimké, edited by Carolivia Herron. Schomburg Library of Nineteenth-Century Black Women Writers. New York: Oxford University Press, 1991.

Studies of Angelina Weld Grimké's Works

Brown-Guillory, Elizabeth. "Disrupted Motherlines." In *Women of Color: Mother-Daughter Relationships in 20th-Century Literature*, edited by Elizabeth Brown-Guillory, 188–207. Austin: University of Texas Press, 1996.

Hirsch, David. "Speaking Silences in Angelina Weld Grimké's 'The Closing Door' and 'Blackness.'" *African American Review* 26 (1992): 459–74.

Honey, Maureen. *Shadowed Dreams: Women's Poetry of the Harlem Renaissance*. New Brunswick: Rutger University Press, 1989.

Hull, Gloria T. *Color, Sex and Poetry: Three Women Writers of the Harlem Renaissance*. Bloomington: Indiana University Press, 1987.

———. "Under the Days: The Buried Life and Poetry of Angelina Weld Grimké." In *Home Girls: A Black Feminist Anthology*, edited by Barbara Smith, 73–81. New Brunswick: Rutgers University Press, 1983.

Krasner, David. "Walter Benjamin and the Lynching Play: Allegory and Mourning in Angelina Weld Grimké's *Rachel*." *Text and Presentation* 18 (1997): 64–80.

Meier, Joyce. "The Refusal of Motherhood in African American Women's Theater." *Mellus* 25 (2000): 117–39.

Miller, Ericka M. *The Other Reconstruction: Where Violence and Womanhood Meet in the Writings of Wells-Barnett, Grimké, and Larsen*. New York: Garland, 2000.

Miller, Jeanne-Maria. "Angelina Weld Grimké: Playwright and Poet." *CLA Journal* 21 (1978): 513–24.

Schroeder, Patricia R. "Remembering the Disremembered: Feminist Realists of the Harlem Renaissance." In *Realism and the American Dramatic Tradition*, edited by Wiliam W. Demastes, 91–106. Tuscaloosa: University of Alabama Press, 1996.

Stephens, Judith L. "Anti-Lynch Plays by African American Women: Race, Gender, and Social Protest in American Drama." *African American Review* 26 (1992): 329–40.

Storm, William. "Reactions of a 'Highly-Strung Girl': Psychology and Dramatic Representation in Angelina W. Grimké's *Rachel*." *African American Review* 27 (1993): 461–71.

Upton, Elaine Maria. "A Word Made Flesh Is Seldom: A Conversation between Certain Poems of Emily Dickinson and Angelina Weld Grimké." *Dickinson Electronic Archives*. 1999. http://jefferson.village.virginia.edu/dickinson/titanic/upton3.

Young, Patricia A. "*Mara*: A Tale of Seduction and Slaughter." *Literary Griot* 6 (1994): 11–25.

———. "Shackled: Angelina Weld Grimke." *Women and Language* 15 (1992): 25–31.

Gloria A. Shearin

ROSA GUY (1925–)

BIOGRAPHICAL NARRATIVE

Rosa Guy (née Cuthbert), novelist, playwright, and editor, was born in Trinidad on September 1, 1925. In 1932 she and her family moved to the United States. Her mother died two years later and Guy and her sister were sent to live with their cousins. After their father died in 1937, Guy and her sister lived in an orphanage and then in foster homes in Harlem, New York. This upheaval in her childhood, and experiences in Harlem, is visible in many of her writings. After leaving school at age fourteen, she began working in factories. She married in 1941, and in 1942 had her only child, Warner. Guy's involvement with civil rights and writing became more established due to her association with the American Negro Theatre during World War II and with her studies at New York University. As a founding member of the Harlem Writers Guild in the late 1940s, along with Maya Angelou and Sarah Wright among others, Guy is an influential historical figure in the arts in the United States. She writes for adults, young adults, and children.

MAJOR WORKS

Her first novel, *Bird at My Window* (1966), is set in Harlem in the 1950s and offers an indictment of racism and poverty through the disintegration of its central character, Wade Williams. The reasons for his slide from being a brilliant school pupil to being unemployed and murderous at the age of thirty-eight are explained with his memories of the past. His wings are seen to have been clipped by institutional racism and poverty, and so, the novel critiques the influence of his environment and challenges his restricted freedom. Wade, who fought in World War II for the United States and helped to liberate France, is an emblem for the hypocrisy of racism. He is depicted as constrained throughout his childhood and adult life at home, and has yet fought for the freedom of others in Europe. The themes of racism and lack of choices are revisited by Guy repeatedly, as with *The Disappearance* (1979) and its sequel *New Guys around the Block* (1983). In these two novels, Imamu Jones survives in Harlem, and Guy, once again, exposes the devastation of an African American family through a central male character. The external influences of alcohol and drugs are vilified as available poisons. The taking of these is written of as the symptom (rather than the cause) of institutionalized inequality.

In her paper, "The Human Spirit," Guy reiterates her criticism of the United States, which she argues is a "playland" of greed. She explains this as such: "we play: society crumbles" (132). Guy's faith in the human spirit is evident in her fiction and this paper, but she is also unafraid to make her readers face the harsh realities of urban living in late-twentieth-century United States.

CRITICAL RECEPTION

Considering Guy's prolific output, relatively little has been written about her. She is, however, included in *Contemporary Lesbian Writers of the United States: A Bio-Bibliographical Critical Sourcebook*. Critical reception of her work has been positive; for example, she was awarded the American Library Association's Notable Book Award for *The Friends*. She has also received the Coretta King Award and an Outstanding Book of the Year citation in the *New York Times*. Furthermore, *Once on This Island* (which is the musical version of *My Love, My Love*) was nominated for eight Tony Awards. *My Love, My Love* is set on a Caribbean Island and is a reworking of Hans Christian Andersen's *The Little Mermaid*.

BIBLIOGRAPHY

Works by Rosa Guy

And I Heard a Bird Sing. London: Gollancz, 1987.
Billy the Great. London: Gollancz, 1991.
Bird at My Window. Philadelphia: Lippincott, 1966.
The Disappearance. London: Macmillan Education, 1979.
Edith Jackson. New York: Viking Press, 1978.
The Friends. New York: Holt, Rhinehart & Winston, 1973.
"The Human Spirit." In *Caribbean Women Writers: Essays from the First International Conference*, edited by Selwyn R. Cudjoe. Wellesley: Calaloux Publications, 1990.
A Measure of Time. New York: Holt, Rhinehart & Winston, 1983.
My Love, My Love or The Peasant Girl. New York: Holt, Rhinehart & Winston, 1985.
New Guys around the Block. London: Gollancz, 1983.
Paris, Pee Wee and Big Dog. London: Gollancz, 1984.
Ruby. New York: Viking, 1976.
The Sun, The Sea, A Touch of Wind. New York: Dutton, 1995. (First U.S. edition, 1985.)

Study of Rosa Guy's Works

Eastman, Beva. "Rosa (Cuthbert) Guy." In *Contemporary Lesbian Writers of the United States: A Bio-Bibliographical Critical Sourcebook*, edited by Sandra Pollock et al. Westport, CT: Greenwood Press, 1993.

Julie Ellam

BEVERLY GUY-SHEFTALL (1946–)

BIOGRAPHICAL NARRATIVE

Beverly Guy-Sheftall, an activist and a contributor to black feminism, was born in 1946 in Memphis, Tennessee. Growing up in the Jim Crow south has profoundly shaped her personal, professional, and civic life. Until her parents separated when she was eleven years old, Guy-Sheftall and her two younger sisters lived with both parents who worked, at least for part of their careers, as teachers. She credits both her parents and her maternal grandparents for providing a foundation for her progressive attitudes on race and gender, particularly her mother Ernestine Varnado Guy, whom Guy-Sheftall refers to as "the first feminist [she] ever knew" (Duplessis and Snitow, 485). Evidently, the value of education in nurturing individuality and self-reliance did not escape Guy-Sheftall who graduated from high school with honors before enrolling at Spelman College in Atlanta at age sixteen.

While a student, Guy-Sheftall made her own efforts to understand and revise race and gender constructions. She earned a B.A. in English with a minor in secondary education from Spelman College in 1966. She completed a master's thesis on Faulkner's treatment of women at Atlanta University in 1970, and continued to pursue her growing interest in women's studies in the Graduate Institute of the Liberal Arts at Emory University, where, in 1984, she completed her dissertation "Daughters of Sorrow: Attitudes toward Black Women, 1880–1920." She shared her interest and growing knowledge of feminist issues with her students, first at Alabama State University, then at Spelman College, where she has been working since 1971. She is now Anna Julia Cooper Professor of women's studies at Spelman College and teaches graduate courses at Emory University's Institute for Women's Studies.

A prolific scholar, outspoken activist, and highly sought-after speaker, Beverly Guy-Sheftall has established herself as an authority on black feminist scholarship. In these roles, as well as in her capacities as coeditor of the now-defunct *Sage* (1983–1995), a scholarly journal addressing issues affecting black women, (cofounded with Patricia Bell-Scott), and as founding director of Spelman College's Women's Research and Resource Center, Guy-Sheftall has developed forums for a much wider audience to participate in the burgeoning field of black feminism.

MAJOR WORKS

Guy-Sheftall's oeuvre includes many firsts: the first anthology on black women's literature; the first anthology of African American feminist thought; and the first anthology of African American men's writings on the subject of race, gender, and sexuality. Her consistency as a trailblazer springs from her resolve to write and speak forcefully and unapologetically about controversial issues, particularly those that challenge historical and social constructions of race, class, gender, and sexuality. Her work has sought to offer alternative perspectives and to invite reexamination of entrenched views within academic and popular discourse. As a result, much of Guy-Sheftall's work is directly involved with the recovery and reclamation of bodies of literature that have gone unacknowledged by the canon of African American and women's writing or with the often contentious critique of an African American racial solidarity that neglects and negates issues of gender and sexuality. By the late 1990s, Guy-Sheftall had contributed several important works to the field of black feminism, including *Sturdy Black Bridges: Visions of Black Women in Literature*, coedited with Roseann P. Bell and Bettye J. Parker (1979); "Daughters of Sorrow: Attitudes toward Black Women, 1880–1920" (1990); *Double Stitch: Black Women Write about Mothers and Daughters* (1991); and *Words of Fire: An Anthology of African American Feminist Thought* (1995).

Guy-Sheftall's most recent work is no less provocative. In 2001, she coedited *Traps: African American Men on Gender and Sexuality*. This anthology offers a broad range of articles that collectively redefine black masculinity by disrupting racial myths and sexual stereotypes. Similarly, Guy-Sheftall's 2003 *Gender Talk: The Struggle for Women's Equality in African American Communities*, coedited with Johnetta B. Cole, contests prevailing attitudes about and actions against black women within African American institutions and popular culture. Like her previous work, this most recent scholarship is grounded historically, situating these contemporary issues in their political, social, and cultural contexts.

No subject is off limits for Guy-Sheftall, who writes about topics as diverse and prescient as the civil rights movement, black nationalism, the Million Man March, hip hop, violence against women and homosexuals, welfare rights, organized labor, healthcare, and AIDS. Guy-Sheftall's attention to these subjects reflects her commitment to black feminism, which incorporates an analysis of gender and sexuality in addition to race and class. Using her platform as a scholar and activist, Guy-Sheftall implores black leaders "to seriously consider issues of gender and sexuality as they try to imagine what it would be like to liberate black people in the 21st century" (Potier 2004). Her body of works argues, in fact, that the discussion of gender and sexuality is as integral as the discussion of race and class to any understanding and revising of the nation's history.

Though having firmly established herself in the academic community, Guy-Sheftall has never been content to confine her research or her critical analyses to academic discourse. Instead, she invites and challenges a wide range of constituencies to recognize and rectify the hegemonic construction of Western feminism and the gender inequality between and within different racial, socioeconomic, and cultural communities. Often, this entreaty is made directly to African Americans. For example, although Guy-Sheftall acknowledges that "both Black women and Black men have been victimized by racism," she adds that "Black people are programmed to focus on the external ways our safety is compromised . . . [b]ut Black women's safety is often threatened by black men, and that's something we don't like to talk about" (Weathers 2003). These types of unsettling revelations have sometimes placed Guy-Sheftall in the midst of controversy, such as when she supported Spelman students' proposed protest against African American rap star Nelly for his misogynistic song lyrics and degrading music videos. Yet, for Guy-Sheftall, the conversation and debate that ensues from such controversy are critical to challenging and changing sexist and homophobic thinking and practices.

CRITICAL RECEPTION

Because of her scholarship and activism, Guy-Sheftall has been recognized with numerous honors and awards, including the Kellogg and Woodrow Wilson fellowships and the Spelman College Presidential Award for outstanding scholarship. Her greatest accomplishment, however, may be her courage and skill in spearheading the long-overdue discussion of the intersecting roles of race, gender, class, and sexuality in this nation's history. In the process, she has helped to rewrite that history.

Criticism of her scholarship bears out this claim. Journalist Janice K. Bryant, in his review of *Words of Fire* in *Journal of Blacks in Higher Education*, laments that the anthology is not a more interesting read because it "showcases black feminist intellectuals, and that is it." She also recognizes that the work is "a solid refutation of feminism as espoused by white women" (112). Most critics recognize this refutation as a remarkable and interesting feat in its own right. For instance, in her review of *Sturdy Black Bridges* for *Library Review*, Women's Studies bibliographer Esther Stineman writes, "So little has been available on the work of black women writers and so much needs to be clarified about what black women have written and the images they have projected that this excellent collection of critical essays, overview articles, interviews and excerpts cannot help but be significant" (1339).

Furthermore, critics applaud Guy-Sheftall's scholarship for its appeal, relevance, and accessibility to a broad audience. Professor of African American and African Diaspora Studies Audrey McCluskey praises the collection of poems, narratives, and essays included in *Double Stitch* as "one that crosses the needlessly rigid line between the truth of scholarship and the truth of personal experience, one that does not sacrifice complexity and depth for sociological formula" (123). Valerie Smith, director of the Program in African American Studies and Woodrow Wilson Professor of literature at Princeton University, refers to Guy-Sheftall as "a path breaking literary and cultural critic" who, along with *Gender Talk* coauthor Johnetta B. Cole, "interweave[s] astute analyses with accounts of their own public and private experiences" (43).

In an *American Visions'* review, Jonetta Rose Barras writes that "*Words of Fire* affirms that, as in the past, the 21st century will not find African-American women hiding behind pastel curtains but rather in the vanguard of the continuing movement for equal rights for all" (32). By all accounts, Beverly Guy-Sheftall is in that vanguard.

BIBLIOGRAPHY

Works by Beverly Guy-Sheftall

"Black Feminism in the United States." In *Upon These Shores: African-American Experience, 1600 to the Present*, edited by William R. Scott and William G. Shade. New York: Routledge, 2000.

"The Body Politic: Black Female Sexuality and the Nineteenth-Century Euro-American Imagination." In *Skin Deep, Spirit Strong: The Black Female Body in American Culture*, edited by Kimberly Wallace-Sanders. Ann Arbor: University of Michigan Press, 2002.

"Daughters of Sorrow: Attitudes toward Black Women, 1880–1920." New York: Carlson, 1991.

Double Stitch: Black Women Write about Mothers and Daughters. With Patricia Bell-Scott. Boston: Beacon Press, 1991.

"Elizabeth Catlett: Making What You Know Best." In *Something All Our Own: The Grant Hill Collection of African American Art*, edited by Grant Hill and Alvia J. Wardlaw. Durham: Duke University Press, 2004.

Finding a Way: The Black Family's Struggle for an Education at the Atlanta University Center. Atlanta: African American Family History Association, 1983.

Gender Talk: The Struggle for Women's Equality in African American Communities. With Johnetta B. Cole. New York: One World/Ballantine, 2003.

"Preface." In *Still Lifting, Still Climbing: Contemporary Black Women's Activism*, edited by Kimberly Springer. New York: New York University Press, 1999.

"Sisters in Struggle: A Belated Response." In *The Feminist Memoir Project: Voices from Women's Liberation*, edited by Rachel Blau DuPlessis and Ann Snitow, 485–92. New York: Three Rivers Press, 1998.

Sturdy Black Bridges: Visions of Black Women in Literature. With Roseann P. Bell and Bettye J. Parker. Garden City, NY: Anchor Books, 1979.

Traps: African American Men on Gender and Sexuality. With Rudolph P. Byrd. Bloomington: Indiana University Press, 2001.

"Where are All the Black Female Intellectuals?" In *Harold Cruse's* The Crisis of the Negro Intellectual *Reconsidered*, edited by Jerry G. Watts. New York: Routledge, 2004.

"The Women of Bronzeville." In *A Life Distilled: Gwendolyn Brooks, Her Poetry and Fiction*, edited by Maria Mootry and Gary Smith. Urbana: University of Illinois Press, 1987.

Women's Studies: A Retrospective: A Report to the Ford Foundation. With Susan Heath. New York: Ford Foundation, 1995.

Words of Fire: An Anthology of African American Feminist Thought. New York: New Press, 1995.

Studies of Beverly Guy-Sheftall's Works

Barras, Jonetta Rose. "Feminist Fire." Rev. of *Words of Fire*, edited by Beverly Guy-Sheftall. *American Visions* 11.1 (February/March 1996): 31–32.

Bryant, Janice K. "Black Women Speak Their Minds." Rev. of *Words of Fire*, edited by Beverly Guy-Sheftall. *Journal of Blacks in Higher Education* 10 (Winter 1995–1996): 111–12.

McCluskey, Audrey T. Rev. of *Double Stitch: Black Women Write about Mothers and Daughters*, edited by Patricia Bell-Scott, et al. *NWSA* 5.1 (Spring 1993): 122–25.

Potier, Beth. "Dangerous Silences: Panel Explores Sexuality in Black Communities." *Harvard University Gazette*. April 29, 2004. Retrieved January 20, 2006. http://www.news .harvard.edu/gazette/2004/04.29/13-afamgender.html.

Smith, Valerie. "Gender Politics in the Black Community." Rev. of *Gender Talk: The Struggle for Women's Equality in African American Communities*, by Johnetta B. Cole and Beverly Guy-Sheftall. *Crisis* (March/April 2003): 42–43.

Stineman, Esther. Rev. of *Sturdy Black Bridges: Visions of Black Women in Literature*, edited by Roseann P. Bell, Bettye J. Parker, and Beverly Guy-Sheftall. *Library Journal* 104.12 (1979): 13–39.

Weathers, Diane. "Black America's Dirty Little Secrets." *Essence* 1 (July 2003): 161–63. *Biography Resource Center*. 2003. Farmington Hills, MI: Thomson Gale. Retrieved January 17, 2006. http://galenet.galegroup.com.eresources.lib.umb.edu/servlet/BioRC (accessed January 17, 2006).

Lynnell Thomas

MADAME EMMA AZALIA SMITH HACKLEY (1867–1922)

BIOGRAPHICAL NARRATIVE

Classical singer, composer, journalist, and author Madame Emma Azalia Smith Hackley's dual legacy is that of preserving the African American spiritual and African American women's dignity. Born on June 29, 1867, to Corilla Beard Smith, a piano/violin teacher, and Henry Smith, a blacksmith, in Murfreesboro, Tennessee, Azalia, as she was called, adopted her mother's enthusiasm for teaching as a means of social uplift. Reared in the Protestant Episcopal Church, Azalia's musical contributions especially emphasized the Episcopalian Church's emphasis upon choral performance of the highest order. She also excelled in piano, voice and pipe organ, first studying under the direction of her mother, in Detroit (racial intolerance in Murfreesboro regarding Corilla Smith's pioneering school for African American children forced the Smith family to relocate). While in Detroit, in 1883, Azalia gained an honors diploma via Central High School. In 1886, she graduated from Washington Normal School.

In Detroit, in 1889, she met Edwin Henry Hackley (1859–1940), an African American attorney, politician, newspaper editor, and native Michigander. The couple eloped in 1894, making their home in Denver, Colorado, where they coedited the *Denver Statesman* (an African American political newspaper containing "The Exponent," Madame Hackley's column regarding women's health and etiquette); joined the powerful Episcopal Church of the Crucifixion; hosted bridge parties and socialized with such African American luminaries as Madame C. J. Walker (who began her million-dollar hair preparations company in the city) and poet laureate Paul Laurence Dunbar. Also, while in Denver, the Hackleys created the Grand United Order of Libyans, a secret organization committed to achieving justice for African Americans through democracy and patriotism. In 1900, Madame Hackley, a coloratura soprano, became the first African American to graduate from the University of Denver with a Bachelor of Music degree. With their organization becoming a lightning rod for racial tension, the couple relocated to Philadelphia in 1901.

Among Madame Hackley's major Philadelphia achievements were creating the People's Chorus, introducing a young Marian Anderson and Roland Hayes to their first audiences, and featuring a unique program of European classical music juxtaposed against arranged African American spirituals—a program format now commonplace in classical music. A pioneer in the area of African Americans in classical music, Madame Hackley's travels paralleled those of African American performers, generally speaking: she nevertheless rode Jim Crow ("Coloreds Only") cars by choice, as she easily could have passed for a white. In fact, she set down much of her writings during long train hauls and while waiting in train stations. Madame Hackley's grueling touring schedule contributed to the dissolution of the Hackley marriage; by 1910, they were divorced.

Following that, Madame Hackley kept her husband's "good name" for protection and relocated to Chicago, the nation's central railroad city.

The Chicago years proved fertile for Madame Hackley. There she started the Hackley Music Publishing Company and the Vocal Normal Institute (1912–1916), a music settlement school for African Americans of modest means. In 1913, she appointed Afro-Canadian composer Robert Nathaniel Dett to the position of director of music at Hampton, thus founding the Music Department at Hampton Institute (now Hampton University). Between 1914 and 1915, she published an advice column for the *New York Age*, called "Hints to Young Colored Artists," which addressed the special concerns of African American classical musicians, particularly with respect to scholarships, touring realities, and travel abroad. In 1916, she published *The Colored Girl Beautiful*. She also toured the United States, Canada, and Europe as vocalist/pianist (establishing herself as the first to arrange African American spirituals for solo voice) and lecturer regarding women's empowerment. While in Paris, in 1918, she composed "Carola (A Serenade)" and appointed herself World War I correspondent, writing columns for the *New York Age* to tell African American readers the fate of their loved ones abroad. In 1920, Madame Hackley traveled to Tokyo, Japan, to introduce African American spirituals during the International Sunday School Convention—a first for Japan, African Americans, and women.

In October 1921, while conducting an African American chorus in Oakland, California, Madame Hackley collapsed, never to regain her physical or mental strength. Transported to Detroit under the loving care of her only sibling, Marietta, she died on December 13, 1922, of a massive brain hemorrhage. Madame Hackley was buried, according to her wish, in an unmarked grave in Detroit. As Madame Hackley made no audio recordings (she refused lucrative recording contracts, as the "catch" was that she would have to betray her African American heritage by "passing" for white), her literary works, ironically, have become her "voice."

MAJOR WORKS

Madame Hackley's best known literary work, *The Colored Girl Beautiful* (1916), is the first etiquette book for African American women. Including such chapter titles as "Deep Breathing," "Vibrations," "Originality," "The School of the Colored Girl Beautiful," "The Religion of the Colored Girl Beautiful," "The Colored Working Girl Beautiful," and "The Colored Mother Beautiful," the book advocates higher education, personal and public health initiatives, and the cultivation of inner beauty, through restraint and thoughtful application of such Christian ideals as purposeful industry, piety, and exalted motherhood. *The Colored Girl Beautiful* is based on lectures that Madame Hackley had given to women students at Tuskegee Institute (now Tuskegee University) in Alabama, at the request of Booker T. Washington. Hackley hawked the hardcover book during her tours, selling 1,000 copies, all below market price, to reach an underserved audience of African American women moving from plantation and domestic jobs to clerical and secretarial work. *The Colored Girl Beautiful* retains its relevance as a literary and historical document regarding the condition of, and possibilities for, African American women.

CRITICAL RECEPTION

The Colored Girl Beautiful (1916) was well received during its initial printing. In *Homespun Heroines*, Hallie Q. Brown mentions the book in her overview of Hackley's career, saying that Hackley "has also contributed to literature in her book titled *The Colored Girl Beautiful*. Madam Hackley's life is a story of lofty purposes and brilliant achievements." As the book's author and primary promoter died only six years after its publication, it lay dormant until the late 1980s. Since that time, the world has witnessed a revival of interest in Madame Hackley's life and works. In 2001, Lisa Pertillar Brevard published *A Biography of E. Azalia Smith Hackley (1867–1922), African-American Singer and Social Activist*, a biography and manuscript recovery project which she began at Smith College in 1989. In discussing *The Colored Girl Beautiful* (as informed by the published work of Brevard), Berg writes, "The popular writer and lecturer E. Azalia Hackley . . . fused Eugenics and New Negro discourses to define the black mother's particularly pivotal role in race building." Barbara Foley finds Hackley's book useful for understanding the African American elite at the beginning of the twentieth century: "For the most part, the offspring of the Negro aristocracy were models of bourgeois conduct, taking their cues from texts such as E. Azalia Hackley's *The Colored Girl Beautiful* (1916)." Moreover, the Harvard University Library Open Collections Program includes the book in its ongoing collection, "Women Working: 1870–1930 "

BIBLIOGRAPHY

Works by Madame Emma Azalia Smith Hackley

"Carola (A Serenade)." Detroit: E. Azalia Hackley, 1918. Reprint, New York: Handy Bros.Music Co., 1953.
The Colored Girl Beautiful. Kansas City, MO: Burton Pub. Co., 1916.
A Guide in Voice Culture. Philadelphia: n.p. 1909.
"Hints to Young Colored Artists." *New York Age* (December 7, 1914–March 1, 1915).

Studies of Madame Emma Azalia Smith Hackley's Works

Berg, Allison. "Fatal Contractions: Nella Larson's *Quicksand* and the New Negro Mother." In *Mothering the Race: Women's Narratives of Reproduction, 1890–1930*. Chicago: University of Illinois Press, 2002.
Brevard, Lisa Pertillar. *A Biography of E. Azalia Smith Hackley (1867–1922), African-American Singer and Social Activist*. New York: Edwin Mellen Press, 2001.
———. *A Biography of Edwin Henry Hackley (1859–1940), African American Attorney and Activist*. New York: Edwin Mellen Press, 2003.
———, ed. *Madame E. Azalia Hackley's The Colored Girl Beautiful (1916)*. New Orleans: Monarch Baby Pub., 2004.
Brown, Hallie Q. "Madame Emma Azalia Smith Hackley: Noted Lyric Soprano." In *Homespun Heroines*, 236. Xenia, OH: Aldine Pub. Co., 1926.
Catalog of the E. Azalia Hackley Memorial Collection of Negro Music, Dance and Drama at the Detroit Public Library. Boston: G. K. Hall & Co., 1979.
Foley, Barbara. "Jean Toomer's Washington and The Politics of Class: From Blue Veins to Seventh-Street Rebels." *Modern Fiction Studies* 42 (Summer 1996): 289–321.

Lisa Pertillar Brevard

VIRGINIA HAMILTON (1936–2002)

BIOGRAPHICAL NARRATIVE

Named after the state from which her grandfather escaped from slavery into freedom, essay and children's writer Virginia Hamilton was born on March 12, 1936, and was raised on a small farm in Yellow Springs, Ohio, that has belonged to her family since the 1850s. She grew up in a large extended family of storytellers aware of the value of their personal experiences and Ohio's centrality to the legacy of both slavery and freedom. Ohio was at the heart of the Underground Railroad; over 50,000 slaves passed through Ohio by crossing the Ohio River into freedom, or settled there after escaping. Her childhood was filled with the stories of escape and daring, and with the personal reminiscences of her family and community. For Hamilton, the "first story," the tale of genesis from which all others proceed, is the story of her grandfather's escape from slavery to freedom. "Every year he sat [his] ten children down and said, 'Listen children, I want to tell you this story of when I ran away from slavery, so slavery will never happen to you'" (Mikkelsen 5). She grew up understanding storytelling as a natural and informal activity and one that was also fundamental to the wholeness of the soul, a way people had of "putting their own flesh and blood in proper perspective" ("Rememory" 637). She became a "teller of tales" because of this legacy, and began writing at a very early age. Hamilton lived at the physical border between slavery and freedom, her knowledge of communal and personal history was grounded in familial myths about the passing on of freedom, and her language derived from a community of folk who learned to be free by "talking themselves into new states of mind" (Mikkelsen 2). Thus, the stories of those crossing the boundary between bondage and freedom—physical, spiritual, cultural, geographical, or political—define her work.

Hamilton wrote throughout high school in Yellow Springs, and after graduation received a full scholarship to study writing at a nearby university, Antioch College. She transferred after three years to Ohio State University, landing finally in New York. There, intent on seeking her fortune, Hamilton focused on her writing and worked at a variety of odd jobs to support herself, including working as an accountant, singing in nightclubs, and playing the guitar for a performance group. She continued to write and study writing, this time at New York's New School for Social Research. There she met her husband, poet Arnold Adoff, whom she married in 1960, and with whom she had two children, Leigh Hamilton Adoff and Jaime Levi Adoff.

While at the New School, a classmate who was working at Macmillan Publishing encouraged her to submit one of her stories as children's literature, and Hamilton's first novel, *Zeely* (1967), was born. Hamilton wrote prolifically for the rest of her life, producing an average of one book a year. After living in New York and Europe for ten years, Hamilton returned to Yellow Springs with her husband and children, purchasing two acres of the family land, upon which she built the home that was her base for the remainder of her life. She was a pioneer in the field of children's literature, consistently producing works that challenged and expanded the form and substance of literature. She died of breast cancer, at her home in Yellow Springs in February 2002.

MAJOR WORKS

Hamilton's work can be roughly divided into three categories: fiction, much of which is innovative, formally daring, and often experimental; her biographies and collections of folklore, what she has called "liberation literature"; and her essays about literature and storytelling, her under-examined contribution to shaping African American literature and literary theory. Hamilton's fiction makes living stories from the buried history of African Americans, an act of writing that she calls "Rememory . . . an exquisitely textured recollection, real or imagined, which is otherwise indescribable" ("Rememory" 633). Privileging the act of recreation as heavily as the "facts" of history has been Hamilton's most magical act. Her works pick apart and reconstruct familiar ideas and symbols, revealing the surprising, enlightening, and sometimes heartbreaking meanings behind the stories her readers think they already know. A story about her grandfather, whose hand was burned closed in a work-related fire, exemplifies this vein of disruption and reconstruction that runs throughout her work: ". . . his hand was a fist with burn scars hidden in the tightly shut palm. I would lace my fingers over his closed fist, and he would lift me up and up and swing me around and around to my enormous delight. After that, the raised black fist became for me both myth and history, and they were mine. Grandpaw Perry was John Henry and High John de Conquer. He was power—the fugitive, the self-made, the closed fist in which I knew there was kept magic" ("Rememory" 673). Claiming and building upon the familiar contemporaneous symbol of African American resistance, she links it to freedom struggle that is at once longer, more intimate, increasingly layered, bound by history, and released into current legibility by an act of reimagination. In her reimaginings, she is unwilling to relinquish the complicated legacy of African American subjectivity. She represents the pain that makes possible the triumph, and the injury at the heart of strength. Hamilton also claims that defiant and complicated symbol for the act of writing and for the work of the African American writer, the "humble crusader locked in a garret room" who "suffers for life, creating all purpose-prose with bruised and delicate hands" ("Rememory" 638). This way of interrogating meaning defines her fiction, particularly the fantasy *The Magical Adventures of Pretty Pearl*, her much-praised *M.C. Higgins the Great*, and *The Justice Trilogy*. Similarly, *The Dies Drear Chronicles—The House of Dies Drear* and its sequel *The Mystery of Drear House*—follow an African American family as they relocate from south to north, retracing the physical route of escape for the enslaved, and moving to a house that was a way station on the Underground Railroad. In these books, Hamilton figures the hidden history of escape as the mystery of a haunting that needs to be uncovered, exposing the reader to the hidden story of black leadership in the Underground Railroad, and by giving an old story an entirely new meaning, showing that history is the real mystery waiting to be solved. Though Hamilton's writings do not explicitly identify her with the freedom struggles of the 1950s and 1960s, they arrive on the tail end of those political movements to offer important critiques and revisions of African American subjectivity, and to interrogate ideas of freedom and cultural transformation.

Her several essays not only examine intimate encounters with writing and storytelling, but also examine the roots of African American writing traditions, literature's cultural functions, and the new uses to which authors might put old fragments of material. Her work probes the ways in which African American lives are bound and shaped by a legacy of oppression and the ways in which those limitations are often exacerbated because histories are buried deep and often lost. In her 1981 essay "Ah, Sweet Rememory!" she coined the term "rememory" as a fundamental strategy within African American writing—six years before the publication of Toni Morrison's *Beloved* propelled that term into widespread use—in order to legitimize a necessary and willed recreation of the past that enables the articulation of what would be otherwise inarticulable. In her 1975 essay "High John Is Risen Again," she argues that reexamining the past might inspire innovations in creative forms, and widen avenues for self-creation. "We who hope to find alternatives to culturally prescribed ways of writing about black and white living," she wrote, "must reach far back and learn to know again and trust the sensibilities of the slave ancestors" (160). One emblem of this rediscovery is the folk hero High John the Conqueror, in whom she sees the possibility of "self-assertion—not necessarily self-sacrifice and self-destruction—and through new art forms wherever possible" (161). Turning such knowledge inside out might reveal, like her grandfather's closed black fist, vital and healing magic.

In the same way that W.E.B. DuBois claimed that the artistic traditions of African America were the very essence of American art and, in fact, constituted its only truly indigenous art forms, Hamilton emphasizes that African American literature is American literature—hence the subtitle of her most revered collection of folklore, *The People Could Fly: American Black Folklore*. She does not make this distinction to reject connections with Africa (which she reverts as well as complicates throughout her work) but rather to foreground and valorize the history and contributions of African lives in the face of an irrevocable breach, and in that way mark the "progress of Black adults and their children across the American hopescape" ("Rememory" 638). Works of reimagined folklore, her "liberation literature," occupied much of her later writing. Her work in folklore is interested in the unique and unprecedented cultural invention that arose from the experience of African peoples in America, across the diaspora. By reclaiming folklore, and proclaiming the merit of "parallel cultures," Hamilton has helped to destabilize the idea of greater and lesser cultures and contributions, and "promises," writes her critical biographer Nina Mikkelsen, "to displace dichotomous thinking about 'mainstream' and 'nonmainstream'" topics and traditions (147).

CRITICAL RECEPTION

Hamilton's work was highly praised and critically successful from its initial appearance on the cultural landscape, and her thirty-five books have won virtually every major award a writer can win, including the Newberry Medal, for which she was the first African American recipient; the Hans Christian Andersen Award, which is the highest honor in children's literature and which recognizes her outstanding body of work; and the National Book Award. In 1995 she became the first children's author to receive the MacArthur Foundation "genius" grant. Her first book, *Zeely*, a young African American girl's coming of age story, was quickly hailed as an important and radical departure from most books about African American children. In contrast to novels that imagine that the problems of segregation and prejudice could be eventually ameliorated by the discovery of the humanness of the African American child despite her color, Hamilton's work dared to assume an African American girl's humanity and examine her growing understanding of her heritage. "Whereas White writers at this time were driven to show equality on terms of similarity," writes Mikkelsen, "Hamilton dared to say that children could be different and still be equal" (10). Hamilton's next two books, *The House of Dies Drear*, which received the Edgar Allan Poe Award for best juvenile mystery of the year, and *The Planet of Junior Brown*, a dystopic novel of urban youth that won the Newberry Honor, cemented her status as an exciting and innovative literary voice and one of America's foremost storytellers. In 1975, she won both the Newberry Medal and the National Book Award for *M.C. Higgins, the Great*, a book that also won more honors and awards than any single children's book.

Hamilton's work has garnered attention in one book-length study, *Virginia Hamilton*, and in numerous scholarly articles and talks. Her work has also inspired and supported one of the largest and longest running conferences on multicultural children's literature, The Virginia Hamilton Conference. Critics of her work cite Hamilton's attention to the stories of African American girls; after the publication of *M.C. Higgins, the Great*, her next eight novels focused solely on African American female protagonists. Her attention to girls as the center of narrative impulse and shapers of modes of discourse and forms of narration has prompted several critical examinations of feminism and feminist theory in her work. Hamilton is widely credited with paving the way for other African American children's authors, in terms of attracting positive critical attention and wider publication. Authors such as Mildred Taylor, Patricia McKissack, Sharon Bell Mathis, and Walter Dean Myers have succeeded her.

Critics also point out affinities with Toni Morrison, in particular the formal strategies that focus on the recovery of what is unspoken and unremembered. Like Morrison, the impact of speaking the unspoken stories on Hamilton's texts is visible within the work as it produces ruptures and discontinuities in time, and as it complicates the use of language. Like Morrison's, Hamilton's works are also deeply tied to a sense of place. Her opus manifests an abiding interest in the relations between African American subjectivity and place, a belief that for African American subjects, claiming a homeplace constitutes a radical political and social act.

The year 1985 heralded a new direction in Hamilton's writing. In that year she published *The People Could Fly*, an illustrated collection of stories from slavery and the first in a series of picture books, including *In the Beginning: Creation Stories from around the World*, *The Dark Way*, *The All Jahdu Storybook*, and *Many Thousand Gone: African Americans from Slavery to Freedom*. These picture books were linked to *Anthony Burns: The Defeat and Triumph of a Fugitive Slave*, and other late novels by their overt focus on liberation, which Hamilton describes as "portray[ing] the individual's and a people's suffering and growing awareness of self in pursuit of freedom" ("Planting Seeds" 676). Her sources for these works were her own family stories, old manuscripts, and the stories told in the Work Progress Administration interviews. Perhaps it would be most accurate to understand that all of her work is liberation literature because such work, as she writes, "not only frees the subject of record and evidence but the witness as well, who is the reader, who then becomes part of the struggle . . . we suffer; and we triumph as the victim triumphs, in the solution of liberation" ("Everything of Value" 375).

BIBLIOGRAPHY

Works by Virginia Hamilton

"Ah, Sweet Rememory!" *Horn Book* (December 1981): 633–40.

The All Jahdu Storybook. Illustrated by Barry Moser. New York: Hartcourt, Brace, Jovanovich, 1991.

"Anthony Burns." *Horn Book* (March–April 1989): 183–85.

Anthony Burns: The Defeat and Triumph of a Fugitive Slave. New York: Knopf, 1988.

Arilla Sun Down. New York: William Morrow, 1976.

The Bells of Christmas. Illustrated by Lambert Davis. New York: Hartcourt, Brace, Jovanovich, 1989.

Bluish: A Novel. New York: Blue Sky Press, 1999.

"Changing Woman, Working." In *Celebrating Children's Books: Essays on Children's Literature in Honor of Zena Sutherland*, edited by Betsy Hearne and Marilyn Kaye. New York: Lothrop, Lee & Shepard Books, 1981.

Cousins. New York: Philomel, 1990.

The Dark Way. Illustrated by Lambert Davis. New York: Harcourt, Brace, Jovanovich, 1990.

Drylongso. Illustrated by Jerry. New York: Hartcourt, Brace, Jovanovich, 1992.

Dustland. New York: Greenwillow Books, 1980.

"Everything of Value: Moral Realism in the Literature for Children." May Hill Arbuthnot Honor Lecture, Richmond, Virginia, May 4, 1993. *Journal of Youth Services in Libraries* 6 (Summer 1993): 363–77.

"Further Notes on a Progeny's Progress." Speech delivered at the Children's and Young People's Meeting of the New Jersey Library Association, May 4, 1968.

The Gathering. New York: Greenwillow Books, 1981.

The Girl Who Spun Gold. New York: Blue Sky Press, 2000.

"Hagi, Mose and Drylongso." In *The Zena Sutherland Lectures, 1983–1992*, edited by Betsy-Hearne. New York: Clarion, 1992.

Her Stories: African American Folktales, Fairy Tales and True Tales. Illustrated by Leo and Diane Dillon. New York: Blue Sky Press, 1995.

"High John Is Risen Again." *Horn Book* (April 1975): 113–21.

The House of Dies Drear. New York: Macmillan, 1968.

In the Beginning. Illustrated by Barry Moser. New York: Hartcourt, Brace, Jovanovich, 1988.

Jaguarundi. Illustrated by Floyd Cooper. New York: Blue Sky Press, 1995.

Jahdu. Illustrated by Jerry Pinkney. New York: Greenwillow Books, 1980.

Junius Over Far. New York: Harper, 1985.

Justice and Her Brothers. New York: Greenwillow Books, 1981.

"The Known, the Remembered, and the Imagined: Celebrating Afro-American Folktales." *Children's Literature in Education* 18 (1987): 67–75.

A Little Love. New York: Philomel, 1984.

The Magical Adventures of Pretty Pearl. New York: Harper, 1983.

Many Thousand Gone: African Americans from Slavery to Freedom. Illustrated by Leo and Diane Dillon. New York: Knopf, 1993.

M.C. Higgins, the Great. New York: Macmillan, 1974.

"The Mind of the Novel: The Heart of the Book." *Children's Literature Association Quarterly* 8 (Winter 1983): 10–14.

The Mystery of Drear House. New York: Macmillan, 1987.

"On Being a Black Writer in America." *Lion and the Unicorn* 10 (1986): 15–17.

Paul Robeson: The Life and Times of a Free Black Man. New York: Harper & Row, 1974.

The People Could Fly. Illustrated by Leo and Diane Dillon. New York: Knopf, 1985.

Plain City. New York: Scholastic, 1993.

The Planet of Junior Brown. New York: Macmillan, 1971.
"Planting Seeds." *Horn Book* (November 1999): 674–80.
"Portrait of the Author as a Working Writer." *Elementary English* (April 1971): 237–40.
A Ring of Tricksters; Animal Tales from America, the West Indies, and Africa. Illustrated by Barry
    Moser. New York: Blue Sky Press, 1997.
Second Cousins. New York: Blue Sky Press, 1998.
Sweet Whispers, Brother Rush. New York: Philomel, 1982.
"Thought on Children's Books, Reading, and Ethnic America." In *Reading Children's Books and
    Our Pluralistic Society,* edited by Harold Tanyzer and Jean Karl, 61–64. Newark: Interna-
    tional Reading Association, 1972.
Time-Ago Lost: More Tales of Jahdu. Illustrated by Ray Prather. New York: Macmillan, 1973.
The Time-Ago Tales of Jahdu. Illustrated by Nonny Hogrogian. New York: Macmillan, 1969.
Time Pieces: The Book of Times. New York: Blue Sky Press, 2002.
"A Toiler, a Teller." In *Many Faces, Many Voices: Multicultural Literary Experiences for Youth:
    The Virginia Hamilton Conference,* edited by Anthony Manna and Carolyn Brodie. Fort
    Atkinson, WI: Highsmith Press, 1992.
W.E.B. DuBois. New York: T. Y. Crowell, 1972.
When Birds Could Talk and Bats Could Sing. New York: Blue Sky Press, 1996.
A White Romance. New York: Odyssey Classics, 1987.
Willie Bea and the Time the Martians Landed. New York: Greenwillow Books, 1983.
"Writing the Source: In Other Words." *Horn Book* (December 1978): 609–19.
Zeely. Illustrated by Simeon Shimin. New York: Macmillan, 1967.

Studies of Virginia Hamilton's Works

Apseloff, Marilyn. "Creative Geography in the Ohio Novels of Virginia Hamilton." *Children's
    Literature Association Quarterly* (Spring 1983): 17–20.
Dickman, Floyd C. "Virginia Hamilton, Conjurer of Tales." *Ohioana Quarterly* (Summer 1985):
    48–54.
Dressel, Janice Hartwick. "The Legacy of Ralph Ellison in Virginia Hamilton's Justice Trilogy."
    English-Journal (November 1984): 42.
Farrell, Kirby. "Virginia Hamilton's Sweet Whispers, Brother Rush and the Case for a Radical
    Existence." *Contemporary Literature* (Summer 1990): 161–76.
Lenz, Millicent. "Virginia Hamilton's Justice Trilogy: Exploring the Frontiers of Consciousness."
    African-American Voices in Young Adult Literature: Tradition, Transition, Transformation
    (1994): 293–310.
Mikkelsen, Nina. "But Is It a Children's Book? A Second Look at Virginia Hamilton's The
    Magical Adventure." *Children's Literature Association Quarterly* 11.3 (Fall 1986): 134–42.
———. *Virginia Hamilton.* New York: Twayne, 1994.
Moore, Opal, and Donnarae MacCann. "The Uncle Remus Travesty, Part II: Julius Lester and
    Virginia Hamilton." *Children's Literature Association Quarterly* 11 (Winter 1986–1987):
    205–10.
Moss, Anita. "Frontiers of Gender in Children's Literature: Virginia Hamilton's Arilla Sun Down."
    Children's Literature Association Quarterly (Winter 1983): 25–27.
———. "Mythical Narrative: Virginia Hamilton's The Magical Adventures of Pretty Pearl." *The
    Lion and the Unicorn: A Critical Journal of Children's Literature* (1985): 50–57.
Nodelman, Perry. "Children's Literature as Women's Writing." *Children's Literature Association
    Quarterly* 13 (Spring 1988): 31–34.
———. "The Limits of Structures: A Shorter Version of a Comparison between Toni Morrison's
    Song of Solomon and Virginia Hamilton's M.C. Higgins the Great." *Children's Literature
    Association Quarterly* (Fall 1998): 45–48.
Quinn, Alice. "Dancing in the Dark." *New Yorker* (December 1995): 132–35; (1996): 132–35.

Russell, David L. "Virginia Hamilton's Symbolic Presentation of the Afro-American Sensibility." *Cross-Culturalism in Children's Literature: Selected Papers from the Children's Literature Association, Carleton University* (May 1987): 14–17.

Sobat, Gail Sidonie. "If the Ghost Be There, Then Am I Crazy?: An Examination of Ghosts in Virginia Hamilton's Sweet Whispers, Brother Rush and Toni Morrison's Beloved." *Children's Literature Association Quarterly* 20.4 (Winter 1995–1996): 168–74.

Townsend, John Rowe. *Written for Children*. New York: HarperCollins, 1992.

Trites, Roberta Seelinger. "I Double Never Ever Never Lie to My Chil'ren': Inside People in Virginia Hamilton's Narratives." *African-American Review* 32.1 (Spring 1998): 147–56

Myisha Priest

LORRAINE HANSBERRY (1930–1965)

BIOGRAPHICAL NARRATIVE

Lorraine Vivian Hansberry, the first African American playwright to have a play produced on Broadway, was born on May 19, 1930, in Chicago. Her parents, Nannie Perry Hansberry and Carl Augustus Hansberry, reared their four children (of which Lorraine was the youngest) in a middle-class, black community in the segregated South Side of Chicago. Thus, Hansberry felt that she existed in a kind of in-between space: "The world in fact is divided in half as it is lived by me," she wrote in her journal, "There are those who think me the liveliest of types. . . . And, still, there are the others, those latter-day images of the children of my youth who found me curious then—and still do. A serious odd-talking kid who could neither jump double dutch nor understand their games, but who—classically, envied them" (*To Be Young* 39). On the one hand, she lived, attended school, and socialized with other African Americans in her community on a daily basis, suffering similar discrimination, fighting for similar rights, and trying to survive white racism. On the other hand, the Hansberrys's economic status as middle class set her apart from a number of their less-fortunate neighbors, who had to fight for every morsel—an experience that young Lorraine could not understand. To her, "they seemed like grownups . . . with their ability to fight back, their fierce independence, their street-smarts. They had *authority*. She, on the other hand, was her family's pet, dressed like a princess to show off her wealth" (Sinnott 22). This kind of upbringing led, perhaps, to a special awareness of the complexities of her own position, and that of other similarly positioned African Americans, in relation to both black and white America.

In addition to the alienation Hansberry sometimes felt with her peers, she experienced alienation from white America, when, in 1938, her family attempted to move into an all-white neighborhood in Chicago, only to be greeted by a brick thrown through the family's window and other harassment. Despite Carl Hansberry's successful efforts to legally end this discrimination—he took his case, with the help of the NAACP, to the U.S. Supreme Court—the family was forced, after only a few months, to move back to the South Side, having been evicted from their home in Washington Park. Hansberry's experiences shaped her understanding of racial discrimination and inequities that continued to plague black Americans in the 1940s and 1950s, even as opportunities for economic upward mobility expanded for some.

After graduating from high school in 1948, Hansberry attended the University of Wisconsin at Madison, where she further developed her interest in both theater and politics. There she took classes in set design and participated in the Progressivist presidential campaign of Henry Wallace, among other political activities. In 1950, however, Hansberry decided to leave the university, finding that she was more interested in pursuing her career as a writer. Later that year, she moved to New York City, writing articles for *Young Progressives of America* magazine. In 1951, her success as a journalist led her to a full-time position at *Freedom* magazine, an alternative to the mainstream white-run presses that focused on informing the black community about things that were of interest to them. In 1952, Hansberry was named associate editor of the magazine and at the same time became even more involved in activism for causes that included the peace movement, the black civil rights movement, and the movement for independence in Africa (a topic that she had studied since childhood).

Hansberry retired from her full-time position with *Freedom* when she married fellow activist Robert Nemiroff on June 20, 1953, though she continued to contribute to the magazine. During the next few years, Hansberry continued to work, to write for magazines, and to participate in the life of Greenwich Village, where she and Nemiroff lived. During this time she also worked on what was to be her most famous play, *A Raisin in the Sun*, which, after a good deal of struggle, opened on March 11, 1959, to rave reviews. Hansberry received the New York Drama Critics' Circle Award for Best American Play on May 4, 1959. The play ran successfully for nine months on Broadway, and Hansberry was commissioned to write a screenplay for a film version of *Raisin*, which premiered in 1961. After her early success, Hansberry continued to work on several plays and projects, including a script completed for NBC-TV, called *A Drinking Gourd*. Ultimately, the play was never aired because the series was conceived to be too controversial and potentially alienating to southern viewers. Hansberry also began work on *Les Blancs* and *The Sign in Sidney Brustein's Window*. During this time Hansberry became increasingly involved in the civil rights movement, becoming friends with James Baldwin and other artist-activists. She was part of a delegation of black artists and activists who met Attorney General Robert F. Kennedy in May of 1963 to discuss the need for laws and policies that would reverse the continued discrimination against African Americans. With regard to the civil rights movement, Hansberry wrote: "Negroes must concern themselves with every single means of struggle: legal, illegal, passive, active, violent and non-violent. That they must harass, debate, petition, give money to court struggles, sit-in, lie-down, strike, boycott, sing hymns, pray on steps— and shoot from their windows when the racists come cruising through their communities" (*To Be Young* 213–14). Hansberry's commitment to the racial struggle in America was under way.

Unfortunately, she would not live to see those struggles through, for, in June of 1963, Hansberry was diagnosed with intestinal cancer and was submitted to surgeries and radiation treatment over the next two years. In March of 1964, Hansberry divorced Nemiroff, though he continued as a presence in her life and became the literary executor of her estate. In October of that year, *The Sign in Sidney Brustein's Window* opened on Broadway to mixed reviews. The show was nearly forced to close down after its first week, but many rallied around the play, supporting it monetarily and ultimately enabling it to run 101 days. The play closed on January 12, 1965—the day that Hansberry died of cancer.

Though Hansberry left no other completed plays after her death, she did leave drafts of several pieces that were later edited and (in some cases) completed by Robert Nemiroff. In 1969, Nemiroff produced the play *To Be Young, Gifted, and Black* along with a companion book that detailed some of the events and writings of Hansberry's life, and in 1970 *Les Blancs* (completed and edited by Nemiroff) opened on Broadway. In addition, Nemiroff wrote and produced a musical version of *A Raisin in the Sun* (called *Raisin*) in 1973. *A Raisin in the Sun* has seen a number of new productions, which included a 1989 uncut television version with Danny Glover and Esther Rolle. In 2004, a fifteen-week revival of the play opened on Broadway. The revival earned Phylicia Rashad and Audra McDonald Tony Awards for Best Actress in a Play and Best Featured Actress in a Play, respectively. The persistent popularity of this play testifies to the fact that, though Hansberry's life was short, the art she created continues to impact Americans into the twenty-first century.

MAJOR WORKS

Lorraine Hansberry's major works consist of a handful of plays and a script written for television. The lack of quantity, however, is made up for in breadth and depth in the available works. Her two complete plays, *A Raisin in the Sun* (1959) and *The Sign in Sidney Brustein's Window* (1964), as well as her telescript *A Drinking Gourd* (1959), and her plays edited and completed by Robert Nemiroff, *Les Blancs* (1970) and *What Use Are Flowers?* (1972), cover a variety of topics and show a deep engagement with issues that include modern American racism, the need for intellectuals to commit to social change, a recognition of the realities of the American slave system, the need for African independence, and the need for enlightened humanism. Though each play functions independently, it is possible to see common themes and motifs that run through each.

A Raisin in the Sun tells the story of the Younger family and their struggle to fulfill their ideals in the segregated and racist world of 1950s America. Lena Younger has recently received a 10,000 dollar life insurance check after the death of her husband and is trying to decide how best to use the money to help the family. Her son Walter wants to use the money to buy into a liquor store, while her daughter Beneatha could use the money toward medical school. The conflict of the play revolves around the various dreams held by members of the family and the ways those dreams become, as in Hughes's poem that begins the play, deferred by the racist, classist, and sexist society that the Youngers inhabit. Lena eventually decides to give most of the money to her son Walter, knowing that he needs it to maintain his sense of dignity and manhood in the face of America's oppression. He is to spend some of the money for his business and save the rest for his sister's education. Meanwhile, Lena reserves the rest of the money for a down payment on a home for the family to move into. Unfortunately, the house she buys is located in an all-white neighborhood and the family must choose between being bought out by a member of the neighborhood "welcoming committee" who feels that the races would get along better by being separate, or maintaining their integrity and facing possible harassment by the community into which they will move. The play culminates with Walter, having been duped out of his and his sister's money, standing up to the racism of Lindner and the welcoming committee. In the final scene, Walter tells Lindner, "We are very proud . . . and we have decided to move into our house because my father— my father—he earned it for us brick by brick. . . . We don't want your money" (1075). Thus, the play ends on a note of pride and hope for the African American community working to achieve equality.

The Sign in Sidney Brustein's Window focuses on the lives of Jewish intellectual Sidney Brustein and his "all American" wife Iris living in the bohemian world of Greenwich Village. Sidney's struggle to find meaning in political struggle is the center-piece of the play as is the sign that hangs in his apartment window, declaring "CLEAN UP COMMUNITY POLITICS Wipe Out Bossism VOTE REFORM" (34). An idealist who has lost his ideals, Sidney is a failed businessman and faces a slowly deteriorating marriage. Despite his failure, Sidney attempts to carry on with a newspaper, which he decides will be entirely apolitical. Nevertheless, when his friend Wally asks him for help on his Reform campaign, Sidney volunteers. He is soon disillusioned by his friend and finds himself back where he started. The sign in his window, then, becomes ironic when Sidney realizes that his friend Wally will become corrupt just like the bosses he ran against.

Hansberry dedicated the play partly to "the committed everywhere," and this dedication highlights the conclusion that Sidney comes to at the end of the play, where he declares his belief that "men change every day and that rivers run and that people wanna be better than they are and that flowers smell good and that I hurt terribly today, and that hurt is desperation and desperation is—energy and energy can *move* things . . ." (142). This declaration signals Sidney's willingness to commit himself to change, both politically and personally. Though the sign initially seems to mock Sidney, it later helps him to realize his duty to fight the status quo despite the problems of individuals like Wally who become corrupted by the system. Thus, the play ends on a hopeful note for the state of the intellectual, the one who will not give in to the demands of a corrupted society, but who sees the potential for change.

Though *Les Blancs* is a lesser-known play, its dramatic focus is extremely important for understanding the kind of commitment that Sidney Brustein urges at the end of his play. Set in a fictional African nation, *Les Blancs* tells the story of Tshembe, an African man living in England who has come home to bury his father. When he arrives home, he finds that his brothers, Eric and Abioseh, have become embroiled in the movement for independence, though each expresses his resistance differently. Taking place mostly on the premises of a medical mission, the play juxtaposes not only the attitudes of the three brothers, but also the attitudes of the doctors working in the mission, their servants, and a visiting American newspaperman. The presence of the American journalist, constantly interested in "picking the brains" of Tshembe, also reveals the complicity of the so-called American liberals who purport to help and yet continue to be part of the imperial problems of Africa. Through these characters, the play explores the complexity of the African situation in which they must overthrow their colonial oppressors violently, while recognizing the ways that their lives are variously intertwined with the colonial culture from which they seek freedom.

This duality is an issue that arises for Tshembe, a former revolutionary who, like Sidney Brustein, has become disillusioned with the political process and seeks only comfort and peace in his life in England with his European wife and his children. When he finds, however, that his brother Abioseh has devoted himself to becoming a priest for the colonial religion, and that Eric, a brother sired by a European officer and his own mother, has taken to alcoholism and inertia, he finds the courage to act on behalf of his people. Tragically, Tshembe is forced to kill Abioseh in an effort to protect the movement for independence. As in Hansberry's *A Raisin in the Sun*, this play attempts to represent Africa and Africans in less stereotypical ways and shows Hansberry's interest in the connections between the struggles of African Americans and Africans worldwide.

Hansberry's *A Drinking Gourd*, though never produced, emphasizes many of the themes picked up both in her writing and in subsequent works by other writers examining the slavery experience. *Gourd* studies the lives of slaves working on the Sweet plantation just before the Civil War. The play depicts various characters' responses to the volatile situation facing the south with regard to its status in the Union and to its institution of slavery. By representing not only the points of view of the plantation owners of different generations (contrasting, for instance, Hiram's view of slavery with his son Everett's view), but also poor white farmers and black slaves, Hansberry is able to point to the complex forces that make the institution a part of southern life at the time.

While Rissa (Hannibal's mother) attempts to work hard to make a difficult life a bit easier for her son, Hannibal sees only the need to escape to the north. In order to follow this dream, Hannibal tricks the Sweets's younger son Tommy into giving him reading lessons. Upon discovering the two studying in the woods, Everett orders Zeb Dudley, the poor white overseer, to cut out Hannibal's eyes. When an ailing Hiram finds out about his son's actions, he goes to Rissa in an attempt to gain her absolution. She refuses and he dies outside the slave quarters, vainly crying for help. In the end, Hannibal does escape the plantation with Rissa's help, taking Sarah, his beau, and his nephew Joshua along. The play does not reveal their fate, but it is clear that, as Hiram states upon hearing that the south is going to war, "The South is lost. . . . A way of life is over. The end is here and we might as well drink to what it was" (213).

The last major work written by Hansberry was the play *What Use Are Flowers?* a story of an elderly hermit, who, having taken off to the woods for twenty years in order to escape man's folly, comes out only to find a wasteland populated only by a group of wild children. Setting about the work of teaching these children how to be civilized human beings, the hermit, a former English teacher, is forced to start from scratch, teaching them about speech, fire, and, eventually, beauty. In the end he finds this concept—beauty—most difficult to teach and despairs of ever civilizing the children. After his death, however, it seems that the children have gained some lessons about the "use" of flowers, which are, as he says in his final speech, "infinite" (261). The children, however, have yet to discover the infinite uses because they have yet to experience death, the end of infinity. The play is, in a way, highly philosophical, as it posits many important questions about the value of art to society. At the same time, it reflects a very real fear of the time—a fear that humankind would destroy itself in nuclear holocaust. Nonetheless, *Flowers* refuses despair and calls for a reevaluation of the status quo.

Hansberry's work is tied together by the theme of the need for understanding. In each play, the central conflicts revolve around a lack of understanding. *A Raisin in the Sun*'s emphasis on intergenerational lack of understanding (as between Mama and Beneatha and Walter) highlights the way that Hansberry will apply this lack of understanding into the larger circle of race relations in the United States. Just as Mama fails (at first) to see Walter's point of view on the issue of race, white America has continually failed to understand the black American family. The play, then, tries to give the audience (both white and black) an understanding of the life situation of this particular group of black Americans struggling to make their way in a hostile situation. This kind of understanding is also vital to Hansberry's second play, *Sidney*, which shows a series of characters, all of whom seem to have no knowledge of the lives of the others. Thus, misunderstandings constantly arise—between Sidney and Iris, between David and Alton, and between Wally and Sidney. All these misunderstandings lead to the ultimate change that will take place at the end of the play when Sidney finally understands what that sign in his window represents—commitment. Likewise, *Les Blancs* offers a tale of the white American journalist and the black Anglo-African who cannot, despite all their talking, come to a sense of a common understanding, even at the end of the play. In *Gourd* we find misunderstandings constantly near the surface. The fact that the poor whites and the enslaved blacks cannot band together to overthrow the mutually oppressive system that hurts them both shows the power of the kinds of misunderstandings that are deliberately cultivated to keep the rich in power.

A notable motif in Hansberry's work is the link that she makes among people of various cultures and backgrounds in terms of their oppression. That is, Hansberry is willing to posit the oppression of women alongside the oppression of blacks as well as homosexuals. Before the term came into being, Hansberry was using the feminist concept of intersectionality. For instance, in *Raisin*, audiences may find themselves aligned not only with Walter, but also with the women in his life, who are forced to work and scrape in sometimes even more menial jobs than the men. Ruth, in particular, is a subject of sympathy, with her need to sacrifice for her family and her lack of time to develop her own talents and potential while often being held responsible for Walter's state: "That is just what is wrong with the colored woman in this world," Walter tells Ruth. "Don't understand about building their men up and making 'em feel like they somebody. Like they can do something. . . . We one group of men tied to race of women with small minds!" (1044). Part of Walter's journey by the end of the play is to gain some understanding of his wife and her situation in the world, and the play asks its audience to recognize the ways that each character struggles for his or her own humanity with obstacles that are overlapping but not identical.

Hansberry's work does not just stop with recognizing the multiple identities of the various characters, but also analyzes their problems not simply as personal but as a part of the larger institutions that maintain the status quo. An example of this is her work on *Sidney* as well as in *Les Blancs* and in *Gourd*. In each of these plays she highlights the ways that each member of the community under examination is subject to the larger forces of the societies in which they reside. Thus, Sidney's aims for genuine political change get wrapped up in the corruption of the American political machine after his candidate, Wally, gets elected. Likewise, *Les Blancs* presents the problems of colonialism and imperialism as central factors in the conflicts among and within the characters represented, just as the institution of slavery shapes each of the characters in *A Drinking Gourd*, whether slave, master, or poor white. This kind of prescience, a quality that existed both in her literary works and in her nonfiction writings and speeches, makes the study of Hansberry relevant for scholars trying to understand the continued oppression of many groups of people throughout the world.

CRITICAL RECEPTION

Generally, critical reception of Hansberry's work has been mixed and has changed over time. Though her first work was generally well received at the time of its opening and was undoubtedly a success as evidenced by its long run on Broadway, it too had its detractors. After the initial general critical reception that created the fame and prestige of the playwright, there was a backlash against her among critics who, citing her middle-class background, called her a sellout and not radical enough for the coming black freedom movement. The opening of *Sidney* did nothing to alleviate this criticism, since the play addresses a very select group of artists and intellectuals and touches only tangentially on the plight of black Americans. Later critics recognized the error of these characterizations, noting the civil rights work Hansberry involved herself in at an early stage in the movement as well as the complexity and commitment she brought to her plays, including the plays that were performed and published by her literary executor Robert Nemiroff after her death.

In 1979 *Freedomways* magazine devoted a special issue to Hansberry's work. Though often focused on *Raisin*, this issue contains articles on Hansberry's aesthetics in relation to her political commitments, representing a revision of how she had been viewed by earlier black activists. In his introduction, Jean Bond writes:

[S]he did not believe that a sharp dichotomy exists between art and propaganda. She asserted that all plays have a message, despite the fact that those which uphold the validity of such conventional ideas as monogamy, capital punishment or militarism are rarely discussed as "message" plays. She felt that plays expressing radical views are stigmatized as propagandistic simply in order to derogate what they have to say. (188–89)

In addition to the praise heaped on Hansberry's work by many critics within the pages of the magazine, we also find Adrienne Rich's "The Problem with Lorraine Hansberry," in which she questions the legitimacy of the versions of Hansberry's plays and life that have been propagated. Using Hansberry's possible lesbianism as a starting point, Rich questions how the writings of Hansberry, as a result of her shortened life, may have been modified to come across as less militant and openly feminist than they turned out to be under the guardianship of Robert Nemiroff. These issues have continued to be relevant in the evaluation of Hansberry's work, as new generations of critics have attempted to grapple with Hansberry's work and legacy.

Full-length studies on Hansberry's works are worth reading for their emphasis on her work as a whole rather than on her first and most famous play alone. In general, these works emphasize the ways that Hansberry was both of her time and ahead of her time, creating worlds on the stage that carefully balanced the need for realistic portrayals of life as it was for black Americans (and other oppressed groups) at the time with the need for a future-oriented and action filled approach to the problems presented in the plays themselves. As Steven Carter notes, "However richly or unpredictably drawn... Hansberry's characters are never viewed in isolation as singular or psychologically unique, but always as social beings interacting with society. And because of her respect for the complexity of both people and their society, she became keenly alert to the multiplicity of motives involved in each action" (15 16). This recognition of complexity led to calls for action on behalf of oppressed peoples in a number of Hansberry's plays. In addition, later critics have focused on Hansberry's place within the canon of American drama, noting her influence on future playwrights and the way she molded the protest play form to suit her particular aims. In most recent criticism of Hansberry's work we find a greater appreciation for the talent she possessed as well as her prescience in understanding the coming of the black freedom movement, the decolonization of Africa, the feminist movement, as well as the continued problems that would beset Americans who have yet to understand some of the lessons she sought to teach.

BIBLIOGRAPHY

Works by Lorraine Hansberry

A Drinking Gourd. 1959. In *Lorraine Hansberry; The Collected Last Plays*, edited by Robert Nemiroff. New York: New American Library, 1983.

Les Blancs. 1970. In *Lorraine Hansberry: The Collected Last Plays*, edited by Robert Nemiroff. New York: New American Library, 1983.

A Raisin in the Sun. 1959. In *Stages of Drama: Classic to Contemporary Theater*, edited by Carl H. Klaus, Miriam Gilbert, and Bradford S. Field, Jr., 1040–81. Boston: Bedford/St. Martin's, 2003.

The Sign in Sidney Brustein's Window. New York: Random House, 1964.

To Be Young, Gifted and Black: Lorraine Hansberry in Her Own Words. Adapt. Robert Nemiroff. Englewood Cliffs, NJ: Prentice Hall, 1969.

Toussaint (A Work in Progress). 1961. In *9 Plays by Black Women*, edited by Margaret B. Wilkerson, 51–66. New York: New American Library, 1986.

What Use Are Flowers? A Fable in One Act. 1972. In *Lorraine Hansberry: The Last Collected Plays*, edited by Robert Nemiroff. New York: New American Library, 1983.

Studies of Lorraine Hansberry's Works

Bond, Jean Carey, ed. *Lorraine Hansberry: Art of Thunder, Vision of Light. Freedomways* 19.4 (1979, special issue): 183–304.

Carter, Steven R. *Hansberry's Drama: Commitment amid Complexity*. Urbana: University of Illinois Press, 1991.

Cheney, Anne. *Lorraine Hansberry*. Boston: Twayne, 1984.

Effiong, Philip Uko. *In Search of a Model for African American Drama: A Study of Selected Plays by Lorraine Hansberry, Amiri Baraka, and Ntozake Shange*. Lanham, MD: University Press of America, 2000.

Gavin, Christy, ed. *African American Women Playwrights: A Research Guide*. New York: Garland, 1999, 61–127.

Grant, Robert Henry. "Lorraine Hansberry: The Playwright as Warrior-Intellectual." Ph.D. Diss., Harvard University, 1982.

Sharadha, Y. S. *Black Women's Writing: Quest for Identity in the Plays of Lorraine Hansberry and Ntozake Shange*. New Delhi: Prestige Books, 1998.

Sinnott, Susan. *Lorraine Hansberry: Award-Winning Playwright and Civil Rights Activist*. Berkeley, CA: Conari, 1999.

Kelly O. Secovnie

JOYCE HANSEN (1942–)

BIOGRAPHICAL NARRATIVE

Joyce Hansen is a writer of young adult literature and historical fiction. She was born on October 18, 1942, in New York City to Austin Victor, a photographer, and Lillian Dancy Hansen. While growing up in the Bronx, she developed an affinity toward books and reading. Hansen's interest in literature continued through her educational career, in which she earned a B.A. in English from Pace University in 1972 and an M.A. in English Education from New York University in 1978. In 1973, she became an English teacher in a New York City school. Through this teaching experience, she realized the positive effects literature has on students. Hansen then decided to write particularly for young readers and include characters with whom they could identify.

Hansen married Matthew Nelson on December 18, 1982, and in 1987 became a mentor and teacher at Empire State College in Brooklyn, New York. She retired from the teaching profession in 1995, yet continues to write full time. Hansen lives with her husband in West Columbia, South Carolina.

MAJOR WORKS

Hansen wrote her first novel, *The Gift-Giver*, in 1980. It was quickly followed by two more novels, *Home Boy* (1982) and *Yellow Bird and Me* (1986), the sequel to *The Gift-Giver*. After *Yellow Bird and Me*, Hansen explored the new genre of historical fiction in *Which Way Freedom?* (1986), *Out from This Place* (1988), *I Thought My Soul Would Rise and Fly: The Diary of Patsy, a Freed Girl* (1997), *The Captive* (1994), and *The Heart Calls Home* (1999). Hansen continued her writing transition with the nonfiction text *Between Two Fires: Black Soldiers in the Civil War* (1993) and *One True Friend* (2001), the continuation of *Yellow Bird and Me*.

Hansen frequently draws upon her experiences when writing her novels. In *The Gift-Giver*, she reconstructs her positive upbringing by reinforcing the values of acting responsibly, self-determination, and showing commitment to one's family. Although Hansen uses the actual murder of a New York City student by a young Jamaican boy as the basis for *Home Boy*, she returns to inspirational themes in *Yellow Bird and Me* and *One True Friend* by emphasizing the triumph of overcoming hardships and the importance of friendship.

Hansen observes the history of slavery in the trilogy *Which Way Freedom?*, *Out from This Place*, and *The Heart Calls Home* by depicting the struggles of two slaves, Obi and Easter, before and after the Civil War. She describes the African Americans who fought in the Northern Army and Confederate Army in *Between Two Fires: Black Soldiers in the Civil War*. By using letters, speeches, and other documents from the time period, Hansen shows how African Americans fought against prejudice and fought for freedom. Her illustrations of slaves are also authentically incorporated in *I Thought My*

Soul Would Rise and Fly: The Diary of Patsy, a Freed Girl and *The Captive*. Both texts illustrate the lives of young slaves who yearn to be free.

CRITICAL RECEPTION

Joyce Hansen's works have been highly praised by critics for her realistic characters and incorporation of historic events. She has won the Parents Choice award for *Yellow Bird and Me* in 1986 and the Coretta Scott King Award for literature four times. For her outstanding literary contributions, Hansen also garnered the Children's Book Award by the African Studies Association in 1995. She continues to be the subject of numerous articles to the delight of her readers.

BIBLIOGRAPHY

Works by Joyce Hansen

Between Two Fires: Black Soldiers in the Civil War. New York: Franklin Watts, 1993.
The Captive. New York: Scholastic, 1994.
The Gift-Giver. Boston: Houghton Mifflin, 1980.
The Heart Calls Home. New York: Walker & Company, 1999.
Home Boy. Boston: Houghton Mifflin, 1982.
I Thought My Soul Would Rise and Fly: The Diary of Patsy, a Freed Girl. New York: Scholastic, 1997.
One True Friend. New York: Clarion, 2001.
Out from This Place. New York: Walker, 1988.
Which Way Freedom? New York: Walker, 1986.
Yellow Bird and Me. Boston: Houghton Mifflin, 1986.

Studies of Joyce Hansen's Works

Berger, Laura Stanley, ed. *Twentieth-Century Children's Writers.* Detroit: St. James Press, 1995.
Moore, Opal, and Donnarae MacCann. "On Canon Expansion and the Artistry of Joyce Hansen." *Children's Literature Association Quarterly* 15.1 (1990): 32–37.
Senick, Gerard J., ed. *Children's Literature Review.* Detroit: Gale, 1990.
Stone, James. "The Coming of Age of the Civil War Novel." *Social Studies* 95.1 (January/February 2004): 40–45.
Tolson, Nancy D. "Regional Outreach and an Evolving Black Aesthetic." *Children's Literature Association Quarterly* 20:4 (1995–1996): 183–85.

Dorsia Smith

FRANCES ELLEN WATKINS HARPER (1825–1911)

BIOGRAPHICAL NARRATIVE

Harper, a poetess, novelist, and essayist, was born on September 24, 1825, to a free black mother in Baltimore, Maryland. Her mother passed away when she was approximately three years old, and Harper subsequently became the ward of her uncle, Rev. William Watkins, a well-known and respected teacher and activist. Her uncle and the education that she received at the school he founded profoundly influenced her. Harper attended the William Watkins Academy for Negro Youth until the age of thirteen. She then took a domestic job with the Armstrong family, during which time she continued to educate herself and spent time developing essays, poetry, and prose. Unfortunately, there is a dearth of public or private documentation on Harper's early years. Harper did not keep a diary and, consequently, much of what is known about her personal life is derived from William Still's *The Underground Railroad*. References suggest that Harper's early years were particularly difficult, though the exact nature of those difficulties is not specified.

At the age of twenty, Harper published her first volume of poetry, *Forest Leaves* (1845). Sadly, there are no extant copies of this work. Harper received training as a seamstress and afterward took on various jobs teaching embroidery and sewing, which she ultimately did not find fulfilling. In 1854, she published *Poems on Miscellaneous Subjects*, which sold more than 10,000 copies. During the same year, she acquired a job with the Maine Anti-Slavery Society as a traveling lecturer, thus beginning her career as a public speaker. Her dedication to the antislavery cause was undoubtedly prompted by the sense of racial responsibility and political activism encouraged by her uncle and the discrimination that she faced. Additionally, she was provoked by the death of a man who violated a law passed in 1853 that prohibited free blacks from entering Maryland with the threat of enslavement. A free black man unwittingly broke the law and was enslaved. He attempted to escape, but was recaptured and died soon after. The incident contributed to her deep commitment to the cause.

In 1860, she married Fenton Harper and subsequently mothered one child, Mary. Her husband died only a few years later, in 1864. Shortly after his death, Harper returned full time to her public speaking and writing careers. Harper spoke on behalf of and was active in numerous organizations and movements dedicated to progressive political change and social justice, including the Underground Railroad, the National Association of Colored Women, the American Equal Rights Association, and a variety of state Anti-Slavery Societies. In 1909, Harper's daughter, Mary, who had never married and lived with her mother, died. Harper died shortly thereafter, in 1911, from heart disease.

MAJOR WORKS

Throughout her life, Harper published numerous volumes of poetry and prose as well as novels, including *Forest Leaves* (1845), *Poems on Miscellaneous Subjects*

(1854/1857), *Minnie's Sacrifice* (1869), *Sketches of Southern Life* (1872), *Sowing and Reaping* (1876–1877), *Trial and Triumph* (1888–1889), *Iola Leroy; or, Shadows Uplifted* (1892) and *The Martyr of Alabama and Other Poems* (c. 1895). She was also a frequent contributor to newspapers and magazines. Not surprisingly, the topics Harper wrote about dealt with the issues of social justice to which she had dedicated her life. She wrote extensively about the institution of slavery and, following abolition, her work reflected the Reconstruction era and the rampant racism that continued to plague the lives of African Americans. Biblical stories and allusions to Judeo-Christian values can be found throughout her work, and a frequent theme of her poems was the employment of moral integrity and perseverance to overcome the multiple oppressions plaguing the downtrodden in the United States. She also wrote about temperance and the struggles faced by women in U.S. society. *Iola Leroy*, for example, is a story about a freeborn mulatta who struggles to survive the racism and sexism that permeated nineteenth-century American society.

Additionally, Harper's political essays, many of which were texts of speeches she had given during her speaking tours, were published in Christian, feminist and anti-slavery publications. For example, Harper's speeches, "We are all Bound Up Together" and "Woman's Political Future" were published in the *Proceedings of the Eleventh National Woman's Rights Convention* (1866) and *The World's Congress of Representative Women* (1894), respectively. Harper's work offers insightful critiques of the white patriarchal power structure that existed in nineteenth-century U.S. culture and its effect on African Americans, women, and biracial people.

CRITICAL RECEPTION

Any consideration of the critical reception of works produced by nineteenth-century African American women must take into account white patriarchal hegemony and the double oppression that African American women faced during the period. These obstacles often relegated the work of African American women writers to the margins and to obscurity. Despite these barriers, Harper's work enjoyed much popular success among African Americans and whites during her time period. Indeed, William Still states that she was the most prominent African American poet of the nineteenth century. Certainly, this was an amazing achievement during the period. Yet, the literary critics of the early twentieth century were not generous in remembering Harper's work, reproaching her poetry for its sentimentality and errors of metrical construction, and consigning it to footnotes. Consequently, much of Harper's work went out of print. However, recognizing the important cultural and historical yield of Harper's literary contributions, feminist literary scholars of the late twentieth and early twenty-first centuries have begun the work of recontextualizing and restoring Harper's literary legacy. Authors such as Frances Smith Foster, Shirley Wilson Logan, Melba Boyd, Hazel Carby, and Carla L. Peterson have made significant strides in the resurrection of Harper's lifework. These authors have emphasized the important cultural work Harper's writings achieved through their focus on political activism and social justice, their ability to speak directly to the needs of the audience, and their feminist underpinnings.

BIBLIOGRAPHY

Works by Frances Ellen Watkins Harper

Iola Leroy, edited by Hazel Carby. Boston: Beacon Press, 1999.
Minnie's Sacrifice, Sowing and Reaping, Trial and Triumph: Three Rediscovered Novels, edited by Frances Smith Foster. Boston: Beacon Press, 1994.

Studies of Frances Ellen Watkins Harper's Works

Boyd, Melba. *Discarded Legacy: Politics and Poetics in the Life of Frances E. W. Harper 1825–1911*. Detroit, MI: Wayne State University Press, 1994.
Carby, Hazel. *Reconstructing Womanhood: The Emergence of the Afro-American Woman Novelist*. New York: Oxford University Press, 1987.
Foster, Frances Smith, ed. *A Brighter Day Coming: A Frances Ellen Watkins Harper Reader*. New York: The Feminist Press at The City University of New York, 1990.
Lauter, Paul, ed. *The Heath Anthology of American Literature*. Boston: Houghton Mifflin, 1998.
Logan, Shirley Wilson. *We Are Coming: The Persuasive Discourse of Nineteenth-Century Black Women*. Carbondale: Southern Illinois University Press, 1999.
———. *With Pen and Voice: A Critical Anthology of Nineteenth-Century African-American Women*. Carbondale: Southern Illinois University Press, 1995.
Peterson, Carla L. "'Whatever Concerns Them, as a Race, Concerns Me': The Oratorical Careers of Frances Ellen Watkins Harper and Sarah Parker Redmond." In *"Doers of the Word": African American Women Speakers and Writers in the North (1830–1880)*, edited by Carla Peterson, 119–45. New Jersey: Rutgers University Press, 1995.
Still, William. *The Underground Railroad*. Medford, NJ: Plexus Publishing, 2005.

Valerie Palmer-Mehta

JUANITA HARRISON (1887–19??)

BIOGRAPHICAL NARRATIVE

Juanita Harrison, autobiographer, was born into a working-class family in Columbus, Mississippi, in 1887. She left school at an early age to begin working and never completed her formal education. Harrison left Mississippi at the age of thirty and traveled throughout the United States, working at different service jobs. She saved her money and invested it wisely, until in 1927 her interest income was $200 a year. She used this income to travel around the world, supplementing it with work as a servant when necessary.

Mildred Morris, daughter of an American family who employed Harrison in Paris, encouraged her to write about her travels and later served as her editor. Two excerpts from Harrison's travel writings were published in the *Atlantic Monthly* in 1935, and were so well received that Macmillan published her collected travel writings in book form in 1936 as *My Great, Wide, Beautiful World*. This book chronicles Harrison's travels throughout Europe, the Middle East, India and Ceylon, Japan and China. Harrison settled in Hawaii in 1936 but continued to travel; she made extensive journeys through Latin America in the 1940s and 1950s, but did not publish further about her experiences. Very little is known about Harrison outside the information contained in her writings, and almost nothing about her later years; even her date of death is unknown. The last certain information about Harrison is that she applied for a new passport in 1950, intending to travel to Bolivia, and that she was single and childless at that time.

MAJOR WORKS

Juanita Harrison's fame rests on her single book, *My Great, Wide, Beautiful World* and on excerpts from it published in the *Atlantic Monthly* in 1935. *My Great, Wide, Beautiful World* consists of more than 200 journal entries recording her impressions of the people, places, and things she observed during her travels. Harrison's lack of formal education is evident in her nonstandard spelling and use of the English language, although her meaning is generally clear and her observations frequently pungent. For instance, this is her impression of London: "The 4 most popular things in London are Fogs bad weather bad colds and chilblains the most rarest thing is the Sun" (13).

My Great, Wide, Beautiful World would be interesting if it were only a travelogue, but in fact it is much more. Because she was a working-class woman and continued to work as a servant from time to time while traveling, Harrison brought a seldom-represented point of view to the great sights of the world, whether the Houses of Parliament in London or the Taj Mahal in India. Equally as interesting were her descriptions of how people reacted to her as an African American woman traveling alone. Because her appearance was racially ambiguous and she was multilingual, when traveling abroad Harrison was able to step outside the racial categorizations enshrined into law in her native Mississippi. Harrison, who is described in the introduction to *My Great, Wide, Beautiful World* as olive-skinned and as having braided black hair, was amused at the number of different racial/ethnic identities ascribed to her in different countries, including Arabic, Jewish, Chinese, Spanish, Anglo-Indian, Greek, and Cuban. She commented that she was not concerned about what ethnicity other people assumed her to be, but was "willing to be whatever I can get the best treatments at being" (75).

CRITICAL RECEPTION

My Great, Wide, Beautiful World was a popular success, going through nine editions in ten months. It was reissued with a new introduction in 1996 as part of the series *African American Women Writers, 1910–1940*, edited by Henry Louis Gates, Jr. However, Harrison's work has not attracted the academic or critical attention it deserves, perhaps because her life and work are so exceptional that they do not fit easily into the standard categories used to describe female and African American writers.

BIBLIOGRAPHY

Work by Juanita Harrison

My Great, Wide, Beautiful World, edited by Mildred Morris. New York: Macmillan, 1936. Reprint in, with an introduction by Adele Logan Alexander, *African American Women Writers, 1910–1940*. New York: G. K. Hall & Co., 1996.

Studies of Juanita Harrison's work

Alexander, Adele Logan. "Introduction." In *My Great, Wide, Beautiful World. Juanita Harrison. African American Women Writers, 1910–1940*, xv–xxviii. New York: G. K. Hall & Co., 1996.
Halverson, Cathryn. "'Betwixt and Between': Dismantling Race in My Great, Wide, Beautiful World." *Journal x* 4.2 (Spring 2000): 133–57.
———. *Maverick Autobiographies: Women Writers and the American West, 1900–1936*. Madison: University of Wisconsin Press, 2004.

Sarah Boslaugh

SAFIYA HENDERSON-HOLMES (1950–2001)

BIOGRAPHICAL NARRATIVE

Born Sharon E. Henderson to Esther and Chet Henderson on December 30, 1950, in Bronx, New York, poet Safiya Henderson-Holmes was an alumna of New York University (B.A.), City College of New York (M.F.A.), and pursued post-Master's work at Columbia University's Teacher's College. Henderson-Holmes was actively involved in Poets and Writers, Art Against Apartheid, MADRE, and National Council of American/ Soviet Friendship. She succumbed to cancer on April 8, 2001, and is survived by her husband, Preston Holmes, and daughter, Naimah.

MAJOR WORKS

Henderson-Holmes's objective of discussing the political realities in the lives of women is best expressed in her first publication, *Madness and a Bit of Hope*. Her collection *Daily Bread* also focuses on the marginalized, giving voice to those who are silenced by their status occupying society's fringe, such as children in dysfunctional families, rape victims, and immigrant women.

After attending a public reading of her work, in a 1995 *Amsterdam News* article, journalist Risasi-Zachariah Dias commented that Henderson-Holmes's "eloquent yet stinging, poignant poetic words pierce souls. [Her] poems are electrifying and volatile, yet soothing." Described by Dias as "positive, fiery, revolutionary," both of Henderson-Holmes's poetry collections address the social conditions paramount in American society. While using her writing to deconstruct paradigms and ideologies, her poems are rife with symbolism, irony, and sarcasm, encouraging personal introspection, social change, and an enlightened sense of community consciousness. In a February 2000 *New York Beacon* article, famed writer/poet June Jordan comments that "Safiya Henderson-Holmes gives us spine and joy and the grace of laughter with the sweetness of spirit—with a surety of craft that cannot fail to swell and, rising, captivate the open political heart of America."

CRITICAL RECEPTION

Critical analyses of Henderson-Holmes's writings are quite scarce; however, she was quite popular in the New York City poetry community. Although her commercial notoriety can be arguably considered as obscure, in affirmation of her writing talents, Henderson-Holmes is widely anthologized and extensively published. In addition, she was the recipient of many awards and fellowships. During her career, she received two Goodman City College of New York Awards (1982), a Northstar Grant (1983), the CAPS Poetry Fellowship (1983), the New York Foundation for the Arts (NYFA) Poetry Fellowship (1986), the Fannie Lou Hamer Achievement Award (1987), a Summer Residency at the Blue Mountain Center (1988), a Summer Residency at the Cummington

Colony and the Community School of the Arts (1989–1991), the Poetry Society of America (PSA) William Carlos Williams Award (1990), and a MacDowell Fellowship (1992).

Henderson-Holmes's collection *Madness and a Bit of Hope* garnered her the William Carlos Williams Award. In her "Essay About Triangle Fire Poetry," Janet Zandy asserts that in Henderson-Holmes's poetry, there exists "a genuine vein of contemporary working-class women's literature." In a 1997 book review, David Earl Jackson of the *Tri-State Defender* writes that Henderson-Holmes "can catch and stay in the groove of a poem . . . making the reader marvel at her display of the language, where the words and the feelings get all jumbled up in a tangled web of therapy and testimony." The therapeutic and cathartic qualities of her writing are more prevalent in her later publications. Because of her diagnosis with a rare cancer, Henderson-Holmes's later writings address the issues of body image, mortality, and the experience of illness. The most noteworthy of the works she created during her final years is "Seeing in Colors," which is a series of intimate reflections inspired by her struggle with the cancer to which she ultimately succumbed. For this collection, in 1999, Henderson-Holmes won an NYFA Fellowship.

BIBLIOGRAPHY

Works by Safiya Henderson-Holmes

Daily Bread. New York: Harlem River Press/Writers and Readers Publishing, Inc., 1994.
Madness and a Bit of Hope. New York: Harlem River Press/Writers and Readers Publishing, Inc., 1990.
Racing and (E)Racing Language: Living with the Color of Our Words, edited with Ellen J. Goldner. New York: Syracuse University Press, 2001.

Studies of Safiya Henderson-Holmes's Works

"Safiya Henderson-Holmes: Patent Leather." *New York Beacon* 7.7 (2000): 23.
Dias, Risasi-Zachariah. "Newark Presents Series of Black Women Writers." *New York Amsterdam News* 86.44 (1995): 21.
Jackson, David Earl. "Poem Crazy All Over Again . . ." *Tri-State Defender* 46.32 (1997): 1B.
Murray, Madeline. "Daily Bread." *Quarterly Black Review of Books* 2.3 (1995): 10.
Zandy, Janet. "Fire Poetry on the Triangle Shirtwaist Company Fire of March 25, 1911." *College Literature* 24. 3 (Oct. 1997): 33–54.

Shamika Ann Mitchell

CAROLIVIA HERRON (1947–)

BIOGRAPHICAL NARRATIVE

Carolivia Herron, poet and short fiction writer, was born in Washington, D.C., in 1947 and attended local public schools. Herron's cultural interest and the traumatic experience of her brother's death at age three inspire her artistry. She became active in events, programs, and initiatives involving African and Judaic heritage. She had her Bat Mitzvah in 1995 and is the founding member of Jews of African descent.

Herron has taken her inquiry and investigation of cultural nuances into the halls of the academy. She received a B.A. in English from Eastern Baptist College (now Eastern College) in St. Davids, Pennsylvania, an M.A. in English from Villanova University, an M.A. in creative writing from the University of Pennsylvania, and a Ph.D. in comparative literature and literary theory from the University of Pennsylvania. She has taught across a broad spectrum of institutions from New England to the Congo: Brandeis, Harvard, Hebrew College in Brookline, Mount Holyoke, Radcliffe College, William and Mary College, Carlton College, Congo, Brazaville, and the Republic of Congo.

Currently, Herron is engaged in projects that concretize her interests as a writer and developer of multimedia, including her work-in-progress, a multimedia book, *Asenath and Our Song of Songs*.

MAJOR WORKS

Carolivia Herron's works, fiction and scholarship, add to the corpus of African American women's literature. She enters the circle of African American women focusing on themes such as family, cultural heritage, history, self-determination, hope, grief, and laughter offering universality. Her inquiry reproduces the sociocultural and sociohistorical experiences of her kin—real and fictive. Herron examines the richness of cultural traditions, specifically orality. Her cache of understanding for preserving rich, Africanist traditions, from "call and response" to "familial teasing" as demonstrated in *Nappy Hair*, invite inquiries that trouble assumptions within communities regarding the celebration of blackness.

Herron's work is a delicate yet punctuated intertexuality among the canonical wells of biblical, Western, and Africanist literary traditions. For example, *Nappy Hair* evokes childhood and adulthood memories—yet, hair stories transcend age, ethnicity, and even gender, while simultaneous investigation into subjectivities occurs. Likewise, investigations of patriarchal and feminist ideologies in *Thereafter Johnnie* and the "poetic canon" of *Selected Works of Angelina Weld Grimké* contribute to critical discussions regarding race, gender, class, sexuality, and color.

Carolivia Herron's poignant attention to the lives, theories, and research of self and others captures and edifies the lived experiences of African Americans. Whether writing about elders, ancestors, or children or introducing homoerotic works, her authorship reveals a historical backdrop of experiences—some marginalized and some decentered. Herron's use of multiple genres adds to the multiple dimensions and complexities of life experienced in her works. Through Herron, readers can transcend the boundaries of their community.

Herron has contributed to multiple anthologies and written articles based on her cultural and experiential knowledge.

CRITICAL RECEPTION

Herron's major works considered incendiary by some, or comical by others, contextualize ways black women examine and research their lives. That Herron contributes to the social, communicative, political, sexual, socioeconomic, philosophical, and cultural discourses of dual cultures—African and Judaic—offers dimensions from alternate vantage points. From *Thereafter Johnnie* to *Nappy Hair* created tenuous assumptions among and between those inside and outside of academe, she defends her book as a contribution to the canon of works celebrating blackness.

Whether in response to *Nappy Hair* (or not), feminist scholar bell hooks wrote and depicted a different view to hair and dialect in *Happy to Be Nappy*. At the base of hooks's scholarship is representation of African Americans, based upon her earlier work related specifically to hair and representation. Both books serve as a reminder that hair politics, like dialect and color, particularly in African American communities, produces a profusion of commentaries.

BIBLIOGRAPHY

Works by Carolivia Herron

Early African American Poetry. New York: Columbia University Press, 1993.
Nappy Hair. New York: Knopf/Distributed by Random House, 1997.
"The Old Lady." In *Afrekete*, edited by Catherine E. McKinley and Joyce DeLaney. New York: Doubleday, 1995.
Selected Works of Angelina Weld Grimké. New York: Oxford University Press, 1991.
"That Place." In *Children of the Night: The Best Short Stories by Black Writers 1967 to the Present*, edited by Gloria Naylor. Boston: Little, Brown Publishers, 1995.
Thereafter Johnnie, 1st ed. New York: Random House, 1991.

Studies of Carolivia Herron's Works

Frazier, Kermit. "Heads of Joy." *New York Times Book Review* (November 21, 1999). http://www.nytimes.com/books/99/11/21/bib/991121.rv143629.html.
Frost, Jennifer. *Race Experts: How Racial Etiquette, Sensitivity Training, and New Age Therapy Hijacked the Civil Rights Revolution*, by Elizabeth Lasch-Quinn. *Journal of Social History* 37.1 (Fall 2003): 235–38.
hooks, bell. *Black Looks: Race and Representation.* Boston: South End Press, 1992.
———. "Straightening Our Hair." In *Reading Culture: Contexts for Critical Reading and Writing*, edited by Diana George and John Trimbur, 290–99. New York: HarperCollins, 1992.
Lester, Neal A. "Nappy Edges and Goldy Locks: African-American Daughters and the Politics of Hair." *The Lion and the Unicorn* 24.2 (2000): 201–24.

————. "Nappy Happy: A Review of Carolivia Herron's Nappy Hair and bell hooks' Happy to be Nappy." *Annotated Bibliography: Children's Folklore Review* 22.1 (1999): 45–55.
Savery, Pancho. *Teaching African American Literature: Theory and Practice*, by Maryemma Graham, Sharon Pineault-Burke, and Marianna White Davis. *African American Review* 34.3 (Autumn 2000): 525–27.
Tuhkanen, Mikko. "Of Blackface and Paranoid Knowledge: Richard Wright, Jacques Lacan, and the Ambivalence of Black Minstrelsy." *Diacritics* 31.2 (2001): 9–34.
Wiley, Ralph. "Racial Astigmatism is a Crossover Condition." *New Crisis* 105.6 (1998): 34–35.

Rachelle D. Washington

FRENCHY JOLENE HODGES (1940–)

BIOGRAPHICAL NARRATIVE

Writer of poetry and short fiction, Frenchy Jolene Hodges, an exponent of folk values, was born on October 18, 1940, in Dublin, Georgia. She grew up on a farm in the rural south. At eighteen she left home to study at Fort Valley State College. After obtaining her B.S. in 1964, she worked for two years in Georgia, and then migrated north to Detroit, where she taught English and creative writing in the inner city high schools. In Detroit she established contacts with the influential Broadside Press, which published her first and best-known chapbook *Black Wisdom* (1971). When in 1972 she received Atlanta University's fellowship to attend their master's program in Afro-American studies, she used her contacts to write a master's thesis on "Dudley Randall and the Broadside Press." After becoming a mother of twins in late 1970s, she settled in Atlanta, where she continued her teaching career.

During her early years in Detroit, Hodges was also an actress. Her most successful performances include "Who's Got His Own" at Concept East Theater, "Little Old Ladies" at Detroit Repertory Theater, and "Mojo, a Black Love Story" by Alice Childress at DSACE Theater. Her acting influenced her poetry readings; in the 1970s she claimed to be the only Broadside author who performed her poems accompanying herself on a guitar.

Hodges's creative activity in the 1970s turned out to be at once the peak and the end of her artistic career. In 1975 she published two more chapbooks, *Piece De Way Home* and *For My Guy*, both with Tibi Productions. In 1979 *Ms.* magazine published her first and only short story, "Requiem for Willie Lee." The story was later reprinted in a collection of best *Ms.* fiction and has since appeared in many anthologies of African American women writers. However, Hodges herself has withdrawn from the literary and artistic scene.

MAJOR WORKS

Hodges's "Requiem for Willie Lee" is by far the most frequently anthologized of her works, and its title character is commonly compared to Bigger Thomas in Richard Wright's *Native Son*. The story is a black schoolteacher's account of an armed robbery she witnesses in a seaside resort. Although the black robber is as threatening to the teacher as to the resort's white clientele, she alone seems to be able to recognize him as a wounded human being, and to discover through him the failure of her educational mission. Highlighting class differences between the teacher and Willie Lee, the story culminates in a scene of reconciliation, when the narrator's and the robber's fates become symbolically united.

The second most anthologized of Hodges's works, the poem "Belle Isle," shares with "Requiem" the sense of care for communal values and mutual recognition, which help African Americans cope with unstable reality. Hodges describes Belle Isle, a park in

Detroit, as a place that performs the same role for the city's black population as the one played by front porches in the southern culture. Despite poverty, the communal ideals enable African Americans to transplant southern sensibility into the northern urban landscape.

Many other poems by Hodges express her appreciation for the folk values and idiom. She frequently uses blues structures and explores poetic tensions, which are born from the juxtaposition of "proper" English with vernacular forms. A similar kind of juxtaposition can be found in her use of naive or uneducated speakers to articulate political criticism, for example, in the poems "Innocent Questions" and "Listen, I'se Talking to You, Lawd," devoted to Martin Luther King's assassination. Some of Hodges's poems convey criticism of the vernacular culture itself, describing the ways in which the culture limits a young woman's identity ("I Was a Good Kid" and "Portrait of My Father").

CRITICAL RECEPTION

Because the volume of Hodges's work is modest, she has received scant critical attention. Still, the presence of her fiction and poetry in contemporary anthologies proves that many editors find her contribution to African American literature significant.

BIBLIOGRAPHY

Works by Frenchy Jolene Hodges

Black Wisdom. Detroit: Broadside Press, 1971.
For My Guy: Poems. Detroit: Tibi Productions, 1975.
Piece De Way Home. Detroit: Tibi Productions, 1975.
"Requiem for Willie Lee." *Fine Lines: The Best of Ms. Fiction*, edited by Ruth Sullivan, 153–64. New York: Scribner, 1982.

Studies of Frenchy Jolene Hodges's Works

Donlon, Joycelyn Hazelwood. *Swinging in Place: Porch Life in Southern Culture*. Chapel Hill and London: University of North Carolina Press, 2001.
Sullivan, Ruth. "Frenchy Hodges." In *Fine Lines: The Best of Ms. Fiction*, edited by Ruth Sullivan, 152. New York: Scribner, 1982.
Washington, Mary Helen. "Frenchy Hodges." In *Black-Eyed Susans/Midnight Birds*, edited by Mary Helen Washington, 209–10. New York: Anchor Books, 1990.

Katarzyna Iwona Jakubiak

BELL HOOKS (1952–)

BIOGRAPHICAL NARRATIVE

bell hooks, a well-known writer of poems and plays, was born Gloria Watkins in 1952 in Hopkinsville, Kentucky, the home of an unusual number of black intellectuals, thinkers, and Rhodes scholars. The middle one of seven children, hooks had power and privileges that none of her other five sisters had. That difference played a significant role in shaping hooks's views about gender and patriarchy, especially in African American families. Her mother worked as a maid in white people's houses in the segregated town—the Watkins family lived in an all–African American neighborhood near the mother's parents, and the children attended all–African American schools until they went to the high school. Early on, school and the southern African American Baptist church that her family attended allowed hooks to find her public voice through talent contests and presentations. She formed her notion of being an intellectual in the racially segregated world she grew up in, largely because her teachers recognized that she was gifted and encouraged her to do something with her knowledge. Part of her never-ending search for knowledge has led her to explore Buddhism in her later life.

After receiving a scholarship from her church, hooks graduated from Stanford University with a B.A. in English literature in 1973, before moving to the University of Wisconsin to receive her master's in 1976, followed in 1983 by her Ph.D. in American literature from the University of California, Santa Cruz, where she wrote her dissertation on Toni Morrison. While at the University of California, she began a fifteen-year relationship with a tenured professor who nurtured her and encouraged her writing. She has taught at Yale as an assistant professor of African and Afro-American studies and English, and at Oberlin College as an associate professor of English and women's studies. She was distinguished professor of English at the City College in New York City from 1993 to 2004. Currently, she has returned to her roots to teach at Berea College in the foothills of Appalachia as their distinguished professor in residence.

MAJOR WORKS

Part of understanding the writer involves addressing the pseudonym that she writes under. As hooks explains in an interview for *Talking Leadership: Conversations with Powerful Women*, she initially got the name "bell hooks" because she was an outspoken child who cursed a lot like her great-grandmother on her mother's side, who was named "Bell Hooks" (White 102). An interview with hooks conducted by Sarah Liss for *Now Online* magazine parenthetically notes that hooks uses lowercase letters for her pseudonym "to challenge authorial authority." The hooks entry for *Voices from the Gaps: Women Writers of Color* supports this interpretation by stating that "both the decapitalization and the pseudonym itself are attempts to take the reader's focus away from the author and place it on the content of the work" (Hua n.p.).

In an interview with the South End Press Collective, hooks describes Lorraine Hansberry and James Baldwin as her literary mentors, because both writers "were people who loudly proclaimed that there is no art that is politically neutral" (*Talking about a Revolution* 50). However, a 1995 interview on *Booknotes* also adds Emily Dickinson to her list of influences. In fact, although known today primarily as a feminist scholar, hooks started her career writing poetry and plays. Her first book, which bears the name "bell hooks" as author, was a collection of political poems called *And Then We Slept* published in 1978. She quickly shifted her focus to the feminist movement that, at the time, was claiming women would be liberated if they worked—an assertion that ran counter to her own observations of the women she had known while growing up. Over the intervening years, hooks's writings have put the spotlight on many current social issues, including race, gender, sex, class, and sexual orientation, frequently addressing several issues at the same time because she believes them interconnected. This blend of concerns appears, for example, in her 1996 memoir *Bone Black: Memories of Girlhood*, among other works.

Ever since her undergraduate years, hooks has been challenging the prevailing stereotypes about black women and the nature of their lives. The subtle sexism found in the black liberation movement, for example, provided the topic for her 1981 book *Ain't I a Woman: Black Women and Feminism*, which positions the struggle within the feminist movement itself because, according to the publisher, "race, class and sex are immutable facts of existence." This book had its genesis in her undergraduate work at Stanford, but it underwent eight years of refining and polishing before it was finally published. At the time, the book was not well received because feminists were not ready to recognize class and racial differences in women.

In her 1995 book *Killing Rage: Ending Racism*, hooks uses the image of a flag created by Emma Amos, a black woman artist, for the front cover, even though hooks generally avoids nationalism and the dialogue associated with nationhood in her writing. This book is her attempt to deal with the pain caused by racism and white supremacy, allowing the female voice to enter into that discussion while imagining a world without racism, as hooks offers positive plans for the future instead of dwelling in the patriarchal models of the past. The book extends the ideas of her 1993 book *Sisters of the Yam: Black Women and Self-recovery*, which takes such a different approach that it reaches white women and black men as well. The book examines leadership and the stress that positions of leadership bring into lives. She uses a self-help approach to help readers unlearn racism and sexism as they strive to heal themselves.

Since 1999, hooks has written four books for children, three of them in collaboration with Christopher Raschka as illustrator. These books portray African American children as they see themselves and as others see them. For example, *Happy to be Nappy* celebrates the beauty of nappy hair using joyful poetry that is meant to be read out loud, thereby reflecting, according to Liss, "a jazzy idiom that recalls Harlem Renaissance poets like Gwendolyn Brooks." Similarly, *Be Boy Buzz* celebrates what it means to be a boy with all of the energy associated with boyhood.

CRITICAL RECEPTION

Although her work has been translated into Italian, Chinese, and Japanese, it has not been well received in segments of the African American male community. For example, Joseph Anderson's editorial for the *Black Commentator* observes that hooks tends to focus on "Black (especially male) psychopathology" when she could be placing the focus on self-esteem, especially when she was promoting her 2003 book *Rock My Soul: Black People and Self-Esteem*. A significant portion of his argument centers on the premise that hooks asserts that the self-hatred she finds characteristic of black males has "widespread sexual abuse" at its core, although she would never make similar assumptions about sexism in various groups of white males having a basis in their feelings of inferiority. For these perceived shortcomings, Anderson finds hooks as detrimental to the African American cause.

Considered by some critics as radical or antiwhite, hooks spells "Black" with a capital letter, yet spells "white" using the lowercase, especially when she is critiquing the capitalistic white patriarchs whose opinions have dominated so many of these current issues. She has been the subject of major theoretical reference for four dissertations over the past few years. Most of the critical use of her work has centered around using her ideas about race, gender, patriarchy, and education in support of the analysis that the critic is doing on the topic.

BIBLIOGRAPHY

Works by bell hooks

Ain't I a Woman. Black Women and Feminism. Boston: South End Press, 1981.
All about Love: New Visions. New York: William Morrow, 2000.
And Then We Slept: Poems. Los Angeles: Golemics, 1978.
Art on My Mind: Visual Politics. New York: New Press/Norton, 1995.
Be Boy Buzz. With illustrations by Christopher Raschka. New York: Hyperion Books for Children, 2002.
Black Looks: Race and Representation. Boston: South End Press, 1992.
Bone Black: Memories of Girlhood. New York: Henry Holt, 1996.
Breaking Bread: Insurgent Black Intellectual Life. With Cornel West. Boston: South End Press, 1991.
Communion: The Female Search for Love. New York: William Morrow, 2002.
Feminism Is for Everybody: Passionate Politics. Cambridge, MA: South End Press, 2000.
Feminist Theory from Margin to Center. Boston: South End Press, 1984.
Happy to Be Nappy. With illustrations by Christopher Raschka. New York: Hyperion Books for Children, 1999.
Homemade Love. With Shane Evans. New York: Hyperion Books for Children, 2002.
Killing Rage: Ending Racism. New York: Henry Holt, 1995.
Outlaw Culture: Resisting Representation. New York: Routledge, 1994.
Reel to Real: Race, Sex, and Class at the Movies. New York: Routledge, 1996.
Remembered Rapture: The Writer at Work. New York: Henry Holt, 1999.
Rock My Soul: Black People and Self-Esteem. New York: Atria Books, 2003.
Salvation: Black People and Love. New York: William Morrow, 2001.
Sisters of the Yam: Black Women and Self-recovery. Boston: South End Press, 1993.
Skin Again. With illustrations by Christopher Raschka. New York: Hyperion Books for Children, 2004.
Talking Back: Thinking Feminist, Thinking Black. Boston: South End Press, 1989.
Teaching Community: A Pedagogy of Hope. New York: Routledge, 2003.
Teaching to Transgress: Education as the Practice of Freedom. New York: Routledge, 1994.
We Real Cool: Black Men and Masculinity. New York: Routledge, 2004.
Where We Stand: Class Matters. New York: Routledge, 2000.
The Will to Change: Men, Masculinity, and Love. New York: Atria Books, 2004.

A Woman's Mourning Song. New York and London: Harlem River Press, 1993.
Wounds of Passion: A Writing Life. New York: Henry Holt, 1997.
Yearning: Race, Gender and Cultural Politics. Boston: South End Press, 1990.

Studies of bell hooks's Works

Anderson, Joseph. "Right Hook at the Bell! Bell Hooks' Black Male-bashing." *Black Commentator* 46.5 (June 2003). Date accessed January 7, 2005, www.blackcommentator.com.

Bauer, Dale M. "Professing Women and the Classroom Crisis." *Reader: Essays in Reader-Oriented Theory, Criticism, and Pedagogy* 45 (2001): 58–72.

Bauer, Michelle. "Implementing a Liberatory Feminist Pedagogy: bell hooks's Strategies for Transforming the Classroom." *MELUS: The Journal of the Society for the Study of the Multi-Ethnic Literature of the United States* 25.3–4 (2000): 265–74.

Bowen, Barbara, and Anthony O'Brien. "Renewing Feminism: An Interview with bell hooks." *Found Object* 2 (1993): 1–19.

Butler, Judith. "Gender Is Burning: Questions of Appropriation and Subversion." In *Dangerous Liaisons: Gender, Nation, and Postcolonial Perspectives*, edited by Anne McClintock, Aamir Mufti, and Ella Shohat. Minneapolis: University of Minnesota Press, 1997.

Cobb, Michael L. "bell hooks (1952–)." In *African American Autobiographers: A Sourcebook*, edited by Emmanuel S. Nelson. Westport, CT: Greenwood Press, 2002.

Crawford, Ilene Whitney. "Out of the Heart of Darkness toward a New Rhetoric of Emotion." Ph.D. Dissertation, University of Wisconsin, 2000.

Donovan, Kathleen McNerney. "Coming to Voice: Native American Literature and Feminist Theory." Ph.D. Dissertation, University of Arizona, 1994.

Edelstein, Marilyn. "Resisting Postmodernism: Or, 'A Postmodernism of Resistance': bell hooks and the Theory Debates." In *Other Sisterhoods: Literary Theory and U.S. Women of Color*, edited by Sandra Kumamoto Stanley. Urbana: University of Illinois Press, 1998.

Florence, Namulundah. *bell hooks' Engaged Pedagogy: A Transgressive Education for Critical Consciousness.* Westport, CT: Bergin & Garvey, 1998.

Fox, Tom. "Literacy and Activism: A Response to bell hooks." *JAC: A Journal of Composition Theory* 14.2 (1994): 564–70.

Green, Kathleen. "Stress Management Ideology and the Other Spaces of Women's Power." In *Hop on Pop: The Politics and Pleasures of Popular Culture*, edited by Henry Jenkins, Tara McPherson, and Jane Shattuc. Durham, NC: Duke University Press, 2002.

Hayes, Robin Donna. "Virginia Woolf's Treatise on Education: 'Three Guineas.'" Ph.D. Dissertation, University of North Carolina, 2002.

Hua, Julia. "bell hooks." In *Voices from the Gaps: Women Writers of Color*. Department of English, University of Minnesota, 2003. Accessed January 7, 2005, http://voices.cla .umn.edu/.

Jones, Lisa. "Rebel without a Pause." *Village Voice Literary Supplement* 109 (1992): 10.

Lamb, Brian, ed. "bell hooks." In *Booknotes: America's Finest Authors on Reading, Writing, and the Power of Ideas*, 62–65. New York: Random House-Times Books, 1997.

Liss, Sarah. "bell hooks: African-American Feminist Icon Fights Fascism with Love." *Now Online Edition*, May 13, 2004, http://nowtoronoto.com/issues/2004-05-13/cover_story.php (accessed January 7, 2005).

McKee, Patricia. "Geographies of Paradise." *New Centennial Review* 3.1 (2003): 197–223.

Moore, Suzanne. "bell hooks Talks to Suzanne Moore." *Wasafiri: Journal of Caribbean, African, Asian and Associated Literatures and Film* 27 (1998): 12–16.

Mussatt, David. "Re-Embodying the Disembodied: A Personal Reflection on Critical Pedagogy and the Use of Anthologies in the Classroom." *Schuylkill: A Creative and Critical Review from Temple University* 3.1 (2000): 63–76.

Olson, Gary A. "bell hooks and the Politics of Literacy: A Conversation." In *Philosophy, Rhetoric, Literary Criticism: Interviews*, edited by Gary A. Olson. Carbondale: Southern Illinois University Press, 1994.

Roux, Nicole Aimée. "Combating Nihilism and Classism in the African-American Community from a Black Feminist Perspective." In *The Image of the Twentieth Century in Literature, Media and Society*, edited by Will Wright and Steven Kaplan. Pueblo, CO: Society for the Interdisciplinary Study of Social Imagery, University of Southern Colorado, 2000.

Talking about a Revolution: Interviews with Michael Albert, Noam Chomsky, Barbara Ehrenreich, bell hooks, Peter Kwong, Winona LaDuke, Manning Marable, Urvashi Vaid, Howard Zinn, 39–52. Cambridge, MA: South End Press, 1998.

Third World Viewpoint. "Challenging Capitalism & Patriarchy: Third World Viewpoint Interviews bell hooks." *Z Magazine* 8.12 (1995): 36–39.

Thomson, Clive. "Culture, Identity, and the Dialogic: bell hooks and Gayatri Chakravorty Spivak." In *Dialogism and Cultural Criticism*, edited by Clive Thomson and Hans Raj Dua. London: Mestengo, 1995.

Townes, Shawn Adrienne. "Black Woman Warrior: A Rhetorical Biography of bell hooks." Ph.D. Dissertation, Ohio University, 2000.

Vega-González, Susana. "The Dialectics of Belonging in bell hooks' *Bone Black: Memories of Girlhood*." *Journal of English Studies* 3 (2001–2002): 237–48.

Walker, Joseph S. "When Texts Collide: The Re-Visioning Power of the Margin." *Colby Quarterly* 35.1 (1999): 35–48.

Watkins, James Ray, Jr. "Hypertextual Border Crossing: Students and Teachers, Texts and Contexts." *Computers and Compositions: An International Journal for Teachers of Writing* 16.3 (1999): 383–94.

White, Deborah Gray, Charlotte Bunch, and Harriet Davidson. "bell hooks." In *Talking Leadership: Conversations with Powerful Women*, edited by Mary S. Hartman, 99–116. New Brunswick, NJ: Rutgers University Press, 1999.

Peggy J. Huey

PAULINE ELIZABETH HOPKINS (1859–1930)

BIOGRAPHICAL NARRATIVE

A pioneer figure in African American women's journalism and a notable novelist and essayist, Pauline Elizabeth Hopkins was born in Portland, Maine, in 1859 to free parents of color. Her mother, Sarah Allen, came from a Boston family that had brought forth ministers of repute, such as Nathaniel Paul and Thomas Paul, founders of Baptist churches in Boston. Not much is known about Hopkins's biological father. In a brief autobiographical sketch that she published in the *Colored American Magazine* in June 1901, Hopkins says she moved to Boston when she was young, attended public schools there, and graduated from Boston is Girls' High School. The pride she took in her mother's side of the family and in their Boston heritage comes across in the sketch through her emphasis on the possible contacts her mother's family might have had with such figures of renown as William Lloyd Garrison and Frederick Douglass.

The first extant record of Hopkins's literary endeavor shows her receiving a ten-dollar prize at an essay contest sponsored by the Congregational Publishing Society of Boston and William Wells Brown when she was fifteen years old. The essay, "The Evils of Intemperance and Their Remedy," is now held at the Fisk University Library Special Collections. In 1879, Sarah Allen married William A. Hopkins and Pauline started signing her works "Pauline E. Hopkins" instead of "Pauline E. Allen." A native of Alexandria, Virginia, William Hopkins moved to Boston after having served in the Civil War in the Grand Army of the Republic.

Hopkins's first work that received public notice is a musical drama, *Slaves' Escape; or, The Underground Railroad*, which she copyrighted in 1879. The title was soon changed to *Peculiar Sam; or, The Underground Railroad* and was performed by Hopkins's Colored Traubadours, which included Pauline Hopkins, Sarah Allen, William Hopkins, a chorus of jubilee singers, and singers such as Sam Lucas and sometimes the Hyers Sisters. The performance traveled to parts of the Midwest before returning to Boston. A few other plays, though they either went unpublished or fell out of circulation, also attest to Hopkins's early aspirations as a playwright. *One Scene from the Drama of Early Days*, presumably written before *Peculiar Sam*, dramatizes the biblical story of Daniel in the lion's den; *Aristocracy* or *Colored Aristocracy*, performed by the Hyers Sisters Concert Company in 1877, is lost; and only a few pages remain of *Winona*, a five-act play.

In the early 1890s, while still performing at recitals and concerts and giving public lectures on black history, Hopkins also looked for a way to support herself. She studied stenography, passed the civil exam, and first found employment as a stenographer with Henry Parkman and Alpheus Sanford, both influential Republicans, in 1892. She was a stenographer in the Bureau of Statistics from 1895 to 1899. In her late years, she turned to stenography also for subsistence.

The first installment of *Hagar's Daughter*, dated 1891, indicates that Hopkins could have been writing as she learned stenography, but it was really with her involvement in the *Colored American Magazine* that she saw an increased opportunity to write and publish. The five years from 1900 to 1904 were Hopkins's most prolific years as a writer. The *Colored American Magazine* was published by the Colored Cooperative Publishing Company, which also published Hopkins's first novel, *Contending Forces: A Romance Illustrative of Negro Life North and South*, in 1900. The September, 1900 issue of the *Colored American Magazine* advertised the novel as "a race work dedicated to the best interest of the Negro everywhere." Starting with the short story "The Mystery within Us" in the May 1900 issue, Hopkins published numerous essays, editorials, and short stories in the magazine. All three of her serial novels—*Hagar's Daughter: A Story of Southern Caste Prejudice* (1901–1902), *Winona: A Tale of Negro Life in the South and the Southwest* (1902), and *Of One Blood; or, The Hidden Self* (1902–1903)—were serially published in the *Colored American Magazine*.

Hopkins's editorial position changed from the editor of the women's column in 1900 to the literary editor of the magazine in 1903. She was dedicated to making the magazine a venue for colored writers, who have difficulty placing their works in the mainstream presses, to publish. Hopkins herself published frequently in the magazine, sometimes two or three pieces in a single issue, using the pen names Sarah A. Allen and Shirley J. Shadrach as well as her own name. The use of pen names was probably a strategy Hopkins adopted to avoid having her name appear too frequently in the magazine. In 1904, around late April and early May, the *Colored American Magazine* was bought by Fred R. Moore, who became the editor. His editorial policies were at variance with those of Hopkins and she was forced to leave the magazine.

While Hopkins still lectured and published after leaving the magazine, the departure marked a turning point in her literary career. In late 1904 and early 1905, she published a couple of pieces in the *Voice of the Negro*, a leading African American journal in the south, including the serial piece, "The Dark Races of the Twentieth Century." Though she was introduced as "one of our regular contributors" in the November 1904 issue of *Voice of the Negro*, Hopkins stopped publishing in the magazine after July 1905 for reasons unknown. In 1905, she self-published a historical treatise, *A Primer of Facts Pertaining to the Early Greatness of the African Race and the Possibility of Restoration by Its Descendants—with Epilogue*. Hopkins attempted a comeback to the literary scene as the editor of *New Era* magazine with Walter Wallace, a former colleague from the *Colored American Magazine*, but the magazine ceased publishing after two issues.

Hopkins's later years, from 1916 to 1930, were spent in obscurity. The tragic accident that caused her death provides a sad finale to the toils of a talented colored woman who bravely strove to make a literary career for herself at a time when both her race and her gender placed limitations on her. Hopkins was brought in to the Cambridge Relief Hospital when the flannel bandages she was wearing because of her neuritis accidentally caught fire. She died on August 13, 1930, at the Cambridge Relief Hospital after suffering from severe burns and was buried in Garden Cemetery, Chelsea, Massachusetts. She was working at the Massachusetts Institute of Technology as a stenographer when she died.

MAJOR WORKS

Hopkins's most well-known work is her first novel, *Contending Forces: A Romance Illustrative of Negro Life North and South* (1900). The only work that was published in book form during her lifetime, *Contending Forces* contains an array of themes, motifs, and novelistic strategies that appear again and again in her works. The curt yet forceful dedication of the novel, "for humanity," conveys her lifelong dedication to better the conditions of the "proscribed race," the term she often used to refer to African Americans. The mystery of veiled identities, which recurs in her serial novels, drives the plot and creates a map of relations among the characters. Though Hopkins has been criticized for focusing on light-skinned, mixed-race characters, light-skinned heroines function as the embodiment of racial violence and the means to expose racial prejudice in *Contending Forces*. The beautiful, light-skinned heroine, Sappho Clark, is abducted, raped, and sold into prostitution by her colored father's half-brother, who is white. The drama of "contending [social] forces" in the strife for racial equality evolves around the figure of the female outcast who reenters the social world and acquires both the friendship of Dora Smith and the love of her brother, Will Smith (256).

In many aspects, the novel speaks to a burgeoning middle-class black audience who were invested in improving their lives both economically and culturally. The Smiths, who run the boardinghouse where Sappho lives, represent an emerging black middle class. Debates over education and the right to vote that take place between Arthur Lewis and Will Smith reflect the debates of Hopkins's time between Booker T. Washington and W.E.B. DuBois. While she is careful not to reduce the debates into a matter of choice between Washington and DuBois, Hopkins works into her novel the complex meaning of uplift for African Americans with a farsightedness that made it possible for her to weigh the immediate gains of an accommodationist politics against the long-term goal of achieving social equality on all fronts. The Sewing Circle led by Mrs. Willis parallels the black women's club movement in its foregrounding of the women's role for the advancement of the race.

Resorting to the genre of romance and using the domestic sphere to reflect on social issues and political concerns are strategies Hopkins employed again in *Hagar's Daughter: A Story of Southern Caste Prejudice* (1901–1902). With the first part set in Charleston, South Carolina, and the second part set in the nation's capital, Washington, D.C., the novel likewise explores race prejudices that span the north and the south through the life of a mixed-race heroine and her daughter. Arguably the most driving mystery of Hopkins's works, the novel runs through a breathless sequel of blackmail and murder to finally rescue the innocent that has been put on trial and bring together Hagar's broken family. The fact that Jewel, Hagar's daughter, loses her lover who has an ingrained sense of racial difference, indicates that Hopkins was skeptical to the question of whether romantic love transcends racial prejudices. In fact, Hazel Carby sees Cuthbert Sumner, Jewel's lover, as Hopkins's critique of "the ambivalence and limits of white liberalism and New England philanthropy" (xli).

Hopkins explores the dynamics of interracial romance with a romantic triangle made up of a mixed-race woman, a black man, and a white Englishman sympathetic to abolition in *Winona: A Tale of Negro Life in the South and the Southwest* (1902). The only novel by Hopkins that deals with the pre–Civil War period exclusively (Wallinger 190, Carby xliii), *Winona* also offers Hopkins's first black male hero in the figure of Judah, the adopted son of Winona's white father (Carby xlii). Stories of John Brown and the Free Soil Movement in Kansas are adapted in the novel as Hopkins uses abolitionism and a distant past to think about contemporary social and political issues.

Of One Blood; or, The Hidden Self (1902–1903) stands out as the only novel by Hopkins that has a mixed-race male protagonist passing for white and that has the protagonist travel out of the United States to Africa. Hopkins's interest in black history, and more specifically in Ethiopianism, finds expression in the novel as Reuel Briggs goes on an excavation expedition to the ancient city of Meroe in Africa only to find out that he is the chosen one to restore the former glory of the race. Historical imagination is infused with fantasy as the haunting legacy of slavery ultimately discloses all three characters involved in the romantic triangle—Reuel, Dianthe Lusk, and Aubrey Livingstone—as siblings. Hopkins probes the ideas of heritage and blood in all of her novels. In *Of One Blood*, though, the reflection takes a singular, transnational turn.

CRITICAL RECEPTION

Ann Shockley calls Pauline Hopkins "[o]ne of the most neglected early black women writers" in her short biographical essay of Hopkins (22). The subtitle of Shockley's essay, a "biographical excursion into obscurity," probably best characterizes the historical amnesia that Hopkins was faced with until recently. Richard Yarborough takes note of this when he compares the fate of Hopkins with those of her male contemporary writers such as Paul Laurence Dunbar and Charles Chesnutt (xxviii). Despite the fact that she wrote no less and no worse than Dunbar and Chesnutt, Hopkins did not receive commensurate recognition from the literary circles in her time and for long after her death. Fortunately, there has been a significant recovery of African American women's writing produced between 1890 and 1910 since the 1980s. Along with Anna Julia Cooper and Frances Harper, Pauline Hopkins is one of the valuable women writers rediscovered in this process (Gates, "Foreword," xvi).

The Schomburg Library of Nineteenth-Century Black Women Writers has firmly put back into circulation *The Magazine Novels of Pauline Hopkins* and *Contending Forces*. From 1985, when Claudia Tate called her "our literary foremother" and on, Hopkins has received ample critical attention from scholars and critics interested in African American journalism, domestic ideology, women's narrative strategies, and changing definitions of race. The publication of *Pauline Hopkins: A Literary Biography*, the first critical biography on Hopkins, in 2005 may be taken as a sign that Pauline Hopkins now occupies an incontestable place in American literary history.

BIBLIOGRAPHY

Works by Pauline Elizabeth Hopkins

Contending Forces: Salem, NH: Ayer Co. Pub. 1900.
The Magazine Novels of Pauline Hopkins, edited by Henry Louis Gates, Jr. The Schomburg Library of Nineteenth-Century Black Women Writers. New York and Oxford: Oxford University Press, 1988.
A Primer of Facts. Appended in Pauline E. Hopkins: A Literary Biography. Athens: The University of Georgia Press, 2005.

Studies of Pauline Hopkins's Works

Ammons, Elizabeth. *Conflicting Stories: American Women Writers at the Turn into the Twentieth Century*. New York and Oxford: Oxford University Press, 1991.
Campbell, Jane. "Hopkins, Pauline Elizabeth (1859–1930)." In *Black Women in America: A Historical Encyclopedia*, vol. I, edited by Darlene Clark Hine et al., 577–79. Brooklyn: Carlson, 1993.

Carby, Hazel. "Introduction." In *The Magazine Novels of Pauline Hopkins*, edited by Henry Louis Gates, Jr., xxix–l. The Schomburg Library of Nineteenth-Century Black Women Writers. New York and Oxford: Oxford University Press, 1988.

Gillman, Susan. *Blood Talk: American Race Melodrama and the Culture of the Occult*. Chicago and London: The University of Chicago Press, 2003.

Gruesser, John Cullen, ed. *The Unruly Voice: Rediscovering Pauline Elizabeth Hopkins*. Urbana and Chicago: University of Illinois Press, 1996.

Shockley, Ann Allen. "Pauline Elizabeth Hopkins: A Biographical Excursion into Obscurity." *Phylon* 33 (Spring 1972): 22–26.

Tate, Claudia. *Domestic Allegories of Political Desire*. New York: Oxford University Press, 1992.

Wallinger, Hanna. *Pauline Hopkins: A Literary Biography*. Athens: The University of Georgia Press, 2005.

Yarborough, Richard. "Introduction." In *Contending Forces: A Romance Illustrative of Negro Life North and South*, edited by Henry Louis Gates, Jr., xxvii–xlviii. The Schomburg Library of Nineteenth-Century Black Women Writers. New York and Oxford: Oxford University Press, 1988.

Jeehyun Lim

ZORA NEALE HURSTON (1891–1960)

BIOGRAPHICAL NARRATIVE

Zora Neale Hurston, a leading novelist, dramatist, folklorist, and short fiction writer, during the Harlem Renaissance, was born on January 7, 1891, in Notasulga, Alabama, the daughter of John and Lucy Potts Hurston. When she was very young, the family moved to the all-black town of Eatonville, Florida, where Hurston grew up. Eatonville became a fixture in her artistic vision, and much of her work is set there. Many of her characters as well are based on Eatonville persons and many of her fictive situations are drawn from real-life occurrences there.

As a child, Hurston lived a rather carefree and happy life surrounded by a large family, including her grandmother. Her father was a local minister and mayor of Eatonville; her mother was a schoolteacher. Hurston received her early education at the Hungerford School in Eatonville, a normal school patterned on the model of Booker T. Washington's Tuskegee Institute. Her later schooling took place at a boarding school in Jacksonville, Florida, until she left school altogether after her mother's death and her father's remarriage.

For a time, Hurston lived with relatives, did a variety of odd jobs, and ultimately obtained work as a lady's attendant in a traveling show. When the show reached Baltimore, Maryland, Hurston left the show and entered the high school department of the Morgan Academy (now Morgan State University). Upon completion of her high school diploma, Hurston entered Howard University in Washington, D.C. While a student at Howard, Hurston studied English with the noted scholar Lorenzo Dow Turner and took classes with Dr. Alain Leroy Locke, the first black Rhodes scholar who taught literature and philosophy at Howard and also advised the literary magazine. While it is not known exactly when Hurston began writing, she had managed to place several poems in Marcus Garvey's newspaper, the *Negro World*, and enjoyed the publication of her first short story, "John Redding Goes to Sea," in the 1921 issue of *Stylus*, the Howard University literary magazine. In addition, Hurston published several works in the annual yearbooks for Zeta Phi Beta Sorority, which she joined while at Howard. Impressed by her creative abilities, Alain Locke brought her to the attention of Charles S. Johnson, editor of *Opportunity* magazine, the official publication of the National Urban League. *Opportunity*, along with the NAACP's the *Crisis* magazine, was instrumental in jumpstarting the Harlem Renaissance by sponsoring literary contests to identify and foreground young African American writers and provide them with publishing venues for their works. Hurston moved to New York, where she soon became a prize-winning author and one of the Harlem Renaissance's most celebrated personalities.

Throughout the remainder of the 1920s Hurston's reputation grew. She published a number of important short stories, including two of her most well-known works, "Spunk" and "Sweat." She also published several short plays and presented several "revues"—programs that featured folk music, dance, and storytelling, told in dialect, in an effort to recreate and celebrate black folklife as she knew it from growing up in the south. In addition, Hurston entered Barnard College, the women's division of Columbia University, on a scholarship. There she studied anthropology with the famed Franz Boas and began her work as a collector of African American folklore. She became the institution's first black graduate in 1928.

In the early 1930s, Hurston turned to the novel as her preferred artistic form, beginning with the publication of *Jonah's Gourd Vine* in 1934. The story, loosely based on her parents' lives, confirmed Hurston's mastery of dialect writing and further established her as a leading voice in African American fiction. In 1935, Hurston published *Mules and Men*, a collection of folklore she had collected during her expeditions to the south. Although it was an artistic rather than a scientific presentation of her research, the book nevertheless gained for Hurston an appreciative audience. In 1937, Hurston published her most important work, the novel *Their Eyes Were Watching God*. This novel, destined to become a classic in African American and women's fiction, was published to mixed reviews, but even the stingiest reviewer had to acknowledge that Hurston was a master of her art.

In 1938, a second collection of folklore, *Tell My Horse*, appeared. Unlike *Mules and Men*, *Tell My Horse* focused largely on folklore and folklife in Haiti. Hurston closed out the busy 1930s with the publication of a third novel, *Moses, Man of the Mountain*, in 1939. A retelling of the Moses myth from an African American perspective, the novel often shows Hurston at her comic best.

Hurston began the 1940s with the same energy that she closed the previous decade with by publishing an autobiography, *Dust Tracks on a Road*, in 1942. An unconventional autobiography, it revealed little about her personal life, but did offer her opinions on any number of other matters. With the publication of *Seraph on the Suwanee* in 1948, Hurston's career came to a painful and unfortunate close. Though she lived for more than a dozen years more, she was never able to recapture her own artistic energy or the interest of publishers in her work.

Throughout the 1950s, Hurston's life was in constant decline. She was discovered working as a maid in the early 1950s and wrote only occasionally, oftentimes for black newspapers like the *Pittsburgh Courier*. Though she continued to write, most of her work was rejected by publishers. Hurston soon began to suffer from the ravages of hypertension and advanced age and suffered a series of strokes. The last stroke, late in 1959, left her debilitated and she entered a welfare home in Fort Pierce, Florida, where she died penniless in 1960. After a funeral, paid for largely with solicited funds, Hurston was buried in an unmarked grave in Fort Pierce's Garden of Heavenly Rest. A marker was erected in the early 1970s by Alice Walker, who called her "a genius of the South."

MAJOR WORKS

Hurston came to critical notice during the 1920s with the publication of a number of short stories. These stories often had a southern setting; in fact, many of them were set in Eatonville, Florida, and were peopled with characters whom Hurston had known while growing up there. Her first published story was titled "John Redding Goes to Sea." It appeared in *Stylus*, the Howard University student literary magazine, for 1921. It is the story of a young man, John Redding, who puts his dreams on hold while he lives up to the expectations of his mother and wife by staying at home and being the dutiful son and husband. The Florida setting, strong elements of folklore and folklife, and the prominence of a theme that Hurston was to use repeatedly make this an important first story.

Although "John Redding Goes to Sea" has a predictable plot, the story does much to establish Hurston as an artist who has a keen ear for dialect speech patterns and a sharp eye for character traits.

Two other stories published during the middle 1920s, "Spunk" and "Sweat," are among Hurston's finest stories. "Spunk" is the story of a bold, brassy, uncompromising individual, Spunk Banks, whom Hurston admires because he has *spunk*, an attitude toward life that Hurston herself held. Having been encouraged by her mother to "jump at the sun," Hurston clearly admired those who dared to demand to be accepted on their own terms. Spunk Banks is by no means a positive character in the usual sense. Indeed, he is a philanderer who preys upon a weak Joe Kanty not only because Spunk wants Joe's wife Lena, but also because he knows that Joe does not have the courage to challenge him. Spunk parades around town, even in Joe's presence, with Lena on his arm, much to the displeasure of the townsmen. When Joe does muster up the courage to demand that Spunk leave Lena alone, Spunk kills Joe with a pistol. Spunk suffers revenge by being cut with a circle saw at the sawmill where he works. In his dying breath, he blames it on Joe's making an appearance as a black bobcat and pushing him into the saw. This inclusion is more evidence of Hurston's use of African American folk beliefs and how they inform the everyday lives of the people. As well, Hurston presents the vibrant community of Eatonville and foregrounds the interactions among its residents as they go about their individual and communal lives.

"Sweat," published in 1926, is arguably Hurston's finest short story. It is the story of Delia Jones, a long-suffering washerwoman who suffers verbal, emotional, and physical abuse from Sykes Jones, her brutish husband of fifteen years. This story, too, is set in Eatonville, with the townspeople gathered on Joe Clarke's store porch serving as a backdrop and moral voice for the story. Delia works all week long, including Sundays, to earn money by washing clothes for white customers. When the story opens on a Sunday evening following church services, Delia is sorting clothes to soak for the next day's wash. Sykes, considering Delia and her work with great disdain, preys upon her fear of snakes by letting his bullwhip slither down her back. An argument ensues and Sykes makes his usual threats and insults.

It soon becomes clear that Sykes wants to make Delia so uncomfortable that she will leave her home, but Delia firmly informs him that she has worked long and hard for that house and has no intentions of leaving it to him and his mistress, a large, dark woman aptly named Bertha. Sykes further resolves to frighten Delia into leaving by placing a large rattlesnake in a box just outside the door to the house, an act that the community clearly does not approve of. When Delia grows accustomed to the snake and its mere presence no longer frightens her, Sykes takes his determination to rid himself of his wife a step further by placing the snake in the clothes hamper where he knows Delia will reach to sort her wash. Delia, however, discovers this trap in time to save herself and escapes the house unharmed.

Sykes, though, is not as lucky. In an ironic twist, Sykes stumbles into the house with a hangover from a night of carousing and falls into the clutches of the snake that bites him. Whether paralyzed from fear of the snake or hatred of her husband, Delia is unable or unwilling to come to Sykes's aid. He dies, knowing that Delia is fully aware of his dying and that she is refusing assistance.

"Sweat" offers a number of tragic dimensions, not the least of which is Delia's transformation from an essentially good, Christian woman to one who refuses to offer compassion to the dying, although we certainly understand the reasons for her refusal.

"Sweat" also plays on the folk adage that the trap you set for others may just as well ensnare you. This truism is particularly applicable to Sykes, a ne'er-do-well who is intent on destroying a good woman in favor of one who has few if any admirable qualities. The story further shows Hurston's adept handling of a familiar setting, familiar characters, and familiar dialect. Although Hurston was sometimes accused of pushing off folklore as imaginative literature, "Sweat" demonstrates her growing expertise in developing dramatic characters and sustaining credible action throughout the plot.

Another important short story is "The Gilded Six-Bits," published in 1933 in *Story* magazine. This story also pivots on the relationship between a black man and woman, but instead of pivoting on hatred as in "Sweat," "The Gilded Six-Bits" posits the enduring and healing power of love. Joe and Missie May Banks are a young couple clearly in love as the story opens. They frolic in their youthful expressions of love and lust, and everything around them is clean, bright, and fresh. A trip to a newly opened ice-cream parlor, however, proves disastrous for the couple. Both Joe and Missie May succumb to their own naiveté and are taken advantage of by a newcomer in town, Otis D. Slemmons, who seduces Joe emotionally and Missie May physically. One night Joe comes home early from work and discovers Missie May and Slemmons in a compromising position. Slemmons barely escapes with his life, and Missie May says in her own defense that she was doing it for Joe's sake. Joe is both hurt and incredulous.

Joe's attitude toward Missie May changes dramatically. For a while, he acts as if nothing is the matter, and then in a moment of physical attraction they make love. Much to Missie May's horror, Joe pays her for her services with the gold-plated coin that he snatched from Otis Slemmons on the night of their altercation. Missie May is devastated and, to add more to her fears of losing Joe, she discovers she is pregnant.

In the conclusion of "The Gilded Six-Bits," Joe acknowledges that the child Missie May has borne is his; according to his own mother who served as midwife for the child, the child is the "spitting image" of Joe. Because they love each other, and because they now have a child that serves as a bridge between the two of them, Joe and Missie May are able to reconcile their differences and resume their lives together just as much in love as before. Once again, Hurston shows herself as a clever manager of artistic detail. As well, she has drawn superb characters and has plotted the action with extreme care.

"The Gilded Six-Bits" not only solidified Hurston's reputation as a talented short story writer, but it also launched her career as a novelist. In response to an editor's query as to whether she might have a novel in the making, Hurston, ever the opportunist, responded in the affirmative and set about writing what became her first novel, *Jonah's Gourd Vine* (1934). This novel is based loosely on the story of her parents, John and Lucy Potts Hurston (Pearson in the novel), and, as such, provided Hurston the opportunity to demonstrate that she could handle the longer narrative inasmuch as she had already mastered the short story. Also, writing the novel gave Hurston the opportunity to reconcile some of her feelings about her father's philandering.

Jonah's Gourd Vine opens in southern Alabama shortly after slavery and concerns the coming-of-age of John "John-Buddy" Pearson, a mulatto field hand known for his physical prowess and his big voice. His father is not known, but is suspected to be the white landowner. This suspicion, coupled with his stepfather's brutal treatment of John-Buddy's mother, causes considerable difficulty in the household. As John Pearson grows into a handsome young man, many young women seek him out, but he is attracted to Lucy Potts, the young daughter of the land-owning Potts family. After they marry, against the advice and preference of the Potts family, John-Buddy goes to Eatonville,

Florida, an emerging all-black town, and soon sends for his wife and children to join him. Although Pearson works to support his family, he is unable to contain his sexual appetite and is often involved with other women. Lucy is aware of his philandering but often suffers in silence.

After a particularly pointed confrontation over his many affairs, John, in a fit of guilt, gives himself over to God and promises to do better. Assisted by his wife, he becomes the pastor of a local Baptist congregation. For a while, all seems to have changed, but then John Pearson falls victim to his previous sexual urges. Subsequently, his long-suffering wife becomes ill and dies, and his life and the lives of his children are thrown into greater turmoil. Shortly after Lucy's death, John marries a woman with a questionable reputation and further damages what is left of his paternal relationship with his children.

Sometime later, again responding to the guilt over the ill treatment of his now dead wife Lucy, and his less than supportive role as a father to his children, Rev. Pearson beats his new wife, blaming her for his many failures and shortcomings, and sets in motion his dismissal as the pastor of the church. He later leaves town, having felt the wrath of those whom he has betrayed.

John Pearson travels to a neighboring city where he hires himself out as a carpenter. He meets a widow and they subsequently marry. With her assistance, John becomes the pastor of another church and grows into a powerful Baptist leader on both the local and statewide levels. For a time, all of his past indiscretions seem to have disappeared and John actually prospers in the company of his new wife and the people of Zion Hope Baptist Church. However, on a trip back to Eatonville to visit old friends, John finds himself enamored of a young woman who awakens in him those same old urges. Although he is warned against pursuing these feelings by one of his old friends, it is as if John cannot help himself. In the aftermath of the affair, however, as John Pearson is reeling from the guilt of betraying yet another good and supportive wife and, no doubt, remembering his betrayal of his first wife as well, he is struck and killed by a train.

Besides being a compelling story, *Jonah's Gourd Vine* demonstrates that Hurston can ably manage a longer narrative. The pace of the events is particularly well handled and she maintains a remarkable consistency in point of view, particularly when one considers that this must have been an especially difficult story to write. Of course, the fact that Hurston's recounting of her parents' lives was, at best, barely fictionalized gave critics reason to be stingy in their reception of her first novel. However, there is so much that is done well, including the handling of the dialect, the detailed presentation of the physical settings, the precise, nonjudgmental capturing of the lives of the black folk of the rural south, and the careful and refreshing placement of humor and pathos throughout the work that it made for a work to be reckoned with even by the most demanding of critics.

In 1935, Hurston published *Mules and Men*, a book of folklore that she collected from throughout the south while she was a student at Barnard College and was employed briefly by Dr. Carter G. Woodson's Association of the Study of Negro Life and History. Because she elected to present her findings artistically instead of from a social science perspective, *Mules and Men* is quite a different kind of collection of folklore. Because Hurston immerses herself in both the collection and the reporting of her findings, *Mules and Men* indeed reads like a collection of stories. In fact, Hurston was frequently criticized for presenting folklore as fiction. As narrator of the collection, Hurston establishes herself as part and parcel of the larger community from which she collects these tales. This act gives her greater authority to comment on African American folklore and folklife as not just a subject for the social scientist, but as a vibrant entity deserving both attention and respect. Because Hurston was interested in the black disapora, she also forayed into Haiti, Jamaica, and South America to uncover African retentions and particular cultural phenomena of these native populations. These trips to the Caribbean and South America provided the material for her second collection of folklore, *Tell My Horse*, published in 1938.

Their Eyes Were Watching God, without question Hurston's most important and best-known work, appeared in 1937. Although it is a post–Harlem Renaissance work, it nevertheless captures Hurston's lifelong concern with the presentation of the life of the folk, or, as she aptly phrased it, "the Negro farthest down." Written in a very short time frame, as is most of Hurston's best work, *Their Eyes* concerns the life of Janie Crawford and her quest for freedom and womanhood.

The novel opens in West Florida in the years following the Emancipation. Janie Crawford, who never knew her mother and father, has been raised by her now aging maternal grandmother whom she refers to as Nanny. The narrative opens on a beautiful spring day. As Janie observes the business of nature, with honeybees pollinating pear blossoms, she experiences her sexual coming-of-age. In an attempt to divert her attention from the flirtatious young Johnny Taylor, Nanny announces that she has decided to marry Janie off to a much older man, Logan Killicks, who owns considerable property and his own house. Although Janie protests against the selection of her husband, she ultimately acquiesces in the face of a determined Nanny who tells her she wants her to have "protection." These early episodes constitute the first of Janie's accepting the dreams of others as her own and also set in motion her life of disappointment until she seizes the opportunity to live her own life according to her own terms.

Janie's marriage to Logan Killicks is doomed from the beginning. Janie has no intention of becoming a farm worker, and when Killicks goes to a neighboring town to purchase a mule for her to plow with, Janie knows that it is just a matter of time. In the meanwhile, Joe Starks enters the picture. He is from Georgia and is passing through West Florida on his way to Eatonville, Florida, where he has heard the residents are in the process of starting an all-black town. With little persuasion, he convinces Janie to join him, which she does, leaving Logan Killicks behind and casting her lot with Joe Starks who has dreams of his own.

When Joe and Janie arrive in Eatonville, they find only the rudiments of a town, but this gives Joe the opportunity to put his considerable and varied business skills to work, and soon he becomes the "big voice" around town, indeed, the mover and shaker in Eatonville. He establishes a general store and a post office and goes about developing Eatonville into a real town. As Joe prospers and becomes more influential, he becomes mayor of the town and announces that Janie is now "Mrs. Mayor Starks," an identity that she neither relishes nor understands fully. What Janie does realize is that this distinction separates her from the regular folk of the town and she begins to feel isolated. Then, too, there is no room for Janie's own dreams in this scheme of things and she begins to feel unfulfilled.

The years draw on and Joe continues to be financially successful even though his health begins to fail. Because Janie is considerably younger than Joe, she holds on to a degree of youth that Joe cannot appreciate and he takes all of his frustrations out on Janie by being both verbally and physically abusive. When he dies, they are estranged even though they still share the house. Janie goes through a brief period of mourning and then elects to move on with her life.

Shortly after Joe Starks's death, Janie is visited at the store by a much younger man, Vergible "Tea Cake" Woods, who begins to woo her. Despite her neighbors' warnings that Tea Cake is only after her money, Tea Cake and Janie soon leave Eatonville for Jacksonville, where they are married, and later move to the Everglades to live and work among the migrant workers. Theirs is a youthful sort of love—they live fast, work hard, and love as hard as they work. When their lives are disrupted by a powerful hurricane, Janie learns the true meaning of love and loss. While trying to save Janie's life, Tea Cake is bitten by a rabid dog and descends into madness. In his derangement, he tries to kill Janie and she shoots him in self-defense.

After she is acquitted by a jury of white men, Janie decides to return to Eatonville to live out the rest of her life. While she is met with scorn and derision from some of the older women of the town, her "kissing-friend," Phoeby, receives her with open arms. It is to Phoeby that Janie tells the story that forms the novel.

Their Eyes Were Watching God is a masterpiece of fiction. It is cleverly plotted and infused with emotion on every page. The characters are realistic, as are the situations, and Hurston handles both with exceedingly great care. In addition, the book is made great by many of the best elements of Hurston's previous works—an expert rendering of dialect speech, a careful and precise inclusion of elements of black folklore, a heartfelt appreciation of the lives of black folk, a comfortable knowledge of setting and a deep sense of place, and a careful balance of humor, tragedy, and pathos that propel the narrative forward in a way that few have matched.

In 1942, Hurston published *Dust Tracks on a Road*, an autobiography. While it did not meet the expectations that most readers have for autobiography, it is significant because it was one of very few autobiographical statements written up to that point by an African American woman. While it revealed very little about Hurston's personal life, it did catalog her attitude toward a number of issues and concerns, including how black people are regarded by whites and by each other. The original manuscript of *Dust Tracks* also included Hurston's critiques of America's imperialist behavior, but these were removed from the book by the publisher in the aftermath of the bombing of Pearl Harbor in 1941. The sections that were removed have since been restored and thus provide a more complete reflection of Hurston's views. Even without these sections, though, *Dust Tracks* won the Anisfield-Wolf Award given by the *Saturday Evening Post* for the most significant work published in the area of race relations.

Hurston published two other novels, *Moses, Man of the Mountain* (1939) and *Seraph on the Suwanee* (1948). *Moses, Man of the Mountain* continues Hurston's interest in biblical lore and in an African presence in the Bible, while one of the most significant aspects of *Seraph on the Suwanee* is that its principal characters are white southerners. While these works round out Hurston's canon, neither of them reaches the magnificence of *Their Eyes Were Watching God* and the early short stories. Although Hurston continued to write until her last years, she published very little after 1950.

CRITICAL RECEPTION

While Hurston was recognized as a leading personality by her contemporaries of the Harlem Renaissance, there is not a large body of criticism available from the early period of her career. This is due in part to the fact that literary criticism, as we know it today, was still a fledgling industry; thus, many writers received only scant mention in an occasional review and received very little sustained study. Those critics and reviewers who did write about Hurston were often ambivalent: they recognized her energy, but they were often unsure what to make of her use of dialect, her southern folk settings, her characters drawn from "the Negro[es] farthest down," or her humor. Many were put off by her portrayals of characters and situations that they would just as soon forget in a time when they were trying to be recognized for their *American-ness* instead of their *blackness*. Richard Wright was particularly dismissive of Hurston's talent, complaining that she seemed more of a minstrel type who was intent on entertaining white people instead of advancing the cause of African Americans. Likewise, Alain Locke was critical of her use of folklore. It is clear that whatever merit these two critics' positions may have, they sought to diminish Hurston's contributions because she would not follow their separate agenda for black writing.

For many years following the 1930s, the critics were largely silent on Hurston. When she died in 1960, for example, her works were out of print and very little was known about her or her work. In the early 1970s, critic Larry Neal wrote a new introduction to *Jonah's Gourd Vine* that attempted to rescue Hurston from oblivion, but it was not until a few years later that novelist Alice Walker launched a full-scale Hurston revival with an essay titled "Looking for Zora," published in *Ms.* magazine. Over the span of the last three decades, not only has Hurston been rescued from oblivion, but she has also been afforded a prime seat at the table where the best of the world's literature is served. It is difficult to imagine in this day and time that Hurston was ever forgotten or unheard of. Her works are centerpiece to any number of literary canons, from Harlem Renaissance literature to African American literature in general, to women's writing, to American and world literature proper, to all points between and among these lines of demarcation. It is difficult to find a college literature course that does not include some Hurston material. This is particularly true of *Their Eyes*, now regarded as a classic novel of American literature. Another telling factor is the number of sustained studies of her work that are produced by graduate students in this country alone. For example, up until 1981, only ten doctoral dissertations focused on Hurston's work; by the one-year period of 1993–1994, there were twenty-six such dissertations that focused on her work, and the numbers have remained consistently high for every year after that. Clearly, Hurston's work has been scrutinized from every possible vantage point and has not come up lacking in critical regard.

Similarly, there are a number of scholarly works that are published by academics and activists alike, and Hurston herself is celebrated in any number of ways, including an annual festival of the arts held in Eatonville each January, having her name attached to a foundation that supports young writers, being the subject of several plays, and so on. For a writer who came from rather humble beginnings, who struggled mightily to carve a place for herself in the world, and who died nearly forgotten, this recent restoration to a place of critical honor in the literary world certainly speaks volumes for her writing and for the person she was.

BIBLIOGRAPHY

Works by Zora Neale Hurston

"Color Struck." *Fire!! A Quarterly Devoted to the Younger Negro Artists* 1.1 (1926): 7–14.
The Complete Stories. Introduction by Henry Louis Gates, Jr., and Sieglinde Lemke. Afterword by Henry Louis Gates, Jr. New York: HarperCollins, 1995.

Dust Tracks on a Road. 1942. Reprint, 2nd ed., edited by Robert Hemenway. Urbana: University of
    Illinois Press, 1984.
Jonah's Gourd Vine. 1934. Reprint, New York: Harper & Row, 1990.
Mule Bone: A Comedy of Negro Life. New York: HarperCollins, 1991.
Mules and Men. 1935. Reprint, Bloomington: Indiana University Press, 1978.
Their Eyes Were Watching God. 1937. Reprint, Urbana: University of Illinois Press, 1978.

Studies of Zora Neale Hurston's Works

Bloom, Harold, ed. *Zora Neale Hurston*. New York: Chelsea, 1986.
Boyd, Valerie. *Wrapped in Rainbows: The Life of Zora Neale Hurston*. New York: Scribner, 2002.
Carby, Hazel V. *Reconstructing Womanhood: The Emergence of the Afro-American Woman
    Novelist*. New York: Oxford University Press, 1987.
Chinn, Nancy, and Elizabeth E. Dunn. "'The Ring of Singing Metal on Wood': Zora Neale
    Hurston's Artistry in 'The Gilded Six-Bits.'" *Mississippi Quarterly* 49 (Fall 1996): 25–34.
Crabtree, Claire. "The Confluence of Folklore, Feminism and Black Self-Determinism in
    Zora Neale Hurston's *Their Eyes Were Watching God*." *Southern Literary Journal* 17.2
    (1985): 54–66.
Harris, Trudier. *The Power of the Porch: The Storyteller's Craft in Zora Neale Hurston, Gloria
    Naylor, and Randall Kenan*. Athens: University of Georgia Press, 1996.
Hemenway, Robert E. *Zora Neale Hurston: A Literary Biography*. Urbana: University of Illinois
    Press, 1977.
Hill, Lynda Marion. *Social Rituals and the Verbal Art of Zora Neale Hurston*. Washington, DC:
    Howard University Press, 1996.
Jones, Evora. "Ascent and Immersion: Narrative Expression in Their Eyes Were Watching God."
    CLA Journal 39.3 (March 1996): 369–79.
Kaplan, Carla, ed. *Zora Neale Hurston: A Life in Letters*. New York: Doubleday, 2002.
Lowe, John. *Jump at the Sun: Zora Neale Hurston's Cosmic Comedy*. Urbana: University of
    Illinois Press, 1994.
Lupton, Mary Jane. "Zora Neale Hurston and the Survival of the Female." *Southern Literary
    Journal* 15.1 (1982): 45–54.
Plant, Deborah. *Every Tub Must Sit on Its Own Bottom: The Philosophy and Politics of Zora Neale
    Hurston*. Urbana: University of Illinois Press, 1995.

Warren J. Carson

ANGELA JACKSON (1951–)

BIOGRAPHICAL NARRATIVE

A twenty-first-century poet, playwright, essayist, and novelist, Angela Jackson was born in Greenville, Mississippi, as the fifth of nine siblings, and raised in Chicago, Illinois. Before her discovery of her penchant for constructing urban paintings from a puzzle of words, a medical career seemed to be her destiny. Living on the southside of Chicago, Jackson traveled north once again to Northwestern University on a premedical scholarship. Surreptitiously, after meeting visiting professors Margaret Walker and Hoyt W. Fuller, she became captivated by African American literature and soon learned her own extraordinary ability to invent metaphors and similes. Stepping through the urban landscapes of the southside of Chicago, she began to paint word pictures of the surroundings and the people—allowing outsiders to view their inner longings, failures, dignity, and desires.

In the summer of 1970, Jackson joined Fuller's workshop, Organization of Black American Culture (OBAC), the first African American writers workshop of its kind in the United States. This organization was intent on developing not only talented African American writers, but also critics of African American literature. Focused on the close adherence to a Black Aesthetic that used the language of the community in new ways, Jackson cites this workshop as the greatest influence on her growth as a writer. She explains: "Our work is in the Word. No place is more sacred or serious. . . . We speak the words. And that is why OBAC is. To consistently search for the clarity inside our experience, to seek the untouched magnificence, the rueful but striving imperfection of our moments in time. . . . We seek to identify and exalt the peculiar movement and music of our experience" (*Nommo* 26).

According to Jackson, writers and critics were "workers," employing their words in a way that would change things. As a guest contributor to *Nommo*, a collection of the works of OBAC members for twenty years, Houston Baker, Jr., explains, "The function of the artist and critic alike was to craft and to celebrate inspiring images of Black life" (317).

Accepting this Black Aesthetic as a young member of OBAC, Jackson hails Hoyt W. Fuller as her mentor. Soon, one of the youngest writers in the workshop would become a sought-after reader of her work as she performed song and jazz rhythms in her readings. In the years following Fuller's death, Jackson continued to share her talent and critiques in the workshop, becoming a guiding beacon of inspiration for countless writers.

MAJOR WORKS

Angela Jackson uses her lyrics to sing of the southside neighborhood she inhabits as she tells the stories of love, poverty, pride, and everyday life of the people who walk the streets. Her dedication to revealing these inspiring images often means highlighting and

naming traditional ideas. Her collection of poetry *The Man with the White Liver* introduces a term used by the generation before her to describe a man with an enormous
sexual appetite. Like Zora Neale Hurston, Jackson strives to document African American language and lies (as storytelling embellishments have been called) through the
memoryhouse of her work.

Only four years after joining OBAC, Jackson published her first poetry collection,
Voodoo/Love Magic. Here Jackson reveals a keen interest in African tradition as divining
sticks, Yoruba masks, ancestors, Nigerian oil, griots, and more parade across her lines as
naturally as the tambourine sounds flowing from storefront churches and blues vocals
bursting out of the doors of local taverns. Voodoo, or hoodoo (as it has been termed in
the southern United States, where many of the African traditions still exist) define the
"hex" as a magic potion, herb, or animal part that when combined with certain words
could work magic. The opening poem of Jackson's first collection, "Voodoo/Love
Magic," pledges such a hex as an African American woman's personal *mojo*. Similarly,
Jackson's play *Shango Diaspora* presents a woman's seduction cloaked in West African
references and images. Jackson's poems "In Her Solitude: The Inca Divining Spider"
and "Arachnia: Her Side of the Story" portray the spider as a mystic weaver, tough and
persistent in its ability to protect itself. The web it weaves becomes a place for renewal,
chance, mystery, and cunning.

Celebrating the physical beauty African American men were said to enjoy in the
women they loved, she borrows from Haki Madhubuti and calls on the "Woman with
Water/Melon Thighs" (*Voodoo* 16). Another poem, titled "A Summer Story," witnesses
the speaker's actions as her cousin takes this little girl, dirty from exhaustive play, and
shows her to herself. "[P]retty big dimples" accent her face and her cousin's ability to
create a new vision (*Voodoo* 9).

Although strong women and positive men find their stories in Jackson's poetry, she
does not sidestep the negative threat of community disunity. In her poem "Because We
Failed: For a Child Who Died from an Overdose of Heroin," she blames the community's
apathy for the loss of a child.

In addition to six collections of poetry, Jackson has published chapters of a novel in
progress, *Treemont Stone*. Through these peeks into a more sustained work of art, the
narrator introduces the reader to the people in her neighborhood who sit outside on
summer nights: "Mr. Rucker who was the drunkman, Uncle Blackstrap who was the
junkman, Miss Ross who was Eddie's mother and no one's wife, Miss Wilson who was
the head lady, my father who was the good man you better not mess with his kids, my
mother who was the sun" (*Chicago Works* 93). Jackson vividly describes individuals
within a collective of African American men, women, and children who share a precarious existence. Yet it is not their oppression that Jackson illuminates, but rather their
dignity, individuality, and inventiveness. Young women play double Dutch, a game as
affordable as the cost of a clothesline that serves as a jump rope. Jackson describes
Halloween as a time when "[s]pirits were being loosed, crossing bridges into matter and
climbing stairs" (*Breaking Ice* 353). And there was a "witch" who "rode no broom; she
wore one, more or less, upon her head . . . blond hair [that lay on her neck] like Des-
demona, the watermelon man's horse's mane" (353).

African Americans living in housing projects and those in neighborhoods that
surround them make their way through the cold winters of Chicago, "learn[ing] new
walks that leaned against the Hawk," as Chicago winds are named. But the children who
were being raised in those housing projects, enduring the cold wind, "came out like

clear, separated cubes of ice—hard and harder" (*Chicago Works* 96). The "other boys *boiled* into manhood" (97). And all the children of the neighborhood had to deal with a child beaten and confined to a slow withering away as his oncoming death matures his two friends as they tenderly protect him from the insult of his demise. In the excerpts from her novel, Jackson tells this story through the eyes of children, using the subtle nuances that define their innocence. Yet this is not a book for children. Exceptionally skilled in the art of storytelling, Jackson leaves adults rubbing their chins, lost in contemplation.

CRITICAL RECEPTION

Jackson has been praised for the precision of her metaphors, her fresh rendering of Chicago's southside community, and her fusion of southern roots and urban tenement life. She is described as a writer of enormous depth who incorporates jazz rhythms and pauses in original ways.

In response to her collection of poems *And All These Roads Be Luminous*, reviewer Kalamu ya Salaam states, "Whether cleaning fish or dusting the furniture, catching a train or leaping across rooftops, Angela accurately reads what's really going on inside of us" (http://aalbc.com/books/poems.htm).

Angela Jackson has been the recipient of numerous awards, and her work has appeared in many literary magazines, such as *First World*, *Triquarterly*, *Open Places*, *River Styx*, and *Callaloo*. A prolific writer with an extraordinary talent, Jackson dedicates her vision to the people around her and a preservation of their everyday beingness.

BIBLIOGRAPHY

Works by Angela Jackson

And All These Roads Be Luminous. Evanston: Northwestern University Press, 1998.
"The Blue Rose." In *New Chicago Stories*, edited by Fred Gardaphè. Chicago: City Stoop Press, 1990.
Dark Legs and Silk Kisses: The Beatitudes of the Spinners. Evanston: Northwestern University Press, 1993.
"From Treemont Stone." In *Chicago Works*. Chicago: The Morton Press, 1990.
The Greenville Club. Chapbook, 1977.
The Man with the White Liver. New York: Contact II Publications, 1987.
Shango Diaspora. A play. 1980.
Solo in the Boxcar Third Floor E. Chicago: OBAhouse, 1985.
"Treemont Stone." In *Breaking Ice*, edited by Terry McMillan. New York: Penguin Books, 1990.
Voodoo/Love Magic. Chicago: Third World Press, 1974.
When the Wind Blows. A play. 1984.
Witness! A play. 1978.

Studies of Angela Jackson's Works

Harris, Trudier, and Thadious M. Davis, eds. *Dictionary of Literary Biography*, vol. 41. Detroit, MI: Gale Research Co., 1985.
Parks, Carole A., ed. *Nommo: A Literary Legacy of Black Chicago (1967–1987)*. Chicago, IL: OBAhouse, 1987.

Peacock, Scot, ed. *Contemporary Authors*, vol. 176. Farmington Hills, MI: Gale Research Co., 1999.

Quashie, Kevin Everod, R. Joyce Lausch, and Keith D. Miller, eds. In *New Bones: Contemporary Black Writers in America*. Old Tappan, NJ: Prentice Hall, 2001.

Judy Massey Dozier

ELAINE JACKSON (1943–)

BIOGRAPHICAL NARRATIVE

Elaine Jackson, a well-known playwright, was born in Detroit in 1943 to Essie and Charles Jackson. After graduating from Wayne State University, where she majored in speech and education, she moved to the West Coast to pursue an acting career. As an actress she eventually performed in more than forty plays in Michigan, California, and in Off-Broadway productions in New York, such as Douglass Turner Ward's Negro Ensemble Company's *Liberty Call (1975)*.

Jackson initially began writing plays as a means of creating roles for herself. However, she eventually turned to writing full time and won a Rockefeller Award for Playwriting in 1978–1979, the Langston Hughes Playwriting Award in 1979, and a National Endowment for the Arts Award for playwriting in 1983. She also served as playwright in residence at the Lake Forest College in Illinois in 1990 and at her alma mater Wayne State University in 1991. Currently, she lives with her husband and son in New York City, where she teaches high school theater and playwriting.

MAJOR WORKS

Elaine Jackson's plays—including *Toe Jam* (1971), *Cockfight* (1976), *Paper Dolls* (1979), *Birth Rites* (1987), and *Afterbirth* (1984)—articulate problems associated with African American females who must compare themselves to standards of white Eurocentric beauty designed to create self-hatred in them. Her work is a philosophical frontal assault on the white Eurocentric standards of beauty that dominate the American stage, as well as television and films. Her plays also speak passionately to the issues surrounding growing up black and female in the United States.

Toe Jam's protagonist is a young African American girl who is in search of her own identity. She tries to escape from the sordidness of ghetto life by dreaming of herself as a great actress-poet-playwright. While *Cockfight* on a surface level looks at the dissolution of a marriage, it actually closely examines the deeper conflicts that sometimes emerge in romantic relationships between black women and men in American society from a feminist point of view.

Jackson's most widely known play is *Paper Dolls*. The protagonists of *Paper Dolls* are two 1930s African American beauty contest winners, Miss Emancipation and her runner-up, who at one time attempted to launch Hollywood film careers. However, when they tried to get movie roles, they were forced to confront the bitter realization that Hollywood had yet to discover them as anything other than Aunt Jemimas. An insensitive film director tells them that, as black actresses, if they want roles in Hollywood, then they better learn to tap dance.

In a series of flashbacks, Margaret-Elizabeth, the more flamboyant of *Paper Dolls*'s two protagonists, drags a reluctant and muted Lizzie through the embarrassing events of their unfulfilled lives, insistent on changing the ending. The play's humor capitalizes on the sibling-like rivalry between the two former "Negro beauties"—women who ultimately embrace themselves and each other as who they truly are: strong black women. Just like the protagonist in Jackson's earlier play, *Toe Jam*, in *Paper Dolls* Margaret is acutely aware of herself as an actress and becomes fed up with being forced into socially scripted dramas. She is incensed at a white artist's negative portrayal of a black woman as an Aunt Jemima, berating her for "missing the rhythm, vitality, and color intensity of the black model."

CRITICAL RECEPTION

Derrick C. Lewis observes in his article "Paper Dolls, Real Women, True Beauty" that *Paper Dolls* is a play that takes a look at black females' attempts to obtain a "right look" that exposes them to easy exploitation. He says that it takes a bite out of the standard Hollywood assumptions of beauty, one that does not accommodate the natural beauty of the black female. (10).

Dana A. Williams says in *Contemporary African American Female Playwrights* that "*Paper Dolls* is a two-act drama that examines the standards of beauty that are set by the American entertainment industry and the negative effects these standards have on black women" (59).

In *The Oxford Companion to African American Literature*, William Andrews notes that Jackson's work, whether dealing with endings or beginnings or redefining spaces in between, further opened the stage door for black playwrights and helped set a standard in mainstream theater for richly textured portrayals of black characters and their stories (392). Andrews also emphasizes that Jackson embraced this task because she emerged as a black female playwright in the 1970s, a socially and politically dynamic moment in the nation's history and a "renascence" decade for African American theater (391).

Margaret B. Wilkerson, the editor of *9 Plays by Black Women*, finds that "the destruction of innocence in the world of black girls and women is also a recurring theme in Jackson's work (348). In her commentary on Jackson's playwriting and the Black Power Movement, Wilkerson notes that although most of the African American plays of this period tended to dwell upon male identity and social confrontation, Jackson's *Toe Jam* became a popular choice at community theaters, colleges, and universities, especially in San Francisco's Bay Area, where several theaters produced the play in the same season. It was eventually anthologized in King and Milner's *Black Drama Anthology*, a seminal collection of works by twenty-two black dramatists (348).

Elizabeth Barnsley Brown contends in her dissertation, "Shackles on a Writer's Pen," that African American female playwrights like Elaine Jackson are healing the deleterious effects of past constructions of race and gender, manipulating a multiplicity of discourses in order to subvert the dominant "Master" discourse or script. Like Wilkerson, she feels that Jackson's playwriting emerged as an important and resonant black female voice during the aforementioned black power period. In "Screening the Camera's Eye: Black and White Confrontations of Technological Representation," Timothy Murray finds in Jackson's African American theater a complexity of technological confrontation exacerbated by plays that suggest that the marvelous "technicolors" of American media have yet to escape from their white-against-black fundamentals.

BIBLIOGRAPHY

Works by Elaine Jackson

Afterbirth (1984), unpublished.
Birth Rites (1987), unpublished.
Cockfight (1976), unpublished.
Paper Dolls (1979). In *9 Plays By Black Women*. Ed. Margaret Wilkerson. New York: New American Library, 1986.
Toe Jam (1971). In *Black Drama Anthology*. Ed. Woodie King and Ron Milner. New York: New American Library, 1971.

Studies of Elaine Jackson's Works

Andrews, William, ed. *The Oxford Companion to African American Literature*. New York: Oxford University Press, 1997.
Brown, Elizabeth Barnsley. "Shackles on a Writer's Pen: Dialogism in Plays by Alice Childress, Lorraine Hansberry, Adrienne Kennedy, and Ntozake Shange." Ph.D. Dissertation, University of North Carolina, 1996.
Janifer, Raymond. "The Black Nationalistic Aesthetic and the Early Fiction of John Edgar Wideman." Ph.D. Dissertation, Ohio State University, 1996.
King, Woodie, and Ron Milner, eds. *Black Drama Anthology*. New York: Penguin Books, 1971.
Lewis, Derrick. "Paper Dolls, Real Women, True Beauty." *Michigan Citizen*, February 9, 1991, 8.
Murray, Timothy. "Screening the Camera's Eye: Black and White Confrontations of Technological Representation." *Modern Drama* 28.1 (1985): 110–24.
Partnow, Elaine T. *The Female Dramatist: Profiles of Women Playwrights from the Middle Ages to Contemporary Times*. New York: Facts on File, 1998.
Peterson, Bernard L, ed. *Contemporary Black American Playwrights and Their Plays: A Biographical and Dramatic Index*. New York: Greenwood Press, 1988.
Wilkerson, Margaret B., ed. *9 Plays by Black Women*. New York: New American Library, 1986.
Williams, Dana A. *Contemporary African American Female Playwrights*. Westport, CT: Greenwood Press, 1998.

Raymond Janifer

MAE JACKSON (1946–)

BIOGRAPHICAL NARRATIVE

A prolific fiction writer, poet, playwright, letter writer, grant writer, and activist, Mae Jackson has accomplished much in her sixty years of life. Born on January 3, 1946, near her father's home in Arkansas, Mae Jackson moved from Arkansas to New Orleans with her mother when she was only nine months old. She lived in the Mardi Gras City for twelve years before moving to Brooklyn, New York, where she continues to reside.

Advocating for human rights is what Mae Jackson does. As a teenager, she loved to go through Harlem smoking cigarettes and trying to get into the Apollo Theater. She would walk into the Chock Full of Nuts coffee shop and see Jackie Robinson, while Malcolm X preached outside of Michelle's Bookstore—a place that Jackson remembers had "books all about black folks, stacked from the floor to the ceiling."

MAJOR WORKS

Malcolm X's family is the subject of Jackson's 1997 essay, "The Fire Next Time—Lessons of the Shabazz Tragedy." In the essay, Jackson writes about Malcolm X's twelve-year-old grandson who sets fire to his grandmother's apartment. The fire ultimately claims the life of Malcolm's widow. In exploring the causes of the boy's actions, Jackson poignantly writes:

What can I claim for my generation? We did not have the type of revolution we'd hoped for. We set fire to inner cities, but we didn't use those fires to purify ourselves. And maybe it's because we didn't want to hear Malcolm after all. We didn't want to take that next step that an oppressed people must take if they are to ever be free. We wanted a little bit of change and were willing to settle for white people liking us enough to stop killing us.

Her 1999 essay, "Killing of Amadou Dillou— -One Mother Hears Another Mother's Cry of Pain," is about the tragic shooting of Guinea immigrant Amadou Dillou. Dillou was standing unarmed in a New York City doorway when four police officers opened fire on him. They fired forty-one shots, nineteen of which struck Dillou. The policemen mistook Dillou for an armed suspect. After the shooting, many in the African American community stated that it was racially motivated. This "history of racism" is what Jackson writes about in the essay: "I know the truth. I also know history. But even if I did not know truth or history, common sense tells me what my mother knew—no people are freed by mere words, or desire. They are freed when they 'recognize the extent of their oppression and organize against it.'"

Can I Poet with You (1969) is a twenty page book of poetry that includes poems on topics such as African American culture, struggles, concerns and language.

CRITICAL RECEPTION

Although Jackson's works have not been the subject of criticism, it has been reproduced in several literary journals and books.

BIBLIOGRAPHY

Work by Mae Jackson

"Killing of Amadou Dillou—One Mother Hears Another Mother's Cry of Pain." *Pacific News Service*, February 17, 1999. http://www.pacificnews.org/jinn/stories/5.04/990217-dillou.html. Accessed January 3, 2005.
"The Fire Next Time—Lessons of the Shabazz Tragedy." *Pacific News Service*, July 11, 1997. http://www.pacificnews.org/jinn/stories/3.15/970711-shabazz.html.
Can I Poet with You. Detroit, MI: Broadside Press, 1969.

Studies of Mae Jackson's Work

Bell, Roseann, Bettye J. Parker Smith, and Beverly Guy-Sheftall. *Sturdy Black Bridges: Visions of Black Women in Literature*. Garden City, NY: Anchor Press/Doubleday, 1979.
Foster, F. S. "Changing Concepts of the Black Woman." *Journal of Black Studies* 3.4 (1973).
Thompson, Julius E. *Dudley Randall, Broadside Press, and the Black Arts Movement in Detroit, 1960–1995*. Jefferson, NC: McFarland & Company, Inc., 1999.

Heather Hoffman Jordan

MATTIE JANE JACKSON (1843–?)

BIOGRAPHICAL NARRATIVE

Mattie Jane Jackson, who deals with her era's historical literacy, was born in 1843 in St. Charles County, Missouri. Jackson is most well known for her 1866 publication *The Story of Mattie J. Jackson; Her Parentage—Experience of Eighteen Years in Slavery—Incidents During the War—Her Escape from Slavery. A True Story.* Her narrative was written, according to its preface, to "gain sympathy from the earnest friends of those who have been bound down by a dominant race in circumstances over which they had no control." This is the primary document of Jackson's life and history, and little is known of her outside the personal narrative.

MAJOR WORK

In recounting her life, Jackson lists her ancestors as well as her slave owners, witnessing the conflicting yet inextricable ties that construct her sense of self in history. When Jackson was three years old, her father, a slave and a preacher, was sold away from the family, yet made his escape to a free state before he could be moved. Two years later, and after the death of her oldest daughter, Sarah Anne, Mattie's mother Ellen Turner and her two remaining children, Mattie Jane and Esther J., attempted an escape themselves. They traveled for two days undetected but were captured when an advertisement describing them reached Illinois just before they did. They were taken to a trader's yard where they were bought by William Lewis, owner of a tobacco factory outside St. Louis.

Jackson writes that four years later her mother married George Brown, a foreman for the Lewis tobacco company, and she had two sons as a result of this union. In an act of resistance to being improperly treated, Brown made his escape to Canada. Soon after he left, Jackson's youngest half brother "was taken sick in consequence of being confined in a box [her] mother was obliged to keep him" in. The boy never recovered and died at the age of two.

Jackson spent most of her young adult years surviving numerous beatings, making several failed escape attempts, and enduring incidents of severe abuse. In 1863, at the age of twenty, she was sold from her family. The conditions of her new residence, with Captain Ehpraim Frisbee, were deplorable. There was never enough heat and the work days were fourteen hours long. After six months and many escape attempts, Jackson finally secured her freedom. Jackson's sister, Esther J., also referred to in the text as Hester, escaped to the free state but was never heard from again. Jackson's mother, during her seventh escape attempt, and after forty-three years as a slave, also secured her freedom.

After securing their freedom, Ellen Turner married Mr. Adams and Jackson moved to Lawrence, Massachusetts to live with her stepfather George Brown and his wife, Dr. L. S. Thompson, who ghost wrote *The Story of Mattie Jane Jackson*. In recognition of the power that language holds in the construction of an autonomous self, and the ways that literacy negotiates that self to the larger society, Mattie writes, "Manage your own secrets, and divulge them by the silent language of your own pen." Jackson's memoir sustains many elements of traditional slave narratives, such as paralleling her geographical path with the chronological events that led to the culmination of her freedom. As well, her narrative style and structure contain a religious foundation that concludes in the final chapter's exhortation on the importance of utilizing Christianity to triumph over the evils of slavery. Jackson's narrative not only concerns itself with a personal rendering of the historical travesties of slavery, but also dialogues with the narrative structure, literary style, artistic and political perspectives, and aesthetic engagement of her era's historical literacy. Jackson seems well aware of the larger discourse into which she is entering, and her voice is a distinct presence in the slave narrative genre.

CRITICAL RECEPTION

Despite the historical value and literary quality of her work, there is no criticism written about the narrative. A copy of the manuscript is held at the University of Chapel Hill, North Carolina, in the "Documenting the American South" collection. In Jackson's honor, there is The Mattie Jackson African American Center, which houses special editions and rare books, located in Miles College in Fairfield, Alabama.

BIBLIOGRAPHY

Work by Mattie Jane Jackson

"The Story of Mattie Jane Jackson; Her Parentage——Experience of Eighteen Years in Slavery—Incidents During the War——Her Escape from Slavery." In *Six Women's Slave Narratives*, edited by William Andrews. New York: Oxford University Press, 1998.

Study of Mattie Jane Jackson's Work

Morgan, Tabitha Adams. "Women's Urban Identity and Cultural Production: Reading the Texts of Ghetto Regionalism in Lydia Maria Child and Mattie Jane Jackson." Paper given at the Catherine Maria Sedgwick Society Symposium, New York City, 2005. Unpublished paper.

Tabitha Adams Morgan

REBECCA COX JACKSON (1795–1871)

BIOGRAPHICAL NARRATIVE

Rebecca Cox Jackson's public life began when she was 35 years old after a spiritual rebirth led her to become a religious leader. Jackson was born in Horntown, Pennsylvania, just outside of Central Philadelphia, one of four children. Her eventual transformation from seamstress and homemaker to visionary was unanticipated because as she often said she was the only child of her mother that "had no learning." Her primary responsibility was to take care of her two younger siblings and her elder brother Joseph's six children.

Joseph, a minister and widower, helped Jackson read the Bible and write letters until a thunderstorm in 1830 changed all that. Because Jackson was afraid of storms, she weathered them through prayer. During a pivotal storm, her prayers were answered in the form of three divine gifts: the ability to read, the gift of healing others, and the gift of power— -a prophetic ability to control weather and read the intentions of others. She details these miracles in "Gifts of Power," an autobiography that was not widely published until over a century later. As she honed these gifts, she began to reconcile her Bible-based African Methodist Episcopal upbringing with a more female-centered and abstinence-based theology that compelled her to eventually leave her husband and become an itinerant preacher.

When she encountered a small religious fellowship of Shakers called the Little Band in 1836, Jackson believed she had found a faith she could practice and preach, even as some Methodist preachers and other detractors tried to thwart her efforts.

Despite the fact that Jackson was not officially affiliated with the Shakers or any other institution until late in her life, she eventually became Mother Rebecca Jackson. With her devout companion Rebecca Perot, she founded the Philadelphia Out-Family, a branch of black Shakers that outlived her by forty years. She died from a stroke in 1871.

MAJOR WORKS

Jackson's journals are preserved in her autobiography, *Gifts of Power: The Writings of Rebecca Jackson, Black Visionary, Shaker Eldress*. The book chronicles her extraordinary experiences as an unconventional woman of God in antebellum America. Through her journal writings, Jackson demonstrates how she relied solely on her independence and faith despite isolation, sickness and uncertainty. *Gifts of Power* serves as a testament to the power of one woman's faith and vision.

Despite its strength, *Gifts of Power* is sometimes tedious and hard to follow. The writings are not in chronological order, which makes it difficult to distinguish Jackson's visions from her real world experiences. Furthermore, for all of her description of her dreams and travels, there is not much discussion of her estranged husband Samuel, or much description of those closest to her, including Rebecca Perot.

CRITICAL RECEPTION

Only a few critical analyses have been written about Jackson, as she is not widely known. In Joanne Braxton's view, her obscurity may have been related to the tension between Jackson's inner voice and the voices of those around her who might have been educated in the African Methodist tradition and could not envision a space for a woman who relied solely on the voice of God in contrast to the voices of external spiritual advisors. Braxton explains that Jackson's reliance on her visionary experiences and dreams are not supposed to be analyzed by today's standards or by psychological inquiry, but should be viewed as one black woman's need to steadfastly pursue her visions. She also notes that testimonies like those of Jackson and other early nineteenth-century black women memoirists set the stage for the better known works of Harriet Tubman and Sojourner Truth.

BIBLIOGRAPHY

Work by Rebecca Cox Jackson

Gifts of Power: The Writings of Rebecca Jackson, Black Visionary, Shaker Eldress. Ed. Jean McMahon Humez. Boston: University of Massachusetts Press, 1981.

Studies of Rebecca Cox Jackson's Work

Braxton, Joanne M. *Black Women Writing Autobiography: A Tradition Within A Tradition*. Philadelphia: Temple University Press, 1989.
Williams, Richard E. *Called and Chosen: The Story of Mother Rebecca Jackson and the Philadelphia Shakers*. Metuchen: The Scarecrow Press, Inc. and The American Theological Library Association, 1981.

Joshunda Sanders

HARRIET ANN JACOBS (1813–1897)

BIOGRAPHICAL NARRATIVE

Harriet Jacobs was born in 1813 in Edenton, North Carolina, to Elijah Jacobs and his wife Delilah, both of whom were slaves. Despite her parents' slave status, she spent her first six years as a free child in her family home. Upon her mother's death, she learned of her slave status and was delivered over to Margaret Horniblow, a mistress who treated her kindly and taught her to read and write. Although it was hoped that Horniblow would eventually free Harriet, she bequeathed the slave to her niece Mary Matilda, the three-year-old daughter of Dr. James and Mary Norcom.

After Horniblow's death in 1825, Jacobs moved to the Norcom household. After she reached adolescence, Jacobs became the subject of Dr. Norcom's predatory, sexual advances. In an attempt to take control of her life, Jacobs began a relationship with Samuel Sawyer, another powerful white man in the community. Sawyer, an attorney who would later become a U.S. Congressman, fathered the slave's two children. Jacobs hoped her relationship with Sawyer and the resulting pregnancies would provoke Norcom to sell her. The outraged doctor, however, refused to relinquish control, even after his jealous wife removed Jacobs from their home. Norcom's persecution of Jacobs continued despite the separation. When she refused to move to a house that he built for her, Norcom sent Jacobs off to work on his family plantation in Auburn.

On the plantation, Jacobs finally resolved to escape. Learning her children were to be brought to Auburn to be "broken in," Jacobs decided to flee north, hoping that the children's father would purchase and liberate them. Things did not work out entirely as planned. Sawyer bought his children but broke his promise to free them. And while Jacobs successfully escaped from the Norcoms in 1835, she would not arrive in the free north for more than half a decade. Finding it difficult to safely escape her hometown or to sever family ties, Jacobs hid for almost seven years in a tiny crawlspace over the house where her grandmother and children lived. Here, she suffered from sensory deprivation and muscular atrophy; she also felt acute distress from being unable to act as a mother to her children. In 1837, Sawyer removed Jacobs's daughter, Louisa, from the home, bringing the girl to Washington, D.C., to live with him. To Jacobs's horror, Sawyer eventually sent their daughter into service to a cousin in Brooklyn.

In 1842, an opportunity for escape arrived, and Jacobs fled north. She soon located her daughter in Brooklyn and arranged for her son, Joseph, to be sent to her brother in Boston. Jacobs could not, however, establish a family home, having neither the legal power to remove Louisa from service nor the financial resources to care for her children. To support herself, Jacobs worked in the New York home of magazine editor Nathaniel Parker Willis, caring for the children from his first and second marriages. Until his death, Norcom continued to pursue Jacobs, making several unsuccessful trips north to recapture her. In 1852, Norcom's daughter, Mary Matilda Messmore, arrived in New York with her husband to reclaim Jacobs. Nathaniel Willis's second wife, Cornelia, came to the aid of her valued employee, paying the Messmores 150 dollars to free Jacobs. While she was relieved, Jacobs bitterly resented that payment was necessary to obtain her legal freedom.

In between employment at the Willis home, Jacobs worked with her activist brother, managing an abolitionist reading room in Rochester, New York. Here, she became acquainted with Amy Post, who encouraged her to write her life story. Although anxious to help the abolitionist cause, Jacobs was reluctant to publish the details of her sexual history, and it would be many years before she began the project. In 1853, Jacobs sought to collaborate with Harriet Beecher Stowe to produce a dictated slave narrative, but negotiations ended bitterly. Resolving to tell her own story, Jacobs spent five years writing her memoir by night, while caring for the Willis family by day. Getting the story to print proved difficult for the escaped slave. Jacobs could not find a publisher until Lydia Maria Child agreed to edit the work and write an introduction for the text. *Incidents in the Life of a Slave Girl, Written by Herself* came to print in America in 1861, and was republished in England the following year.

Jacobs lived a long and productive life after the publication of *Incidents*. During the Civil War, she worked in Washington D.C., and Virginia, collecting and distributing clothing and medical supplies for the "contrabands"—southern black refugees who sought aid across Union lines. She later established a free school for the contrabands. During Reconstruction, she continued her relief efforts for southern blacks, working primarily in Georgia. Suffering from declining health and financial circumstances in her final years, Jacobs struggled to support herself by running boarding houses. On March 7, 1897, Harriet Jacobs died in Washington, D.C.

MAJOR WORK

Harriet Jacobs's single text, *Incidents in the Life of a Slave Girl*, is an autobiographical work in the tradition of the American slave narrative. Using the pseudonym Linda Brent, Jacobs details her life from early childhood through her escape north and her attainment of legal freedom. *Incidents* separates itself thematically from male-authored slave texts by focusing on the distinctive concerns of the female slave. Articulating the unique suffering of slave women, Jacobs writes, "Slavery is terrible for men; but it is far more terrible for women. Superadded to the burden common to all, *they* have wrongs, and sufferings and mortifications peculiarly there [sic] own" (77). Throughout the text, Jacobs focuses specifically on the sexual exploitation of the female slave and explores the emotional complexity of slave motherhood.

Like other slave narratives, Jacobs's text is underwritten by the testimony of prominent white citizens. In the introduction and appendix of *Incidents*, Lydia Maria Child and Amy Post attest to the narrative's accuracy and vouch for the author's character. Despite these testimonials, Jacobs takes ownership of her narrative in the preface to the work, underscoring that "the narrative is no fiction" and articulating her own women-centered abolitionist mission: "I do earnestly desire to arouse the women of the North to a realizing sense of the condition of two millions of women in the South, still in bondage . . ." (1).

Although *Incidents* has been widely studied as a female slave narrative, one of the most critically interesting aspects of the work is its complex amalgamation of literary genres. In addition to its use of the slave narrative, Jacobs's text deploys conventions of autobiography, sentimental and domestic fiction, the seduction novel, and abolitionist literature.

Critics have also noted that Jacobs speaks in multiple, often contradictory, voices throughout *Incidents* and that the text is riddled with elisions and contradictions. This is nowhere more evident than in Jacobs's treatment of her sexual history with Samuel Sawyer. On the one hand, Jacobs repents for her sexual impropriety, begging the audience's "pity" and "pardon," for the affair (55). On the other hand, she exonerates herself of any sexual indiscretions and boldly instructs her white audience that "the slave woman ought not to be judged by the same standards as others" (56). Similarly, Jacobs's narration both valorizes and critiques the idealized domestic and maternal values of the era. While Jacobs depicts herself as a heroic slave mother in *Incidents*, she ultimately flees without her children, refusing to let her captors use her maternal affections to "fetter" her "to the spot" (93). The text's multiple voices and inconsistencies reflect not only the author's complex subjectivity but also reveal Jacobs's conflicted relationship with her culture's ideals of maternity, domesticity, and sexual behavior for women.

CRITICAL RECEPTION

For much of the twentieth century, *Incidents in the Life of a Slave Girl* was ignored by historians and literary critics alike because it was suspected to be a work of sentimental fiction, one most likely created by its named editor, Lydia Maria Child. In the 1980s, however, Jean Fagan Yellin authenticated Jacobs as the author of *Incidents*, established the limited nature of Child's editorial work, and documented the historical veracity of the memoir. After Yellin's publication of a new edition of *Incidents* in 1987, the work has garnered much critical attention and has become a staple of nineteenth-century American literary studies.

In the wake of Yellin's scholarship, critical studies have been preoccupied with the literary innovations that flow from Jacobs's unique position as a nineteenth-century female slave and author. Specifically, critics are interested in Jacobs's adoption and adaptation of various literary genres. Mary Helen Washington, Joanne Braxton, and Frances Foster, for example, analyze *Incidents* as a slave narrative, documenting how Jacobs's text breaks the conventions of similar, male-authored works such as *Narrative of the Life of Frederick Douglass*. Such scholarship has led to a reevaluation of the distinctly gendered definitions of the genre that had formerly been used.

Jacobs's deployment of sentimental strategies to appeal to her white, northern audience has also been widely studied. Many critics have noted that Jacobs does not simply adopt the conventions of the sentimental novel. Hazel Carby, for example, argues that Jacobs's narrative actually critiques the cultural ideals of womanhood upon which much nineteenth-century sentimental fiction is based. Others such as Elizabeth C. Becker, Caroline Levander, and Krista Walter explore how Jacobs specifically challenges the domestic ideology of sentimental novels.

Incidents has been studied in relation to other popular genres as well. Beth McClay Doriani and Johnnie M. Stover analyze Jacobs's work in relation to conventions of autobiography. Franny Nudelman documents how *Incidents* relies on the form and formulas of abolitionist literature. Finally, Jennifer Rae Greeson explores Jacobs's work in relation to the conventions of urban gothic fiction.

In 2004, Jean Fagan Yellin published a new biography, *Harriet Jacobs: A Life*. The study, which gives new insight into Jacobs's relationships with Norcom and Sawyer and details her work during the Civil War and Reconstruction, will likely reenergize scholarship surrounding *Incidents in the Life of a Slave Girl*.

BIBLIOGRAPHY

Work by Harriet Ann Jacobs

Incidents in the Life of a Slave Girl, Written By Herself. 1861. Reprint, edited by Jean Fagan Yellin. Cambridge: Harvard University Press, 1987.

Studies of Harriet Jacobs's Work

Braxton, Joanne M. *Black Women Writing Autobiography: A Tradition within a Tradition.* Philadelphia: Temple University Press, 1989.

Carby, Hazel. *Reconstructing Womanhood: The Emergence of the Afro-American Woman Novelist.* Oxford: Oxford University Press, 1987.

Foster, Frances Smith. *Written by Herself: Literary Production by African-American Women 1746–1892.* Bloomington: Indiana University Press, 1993.

Fox-Genovese, Elizabeth. "My Statue, Myself: Autobiographical Writings of Afro-American Women." In *The Private Self: Theory and Practice of Women's Autobiographical Writings,* edited by Shari Benstock. Chapel Hill: The University of North Carolina Press, 1988.

Garfield, Deborah M., and Rafia Zafar, eds. *Harriet Jacobs and Incidents in the Life of a Slave Girl: New Critical Essays.* New York: Cambridge University Press, 1996.

Greeson, Jennifer Rae. "The 'Mysteries and Miseries' of North Carolina: New York City, Urban Gothic Fiction, and *Incidents in the Life of a Slave Girl.*" *American Literature* 73.2 (2001): 277–309.

Levander, Caroline. "'Following the Conditions of the Mother': Subversions of Domesticity in Harriet Jacobs's *Incidents in the Life of a Slave Girl.*" In *Southern Mothers,* edited by Nagueyalti Warren and Sally Wolff, 28–38. Baton Rouge: Louisiana State University Press, 1999.

Nudelman, Franny. "Harriet Jacobs and the Sentimental Politics of Female Suffering." *ELH* 59 (1992): 939–64.

Smith, Valerie. *Self-Discovery and Authority in Afro-American Narrative.* Cambridge: Harvard University Press, 1987.

Stover, Johnnie M. "Nineteenth-Century African American Women's Autobiography as Social Discourse: The Example of Harriet Ann Jacobs." *College English* 66.2 (2003): 133–54.

Walter, Krista. "Surviving the Garret: Harriet Jacobs and the Critique of Sentiment." *ATQ* 8.3 (1994): 189–210.

Washington, Mary Helen. *Invented Lives: Narratives of Black Women, 1860–1960.* Garden City, NY: Doubleday, 1987.

Yellin, Jean Fagan. *Harriet Jacobs: A Life.* New York: Basic Civitas Books, 2004.

Mary McCartin Wearn

AMELIA E. JOHNSON (1858–1922)

BIOGRAPHICAL NARRATIVE

Novelist, short-fiction writer, poet, and editor Amelia Etta Hall Johnson was born in Toronto, Canada, in 1858. After her education in Montreal schools, Johnson moved to Boston in 1874. There she met and married Rev. Harvey Johnson, the author, activist, and famed minister of the Union Baptist Church. They had three children, a daughter and two sons. Johnson died in the spring of 1922.

MAJOR WORKS

Writing under the name of "Mrs. A. E. Johnson," Johnson is best known for her contributions to children's literature. In fact, Johnson began her literary career regularly contributing poems and short stories for children in *National Baptist*, *American Baptist*, and *Sower and Reaper* magazines, among other periodicals. In 1887 she founded an eight-page monthly magazine, especially for African American females, titled *Joy*, while her *Ivy*, published in 1888, instructed youth about African American history. Her regular contributions to the Baltimore *Sower and Reaper*, called "Children's Corner," is yet another instance of Johnson's sustained interest in children's literature.

In the early stages of her career, Johnson envisioned novels as a means to morally equip and uplift the American and African American community. Johnson published three novels in her lifetime. They include *Clarence and Corinne, or God's Way* (1890), *The Hazeley Family* (1894), and *Martina Meriden, or What Is My Motive?* (1901). *Clarence and Corinne* is a poignant depiction of the agonies and humillations suffered by Corinne and Clarence after their mother's death and their father's abandonment. Though the novel begins on a pessimistic note, it ends with Clarence and Corinne grown and happily married to two childhood friends. With the publication of this book by the American Baptist Publication Society of Philadelphia, white-administered and one of the largest publishing houses of the time, Johnson became the first African American Sunday school fiction writer. And, more significantly, this novel is the second published African American novel.

In *The Hazeley Family*, Johnson through Flora Hazeley, the protagonist, emphasizes, as M. Giulia Fabi observes, "the Christian value and social usefulness of women's 'home-work.'" While *Martina Meriden, or What Is my Motive* is an expansion of her previous themes with a stress on the need for the Christian outlook on life, both novels collectively exemplify Sunday school literature, which R. Frank Taylor in his 1888 essay "Sunday School Literature" defines as "good, wholesome food for thought" and an alternative to "cheap, trashy reading matter."

Johnson's novels foreground the virtues of Christian ways of life, divulge underlying tension between the domestic sphere and Christian orthodoxy, and further portray the issues of African American women. Unlike her contemporaries, Johnson never overtly discusses racial issues, though she always focuses on social problems such as alcoholism and urban poverty. To these ends, Johnson deploys racially neutral characters and thus maintains a healthy indifference to the racial literature.

CRITICAL RECEPTION

Though Johnson was a prominent writer of the late nineteenth century, there is a dearth of critical materials on her works. In a recent attempt to reclaim and record the nineteenth-century African American literary voices, the highly important Schomburg Library, in collaboration with Oxford University Press under the general editorship of Henry Louis Gates Jr., revived *Clarence and Corinne* and *The Hazeley Family*. In her introduction to *Clarence and Corinne,* published in this series, Hortense J. Spillers contends that as a "didactic narrative of the family," *Clarence and Corinne* reflects the social reform ideology of the late-nineteenth-century women's movement. Barbara Christian's introduction to *The Hazeley Family* is also a scholarly attempt to recover and preserve Johnson's writings for posterity. Christian discusses the nonracial characters, domestic idealism, and the feminist themes of the novel.

Claudia Tate's provocative *Domestic Allegories of Political Desire: The Black Heroine's Text at the Turn of the Century,* through contextualizing Johnson's works, examines the relations between political desire and domestic ideology in post-Reconstruction novels. In short, gaining recognition for her literary strategies and thematic concerns Johnson's works offer fascinating insights into the turn-of-the-twentieth-century American and African American society and therefore deserve special attention.

BIBLIOGRAPHY

Works by Amelia E. Johnson

Clarence and Corinne, or God's Way. 1890. Reprint, New York: Oxford University Press, 1988.
The Hazeley Family. 1894. Reprint, New York: Oxford University Press, 1988.
Martina Meriden, or What Is My Motive? Philadelphia: American Baptist Publication Society, 1901.

Studies of Amelia E. Johnson's Works

Christian, Barbara. "Introduction." In *The Hazeley Family* by Amelia E. Johnson. Oxford: Oxford University Press, 1988.
Fabi, M. Giulia. "Johnson, Amelia E." In *The Oxford Companion to African American Literature,* edited by William L. Andrews, Frances Smith Foster, and Trudier Harris, 401. New York: Oxford University Press, 1997.
———. "Taming the Amazon? The Price of Survival in Turn-of-the-Century African American Women's Fiction." In *The Insular Dream: Obsession and Resistance,* edited by Kristiaan Versluys, 228–41. Amsterdam: VU University Press, 1995.
Pegues A. W. *Our Baptist Ministers and Schools.* Springfield, MA: Wiley, 1892.
Shockley, Ann Allen. *Afro-American Women Writers, 1746–1933: An Anthology and Critical Guide.* Boston: G. K. Hall, 1988.
Spillers, Hortense J. "Introduction." In *Clarence and Corinne, or God's Way* by Amelia E. Johnson. Oxford: Oxford University Press, 1988.

———. "Moving on Down the Line." *American Quarterly* 40.1 (1988): 84.

Tate, Claudia. *Domestic Allegories of Political Desire: The Black Heroine's Text at the Turn of the Century.* New York: Oxford University Press, 1992.

Sathyaraj Venkatesan

GEORGIA DOUGLAS JOHNSON (1877–1966)

BIOGRAPHICAL NARRATIVE

Poet Georgia Blanche Camp was born on September 10, 1877, in Atlanta, Georgia, the daughter of Laura (Douglas) and George Camp, both of mixed racial heritages. When she was a young child, her parents separated, and Johnson lived with her mother, attending public schools in Atlanta and finishing Atlanta University's Normal School in 1893. She then served as a teacher in Marietta, Georgia, until 1902 when she left to attend the Oberlin Conservatory of Music. Returning to Atlanta in 1903, she worked briefly as an assistant principal, before resigning to marry Henry Lincoln Johnson, a prominent Atlanta attorney, in September 1903. Although her relationship with her mother had often been difficult, when she married, Johnson chose to use her mother's surname, Douglas, as her middle name. Two sons, Henry Lincoln, Jr. (ca. 1906–1990) and Peter Douglas (1907–1957), were born to the Johnsons before 1910, when the family relocated to Washington, D.C. There Henry Lincoln, Sr., established a law firm and in 1912 was appointed Recorder of Deeds by President Taft. With this appointment, the Johnsons's place in Washington's elite African American society was established.

In spite of her husband's conviction that "a woman should take care of her home and her children and be content with that," Johnson was an extremely prolific writer who published two volumes of poetry, both dedicated to her husband, in spite of his criticism of her efforts: *The Heart of a Woman* (1918) and *Bronze* (1922). In addition, around 1920, Johnson began holding informal gatherings of writers in her home. Her "Saturday Nighters Club" meetings, held regularly until the 1930s, became an important venue for prominent writers to discuss literature and share their work. Her salon participants represented both the younger and older generations of writers, including Gwendolyn Bennett, Langston Hughes, Zora Neale Hurston, and Jean Toomer as well as William Stanley Braithwaite, W.E.B. DuBois, Jessie Fauset, and Alice Nelson-Dunbar.

After Henry Lincoln, Sr.'s death in 1925, Johnson sought employment, mostly in government service, to support herself and finance her sons' education: Henry Jr., to Bowdoin College and Howard University Law School and Peter to Dartmouth College and Howard University Medical School. In spite of the demands of working, Johnson continued to write, enjoying the greater freedom widowhood afforded her. In 1926, her one-act play, *Blue Blood*, won honorable mention in the *Opportunity* drama contest. The next year, her play, *Plumes*, won the first prize in the same competition. That moment represented a high point in Johnson's career. Unable to find a publisher for her third volume of poetry, *An Autumn Love Cycle*, Johnson published it at her own expense in 1928 (as she had the previous two volumes). The Stock Market Crash and Great Depression further limited Johnson's access to publishing opportunities.

In 1935 the Federal Theater Project (FTP) gave Johnson a venue to submit plays of social protest. From 1935 to 1939, Johnson submitted at least five plays to the FTP, none of which were produced. Two of the plays, *Frederick Douglass* and *William and Ellen*

Craft, were historical sketches depicting slaves seeking freedom. Three others focused on the issue of lynching: *Blue-Eyed Black Boy*, *Safe*, and *A Sunday Morning in the South*. Johnson submitted at least two other plays to the NAACP in support of their effort to pass legislation banning lynching. These were also rejected but demonstrate a very important concern in Johnson's writings.

In 1941, Johnson joined a group of black writers called the Writers' Club of Washington, D.C., and attended meetings regularly until the group disbanded in 1960. According to Writers' Club records, Johnson continued to publish poems and short stories in a variety of journals and literary magazines, as well as columns for Negro newspapers. Much of her writings, published under pseudonyms in publications that no longer exist, may forever be lost. Scholar Claudia Tate explains, "This practice was symptomatic of her intense anxiety of authorship, for she was fully convinced . . . that her readers would be more likely to treat her work seriously if she disassociated her black and female self from them" (xxxiii). Her last major work, *Share My World*, a volume of poetry self-published in 1962, included numerous poems written for and shared with friends.

Although Johnson never secured funding for her writing, she continued to write, catalogue her work, and seek literary fellowships well into the 1960s. Using her writing to "sustain her subjectivity and optimistic outlook," Johnson persisted in her efforts even without publishing success (Tate xxxiv). So essential to her was her identity as a writer that, on her deathbed, her friend May Miller soothed her by repeatedly calling her "Poet Georgia Douglas Johnson."

MAJOR WORKS

Georgia Douglas Johnson's varied writings focus primarily on intensely female issues of the heart, African American motherhood, sexual and racial violence, and the experience of mixed-race people. Known primarily for writing traditional poetry of the genteel school, Johnson was regarded as a minor poet of the New Negro era, who was consistently overshadowed by the "masculine literature of the 'New Negro'" (Redding, quoted in Fletcher 153). The reception to her earlier work reflects the "unresolved duality of women of color [who] were expected to identify themselves as either black or female, but never both, [and who sought] an audience in a society that respected neither" (Moses 203).

Her first volume of poetry, *The Heart of a Woman*, described by William Stanley Braithwaite as "intensely female . . . which means more than anything else . . . deeply human," focused primarily on the emotions of women. Written from a race-neutral perspective, *Heart* has been dismissed as sentimental and genteel and criticized for its lack of concern with racial uplift. Claudia Tate argues, however, that Johnson's style "was part of her strategy of 'compensatory conservatism,' which veiled her criticism of racial and gender oppressions behind the demeanor of 'the lady poet'" (xviii). Although unexplored until recently, even early critics like Braithwaite noted a world of "mystery and passion . . . or romantic visions and practical ambitions" just beneath the surface in *Heart* (quoted in Hull 157). In Johnson's era, however, exploring the full implication of such passion would have suggested licentiousness unacceptable in a lady poet.

In a 1941 letter to Arna Bontemps, Johnson reflects, "My first book . . . was not at all race conscious. Then someone said she has no feeling for her race. So I wrote *Bronze*.

It is entirely race conscious." While *Heart* focuses on the heart of the universal woman, *Bronze* reflects "the heart of a colored woman aware of her social problems" and demonstrates the influence Johnson's New Negro salon members had on her writing (Fletcher 156). In *Bronze*, Johnson considers pressing race issues including violence, the experience of mixed race people, and migration north. Of particular interest in *Bronze* is the "Motherhood" section, which considers the special concerns of African American mothers, specifically "the ambivalence of black women . . . bringing children into a society that despised them even before they were born" (Moses 204).

Issues facing African American mothers predominate Johnson's first two plays as well. *Blue Blood* depicts two mothers who, just before the marriage of their son and daughter, discover that both children have been fathered by the same white man. Although this knowledge is uncovered as each mother boasts of her child's superiority to the other because of his or her blue (really white) blood, the play quickly becomes a commentary on the foolishness of African Americans fixating on skin color, which only reflects their own "violation and powerlessness," and on the state of African American women who are victimized sexually but forced to keep silent in order to protect their husbands and sons from being killed trying to protect their honor (Brown-Guillory 13). In *Plumes*, Johnson's most celebrated play, an African American mother with a gravely ill daughter is faced with the choice of spending her last dollar to pay a doctor to perform a surgery that may not cure the daughter or reserving the money to pay for an elaborate funeral (complete with plumed horses) that would demonstrate her love for her child. Here the expression of an African American mother's love is reduced to dollars and cents. Some critics have suggested that the mother allowing her daughter to die without the surgery demonstrates her choosing death rather than allowing her child to suffer in a racist society. Claudia Tate argues, however, that the play "represents the inevitability of death and Johnson's steadfast conviction that only love can preserve human dignity. Thus the mother's final display of love for her daughter is more important than trying to postpone the certainty of death" (lx).

Johnson continued to explore motherhood, violence, and miscegenation in her lynching plays. *Blue-Eyed Black Boy*, for example, depicts a young African American man about to be lynched for innocently brushing against a white woman. The man is saved from death when his mother sends a message and a small ring to the governor advising him that "they goin' to lynch her son born 21 years ago." The governor, remembering his liaison with the mother, sends the militia to save his unrecognized son. *Safe* depicts a mother so traumatized by the lynching of a young African American man on the day she delivers "a fine boy" that she decides to smother her baby to keep him "safe—safe from the lynchers." Both plays were submitted to the Federal Theater Project and rejected, the first called an "incomplete drama" and the second "an utter exaggeration [based on] an absurdity—that they lynch Negro boys 'Down South' for defending themselves" (quoted in Fletcher 160, 161). Interestingly, the two lynching plays Johnson submitted to the NAACP in support of their antilynching legislation, *And Yet They Paused* and *A Bill to Be Passed*, were returned to her because they "all ended in defeat and gave one the feeling that the situation was hopeless" (White, quoted in Stephens 519). These plays, discovered in NAACP papers by Judith Stephens in 1999, have begun a new discussion of Johnson's dramatic works and her significant contributions to this "uniquely American dramatic genre" (519).

CRITICAL RECEPTION

Although one of the most anthologized women poets of the New Negro era, Georgia Douglas Johnson was criticized in her time for being insufficiently concerned with race and was labeled a minor figure when the New Negro era was retheorized by African American scholars in the 1960s and 1970s. Overshadowed then by young writers whose black nationalist stance made them more easily reclaimed during the 1960s and 1970s, Johnson has until recently been consigned to the "old negro" generation that preceded the new (Tate xxi, xxii). In more recent years, however, Johnson has herself been recovered and recognized as "one of the first black feminist poets and the most prolific black women playwrights of the Harlem Renaissance" (Brown-Guillory 12). Her work formed a bridge between the genteel age and the age of the New Negro, presented the emotions and experience of women as valid subjects of literary creation, and depicted dramatically how the evils of American society disempowered, victimized, and paralyzed black women in their roles as mothers and lovers.

BIBLIOGRAPHY

Works by Georgia Douglas Johnson

An Autumn Love Cycle. Introduction by Alain Locke. New York: Vinal, 1928.
Blue Blood. In *The Plays of Georgia Douglas Johnson: From the New Negro Renaissance to the Civil Rights Movement*. Ed. Judith L. Stephens. Urbana: University of Illinois Press, 2006.
Blue-Eyed Black Boy. In *Wines in the Wilderness*, edited by Elizabeth Brown-Guillory. New York: Praeger, 1990.
Bronze: A Book of Verse. Introduction by W.E.B. DuBois. Boston: Brimmer, 1922.
Frederick Douglass. In *The Plays of Georgia Douglass Johnson: From the New Negro Renaissance to the Civil Rights Movement*. Ed. Judith L. Stephens. Urbana: University of Illinois Press, 2006.
The Heart of a Woman and Other Poems. Introduction by William Stanley Braithwaite. Boston: Cornhill, 1918.
Plumes. In *Plays of Negro Life: A Sourcebook of Native America Drama*. Ed. Alain Locke and Montgomery Gregory. New York: Harper, 1927.
Safe. In *Wines in the Wilderness*, edited by Elizabeth Brown-Guillory. New York: Praeger, 1990.
The Selected Works of Georgia Douglas Johnson. Introduction by Claudia Tate. New York: Hall, 1997.
Share My World: A Book of Poems. Washington, DC: Author, 1962.
A Sunday Morning in the South. In *Black Theatre, USA: Plays by African Americans: The Recent Period, 1935–Today*. Ed. Ted Shine and James V. Hatch. New York: The Free Press, 1974.
William and Ellen Craft. In *The Plays of Georgia Douglas Johnson: From the New Negro Renaissance to the Civil Rights Movement*. Ed. Judith L. Stephens. Urbana: University of Illinois Press, 2006.

Studies of Georgia Douglas Johnson's Works

Bower, Martha Gilman. *"Color Struck" under the Gaze: Ethnicity and the Pathology of Being in the Plays of Johnson, Hurston, Childress, Hansbury, and Kennedy*. Westport, CT: Praeger, 2003.
Brown-Guillory, Elizabeth. *"Wines in the Wilderness": Plays by African American Women from the Harlem Renaissance to the Present*. Westport, CT: Greenwood Press, 1990.

Fletcher, Winona. "From Genteel Poet to Revolutionary Playwright: Georgia Douglas Johnson." *Theatre Annual* 30 (1985): 41–64.

———. "Georgia Douglas Johnson." In *Afro-American Writers from the Harlem Renaissance to 1940. Dictionary of Literary Biography 51*, edited by Trudier Harris and Thadious Davis, 153–64. Detroit: Gale, 1987.

Hull, Gloria T. *Color, Sex and Poetry: Three Women of the Harlem Renaissance.* Bloomington: Indiana University Press, 1987.

Moses, Lorraine Alena, and Ruth Elizabeth Randolph, eds. "Georgia Douglas (Camp) Johnson." In *Harlem Renaissance and Beyond*, 201–8. Boston: Hall, 1990.

Shockley, Ann Allen. *Afro-American Women Writers, 1746–1933: An Anthology and Critical Guide.* Boston: Hall, 1988.

Stephens, Judith. "'And Yet They Paused' and 'A Bill to be Passed': Newly Recovered Lynching Dramas by Georgia Douglas Johnson." *African American Review* 33.3 (Fall 1999): 519–22.

Tate, Claudia. "Introduction." In *The Selected Works of Georgia Douglas Johnson*, edited by Henry Louis Gates. New York: Hall, 1997.

Wall, Cheryl. *Women of the Harlem Renaissance.* Bloomington: Indiana University Press, 1995.

Maria J. Rice

HELEN JOHNSON (1906–1995)

BIOGRAPHICAL NARRATIVE

Helen (Helene) Johnson's career as a poet was brief but sparkling. She moved to Harlem during the late 1920s and befriended some of the luminaries of the Harlem Renaissance such as Zora Neale Hurston and Wallace Thurman. She published only thirty-four poems in nine years, but some of her poems are among the best known of the Harlem Renaissance.

Born in 1906 in Boston, Johnson was raised in a woman-dominated household that her daughter would later refer to as a "family collective," which also included eight aunts and two cousins. Despite financial restrictions, the family always provided the cousins with the best educational and cultural opportunities available.

Johnson attended Boston University and joined a local literary club. In 1925, she began publishing her work and entering it in contests such as the *Opportunity* competition. She won honorable mention in poetry in 1926, and she and her cousin Dorothy West traveled to New York to participate in the awards dinner. In 1927, the cousins moved to Manhattan and took classes at Columbia University, but Johnson's real education came in her exposure to the vibrant cultural life of Harlem.

Johnson and West were well liked because of their youth and unaffected innocence. Zora Neale Hurston often subcontracted work to them and let them stay in her apartment while she was traveling. Johnson worked on both the new magazines *Fire!* and *Harlem*, both which lasted only one issue.

In 1933, Johnson married and dropped out of the literary world. Although she did occasionally contribute to *Opportunity, Saturday Evening Quill*, and *Challenge*, she did not otherwise publish her work after 1935. Her daughter was born in 1940, and Johnson devoted herself to raising her child. According to her daughter, she wrote creatively every single day of her life, and, thanks to a new collection of her work, scholars now may read some of her unpublished poems, many of which she wrote while retired and living in Greenwich Village in New York City, where she died in 1995.

MAJOR WORKS

Johnson's career peaked during the Harlem Renaissance, a literary and artistic movement that celebrated African American life and culture. The primary themes of Harlem Renaissance art were racial pride, primitivism, social protest against racism, optimism about the future, influence of jazz and blues, and disillusionment with urban experience.

Johnson's poems typify many of these themes, and she is best known for her poems celebrating racial pride. Her most famous poems, "Sonnet to a Negro in Harlem," "Bottled," and "Poem" each center on a single African American man portrayed as a figure of magnificence, beauty, and admiration. These poems also demonstrate Johnson's ability to move comfortably between traditional poetic forms, such as the sonnet, and informal poetic diction. "Sonnet" uses a traditional poetic form to convey Johnson's feelings toward her unconventional subject, feelings of admiration, awe, and attraction. On the other hand, "Poem" is a free-verse poem, and the colloquial diction and playful tone effectively suggest the speaker's affection for the subject of the poem.

"Bottled" was Johnson's most high-profile poem, appearing in *Vanity Fair* in May 1927. As in "Sonnet" and "Poem," the speaker is observing a male figure, a street performer, comparing the street performer to a bottle of sand from the Sahara. Neither is in its natural environment, and, as a result, each has become an object of curiosity whose beauty cannot be fully appreciated. The colloquial speech patterns of the speaker capture her evolving feelings while watching the performance, from amazement to pride to awareness. This poem focuses on Johnson's belief that concepts of beauty and value are not intrinsic but socially constructed and context dependent.

Johnson's early poems, which earned her attention from critics such as James Weldon Johnson and Robert Frost, relied on natural imagery, which, later in her poetic career, took on more sexual overtones. Her first published poem, "Trees at Night," is typical of poems in this style, and the references to "ink," "stenciled," and "printed" suggest the ways that nature is God's work of art; in the same way the poem is the creation of the poet. A poem Frost admired, "The Road," won an *Opportunity* award (honorable mention) and is a straightforward comparison of the black race to a road, its "trodden beauty" similar to African Americans' "trodden pride."

"Summer Matures" and "What Do I Care for Morning?" on the other hand, use natural imagery to evoke more sexual connotations. "Summer Matures," with its allusions to love poet Sappho, describes a "swooning night" of sensual possibility. "What Do I Care for Morning?" also refers to night as a time of sexual possibility, "yielding and tender," in opposition to the cool, clear light of morning.

One prevailing theme in Harlem Renaissance writing involved the perceived conflict between the primitivistic passion of African Americans and the spiritually deadening effects of contemporary Christianity. Johnson addressed this theme as well. "Regalia" portrays a working-class man whose colorful lodge uniform temporarily confers upon him a social status and an inner joy and pride that his position as janitor does not. Unfortunately, his minister criticizes his pleasure in his "regalia" as "vanity." When the minister dies, the man puts on his regalia only to have the minister's words come back to haunt him, taking away his pleasure in the uniform. Similarly, "Magula" (Mitchell notes that this is Johnson's original spelling, and subsequent reprintings of the poem have misspelled the title) describes a young woman being tempted by a "man with a white collar," whose creeds "will not let you dance." The poem is an exhortation to the reader to appreciate the value of Magula's world, "a pulsing riotous gasp of color," and resist any attempts to repress that sensuality.

Johnson's later poems reflect more socially conscious themes. "Rootbound," an unpublished poem collected and published for the first time after Johnson's death, is about a man who is tired of the restrictions of America, so he plans his escape to another country. At the last moment, he reconsiders his choice, affirming his commitment to the America his ancestors lived in and fought for. These later poems share with the earlier poems a validation on the inner worth and dignity of all people, African American and white, rich and poor, young and old. Johnson's most delightful unpublished poem reflects giddily on an older woman's crush on a young man. The poem effectively uses rhyme to establish the speaker's excitement, attraction, and tongue-in-cheek self-deprecation of herself for her futile, unrequited feelings. Comparing this poem to those she wrote fifty years earlier reveals that the unreserved pleasure and playfulness of Helen Johnson's poetry remained unchanged throughout her writing career.

CRITICAL RECEPTION

Although Helen Johnson's work won *Opportunity* awards in poetry four times, and several of her poems were included in such well-respected anthologies as *Carolling Dusk*, edited by Countee Cullen, and *The New Negro*, edited by Alain Locke, it has not received much critical attention. In *The Book of American Negro Poetry*, James Weldon Johnson writes that Johnson "possesses true lyric talent.... She has taken the very qualities and circumstances that have long called for apology or defense and extolled them in an unaffected manner."

Johnson's work is anthologized in few of the major collections of black poetry, though Blyden Jackson and Louis Rubin (*Black Poetry in America*) and Eugene Redmond (*Drumvoices*) call attention to her talent. Even with the renewal of interest in African American women writers in the 1980s and 1990s, few scholars showed interest in Johnson's work, one notable exception being Verner D. Mitchell, whose 2000 collection *This Waiting for Love* compiles all Johnson's poetry, published and unpublished, as well as additional biographical information, letters, and photographs to provide the most complete picture yet of Johnson's life and work.

Critics such as Nina Miller, who has written on modernist women's poetry, are rediscovering Johnson's unconventional poems and situating them in their context in the Harlem Renaissance. Miller goes a step further to position Johnson's poems as examples of an avant-garde feminine aesthetic that asserted the prominence of female subjectivity in the male-dominated movement.

BIBLIOGRAPHY

Works by Helen Johnson

"Bottled." *Vanity Fair* (May 1927).
"Fiat Lux." *Messenger* (July 1926).
"Fulfillment." *Opportunity* (June 1926).
"Futility." *Opportunity* (August 1926).
"Goin' North," "Rootbound," "Foraging," "He's about 22. I'm 63," "A Moment of Dignity," "Time after Time," "War," "War——Part II," "The Street to the Establishment," "For Jason," "A Boy Like Me," "The Whimsy of It All," and "The Quest." In *This Waiting for Love*, edited by Verner D. Mitchell. Amherst: University of Massachusetts Press, 2000.
"I Am Not the Proud," "Invocation," "Regalia," "Remember Not," "Rustic Fantasy," "Why Do They Prate?" and "Worship." *Saturday Evening Quill* (April 1929).
"Let Me Sing My Song." *Challenge* (May 1935).
"The Little Love." *Messenger* (July 1926).
"Love in Midsummer." *Messenger* (October 1926).
"Magula." *Palms* (October 1926).
"Metamorphism." *Opportunity* (March 1926).
"A Missionary Brings a Young Native to America" and "Cui Bono?" *Harlem* (November 1928).
"Monotone." *Opportunity* (September 1932).
"Mother." *Opportunity* (September 1926).

"My Race." *Opportunity* (July 1925).
"Night." *Opportunity* (January 1926).
"Plea of a Plebian." *Opportunity* (May 1934).
"Poem," "What Do I Care for Morning?" and "Sonnet to a Negro in Harlem." *Carolling Dusk* (1927).
"The Road." In *The New Negro*, edited by Alain Locke. New York: Simon and Shuster, 1927.
"Sonnet [Be Not Averse to Beauty]." *Opportunity* (December 1931).
"Sonnet [Wisdom May Caution]." *Opportunity* (March 1932).
"A Southern Road." *Fire!!* (November 1926).
"Summer Matures." *Opportunity* (July 1927).
"Trees at Night." *Opportunity* (May 1925).
"Vers de Societe." *Opportunity* (July 1930).
"Widow with a Moral Obligation." *Challenge* (March 1934).

Studies of Helen Johnson's Works

Bryan, T. J. "Women Poets of the Harlem Renaissance." In *Gender, Culture and the Arts*, edited by Ronald Dotterer and Susan Bowers. Selinsgrive, PA: Susquehanna University Press, 1993.
Ferguson, SallyAnn H. "Dorothy West and Helene Johnson in Infants of the Spring." *Langston Hughes Review* 2.2 (1983): 22–24.
Griffin, Barbara L. J. "Helene Johnson (1906–1995)." In *African American Authors, 1745–1945: A Bio-Bibliographical Critical Sourcebook*, edited by Emmanuel S. Nelson, 290–96. Westport, CT: Greenwood Press, 2000.
Honey, Maureen, "Introduction." In *Shadowed Dreams: Women's Poetry of the Harlem Renaissance*, edited by Maureen Honey. New Brunswick: Rutgers University Press, 1989.
Miller, Nina. *Making Love Modern: The Intimate Public Worlds of New York's Literary Women*. New York: Oxford University Press, 1998.
Mitchell, Verner D., ed. *This Waiting for Love: Helene Johnson, Poet of the Harlem Renaissance*. Amherst: University of Massachusetts Press, 2000.
Patterson, Raymond. "Helene Johnson." In *Dictionary of Literary Biography*, vol. 51, edited by Thadious Davis and Trudier Harris. Detroit: Gale, 1987.

Wendy Wagner

GAYL JONES (1949–)

BIOGRAPHICAL NARRATIVE

Gayl Jones, a writer of drama novels and essays, was born in Lexington, Kentucky, on November 23, 1949, to Franklin and Lucille Jones, the former a cook and the latter a housewife and aspiring writer. She attended Connecticut College, receiving a B.A. in English in 1971. Jones then enrolled at Brown University, where she earned an M.A. (1973) and a D.A. (1975) in creative writing.

Upon graduation from Brown, Jones accepted a full-time tenure-track position at the University of Michigan, Ann Arbor. She taught there from 1975 until 1983, having achieved tenure. Jones met and married Robert Higgins, who adopted her surname, while teaching at Michigan. In 1983, she resigned from her professorship at Michigan.

From 1983 to 1998, turmoil and tragedy characterized Jones's life. After her resignation from Michigan, Jones and Higgins (Jones) left the United States and lived in Europe, mainly France, until their return in 1988 to care for her mother in Kentucky, who was ill with cancer and subsequently died in 1997.

In 1998, an intermittent conflict between Higgins and local authorities, over alleged racial injustices related to the hospital care of Jones's mother, escalated into a violent confrontation between the Joneses and law enforcement. The confrontation culminated in Higgins's suicide and Jones's hospitalization for psychiatric examination. Jones's whereabouts are unknown currently; it is assumed that she continues to reside in Kentucky.

MAJOR WORKS

Jones writes, in the essay titled "About My Work," that she is "interested in the psychology of characters—and the way(s) in which they order their stories– their myths, dreams, nightmares, secret worlds, ambiguities, contradictions, ambivalences, memories, imaginations, their 'puzzles'" (233). Indeed, her early work proffers both stark and brutal accounts of African American women whose psyches, lives, and choices reflect and contradict the desolation of accumulated sexual and racial exploitation and physical abuse. Reflecting her interest in the African presence in the Americas, Jones often, directly and indirectly, reveals the legacy of institutional slavery and other forms of subjugation on the relationships of the people of the African diaspora. Her work is concerned with the harsh realities of African American life, especially for women, revealing the excoriated terrain of intimate relationships.

Nevertheless, the female protagonists of her novels are not paralyzed victims of a system that renders them doubly oppressed because of their gender and race. Rather, Jones's novels "dismantl[e] the social structures and discourses that necessitate the positioning of the black female subject" (Robinson 135). The protagonists of her novels have been denied access to a fixed "identity," a position that they might occupy safely and unproblematically, because of the legacy of slavery and systematic violence and oppression. Subsequently, these women speak and act against the discourses that marginalize them by utilizing the marginal spaces of psychosexual violence and oppression to forge an identity that is neither *self* (a representation of the oppressor), nor *other* (a naturalized composite of the oppressed). Jones's heroines exist outside the normative categories of *self* and *other*—both as tragic and redemptive figures—they refuse, often to their own psychic and physical detriment, to embrace the hegemonic and homogeneous representations of themselves by which the dominant society attempts to circumscribe them.

Corregidora, Jones's first novel, rendered dually by first-person narration and internal dialogue, considers the psychosexual effects of slavery and physical and sexual abuse on the life and relationships of a contemporary black woman. Ursa Corregidora is a descendent of Corregidora, "the Portuguese slave breeder and whore monger," who fathered both her grandmother and mother (9). She sings the blues in a Kentucky nightclub, where she attracts the unsolicited attention of men. Ursa is married to Mutt, a man driven to violence as a result of his jealousy over the attention she garners at the nightclub.

In a jealous rage, Mutt throws Ursa down a set of stairs; consequently, Ursa has a hysterectomy. This is significant not only as a sign of the ravages of physical abuse in a sexual relationship, but also because of the dictate Ursa received from her mother and grandmother to "make generations" in order to expurgate the terrible wound inflicted upon their family by institutionalized rape. After leaving the hospital, Ursa separates from Mutt. She then begins to date and eventually marry Tadpole McCormick, the owner of the nightclub where she sings. Ursa divorces Mutt and then marries Tadpole. This relationship, too, is consigned to failure because of Tadpole's infidelity.

Eva's Man, Jones's second novel, retains her concern for the psychosexual effects of brutality. Eva Medina Canada is the emotionally desolate protagonist of this novel. She has been incarcerated for the murder and mutilation of a male acquaintance. While in prison, Eva recounts her personal history, which is replete with episodes that chronicle the exploitative world that has shaped her psychologically. She reveals childhood sexual violations, early consciousness of her mother's adultery and promiscuity, confrontations with the whores of the slums in which she matured to adulthood, and her eventual and hesitant emulation of the sexual profligacy she witnessed as a young girl. In this fragmented narrative, Eva neither provides a tangible motive for the crime of which she has been accused, nor does she express remorse or a desire for rehabilitation. She has become the depravity that has surrounded and was perpetrated against her by those close to her in proximity and relation. Yet, the first-person narrative humanizes Eva; simultaneously, she becomes more than and exists outside of her crime.

Liberating Voices: Oral Tradition in African American Literature, Jones's collection of critical essays, is a "transhistorical, transcultural critical survey of literature," which seeks to delineate "the movement from the restrictive forms . . . to the liberation of voice and freer personalities in more intricate texts" in African American literature (Bell 248). The text contains fifteen chapters, which examine the works of authors from Langston Hughes to Toni Morrison.

The Healing, Jones's first post-European novel, focuses on Harlan Jane Eagleton, a traveling faith healer and wife of an anthropologist, among other vocations. Jones's novel is a meditation on contemporary African American culture and life using the vernacular voice of its narrator, Harlan. In the novel, Harlan transgresses and comments on the hierarchical relationship between black vernacular speech and literary language, and non-English languages and American English dialect.

Mosquito, Jones's most recent novel, "offers a metadiscourse on stereotyping, where racial clichés are rehearsed, repeated, and ridiculed without apology." The novel "challenges the traditional hierarchical assumptions" of "narration by reimagining the spatial and temporal dimensions of the novel" (Bramen 127, 129). Mosquito, the novel's narrator and protagonist, acquired her name from a childhood allergic reaction to an insect bite. She discovers Maria Barriga, a Mexican, hiding in the back of her truck. Mosquito transports Maria to safety by taking her to the local leader of the Sanctuary Movement, Father Ray, with whom she has an affair. Unexpectedly, Mosquito is swept into the movement, which is referred to as the New Underground Railroad. The events of the aforementioned "plot" operate in tandem with image-laden passages of Mosquito's thoughts and experiences, which include her friendship with Delgadina, a Chicana intellectual bartender, and letters from Monkey Bread, an acquaintance from Kentucky, who is the personal assistant to a movie star.

CRITICAL RECEPTION

In spite of the defiant female characters at the center of her works, cultural and feminist critics, until recently, have tended to avoid Jones's work because of the complicated and unflattering portrayal of women, in general, and African American women, in particular. Indeed, in the *New York Times Book Review*, June Jordan notes, regarding *Eva's Man*, that "[t]here is the very real upsetting accomplishment of Gayl Jones in this, her second novel: sinister misinformation about women—about women, in general, about black women, in particular." Furthermore, Jordan describes *Eva's Man* as "the blues that lost control. This is the rhythmic lamentation of one woman, Eva Medina, who is nobody I have ever known."

Nonetheless, in spite of this reception, Jones's work has been celebrated by literary luminaries such as James Baldwin, Maya Angelou, John Updike, and Toni Morrison. Indeed, Updike comments about *Corregidora*, that "[o]ur retrospective impression of [the novel] is of a big territory— the Afro-American psyche—rather thinly and stabbingly populated by ideas, personae, hints. Yet that such a small book could seem so big speaks well for the generous spirit of the author, unpolemical where there has been much polemic, exploratory where rhetoric and outrage tend to block the path." Commenting on Jones's rigorous refusal to make moral or political judgments of her characters, Keith Byerman asserts that "[t]he authority of [Jones's] depiction of the world is enhanced by [her] refusal to intrude upon or judge her narrators. She remains outside of the story, leaving the reader with none of the usual markers of a narrator's reliability."

Regarding Jones's later works, critical reception has been mixed. Often it is limited, disrupted, and distorted by excessive attention to the tragic circumstances that characterized her life in the years from 1983 to 1998. Jones's collection of critical essays, *Liberating Voices: Oral Tradition in African American Literature*, has been lauded for its reaffirmation of the proposition that "the foundation of every literary tradition is oral, whether it is visible or invisible in the text" (2). However, Bernard W. Bell writes that in spite of the profundity of this proposition and of the pioneering nature of Jones's work, as the "first critical survey by a contemporary black woman writer that attempts an extended comparison of the oral foundation of African American literature with those of non-African American literatur[e]," the text "provides a provocative and important yet inadequate, misleading map of the oral or vernacular tradition in African American literature."

Concerning the novel *The Healing*, Marcie Hershman writes that while Jones's early work was "bull's eye directed and tersely expressed, [her late work] now comes across as expansively detailed and moving in circles away from its subject." Valerie Sayers comments that "[i]n loosening the tight control she exercised over her earlier fiction," sometimes Jones leaps the chasm and sometimes she takes a nose dive, but on the whole the dares are worth her trouble and ours."

In general, critics have been bewildered and, at times, unkind in their responses to Jones's most recent novel, *Mosquito*. Eleanor J. Bader describes the tome as both "exhausting and exhilarating." James A. Miller cautions that, for select readers, "this work, like a mosquito, will buzz along—nagging, irritating, provoking, exasperating," because it is "long-winded, disassociative, plotless, cutesy, full of hairsplitting deconstructive debates." Henry Louis Gates describes the novel as a "late-night riff by the Signifying Monkey, drunk with words and out of control, regurgitating half-digested ideas taken from *USA Today*, digressing on every possible subject." Disagreeing with most critics, Greg Tate writes that "[w]hen white boys write books as cunning and convoluted as this one we call them postmodern, experimental, exemplars of the literature of exhaustion." Carrie Tirado Bramen agrees with Tate, writing that "[t]his same seriousness should also be applied to this 'maddening tale,' which encourages the reader to rethink the conventions of racial representation by radically challenging the conventions of narration" (129).

BIBLIOGRAPHY

Works by Gayl Jones

Chile Woman. New York: Shubert Foundation, 1974.
Corregidora. Boston: Beacon, 1975.
Eva's Man. Boston: Beacon, 1976.
The Healing. Boston: Beacon, 1998.
The Hermit-Woman. Detroit: Lotus, 1983.
Liberating Voices: Oral Tradition in African American Literature. Cambridge: Harvard University Press, 1991.
Mosquito. Boston: Beacon, 1999.
Song of Anninho. Boston: Beacon, 1981.
The White Rat. New York: Random House, 1977.
Xargque and Other Poems. Detroit: Lotus, 1985.

Studies of Gayl Jones's Works

Allen, Donia Elizabeth. "The Role of the Blues in Gayl Jones's *Corregidora*." *Callaloo* 25.1 (2002): 257–73.
Bell, Bernard. "The Liberating Literacy and African American Vernacular Voices of Gayl Jones." *Comparative Literature Studies* 36.3 (1999): 247–58.
Bramen, Carrie Tirado. "Speaking in Typeface: Characterizing Stereotypes in Gayl Jones's *Mosquito*." *Modern Fiction Studies* 49.1 (2003): 124–54.
Clabough, Casey. "Afrocentric Recolonizations: Gayl Jones's 1990s Fiction." *Contemporary Literature* 46.2 (2005): 243–73.
Coser, Stelamaris. *The Literature of Paule Marshall, Toni Morrison, and Gayl Jones*. Philadelphia: Temple University Press, 1995.

Evans, Mari, ed. *Black Women Writers: Arguments and Interviews*. London: Pluto, 1983.

Goldberg, Elizabeth Swanson. "Living the Legacy: Pain, Desire, and Narrative Time in Gayl Jones' *Corregidora*." *Callaloo* 26.2 (2003): 446–72.

Horvitz, Deborah. "'Sadism Demands a Story': Oedipus, Feminism, and Sexuality in Gayl Jones's *Corregidora* and Dorothy Allison's *Bastard out of Carolina*." *Contemporary Literature* 39.2 (1998): 238–61.

Robinson, Sally. *Engendering the Subject: Gender and Self-Representation in Contemporary Women's Fiction*. Albany: State University of New York Press, 1991.

Rushdy, Ashraf H. A. "'Relate Sexual to Historical': Race, Resistance, and Desire in Gayl Jones's *Corregidora*." *African American Review* 34.2 (2000): 273–97.

Tate, Claudia, ed. *Black Women Writers at Work*. New York: Continuum, 1984.

Willingham, Kathy G. "*Corregidora*: Retelling (Her)Story." *Style* 35.2 (2001): 308–20.

Helen Doss

JUNE JORDAN (1936–2002)

BIOGRAPHICAL NARRATIVE

June Jordan was a poet, novelist, journalist, biographer, dramatist, and committed activist. One of the fiercest and most compassionate voices of the twentieth century, as well as one of its most prolific writers, Jordan published over twenty-eight books of poetry, children's stories, and collections of political essays and lectures. A prominent artist and organizer since the 1960s, Jordan played a significant role in the development of African American artistic, social, and political movements, advocating in particular for the rights of women and urban youth.

Jordan was born in Harlem, New York, on July 9, 1936, and lived most of her childhood in the Bedford-Stuyvesant section of Brooklyn. She was the only child of Granville Ivanhoe Jordan and Mildred Maud (Fisher) Jordan, who came separately to the United States from Jamaica. Her father—an often violent man who projected his ambitions onto his daughter—compelled her at an early age to read broadly and memorize passages from classical texts. This had an edifying impact on Jordan's intellect, and she began writing her own poetry by the time she was seven years old. She describes the complex trials of her early life in her short memoir, *Soldier: A Poet's Childhood* (2000), which she dedicated to her father.

After a year at Brooklyn's Midwood High School, where she recalls being the only black student, Jordan's father transferred her to the Northfield School for Girls in Gill, Massachusetts, where she was again immersed in an all-white environment but in the context of which she was able to construct her consciousness as an African American and a writer. In 1953 she graduated high school and entered Barnard College in New York City, where she met Michael Meyer, a white Columbia University student, whom she married in 1955. Subsequently, she left New York to accompany Meyer to the University of Chicago, where he would pursue graduate study in anthropology. She also enrolled at Chicago but within a year returned to Barnard where she stayed until 1957. In 1958 Jordan gave birth to a son, Christopher David Meyer, for whom she assumed full responsibility, working as a freelance writer, urban planner, and production assistant. The couple finally divorced in 1965.

Jordan's poetry and essays entered the public eye in the 1960s through publication in a number of periodicals, including *Esquire,* the *Nation, Partisan Review, Essence,* the *Village Voice,* and the *New York Times*, among others. Her novel, *His Own Where* (1971), was a National Book Award finalist. She also received a Rockefeller Foundation grant in 1969, a Yaddo fellowship in 1979, the National Association of Black Journalists Award in 1984, and fellowships from the New York Foundation for the Arts and the National Endowment for the Arts. In 1998, Jordan received the Lifetime Achievement Award from the National Black Writers' Conference. By the year 2000, Jordan was still publishing frequently, editing collections of poetry and regularly contributing sharp political essays to the *Progressive* magazine.

Jordan maintained a long and distinguished career as a college professor, beginning in 1966 as an instructor of English at the City University of New York, then at Connecticut College and Sarah Lawrence College. From 1974 to 1975 she was a visiting professor of English and Afro-American studies at Yale. She earned tenure at the State University of New York at Stony Brook in 1982, and finally became professor of Afro-American studies and women's studies at the University of California, Berkeley, in 1989. There she established the ongoing *Poetry for the People* program through which college students learn to teach creative writing as a form of self-expression and empowerment.

June Jordan died of breast cancer on June 14, 2002, in Berkeley, California.

MAJOR WORKS

Jordan's poetry reveals her early engagement, as part of her father's fierce discipline, with the works of Shakespeare and Paul Laurence Dunbar, and also suggests stylistic impulses reminiscent of Walt Whitman, Langston Hughes, Margaret Walker, and Robert Hayden, whom she studied. These influences are present in Jordan's work, but hers is a unique voice that consistently and artfully weaves her personal experiences as a political activist, educator, and a bisexual African American woman with love, fury, confession, and commentary. Her artistic range encompasses the intimate, the local, and the transnational—from love poems and poems about sexual freedom such as those found in *Haruko/Love Poetry* (1993), an arc that charts a poet's cross-cultural relationship in the style of Browning and Neruda, to pieces such as "Poem about My Rights" (*Passion* 1980), which rages at the injustices of rape, apartheid, and ethnic cleansing, linking personal experiences to global issues within the sphere of one poem and one poet's consciousness.

Jordan's published body of prose—which includes children's books, letters, essays, and a novella—is likewise intersectional in its substance and themes. *His Own Where* (1971), a short novel for adolescents, was awarded the Prix de Rome in Environmental Design for its innovative translation of architecture and urban planning into fiction. The novella looks at the problem of African American identity and public space and envisions practical, community-centered methods of environmental planning, and also illustrates Jordan's attuned adaptation of African American speech in her writing. The inclusion of "Letter to Michael" in *Civil Wars* (1981), Jordan's first collection of essays, allows the author to use a private genre to deploy a public appeal. Describing the 1964 Harlem Riots to her estranged ex-husband in an ostensibly private prose style, the letter challenges public perception of the ordeal by divulging a witness's account of the violence perpetrated by public officials against African Americans, testifying, most importantly, to the resolve and resilience of the Harlem community.

In the communities where she worked Jordan was both citizen and witness, but it was through her role as an intellectual that she conveyed her visions for new strategies in civil rights work that are inclusive and nurturing, governments that are effective and democratic, and a society that derides ignorance so that it can thrive in its understanding of difference and potential for equality. In her oft-quoted essay from *Technical Difficulties* (1992), "A New Politics of Difference," Jordan confronts the complex imbrications of race, class, sexuality, and family, and contests the "exploitation of the human domain of sexuality for power." By rhetorically providing links among forms of oppression based on sexuality, race, and gender, she cultivates a context for struggle marked by its global complexity and potential for coalition: "Freedom is indivisible," she writes, "or it is nothing at all besides sloganeering and temporary, short-sighted, and short-lived advancement for the few."

Selections of Jordan's latest essays and lectures open the latest collection, *Some of Us Did Not Die*, in which the multiplicity of her social and intellectual commitments become her trademark. These essays take on the form of short, topical, occasional discussions dealing with everything from ancient poetic forms ("A Far Stretch Well Worth the Effort"), controversies surrounding the 2000 U.S. presidential election ("The Invisible People: An Unsolicited Report on Black Rage"), her views on Palestine over a number of decades, and commemoration of important civil rights events and news items of social weight. In "Update on Martin Luther King, Jr., and the Best of My Heart," the question of universal equality as articulated by the late civil rights leader is Jordan's central concern as she describes the imaginative magnitude of a democracy built on a basis of common self-interest as opposed to "American delusions illusions of autonomy, American delusions of individuality" (*Some of Us Did Not Die* 112)—a national paradox she presents in her 1986 lecture, "Waking Up in the Middle of Some American Dream."

Jordan's body of work is characterized by its contribution to multiple genres and its socially informed style of literary expression—significant practices in contemporary African American intellectual work that are also exemplified by writers like Paule Marshall and Alice Walker. Jordan's rendering of spoken African American English in both her poetry and prose illustrates her participation in an oral literary tradition also practiced by Nikki Giovanni and Amiri Baraka. The breadth of Jordan's subject matter, particularly in her poetry, is akin to the work of Rita Dove and Gwendolyn Brooks, insofar as a theme can be built on both domestic and international causes, both intimate and public concerns. Although Jordan's eloquent and accessible style is often motivated by sincere anger, her ultimate message is invariably infused with optimism and an indefatigable devotion to justice.

CRITICAL RECEPTION

In her long career as primarily a poet and a journalist, Jordan never concentrated her talent into a singular literary *tour de force* of the sort that define many foremost African American writers. Instead, Jordan's work has appeared over a span of decades, often quite pointedly coinciding with major events in U.S. culture. In an essay published in a 1999 issue of the *African American Review*, Scott MacPhail gives an account of June Jordan's ambivalent, often misunderstood, role among black intellectuals since the 1960s, particularly as portrayed by the mainstream press. Jordan has often been sidelined, he argues, precisely because she challenges both African American and women's movements to extend the boundaries of identity politics, or abandon such a project altogether in favor of a new politics of race, gender, sexuality, and transnational action. Included in MacPhail's genealogy of "new black intellectuals" are Alice Walker and Toni Morrison, both of whom have publicly lauded Jordan's canon of work, the latter praising Jordan as "our premier black woman essayist" ("After Identity," Erickson 132).

Jordan's work, like the author herself, resists easy classification. Her aesthetic practices, the subjects of her essays, and her interdisciplinary approach to intellectual production all consistently exhibit, as Peter Erickson writes, an "absolute refusal to be confined by fixed categories of identity." Jordan's essays exhibit a "rigorous scrutiny of democracy" that is fueled by her "transcendent human vision of political coalitions formed across racial lines" ("After Identity," 132). Indeed in literary studies Jordan's work is often examined as a coalitional site and considered in relation to poets such as Adrienne Rich, Ntozake Shange, and Elizabeth Bishop. Her contribution to African American culture in particular, however, is crucial to many critics. In her 1981 review of *Civil Wars*, Toni Cade Bambara likened Jordan's body of work to an achievement comparable to W.E.B. DuBois's *Dusk of Dawn: An Essay Toward an Autobiography of a Race Concept,* published in 1940.

The wide range of Jordan's ideological pursuits illustrate the central ethics of self-determination that are not at odds with her belief in the establishment of justice through communal action and coalitional politics. Jordan's artistic and social vision is comprehensive, engendered by her concurrent participation in antiracist and antihomophobic social movements, and evidenced by her refusal to be confined by identity politics. Having surfaced as a political commentator, activist, and a working artist at a time when liberation movements were often divided from within by conflicting aims, Jordan's work implements a mode of intersectional human rights discourse that has been influential to the African American movement and U.S. feminism and has become a standard for independent, democratic thought in the twenty-first century.

BIBLIOGRAPHY

Works by June Jordan

Affirmative Acts: Political Essays. New York: Anchor Books, 1998.
All These Blessings. Play complete in 1988, unpublished.
Bang Bang Uber Alles. Produced in Atlanta, GA, 1986, unpublished.
Bobo Goetz a Gun. Willimantic, CT: Curbstone Press, 1985.
The Break. Produced in New York, 1984, unpublished.
Campaigns: Selected Poems. London: Virago Press, 1989.
Civil Wars. Boston: Beacon Press, 1981.
Dry Victories. New York: Holt, 1972.
Fannie Lou Hamer. New York: Crowell, 1972.
For the Arrow That Flies by Day. Produced at the Shakespeare Festival, New York, April 1981, unpublished.
Freedom Now Suite. Produced in New York, 1984, unpublished.
Haruko/Love Poetry: New and Selected Love Poems. London: Serpent's Tail, 1993.
High Tide—Marea Alta. Willimantic, CT: Curbstone Press, 1987.
His Own Where. New York: Crowell, 1971.
I Was Looking at the Ceiling and Then I Saw the Sky. Produced at Lincoln Center, New York, 1985, unpublished.
In the Spirit of Sojourner Truth. Produced at Public Theater, New York, May 1979, unpublished.
Kissing God Goodbye: New Poems. New York: Doubleday, 1997.
Living Room: New Poems. New York: Thunder's Mouth Press, 1985.
Moving towards Home: Political Essays. London: Virago Press, 1989.
The Music of Poetry and the Poetry of Music. Produced in New York and Washington, DC, 1984, unpublished.
Naming Our Destiny: New and Selected Poems. New York: Thunder's Mouth Press, 1989.
New Days: Poems of Exile and Return. New York: Emerson Hall, 1973.
New Life: New Room. New York: Crowell, 1975.

Okay Now. New York: Simon and Schuster, 1977.

On Call: Political Essays, 1981–1985. Boston: South End Press, 1985.

Passion: New Poems, 1977–1980. Boston: Beacon Press. 1980.

Soldier: A Poet's Childhood. New York: Basic Books, 2000.

Some Changes. New York: Dutton, 1971.

Some of Us Did Not Die: New and Selected Essays of June Jordan. New York: Basic/Civitas Books, 2002.

Soulscript: A Collection of Classic African American Poetry. 1970. Reprint, New York: Harlem Moon, 2004.

Technical Difficulties: African American Notes on the State of the Union. New York: Pantheon Books, 1992.

Things That I Do in the Dark: Selected Poetry. New York: Random House, 1977.

The Voice of the Children. Editor. New York: Holt, 1970.

Who Look at Me. New York: Crowell, 1969.

Studies of June Jordan's Works

Bambara, Toni Cade. "Chosen Weapons." *Ms.* (April 1981): 40–42.

Brogan, Jacqueline Vaught. "From Warrior to Womanist: The Development of June Jordan's Poetry." In *Speaking the Other Self: American Women Writers*, edited by Jeanne Campbell Reesman, 198–209. Athens: University of Georgia Press, 1997.

———. "Planets on the Table: From Wallace Stevens and Elizabeth Bishop to Adrienne Rich and June Jordan." *Wallace Stevens Journal* 19.2 (Fall 1995): 255–78.

DeVeaux, Alexis. "A Conversation with June Jordan." *Essence* (September 2000): 102.

Erickson, Peter. "After Identity: A Conversation with June Jordan." *Transition: An International Review* 63 (1993): 132–49.

———. "Putting Her Life on the Line—The Poetry of June Jordan." *Hurricane Alice: A Feminist Quarterly* 7.1 (Winter–Spring 1990): 4–5.

Freccero, Carla. "June Jordan." In *African American Writers*, edited by Valerie Smith, 443–60. New York: Scribner's, 1991.

Harjo, Joy. "An Interview with June Jordan." *High Plains Literary Review* 3.2 (Fall 1988): 60–76.

Heflin, Kyla. "June Jordan." In *Contemporary American Ethnic Poets*, edited by Linda Collum, 151–54. Westport, CT: Greenwood Press, 2004.

Johnson, Ronna C. "June Jordan." In *The Concise Oxford Companion to African American Literature*, edited by William L. Andrews, Frances Smith Foster, and Trudier Harris. New York: Oxford University Press, 1997.

Joyce, Joyce Ann. "June Jordan." In *The Heath Anthology of American Literature*, 4th ed., edited by Paul Lauter et al., 2632–39. Boston: Houghton Mifflin, 2002.

MacPhail, Scott. "June Jordan and the New Black Intellectuals." *African American Review* 33.1 (Spring 1999): 57–71.

Nelson, Jill. "A Conversation with June Jordan." *Quarterly Black Review of Books* 1 (May 1994): 50–53.

Roy Pérez

ELIZABETH HOBBS KECKLEY (1818–1907)

BIOGRAPHICAL NARRATIVE

Elizabeth Hobbs Keckley was born in 1818 to Agnes Burwell Hobbs, a slave, and Armistead Burwell, her slave owner, in Dinwiddie Court-House, in Virginia. Although the married Armistead Burwell fathered Elizabeth, the enslaved Agnes was the wife of another slave, George Pleasant Hobbs, who loved and accepted Elizabeth. Both Agnes and George were literate (Fleischner 29). Keckley fondly remembered George Pleasant Hobbs as a loving father forced to live and labor on another farm, who referred to her as "Little Lizzie," wanted her educated, and visited on holidays, until he was sold away from the neighborhood. He tried to maintain his familial connection with letters to Agnes. His communication stopped in 1839.

MAJOR WORK

Elizabeth Hobbs Keckley's only work is *Behind the Scenes or Thirty Years a Slave, and Four Years in the White House* (1868). In this work she recounts her experiences as a slave.

Among young Keckley's first official duties as a slave, of four years old, is to care for her master's infant daughter. She is to rock the cradle, keep flies off, and prevent the baby from crying. Keckley's enthusiasm for rocking the cradle causes the infant to be tossed to the floor and leads to her first violent punishment. Keckley writes that it was the severity of her lashing that caused her to remember the brutality of the event. Sadly, she writes, "This was the first time I was punished in this cruel way, but not the last" (Keckley 21).

Ten years later, at about the age of fourteen, Keckley is sent to live with her master's eldest son, a Presbyterian minister—Robert Burwell—and his young cruel wife—Anna. Keckley finds that she is to do the work of three servants and is underappreciated by the mistress. Anna, after several years sensing what she characterizes as "stubborn pride" in Keckley, asks the overseer Bingham to gain control over Keckley. Bingham requests that she join him in the study. Once inside the study, Bingham demands that Keckley remove her dress to accept a flogging. The fully developed, eighteen-year-old Keckley responds, "No, Mr. Bingham, I shall not take down my dress before you. Moreover, you shall not whip me unless you prove the stronger. Nobody has a right to whip me but my own master, and nobody shall do so if I can prevent it'" (Keckley 33). Although she loses the fight and is savagely beaten, she demands to know why, maintains her defiance of wrongs against her, and preserves her pride and rebellious spirit. Though she is subjected to more beatings, eventually, Bingham decides it is a sin to beat her further and asks Keckley's forgiveness, and according to her "was never known to strike one of his servants from that day forward" (37).

Keckley reveals that as a result of being raped for four years by an unnamed white man, she gives birth (1842) to her only child, whom she names after her lost father, George. She leaves North Carolina and returns to Virginia as a slave for one of her master's daughters (Ann Burwell Garland) and her husband. It is during this time that she hones her abilities as a seamstress and dressmaker.

It is in Virginia that Elizabeth meets her husband James Keckley. Initially she declines his marriage proposal because she refuses to give birth to another child who will suffer the violent and senseless existence of American slavery. However, when Keckley believes he can secure freedom for both her and her son, George, she consents to wed James, who claims to be a free man. After their marriage, in 1852, she discovers that James is a slave who battles other difficulties, and their marriage is brief.

When the master's family talks of letting aged Agnes go, Keckley appeals to Mr. Garland to allow her to earn money to support her mother's upkeep. Consequently, she gains a reputation as a fine seamstress and dressmaker to affluent women in St. Louis. Keckley states, "With my needle I kept bread in the mouths of seventeen persons for two years and five months" (45). As a result of Keckely's work, Agnes remains with her enslavers until her death in Vicksburg, Mississippi, in 1857.

On August 10, 1855, 1,200 dollars is paid to secure the freedom of both Elizabeth and her sixteen-year-old son, George. Elizabeth later repays her slave ransom to her patron.

By the spring of 1860, James Keckley is dead and Elizabeth forms a school in Baltimore, Maryland, to teach young colored women her system of sewing. After six weeks she becomes disappointed and moves on to Washington. Once in Washington, Keckley begins to develop an impressive cliental of influential women eager to have her sew their dresses and this enhances her entrepreneurial endeavors. Keckley lets it be known that she wants to secure a sewing position in the White House. Among others, she becomes modiste to Varina Howell Davis, wife of Jefferson Davis, and also privy to Davis's political meetings and the upcoming strategies of the Civil War. Although Mrs. Davis wants Keckley to come south with her family, she is determined to "work for the ladies of the White House" (Keckley 76).

Keckley's insight, resolve, ability, and reputation as a dress designer gain her introduction to Mrs. Lincoln and entrance into the White House. The friendship between Keckley and Mary Lincoln extend beyond the White House years.

Keckley becomes acquainted with many prominent individuals and her concern for the advancement of African Americans leads her to use these connections to their benefit. For example, she is instrumental in introducing Sojourner Truth to President Lincoln. Notably, she serves as an activist concerned with the freedom of colored people and their acclamation to living free lives. In 1862, she starts and leads the First Black Contraband Relief Organization. At Wilberforce University, in Xenia, Ohio, she heads the Department of Sewing and Domestic Science Arts in 1892.

In 1907, Elizabeth Hobbs Keckley died in her sleep at the National Home for Destitute Colored Women and Children, a Washington institution she helped create earlier.

CRITICAL RECEPTION

At the time of its publication, much controversy surrounded *Behind the Scenes or Thirty Years A Slave, and Four Years in the White House*. Before its publication, her publisher (Carleton and Company) offered favorable advanced reviews of her narrative. However, its publication caused a rift in Keckley's relationship with Mary Lincoln and caused Lincoln's son Robert to campaign to have the narrative withdrawn from publication.

After its publication, many individuals were outraged that a colored woman, former slave, and former dressmaker of the Lincolns, would dare to reveal details of her life, the lives of the Lincoln family, and suggest that she was a friend and confidante to Mrs. Lincoln. As a result, *Behind the Scenes* and Keckley were mocked and renounced by the press. Most cruelly, Keckley was insulted and ridiculed with a parody titled *Behind the Seams; by a Nigger Woman who took work in from Mrs. Lincoln and Mrs. Davis*, and the author was designated with an "X" for "Betsey Kickley (nigger)" (The National News Co., New York, 1868—Fleischner 317).

Despite the aforementioned criticism, Elizabeth Hobbs Keckley and her nineteenth-century narrative, *Behind the Scenes*, occupy a necessary and critical place in United States presidential history, African American women's history, and African American literature. For example, James Olney characterizes *Behind the Scenes* as a memoir more than a slave narrative or autobiography because Keckley's focus goes beyond personal details to "external events and figures who occupy some important place in the affairs of the world" (xxxiii). Although *Behind the Scenes* includes outside events, one certainly gets a sense of the concerned and kind woman warrior known as Elizabeth Hobbs Keckley.

BIBLIOGRAPHY

Work by Elizabeth Hobbs Keckley

Behind the Scenes or Thirty Years a Slave, and Four Years in the White House. 1868. Reprint, New York. Oxford University Press, 1988.

Studies of Elizabeth Hobbs Keckley's Work

Fleischner, Jennifer. *Mrs. Lincoln and Mrs. Keckley: The Remarkable Story of the Friendship between a First Lady and a Former Slave.* New York: Broadway Books, 2003.

Foster, Frances Smith. "Romance and Scandal in a Postbellum Slave Narrative: Elizabeth Keckley's *Behind the Scenes.*" In *Written by Herself: Literary Production by African American Women, 1746–1892*, 117–30. Bloomington: Indiana University Press, 1993.

Olney, James. "Introduction." In *Behind the Scenes or Thirty Years a Slave, and Four Years in the White House*, xxvii–xxxvi. New York: Oxford University Press, 1988.

Regina V. Jones

ADRIENNE KENNEDY (1931–)

BIOGRAPHICAL NARRATIVE

Adrienne Kennedy, playwright and educator, was born Adrienne Lita Hawkins on September 13, 1931, in Pittsburgh, Pennsylvania. Her mother, Etta Haugabook Hawkins, was a schoolteacher and her father, Cornell Wallace Hawkins, was a social worker and the executive secretary of the YMCA. When Kennedy was four years old, the family moved to Cleveland, Ohio, where she remained until she married Joseph C. Kennedy in 1953. Her parents were among the prominent African American citizens of Cleveland, and Kennedy was very interested in their lives and the community around them. She was particularly fascinated by her mother, a beautiful woman, about whom Kennedy says, "She told me stories about her life in Georgia, which would one day sound remarkably like the monologues spoken by the characters in my plays" (*People* 12). Kennedy's maternal grandfather was a wealthy white peach grower, and this fact may also have influenced the course of her writing, making her interested in exploring the psyche of the mulatto characters that inhabit her dramatic world. During her childhood, she made frequent visits with her parents and her younger brother to Montezuma, Georgia, where most of her relatives, African Americans and whites lived. Images of Montezuma from her childhood memories persist in her work, and she recalls these in *People*: "Montezuma, Georgia looked to me like the drawings we were given in Sunday school of Jerusalem, the golden and red and white colors of the landscape, the processions of people walking on the road coming from the fields, walking to church" (85). Her mixed ancestry also inculcated in her a lifelong fascination with England. Again in *People*, she says, "My mother often said that most of the white people of Montezuma's families came from England. . . . I became very interested in 'England' " (22).

After her marriage, Kennedy moved to New York with her husband and joined a creative writing course at Columbia University (1954–1956). She had started writing plays and fiction, and her early work, such as "Pale Blue Flowers" (unpublished), was influenced by, and was indeed, as she later said, imitative of, the plays of Tennessee Williams. Other important influences on her were the plays of Chekhov and Lorca. She traveled to Europe and East Africa with her husband and this experience changed the direction of her work. Although she had grown up with significant exposure to African American literature and culture through her parents, her travels to Africa opened new perspectives to her and she says, "Not until I bought a great African mask from a vendor on the streets of Accra, of a woman with a bird flying through her forehead, did I totally break from realistic-looking characters" (*People* 121). Her first story, "Because of the King of France," was published in *Black Orpheus: A Journal of African and Afro-American Literature* (1963), a West African journal in which Soyinka and Achebe were also being published in the 1960s. She read many African writers and identified with them: "Chinua Achebe, Amos Tutuola, Wole Soyinka, Eufua Sutherland, Lawrence Durrell. . . . Now that I was going to be published in *Black Orpheus*, I was joined to these writers and I wanted to read their work" (*People* 121). Kennedy wrote *Funnyhouse of a*

Negro and *The Owl Answers* during her stay in Accra and Rome. When she came back to New York in 1962, she had two children, Joseph and Adam, and two completed plays in her suitcase. *Funnyhouse* was a powerful introduction of Adrienne Kennedy to the New York Off-Broadway theater world.

Since then, she has written some fifteen one-act plays, a highly acclaimed auto-biographical work, *People Who Led to My Plays*, a novella, and various semiautobiographical prose pieces. Besides winning the Obie Award thrice, she has also received the American Book Award, American Academy of Arts and Letters Award, the Pierre LeComte duNouy Foundation Award, and has also earned several grants and fellowships including the Guggenheim and the Rockefeller. She has taught drama and playwriting at various universities including New York University, Yale University, University of California at Berkeley, and Harvard University. In 1992, the Great Lakes Theatre Company organized a month-long celebration of her work. In 1995–1996, Signature Theatre Company selected her as their playwright of the fall season and produced seven of her plays. She is one of the only five African American playwrights to be included in *The Norton Anthology of American Literature* (third edition). She has been commissioned to write plays for, among others, the Public Theater, Jerome Robbins, Mark Taper Forum, Juilliard, Lincoln Center, and the Royal Court in England.

MAJOR WORKS

Kennedy's powerful antirealistic and nonlinear one-act plays employ surrealistic and often nightmarish imagery, fragmented characters, and a nearly ritualistic repetition of dialogue. She had tried to work with simultaneous use of different settings and perspectives in her short stories earlier, but in her plays, she broke free from the conventions of naturalistic and realistic drama and experimented radically with form and character delineation. It was a radical breakthrough for her when her characters began to have other personas. The use of masks and personas made it possible for her to use historical people as extensions of the main character, thus bringing apparently unconnected but deeply formative areas of experience across the boundaries of race, gender, and culture within the space of individual experience. Although Kennedy has claimed that her work is primarily autobiographical, dealing with inner, psychological confusions stemming from childhood, these personal questions in her plays widen out in space and time to carry the weight of historical and cultural issues concerning women and people of color.

Funnyhouse of a Negro is an intense and deeply moving play about the life of Negro Sarah, who longs to become a "more pallid Negro than I am now," and whose "only defect is that I have a head of frizzy hair" (*The Adrienne Kennedy Reader* 14). Queen Victoria, Duchess of Hapsburg, Jesus, and Patrice Lumumba are each "One of Herselves." The other characters in the play are The Mother, Landlady who is "Funnylady," and Raymond, who is "Funnyman." In terms of chronological sequence, the play seems to begin just a little before the end when Sarah hangs herself. In her first appearance, we see her already with a hangman's rope about her neck, and at the end we see her hanging figure on the stage. In between, we catch disjointed but highly suggestive glimpses of Sarah's life and her multiple selves. The incidents repeatedly recalled in the play revolve around Sarah's African American father and mulatto mother. In Africa, he starts to drink and one night "rapes" his wife. The child of this rape is Sarah, who has yellow skin and no glaring negroid features. After Sarah's birth her mother suffers a breakdown and has to be sent to an asylum. There are various versions of the father's fate after his return: Sarah confesses that she bludgeoned him to death, Landlady says that he hanged himself in a Harlem hotel, and Raymond claims that the man is alive and that he is a doctor, married to a white woman. Since all the events are reported by the characters and do not take place on the stage, they have no verifiable, objective reality. Kennedy's plays problematize the idea of a consistent and structured "reality" by playing with continually transforming personas and shifting perspectives.

In *The Owl Answers*, Kennedy continues her experiments with fragmented identities and gives multiple personas to nearly all the characters in the play. The protagonist, Clara, a mulatto and a bastard, is confounded by the cultural, racial, and religious contradictions of her existence and turns into an owl at the end.

Two short plays, *A Rat's Mass* and *A Lesson in Dead Language*, express an obsessive fear of heterosexuality, rape, and guilt caused by menstruation. *A Lesson in Dead Language* conflates the menstrual flow of blood with revenge for the mythical and historical acts of the killing of Jesus and Caesar. Big, red stains of blood on the back of the characters' white dresses are the sign of guilt and punishment seen in female terms. In *Rat's Mass*, the characters appear as rats: Brother Rat with a rat's head and a human body, and Sister Rat with a rat's belly and a human head. Their repetitive comments gradually conjure up the image of a traumatic experience that both are trying to overcome—that of the rape of Sister Rat by Brother Rat, because of which Sister Rat has a mental breakdown and has to be taken to the mental asylum. This act was supposedly instigated by Rosemary, the girl with worms in her hair, who looms menacingly over the experiences of Brother and Sister Rat. Having exploited Brother Rat's love for her to force him into incest and the consequent guilt and horror, she suggests that he put a bullet to his head. The play employs Christian images to suggest a fall into the state of sin and also refers to the coming of Nazis. In both these plays, interestingly, the threatening figures are those of women, the White Dog in *A Lesson* and Rosemary in *A Rat's Mass*.

Sun: A Poem for Malcolm X Inspired by His Murder and *an Evening with Dead Essex* testify to Kennedy's involvement with the issues of race relations and the larger political questions in the 1960s. Commissioned and produced by the Royal Court Theatre, *Sun* is a short expressionistic work that combines visual imagery, poetry, body movement, sound, lighting, and screen projections to create choreographed dramatic poetry that speaks in a highly symbolic language. *An Evening with Dead Essex* is much more explicit and direct in its political commentary. The play is based on the magazine reports and stories about the gunning down of Mark Essex by the police in New Orleans on the roof of a motel with more than a hundred bullets in his body. Kennedy uses the Vietnam War news headlines, statements about President Nixon and Secretary of State Henry Kissinger, and references to American soldiers stationed in Europe to underscore her comments on the meaning of Essex's actions and his death. In an interview with Paul Bryant-Jackson and Lois More Overbeck, Kennedy remarked that she saw him as a "victim and a hero," saying that "I feel tremendous rage against American society. I feel like Mark Essex" (Bryant-Jackson and Overbeck 8).

A Movie Star Has to Star in Black and White is a brilliant interweaving of cultural history, autobiographical narrative, and an implied ideological commentary on the Western constructions of race and gender. Hollywood films and stars are appropriated by Kennedy to play roles evocative of their roles in the films and also to become mouthpieces narrating the lives of the African American characters in the play. Marlon Brando, Paul Henry, Montgomery Clift, Jean Peters, Bette Davis, Shirley Winters, and Columbia Pictures Lady recreate visual images from their films *Now Voyager*, *Viva Zapata!*, and

A Place in the Sun, while the narrative revolves around the lives of Clara, The Mother, The Father, and The Husband. Kennedy reverses the phenomenal power of popular icons to be the focus of everyone's desire and instead makes the movie stars compulsively live out the details of her protagonist's life. In a further twist that is common in Kennedy's work, the details of Clara's life often echo the details of Kennedy's life, always mapping life on to art, blurring the divide between the two. In *A Movie Star*, for instance, Clara/ Jean Peters is a writer of a play called *A Lesson in Dead Language*, and a play "about a girl who turns into an owl (*The Owl Answers*). Not only do Kennedy's characters repeat each others' lines within a given play, but there is also repetition across plays, such as Jean Peters repeating Clara Passmore's lines from *The Owl Answers*. Such intertextuality creates connections of mood and images, suggesting a continuity of concerns across plays, building a unique body of work in which parts flow into one another and characters evoke and resonate not only with each other but also with the autobiographical details of the playwright's life.

The plays published as *The Alexander Plays* in 1992 include *She Talks to Beethoven*, *The Ohio State Murders*, and *The Film Club*. Kennedy began her literary career in the 1960s when black nationalism was at its peak, but she consistently kept herself out of any kind of political activism. Nevertheless, Kennedy was deeply affected by the contemporary political, social, and cultural upheavals in America and Africa, and her literary and dramatic aesthetics were formed by the dissonance caused by these events. Instead of writing militant, didactic plays, in her early work she sought to grapple with her inner, psychological confusion and conflicts. However, in *She Talks to Beethoven*, Kennedy goes back to the 1960s and locates her play in the midst of a nationalist movement and shows the artists and the artistic process embroiled in social and political turmoil. *She Talks* is an intricately woven piece in which a number of contexts are embedded one within the other, contexts that are widely removed chronologically but have innumerable strands connecting them. It brings into conjunction a mythic time in which the story of Beethoven's opera "Fidelio" is set, Beethoven's Vienna of the 1820s with the Napoleonic war in the background, the newly liberated but politically troubled Ghana of 1961, and the contemporary African American world in which Kennedy is writing. Each of these contexts reverberates on the other, commenting, enlarging, and enriching the central concern of the play, which is the relationships between the aesthetic, the social, and the political. In *The Ohio State Murders*, Suzanne Alexander in the present is a "well-known black writer" visiting Ohio State University to give a talk on "the violent imagery" in her work. The younger Suzanne, whose story forms the body of the play, is the "young writer as a student attending Ohio State" (*Alexander* 26). The narrative is constructed by the alternating voices of Suzanne in the present and as a student in 1949–1950. The dates are relevant because when Suzanne attended the Ohio State University, the 1955 Supreme Court ruling declaring discrimination in education as unconstitutional was still to come. Hence, as a student, Suzanne encounters racial discrimination in various forms. Suzanne, the writer, traces the tragic events in her life at the campus in response to the invitation by the "Chairman": "we do want to hear about your brief years here at Ohio State but we also want you to talk about violent imagery in your stories and plays" (27). The play appears highly self-reflexive as the protagonist, Suzanne Alexander, responds to a question that may well be asked about Adrienne Kennedy's plays, the source of the violent imagery in her work.

Kennedy's memoir, *People Who Led to My Plays*, written in a highly original form of short entries, brings together innumerable small and big influences, people, and events that shaped her life and writings. *June and Jean in Concert* is a theater piece with music, in which she reworks material from *People* into a dramatic form. *Deadly Triplets* combines a mystery in novella form and journal writing based on Kennedy's experiences in London from 1966 to 1969. The prose pieces *A Letter to Flowers* and *Sister Etta and Ella* again creatively use material from Kennedy's own life. *Sleep Deprivation Chamber*, coauthored with her son Adam, records her quest for justice following the beating of Adam by racist police officers. In *Motherhood 2000*, Kennedy again wrestles with her anger at the unjust beating of her son in the form of a miracle play and ends with an apocalyptic scene in which the character called Mother/Writer strikes the policeman in the head with a hammer.

CRITICAL RECEPTION

Werner Sollors, the editor of *The Adrienne Kennedy Reader,* succinctly evaluates the scope and the depth of Kennedy's works thus:

Adrienne Kennedy's work . . . has affinities to the work of Sam Shepard, Amiri Baraka, Ntozake Shange, Arthur Miller, Edward Albee, and Wole Soyinka. Simultaneously, it echoes the entire dramatic tradition, from Greek tragedy to theatre of the absurd, from Euripides to Shakespeare, and from Chekhov to Tennessee Williams. Inspired by the themes of Hollywood movies and by cinematic techniques, Kennedy's highly acclaimed and frequently staged works have been praised as surrealistic dream plays, hauntingly fragmentary and nonlinear lyrical dramas, high points in the development of the American one-act play, and dramatic harbingers of feminist themes in contemporary Black women's writing. (*The Adrienne Kennedy Reader* vii)

In the 1960s and early 1970s, the brilliance and the raw intensity of Kennedy's work were recognized and her plays were produced by Off-Broadway theaters. Edward Albee, Michael Kahn, Joseph Chaikin, Joseph Papp, Robbie McCauley, Gerald Freedman, and Ellen Stewart are some of the theater people who have produced and directed her work. Her work was also embraced by the European Avant-garde and was performed in London and Paris. The international academic community responded to her writings and she began to be read and taught in countries as far apart as India, Nigeria, and Norway.

The complexity of Kennedy's work was evident from the beginning. The multiplicity of contexts to which her work belongs is evident in *Intersecting Boundaries*, which contains essays that evoke divergent theatrical, dramatic, and literary contexts: the European Avant-garde movements such as Symbolism, German Expressionism, and the Absurd; West African ritual; African American women's writing; the transcendentalism of Whitman and Emerson, and so on. In her early plays, one of the most problematic areas of experience for the characters as well as for the reader/audience is the status of "reality." Even in terms of psychological realism, the plays do not have a stable text or subtext. Her protagonists are invaded by ideas, images, and stimuli with no boundaries to help them distinguish the self from the outer world. The multicultural and multiracial characters and themes of her work were not fully amenable to the black nationalist focus, and her relationship with the Black Arts Movement in the 1960s was a little problematic. Her plays, nonetheless, remain extremely powerful dramatizations of contemporary social and political issues including race relations and its psychological consequences for the people of color. She has brought a new intensity and power to the one-act form, and her influence has been acknowledged by younger playwrights such as Ntozake Shange and

Suzan-Lori Parks. Today, Kennedy is recognized as a major American playwright who broke free from the dominant conventions of realism and naturalism and gave a new dimension to American and African American drama.

BIBLIOGRAPHY

Works by Adrienne Kennedy

Adrienne Kennedy in One Act. Minneapolis: University of Minnesota Press, 1988.
The Adrienne Kennedy Reader. Introduction by Werner Sollors. Minneapolis: University of Minnesota Press, 2001.
The Alexander Plays. Minneapolis: University of Minnesota Press, 1992.
Cities in Bezique: Two One-Act Plays. New York: Samuel French, 1969.
Deadly Triplets: A Theatre Mystery and Journal. Minneapolis: University of Minnesota Press, 1990.
The Lennon Play: In His Own Write. London: Cape, 1968.
People Who Led to My Plays. New York: Knopf, 1986.
Sleep Deprivation Chamber: A Theatre Piece. With Adam P. Kennedy. New York: Theatre Communications Group, 1996.

Studies of Adrienne Kennedy's Works

Barnett, Claudia. "'This Fundamental Challenge to Identity': Reproduction and Representation in the Drama of Adrienne Kennedy." *Theatre Journal* 48.2 (1996): 141 55.
Benston, Kimberly W. "'Cities in Bezique': Adrienne Kennedy's Expressionistic Vision." *CLA Journal* 20 (1976): 235–44.
Bryant-Jackson, Paul K., and Lois More Overbeck, eds. *Intersecting Boundaries: The Theatre of Adrienne Kennedy*. Minneapolis: University of Minnesota Press, 1992.
Carbone, Melissa. "The Concomitant Forces of Placement: Re-Placing the African-American Woman in Adrienne Kennedy's *Funnyhouse of a Negro* and *Ohio State Murders*." *Text & Presentation: the Journal of the Comparative Drama Conference* 14 (1993): 5–9.
Curb, Rosemary K. "Fragmented Selves in Adrienne Kennedy's *Funnyhouse of a Negro* and *The Owl Answers*." *Theatre Journal* 32 (1980): 180–95.
Diamond, Elin. "Rethinking Identification: Kennedy, Freud, Brecht." *Kenyon Review* 15.2 (1993): 86–99.
Kintz, Linda. "The Sanitized Spectacle: What's Birth Got to Do with It? Adrienne Kennedy's *A Movie Star Has to Star in Black and White*." *Theatre Journal* 44.1 (1992): 67–86.
———. *The Subject's Tragedy: Political Poetics, Feminist Theory, and Drama*. Ann Arbor: University of Michigan Press, 1992.
Kolin, Philip C. "Orpheus Ascending: Music, Race, and Gender in Adrienne Kennedy's *She Talks to Beethoven*." *African American Review* 28.2 (1994): 293–312.
McDonough, Carla J. "God and the Owls: The Sacred and the Profane in Adrienne Kennedy's *The Owl Answers*." *Modern Drama* 40.3 (1997): 385–402.
Oha, Obododimma. "Her Dissonant Selves: The Semiotics of Plurality and Bisexuality in Adrienne Kennedy's *Funnyhouse of a Negro*." *American Drama* 6.2 (1997): 67–80.
Shafee, Syed Ali. "Probing the African-American Psyche: A Study of the Protagonists of *Funnyhouse of a Negro* and *Les Blancs*." *Indian Journal of American Studies* 24.2 (1994): 83–88.
Shinn, Thelma J. "Living the Answer: The Emergence of African American Feminist Drama." *Studies in the Humanities* 17.2 (1990): 149–59.
Sollors, Werner. "Owls and Rats in the American Funnyhouse: Adrienne Kennedy's Drama." *American Literature* 63.3 (1991): 507–32.

Tener, Robert L. "Adrienne Kennedy's Portrait of the Black Woman." *Studies in Black Literature* 6.2 (1975): 1–5.
Zinman, Toby Silverman. "'In the Presence of Mine Enemies': Adrienne Kennedy's *An Evening with Dead Essex*." *Studies in American Drama* 6.1 (1991): 3–13.

Nita N. Kumar

JAMAICA KINCAID (1949–)

BIOGRAPHICAL NARRATIVE

Jamaica Kincaid, a successful novelist, was born as Elaine Cynthia Potter Richardson in St. John's, the capital of the Caribbean island of Antigua, on May 25, 1949. While Kincaid lived in Antigua, the island was still a British colony, and this firsthand experience of colonialism left a deep trace in her future writing.

Kincaid's family was an ordinary one with her stepfather, a carpenter, earning decent money when there was work, and her mother taking care of the house; Kincaid's biological father was never a part of her life. Until the age of nine, Kincaid felt happy and loved as an only child, but when her mother gave birth to her three brothers in rapid succession, her world changed. Kincaid felt that her mother's love shifted to her younger brothers and she deeply resented both the loss of her mother's affection and her new obligations in helping her mother take care of the babies.

Kincaid's adolescent years were traumatic not only because of the paradise lost at home, but also because of her growing resentment toward the colonial system and the attempts both at home and at school to turn her into a proper middle-class Afro-Saxon girl. While people around her easily accepted themselves as Britons, Kincaid thought they were slaves. Her rebellion took the form of withdrawal into literature, and Kincaid read obsessively, mostly nineteenth-century British literature. At school, she was one of the brightest pupils in class, disliked and bullied by her classmates.

At the age of thirteen, when Kincaid was preparing for exams that would open the way to higher education, her parents removed her from school. Her stepfather had been sick and Kincaid was expected to help her mother at home with taking care of her three little brothers. For Kincaid that meant foregoing the dreams of a university education, and she started resenting both her mother and her brothers for taking away the only thing she enjoyed doing—reading.

In 1965 Kincaid's family heard of an opportunity for Kincaid to go to New York and work for a family with kids as an au pair. Since her father was still sick and the family was in financial trouble, they expected Kincaid to support them until things became better. Kincaid left Antigua at the age of seventeen; the next time she saw her hometown was in 1986, twenty years later.

Upon her arrival in New York, Kincaid eventually began an au pair job, for *New Yorker* writer Michael Arlen, his wife, and their four kids. She stayed with them for three years and later described her experiences in her novel *Lucy*.

While working for the Arlens, Kincaid obtained a high school equivalency diploma and took courses in photography, but her attempt to obtain a college diploma was unsuccessful despite the full scholarship she received. Having tried several low-paying jobs, Kincaid started to write as a freelancer, and in the early seventies made herself a reputation with the "When I Was Seventeen" series produced for *Ingenue* magazine. Around this time she adopted the pseudonym Jamaica Kincaid, which reflects her Caribbean origins.

In 1974 her first short story appeared in the *New Yorker*, where she also worked as a staff writer till 1995. Writing for the *New Yorker* was good schooling for Kincaid professionally; her success as a magazine writer inspired her to try her hand at fiction.

Kincaid's first collection of stories, *At the Bottom of the River*, was published in 1983 and included stories earlier published in the *New Yorker*. In 1985 she published her first novel, *Annie John*, written while Kincaid was pregnant with her first child from a marriage to composer Allen Shawn, son of *New Yorker* editor-in-chief William Shawn. The same year the family moved to Vermont, where Kincaid's husband was offered a teaching position at Bennington College.

In 1986 Kincaid returned to Antigua for the first time in twenty years. She was disappointed with the changes that had taken place since the country obtained independence, as she saw no sign of political or economical improvement. The second blow she received in her home country was her unsuccessful attempt at reconciliation with her mother. Kincaid described her visit in *A Small Place* (1988).

In 1990 Kincaid published her second novel, *Lucy*, considered by many a sequel to *Annie John*. About the same time, after her mother's visit to Vermont, Kincaid had a nervous breakdown and sought help in psychotherapy. She did not publish for three years until 1993, when her third novel, *The Autobiography of My Mother*, started appearing in installments in the *New Yorker*. The full text of the novel was published in 1996. Shortly after its publication, Kincaid left the *New Yorker*, following a conflict with the editor Tina Brown.

In 1997 Kincaid published another autobiographical narrative, *My Brother*, based on the story of her brother's death due to AIDS. Although Kincaid lost connection with her family during the years she lived in the United States, she helped him during his illness because both homosexuality and AIDS bore a stigma in Antigua.

Living in Vermont, Kincaid became a passionate gardener and made gardening her way of life. She channeled her new knowledge and experience into writing and produced a series of articles, the first of which were published in *New Yorker* before she left it. In 2001 these articles appeared as a book under the title *My Garden*.

Since 1994 Kincaid has been teaching literature and creative writing in the Department of African and African American Studies at Harvard University. She is recognized as a modern classic, with her work widely anthologized and included in course curriculums on literature and writing all over the country. With numerous articles about her work and two books of biography, Kincaid holds a prominent place in American literature of today.

MAJOR WORKS

Kincaid's first book, *At the Bottom of the River*, is a compilation of short stories previously published in magazines, in particular the *New Yorker*, and one new story. In these stories Kincaid attempts to recreate the atmosphere and the mood of her Caribbean childhood using a vague, experimental style and mixing dream and reality in a plot-lacking narrative. The first story of the collection, "Girl," is perhaps the most known one. Written as a mother's set of instructions to her teenage daughter, only twice interrupted by the girl's own voice, the story not only creates two vivid characters, but also presents a critique of the mother's attempt to mold her daughter into an exemplary Saxon middle-class young lady, suppressing and corrupting the daughter's personality. This one-page story clearly outlines the themes that Kincaid pursues in her subsequent writing: oppression and domination within one's family, a complex love-hate mother-daughter relationship, and political and cultural power struggles of the colonized against their colonizers. Even Kincaid's most recent pieces on gardening reflect her favorite domination theme: transplanting the plants from their native soil to the foreign lands serves as a mechanism of suppression and conquest.

Kincaid's first novel, *Annie John* (1985), consists of eight chapters that were initially published as stories in the *New Yorker*. Although their themes are reminiscent of *At the Bottom of the River*, the language is more accessible and the ideas are less puzzling to the general reader, which explains the novel's immediate success. The story is clearly autobiographical, written in the genre of *Bildungsroman* that typically traces the spiritual, moral, psychological, or social development and growth of the main character from childhood to maturity. Since the eight chapters of the novel were initially published as self-contained stories, the novel lacks a tight plot. The unifying element of the novel is the protagonist's voice and powerful presence through which the events are filtered. With the chapters arranged chronologically, from the time Annie is a young girl of ten till the time she leaves Antigua at the age of seventeen, the novel covers seven years.

Annie's story narrates her expulsion from paradise: her early closeness to her mother and mutual adoration gives way to hatred and lack of understanding as the girl approaches adolescence. Annie rejects her mother's British middle-class values, conventionality, and acceptance of the colonial hierarchy. Through her resistance to her mother's domination, Annie tries to create her own character and individuality. Her bitterness sometimes seems exaggerated, but it is the only way Annie can sever connections with the system that enslaves her. At the end of the novel Annie leaves for England, not because she is eager to see new places, but because putting distance between herself and her mother, between herself and Antigua, is the only way for her to preserve her newly found identity and escape enslavement for life. Significantly, in the parting scene, when Annie's mother embraces her, Annie feels that she is suffocating.

A Small Place (1988), Kincaid's nonfiction book, thematically connects to *Annie John* through addressing the issues of colonialism in her native Antigua. However, while the general tone of *Annie John* is one of sadness with its insights mediated through the eyes of a teenager, *A Small Place* strikes by its grown-up relentlessness and uncompromising severity in judging the Antiguan government for the mismanagement of the island as well as industrialized countries for their now covert exploitation of the Antiguan people. The generic tourist, whom Kincaid addresses directly in the first section of the book, is guilty of perpetuating poverty and racism in Antigua. The second part of the book takes the reader back to the times when Antigua was under the British rule, subject to racism and exploitation. Returning to present-day Antigua in the third part, Kincaid invites the reader to face the most important issue of whether the changes brought about after the country gained independence made it into a better place. Kincaid's answer is an emphatic "no." *A Small Place* is a book filled with anger and indignation, calling for the American and British audience to recognize the harm they bring to her country and for the Antiguans to resist corruption and imperialist exploitation.

Kincaid's next novel, *Lucy*, published in 1990, picks up the story where it was dropped in *Annie John*, except that the protagonist's name is now Lucy and she arrives in the United States and not England to work as a nanny for a well-to-do American family. *Lucy* has the same publication history as *Annie John*, first appearing as five independent stories in the *New Yorker*, but it shows more tightness and coherence in its plot and works better as a continuous narrative. It is Kincaid's first novel set outside of Antigua, in New York, and it covers a year of the protagonist's life.

Confronted with a foreign culture and overwhelmed by the lights of a big city, Lucy, a young Caribbean girl, attempts to preserve her identity against her mother's still powerful influence from Antigua and her employer's well-meaning but destructive efforts to mold her into something she is not. The friendliness of the American people Lucy meets is corrupting and her main quest is to resist Mariah, her employer, in the same fashion that she resisted her own mother. At the end of the novel, Lucy leaves her surrogate mother Mariah and finds solace and satisfaction in her newly acquired ability to be her own mistress, to be by herself, in her own apartment, content with her solitude. In *Lucy*, the familiar themes of domination, hierarchy, and power struggles between the oppressor and the oppressed are enriched by the profound discoveries of interconnectedness of race, class, and gender.

For several years after the publication of *Lucy*, Kincaid was working on her next novel, *The Autobiography of My Mother*, published in 1996. The novel became Kincaid's most controversial writing, depicting a character who many readers find unsympathetic and difficult or even disturbing. Kincaid bases Xuela, the protagonist, on her mother and attempts to explore what her mother's life would have been if she had not left Dominica for Antigua and had not had children. *The Autobiography* narrates the story of the motherless and childless Xuela from birth till her old age, raising the familiar issues of mother-daughter relationship, oppression within the family and, parallel to it, under the colonial rule, self-destructiveness and a search for identity.

Kincaid's second book of nonfiction, *My Brother* (1997), presents an autobiographical account of Kincaid's relationship with her brother Devon Drew. While her other books were also based on autobiographical material, they were nevertheless fictionalized; *My Brother*, on the other hand, is written as an actual account of her brother's struggle in a society where being homosexual is a stigma and where contracting AIDS means an ignoble and fast death. Thematically, the book is linked to Kincaid's other writing in raising the issues of oppression and dominance, injustice and exploitation, corruption and hypocrisy.

Similar to *The Autobiography of My Mother*, *Mr. Potter* (2002) is a fictional memoir, this time of Kincaid's biological father, Roderick Potter. Told by his illegitimate daughter, Elaine Cynthia Potter, that is, Jamaica Kincaid herself, the novel, as all Kincaid's writings, is as much about her father as about herself and her attempt to come to terms with her family and her past. Kincaid's rage against her father is open and uncompromising, reminiscent of Kincaid's real and fictionalized love-hate relationship with her mother in her other novels.

My Garden, Kincaid's book compiled of her essays on gardening, is a logical continuation of her previous work. In this book Kincaid attempts to weave her gardening experience in her Vermont home into the complex fabric of philosophical and psychological issues. Comparing gardening in Antigua and Vermont allows Kincaid to address the familiar issues of colonialism and forced transplanting of cultures, the scourge of colonial domination, and the resistance to it. Looking through the lens of gardening, and grounding her work in the long-standing tradition of English and American garden-writing, Kincaid explores her favorite themes of motherhood, home, power, and possession. In a similar vein, Kincaid's highly introspective book, *Among Flowers: A Walk in the Himalaya*, published in 2005, an account of her travel, uses the search for rare plants as a starting ground for the author's meditations on life, people, and nature.

CRITICAL RECEPTION

Kincaid's reception in the United States was immediate and enthusiastic. Her successful career as a novelist was prepared by her long-time collaboration with the *New Yorker*, where she originally published most of her writings. Starting with her first book, *At the Bottom of the River*, critics hailed her as one of the most promising and important writers of the 1980s. Though some critiqued the novel for its vagueness and inaccessibility to a general reader, it won public acclaim and received the Morton Dauwen Zabel Award of the American Academy and Institute of Arts and Letters and was nominated for the PEN/Faulkner Award. Kincaid's second novel, *Annie John*, became a literary sensation, ending among the three finalists for the Ritz Paris Hemingway Award. *A Small Place*, on the other hand, received a mixed response. Robert Gottlieb, the editor of *New Yorker*, considered it too critical and refused to publish it. Neither was the book well received in Antigua, from where Kincaid was unofficially banned for years for her open critique of the Antiguan government. *Lucy*, Kincaid's next novel, received a favorable reception and was highly praised for its masterful constructing of a girl's complex identity; however, Kincaid's colleagues accused her of what they saw as exposing the life of her former employer, Michael Arlen and his wife, as their marriage broke up. *The Autobiography of My Mother* solidified Kincaid's position as a writer. It was nominated for the National Book Critics Circle Award in fiction, was a finalist for the PEN/Faulkner Award, and received the Cleveland Foundation's Anisfield-Wolf Award as well as the Boston Book Review's Fisk Fiction Award.

Kincaid's books on gardening, while praised by some critics for their lyrical dreaming meditative style, are at the same time criticized for the author's self-indulgence and self-absorption as she burdens the narrative with tedious accounts of various nurseries and their services and reproduces lists of catalogued plants.

All Kincaid's work is openly autobiographical, as commented on by critics and acknowledged by the author herself: "I've never really written about anyone except myself and my mother. . . . I'm just one of those pathetic people for whom writing is therapy" (Listfield 82). Through creating and recreating her story, Kincaid produced a body of literature that placed her among the most important and provocative American writers.

BIBLIOGRAPHY

Works by Jamaica Kincaid

Among Flowers: A Walk in the Himalaya. New York: National Geographic, 2005.
Annie John. New York: Farrar, Straus & Giroux, 1985.
At the Bottom of the River. New York: Farrar, Straus & Giroux, 1983.
The Autobiography of My Mother. New York: Farrar, Straus & Giroux, 1996.
Lucy. New York: Farrar, Straus & Giroux, 1990.
Mr. Potter. New York: Farrar, Straus & Giroux, 2002.
My Brother. New York: Farrar, Straus & Giroux, 1997.
My Garden. New York: Farrar, Straus & Giroux, 2001.
A Small Place. New York: Farrar, Straus & Giroux, 1988.

Studies of Jamaica Kincaid's Works

Bouson, Brooks. *Jamaica Kincaid: Writing Memory, Writing Back to the Mother.* New York: State University of New York Press, 2005.

Covi, Giovanna. "Jamaica Kincaid and the Resistance to Canons." In *Out of the Kumbla*: *Caribbean Women and Literature*, edited by Carol Boyce Davis and Elaine Savory Fido, 345–54. Trenton, NJ: Africa World Press, 1990.

Donnell, Alison. "Dreaming of Daffodils: Cultural Resistance in the Narratives of Theory." *Kunapipi* 14.2 (1995): 45–52.

Ferguson, Moira. *Jamaica Kincaid: Where the Land Meets the Body.* Charlottesville: University Press of Virginia, 1994.

Listfield, Emily. "Straight from the Heart." *Harper's Bazaar* (October 1990): 82.

Paravisini-Gebert, Lizabeth. *Jamaica Kincaid: A Critical Companion.* Westport, CT: Greenwood Press, 1999.

Simmons, Diane Ellis. *Jamaica Kincaid.* New York: Twayne, 1994.

———. "The Rhythm of Reality in the Work of Jamaica Kincaid." *World Literature Today* 68.3 (1994): 466–72.

Maria Mikolchak